The Development of Trade Unionism in Great Britain and Germany, 1880–1914

The Development of Trade Unionism in Great Britain and Germany, 1880–1914

Edited by

WOLFGANG J. MOMMSEN

and

HANS-GERHARD HUSUNG

THE GERMAN HISTORICAL INSTITUTE

GEORGE ALLEN & UNWIN

London

Boston   Sydney

© George Allen & Unwin (Publishers) Ltd, 1985
This book is copyright under the Berne Convention.
No reproduction without permission. All rights reserved.

George Allen & Unwin (Publishers) Ltd,
40 Museum Street, London WC1A 1LU, UK

George Allen & Unwin (Publishers) Ltd,
Park Lane, Hemel Hempstead, Herts HP2 4TE, UK

Allen & Unwin, Inc.,
Fifty Cross Street, Winchester, Mass. 01890, USA

George Allen & Unwin Australia Pty Ltd,
8 Napier Street, North Sydney, NSW 2060, Australia

First published in 1985

British Library Cataloguing in Publication Data

The Development of trade unionism in Great Britain and Germany,
1880–1914.
1. Trade-unions – Europe – History – 19th century. 2. Trade-unions –
Europe – History – 20th century
I. Mommsen, Wolfgang J. II. Husung, Hans-Gerhard. III. German
Historical Institute
331.88′094 HD6657
ISBN 0-04-940080-0

Library of Congress Cataloging in Publication Data
Main entry under title:

The Development of trade unionism in Great Britain and Germany,
1880–1914.
Includes index.
1. Trade unions – Great Britain – History. 2. Trade unions – Germany –
History. I. Mommsen, Wolfgang J., 1930–   . II. Husung, Hans-Gerhard.
III. German Historical Institute in London.
HD6664.D48 1985   331.88′0941   84-28235
ISBN 0–04–940080–0 (alk. paper)

Set in 10 on 11 point Times by Computape (Pickering) Ltd, N. Yorkshire
and printed in Great Britain by Mackays of Chatham, Ltd.

Contents

Introduction

Wolfgang J. Mommsen

The contributions to this volume are based on papers presented at a conference held in 1981, organized by the German Historical Institute in London in conjunction with the *Politsche Akademie Tutzing*. The objective was to pave the way for a comparative analysis of the development of trade unions in Germany, Great Britain and France. Largely for editorial reasons, however, this volume deals only with German and British trade unions.

The history of the labour movement is usually seen within the framework of national histories, rather than as a transnational phenomenon (with some notable exceptions, which are also represented in this collection). Of course, many good reasons can be found for focusing on one country. Despite many general trends common to all the major European countries, the specific political, economic and social conditions under which efficient trade union organizations developed differed widely from country to country. This is particularly true of Germany and Great Britain. The development of trade unions was determined largely by political factors in Imperial Germany, where an independent labour movement of a socialist nature was established as early as the 1860s. This movement represented a fundamental challenge to the existing social order, refusing on principle to co-operate with the bourgeois political parties and in particular with the Progressive Liberals. Its inception was crucial for the direction taken by trade unionism in Imperial Germany. The historical roots of the trade unions go back to the eighteenth century, but given the slow start of German industrialization, they did not get beyond their initial stages until after the turn of the century. After the Party Congress in Gotha in 1875, at which August Bebel's *Sozialdemokratische Arbeiterpartei* (SDAP) and the *Allgemeine Deutsche Arbeiterverein* (ADAV) founded by Ferdinand Lassalle were united, the Free Trade Unions became increasingly dependent on the Social Democratic Party, while the Liberal Hirsch-Duncker and the confessional unions attracted only modest support from the workers. The state authorities' attempts if not to suppress the socialist workers' movement then at least to prevent it from exercising any political influence profoundly affected the trade union movement too. Thus in Imperial Germany the unions were forced to enter the political arena and opt for a political party. In Britain, by contrast, the unions had been able to develop relatively freely since the early nineteenth century, without much direct government interference. Until the turn of the century, therefore, there was little reason for them to adopt a political profile. For a long time the political interests of their members were represented by the established bourgeois parties, in particular the Liberal Party whose radical wing was keen to cultivate the labour vote. Not until after the famous Taff Vale ruling in 1900–1, which was a severe blow to trade union immunities, and a series of subsequent court rulings similarly hostile to the unions, did they seek political representation of their own. They founded the Labour

Representation Committee from which, within a few years, emerged the Labour Party as we know it today. This development is reflected in the special relationship, which has survived to our own time, between the unions represented in the Trades Union Congress and the Labour Party. This party always was, and still is, to some degree dependent on the trade unions, whereas in Germany it was the other way around.

Against this background, German historiography has traditionally paid more attention to the political activities of the trade unions than to their role in industrial relations. In other words, the history of trade unions in Germany has as a rule come to be seen as an integral part of the history of social democracy. By contrast, issues like union organization, the effectiveness with which they promoted the interests of workers vis-à-vis employers, union membership and the relationship between union officials and the rank and file on the shop floor have been relatively neglected. British historians have approached the subject in an entirely different way. Given the more liberal political system which made independent political representation of the working class superfluous, at least initially, the history of the trade unions has always been regarded as by and large equivalent to that of the labour movement.

By the 1880s British workers were already highly unionized, judged by continental standards. Generally, British unions were fairly successful in obtaining lasting improvements in the standard of living and in the working conditions of industrial labour. They achieved this by confronting employers over wages and working conditions, and forcing them to make concessions in these areas. However, subsidiary organizations also played an important part in this: the Friendly Societies provided assistance to the needy on the basis of solidarity; various kinds of social welfare associations were run on a voluntary basis; labour exchanges organized by the unions rather than by entrepreneurs or the government helped to reduce unemployment and to rationalize the labour market; co-operative associations sought to provide cheaper food and commodities. All this speaks for itself. Since the failure of the Chartist movement, if not before, the struggle for the emancipation of the working class had largely shifted to the level of union activities. The top echelon of workers, the often cited 'labour aristocracy', and the skilled craftsmen representing the 'respectable working class' had gradually succeeded in considerably improving their working conditions. This was possible because they had to a large extent gained actual control of production processes at factory level. However, this form of union organization, which gave the 'labour aristocracy' a kind of hegemony on the shop floor at any rate, favoured craft unions rather than industrial or general unions. It often went hand in hand with extremely restrictive practices excluding unskilled or semi-skilled workers from union membership. The sort of class-consciousness which developed among the upper levels of the working class thus did not entirely lack elitist features. But it also reflected a considerable degree of awareness on the part of these groups that they were essential to the production process, both as far as other groups of workers were concerned, and from the point of view of capitalist society as a whole.

These brief remarks may suffice to explain how the different conditions under which trade unions developed in the two countries have led German and British labour historians to approach their subject from rather different vantage-points. But it can no longer be doubted that a careful analysis of conditions in the lower echelons of union organization and on the shop floor in both countries will reveal that they were not as different as has long been assumed. Research in the two countries is thus increasingly converging, as far as methods and issues are concerned. For some years now historians in the Federal Republic of Germany have been devoting more attention to the institutional factors which governed union activities. They are examining in detail the role of the unions on the shop floor, rather than limiting themselves to looking at union activities within the political arena. As a result, the relationship between union officials and the rank and file, or to express it in terms very much in vogue today, the *Basis*, is increasingly being highlighted. What has emerged is that the socialist Free Trade Unions, organized under strong, almost authoritarian leadership, in fact encompassed only a fraction of the workforce. Their members were to be found mainly among the upper strata of skilled workers, while most of the workers employed in the huge plants of the coal and steel industry were not reached by the unions at all, not to mention those who, like the railway workers, were legally prevented from forming trade unions. In view of these findings, a different approach seemed called for. It proved to be more fruitful initially to look at the conduct of the working class in terms of growing social differentiation among the workforce than to analyse it in terms of political or ideological allegiances. The British trade union movement was never split into unions of different political persuasions, as was the German movement. On the other hand, it was much more fragmented, and at least at first sight, much less effectively organized than its German counterpart. In Britain, there existed an enormous variety of specialized trade unions, based on particular skills rather than on trades, which consciously identified with the traditions of the older craft unions. Highly skilled workers, who thought of themselves as craftsmen rather than as ordinary members of the working class, played a key role in running union affairs. Accordingly, their mentality tended to be rather traditionalist. But surprisingly, the picture is not strikingly different for Imperial Germany, apart from the fact that the Free Trade Unions more or less considered themselves an integral part of the social democratic movement. There too an élite of well-paid skilled workers, who were fully aware of the importance of their position and could be considered a sort of 'labour aristocracy', dominated union affairs until the First World War and even later.

In the late 1880s and early 1890s unionization in both countries took a big leap forward. New mass unions were founded in the wake of a series of spectacular mass strikes. Groups of workers such as the dockers, who had previously been largely unorganized, were recruited. Other groups of unskilled and semi-skilled workers, also largely unorganized, now joined the more traditionally oriented unions – known as the old unions – in substantial numbers. The explosive growth of the New Unionism in Great Britain is usually interpreted as a direct result of the great London dockers' strike. (It is worth noting that this strike had German parallels in the big miners' strike in the Ruhr in 1889, and in the Hamburg dockers' strike of

1896–7.) Its impact on British unionism was remarkable, and contributed to the rapid success of the New Unionism. The new mass unions succeeded in recruiting large numbers of members among previously unorganized groups of workers, but it should not be overlooked that these new membership levels could not be maintained. The old unions, especially those founded in the early 1870s, and the traditional craft unions also experienced an extraordinary expansion during this period. In other words, all unions, new and old alike, managed to consolidate their hold on the labour force as a whole. It was the old unions, not the New Unions of semi-skilled and unskilled workers, which continued to set the tone. In much the same way as before, they and not the New Unions represented the bulk of the labour force, in so far as it was unionized at all. The step forward taken almost simultaneously by the union movement in both countries was furthered in Imperial Germany by the revocation in 1890 of the *Sozialistengesetz* (Anti-Socialist Law), which had imposed severe restrictions on union activities. On the other hand, employers now felt it necessary to create special employers' organizations in order to check the growing power of the union movement. They also established 'yellow' unions, which could be used as a convenient strike-breaking force. In addition, employers appealed to the government to contain unionized labour by passing legislation to minimize the scope of union activities in general, and strike action in particular.

This chain of events in the two countries under consideration provides the backbone of the essays collected here. They all deal with the sudden upsurge of trade unionism in the 1880s, and examine the factors which made it possible. Initially, the New Unionism itself must be described. Does it really deserve such a prominent place in the history of the union movement in Great Britain? What impact did it have on trade unionism in Imperial Germany, and indeed in Europe as a whole? These and other issues are dealt with in the first section, 'The New Unionism in a European Context', which is opened by Eric J. Hobsbawm. He masterfully surveys the history of the New Unionism, looking at the great spurt of the late 1880s and early 1890s in the context of the European labour movement before the First World War. He points out that the expansion of unions was not a continuous process, but took place in waves, against the background of a rapidly changing economy and the vicissitudes of the labour market. Similarly, Sidney Pollard suggests that the growth of the unions must be seen in the context of economic cycles; although the upsurge of unionism in Britain had already begun at the lowest point in the recession of 1886, it reached its climax with the dockers' strike in 1889, largely corresponding to fluctuations in the economy. It emerges that the New Unionism represented only one of three consecutive spurts in unionization, the first one having taken place already in the early 1870s. Hence the great upsurge in unionism in the years after 1889 cannot be attributed primarily to the heroic efforts of the grand old men of the New Unionism, such as Tom Mann, Ben Tillett and John Burns. It was certainly no accident that the breakthrough of the New Unionism on a broad front coincided with the very end of the Great Depression. The New Unions could take full advantage of conditions generally favourable to trade union activity during the subsequent phase of economic recovery. When this climate changed during the next economic recession, the impressive membership gains could not be maintained by the New Unions nor, to a lesser degree, by the old unions. Hobsbawm and Pollard point out that it was only in the last few years before the First World War that union organization once again took a dramatic leap forward. This time, under the exceptional conditions created by the First World War, it was possible to consolidate membership gains permanently.

In the second section, 'Strike Movements in Europe: A Comparative Analysis', James E. Cronin and Friedhelm Boll examine the great strike waves which occurred between 1870 and 1914, and their impact on the history of unionism in Europe. The comparisons they draw between strike patterns in Great Britain and Imperial Germany during this period are based on quantitative analyses of strike movements. Cronin's and Boll's analyses of strike movements build on an approach pioneered by Edward Shorter and Charles Tilly. These earlier attempts come under close scrutiny, and are criticized for approaching the subject in a far too generalized manner, and drawing conclusions from aggregate data which do not always hold water when analysed in a more detailed fashion. Cronin and Boll demonstrate that in many cases strikes formed the nucleus of union organization, or at least provided an important stimulus for membership growth. Thus in Britain and Germany alike, the mass strikes of the 1880s and early 1890s produced mass unions of a new type. Conversely, strikes which failed could result in severe setbacks for working-class organization. John Lovell's analysis of the great London dockers' strike of 1889 and Michael Grüttner's essay on the Hamburg dockers' strike of 1896–7 show that although the methods of the two strikes were very different, they developed many of the same features. For the first time, unorganized sections of the workforce, which did not even have regular employment, were effectively mobilized in the struggle for improved working conditions.

Despite the importance of strikes for the development of unions, a variety of other explanatory patterns are used to outline the long-term cycles typical of the way in which unionization progressed in the period under discussion. Solely economic explanations which view union organization as directly dependent on cyclical economic movements, or which detect correlations between unionization and fluctuations in price levels, would appear to be not fully satisfactory. The same can be said of narrow political interpretations which tend to see the growth of unionism as a direct result of the activities of working-class leaders, or of a rise in working-class consciousness. This is even more the case as factors external to the trade union movement and beyond its control played an important role, especially in Imperial Germany. It should be taken into consideration that the relaxation of repressive legislation, in particular the revocation of the Anti-Socialist Law in 1890, meant that the Free Trade Unions were from now on able to develop more freely and dynamically. There was also a noticeable shift in public opinion in favour of the working class; during the dockers' strike in Hamburg in 1898 and the great miners' strike in the Ruhr in 1905 the public clearly sympathized with the unions rather than with the entrepreneurs, enforcing a certain moderation in governmental attitudes towards the unions. Even so, it is undoubtedly true that the working class in Wilhelmine Germany remained highly underprivileged, participating only moderately in the increasing wealth of the nation. This fact provided a perennial impetus for rallying more and more workers behind the unions; the recruiting of new workers to the unions thus went on almost continuously, largely independent of the ups and downs in the economy. Recently, however, historians have tended to explain the considerable progress made by trade union organization less as an awakening of working-class consciousness or as the consequence of improved political conditions, than in terms of qualitative changes in the methods of industrial production which were introduced as a result of technological modernization.

These and related problems are discussed in the section 'Industrial Modernization, Politics and Trade Union Organization'. Two case studies, one of the Amalgamated Society of Engineers, the other of the Railwaymen's Union, deal with the key issue here: what did technological innovation, and the changes in the organization of work associated with it (often involving the replacement of skilled workers by semi-skilled or unskilled workers), mean for trade union organization? Particular attention is paid to the increasing differentiation of the workforce, that is, the emergence of distinct groups of workers with different economic interests, which resulted from changes in the organization of work. Richard Price argues that under these circumstances the main objective of the unions was to defend the workers' traditional control of production processes on the shop floor, regardless of the introduction of new machinery. This view has not, however, gone unchallenged, as Alastair Reid's contribution to this volume shows. But in any case, the change-over from the old and comparatively elitist craft unions to the New Unions was certainly a more continuous process than historians have usually assumed. In the British case at least, the slowly emerging working-class culture was not conducive to militant unionism; it pointed more to a policy of compromise and moderation. German historians, on the other hand, emphasize the moderating effects which the highly organized union bureaucracies had on the conduct of day-to-day business; they were certainly not interested in rash strike action which might cost them dearly or even endanger the organization. Particular attention is also given to the specific political conditions under which unions had to operate. In view of continuous government repression, the Free Trade Unions came to see themselves, and to present themselves to the workers, primarily as working-class organizations engaged in a permanent struggle against the bourgeoisie and the state alike, while the Liberal and Christian union organizations were relegated to marginal significance. This was also reflected at the organizational level. As Klaus Tenfelde rightly points out, the very fact that the trade unions had to operate under relatively backward political and legal conditions in Germany forced them from the start to transcend the level of individual craft unions in order to strengthen their political foothold against the authorities and the entrepreneurs alike. In Britain, by contrast, the traditions of the craft unions, which in the past had organized only trades with some degree of control over actual production processes, remained alive in the trade union movement. This was the case even after the emergence of the New Unions, which served as a rallying point for unskilled and semi-skilled workers.

Given the fundamental differences in the conditions under which trade unions had to operate in Britain and Germany, it is not surprising that the relationship between union leaders and rank and file took on a rather different character in each of the two countries. This is reflected in the fundamental issue of strategy. Should priority be given to militant strategies designed ultimately to get rid of the established political system altogether, and perhaps capitalism as well, or to strategies geared merely to gaining improvements in wages and working conditions? Union leaders in Germany on the whole succeeded in securing the loyalty of the rank and file, partly by emphasizing the need for discipline in the fight against the bourgeoisie. None the less, serious conflicts occurred frequently between trade union officials and the men on the shop floor; the latter often proved far more willing than the leaders to adopt radical measures. In Britain such conflicts were relatively rare, largely because of the key role played by craft unions, which managed to maintain close ties with the workers on the shop floor; even so, tension between the union leadership and the rank and file developed often enough.

In the last decade before the First World War a wave of working-class unrest swept across both Germany and Britain with considerable momentum. Again, bitter labour disputes involving large numbers of workers broke out, often taking on a political dimension, not least because of the authorities' reactions. It is worth noting that in spite of different long-term conditions, this wave of unrest, reaching proportions hitherto unknown, occurred at roughly the same time and bore surprisingly similar features in both countries.

These violent mass strikes were, however, in a way the exception to the rule. In general, the unions were geared more towards almost bureaucratically negotiating wages and working conditions. When union activities were rationalized, the leadership was prone to lose contact with feelings on the shop floor. This was also to some degree a result of government legislation which attempted to restrict strikes by means of a finely spun legal net. These issues are discussed by John Saville, Jonathan Zeitlin and Klaus Saul. They are especially concerned with the changing nature of the relationship between employers, unions and government authorities during the period between 1880 and 1914. It is hardly surprising that Saville and Zeitlin give particular attention to the role of the entrepreneurs, as ever since 1875 government policy in Britain in theory if not in practice had been based on the idea that both sides in industry should be treated equally, while the state was to remain neutral. It was under the impact of the great strike movements of the late 1880s, however, that the government became increasingly worried about the apparently ever-growing power of the unions. To some it seemed to pose a threat to the very fabric of society. The government therefore came to favour the introduction of conciliation or arbitration boards to facilitate a peaceful solution of industrial conflicts. But on the whole, the authorities abstained from interfering in labour relations.

The same cannot be said of the courts. It was a court ruling against the trade unions in the Taff Vale decision of 1900–1 which initiated a spectacular departure from established practice in the British trade union movement. The trade unions decided that the working class needed independent political representation in Parliament in order to be able to seek redress for this decision. By 1906, however, the previous law regarding strike action and trade union activities had been restored. With only a few exceptions, labour relations continued to be free from direct government control of any kind. Conditions in the labour market, not government interference, determined the success or failure of union struggles, and of entrepreneurs' attempts to reduce wages or to take away workers' traditional rights on the shop floor when they stood in the way of technical innovation. But this is not to say that under existing social and political conditions employers fared better than the unions. Ever since the 1880s, and increasingly since the turn of the century, employers had been trying to abolish the control exercised by small groups of highly skilled workers over the division of labour on the shop floor. Naturally these attempts often met with bitter resistance from the work-force. This aspect comes out particularly well in Zeitlin's study of labour relations in the British engineering industry. Finally, it must be mentioned that by the turn of the century employers had begun to form their own organizations for the specific purpose of fighting union power more effectively. Thanks to their stronger organization, the entrepreneurs were eventually fairly successful in preventing further rises in real wages. Real wages had stagnated since about 1900 in Britain, and to a lesser extent in Germany also.

By and large, no comparable studies of this sort have been undertaken in the Federal Republic of Germany. But there can be little doubt that during the period we are dealing with here, labour relations were far more backward in Imperial Germany than in Britain. Before the turn of the century, neither employers nor government were in the least prepared to recognize the unions as equal partners, in principle or in practice. Depending on the situation and on conditions in individual sectors of industry, they vacillated between outright repression and tacit recognition of the unions; only occasionally were employers willing to acknowledge them formally as equal partners legitimately representing the interests of their workforce. Up to 1914 employers were not ready to contemplate a wholesale transition to collective bargaining although it was already being practised in certain sectors of industry. Friedrich Naumann, who pleaded passionately for collective agreements as the key to industrial peace, found little support for collective bargaining in his own party, the Progressive Liberals, let alone among the industrialists.

In addition to employers' hostility, the Free Trade Unions faced much more government repression than did their counterparts in Britain. They were confronted with court rulings designed to subject strikes to stringent legal restrictions, if not to outlaw them altogether. Government authorities did everything in their power to prevent the spread of unionization. For instance, they did not allow railwaymen to organize, ostensibly for reasons of national security, nor did they tolerate the formation of agricultural workers' unions. While a growing number of social reformers in the

Reichstag favoured a liberal policy vis-à-vis the trade unions, the government remained committed to an anti-union strategy. Therefore it was not prepared to give union representatives a share in the administration of social insurance and welfare institutions. Eventually, however, it had to give way in the case of compulsory accident insurance, where trade union representatives were allowed to represent the workers on the joint administrative boards. Under these circumstances, the employers on the whole managed to maintain their right to manage vis-à-vis the workforce. The huge plants of the iron and steel industry in particular were notorious for their rigid control of the workers. Neither here nor in the new chemical and electrical industries did trade unions have much of a say. The high turnover rate among workers in these industries made it especially difficult to recruit them for the union movement. There can be little doubt that the preconditions for union activities were in general much more favourable in Britain than in Imperial Germany, however proud the German Free Trade Unions might be of their disciplined armies of followers. Not unnaturally, liberal social reformers like Lujo Brentano considered Britain an example for Imperial Germany to follow.

It is therefore not surprising that the essays by Jay M. Winter and Hans Mommsen, which round off this volume, strike totally different chords in their analyses of the relationship between the unions and the political labour movements. In Britain, the Trade Union Congress exercised hegemony over the slowly emerging Labour Party. At least for the time being, the unions were the main guardians of working-class interests, and the Labour Party no more than their political arm. In Imperial Germany, the opposite was the case. The Free Trade Unions were seen by the workers, and at least in part by union officials themselves, as a subordinate element in the German labour movement, of which the Social Democratic Party enjoyed undisputed leadership. The Free Trade Unions in principle accepted the 'primacy of the political movement'. Nevertheless they gradually developed into more than merely subsidiary organizations of the Social Democratic Party. Step by step, they established themselves as equal partners. Trade union leaders approached the problems of the day in a remarkably pragmatic way, and while in theory they continued to subscribe to the ideology of socialist class struggle, in practice they tended increasingly towards social compromise and fair dealing with management. If a satisfactory wage agreement could not be reached by negotiation, they did not hesitate to call for well-organized strike action; but they concentrated on strikes that would achieve concrete goals which were within reach, rather than challenging the existing capitalist order as such. They would have nothing to do with political strikes. The Free Trade Unions were clearly opposed to exposing the highly developed union organizations to the danger of repressive governmental action or indeed forfeiture by embarking on risky political strikes, which they regarded as at best only of symbolic value.

In spite of substantial differences, unions in both Britain and Germany largely distanced themselves from revolutionary socialism or, more often, from socialist positions which adopted a revolutionary posture without being prepared to wage an all-out revolutionary struggle. In political matters, the unions as a rule followed a defensive strategy. They were primarily interested in maintaining, and if possible furthering, advances made in the field of welfare policy. In addition, they strove to retain their previously established control over the organization and division of labour on the shop floor. The adoption by the unions of a rather defensive stance is understandable if it is remembered that only a fraction of the British industrial and agrarian working class was organized in unions at this time; in Imperial Germany the proportion was even smaller. Nevertheless, between 1880 and 1914 the foundations were laid for a system of industrial relations and union representation which has become an integral part of Western industrial society.

The essays collected in this volume offer a comprehensive survey of present research into the history of both British and German trade union movements before the First World War. They inform the reader about the great variety of research strategies and explanatory models now being applied to labour history. Although there is still much to be done before a full comparative assessment of the history of German and British trade unionism can be undertaken, this book undoubtedly paves the way for a better understanding of the different traditions, and in particular, the different organizational structures which have determined the character and policies of both trade union movements to this day. It is hoped that this volume will have a fruitful impact on future research in labour history; the wide divergence in the approaches and explanatory models with which British and German labour historians tackle their problems may well prove to be an advantage rather than a drawback.

Finally, we are indebted to all those who have helped to bring about the publication of this volume. First of all, we would like to thank Professor Manfred Hättich, Director of the *Politische Akademie Tutzing*, who made it possible to hold the conference at which these papers were first presented in the hospitable atmosphere of the *Akademie* near the Starnbergersee. We would also like to express our thanks to the translators of the German papers, Cathleen S. Catt, Stephen Conn, Helen Pridt, Simon Steyne and Chris Urban, and in particular to Dick Geary for his invaluable help in revising the texts. We are grateful to Angela Davies for editorial assistance, including the preparation of the index. Finally, thanks are due to the staff of the German Historical Institute for their assistance.

Part One

The New Unionism in a European Context

1 The 'New Unionism' Reconsidered

ERIC J. HOBSBAWM

I

As applied to its period of origin, the 1880s and early 1890s, the term New Unionism suggests three things to a British labour historian. First, a new set of strategies, policies and forms of organization for unions, as opposed to those associated with an already existing 'old' trade unionism. It suggests, in the second place, a more radical social and political stance of unions in the context of the rise of a socialist labour movement; and finally, the creation of new unions of hitherto unorganized or unorganizable workers, as well as the transformation of old unions along the lines suggested by the innovators. Consequently it also suggests an explosive growth of trade union organization and membership. The dock strike of 1889 and its aftermath illustrate all these aspects of the New Unionism, and it therefore provides the most popular image of the entire phenomenon. It is interesting that the very similar union upsurge and transformation of 1911–13 has never generated any similar label, though it was quite as innovative and much more radical. This indicates that even at the time it was regarded as a continuation, or a second instalment, of the process initiated in 1889. This in fact seems to be the best way to see it.[1]

A comparative study of New Unionism in various countries during the period 1890–1914 implies that there were comparable trade union developments in them. Now the British case was at this time unique in Europe in one respect. Here there was an already established and significant 'old' unionism, rooted in the country's basic industries, to combat, transform and expand. This was notably not the case in the other country of old industrialism, Belgium. In Germany the Free Trade Unions, though they had multiplied their membership almost fourfold since 1889, had by 1900 just about reached a numerical strength comparable to the 'old unions' of Britain in 1887 (680,000 as against 674,000). In short, the continental New Unionism of the late nineteenth century was new chiefly in as much as it established trade unions as a serious force, which they had not hitherto been outside some localities and the occasional craft trade such as printing and cigar-making. To this extent the New Unionism of Britain is *sui generis*.

Thus on the continent unionism developed simultaneously with the mass political labour movement and its parties, and largely under their impulsion. Its major problems arose when it became sufficiently massive to discover that the policies of trade union leaders, however socialist, could not be entirely congruent with the policies of the political leadership of socialist parties. Union membership probably grew faster than party membership and eventually exceeded it in size, except in such countries as Bohemia and Finland where the party consistently had more members than the unions, presumably because of the local impact of national sentiment. However, the party electorate greatly outnumbered union membership, except in Denmark up to 1913.[2] On the other hand, in Britain the Labour Party was itself a creation of the unions, and before 1914 the total vote for all labour and socialist candidates, whatever their affiliations, never amounted to more than perhaps 20 per cent of union membership,[3] while in Germany, even after the unions had grown to a larger size and, according to some, density of organization, than in Britain, the Social Democratic vote was about double the membership of all unions of whatever ideological persuasion, omitting only the organizations of salaried employees.[4]

In certain crucial respects the New Unionism of Britain and continental countries are therefore not comparable. On the other hand there are analogies between the British and continental cases, in so far as the mass extension of unionism raised problems of strategy and organization which had not previously arisen. Moreover, in some respects all trade union movements experimented with the same solutions to these problems, though the British pattern, which was eventually to supplement a broadened craft unionism primarily by general unions, was not paralleled on the same scale in continental Europe. Conversely, neither the policy of forming the union movement into a relatively small number of comprehensive organizations covering entire industries (industrial unionism), nor the formation of local inter-occupational bodies such as *bourses du travail* or *camere del lavoro* was notably successful in Britain.

Britain and the continent are also directly comparable, in so far as initiative and ideas in the union movement came largely from the radical, and indeed theoretically revolutionary, left, though naturally in Britain the bulk of the leadership in older unions were not socialists and still less revolutionaries. Still it is important to insist against sceptics like Hugh A. Clegg, Alan Fox and A. F. Thompson[5] on the disproportionately large role of the numerically small socialist movement in the British unions, particularly from the middle 1890s. The total membership of all socialist organizations in the middle of that decade may be generously estimated at not more than 20,000, and their paid-up membership at the time of the foundation of the Labour Representation Committee cannot have been more than perhaps 10,000, since they themselves only claimed 23,000.[6]

Some of this British left – the Marxists and later the syndicalists – were undoubtedly guided by international ideologies and strategies, and conversely, British trade union experience was taken note of on the continent. That movements in one industrial country thus claimed to be influenced by the experience, the ideologies and strategies of others, is itself evidence for some comparability, even though it may be doubted whether British union history would have been significantly different if nobody in Britain had heard of revolutionary syndicalism, or continental union developments would have been notably different if nobody in France or Germany had been acquainted with the British term 'ca'canny' (go-slow).[7] However, such foreign or international models were not always mere colourful labels which national activists stuck on bottles containing strictly native beverages. The international Marxism of the 1880s had little to say about trade unions, except to demand comprehensive class organization and warn against craft exclusiveness, but from about 1906 the British objective of rationalizing trade union structure along the lines of industrial unionism was certainly derived from ideas and experiences drawn from, or acquired, abroad. In any case the fact that union leadership and activism in this period were so widely identified with social-revolutionary movements, and that trade unionism also came to develop its own international organizations, is itself significant.[8] It must affect the historical assessment of certain novel forms of action, occurring internationally and much debated, such as general strikes.

The most easily comparable aspect of New Unionism is the general pattern of trade union growth through discontinuous leaps or explosions.[9] Such leaps occurred in most European trade union movements during the period from the 1880s up to the First World War, though not necessarily at the same time. If Britain and Germany both experienced such a leap in 1889–90 – both increased by about 90 per cent during this brief period, though the British movement from a base five times as large as the German – there is no British equivalent to the major continental leaps of 1903–4 (Norway, Sweden, Switzerland, Holland), and of 1905 (Austria). Conversely, there is no real continental equivalent to the great British explosion of 1911–13. This should warn labour historians against assuming too close a correlation between trade union expansion and cyclical economic fluctuations, national or international.

However, perhaps there is not much point in stressing the obvious, namely, that trade union growth at a certain stage must be discontinuous. Only when unionism in a country has been recognized and institutionalized, or when it has reached a density, by voluntary recruitment or compulsory membership, which only leaves room for marginal growth or expansion and contraction in line with the changing size of the labour force, can the curve of union growth be expected to be smooth and gentle. In no country and no industry (with rare exceptions such as British coalmining just before 1914) had this stage been reached in 1880–1914. Growth must be discontinuous under these circumstances, because if unions are to be effective they must mobilize, and therefore seek to recruit, not numbers of individuals but groups of workers sufficiently large for collective bargaining. They must recruit in lumps.

II

The year 1889 unquestionably marks a qualitative transformation of the British labour movement and its industrial relations. Between the great dock strike and the First World War effective and permanent employers' organizations were formed on a national scale, such as the Shipping Federation, the Engineering Employers' Federation and the Newspaper Proprietors' Association. Britain experienced the first nationwide and national

Table 1.1   *Ranking List of the Ten Largest Unions, 1885 and 1893*

1885	1963
Amalgamated Society of Engineers	Transport and General Workers' Union
Durham Miners' Association	Amalgamated Union of Engineering
United Society of Boilermakers	Workers
and Iron and Steel Shipbuilders	National Union of General and Municipal
Amalgamated Society of Carpenters	Workers
and Joiners	National Union of Mineworkers
Amalgamated Association of	National Union of Shop, Distributive &
Operative Cotton Spinners	Allied Workers
Amalgamated Society of Tailors	National Association of Local Government
The Northumberland Miners'	Officers
Mutual Confident Association	National Union of Railwaymen
Friendly Society of Ironfounders	Electrical Trades Union
Friendly Society of Operative	National Union of Teachers
Stonemasons	National Union and Public Employees
National Union of Boot and Shoe	
Operatives	

industrial disputes and collective bargains, the first interventions of central government in labour disputes, and indeed the creation of government offices designed to take care of the now constant interest of government in these matters. For during this period the first expressions of political concern about the possible effects of strikes and unions on the competitive position of the British economy were voiced. The appearance of a national Labour Party consisting essentially of trade union affiliates, and the welfare legislation of the years before 1914, are familiar to all.

So far as the unions themselves are concerned, the most striking difference lies not so much in the increased size and changed composition of the movement, but probably in its economic effects. Broadly speaking, before about 1900 trade unionism served, if anything, to widen wage-differentials between different groups of workers. After 1900, and especially after 1911, it contributed to the progressive narrowing of such differentials.[10] Nevertheless, the actual innovations in trade union structure and industrial or occupational distribution are not to be overlooked. If the list of the largest unions in 1885 is compared with that of 1963 as recorded by the Royal Commission on Trade Unions and Employers' Associations of 1965–8, it becomes apparent (see Table 1.1) that only one of the ten largest unions of 1885 was still in the list eighty years later – the Amalgamated Engineers. Conversely, seven of the ten largest unions of 1963 were founded, or are the lineal descendants of new unions founded during the period 1880–1914: the ancestors of the Transport and General Workers, General and Municipal Workers, National Union of Mineworkers and Electrical Trades Union were born in 1888–9, of the Shop, Distributive and Allied Workers in 1891, one of those of the National Union of Railwaymen in 1889, and the National Association of Local Government Officers in the 1900s.

A new era in labour relations and class conflict was clearly opening. The shock of 1889 was temporary, but it precipitated permanent changes in attitude not only among unions but among employers, politicians and government administrators as well, and it encouraged or even compelled them all to recognize the existence of transformations which had already taken place below the horizon of collective visibility. To this extent the shock of 1889 was probably more effective than the much larger and more lasting explosion of 1911–13. That later upheaval added one-and-a-half million members (or 66 per cent) to the forces of unionism and was accompanied by 3,165 strikes totalling 60 million man-days lost in three years: a far greater concentration of industrial conflicts than in any previous period of the same length. The absence of adequate statistics before 1892 makes it impossible to measure the impact of the years 1889–90, but the membership of the TUC increased by 650,000 (80 per cent) between 1888 and the peak year of 1890, with about 2,400 stoppages and 11 million man-days lost in 1889 and 1890.[11] However, unlike the membership acquired in 1911–13, more than a third of the new membership of 1888–90 had been lost by 1893, largely by the collapse of most of the New Unions of 1889. Their relative weight in the organized labour movement – impossible to estimate precisely given the absence of reliable official membership figures before 1892 and indeed the unreliability of the New Unions' own statistics – was pretty certainly rather larger for a moment in 1889–90 than in 1911–13, but the mean size of strikes was at most a quarter of that in 1911–13, though the number of strikes per year was substantially larger. Many strikes in 1888–90 were not recorded at all.

The size and impact of the 1889 shock was unexpected, but not in retrospect surprising. When industrial discontents have, for one reason or another, accumulated without being able to unload their charge of tension, the consequent outburst is almost inevitably large and dramatic, all the more so because in such situations the demonstration effect of the initial struggles is spectacular, especially if they are successful. The outbreak of mass unionism in Brazil and Poland in recent years illustrates this effect. On the whole the strikes of 1889 were extremely successful: of 1,051 whose outcome is known only 20 per cent were lost, 45 per cent were victorious, the rest settled by compromise.[12] This was partly because the moment of the trade cycle was well chosen for union demands, partly because in the pace-setting industries of the 1889 outburst, waterside labour and the gas industry, the mechanism which accumulated tension also created, or coincided with, unusual bargaining strength among the workers. For the gas industry the arguments put forward several years ago still stand.[13] As for water transport, 1889 was a record year both for outward and homeward freight rates, which explains why this was a good year for the young seamen's union to launch its national attack on a highly competitive industry. It was only defeated in Liverpool by the common front of the sixteen Atlantic liner companies, sufficiently small in number to concert their action.[14] As for the dockers, John Lovell has demonstrated how inflammable was the combination in London of a rapidly growing traffic, essentially loaded and unloaded by speeding up labour that operated by primitive manual methods, with pressure on the dock companies' profits which made them attempt actually to cut labour costs.[15] At least the first of these two factors applied to most British ports. In short, employers had for many years relied on squeezing workers, who now found themselves both relatively more indispensable and confronting employers who could not afford to face the cost of lengthy disputes.

John Mavor, who analysed the Scottish railway strike at the time, summarizes the position. 'The strike', he thought, 'is best described as a revolt of labourers against the inefficient organisation of their industry.' The Scottish railways had grown too rapidly, without either adapting their structure or modernizing their equipment, meanwhile indulging in cutthroat competition between their two main lines. 'There is not', observed Mavor, 'an unlimited number of highly skilled artisans from which efficient workers may be promptly drawn. The artisan class has come to consist of a great number of strata, skill being specialised highly, and even localised on each plane. This gives an increasing amount of power to certain strata of artisans. . . . The widely extended paralysis caused by a strike of at most 9,000 men was a significant and serious circumstance.' In fact, though the companies fought the dispute to a finish and destroyed the union, they could not afford to sack the strikers en masse; only a little over 500 men of all grades in three railway companies were victimized.[16]

Such was the situation in established industries and occupations. In so far as the New Unionism was the organization of unions in *new* industries and occupations, it was as yet largely symbolic. It symbolized the future, the shape of things to come. In this sense the beginnings of white-collar, distributive trades' and public service unionism or the foundation of the Electrical Trades Union are significant. In the short run such unions, in so far as they survived, were as yet neither large nor successful.

Two conclusions can be drawn from this brief analysis. First, that the unions and strikes may have been 'new', but they were provoked by the fact that industry was the opposite of new. It had, by and large, kept pace with expansion not by modernization and rationalization, but by increasing the exploitation of its labour force in the old way. Rationalization was sometimes the response to the shock of 1889–90, not the other way round. No doubt the pressure on prices and profits during the long years of the Great Depression encouraged such a policy, while at the same time depression made organized labour disinclined to offensive action, and postponed any revival of unionism in industries which had been briefly organized during the great boom of the early 1870s, but had been unable to maintain organization. The first battles of the future New Unionists in the mid-1880s had been precisely against this defensiveness of the old unions. As Tom Mann said in 1886, 'the true Unionist policy of aggression seems entirely lost sight of'.[17] And when the moment of successful aggression came, the example of success, or even the sight of hitherto inactive and demoralized workers going on strike, had a snowball effect.

However, there is a second conclusion. The lasting success of new unions or of union expansion depended on the readiness of employers to accept them. As it happened, British employers were quite prepared in principle to do so. Of the employers' suggestions for preventing or settling disputes which the Board of Trade collected in 1889–90, only 20 per cent were hostile to unions or intransigent, and this percentage tended, if anything, to diminish over the next four years.[18] The attitude of the civil service was, as we know, favourable to a strong but moderate trade unionism. On the other hand large employers, or those capable of co-ordinated action, were in a position to counter-attack or resist 'old' or New Unions if these went beyond what they thought they could tolerate or afford. A balance was normally recognized by both sides, but a major explosion of trade unionism inevitably disturbed it in four ways.

First, it extended unionism to industries or types of workers to which or whom the old and essentially localized and sectional form of collective bargaining hitherto dominant, was inapplicable. Thus on the docks unions had either to be mass closed shops or confined to small bodies of specialists, while on the railways the unit of negotiation was normally neither a single plant nor a locality, but ideally, the entire rail system of a company. Second, sudden and uncontrolled unionization could affect the labour process, either by lowering productivity or by cutting into managerial functions. Old unionists might intensify restrictive practices, inexperienced and undisciplined new unionists might simply work less hard – a very real problem in the London docks of 1890. Third, a vast extension of unionism brought to the fore issues which were by definition *national*, such as the Eight-Hour Day or the principle of mechanization. Such issues were seen to require co-ordinated action by both sides as soon as unions were sufficiently widespread and extensively organized. Thus by 1893 even a simple wage reduction in the coalmines implied a simultaneous nationwide dispute, since the major coalfields (outside Wales, Scotland and the north-east) were now co-ordinated in the new Miners' Federation of Great Britain. Fourth, the sheer scale of such disputes had no precedent. Thus *The Times* commented, in 1890, apropos of a brief and successful wage-strike by the Miners' Federation, that 'twenty or even ten years ago it would have been out of the question for 300,000 workmen to combine so perfectly as to stop work at one moment and to resume it at another'.[19]

A counter-attack, spearheaded by large or newly federated employers, was therefore bound to develop, and it did so from 1890. It wiped out most of the New Unionism, and thus made a second and delayed instalment of the expansion inevitable. It was, after all, hardly conceivable that an industry like the railways would permanently remain without effective unions, except perhaps those of engine-drivers. For two reasons that second instalment largely took the form of a revival or expansion of the New Unionism of 1889, or of others formed along similar lines from time to time thereafter. First, because few attempts were made to eliminate unions altogether or to deny their right to exist. Nobody negotiated with the Amalgamated Society of Railway Servants and still less with the enfeebled General Railway Workers' Union, but they were not banned, and therefore capable of rapid expansion when occasion arose. They could therefore grow slowly, occasionally expanding and relapsing as in 1897 when the so-called 'all-grades movement' briefly doubled their numbers. Second, because of the discovery of the device of the 'general union' which established its capacity to survive, not as an all-embracing union of unspecialized labourers, but as a changing conglomerate of miscellaneous local and regional groups of workers in particular industries, occupations and plants.[20]

However, the second instalment differed significantly from the first. In the first place, it organized not only the empty spaces in the existing Victorian industries, but also new, technically and organizationally transformed industries. This is very clear in the metal sector. Of the million members added to the TUC between 1910 and 1914, about 200,000 were in the Amalgamated Engineers and in the Workers' Union which, as Richard Hyman has shown, was primarily a body of semi-skilled engineering workers.[21] Even without counting this union, the numbers in the metal, engineering and shipbuilding unions rose by 50 per cent between 1910 and 1913. In the second place, the economic and political setting of unionism had meanwhile changed fundamentally. Bargaining was increasingly industry-wide and industrial conflicts interlocked, not only because employers drew together when faced with co-ordinated unions, but because industry itself, and indeed all sectors of the industrial economy, were increasingly seen as strategically interlocked. Without entering into the debate on how far Lenin's analysis of monopoly capitalism applied to pre-1914 Britain, it is hard to deny that British capitalism between 1890 and 1910 grew in scale, and became more tightly structured in its organization than it had been in the 1880s. In short, while the outbreak of 1889 had consisted largely of a wave of local and generally not very large strikes propagated by chain reaction, the 1911 outburst was dominated by national confrontations, or battles deliberately engaged by national armies, as Lord Askwith's Memoirs vividly demonstrate.[22] The cotton industry, stronghold of the old localism and individualism, illustrates this transformation very clearly.

The sensitiveness of government to labour disputes underlined and intensified this national and organized dimension of industrial conflict. Quite apart from the fact that employees in the rapidly growing public sector – as yet in local rather than central government employment – had become increasingly involved in trade unionism since 1889,[23] public authorities had three reasons for intervening in, and therefore shaping, the pattern of trade unionism. They now operated under a largely working-class electorate, whose pressures and demands they had to take account of, if only in order to prevent the class polarization of British politics. They had for the first time to confront the problem of how to meet a general disruption of the economy or of national life by national disputes in particular industries, and especially in transport and coal. And from the 1890s on they were increasingly aware of the relative vulnerability of the British economy to foreign competition. British labour and industrial relations began to be regarded as a relevant aspect of British 'national efficiency'. This had not been so before 1880.[24] From 1893 on, and especially after 1906, central government intervention in large disputes became a regular incident in the industrial drama, and since its major objective was rapid settlement, its net effect was to strengthen trade unionism, if only by providing it with official recognition. It might be added that the government's wider social programme had the incidental effect of providing new or weak unions with the means of surviving defeat. The National Insurance Act allowed them to acquire the advantages of Friendly Societies without high subscriptions, and therefore provided workers with a reason for maintaining membership. The war made this integration of unions into the administrative system permanent. Trade unionism in agriculture had virtually been wiped out after the 1870s, and was again destroyed after the 1889 explosion. It was not very strong in 1914, but it has never disappeared from the scene since then.

The novelty of the new phase is reflected in the differences between the strategies of union reform in 1889 and 1911. In both cases the object of the reformers, largely drawn from the contemporary left or ultra-left, was to replace defensive by aggressive, sectional by class unionism. However, in the 1880s the alternative was extremely vague, as indeed was the strategy to achieve it; perhaps naturally so in view of the extreme paucity of socialist thinking about trade unionism. In retrospect the reforming programme appears to have consisted of three points. First, New Unions were to be created for hitherto unorganized labour, either consisting of the generally unskilled, believed to be mobile and interchangeable, or the occupationally more specialized for whom suitable occupational unions might be found. Second, the membership of existing craft unions should be extended to embrace the less skilled grades and negotiate for all; and third, the struggles of different groups of workers should be co-ordinated locally through trades councils and nationally through a radicalized TUC as well as through political action in favour of uniform and generally applicable demands such as the Legal Eight-Hour Day. The most significant result of this programme was the invention of the 'general union', but in a form which had been neither intended nor predicted, and which did not demonstrate its full potentialities until after 1911. By and large, the attempts to broaden the old craft unions failed. The TUC did not stay radicalized for long, and the Trades Councils, whose expulsion from the TUC in 1895 marks the end of the radical phase, remained on the fringes of trade unionism. Indeed, they probably played a less active role in the second expansion than they had in the first.

The second phase, on the other hand, was inseparably linked with conscious and well-considered attempts to rationalize and reform trade union structure and strategy, the former mainly by amalgamation and federation ideally aiming at one union for each industry. The attraction of industrial unionism for its main spokesmen, like that of the general unionism of 1889, may initially have been political. It could be seen as a version of class unionism against sectionalism, or even as a preparation for the syndicalist society of the future. However, the extent to which trade union structure and strategy were debated for the twenty years after 1906, the wave of actual federations and amalgamations which took place, the experiments in joint national union strategy and battle from the Triple Alliance of 1914 to the General Strike, suggest that the stimulus for reform was by no means only ideological. 'Old' and New Unions now plainly felt the need to adapt themselves to conditions of industrial action which they recognized as new. This did not produce any significant general shift towards industrial unionism. In spite of the enthusiastic and persistent advocacy of this pattern of organization by the left, and even the occasional commitment of the TUC to it, as at Hull in 1924, the reorganization of the British union movement along industrial lines was and has remained an unrealistic aspiration. However, about the major advances of the reform movement after 1911 there can be no doubt at all. The British trade unions were largely restructured, even though some of the major amalgamations did not take place until after the war, when the decline in union membership made rationalization more urgent.

III

A comparative approach reveals that the question of trade union structure arose, and was hotly debated, in all countries, but solved in very different ways. One major division is between countries which firmly opted for an essentially national unionism, with whatever concessions to local autonomy were necessary, and those which opted for localism or federalism, except in industries like the railways where it would not have made sense at all. The local and federal option, which clearly prevailed in France and Italy, was ideologized by anarchist and syndicalist thinkers, but essentially it represented the apparent irrelevance of the national economy for collective bargaining, or conversely, the potential strength of a purely local unionism, which is not to be underestimated in certain circumstances. Thus building unions in the United States have always flourished by establishing local craft monopolies, since the building and public works market of American cities is largely autonomous. Again, economic general strikes or extensive local sympathy strikes with one occupational dispute, are most likely to occur in towns – most typically port towns – whose economy is, as it were, topographically determined. Hence in the early 1900s such strikes occurred typically in such cities as Trieste (1902), Marseilles (1904), Genoa (1904), Barcelona (1902), Amsterdam (1903).[25] The relative insignificance of the national dimension in a country like France is shown by the fact that, according to *Confédération Générale du Travail* (CGT) statutes, the minimum number of (local) unions needed to form a national federation was no more than three.[26] It is clear that in countries like Britain and Germany the local option took second place to the national and regional option, though the degree of centralization envisaged was variable, and that achieved was much smaller in practice than in theory.

The second major issue was between craft or occupational unionism and various forms of more comprehensive organization covering a number of crafts or grades of skill within one industry, or more generally. The ideological history of 'industrial unionism' remains to be written. There is not even as yet an adequate history of the very concept of the specific 'industry' or of what led socialists, no doubt following official statisticians and others, to draw up a list of unions each of which was to be ideally coextensive with the appropriate 'industry', all of whose workers it was designed to organize. What – to mention the most systematic effort of this kind – led the Austrian socialists to envisage just sixteen industries, some-what inconsistently selected?[27]

However that may be, it is obvious that the struggle for a more com-prehensive union structure was universal and directed primarily against craft and other sectionalism and its 'trade consciousness'. Outside Britain this sectionalism was primarily confined to old handicraft occupations. To the extent that all unionism before about 1890 was 'old unionism', the problems faced in all countries were similar, though the solutions could be highly specific. In certain cases craft unionism could work successfully even in the most patently 'industrial' industries, as on the American railroads where a complex of thirty-two unions, fourteen of them of major significance, covered the industry in 1940. Conversely, under certain circumstances even a trade as enormously proud of craft status as the Amalgamated Society of Engineers could call for a more comprehensive recruitment of the occupa-tional labour force – for instance in Western Australia, as distinct from all other parts of the world.[28]

While a more comprehensive unionism advanced everywhere, it did not entirely succeed anywhere. Neither craft unions nor their correlative, labourers' or general or indiscriminate 'factory workers'' unions dis-appeared totally, even in countries with strong national trade union centres committed to industrial unionism. All union movements thus developed as a mixture of narrower or wider craft/occupational unions, of industrial unions coexisting with them or absorbing them, and of general unions – but in different combinations. In the British mix industrial unions were not important, except for mining and railways. In the Norwegian mix general unions were temporarily dominant, though eventually (1954) they were to cover no more than 5 to 6 per cent of union membership,[29] whereas in Britain they became increasingly important, especially when considering that the recent tendency to form conglomerate unions (as by the merger of the engineering union with foundryworkers and draughtsmen, the elec-tricians with the plumbers) is essentially similar to general unionism. In Austria general unions were absent. More examples could be added.

Thus the Norwegian union movement, committed to industrial unionism since 1923, in 1954 consisted of forty-three unions some of which can only be described as craft societies, for example, the Lithographic and Photo-engravers. The locomotive men organized themselves separately from the railway workers and the bricklayers separately from the building workers. And of course there was the Union of General Workers too. Industrial unionism has met considerable resistance even within the metalworking industry, where the internal pressures to build industry-wide unions in the twentieth century have almost everywhere been stronger than in any other industry except railways, coalmining and government employment.[30] Most unionism has remained mixed. In this respect there is a certain parallelism between the British and continental movements.

The most comprehensive industrial unions, leaving aside mines, railways and the public sector, were those founded and structured from outside and above, in effect as frameworks for subsequent expansion – like the Metal-workers' Federation in Italy which, before 1914, was nationally negligible.

Evidently this implied both an influential working-class party and absent or relatively weak earlier trade unions. The formation of general textile workers' unions, such as were common elsewhere, could hardly have been envisaged in Britain, where cotton had long been organized on its own. The relative success of industrial unionism elsewhere and its failure in Britain are thus largely explained.

For the same reason, general unions, though not absent in Europe, lacked the scope for development they had in Britain. Where most organizable workers could be fitted, if they wanted to, into some already notionally existing national union, there was room for genuinely unclassifiable labourers' unions or for workers in factories who could not be readily attached to some already classified union. Such bodies existed in Germany, Sweden, Denmark and Norway, but unlike the British general unions they were residual. As soon as enough workers had been organized in the relevant branches of activity, separate industrial unions – for example, those of sawmill workers or paper and pulp workers – could be hived off the general association. The strength of the British general unions lay in their ability to penetrate any and every industry in the absence of any other kind of union which could fill the spaces deliberately left empty by the refusal of craft unions to fill them. Quite often they would generate de facto industrial unions, but there was no particular reason why these should separate from the general unions within which they formed separate sectors or trade groups, such as the dockers in the Transport and General Workers' Union.

But why did industrial unions progress on the continent, unlike in Britain, in spite of the already observed reluctance of skilled and craft groups, which was very marked, especially in the 1890s? For these groups, after all, still formed the natural nucleus of unionization, and it was among them that the most rapid advances were usually apt to occur. One reason, it may be suggested, was that much apparent 'industrial unionism' or what turned into 'industrial unionism' on the continent, was really the analogue of the so-called 'new model' of the British unions in the 1850s and 1860s. It envisaged essentially the formation of nationwide, relatively centralized, amalgamations of fairly closely associated craft occupations. It is perhaps no accident that the two typical 'new model' unions of mid-Victorian Britain, the Amalgamated Society of Engineers and the Amalgamated Society of Carpenters and Joiners, had their equivalents in the *Deutsche Holzarbeiterverband* (German Woodworkers' Union) and the *Deutsche Metallarbeiterverband* (German Metalworkers' Union), which for most of the 1890s were both the strongest unions in Germany, and the most strongly committed to industrial unionism. However, the case of the metalworkers, or more precisely the machine-builders, suggests another possible reason.

Almost everywhere unions of such workers opted for industrial unionism; or rather the ones which chose this option eventually prevailed. This was because in metalworking the position of the skilled manual craftsmen was increasingly vulnerable and, apart from a few protected enclaves, threatened by the advance of complex machine tools and mass production. Skilled metalworkers were powerful, but not secure. The war years were to demonstrate that in all belligerent countries the armaments industries formed the front line of the industrial class battle. They did so precisely because here mechanization encountered self-confident, combative, often politically conscious skilled men who resisted downgrading. But the fact that the line between the apprenticed skilled craftsmen, the skilled worker who 'picked up the trade', and the new categories of the semi-skilled workers or those with only the narrowest range of skills, became increasingly hazy, made it advisable for unions of skilled metalworkers not only to defend craft exclusiveness, but also to seek to recruit the growing mass of production workers whom they could no longer hope effectively to exclude. The two policies were sometimes in conflict. In Britain rank-and-file resistance to broadening the Amalgamated Society of Engineers into something closer to an industrial union was strong, and a constant brake on the reforming policies of the union leaders.[31] Where craft privilege was less entrenched and powerful, the forces favouring the broadening of the unions were stronger, or rather those resisting it were weaker. The weakness of craft unionism in metals, and the foresight of the continental pioneers of industrial unionism, based on a combination of feeble unions and radical ideology, is demonstrated by the eventual success of continental metalworkers' unions in organizing the motor industry, for example in France and Italy. In the United States this industry was to be organized in the 1930s by a special industrial union, the craft union of skilled 'machinists' having long been extruded from it. In Britain, the organization of the majority of automobile workers was in practice to be left to the general unions, mainly the Transport and General Workers' Union, leaving the unions of skilled workers in a minority; though they had proved in the struggles of the 1890s and 1900s that they were too strong to be overridden. In Italy and France the choice was either between no union or the industrial union of metalworkers, and indeed in Turin the *Federazione Impiegati Operai Metallurgici* won its first major automobile contract in 1906, when it succeeded in organizing 40 per cent of all metalworkers in the city.[32]

The new phase of capitalism thus implied a change in union structure, but also in the distribution of trade unionism. Here also a comparison between the British and continental cases is possible and useful. Where mass unionism established itself – as it had not yet done in France and Italy by 1914, except for the Italian agricultural workers who formed one-third of all trade unionists in 1910[33] – its distribution had by 1914 changed both geographically and industrially.

The general pattern of change shows a growth in the union of transport workers, of factory workers, whether organized in general, industrial or 'factory workers'' unions, the rise of the miners – where these were not already well organized – and the expansion of the metalworkers' unions. Thus in Germany transport, metalworkers and factory workers formed 12 per cent of the membership of the Free Unions in 1896, but almost 39 per cent in 1913. The rise in Britain – from 33 per cent to 39 per cent – was less marked, because metals had already been strongly organized and grew rather slowly, that is, by a little more than 100 per cent between 1892 and 1913, thus concealing the quadrupling of the organized transport workers and the equivalent rise among general workers. In 1888, which is in many ways more comparable to the Germany of the 1890s, transport and general workers had comprised perhaps 8 per cent of British unionists, as against 25 per cent in 1913.[34]

As for the regional distribution, it is clear that the German unions in the early 1900s were weak in the major industrial area of Rhine-Westphalia, with the fluctuating exception of the miners, but that their penetration into this region accelerated after 1907.[35] In Britain the old trade unionism was deeply rooted in the major industrial areas of northern England, though not of Scotland. The only geographical analysis remains that made by the Webbs in 1892, who found – roughly speaking – at least twice the mean density of national unionization in Durham, Northumberland and Lancashire, from 20 per cent to 100 per cent above the mean in the counties of Derby, Gloucester, Leicester, the East and West Ridings of Yorkshire and South Wales, mean density – plus or minus 20 per cent – in Cheshire, Northampton, Stafford, Suffolk, Warwick and Scotland, and below the average everywhere else.[36] Whatever a comparable geographical study for 1913 would show, it seems clear that the union explosion of 1911–13 made disproportionate progress in some hitherto rather weak areas, such as the dynamic new engineering regions of the West Midlands. This area now contained 40 per cent of the strength of the Workers' Union, which now became one of the five or six largest unions in the country.[37]

One final question has already been answered incidentally in the course of this paper, but is worth elucidating clearly. What was the role of the ideologically committed leftists who played so large a part in the union expansions of all European countries during this period? First of all, it must be repeated that neither Marx nor Marxist theory had anything very specific to say about trade union structure and strategy, as distinct from the workers' immediate economic and social demands. And this in spite of the fact that, as Georgee Haupt has shown, the bulk of the continental socialist parties initially developed closer to the British than to the German social-democratic model – or more exactly, closer to the Belgian model, in which the party consisted of a combination of political groups, unions and other labour organizations such as co-operatives. Admittedly the Great Depression of the 1870s and 1880s tended to shift the centre of gravity of most such parties away from the enfeebled unions.[38] Furthermore union strategy derived from socialist theory a general hostility to exclusive, craft, or sectional unionism, but it also increasingly derived strategic ideas from the Marxist analysis of the concentration and mechanization of capitalist production, especially after 1900.

With the rise of both mass unionism and mass working-class parties, socialists who were primarily active in unions became increasingly distinct from socialists who were primarily active in the political party. This was most dramatically evident in trade union movements which, like the French CGT, and anarchist or revolutionary syndicalist bodies in general, specifically rejected political action which was largely confined to electoral efforts, but almost equally evident in movements closely identified with the working-class party, even though a union position was a very helpful springboard for workers who wished to launch themselves into a political career in markedly proletarian parties such as the German Social Democratic Party (SPD); and even though unions might wish, by strengthening their direct representation in parliamentary fractions, to underline their dominant position within the party as in Britain[39] or their increased independence within it as in Germany.[40] This divergence, often accompanied by friction between party and unions, arose chiefly from the functional specialization of both. Whether the union's daily work was or was not conceived as the overthrow of capitalism, it was not the same as the party's activity, which could therefore be seen, according to taste and situation, either as an excessively radical diversion from the unions' bread-and-butter tasks, for instance by calling for political strikes, or as diversionary electoral activity distracting the workers from their direct assault upon the system. But it also arose from the differences within unions, such as the tensions between rank-and-file or local militancy and the increasingly assertive national organizations. Judged by revolutionary criteria, the leaders of national unions or union federations were excessively reformist, as indeed almost all were in theory or practice. This could apply even to syndicalist unions in the eyes of pure anarchists, as witness the struggles, during and after the First World War, between these and the leaders of the anarcho-syndicalist *Confederatione Nacional del Trabajo* in Spain. Leaders were less radical than militants: Verzi, the founder of the Italian Metalworkers' Federation, was expelled from it in 1909 as a reformist, and Buozzi who replaced him, though not the most extreme of moderates, was decidedly no leftist and was to be denounced by the young communists of *Ordine Nuovo*.[41]

In fact revolutionary slogans alone made sense chiefly where unions were too weak to do more than organize the occasional rebellions of the unorganized, or in the preparation of great industrial battles, or as a defence of rank-and-file autonomy, or of localized unionism, against encroaching national bureaucracy and centralized strategy. This could lead to paradoxical situations, as in Britain, where the most socialist in origin of all unions, the Gasworkers', had by 1914 become distinctly moderate, while the rank and file of the far from revolutionary Amalgamated Society of Engineers resisted its socialist General Secretary, George Barnes of the Independent Labour Party, on the basis of the ideology of old craft exclusiveness, before discovering – during the war – a radical left-wing justification for their defence of craft rights. Classifying unions as right or left may make sense in terms of their support of, or opposition to, various political and party programmes and proposals, but, as every student of British trade unionism today knows, things are rather more complex in reality. In general during the period 1880–1914 those unions which were associated with labour and socialist parties and movements, tended to maintain their party identification, in spite of friction between union and party or within unions.

Undoubtedly the role of socialists was important and could be decisive as on the continent where the strength and national presence of mass parties with mass electorates provided a framework into which unions could grow, and thus helped to rationalize union structure. Nevertheless, it can be said that the development of union structure and strategy were largely independent of the prevalent ideology, Marxist, anarcho-syndicalist, or otherwise;

except in as much as political consciousness provided trade union agitators, leaders and activists with confidence, persistence and dynamism. Structure and strategy largely reflected the actual economic and industrial situation in which workers had to organize, and the conditions – including those created by the past history and development of the working class – in which they did so. This is probably the main reason why syndicalism, though its appeal to labour militants and radicals was large and international in the years before 1914, was never really an international movement, as distinct from an internationally useful set of ideas. It naturally made a greater appeal in countries of weak or unstable unionism such as Spain, France and Italy – but also in Scandinavia[42] – than in countries with strong unionism and fairly steady growth such as Germany, Britain and Denmark. It naturally appealed to boom-town industrialization reminiscent of the Wild West, as in the South Wales coalfield or in provincial Norway, where masses of raw workers from the countryside or abroad flooded into a new industry which already had a union framework – unless these greenhorns were themselves organized by bodies opposed to socialism. It probably had a special appeal to workers whose essential frame of reference was the local community as much as, or more than, their industry or occupation; this seemed to have been the case in Spain, Italy and France. Nor should those special cases among local communities, the seaport towns, be ignored: Marseilles, Le Havre, Nantes, Genoa, Livorno, Barcelona, Belfast, Liverpool.[43] The varying appeal of syndicalist ideas can be explained, but it remains true, as Edward Shorter and Charles Tilly have shown, that in France ideological differences account for almost none of the differences in the propensity to strike or the forms of strike action.[44]

So it seems best to distinguish the various union movements of Europe not ideologically, but according to the phase and rate of industrialization they represent. Thus a distinction can be made between countries of weak or backward industrialization, such as France or Italy, countries dominated by the first industrial revolution like Belgium and Britain, and countries rapidly and massively industrializing along more modern lines, such as Germany and Scandinavia. None of them, except for the 'workshop of the world', had developed craft or professional trade unionism which had succeeded in colonizing the basic industries of the country; certainly not Belgium, which perhaps lacked the large skilled sector of Britain. In fact, throughout this period Belgian unions remained unusually weak, barely stronger in 1913 than those of the much less or more recently industrialized Netherlands. Hence none developed the British pattern.

The first group developed no mass unionism in this period, except in the public sector, perhaps in the mines and – a special Italian case – among agricultural workers. It developed fairly strong inter-union local centres of mobilization and cadres of craft workers capable of leading occasional battles. The third group ranged from countries suddenly plunged into a novel industrial development, like Norway, where modern industries were organized by a general union which virtually dominated the entire movement in the 1900s with 50 per cent of total membership before spawning various industrial unions, to countries like Germany, where fairly strong craft-based unions extended their field, before other workers were organized in such unions as those of transport workers and factory workers. Once again, by 1913 this combination of industrial and general unionism dominated the field. Nevertheless, as already observed, in none of these countries was craft unionism eliminated. In the countries forming the latter two groups trade unionism had, by 1913, begun to take its modern shape, allowing for subsequent occupational changes. In none of them, however, had it succeeded in recruiting the majority of workers in any industry as a national whole. Rare exceptions only proved the rule.

The trade union density in Britain, Denmark and Norway at the end of the First World War was to be between twice and three times the percentage of 1913, in Sweden and the Netherlands more than three times, in Belgium almost five times as high. One cannot conclude this survey without observing that in some cases – notably Britain and Germany – the strength of trade unions as a percentage of the labour force was higher than it has ever been since, in others – France, Denmark, perhaps Norway – it was not reached again before the middle or late 1930s. Should the great leap forward of unionism during and after the First World War not be seen as the logical continuation of the pattern of trade union expansion in the period 1880–1914? To this extent the New Unionism of the period before 1914 reached its apogee in 1918–20. In this respect the British and Western European movements are, once again, comparable. And the measure of this remarkable international growth – and temporary radicalization – is also a measure of the historical significance of the phase of union development which is the subject of this book.

Notes: Chapter 1

1 The term New Unionism dates back to the 1880s. cf. *A Speech by John Burns on the Liverpool Congress* (London, 1890), 6.
2 G. Haupt, 'Socialisme et syndicalisme. Les rapports entre partis et syndicats au plan international: une mutation?' in M. Réberioux (ed.), *Jaurès et la classe ouvrière* (Paris, 1981), 29–66 (50).
3 Calculated from data in G. D. H. Cole, *British Working Class Politics, 1832 to 1914* (London, 1941), 228–30, 236–8.
4 G. S. Bain and R. Price, *Profiles of Union Growth: A Comparative Statistical Portrait of Eight Countries* (Oxford, 1980), 170.
5 H. A. Clegg *et al.*, *A History of British Trade Unions since 1889*, Vol. 1 (Oxford, 1964), ch. 7.
6 H. Pelling, *The Origins of the Labour Party 1880–1900*, 2nd edn. (Oxford, 1965), 225 for estimates.
7 cf. the use of this tactic in E. Pouget, *Le sabotage* (Bibliothèque du Mouvement Prolétarien xiii, Paris, n.d.), 5–8 where it is described as *une importation anglaise*.
8 International conferences attended by secretaries of national union federations were held from 1901, an international secretariat existed from 1903, an International Federation of Trade Unions from 1913. By 1912 we have record of thirty-two international trade secretariats for particular branches of unionism. However, such forms of international trade union co-ordination were not of much practical importance.
9 cf. E. J. Hobsbawm, 'Economic fluctuations and some social movements', in idem, *Labouring Men* (London, 1964), 126–57.
10 cf. E. H. Hunt, *Regional Wage Variations in Britain 1850–1914* (Oxford, 1973), 354.

11 For TU membership, B. C. Roberts, *The Trades Union Congress 1868–1921* (London, 1958), 379; for the best strike estimates, Clegg *et al.*, *History of British Trade Unions*, 489.
12 Report on the Strikes and Lock-Outs of 1889, 1890, C. 6176, LXVIII.
13 cf. E. J. Hobsbawm, 'British gas-workers, 1873–1914', in idem, *Labouring Men*, 158–78.
14 Clegg *et al.*, *History of British Trade Unions*, 55–6.
15 J. Lovell, *Stevedores and Dockers: A Study of Trade Unionism in the Port of London, 1870–1914* (London, 1969), ch. 2. cf. also R. Brown, *Waterfront Organization in Hull 1870–1900* (Hull, 1972); E. L. Taplin, *Liverpool Dockers and Seamen, 1870–1890* (Hull, 1974); M. Daunton, 'The Cardiff Coal Trimmers' Union 1888–1912', *Llafur* 3 (1978): 10–23.
16 For the Scottish railway strike of 1890 see Clegg *et al.*, *History of British Trade Unions*, 232–3; P. S. Bagwell, *The Railwaymen: The History of the National Union of Railwaymen* (London, 1963), 139–49; J. Mavor, *The Scottish Railway Strike* (London, 1891). Quotations are from J. Mavor, 'The Scottish railway strike', *Economic Journal* 1 (1891): 204–17 (215).
17 *What a Compulsory Eight-Hour Day Means to the Workers*, cited in E. J. Hobsbawm (ed.), *Labour's Turning Point 1880–1900* (Brighton, 1974), 72.
18 Reports on Strikes and Lock-Outs: for 1889, 1890, C. 6176, LXVIII; for 1890, 1890–1, C. 6476, LXVIII; for 1891, 1893–4, C. 6890, LXXXIII; for 1892, 1894, C. 7403, LXXXI; for 1893, C. 7566, ibid., Table VI.
19 R. H. Gretton, *A Modern History of the English People*, 2 vols (London, 1913), 1: 263. The strike only affected about 100,000 workers, but the exaggeration is itself significant.
20 cf. E. J. Hobsbawm, 'General labour unions in Britain, 1889–1914', in idem, *Labouring Men*, 179–203.
21 R. Hyman, *The Workers' Union* (Oxford, 1971), 38–40.
22 G. R. Askwith, *Industrial Problems and Disputes* (London, 1920).
23 The fashion for municipalizing public utilities and services swelled the number of publicly employed manual workers in this period.
24 Leone Levi in 1877 specifically claimed that he had 'proved . . . that up to 1873 at least the trade and industry of England had not suffered from the many disturbances which have taken place – at least not to any material extent –, and that foreign competition had not gained upon British industry'. L. Levi, *Work and Pay* (London, 1877), 94. For the new attitude see R. Davidson, 'Government administration', in C. J. Wrigley (ed.), *A History of British Industrial Relations 1875–1920* (Brighton, 1982), 159–87 (163, 169).
25 For a useful sketch of US building trade unionism cf. H. A. Millis (ed.), *How Collective Bargaining Works* (New York, 1942), ch. 4, 183–228; for early twentieth-century local general strikes cf. E. Georgi, *Theorie und Praxis des Generalstreiks* (Jena, 1908).
26 M. Leroy, *La coutume ouvrière*, 2 vols (Paris, 1913), 1:387. National unions with branches, as distinct from federations of local unions, were virtually confined in the early 1900s to the French railways and postal service.
27 They were, in alphabetical order as given in the *Handwörterbuch der Staatswissenschaften* (1902 edition), Vol. 4, p. 682, article 'Gewerkvereine': (1) Building, (2) Clothing, (3) Mining, (4) Chemical, (5) Iron and metal, (6) Gas and water, (7) Glass and pottery, (8) Printing and paper, (9) Commerce, (10) Wood, (11) Horn, bone and tortoiseshell, (12) Agriculture, (13) Food and drink, (14) Textiles, (15) Transport, (16) Women's industries.
28 K. D. Buckley, *The Amalgamated Engineers in Australia, 1852–1920* (Canberra, 1970), 212; the reason is suggested on p. 150.
29 E. Bull, *The Norwegian Trade Union Movement* (Brussels, 1956), 46–8, 128–30.
30 For the early difficulties of the French *métallos*, cf. P. Louis, *Histoire du mouvement syndical en France* (Paris, 1920), 191–2; for the logic of industrial unionism as seen by intelligent militants cf. E. Dolléans, *Alphonse Merrheim* (Paris, n.d. [1939?]), 9–11; M. Antonioli and B. Bezza, *La FIOM dalle origini al Fascismo 1901–1924* (Bari, 1978), 17–18.
31 J. B. Jefferys, *The Story of the Engineers* (London, 1945), 137–8, 166.
32 For the 1906 contract cf. P. Spriano, *Storia di Torino operaia e socialista* (Turin, 1972), 136–46; Antonioli and Bezza, *La FIOM*, 719–37, for pre–1914 automobile collective contracts. For France, P. Fridenson, *Histoire des usines Renault* (Paris, 1972), 73–9, demonstrates the contemporary weakness of what was essentially craft unionism in this industry, and the eventual success (1936) of industrial unionism reinforced by communist political organization (p. 268). For the 1912–13 strikes against Taylorism, see C. Gras, 'La

Fédération des Métaux et la crise du syndicalisme révolutionnaire en 1913–1914', *Mouvement Social* (October–December 1971), 92–8. The presence of the British New Unionist Ben Tillett at the strike meetings may be noted.

33 E. Lemonon, *L'Italie économique et sociale (1861–1912)* (Paris, 1913), 406–7.

34 For British unions, Bain and Price, *Profiles of Union Growth*, ch. 2.

35 cf. W. Troeltsch and P. Hirschfeld, *Die deutschen sozialdemokratischen Gewerkschaften. Untersuchungen und Materialien über ihre geographische Verbreitung, 1896–1903* (Berlin, 1907); Haupt, *Socialisme et syndicalisme*, 63–4.

36 S. Webb and B. Webb, *The History of Trade Unionism* (London, 1894), Appendix IV.

37 Hyman, *Workers' Union*, 35, 48.

38 Haupt, *Socialisme et syndicalisme* 33–4. For the Belgian model, see J. Destrée and J. Vandervelde, *Le socialisme en Belgique* (Paris, 1903), 1, ch. 2.

39 In Britain union leaders, particularly among miners, were habitually elected to parliament before 1914, but leaders of cotton workers (Mawdsley, Shackleton), printers (Bowerman), railwaymen (Bell, J. H. Thomas), shipwrights (Wilkie), engineers (Barnes), steelworkers (Hodge), the furniture trades (O'Grady), not to mention the New Unions, stood, or were elected. (For a complete list see Cole, *British Working Class Politics*, Appendix I).

40 W. H. Schröder, 'Sozialstruktur der sozialdemokratischen Reichstagskandidaten 1898–1912', in idem, *Herkunft und Mandat: Beiträge zur Führungsproblematik in der Arbeiterbewegung* (Frankfurt, 1976), 72–96, esp. 94–6.

41 F. Andreucci and T. Detti (eds), *Il movimento operaio italiano: Dizionaro Biografico*, Vol. 1 (Rome, 1974): Buozzi; Vol. 5 (Rome, 1979): Verzi.

42 Swedish union membership in mining and manufacturing rose from 13·7 per cent of the labour force in 1902 to 38·6 per cent in 1907, but fell to 16·3 per cent by 1911 and had only risen to 18·5 per cent in 1913. Bain and Price, *Profiles of Union Growth*, 145.

43 cf. E. Shorter and C. Tilly, *Strikes in France 1830–1968* (Cambridge, 1974) 164–5.

44 ibid., 172.

2 The New Unionism in Britain: its Economic Background

SIDNEY POLLARD

I

The New Unionism cannot be properly analysed without reference to the variety found in the development of different industries in the years around 1889–92 when the British explosion of New Unionism occurred. For no one investigating the economic background can fail to notice the complete lack of congruity between the variety of the workplace experience of different trades, industries and even localities, and the singularity and unity of the trade union phenomenon which it is intended to explain. How can such a variety of multifarious causes lead to the same result in the form of adherence to the New Unionism?

In fact, the matter is even more complex than this. For the phenomena which are to be linked with each other fall into three groups, not two. There is, first of all, an underlying and continuous, even if not regular, upward trend, applying to the whole economy; there is a more irregular trend of rising technology but highly variable economic fortunes, applying separately and very differently to industries and regions; and there are the sudden bursts of trade union advance, of which the New Unionist leap forward of 1889–92 was entirely typical, again covering the industrial scene as a whole. As the juxtaposition of these three will form the main theme to be dealt with here, it will be worthwhile giving a rough outline of each at the outset.

The trend
The late Victorians were, and were conscious of being, on an upward trend along all economic indicators of any significance: national production, exports, real wages, education, and many more. It was not unreasonable to expect a similar long-term rise in the fortunes of trade unions in every industry, albeit with possibly more marked cyclical relapses than were found in other time series. For those who believed that trade unions contributed to the stability and strength of the Victorian economy and society, the growth in numbers and funds and the improved organization and strategies of trade unions seemed a part of the inevitable march of progress. Seen in this light, the New Unionism is not a bump in a level plain but rather a particularly steep section of an upward slope.

The industrial divergences
If the history of trade unions reflects the work experience of wage- and salary-earners, as historians frequently assume, then unionization will take

different forms, and proceed at vastly different speeds, with differing peaks and troughs, in each industry. Thus there are industries with many or few labourers, sometimes employing them directly, sometimes not; others have no crafts, but progression up a ladder, which may be restricted or not, the senior, adult rungs being considered the most promising trade union material; there are industries for which the best strategy is 'closed' unionism, and others in which 'open' unionism offers better opportunities; there are industries employing many women, few, or none; there are sheltered industries and those directly exposed to foreign competition; there are stable and cyclical employments; there are growing, stagnant and declining occupations. The possible and relevant variations are almost endless.

Above all, in as much as mechanization and the structure of the industry itself[1] are held to be major factors influencing the progress of unionization, the installation of machinery and the type of machinery installed, as well as the establishment of a factory system and the consolidation of firms into larger units, will differ widely not only as between industries, but also between regions and individual firms within the same industry. Some workers will find themselves serving near-automatic machinery in huge combines, while others are still plying their needles or hammers at home, working for masters little better off than themselves. Some industries mechanized, as it were, in one go, the breakthrough occurring by a single major technological innovation, while in others a piecemeal process might have extended over a century. Moreover, in one industry mechanization might reduce skills and differentiation among workers, in another it might increase them; in one, it might save labour per unit, but lower costs and broaden the market to such a degree that output rises lead to an extension of employment; in another, the market extension would not be sufficient, and there might be technological unemployment in consequence; in a third, as in coalmining, better technology might merely compensate for the diminishing returns naturally occurring in mines. All these variants were to be found in Britain in the later 1880s.

The big leap forward
Yet the historical fact remains that British trade unions had brief periods when immensely powerful forces seemed to propel workers in all or most industries forward simultaneously, in spite of the profound differences in their experiences and the differing internal logic of their employments. Such leaps forward occurred at fairly regular intervals in 1871–3, in 1889–92 and in 1911–13,[2] the first two being followed in due course by almost equally dramatic declines, whereas the third led directly to the war years when for quite different reasons the upward movement in membership was continued.

The years of discontinuous, bunched trade union advance therefore imposed a kind of rigid grid on the continuous, flexible and variable changes in British industry which were alleged to have influenced them. The spurt of 1889–92 which saw the birth and high point of the New Unionism was one member of that grid. There is an obvious logical weakness in that kind of explanation, almost a paradox. Before turning to the attempt to resolve that paradox, it will be useful to digress in order to deal with another weakness in the traditional story.

II

Recent scholarship has been leading to the inevitable conclusion that the classical picture of events associated with the rise of the New Unionism, and the role of the great London dock strike within it in particular, is largely mythical.[3] There are four main points to the traditional story:[4] (1) that the New Unionism began with the three famous London strikes of 1888–9, those of the match girls, the gas workers and the dockers, the latter providing the main impetus; (2) that the New Unions were made up of unskilled or general workers who had hitherto been thought unorganizable; (3) that workers of this type were unable to afford contributions large enough to pay for friendly benefits, so that funds were used for the purpose of organization and disputes only, which made these New Unions far more militant than the older ones; and (4) that they were also much more strongly politically motivated in the direction of socialist policies, since in the absence of loyalty to a particular trade the members were necessarily more class conscious. Each of these assertions has been challenged by recent findings – as indeed it had by many contemporaries.

The myth that the organization of the unskilled took its beginnings from the London dock strike of August 1889, or possibly the Bryant & May match girls' strike of 1888, has been untenable since A. E. P. Duffy's pioneer article of 1961 at the latest.[5] Even the labourers' unions of the preceding burst of 1871–3 were not the earliest, though it was in those years that they first appeared in larger numbers. Among the most remarkable were the various agricultural labourers' unions, some of which, including the National Agricultural Labourers' Union,[6] survived until the 1890s, and the Amalgamated Society of Railway Servants (ASRS) together with its independent Scottish counterpart (established in 1871 and 1872 respectively) which covered several grades including some clearly unskilled ones. The ASRS has survived in a modified form until the present. Significantly, both of these groups of unions depended initially on middle class and other outside support, as also did the London Dock Strike of 1889.[7] Another important organization was the (London) Labour Protection League of 1871 which survived to be transformed in part into the Amalgamated Stevedores' Society, and in part into the Labour Protection League, South of the River, both of which formed hard nuclei around which the dock strike of 1889 was built.[8] Even the London gas stokers' union had its forerunners in this phase, and the savage sentences of twelve months' imprisonment on five of their leaders after a dispute in 1872 became a *cause célèbre* in the agitation which led to the legislation of 1875. There was also Patrick Kenney's General Labourers' Amalgamated Union, and the wave of organizations among dustmen, shop assistants, Liverpool dockers,[9] cotton porters, omnibus drivers, carmen, a causeway layers' society, and even postal workers and policemen among others. It is of interest that some contemporary opinion pointed to the inherent antagonism between artisans and labourers as a cause of the latter's unionization: 'If the bricklayers strike, they throw not only themselves but their labourers out of employment. It is very natural that these labourers should wish to have a voice ... and the only way to obtain that voice is to make for themselves an organisation similar to that of those Trade Unions.'[10] It is true that few of these survived, and all suffered severe losses of membership after the boom broke; but that applied to the labourers' unions of 1889–92 also.

Nor did the dock strike mark the origins of the wave of New Unionism, but rather the approach to its peak. The rise began in the depth of the slump, in 1886: Tom Mann's *What a Compulsory Eight-Hour Working Day Means to the Workers*, published in that year, has been termed the first manifesto of the New Unions.[11] The National Labour Federation, an organization of semi-skilled workers, was formed in the north-east in 1886, Havelock Wilson's National Amalgamated Union of Sailors and Firemen began its meteoric and at first violent career in 1887 and the Miners' Federation, another union ranging over various grades and definitions of skill, may be said to have been formed in 1888. The ASRS changed from a friendly society into a militant union in the years 1887–91.[12] Branches of the American Knights of Labour, a general union, were established in the mid-1880s and by 1888–9 claimed upwards of 10,000 members in Britain.

In March 1889 the Beckton gas workers, undeterred by failed strikes in 1884 and 1885, struck and formed the first of the classic New Unions, Will Thorne's Gasworkers' and General Labourers' Union. In the north-east, the Tyneside and National Labour Union, founded in February, was destined to become the foundation for another great general union; the building labourers were organized in Leeds in July.

In the docks themselves, there had been not only Ben Tillett's minute Tea Coopers' and General Labour Association dating from 1887 but also the National Amalgamated Labourers' Union (South Wales) in 1888 and the National Union of Dock Labourers (Glasgow and Liverpool) before those August days when the issue of the 'plus' money set the Thames ablaze with the great dock strike, as a result of which the Dock, Wharf, Riverside and General Labourers' Union, the most famous of them all, was founded. By then, even the Battersea laundresses had been swept into agitation and strike.[13] The chronological sequence at least suggests that the London events were part of an ongoing national movement rather than their inspiration.

The definition of skill is surrounded by a similar penumbra of uncertainty. Very few trades had retained their formal pre-industrial apprenticeship, though some, like builders, printers and cutlers, were trying to preserve it with varying degrees of success. In some, notably the engineering and iron and steel shipbuilding trades, it had been introduced recently, but was nevertheless under pressure. Where no such formal barrier as a completed apprenticeship existed, it was difficult to draw the line. We need not go to the well-known and oft-quoted hierarchy of coach-makers[14] for the almost infinite gradations of skill and esteem among British workers; among sailors, within the crews of steel rolling mill or iron blast furnace, it was by no means

clear where skill began, and who therefore, in contemporary language, were
the organizable and who were beyond the pale and could not, according to
the traditionalist 'old' union leaders, be organized. In the coalmines, the
hewers were clearly skilled; but were those engaged in underground transport unskilled? Were the cotton-spinners skilled, and the piecers, let alone
the weavers, unskilled? Are only the footplate men among railway workers
to be accounted skilled? How much skill was needed to operate a shoe-
stitching machine, or a sewing machine? How much was left of a composi-
tor's skill after the introduction of Linotype and Monotype machines? The
issue is further complicated by the fact, increasingly recognized by historians
today, that while skill was an aid in the formation of a union, a union was
equally an aid in defining the notion of skill. 'The Unions did not only defend
"skill", but often created a task which they labelled their "skill". They made
a craft where it had not existed before.'[15]

Even those who formed the core of the classic or general labourers' unions
were by no means an undifferentiated unskilled proletariat. Agricultural
workers, quite apart from the trades of shepherd or carter, recognized in the
1870s by an additional shilling a week, always possessed a variety of skills.
Joseph Arch, for example, was a tolerable carpenter, and a 'good allround
man'.[16] Shipyard platers' helpers, despite their lowly status, possessed vital
skill and experience, and holders-up even managed to fight their way into
the exclusive boilermakers' union in 1882: 'A skilled labourer', according to
one of them, 'is doing work requiring technical knowledge and such men as
those who are doing work, which if it was not done by a labourer would be
done by a mechanic, are skilled labourers. . . . We call a man able to assist a
mechanic a skilled labourer.'[17] Gas stokers were clearly also not without
skill.

In the docks themselves there was a complex hierarchy of skills, the most
differentiated of all being in London. The main distinction was between ship
and shore work, the former being much the more skilled and more dangerous, requiring also the handling of complex equipment. There were dockers
to unload, and skilled stevedores to stow the cargo, while the loading and
unloading from the short-distance vessels along the wharves was done by a
different group of men altogether. Within each set there was specialization
in handling coal, corn, timber and (in Liverpool) salt; there were specialists
for chemicals, orange boxes, tobacco, or frozen meat. On the south side of
the river alone, when Tom Mann came to aid the committee during the great
strike of 1889, he found himself presenting separate claims for the following:
the deal porters; lumpers (outside); stevedores (inside); overside corn
porters; quay corn porters; trimmers and general labourers; weighers and
warehousemen; granary corn porters; and steamship workers. In Liverpool
there were also such specialists as railway bar dockers; hand bushellers of
grain; bag stitchers; and tallymen.[18] Somewhere on the outer fringe of it all
were the genuine unskilled, the wholly casual, or recent arrivals, but the
specialists rising in a hierarchy above them possessed the kind of strength,
skill and experience that would be as hard to replace among them as among
nominally skilled, well-organized trades. Nor were they the dregs of
working class society. James Sexton, the Liverpool docker, had been by

turns sailor, docker, painter and merchant; Ben Tillett, the London leader, had also been to sea both in the Royal Navy and the merchant marine, and had been a shoemaker and a dock manager/foreman in his time. In Sexton's picturesque language, 'although he was classified merely as a casual labourer, the all-round docker of those days [the early 1880s], knowing his business from keelson below to gantling blocks aloft, required the intelligence of a Cabinet Minister . . . the mechanical knowledge and resource of the skilled engineer, and, in addition, the agility and quick-wittedness of a ring-tailed monkey'.[19]

The New Unions, it is true, began with low weekly contributions and minimal benefits, though these could be found among some of the older ones as well. However, this was out of practical necessity rather than because of the principles supported so strongly by such as John Burns and Tom Mann,[20] for several of those that survived soon adopted one or other of the friendly benefits associated with the 'older' unions, requiring appropriate weekly payments.[21]

Similarly, the New Unions appeared aggressive and militant, for most of them originated in disputes; but then, most of the 'old' unions had similarly arisen in labour battles in their turn, and had gone on to maintain their position over the years by militancy and vigilance.[22] In the slump of the mid-1880s, it is true, many of them had become cautious, and some had opted for sliding scale agreements and for arbitration or conciliation schemes. But when the opportunity arose after 1889, several of them returned to militancy and some repudiated their sliding scales, whilst on the other side the New Unions also quickly settled down to peaceful bargaining. Trade unions in coal and cotton, numerically among the most important, had in any case never conformed to the craftsmen's 'model' which is contrasted with the New Unionism. By the late 1890s it would have been hard to discern by their actions which union was New in that sense and which was 'old',[23] and the Workers' Union, at first a pathetically weak society, had to be created specifically in 1898 to salvage some of the alleged spirit of the New Unionism.

Lastly, the political and social attitudes of the two groups are often contrasted: trade-oriented, Liberal, or Lib-Lab in politics, and at times even Conservative, in the case of the 'old'; socialist-inspired and class conscious in the case of the New. There is at first sight much truth in this characterization. By the late 1880s, several of the 'old' TUC stalwarts sat in Parliament as Liberals, while much of the organizational work for the key New Unions was done by socialists. Yet even here, apart from a handful of leading figures, the contrasts fade on closer inspection. The London dockers, to be sure, owe their organization to convinced socialists; but the Glasgow and Liverpool ones were inspired and led by Henry Georgeites. While the drive for the London gasworkers came from socialist leaders, the Birmingham gasworkers, the sailors and the National Agricultural Labourers' Union (NALU) were led by Lib-Labs, and elsewhere trades councils did much of the organizing. In any case, the leading figures, John Burns and Tom Mann, were reared in the stable of the ASE, the most rigid of the 'old' models. By contrast the miners, with all their new-found militancy, were to remain solidly Liberal for a long while yet.

There is in this much wish-fulfilment, for the socialists, mostly young men recruited into newly founded societies, above all the Social Democratic Federation (SDF) and later the Independent Labour Party (ILP) amidst the searing experience of the unemployment of the mid-1880s, expected their zeal to bear fruit in the unions they had had a hand in creating; but their missionary activity was carried out, not in any naturally fertile ground for socialists, but where trade unions happened to be badly needed and potentially organizable. In most of these cases the 'class' idea was a non-starter, for the New Unions quickly showed that they were not general or undifferentiated, still less universal, but firmly anchored in clearly outlined local labour monopolies. The Tyneside labourers' union, for example, soon organized Grimsby dockers, Liverpool, Belfast and Glasgow shipyard labourers, South Yorkshire colliery surface men, Sheffield metal workers, Thames cement workers; and Will Thorne's Gasworkers in Bristol had branches of cotton operatives, pipemakers, boxmakers, sanitary workers and quarrymen, and in Birmingham it had builders' labourers, polishers and grinders, steel toy makers, glass bottle makers and brick-makers. They thus very quickly took on a form not dissimilar to the 'old' trade societies,[24] and it is that which in fact secured their survival; limited to their original 'general' base, New Unions would have died out in even larger numbers after 1893 than in fact they did.

It should be remembered that the 'old' unions were also transformed in those years, and their membership gains in total were very much larger than those of the New. Several of the craft unions became less exclusive in their recruitment, and others, for various reasons, accepted into their pro-grammes that touchstone of the New, the Eight-Hour Day by legislation.[25] Membership of the eleven main skilled unions in metals and shipbuilding rose from 115,000 in 1888 to 155,000 in 1891, and of the ten largest skilled building unions it rose from 57,000 to 94,000 in the same years; the number of affiliated miners probably trebled, and the totals organized in trade unions rose from around 750,000 in 1888 to 1,500,000 in 1892. The figures for the New Unions are less reliable, since they tended to exuberant exagger-ation and in any case, in view of the volatile membership, little meaning can be attached to 'adherence' which might last only a few weeks or months. At their peak in 1890, the nine major societies allegedly totalled 350,000 members; these had by 1892 fallen to 132,000 and in 1896 to a mere 81,000. According to Eric J. Hobsbawm, the general, 'all-grade' and 'new crafts' types of New Unions together totalled 107,000 out of 1,555,000 in 1892–4, or 7 per cent of the trade union membership, and 103,000 out of 1,614,000 in 1895–7, or 6·4 per cent. No calculation ever gave them more than 13 per cent of the TUC affiliation, and after the decision of 1895 to exclude all those individuals who were not working at their jobs, or were full-time trade union officials, and also to exclude the trades council delegations, their direct influence there waned still further. By 1900 only one New Union, the Gasworkers, was among the ten largest.[26]

Nor could their much-vaunted gains be held. Even the London dockers had to accept a form of decasualization which broke the union's power and much of what they had achieved was gradually 'whittled away in the years that followed'. Henry M. Hyndman was not entirely tasting sour grapes when he asserted that 'the dockers as a body were, in some respects, even worse off after the strike than they were before'.[27] In Liverpool also, after initial successes, the dockers were defeated in 1890–1,[28] in Cardiff they were worsted in 1891 and in Hull in 1893. Other New Unions suffered similar reverses.

Although the consequences of these defeats lasted up to twenty years compared with at most twenty months in which the gains were operative, the former figure in the literature much less prominently than the latter. In part, the losses may be explained by the effect of the unions as irritants which called forth equal or even more than proportionate reactions on the part of the employers, of which the Liverpool Employers' Labour Association and the Shipping Federation (both established 1890), the National Free Labour Association (1893) and the Employers' Parliamentary Council (1898), as well as the profit-sharing scheme of the South Metropolitan Gas Company, may serve as examples. In part, however, the critics were correct in pointing out that unions of that type were inherently unstable, fly-by-night and unable to hold the loyalty of their members in the way the craft unions had done, or in other words, that little had changed in principle since the 1870s. Even the newness of the New Unionism seems to have been something of a myth.

Instead there was a general trade union boom among all types of trade unions, such as occurred twenty years earlier and twenty years later, and of which the New Unionism formed but one aspect. Moreover, it was a boom that was to be found, with its local variations, in the evolution of the more developed continental countries also.

III

How could the three forms of historical development be brought together: the trend, the divergences and the bursts? The trend requires little argument. In spite of widespread complaints of a prevailing long-term depression, and the deceleration in the British growth rate (see Table 2.1), there can be no question but that output and incomes were growing throughout the period, and expected to continue to grow. The plans and actions of trade union leaders and their potential members were therefore carried out against a background of rising expectations.

Table 2.1 *Average Annual Growth Rates, Total Gross Product, in Percentages*[29]

	Gross domestic product	Gross national product
1853–73	1·95	2·1
1873–83	1·90	2·0
1883–99	1·85	1·9
1899–1913	1·70	1·9

From peak to peak, national income per head in constant (1913–14) prices rose as follows:[30]

1856	20·54
1866	24·27
1874	30·29
1890	41·19
1898	46·91

Real per capita income therefore doubled within one generation.

How far trade unionists observed the declining trend of those upward series, how far they noted the change in mood from the optimism of Robert Giffen and Leone Levi to the pessimism of Joseph Chamberlain cannot now be established. Few were likely to have paid much attention to the literature, but it may be assumed that while it may have taken some years, probably the whole of the 1850s, for the realities of long-term improvement to have translated itself into working-class expectations, they would certainly have become firmly ingrained by the 1880s.

More immediately relevant, real wages were rising faster even than productivity in our period, a trend which was particularly marked in phases of falling prices, since money wages maintained an upward drift[31] which cannot be divorced, in turn, from trade union pressure.

There was also an increase in the proportions employed in large firms and in factories, with their controlled and inspected conditions, and a shift away from low-paid employment such as agriculture and domestic industry towards higher-paid industries. The gap between employments that were regulated by law or trade union power, and the sweated trades, may or may not have become larger, but it was felt to be less tolerable precisely because general standards were rising.

In parallel with all these changes, trade union membership also registered a secular rise from the mid-century on. Each major burst was followed by a falling back, but there was also a long-term ratchet effect, and membership never fell back quite to the original level, while each rise peaked with higher numbers: around 1 million in 1874, 2 million in 1890 and 4 million in 1913. While those totals hide the divergent experiences of different unions, from the steadily rising numbers of the ASE at one extreme to the switchback history of the miners' unions on the other, the rising trend was general and the survival chances became steadily better.

Behind this rise, in turn, stood the marked upward movement in the legal and social status of trade unions. It was the legislation of 1871 and 1875 in particular which improved their rights out of recognition. On the one hand, the stigma of illegality was definitely removed, protection for union funds was secured and collective action legalized to a more liberal extent; on the other, trade unions were given some remarkable immunities from the consequences of their actions, although the Taff Vale decision of 1901 and some preceding judicial decisions had shown them to be less firmly based than was at first believed.[32] The Employers and Workmen Act of 1875, significantly renamed from the Master and Servant Act which it replaced, put both sides on a comparable legal basis in cases of breaches of contract. The Employers' Liability Act of 1880, again significantly renamed in its amended form of 1896 as the Workmen's Compensation Act, greatly improved the wage worker's chances of compensation in cases of injury at work. This and similar legislation, including above all the almost continuous extension of protective legislation in factories, workshops and mines in those years, was paralleled and in part indeed called forth by the extension of the suffrage to many urban workers in 1867 and rural labourers in 1884, as well as by other electoral reforms.

The movement upwards was not in a smooth line. Occasionally it raced ahead of middle-class opinion or was influenced by sensationalized trade union action, as in the 1860s following some outrages in Sheffield, or in the 1890s following the successes of some of the New Unions, but these were temporary aberrations, always followed by legislation to return the unions to equal or even more favourable positions. Overall the trend was unmistakable: from barely tolerated semi-legality in the 1840s to 'responsible' unionism, welcomed by the better employers in the 1870s and near universal acceptance, with but a few exceptions, notably on the railways, thereafter. The employers who attempted initially to meet the claims of the New Unions by refusing to recognize them at all on principle were thus at variance with a large part of public opinion and thereby seriously weakened their own initial position. By 1909 the wheel was to come full circle as the Trade Boards Act declared, in effect, that where no trade union existed, the state had to step in and create an equivalent in order to secure an acceptable labour market.

Similarly, trade union leaders were converted from bogey-men to respected Members of Parliament, to witnesses and even to members of Royal Commissions and Select Committees. At first merely entered without title when authority dealt with them, they later in the century became 'Mr.' and at its end even 'Esq.', an evolution which put the change in their status in a nutshell.

IV

Many studies see the real causes of the New Unionism in the industrial changes of the period, presumably the 1880s. The problem here is that technical developments, and structural changes within industries flowing from them, proceeded at greatly varying speeds in different trades, firms and regions, and the 1880s were in no way specially marked by a deeper or more far-reaching transformation than other similar periods. No brief foray can do justice to the actual variety of experience, and the following paragraphs can at best only hint at it.

In the London (and some provincial) gasworks a recently introduced technical device, the 'iron man', had speeded work at the cost of harder toil, but the real issue was the twelve-hour shift system, and the spark was an alteration in the weekend change-over which created one continuous eighteen-hour shift. This was in an industry fairly free of cyclical fluctuations and little spare capacity in winter, but with predictable highly seasonal variations in employment, in an entirely protected and monopolistic as well as strongly expanding market: 45,000 gasworkers were enumerated in 1891 against a mere 14,000 in 1861. Beckton gasworks in London and Leeds gasworks were among the chief flashpoints of the New Unionism.[33]

In engineering, changing technology and the growing size of firms have often been linked to trade union developments. However, in spite of the appearance of 'families' of improved machines, as the centre lathe gave way to specialized machines employing millers, slotters, borers, planers, and in turn to single-purpose machines, and ultimately universal turret and capstan lathes using standardized tools, these developments, and the consequent changes in skill, were continuous rather than assignable to a particular breakthrough. Perhaps it was the 1890s when the ASE took in semi-skilled grades (1892), when the bitterness rose in the relations between de-skilled fitters and turners and their labourers[34] and the issue of dilution was brought to a head in the 1897–8 dispute, which saw the critical breakthrough against a background of sharpening international competition; significantly perhaps, the industry played little part in the New Unionism. In shipbuilding, by contrast, the major technical revolution had long since passed when iron and later steel were introduced in place of timber, and a new union, the boilermakers', had taken the place of the shipwrights in the constructive part of the work. There the festering grievances of the unskilled helpers for whom there was no significant change in the 1880s except that the holders-up were admitted to the boilermakers' union came to a head with the New Unionism.[35]

In printing, the new techniques of Linotype setting became an effective threat only in the 1890s, after our key years, but the compositors decided to accept it themselves in the hope of keeping out the lesser skilled men. The industry does not figure in the New Unionism.[36] In boot and shoemaking, however, the later 1880s saw new machinery, involving also team work and further loss of skills, after the introduction of the first machines in the 1860s had led to the breakaway of the machine operators to form a union which later became the National Union of Boot and Shoe Operatives. The confused struggle between London and the provinces which had Northampton as their main centre, and between the hand-made, high-class sector, the machine-made medium sector and the sweated outwork low-quality sector occurred in the years of the New Unionism and may be accounted part of it.[37]

The story of the London docks has often been told. Here was a confusion of rigid demarcations unable to cope with changing circumstances, particularly the growing importance of the steamship which required a faster turnround including much overtime and nightwork though it fluctuated less with the seasons. At the same time, the shift downstream to the new Victoria, Albert and Tilbury docks had left the upstream docks with a declining share of the traffic; the East and West India Docks had gone bankrupt in 1888, and the London and St. Katherine's Docks barely survived. The traffic of the six upstream docks fell from 2,171,000 tons in 1877 and 2,217,000 tons in 1880 to 1,599,000 tons in 1887.

The pressure towards cost reductions and especially wage cuts was therefore great, yet owing to the labour surplus, itself a precondition and a result of the casual, at times hourly employment system, the mechanical equipment was surprisingly primitive right up to 1889. According to Booth, the docks needed in 1891 a fluctuating total of 12,000 to 18,000 men, equivalent to a permanent force of 16,000, yet in fact there were 21,300 attached regularly, plus others floating in and out, so that there were 6,000 too many seeking work there. Matters were made worse by the fact that although the dock companies in London or Liverpool may have been large organizations, the actual employers of dockers were often small, struggling firms. Weekly earnings were among the lowest in London, and conditions in other ports were not dissimilar. The surplus was kept up, despite the growing traffic and therefore growing demand for labour, by an even faster attraction of workers from elsewhere, especially from Ireland, into the docks. The strike of 1889 failed to close the docks to outside labour, as it failed in most of its other long-term aims, but it led to overdue rationalization, and labour saving in London and several out-ports.[38]

The agricultural workers were in a rapidly declining employment; their unions showed a temporary rise in membership, but soon collapsed and showed none of the spirit of the 1870s.[39] On the railways, formerly quietist benefit societies in both England and Scotland were transformed into militant and active unions, but there was no discernible technical or economic change within the system to account for it, and only a background of long-simmering grievances.[40] The coalminers broke through in those years to a permanent national federation with militant policies, though the all-grade, industrial structure of the union, and its politically Liberal tendencies make it difficult to decide whether to include the Miners' Federation of Great Britain among the New Unions. There were no important technical or organizational innovations proceeding in those years, and the industry was among the fastest growers and absorbers of new labour. Between 1887 and 1890 alone it absorbed 103,000 workers, adding 20 per cent to its labour force. The more immediate issues were concerned with the bitter experience of sliding scale wages in the preceding slump years, and the attempt to reduce output by the Eight-Hour Day, though there were differences between the export fields with their particularly rapid rise in sales, and those supplying mainly the home market.[41]

In steelmaking and the iron goods trade in general there was no significant industrial change, but there were some labourers' groups which emerged as constituent branches of larger general unions, and there were the West Midlands nailers organized in 1891–2. The tinplate workers, forming their society in both parts of South Wales in 1886–7,[42] might possibly also be termed a New Union. The occasion was an attempted wage cut, but their new conditions emerged only after 1890, when the protectionist McKinley tariff decimated British exports of tinplate to America.

In cotton, too, there were no significant industrial changes apart from continuous minor improvements, but the unions, especially the aristocratic spinners, all increased their membership in the years of the New Unionism, and the card and blowing room operatives, mostly women, set up their amalgamated union in 1886. Some doublers joined general unions in the 1890s. It is possible to view the weavers' amalgamations formed in the struggles of the 1850s as forerunners of the New Unionism,[43] but this would not help the study of the years around 1890. As in cotton, much of the labour force in wool was female and had therefore a high organizational threshold. The powerloom workers in the West Riding in that branch did not begin to organize until the New Union phase, clearly influenced by the general enthusiasm rather than their specific industrial experience. Tailoring and dressmaking were largely sweated trades and included much female and foreign labour with little muscle. In view of the large number of small units in these branches and the subjective nature of most observations, it is difficult to be certain whether conditions deteriorated between about 1850 when Mayhew described them and around 1890, when they attracted much attention, including the House of Lords Select Committee, or whether the latter reflected higher standards everywhere else. Apart from some small Jewish associations, which again were frequently in non-competing groups, and some short-lived women's groups organized as part of the New Union wave by the Women's Trade Union Association, these workers were for practical purposes outside the range of the unions though some possessed a high degree of skill.[44] Whenever the trade unions in the better or legitimate sections of these trades felt strong enough, as did the tailors in 1892 or the boot and shoemakers noted above, they tried to abolish sweated outwork altogether, but it had a logic of its own and survived.

Tram and omnibus drivers were in a rapidly expanding industry, recruiting from the most diverse sources,[45] but they paid for the security of their employment by low pay and long hours. The sudden outburst of unrest and unionization in several cities in 1889–91[46] must be attributed to the spirit of the age rather than to intrinsic changes within the industry. Among sailors and firemen there arose one of the classic New Unions. Essentially their intention was to achieve job control at the recruiting point on shore, as the only realistic way of regulating the labour market in their industry. However, it would be hard to point to any specific changes in that industry around 1887, when the seamen's agitation took off, other than a slow trend to larger companies and to cartel agreements between them.

The search for links between industrial change and the New Unionism is no more fruitful in other industries. In building, some local labourers' unions are recorded, but no new technology to explain them. In the potteries, the machines conquered in the 1870s and the fairly ineffective National Union of Potters was founded in 1883. Among shop assistants, unionization occurred exactly in line with the New Unionism, the early harbinger appearing in 1887 in Northumberland and more widespread agitation erupting in 1889–91, the two leading unions (in every case in co-operative employment) being formed in 1891;[47] but here, too, no technical or organizational revolution can be discerned.

V

Why, then, the bunching around 1890? Most explanations turn on two developments: the preceding depression, and the boom beginning around 1889. Whereas the slump, with its heavy unemployment and widespread wage cuts, is believed to have radicalized the membership, the boom gave them the muscle to recover their lost ground, and advance beyond it, so that organization seemed worthwhile. Once the bandwagon was rolling, others too climbed on it. Marxists also tend to stress the growth of 'monopoly' in those depression years,[48] but this was a weak plant compared with the United States or Germany. Unemployment was worse than in comparable stages of other cycles and particularly hit the unskilled groups.[49] In certain export industries such as iron and steel and cotton goods, foreign competition became an important threat for the first time, while foreign tariffs were building up. It was stagnating exports, above all, which were holding back British recovery. As profits and investment were low and technology relatively immobile, the downward pressure on costs was strong in the mid-1880s, and in unsheltered industries remained so even in the boom: for most other industrial countries, unlike the United Kingdom, the 1880s had been a more prosperous, progressive decade.[50]

In the boom of 1890–2, while money wages rose, prices tended to rise faster – paradoxically, therefore, real wages per head fell from their peak of 1890 (though the numbers at work rose sharply) so that an edge was given to union militancy. Yet the fall in money wages and the rising unemployment from 1892 on did not intensify trade union adherence, but was accompanied by its decline. The incidence of these changes differed as between industries, but employment in some sectors grew particularly fast, including transport, mining, metals, engineering, building and printing.[51]

The problem with this type of 'cyclical' explanation is that it fits all booms and leaves unexplained why some, and the boom of around 1890 in particular, should have released so much trade union energy and others not. Hobsbawm, who makes this point, picks out the failure of some key trades to share in the boom as a significant factor in locating the trade union leaps forward, but his own pauperism statistics show the levels of 1886–9 to have been much lower than in 1867–72. Nor do relative wage movements help much as an explanation when the trade union bursts of the 1870s and 1910s are also brought into the discussion.[52]

Other studies, particularly in the United States, concerned with the explanation of trade union growth in general, have, like the 'Wisconsin school', linked it with prosperity (workers turning to political means in the depression) or, like Davis and Dunlop, with rising prices or other signs of unsatisfactory performance of the economy.[53] A modern econometric study based on data from Britain, the United States, Sweden and Australia found a positive correlation of union membership growth with rising prices and rising wages, particularly when the two were not growing at the same rate, and a negative correlation with unemployment rates and with the trade union density already achieved. The influence of political events

Table 2.2 *Average Earnings in a Normal Week (1891 = 100)*[54]

	Agriculture	Compositors	Building	Shipbuilding and engineering	Cotton	Coalmining
1886	91	96	96	90	89	70
1889	97	96	99	98	95	87
1890	100	98	100	100	96	99
1891	100	100	100	100	100	100
1894	99	101	103	98	101	88

Table 2.3 *Industrial Production in the United Kingdom (1891 = 100)*[55]

	Iron and steel	Iron and steel products	Shipbuilding	Building materials	Houses, incl. repair	Commercial buildings incl. repair	Other construction	Clothing	Textile finishing	Printing and materials	Chemicals	Electricity	Food manufacture	Gas	Totals (excluding construction)
1886	86	80	37	76	97	49	72	70	81	72	71	75	88	81	80
1889	112	113	110	92	100	113	72	83	91	88	108	87	95	90	98
1890	108	110	104	96	99	135	80	91	96	95	108	91	98	95	99
1891	100	100	100	100	100	100	100	100	100	100	100	100	100	100	100
1894	97	92	89	99	115	60	102	102	94	107	108	133	108	105	99

and social movements could also not be excluded.[56] Can the concentrated burst of around 1890 be explained along those lines?

No uniformity on the wages front is to be expected. The data do not exist to test Hobsbawm's hypothesis that the gap between the aristocracy of labour and the rest widened in these critical years, thus leading to a revolt from below, but it is unlikely that relatives altered much, and in any case, 'old' unions showed membership explosions similar to the New. The classic contemporary statements of the superiority of the labour aristocrat over the labourer and the widest recorded wage differentials date, in fact, from earlier decades rather than from the 1880s.[57] Table 2.2 shows that, apart from coalmining with its sliding scales, changes in earnings in the individual key years tended to be small.

Industrial production, recalculated from the base 1913 = 100 to the base of 1891 = 100, shows much wider fluctuations as well as the expected differences between capital goods and consumer goods, but little can be derived from these series to account for the incidence of the New Unionism (see Table 2.3).

On an international basis, this leap forward has been associated with one demand above all else: the demand for the legal Eight-Hour Day. Inaugurated by Tom Mann in 1886, it most clearly divided the 'old' from the New Unionists in the TUC, and its triumphant acceptance by that body after several earlier rejections in 1890 was one of the high points of the new movement, though the significance of that vote has often been exaggerated. It also links the British trade union revival with the Second International, a series of largely political congresses, and thus emphasizes the political element which tends to be neglected in British insular discussions of the trade union revival but figures more largely on the continent.

Three major aims were combined in this demand. One, which inspired Tom Mann and also several groups of miners, saw in it a means to limit output and thus keep up prices and wage rates.[58] The second was to confirm the gains made over a longer period by strong unions and within large firms and spread them to weaker sections and smaller firms by means of compulsion through legislation. The third placed it within the long-term movement, begun with the early factory legislation and continued with the nine-hour fight of the 1870s, of converting some of the additional incomes into more leisure. Here was one link between the steady, long-term cumulative pressure and its release in sudden bursts of trade union energy.

VI

Can we make sense of the disparate and, at first sight, contradictory data so far? The first question must be this: If the New Unionism, at least in the form of an alleged qualitative difference in one of the regular trade union leaps forward, is largely a myth, and its links with British industrial experience difficult to establish, to put it no higher, how has it managed to survive in the literature for so long?

One answer is undoubtedly that it suited contemporaries of all shades of opinion to present it in the light of a distinct movement, while no one had any reason to call this bluff. Its enemies within the trade union world, the old guard, locked in a battle of principles and personalities with it, fought it with the accusation, among others, that it disgraced the traditions established over the years and cherished by the 'old' unions. George Howell accused its leaders of indulging in 'strikes without reason; in the exercise of brute force, without compunction; and in capitulation without honour'. He and his colleagues were therefore hoping that 'the rise of organization among the less skilled workers [would] be only a mushroom growth, and one which was certain to disappear as soon as the temporary wave of unrest subsided'.[59]

The Webbs, starting up what was for long the mainstream of British labour historiography, had watched the developments at close quarters and had their own reasons for wishing to overemphasize the contrast. They were, in particular, straining the evidence to focus on the socialist leanings of the New Unions as against the Liberalism or the political disinterest of the 'old'.[60]

However, it was the left which hailed the new movement in the most exorbitant manner of all. 'Not since the high and palmy days of Chartism', enthused that stalwart old Chartist George Julian Harney, 'have I witnessed any movement corresponding in importance and interest to the great strike of 1889.'[61] The aged Engels, once more greeting yet another false dawn with pathetically misplaced hopes, was even more impressed:

> The people are throwing themselves into the job in quite a different way, are leading far more colossal masses in the fight, are shaking society much more deeply, are putting forward much more far-reaching demands. . . . Unlike the old trade unions, they greet every suggestion of an identity of interest between capital and labour with scorn and ridicule. . . . The masses are on the move and there is no holding them any more. . . . These unskilled are very different chaps from the fossilised brothers of the old trade unions; not a trace of the old formalist spirit, or the craft exclusiveness of the engineers, for instance; on the contrary, a general cry for the reorganisation of all trade unions in one fraternity and for a direct struggle against capital. . . . [The] arrogant old great trade unions will soon be made to look small. . . .
>
> 'New Unionism' . . . may to a great extent adopt the form of the old Unions of 'skilled' workers, but it is essentially different in character. . . . We now see these Unions taking the lead of the working-class movement generally, and more and more taking in tow the rich and proud 'old' unions.[62]

This revolutionary view of the New Unionism, also held by its most prominent leaders, John Burns, Tom Mann and Ben Tillett,[63] has become the standard interpretation among Marxists and the left generally.

Yet there is more in it than merely the interested views of contemporaries: their remarkable unanimity reflects the current atmosphere, including the atmosphere within the world of labour itself. There was evidently a powerful psychological element in the outburst of the New Unionism which superimposed itself on a 'normal' cyclical trade union revival, and which by its very force strengthened the resolve elsewhere to use the same opportunities for making collective demands and creating new organizations. The psychological moment on such occasions must not be underrated, and even false hopes and mistaken claims of victory can contribute to it.

It seems that the histrionics and the razzmatazz of the great dock strike, little though it availed the workers in the Port of London in the longer run, had a powerful effect on the union awakening elsewhere, call it New Unionism or what you will. Behind the receptiveness for it in a variety of industries lay different experiences, an accumulation of grievances and of technical skills, learning the 'rules of the game' to deal with them,[64] the trauma of the last bout of wage cuts and unemployment, and the growing and hardening realization that after 1875 workers ran fewer personal risks in leading unions and taking part in strikes. The grievances and needs of declining and expanding industries, of those with stagnating and those with revolutionized technology, of the sheltered and those exposed to international competition may well have been different; but the heave of the collective enthusiasm did indeed bunch manifestations that were ready and others that were almost ready but were brought forward in time precisely because of it.

This enthusiasm was remarkable for rousing even the downtrodden, the illiterate, the unorganizable men, even the women in sweated trades. In some localities the very schoolboys and battered wives were moved to organization.[65] This is what captured the imagination of onlookers, but the bunching was marked equally strongly among the 'old' and unregenerate societies: 'Send for John Burns!' cried dissatisfied boot and shoemakers in 1890.[66] The significance of the New Unionism was that it added to the impetus and the strength of revival of all unions, rather than that it created a separate new class of its own.

The handful of inexperienced socialists failed to impose socialism on the British trade union movement at the time, and in retrospect it is evident how slight their chances were of doing so. Similarly, organizational innovations were surprisingly few, apart from the grouping of more or less skilled local trades incongruously within the same 'general' union in place of the unskilled whom the leaders had set out to capture. But on the basis laid then, stronger and more permanent general unions emerged twenty years later, and a socialist programme could be made palatable to the trade union-dominated Labour Party another seven years on.

The framework thus is one of structure and conjuncture. Longer-term, industrially varied economic and technological developments determined the structure. The dockers and their flamboyant leaders provided the conjuncture for the big leap forward, even if not for the victorious establishment of the New Unionism.

Notes: Chapter 2

1 cf. H. A. Clegg, *General Union in a Changing Society* (Oxford, 1964), 7; R. Q. Gray, 'The labour aristocracy in the Victorian class structure', in F. Parkin (ed.), *The Social Analysis of Class Structure* (London, 1974), 19–33 (30).

2 E. J. Hobsbawm, 'Economic fluctuations and some social movements since 1800', in idem, *Labouring Men* (London, 1963), 126–57 (126–7).

3 No wonder that the most thorough of recent historians of that period have had to confess that 'the new unionism stands out as one of the most colourful and baffling phenomena in British trade union history'. H. A. Clegg *et al.*, *A History of British Trade Unions since 1889* (Oxford, 1964), 55.

4 For a slightly different emphasis, see R. Hyman, *The Workers' Union* (Oxford, 1971), 2.

5 A. E. P. Duffy, 'New Unionism in Britain, 1889–90: a reappraisal', *Economic History Review* 14 (1961–2): 306–19.

6 There were some branches even before Joseph Arch opened his campaign. P. Horn, *Joseph Arch (1826–1919), the Farm Workers' Leader* (Kineton, 1971), 44.

7 'There have been few strikes in British history which have been helped by subscriptions from the City, cheered on by stockbrokers and won in an atmosphere of carnival. But all this was true of the dock strike of 1889.' G. Stedman Jones, *Outcast London. A Study in the Relationship between Classes in Victorian Society* (Oxford, 1971), 315.

8 J. Lovell, *Stevedores and Dockers. A Study of Trade Unionism in the Port of London 1870–1914* (London, 1969), 59 and *passim*.

9 e.g. E. L. Taplin, *Liverpool Dockers and Seamen 1870–1890* (Hull, 1974), 17 and *passim*.

10 R. Lowe, 'Trade Unions', *Quarterly Review* 123 (1967): 351.

11 Hyman, *Workers' Union*, 5.

12 P. S. Bagwell, *The Railwaymen. The History of the National Union of Railwaymen*, Vol. 1 (London, 1963), 145.

13 D. Russell and M. Tichelar, *Class Struggles in South London, 1850–1900* (London, 1980).

14 'The body-makers are first on the list; then follow the carriagemakers; then the trimmers; then the smiths; then the springmakers; then the wheelwrights, painters, platers, brace-makers and so on.' W. B. Adams, *English Pleasure Carriages* (London, 1837), 188–9. Similarly, in Cornish mining 'the tributers look with as great contempt upon the tutmen as the tutmen do upon the surface labourers. Indeed, a tributer will be on the point of starvation before he will take tut-work.' From the *Morning Chronicle*, quoted in P. E. Razzell and R. W. Wainwright (eds), *The Victorian Working Class* (London, 1973), 26. For Yorkshire textile workers in the 1880s, in almost identical terms, see B. Turner, *About Myself* (London, 1930), 130.

15 W. H. Fraser, *Trade Unions and Society. The Struggle for Acceptance 1850–1880* (London, 1974), 210. Also H. A. Turner, *Trade Union Growth, Structure and Policy* (London, 1962), 194; G. Crossick, *An Artisan Elite in Victorian London. Kentish London 1840–1880* (London, 1978), 158.

16 J. Arch, *The Autobiography of Joseph Arch* (London, 1966), 38.

17 W. J. Lewington, evidence to the Royal Commission on Labour, 1893, quoted by J. H. Treble, 'The market for unskilled male labour in Glasgow, 1891–1914', in I. MacDougall (ed.), *Essays in Scottish Labour History* (Edinburgh, 1978), 115–42 (119–20).

18 Lovell, *Stevedores and Dockers*, 35 and *passim*; Crossick, *Artisan Elite*, 64 and *passim*; J. Sexton, *Sir James Sexton, Agitator* (London, 1936), 110.

19 ibid., 67; B. Tillett, *Memories and Reflections* (London, 1931).

20 cf. E. J. Hobsbawm (ed.), *Labour's Turning Point 1880–1890* (Brighton, 1974), 72–3.

21 Clegg *et al.*, *History of British Trade Unions*, 93; Clegg, *General Union in a Changing Society*, 28; Hyman, *Workers' Union*, 7; Bagwell, *Railwaymen*, 86; G. Radice and L. Radice, *Will Thorne, Constructive Militant* (London, 1974), 34, 47. See also J. Benson, 'The thrift of English coal miners, 1860–95', *Economic History Review* (1978): 410–18.

22 e.g. Fraser, *Trade Unions and Society*, 224.

23 Clegg *et al.*, *History of British Trade Unions*, 304; R. M. Martin, *T.U.C.: The Growth of a Pressure Group, 1868–1976* (Oxford, 1980), 57; A. E. Musson, *Trade Union and Social History* (London, 1974), 69.

24 E. J. Hobsbawm, 'Economic fluctuations', 127, and idem, 'General labour unions in Britain, 1889–1914', in idem, *Labouring Men*, 179–203 (188, 195); Clegg, *General Union in a Changing Society*, 26–7; B. C. Roberts, *The Trades Union Congress 1868–1921* (London, 1958), 134; Duffy, 'New Unionism', 317; D. Kynaston, *King Labour. The British Working Class, 1850–1914* (London, 1976), 137–43; H. A. Clegg, *General Union. A Study of the National Union of General and Municipal Workers* (Oxford, 1954), 3; Radice and Radice, *Will Thorne*, 14.

25 H. Pelling, *A History of British Trade Unionism* (London, 1976), 101–3; S. Webb and B. Webb, *The History of Trade Unionism, 1660–1920* (London, 1920), 421.

26 Clegg *et al.*, *History of British Trade Unions*, 83, 99; T. Mann, *Memoirs* (London, 1967), 71; Pelling, *History of British Trade Unionism*, 117.

27 K. D. Brown, *John Burns* (London, 1977), 49; H. M. Hyndman, *Further Reminiscences* (London, 1912), 441.

28 Sexton, *Sir James Sexton*, 94–104.

29 W. A. Lewis, *Growth and Fluctuations 1870–1913* (London, 1978), 113.

30 P. Deane and W. A. Cole, *British Economic Growth 1688–1959* (Cambridge, 1967), 329–30.

31 Lewis, *Growth*, 107. Also Deane and Cole, *Economic Growth*, 247, Table 65.

32 J. Saville, 'Trade unions and free labour: the background to the Taff Vale decision', in A. Briggs and J. Saville (eds), *Essays in Labour History* (London, 1960), 317–50.

33 Clegg, *General Union in a Changing Society*, 8 and *passim*; Radice and Radice, *Will Thorne*, 19 and *passim*; Hobsbawm, 'Economic fluctuations', 142, and 'British gas-workers, 1873–1914', in idem, *Labouring Men*, 158–78 (158–66).

34 N. Todd, 'Trade unions and the engineering industry dispute at Barrow-in-Furness, 1897–98', *International Review of Social History* 20 (1975): 33–47; also G. D. H. Cole, *Trade Unionism and Munitions* (Oxford, 1923), 32–46; Crossick, *Artisan Elite*, 78; J. B. Jefferys, *The Story of the Engineers* (London, 1945), 122–5.

35 J. E. Mortimer, *History of the Boilermakers' Society*, Vol. 1 (London, 1973), 110; P. L. Robertson, 'Demarcation disputes in British shipbuilding before 1914', *International Review of Social History* 20 (1975): 220–35; J. Lynch, 'Skilled and unskilled labour in the shipbuilding trade', *Industrial Remuneration Conference Report* (1885), 114–18.
36 J. Child, *Industrial Relations in the British Printing Industry* (London, 1967), 164, 197–201; G. B. Dibbles, 'The printing trade and the crisis in British industry', *Economic Journal* 12 (1902): 1–14; A. E. Musson, *The Typographical Association. Origins and History up to 1949* (Oxford, 1954), 221–33.
37 Clegg *et al.*, *History of British Trade Unions*, 25–6; A. Fox, *A History of the National Union of Boot and Shoe Operatives 1874–1957* (Oxford, 1958), esp. 99 and *passim*; D. Bythell, *The Sweated Trades. Outwork in Nineteenth-Century Britain* (London, 1978), 109–12, 215–16.
38 Stedman Jones, *Outcast London*, 53, 112 and *passim*; E. J. Hobsbawm, 'National unions on the waterside', in idem, *Labouring Men*, 204–30; M. J. Cullen, 'The 1887 survey of the London working class', *International Review of Social History* 20 (1975): 48–60 (59); Lovell, *Stevedores and Dockers*; Taplin, *Liverpool Dockers*; Mann, *Memoirs*, 60 and *passim*; Sexton, *Sir James Sexton*; M. J. Daunton, 'Inter-union relations on the waterfront: Cardiff 1880–1914', *International Review of Social History* 22 (1977): 350–78; L. J. Williams, 'The New Unionism in South Wales 1889–92', *Welsh History Review* 1 (1960–3): 422–5.
39 Webb and Webb, *History of Trade Unionism*, 403; Hobsbawm, *Turning Point*, 88–9; R. Groves, *Sharpen the Sickle! The History of the Farm Workers' Union* (Barnstable, 1949), 83–7; R. C. Russell, *The 'Revolt of the Field' in Lincolnshire* (Lincoln, n.d.), 152–4; Horn, *Joseph Arch*, 191–4, 222; B. W. Robertson, 'The Scottish farm servant and his union: from encapsulation to integration', in I. MacDougall (ed.), *Essays in Scottish Labour History. A Tribute to W. H. Marwick* (Edinburgh, 1980), 90–114 (91).
40 Bagwell, *Railwaymen*, 142, 149; W. H. Marwick, *A Short History of Labour in Scotland* (Edinburgh, 1967), 63; Webb and Webb, *History of Trade Unionism*, 523–5; Williams, 'New Unionism in South Wales', 419–20; Kynaston, *King Labour*, 154.
41 R. Page Arnot, *The Miners. A History of the Miners' Federation of Great Britain 1889–1910* (London, 1949), esp. 68 and *passim*.
42 W. E. Minchinton, *The British Tinplate Industry. A History* (Oxford, 1957), 120.
43 Turner, *About Myself*.
44 E. J. Hobsbawm, 'Trends in the British labour movement since 1880', in idem, *Labouring Men*, 316–43 (321); also B. Webb, *My Apprenticeship* (London, 1926), 331; Bythell, *Sweated Trades*; Fox, *Boot and Shoe Operatives*, 106; Stedman Jones, *Outcast London*; Hobsbawm, *Turning Point*, 90; N. C. Soldon, *Women in British Trade Unions 1874–1976* (Dublin, 1978), 31 and *passim*; E. A. Paterson, in *Industrial Remuneration Conference*, 200 and *passim*; Treble, *Unskilled Male Labour*.
45 Razzell and Wainwright, *Victorian Working Class*, 151–2.
46 Hobsbawm, *Turning Point*, 93; E. L. Taplin, 'The Liverpool tramwaymen's agitation of 1889', in H. A. Hikins (ed.), *Building the Unions. Studies in the Growth of the Workers' Movement in Merseyside 1756–1967* (Liverpool, 1973), 55–76; G. Alderman, 'The National Free Labour Association', *International Review of Social History* 21 (1976): 309–36 (313); Williams, 'New Unionism in South Wales', 418; G. Tate, *London Trades Council, 1860–1950. A History* (London, 1950), 72.
47 W. H. Wharburton, *The History of Trade Union Organisation in the North Staffordshire Potteries* (London, 1931), 177, 192; Sir W. Richardson, *A Union of Many Trades. The History of the Union of Shop, Distributive and Allied Workers* (Manchester, 1980), 16–20.
48 Hobsbawm, 'Trends in the British labour movement', 316–17.
49 Treble, *Unskilled Male Labour*, 131. The suggestion has also been made that some of these groups were becoming restive because of the troubles in Ireland. R. Bean, 'New Unionism in Liverpool 1888–1896', in Hikins (ed.), *Building the Unions*, 99–118 (100).
50 Lewis, *Growth*, 50 and *passim*; H. L. Beales, 'The "Great Depression" in industry and trade', *Economic History Review* 5 (1934): 65–75; S. B. Saul, *The Myth of the Great Depression 1873–1896* (London, 1969), 41–2; A. G. Ford, 'British economic fluctuations, 1870–1914', *Manchester School* 37 (1969): 102; A. E. Musson, 'The Great Depression in Britain, 1873–1896: a reappraisal', *Journal of Economic History* 19 (1959): 199–228 (201–2, 212–13); Taplin, *Liverpool Dockers*, 84–6.
51 Saul, *Myth*, 30–1; Roberts, *Trades Union Congress*, 133; H. Llewellyn Smith and V. Nash, *The Story of the Dockers' Strike* (London, 1890), 42; Clegg *et al.*, *History of British Trade*

Unions, 4–5; B. R. Mitchell and P. Deane, *Abstract of British Historical Statistics* (Cambridge, 1962), 343–5.

52   Hobsbawm, 'Economic fluctuations', 128 and *passim*.

53   G. S Bain and F. Elsheikh, *Union Growth and Business Cycles* (Oxford, 1976), ch. 2.

54   ibid., chs. 4–6.

55   E. J. Hobsbawm, 'The labour aristocracy in nineteenth-century Britain', in idem, *Labouring Men*, 272–315; Crossick, *Artisan Elite*, 108–9; R. Harrison, *Before the Socialists. Studies in Labour and Politics, 1861–1881* (London, 1965), 25–31; K. G. J. C. Knowles and D. J. Robertson, 'Differences between the wages of skilled and unskilled workers 1880–1950', *Bulletin of the Oxford University Institute of Statistics* 13 (1951): 109–27 (111, 119); G. D. H. Cole, *Studies in Class Structure* (London, 1955), 53.

56   Based on A. L. Blowley and G. H. Wood, 'The statistics of wages in the United Kingdom in the 19th century', *Journal of the Royal Statistical Society* 69 (1906): 148–92. Mitchell and Deane, *Abstract*, 350.

57   Lewis, *Growth*, 248–9.

58   Webb and Webb, *History of Trade Unionism*, 393–4; B. McCormick and J. E. Williams, 'The miners and the Eight-Hour Day, 1863–1910', *Economic History Review* 12 (1959–60): 223–6; D. Torr, *Tom Mann* (London, 1936), 18; Duffy, 'New Unionism', 312; Martin, *T.U.C.*, 74; Page Arnot, *Miners*, 107, 126–9, 137; Hobsbawm, *Turning Point*, 101–2; Mann, *Memoirs*, 44 and *passim*.

59   G. Howell, *Trade Unionism, New and Old* (London, 1891), 135, also 164; Cole, *Trade Unionism and Munitions*, 4; also e.g. Mortimer, *Boilermakers' Society*, 119–20; Collison, of the Free Labour Association, made the contrast, if anything, even stronger: Alderman, 'National Free Labour Association', 314.

60   Webb and Webb, *History of Trade Unionism*, esp. 359, 368–70, 383–8.

61   Hobsbawm, *Turning Point*, 85.

62   F. Engels, Letter to Sorge 7 December 1889, to Schlüter 11 January 1890, Preface to 1892 edition of *Condition of the Working Classes*, in *Selected Correspondence . . . Marx and Engels* (London, 1941), 461, 463, 465. Also S. Bünger, *Friedrich Engels und die britische sozialistische Bewegung von 1881–1895* (Berlin, 1962), esp. 168–9.

63   T. Mann and B. Tillett, *The New Trades Unionism* (London, 1890); Brown, *John Burns*, 54.

64   Hobsbawm, *Labouring Men*, 144.

65   Williams, 'New Unionism in South Wales', 417–18.

66   Fox, *Boot and Shoe Operatives*, 108.

Part Two

Strike Movements in Europe:
A Comparative Analysis

3 Strikes and the Struggle for Union Organization: Britain and Europe

JAMES E. CRONIN

I

The importance of strikes in the general evolution of modern labour movements is obvious and well-recognized by historians and students of industrial relations. They seem to represent the form of collective action that workers feel most adept at using, whose tactical logic is understood almost intuitively by working men and women, and which has proved to be as useful and effective as any other style of resistance or contention, and probably the most democratic as well. It should not be surprising, then, that strikes played an absolutely critical role in that primary mobilization of working-class interests that occurred throughout Europe in the quarter century preceding the outbreak of the First World War.[1] Both strikes and union organization increased massively in these years in Great Britain, France and Germany; the value of the strike weapon, particularly the general strike, became a major focus of debate among socialists and syndicalists; and the evident power of strikes to wring concessions from governments and employers led not a few militants to develop a strategy for the emancipation of labour based almost entirely upon the unrestricted use of the strike.

Clearly, some particular factors specific to this historical moment were at work enhancing the role of strikes above and beyond their normal function as the last resort in collective bargaining. The answer, it would seem, lies in the contradiction between the growing capacity for collective action achieved by workers at the workplace and in their communities, and their inability, for various reasons in different countries, to translate this into effective power in industry and government.

II

'Striking has become a disease, and a very grave disease, in the body social', intoned George Phillips Bevan at the beginning of his learned lecture on strikes to the Royal Statistical Society on 29 January 1880.[2] Worse still, the disease 'as yet shows no sign of having run its course', and the concerned statistician could not bring himself 'to believe in any speedy cure', whether 'by legislative measures or any one course of action'. Bevan's subject was the record of industrial disputes during the 1870s, which he compiled in a most

Table 3.1 *Strikes and Strikers in Britain, 1870–1914*

| | Strikes | | Strikers | |
	A (Bevan)[a]	B (Webbs)[b]	C (Official)[c]	C (Official)[c]
1870	30			
71	98			
72	343			
73	365			
74	286			
75	245			
76	229	17		
77	180	23		
78	268	38		
79	308	72		
1880		46		
81		20		
82		14		
83		26		
84		31		
85		20		
86		24		
87		27		
88		37	517	119,000
89		111	1,211	337,000
1890			1,040	393,000
91			906	267,000
92			700	357,000
93			782	599,000
94			929	257,000
95			745	207,000
96			926	148,000
97			864	167,000
98			711	201,000
99			719	138,000
1900			648	135,000
01			642	111,000
02			442	117,000
03			387	94,000
04			354	56,000
05			358	68,000
06			486	158,000
07			601	101,000
08			399	224,000
09			436	170,000
1910			531	385,000
11			903	831,000
12			857	1,233,000
13			1,497	516,000
14			972	326,000

Notes and Sources:

[a] Derived from various newspapers and reports by G. P. Bevan, 'The strikes of the past ten years', *Journal of the Royal Statistical Society* (March 1880): 37.

[b] Collected from strikes mentioned in *The Times* by S. and B. Webb, *The History of Trade Unionism* (New York, 1920), 347n.

[c] Based on the Reports on Strikes and Lockouts published by the Board of Trade from 1888 to 1914.

thorough and useful fashion, and his judgement on this particular era in industrial relations was endorsed by George Howell, who also had recourse to the metaphor from pathology. 'This was a period of strike epidemics, not to occur again, let us hope', wrote Howell on the very eve of the next such epidemic in 1889.[3]

The figures produced by Bevan, and reproduced as part of Table 3.1, are indeed impressive; impressive enough to suggest that the 1870s probably were the years when strikes became the dominant form of workers' collective activity. Though the labour market was buoyant in 1870 – unemployment was only 3·9 per cent, compared with 7·9 per cent in 1868 and 6·7 per cent in 1869 – only thirty strikes were recorded. The figure tripled in 1871, to ninety-eight, and more than that again in 1872, when 343 disputes were noted. The levels of strike activity remained high through the 1870s, as what Thomas Wright called 'the alternation between "flushes" and "crashes"' shifted the balance of tactical advantage back and forth, and so prompted first workers and then employers to press their advantage to the fullest.[4] Indeed, the strike wave of the early 1870s was probably the first of those major explosions of militancy and union organization that have characterized the subsequent history of British industrial relations.[5] Like the waves of 1889–90, 1911–13 and 1919–20, it represented not merely an escalation of overt conflict between workers and employers, but also a shift towards more inclusive organization of less skilled workers, together with an upsurge of rank-and-file activism, a rejection of the cautious advice of established officials and a renewed emphasis upon the efficacy of strike activity.[6] Like later insurgencies, too, it was followed by a substantial counter-attack by employers which succeeded in beating back workers' organization from its furthest and weakest extensions, but which did not manage to turn the clock back to the state of organization existing prior to the strike wave. The modes used to re-establish order within 'the industrial relations system' also exhibited marked similarity during these successive counter-offensives: an odd mix of employer attempts to inflict symbolic defeats upon key groups of workers, together with efforts on the part of union leaders, state officials and enlightened employers to elaborate restrictive conciliation schemes and procedures for resolving disputes.[7]

Despite certain earlier prefigurations, it seems reasonable to regard this pattern as basically novel to the era beginning in 1870. The mark of this new pattern was the advance of workers' organization from a very modest position in 1870 – about a quarter of a million trade unionists were affiliated to the TUC in that year – to the point where in 1920 the bulk of the manual workers, skilled and unskilled, were organized in trade unions whose strength exceeded eight million. This massive achievement, which has yet to be properly appreciated, was accomplished by aggressive worker activity at the point of production which, at its core, involved the strike.[8]

In this sense, the strike truly came into its own as a form of collective action in the 1870s, and the history of both unionism and strikes from 1870 up to the war of 1914–18 is concerned primarily with the spread of each downwards and outwards (and occasionally upwards),[9] to progressively larger sections of the working class. This extension is revealed graphically in

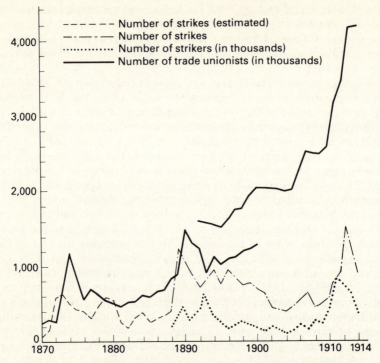

Figure 3.1   *Strikes and Union Organization in Britain, 1870–1914*

Sources: Data on strikes and strikers based on Table 3.1. This figure is reproduced from J. Cronin, 'Strikes, 1870–1914', in C. J. Wrigley (ed.), *The History of British Industrial Relations* (Brighton, 1982).

Figure 3.1, which depicts the number of strikes, of strikers and of trade union members from 1870 to 1914. These graphs suggest the main outlines of the question to be addressed here. Most obviously, organization among workers increased dramatically and consistently throughout the entire period. Strike activity also grew, in the sense that strike propensity was higher across British industry at each successive peak in the curves of strikes and strikers. But the most distinctive aspect of industrial conflict was its tendency to occur in sharp explosions about every other decade. The problem, then, is to explain both the overall and spectacular advance of organization and the way the three great strike waves of 1871–3, 1889–90 and 1911–13 fit into the process.

Before we address the problem directly, it is necessary as a first step to attend to the formulation of the questions. The norm of analysis in traditional labour history has been to focus upon the accumulation of grievances, as if the relationship between the extent and character of oppression and the resistance to it was uniformly close and direct. By now, the sum of research on collective action showing the importance of strength and resources for mobilization ought to allow us to modify that approach considerably, so that the key question becomes not, 'why workers fight?' but rather, 'what allowed for or facilitated the translation of grievance into protest?' It is important, in addition, to recognize that, because the transformation in organization and strikes occurred throughout British industry, the critical factors should themselves be effective at a broad societal level. Therefore, the argument pursued here is based on changes of a structural nature in economy and society that combined to enhance the collective capacity of working men and women to organize and resist.

Before 1870 the social reach of unionism and of strikes was very narrow. Not without reason were unions in this period attacked as the province of the skilled and best-paid of workers. 'It is notorious', one hostile observer wrote, 'that strikes and combinations have been most common amongst those portions of the working population whose wages are highest.'[10] By 1914 this was no longer true in any sense: organization and strike-proneness had become common throughout the working class. The change is recorded in both the geography and the industrial distribution of strikes. In the 1870s, medium-sized towns exhibited the highest strike rates: Barnsley came just after London in the list of strike locations; Manchester saw fewer than Dundee or Merthyr; Sunderland outpaced Birmingham, Bradford, Bristol and Belfast. A similar pattern can be observed during the explosion of the New Unionism and at the turn of the century. This clearly reflected the coming to union organization of operatives in basic industry located in these urban centres of modest size. The pattern shifted after 1900, as many transport and service workers in the large provincial cities and in London finally succeeded in building stable unions and so were able to launch effective strikes. These geographical patterns were manifestations of the continued extension of organization from the craftsmen in the largest cities to the operatives in the factory towns and the miners in their mining villages, and then back to the less skilled workers in the service sectors in the big cities.[11]

The industrial distribution of strikes was similarly broad from 1870 onwards, and broadened further in the years approaching 1914. At its peak the militancy of 1871–3 touched agricultural workers, dockers and other unorganized groups. Among the engineers, too, the unorganized played a major role, as in the Newcastle strike in 1871, where no more than 10 per cent of the strikers were members of the Amalgamated Society of Engineers. From then until 1914, strike propensity was surprisingly evenly spread out in 'the staple industries', as Bevan had noted for the 1870s. Though some groups, like miners, were more prone to strike (for reasons that have been discussed many times over), the really marked divergence between industries visible since the 1920s was much less clear before 1914. And the changes that did occur before 1914 – the slight decline in strikes among builders, the increase among transport workers – confirm the tendency for the differences between industries and between skilled and unskilled to lessen somewhat as organization advanced.[12]

So while strikes broke out and organization deepened among the skilled, the truly novel phenomenon was the enrolment of those without apprenticeships or scarce skills into the labour movement, and it was this that accounted for the truly massive growth in unions and in strike activity throughout the prewar era. Three sets of factors seem most compelling as explanations of this change. First, there was crude demography: the ranks of the 'semi-skilled' and 'unskilled' increased substantially after 1870. This was intimately linked with a second factor: the pattern of industrial development led to increased demand for semi-skilled, as opposed to skilled, labour, and this demand was filled largely, though not exclusively, by an upgrading in the status of unskilled or casual labour. Thirdly, the social ecology of mid-Victorian cities slowly gave way to a more socially segregated pattern of residence during the massive urban growth of 1870–1914. The effect was to create a physical space for the development of a strong and distinctive working-class culture sustained by, and itself helping to sustain, a broad array of social and political institutions that together added substantially to the resources which workers could mobilize on their own behalf.

To document these changes to any substantial degree would necessitate extensive discussion, but one might nevertheless suggest a few reasons for believing them to have been both real and significant. The growth in the ranks of the less skilled is well known, and resulted from an expansion of the number of non-apprenticed workers in trades like engineering, printing, iron and steel, from the development of new industries that required a small number of skilled men for maintenance and much larger numbers of routine workers for production, and from the enhanced economic importance of transport, communication and service.[13] From 1890 the rate of increase of the workforce in these industries exceeded that of manufacturing industry, and added greatly to the amount of stable, semi-skilled employment. Even within manufacturing, there was a steady increase in the size of plant, the ratio of capital per worker and in industrial concentration. However retarded the modernization of British industry, the trends were visible and important, both in new industries and in old established trades, like mining and cotton.[14]

In terms of labour, the net result of such changes was to make work more regular and predictable as well as more tightly controlled and supervised. Scientific management remained more of an ideology than a reality, but even that revealed a greater attention on the part of management to the affairs of production.[15] In some cases, this led to sharp conflicts with the skilled workers, as in engineering, but other factors combined to make such confrontations the exception. For one thing, the process of 'deskilling', as it has been called, occurred more at the level of the class or the entire population than the individual, for individual artisans were kept employed in superior grades of work, in the toolroom or in specialized production rather than displaced. This was guaranteed by the timing of the change in particular, for the diffusion of new equipment could be achieved only during periods of high demand and investment, which meant that labour shortages were also acute.

The skilled were therefore challenged, but by no means defeated or eliminated.[16] The evolution of industrial structure affected the unskilled in an equally contradictory fashion. Jobs came to approximate the norm of factory work, with greater distance between master and men, more bossing and discipline and, ordinarily, a more intensive pace of production. But the greater regularity, rationality and stability of employment provided the material underpinnings for organization and resistance. It took time, naturally, for new unskilled factory hands to acquire what E. J. Hobsbawm has termed the 'habit of solidarity', and in particular for workers in transport and government service to evolve forms of organization appropriate to the scale and style of their employment and to the combined strength of their employers, but by 1914 the process was well advanced.[17]

The impact of developments in the spatial relations of classes is difficult to assess with precision, but seems to have worked in most cases to facilitate militancy. The pattern varied a good deal from place to place, depending upon the nature of local transportation systems, housing and labour markets, but in general it appears that from 1870 to 1914 working-class communities acquired a degree of stability such as to allow for the elaboration of a robust, and partially autonomous, way of life.[18] Intimately linked to this culture, or these locally rooted subcultures, were networks of formal and informal institutions, from adult classes to the friendships of the street and the pub. The emergence of this working-class social and cultural presence in the cities of late Victorian and Edwardian Britain has been documented by several historians, and was, of course, much discussed by contemporaries as well. In both instances, commentary has tended to stress the problems with this new culture – its patriarchal, hierarchical and complacent aspects being deplored by historians, its paganism, cynicism and insularity being attacked by contemporaries. Neither perspective, it can be argued, sufficiently emphasizes the novelty of the development, or the implications for politics and other forms of collective action, for these increasingly solid communities represented a substantial increment to the strength of labour.[19]

The strengthening of independent working-class communities seems to have occurred throughout the country, though the precise set of processes involved varied a good deal. In mining communities, the factors seem to have been the gradual slowing down of migration in older centres which eliminated much of the instability and heterogeneity common during periods of rapid demographic expansion, and, on the other hand, the establishment of a new cultural identity in growing areas like South Wales.[20] For older industrial centres, the process differed. Urban growth after 1870 seems to have centred in the larger towns and cities, rather than in those medium-sized towns that housed so many of the mills of the first industrial revolution. As cities grew, the local 'urban villages' centred on a factory and presided over by a paternalistic employer, as described recently for industrial Lancashire, were submerged in the larger agglomerations of working-class residence that were housing the growing working population.[21] In London, the key seems to have been the spreading out of working-class families into newer settlements from Hackney to the north and from the Thames south.[22] The classic case was Battersea, a centre of Labour voting, trade union membership and left-wing support, but other areas followed not dissimilar paths.[23]

At the point of production and in their communities, therefore, British workers found new sources of strength from 1870 to 1914, and this was particularly important for those who did not possess a certified and marketable skill with which to bargain. When these new resources were combined with a favourable economic conjuncture – that is, a tight labour market – the common result was an outbreak of union activity and strikes. Obviously, a great deal remains to be said about these structural determinants of the balance of power between classes – the role of the state in particular could use further explication – but the foregoing must suffice for present purposes.[24]

III

If secular trends in the structural evolution of economy and society lay behind the great changes in industrial relations, it is nonetheless the case that the pace of development varied considerably from year to year. Both the growth of organization and the increase in strikes were concentrated in three 'great leaps', in 1871–3, 1889–90 and 1911–13. What caused this distinctive clustering of forward movements? The vagaries of the trade cycle are no doubt part of the answer: each of the strike waves occurred when the labour market was most favourable to workers. The wild boom of 1871–3 saw unemployment in the organized trades well below 2 per cent; in the same industries only 2·1 per cent were out of work in 1889–90, compared with 10·2 per cent just two years before; in 1911–13 unemployment averaged just under 3 per cent, whereas double that were out of a job in 1908–9. Clearly, a favourable labour market was something of a precondition for launching a wave of militancy.[25]

A slightly broader view of economic conjuncture suggests a further feature common to these moments of insurgency. If one considers not simply the classic trade cycle of seven to ten years, but also the long waves of roughly half a century through which capitalist development seems to pass, it becomes clear that strikes and organization have tended to come during short-term upswings near the end of each phase of the long wave. The first great British strike wave in 1871–3 came during the speculative climax of the mid-Victorian boom; the New Unionism broke through during the flurry of trade just before the last trough of the Great Depression; and the 'labour unrest' swept Britain near the end of the long Edwardian prosperity. This quite marked pattern suggests a very intimate relation between the *langen Wellen der Konjunktur*, as Kondratiev called them, and labour militancy. It seems, in addition, that long waves are connected with the structural evolution of economy and society which brought about the enhanced capacity for workers' collective action after 1870.[26]

Perhaps the best way to show these links and mediations is to describe briefly the most salient feature of each major outbreak of strikes. Unfortunately, the militancy of 1871–3 is surely the least well documented of such episodes. According to Bevan's count, the number of separate strikes increased from a mere thirty in 1870 to about 350 for 1872 and 1873, an increase of well over ten times. Of these, however, very few find their way into George Howell's list of 'Great Strikes' or a similar list compiled by the Board of Trade in 1889, so our knowledge of most remains scanty indeed. The best known is the engineers' nine hours strike in the north-east in 1871, which seems to have been a stimulant to other workers. Several features stand out in the various accounts of that struggle: the quality of the men's leadership, particularly John Burnett; the fact that most of the strikers were not members of the union; the recalcitrance of the owners and the public support generated by the workers. The demand for a shorter working day was extremely popular, and was widely emulated by workers in other industries. The initiative of the unorganized was also characteristic of the movement elsewhere, and the two often came together, as when 'a massive strike wave' swept Sheffield in 1872, bringing over 1,200 smelters into the union around the demand for a shorter week. The strikes in general reflected a broad attempt to organize unions, and membership in TUC-affiliated societies grew from about a quarter of a million in 1870 to almost 1·2 million in 1874. The growth was particularly concentrated in heavy industry, like engineering and metal working: the ironworkers grew from a mere 476 members in January 1869 to over 35,000 in 1874.[27]

It seems that unions and strikes, though still strongest in the older, skilled

Table 3.2 *Major Participants in Strikes, 1871–3*

Industry or occupation	Number of strikes
Agricultural labourers	3
Bakers	17
Boilermakers	8
Bricklayers	14
Building operators	20
Carpenters and joiners	65
Colliers	87
Cotton hands	19
Dock labourers	15
Engineers and fitters	37
Flax, linen and jute hands	24
Iron workers	44
Masons	31
Nail and chain makers	14
Navvies	5
Painters	8
Plasterers	9
Plumbers	81
Printers and compositors	10
Quarrymen	16
Railway and telegraph employees	13
Shipbuilders	28
Shoe and bootmakers	48
Slaters	11
Tailors	24
All others	232
Total	806

Source: G. P. Bevan, 'The strikes of the past ten years', *Journal of the Royal Statistical Society* (1880): 39–41.

trades, were spreading into basic industry (see Table 3.2). Unskilled 'boys' in shipbuilding, gas-stokers, building labourers, dockers, even agricultural labourers, formed unions and/or struck in the early 1870s in what was by then the furthest extension of organization ever achieved. In 1873 the National Agricultural Labourers' Union claimed 100,000 members in approximately 1,000 branches. Among the miners, it was the South Wales coalfield, which was newer than other fields, rapidly expanding, and previously less well organized, that was the centre of mining militancy. Generally, the strikes of 1871–3, whether in industry or the older trades, were short, small and successful, pushing organization to its furthest limits.[28]

Inevitably, the depression of the late 1870s destroyed much of what had been gained by 1874. Union membership was halved, but still remained almost twice as high as it had been in 1870. The footholds of unionism in agriculture, on the docks and among other unskilled workers were lost, but advances made within industry were more stable. Overall, therefore, this foray into organizing beyond the skilled trades produced mixed results. One obvious weakness was ideological and strategic. The extension of organization downward and outward within the working class was not accompanied by a new set of political ideas, by novel strategic thinking, or what might be termed a new philosophy of labour. Yet clearly the outlook and style of the established unions were not well suited to the needs of the mass of workers.

The inability to maintain the gains of 1871–3 showed the inadequacy of the old unions and the old ideas for the new era of mass organization. In this sense, the Great Depression was a great teacher of labour. The great defeat of 1878, for example, prompted changes in the cotton unions, the fall in product prices gradually disabused the miners and others of the fondness for sliding scales, the railwaymen slowly discovered the need for an 'all grades' strategy, even the engineers toyed repeatedly (if unsuccessfully) with plans for opening membership more broadly, and, most obviously, a new generation of activists came quickly to the conclusion that a broad, inclusive strategy was the key to organizing the unskilled. These ideas and this strategic perspective crystallized in the New Unionist explosion of 1889, but the antecedents go back to the 1870s. It is no doubt true, as George Howell wrote in 1902, that very quickly the novelty of the New Unionism wore off, that the New Unions took on characteristics of the old and vice versa, but the net effect of the movement was nevertheless a major shift in the nature of the labour movement.[29]

Once again, in 1889–90, union membership jumped – from 817,000 in 1888 to 1,470,000 in 1890; the number of strikes increased a comparable amount, from 517 in 1888 to 1,211 in 1889 and just over 1,000 in 1890; while the workers involved grew by still more, from 119,000 in 1888 to just under 400,000 in 1890. As in 1871–3, strikes were relatively short and extremely successful. In 1889–90, 312,000 workers achieved clearcut victories in strikes, a further 254,000 some sort of compromise, while only 143,000 experienced defeat. This is quite a remarkable record, for it is a commonplace in industrial relations that neither side is ordinarily anxious to claim or concede victory or defeat. The industrial spread of strikes was even broader than in 1871–3, with much increased participation by transport workers and by workers in metal, engineering and shipbuilding, and somewhat reduced activity among the mostly skilled building trades. The shift towards heavy industry and towards the less skilled was thus further accentuated. Most significantly, the 1890s seem to have witnessed the first large-scale organization of women workers, mostly in textiles, but also in teaching and other white-collar occupations.[30]

Predictably enough, the wave of 1889–90 was followed by an employers' counter-attack that began during the depression of 1892–3 and continued through the decade. The reaction was notable in several respects. It led to some of the most bitter, and occasionally violent, confrontations in the history of labour, among dockers, miners, engineers, quarrymen, boot and shoemakers and others. More significantly, the employers took the initiative in evolving new forms of organization with which to prosecute their aims. The Shipping Federation and the Engineering Employers' Federation gave the lead in organized strikebreaking, while individual companies pursued the legal attack on unions culminating in the Taff Vale case. The advance in workers' organization thus prompted counter-organization among employers that tipped the balance of forces back in their direction. Lastly, despite the strength of the attack upon labour, union membership remained relatively stable through the 1890s and even began to creep up again after 1896. This was no doubt due to the much improved labour market in the late 1890s, but whatever the cause, it meant that unions kept more of the gains resulting from the New Unionism than they had from the 1871–3 strike wave. The mass organization of industry was gradually taking hold.[31]

The further development of unions and strikes was greatly hindered after 1900 by the combined effects of legal restrictions, which lasted until 1906, strong employer organizations and the uncertain economic climate. The underlying structural weakness of the British economy meant that the upswing beginning in 1896 was much weaker than in other countries, and unemployment from 1901 to 1910 was on average double that of 1896–1900. The numbers unemployed were below 3 per cent during 1898–1900, but consistently above that every year after until the war. Faced with such disadvantages, union strength stagnated, and even declined slightly, from 1900 until 1905. The legislation of 1906, and a reasonably strong demand for labour, allowed a jump in that year, but membership declined again from 1907 to 1909. By 1910 membership had crept over the 2·5 million mark, from which point a rapid rise ensued. Over 1·5 million new members were added during the next three years, as organization was consolidated and extended among transport workers – dockers and railwaymen primarily – and in basic industry.

The 'labour unrest' of 1911–13 was thus, in the first instance, a qualitative breakthrough in the extent of organization achieved despite tough, and quite unrelenting, employer opposition. Inevitably, such a movement had to be led by the rank and file, and often even took the form of a rebellion against the union leaders. Not without reason did Sydney Buxton, President of the Board of Trade, complain in 1911 about 'the serious diminution in the control which the leaders of the men used to exercise over their rank and file'. It was also left to the rank and file, and to various militants, to articulate a new philosophy of mass unionism and direct action. Whether a great many workers grasped the key tenets of syndicalism or not, the syndicalist approach resonated well with the mood of the men and helped to express its essential thrust. The rebellion within the labour movement against the leaders can in a sense be viewed as the critical, preliminary skirmish in the struggle for another, qualitative advance of organization.[32]

The nature of strikes during 1911–13 reinforces this general picture. The spread of unions and of the capacity to strike is revealed both in the mass character of disputes and in their industrial incidence. The size of the average strike increased from 350 during 1889–92 to 780 workers during 1910–13. As in 1889–90, these strikes were immensely successful, 1,135,000 strikers (44 per cent) winning outright victories against employers, 1,080,000 (42 per cent) being involved in compromises and only 363,000 (14 per cent) experiencing clearcut defeats. The pattern of participation revealed a further shift away from skilled craftsmen towards the newer, more 'proletarian' workers in industry and transport, with miners, dockers, railwaymen and textile workers especially prominent.[33]

The transformation wrought by these waves of organizing and strikes by 1914 is perhaps best revealed by the changed role and attitude of the government. The government had become interested in fostering industrial peace in the late 1880s, appointing the Royal Commission on Labour of 1889–92, setting up a Labour Department of the Board of Trade just after this, intervening in the 1893 coal dispute, and actively fostering conciliation from 1896 onward. Faced with employer resistance and not pressed on by any crisis in industrial relations, such efforts languished from about 1897 to 1910. The wave of strikes that broke out in 1911, however, brought government back into the field for good. Troops were sent to Wales in 1910, to Liverpool and other ports in 1911; Lloyd George got involved directly in 1911–12 with the railwaymen and the miners; and throughout the turbulence the government's chief conciliator, George Askwith, was kept continually busy. The net effect of government intervention was problematic – its protection of blacklegs angered workers and assisted employers, but Lloyd George's efforts to mediate were resented almost as much by the employers. By 1913 the government was disillusioned with the results of its efforts, and the outcome of the contests on the docks and the railways remained in doubt, the possibility of major disputes in 1914–15 looming just over the horizon. It is especially unclear just what role government would have played in such confrontations, but it seems unlikely they would have been able to withdraw. By 1914 workers were organized in all the major industries, and their combined action could have dramatic consequences. Government could no longer remain aloof from the day-to-day conduct of industrial relations.[34]

Though the First World War is beyond the scope of this essay, it should be noted, at least by way of postscript, that its primary effect on workers was to spread their organization even further and deeper than it had been in 1914. The battle to establish collective bargaining had therefore been won by 1918, and the conduct of industrial relations permanently altered.[35] This was

Table 3.3 *Strikes, Strikers and Trade Union Membership in France, 1870–1914*

	Strikes	Strikers	Union membership
1870	116	88,200	
71	52	14,100	
72	151	21,100	
73	44	4,900	
74	58	7,800	
75	101	16,600	
76	102	21,200	
77	55	12,900	
78	73	38,500	
79	88	54,400	
1880	190	110,400	
81	209	68,000	
82	271	65,500	
83	181	42,000	
84	112	33,900	
85	123	20,800	
86	195	35,300	
87	194	38,100	
88	188	51,500	
89	199	89,100	
1890	389	119,400	140,000
91	313	108,900	205,000
92	268	45,900	289,000
93	634	172,500	402,000
94	397	54,400	403,000
95	409	46,000	420,000
96	486	49,700	423,000
97	366	68,500	430,000
98	386	81,300	438,000
99	771	117,300	420,000
1900	890	215,700	492,000
01	541	110,800	589,000
02	571	212,400	614,000
03	642	120,300	644,000
04	1087	269,900	716,000
05	849	175,900	781,000
06	1354	437,800	836,000
07	1313	197,500	896,000
08	1109	123,800	957,000
09	1067	177,000	945,000
1910	1517	287,000	977,000
11	1489	228,200	1,029,000
12	1150	270,700	1,064,000
13	1099	226,400	1,027,000
14	685	161,400	1,026,000

Source: All information in this table was derived from E. Shorter and C. Tilly, *Strikes in France, 1830–1968* (Cambridge, 1974), Appendix B, pp. 360–76.

Table 3.4 *Strikes, Strikers and Trade Union Membership in Germany, 1864–1915*

	Strikes (from Steglich)
1864	23
65	30
66	9
67	14
68	14
69	98
1870	79
71	190
72	213
73	223
74	103
75	43
76	41
77	6
78	12
79	3
1880	9

	Strikes	*Strikers*	*Strikes*	*Strikers*	*Free Trade Union Member-ship*	*All union membership (excluding salaried employees)*
	(official figures)		*(General Commission of the Free Trade Unions)*		*(000s)*	*(000s)*
Jan 1889 – June 1890	1,131	394,440				
1890–1			226	38,536		
1891					277·7	343·3
92			73	3,022	237·1	294·9
93			116	9,356	223·5	284·7
94			131	7,328	246·5	313·6
95			204	14,032	259·2	331·9
96			483	128,808	329·2	409·1
97			578	63,116	412·4	513·0
98			985	60,162	493·7	610·9
99	1,364	104,636	976	100,779	580·5	723·7
1900	1,500	131,888	852	115,711	680·4	848·8
01	1,019	60,677	727	48,522	677·5	857·1
02	1,135	64,217	861	55,713	733·2	919·2
03	1,501	120,876	1,282	121,576	887·7	1,079·1
04	1,990	137,240	1,625	135,957	1052·1	1,271·6
05	2,657	526,810	2,323	507,964	1344·8	1,650·0
06	3,626	349,327	3,480	416,043	1689·7	2,055·3
07	2,512	273,597	2,792	281,030	1865·5	2,248·7
08	1,524	112,110	2,052	126,883	1831·7	2,201·8
09	1,652	119,849	2,045	131,244	1832·7	2,211·5
1910	3,228	369,809	3,194	369,011	2017·3	2,435·0
11	2,798	356,163	2,914	325,253	2339·8	2,788·5
12	2,834	481,094	2,825	479,589	2553·2	3,007·1
13	2,464	311,048	2,600	248,986	2573·7	3,023·1
14			1,407	96,681	2075·8	2,436·3

Sources: Sources for strike data are listed in note 36. Data on union membership were taken from G. S. Bain and R. Price, *Profiles of Union Growth* (Oxford, 1980), 133.

what the great waves of militancy of 1871–3, 1889–90 and 1911–13 had been about, although on the surface the demands usually concerned wages, piecework, apprentices and similar narrow, 'economistic' issues. The real issue was power, which is, of course, the essence of the entire history of strikes.

IV

Issues of power were equally central to the evolution of strikes and unions on the continent. Tables 3.3 and 3.4 summarize in statistical form the course of strikes and union membership in France and Germany before the war.[36] These data are slightly more controversial than those for Britain – indeed the greater politicization of industrial conflict in France and Germany finds a direct expression in arguments about strike statistics – but they suffice to show the main trends in both nations. The most casual inspection will reveal that much the same pattern of overall growth obtained in France and Germany as in Great Britain. This suggests strongly that, in general, rather similar processes of class formation and mobilization were operating in all three countries. At the same time, however, a closer examination of the data shows some interesting and important points of divergence in the behaviour of the various indices which highlight substantial differences in the position of labour in British, French and German society.

The similarities are most easily dealt with. Between 1885–90 and 1910–14 the frequency of strikes increased by four-and-a-half times in France, even allowing for growth in the population and the workforce. Simultaneously, union membership increased over seven times, from less than 150,000 in the late 1880s to over a million just before the war. In Germany, membership in the Free Trade Unions grew by a comparable amount, from approximately 278,000 in 1891 to over 2·5 million in 1913, while the number of strikes jumped from less than 200 per year in the early 1890s to more than 2,500 per year during 1910–14. The gross statistical record is thus very close to that of Great Britain where, starting from a somewhat stronger base in the late 1880s, unions and strikes both grew to unprecedented levels by 1913.

It would seem reasonable to argue from this similarity that, as in Britain, workers in France and Germany were gaining increasing strength and organizational capacity both in the community and at work. Indeed, the late industrialization and urbanization of both countries relative to Britain should have meant that those transformations in the nature of industrial organization and urban ecology noted in Britain were even more accentuated in France and Germany. Factories were newer, larger and more technically advanced; cities grew more rapidly and massively, creating in extreme form the physical settings for the emergence of distinct working-class cultures.

In fact, the strength and political significance of working-class communities was notable in both France and Germany, and was reflected in aspects of politics and strikes. Edward Shorter and Charles Tilly have shown, for example, that as much strike activity was co-ordinated on regional as on industrial or occupational lines, by the local *bourses du travail* encompassing all the trades within the commune as often as by the federations that linked up workers in the same trade across local boundaries.[37] Left-wing political activity also achieved important victories when community power was mobilized at municipal elections.[38] In Germany, leftist politics struck deep roots in working-class residential areas, becoming often the basis of community life and thus determining the form and the idiom through which working-class culture was expressed. Much has been written about how the elaboration of a dense network of social institutions, grounded in the neighbourhoods even if linked formally in a national structure, under the auspices of Social Democracy, helped to integrate the Social Democratic Party (SPD) into the political and social life of the empire.[39] But perhaps it would make more sense, or at least equal sense, to reinterpret these practices in more favourable terms, as something which added substantially to the collective strength, as well as to the short-term well-being, of German workers.[40] Just how the building of strong working-class communities affected political and industrial struggle is still far from obvious – even in Britain the precise connections are still not clear[41] – but it surely must have added measurably to workers' economic resources, their sense of collective worth and identity, and to their organizational and social networks.

The transformation of production seems to have had more ambiguous effects upon organization and strikes in France and Germany. It is necessary in this context to distinguish two different components in the economic development of both countries prior to 1914. The most spectacular type of growth involved the development of those new industries – steel, chemicals, electricity and related industries – often taken to represent the core of the 'second industrial revolution'. Production in these industries tended to be more highly rationalized and capital intensive than in the rest of the economy, to be located either in new manufacturing centres or in the suburban belts surrounding the metropolis and other very large cities. The character of the workforces employed in these new sectors differed markedly from other industries too: workers were often recruited from among rural proletarians or from the unskilled urban labourers, with just a sprinkling of skilled craftsmen. Employers in these industries were also different: they were larger, possessed greater capital and hence economic leverage, and often had close links with large-scale, financial interests. These characteristics combined to make it especially difficult in the short term for workers in these new plants to organize and to resist the heavy-handed paternalism practised by their employers. Over the long run, of course, the new technology and the rationalized flow of production would place increased power in the hands of workers on the shop floor and facilitate militancy and organization. Indeed, some few workers were able to grasp their new role in the production process and utilize it effectively quite early on, as seems to have been the case in the Dortmund Union steel strike of 1911. But on balance such workers remained weak throughout most of heavy industry in Germany and in France until after 1914.[42]

Inevitably, however, the growth of these new sectors with their modern techniques and patterns of production spilled over into prosperity for industries organized more traditionally and for the service sector. For these workers, growth meant steadier employment, greater involvement in the market and its attendant uncertainties, increases in the scale of operations, in the social distances between workers and employers and in the amount of supervision and control. But because the details of the production processes were not normally disrupted, the bargaining power of the skilled, and even, to a lesser extent, those without recognized skills, was enhanced; organization proceeded apace and strike activity flourished. Judging from statistics on the industrial distributions of strikes and lock-outs, this type of worker consistently took the lead in strike movements.[43] They also formed the basis of socialist support in both nations.

It would surely be stretching the meaning of the phrase to say that France and Germany were 'dual economies' during this era, but there certainly were marked differences in the ability of various groups within the working class to organize and press their grievances collectively. And these differences, rooted in the changing and varied nature of production, were reflected in the trend of organization and strikes. In France, both union membership and strikes were at very low levels until the mid-1880s, from which point a steady climb ensued. Union strength jumped dramatically in 1889–90, and was accompanied by a strike wave that ended only in 1893. Another jump in strikes occurred in 1899–1900, after which the frequency of conflict remained high until 1914. The peak, however, came in 1906, not, as in Britain, in the immediate prewar years. Union membership increased more regularly and peaked later, rising from 780,000 in 1905 to over a million in 1911. At that point, however, the rising trend of unionization also stabilized, so that from 1911 to 1914 neither strikes nor unionization were increasing.

The fact that both indicators level off so obviously before the war suggests important, underlying weaknesses in the capacity of French workers to form stable unions and wage collective struggles.[44] The key, it seems, was the inability to make any significant breakthrough into the new industries and among the not-so-skilled workers within them. As Bernard Moss has shown, both the industrial and political activity of labour was dominated by skilled workers from the revival of the 1880s onwards, and even by 1914 this had changed but little. The attempted general strike of 1909, for example, failed precisely for want of support among 'modern' factory workers, while the famous strike at Renault on the outskirts of Paris in 1913 was carried on almost exclusively by the handful of skilled workers at the plant.[45] Between 1905 and 1910, it appears, the approximate limits of organization and rank-and-file action among the skilled were reached, and further growth depended from then on upon the mobilization of new, hitherto unorganized, groups of workers. Since this would inevitably entail sharp confrontation with paternalistic employers and with an increasingly unsympathetic state, it would have required novel strategic thinking on the part of activists and new sources of strength for the rank and file of workers, but neither was on the agenda before the onset of war in 1914.[46]

The same problem seems also to have beset the German labour movement. There the first noticeable upsurge came earlier, during the boom years of the *Gründerzeit*, but, of course, in this period it was almost solely the work of the skilled artisans. Activity waned during the depression of the late 1870s and 1880s, but revived in 1889, as it did in France and in Britain. Unions were on the defensive in the early 1890s there as well, but from 1896 membership began to climb steadily and, from 1899, quite steeply. Strikes followed a very similar path, rising from a low level during 1892–5 to a substantially higher one at the turn of the century. As in France, however, the peak of activity came much earlier than in Britain, that is, in 1905–7. Another revival did occur just before the war, but this particular strike wave was not as large as the previous one and was produced by somewhat fewer, though larger, and thus more defensive strikes than that of 1905–7.[47] The pattern of union membership points even more clearly to the largely defensive quality of worker activity immediately prior to the war. The number of unionists stood at about 850,000 in 1900 and rose to more than 3 million in 1912. But in the next year growth ceased, and by 1914 half a million members were lost to the unions.

Much as in France, therefore, the strength of the workers' movement in Germany seems to have reached a sort of limit some years before the war, and not to have been expanding after 1910. Several factors no doubt interacted to produce this depressing result. First, by 1905 German employers were organized into two powerful associations pledged to mutual support in the fight against the Free Trade Unions. They had first come together upon the occasion of the Crimmitschau lock-out of 1903–4, and from then on, most obviously in the mining strike of 1905, played an important part in encouraging and sustaining employers' resistance to workers' attempts to organize.[48] A second factor was the increasing tendency, encouraged by the leaders of the unions, to settle disputes without recourse to strikes. Hartmut Kaelble and Heinrich Volkmann, in their analysis of German strikes from 1891 to 1914, argue that the failure of strikes to continue to grow after 1905 was related to the emergence of 'organized capitalism'. They thus point to the continued growth, even after 1905, of wage movements settled without strikes (*Bewegungen ohne Arbeitseinstellung*) and the emergence of negotiated contracts between employers and unions during the same period as evidence for the institutionalization of conflict.[49]

Yet they also admit that these tendencies, and the latter process in particular, were much more evident in industries dominated by skilled craftsmen and their organizations than in the newer, mass production industries. This suggests that the truly critical factor in limiting the growth of unions and strikes after 1905 was the failure to crack the hold of employers in heavy industry over their workforces. Thus, although the German metalworkers' union had enrolled over half a million members by 1913, few of these were located in the expanding centre of the industry in the Ruhr. And even though there is evidence for a certain amount of unrest and activity among the less skilled before the war, it remained the case that from 1901 to 1913 engineering and metal workers accounted for a smaller percentage of strikes and of strikers than their proportion in their workforce, while miners, builders and woodworkers accounted for substantially more than their 'proper share'. In the end, it would require the imperatives and exigencies of war to bring such workers decisively – and even then not permanently – within the ambit of the organized labour movement.[50]

Overall, then, the balance of forces in France and Germany combined to restrict the spread of organization and to lower workers' capacity for collective action, at least in comparison with British workers. The most telling indicator is union density, which in prewar Germany reached 15 per cent (1913 = 16·4 per cent, 1914 = 13 per cent) and which was no higher than 10 per cent in France. In the United Kingdom, however, the figure was just about 25 per cent. The difference was not simply quantitative but also qualitative, for it meant that in France and Germany unions and strikes remained the province primarily of the skilled workers, with participation by the emerging mass of factory proletarians increasing, but still very minor.[51]

The precise set of reasons for these differences in the strength of workers in the different countries prior to 1914 are still not fully known, and it would be silly to pretend to settle the issue in the brief treatment offered here. Some, like Arno Mayer, would put emphasis upon the successful political regrouping of right-wing forces in alliance with conservative employers in both Germany and France in temporarily halting the advance of labour, and there is certainly a case to be made for the primacy of politics in such matters.[52] Others, like Georges Haupt, seem to view the weakness of labour during 1912–14 as largely a matter of conjuncture.[53] This essay has placed the emphasis primarily upon the distinctive and uneven character of industrial organization in France and Germany which, it is clear, differed significantly from the more complicated and heterogeneous system prevailing in Great Britain. Whatever the ultimate mix of influences, it should be obvious that those long-term structural factors connected with the transformation of the workplace and the community which helped to underpin and sustain militancy and organization were mediated not only by economic conjuncture, which did so much to determine the rhythm of protest, but also by organization and politics.

Notes: Chapter 3

An earlier version of the portions of this essay dealing solely with the British experience appeared as 'Strikes, 1870–1914', in C. J. Wrigley (ed.), *The History of British Industrial Relations, 1875–1914* (Brighton, 1982).

1 E. Shorter and C. Tilly, *Strikes in France, 1830–1968* (Cambridge, 1974), 307, attribute the 'distinctive, mountain-like, rise' in strikes from 1890 to 1920 in France and the rest of Europe to 'the great mobilization of the working classes'; and H. Kaelble and H. Volkmann, in 'Konjunktur und Streik während des Übergangs zum Organisierten Kapitalismus in Deutschland', *Zeitschrift für Wirtschafts- und Sozialwissenschaften* 92 (1972): 513–44 (539), suggest that 'Der Streik war das bevorzugte Kampfmittel in der Organisationsphase der Arbeiterbewegung'.

2 G. P. Bevan, 'The strikes of the past ten years', *Journal of the Royal Statistical Society* 42 (March 1880): 35–54.

3 G. Howell, 'Great strikes: their origin, costs, and results', *Cooperative Wholesale Societies Annual 1889*, 310.

4 T. Wright, 'On the condition of the working classes', *Fraser's Magazine* 4 (October 1871): 427.

5 The importance of strike waves in labour history is stressed generally by E. J. Hobsbawm, 'Economic fluctuations and some social movements since 1800', in idem, *Labouring Men* (London, 1964); and for Britain in J. Cronin, *Industrial Conflict in Modern Britain* (London, 1979), 45–73.

6 One implication of this recurring pattern is that the tension between entrenched union leaders and rank-and-file activists is a long-term, indeed structural, aspect of labour history, not peculiar to any particular moment but to those various periods when workers on the shop floor perceived a possibility of advance beyond what the leaders have come to expect. Ideological factors, generational differences, degrees of bureaucratization and government policy all help to condition and mediate this tension but its roots seem to go much deeper. The evidence for this view is scattered widely throughout the record of labour history, but one might begin the study of the unofficial character of virtually all insurgencies with George Howell. He claimed in 1890 that 'it is perhaps a bold thing to say, but the statement can be made with considerable confidence, that in 90 per cent of the strikes which take place, the men directly concerned are the instigators and promoters, and that the union is the brake on the wheel which prevents too great precipitation, and liability to consequent failure'. See G. Howell, *The Conflicts of Capital and Labour*, 2nd edn (London, 1890), 211. The echoes with more recent complaints are striking.

7 The persistent preference for conciliation in the British system of industrial relations has been stressed especially by F. Wilkinson, 'The development of collective bargaining in Britain to the early 1920s', paper presented to the Shop Floor Bargaining Seminar, King's College Research Centre, Cambridge (March 1981). See also J. H. Porter, 'Wage bargaining under conciliation agreements, 1870–1914', *Economic History Review* 23 (1970): 460–75; and R. Davidson, 'Social conflict and social administration: the Conciliation Act in British industrial relations', in T. C. Smout (ed.), *The Search for Wealth and Stability* (London, 1979), 175–97.

8 For the most recent overview, see E. H. Hunt, *British Labour History, 1815–1914* (London, 1981).

9 On the beginnings of organization among teachers, shop assistants, government workers and others in white-collar jobs after 1880, see Hunt, *British Labour History*, 302.

10 Quoted in G. Potter, 'Trades' unions, strikes, and lock-outs: a rejoinder', *Contemporary Review* 17 (1871): 529.

11 Bevan, 'The strikes of the past ten years', 45; L. H. Lees, 'Strikes and the urban hierarchy in English industrial towns, 1842–1901', in J. Cronin and J. Schneer (eds.), *Social Conflict and the Political Order in Modern Britain* (London, 1982), 52–72.

12 Bevan, 'The strikes of the past ten years', 39–42; Cronin, *Industrial Conflict*, 159–61 and, on mining in particular, 179–83.

13 P. Stearns, 'The unskilled and industrialization: a transformation of consciousness', *Archiv für Sozialgeschichte* 16 (1976): 249–82, is a useful comparative overview. For the date on Britain, see J. A. Banks, 'The social structure of nineteenth century England as seen through the census', in R. Lawton (ed.), *The Census and Social Structure* (London, 1978), 179–223.

14 Hunt, *British Labour History*, 312–13, 331–2. The contrast with the mid-Victorian mix between skilled and casual labour is especially marked. See R. Samuel, 'The workshop of the world: steam power and hand technology in mid-Victorian Britain', *History Workshop Journal* 3 (1977): 6–72.

15 E. Hobsbawm, 'Custom, wages, and work-load', in idem, *Labouring Men*, 344–70.

16 On skill in general, see C. More, *Skill and the English Working Class, 1870–1914* (London, 1980).

17 The situation on the railways posed particularly difficult problems. See G. Alderman, 'The railway companies and the growth of trade unionism in the late nineteenth and early twentieth centuries', *Historical Journal* 14 (1971): 129–52; P. S. Gupta, 'Railway trade unions in Britain, c. 1880–1920', *Economic History Review* 19 (1966): 124–53; and, of course, P. S. Bagwell, *The Railwaymen*, 2 vols (London, 1963).

18 In general, see R. Dickinson, *The West European City* (London, 1961), 463–4; J. P. McKay, *Tramways and Trolleys: The Rise of Mass Transport in Europe* (Princeton, N.J., 1966), 205–25; S. D. Chapman (ed.), *The History of Working-Class Housing* (Newton Abbot,

1971); J. Burnett, *A Social History of Housing* (Newton Abbot, 1978); and J. R. Kellett, *The Impact of Railways on Victorian Cities* (London, 1969).

19 See, for both reactions, S. Meacham, *A Life Apart. The English Working Class* (London, 1977); G. Stedman Jones, 'Working-class culture and working-class politics in London, 1870–1900', *Journal of Social History* 7 (1974): 460–508; and R. Roberts, *The Classic Slum* (Manchester, 1971). For the beginnings of a critique, see J. Cronin, 'Labour insurgency and class formation. Comparative perspectives on the crisis of 1917–1920 in Europe', in idem and L. Siriami (eds), *Work, Community, and Power* (Philadelphia, 1983), 20–48.

20 C. Storm-Clark, 'The miners, 1870–1970: a test case for oral history', *Victorian Studies* 15 (1971): 49–74; Cronin, *Industrial Conflict*, 180–3; and, on Wales, K. O. Morgan, 'The New Liberalism and the challenge of labour', *Welsh History Review* 6 (1973): 288–312.

21 P. Joyce, *Work, Society and Politics. The Culture of the Factory in Later Victorian England* (Brighton, 1980). Whether Joyce has exaggerated the degree of paternalism and supra-class politics of 1850–80 or not, his description of the change after 1880 seems very accurate. As he explains, 'both industry and the town were by the end of the nineteenth century taking on their modern forms, forms marked by the mutual ignorance and antagonism of the classes'. 'The changing ecology of the factory town, and the increased degree of organisation and commercialisation in popular culture combined to enlarge the scope of people's lives, and break the hold of the old communities of work, religion and politics on their daily lives' (p. 342). There is obviously a need for more local, provincial studies of such developments. The ideal would be a study that combined the technical sophistication of R. M. Pritchard's *Housing and the Spatial Structure of the City* (Cambridge, 1976) with the theoretical concerns of Joyce.

22 H. Pollins, 'Transport lines and social division', in R. Glass (ed.), *London: Aspects of Change* (London, 1964), 34–46.

23 See C. Wrigley, 'Liberals and the desire of working-class representatives in Battersea, 1886–1922', in K. D. Brown (ed.), *Essays in Anti-Labour History* (London, 1974), 126–58.

24 On the state, see J. White, '1910–1914 reconsidered', in Cronin and Schneer, *Social Conflict and the Political Order*, 73–95.

25 These statistics were taken originally from the Department of Employment and Productivity, *British Labour Statistics: Historical Abstract 1868–1968* (London, 1971). They also appear, together with extensive strike statistics, in Cronin, *Industrial Conflict*, 206–38.

26 J. Cronin, 'Stages, cycles, and insurgencies: the economics of unrest', in T. Hopkins and I. Wallerstein (eds), *Processes of the World System* (London, 1980), 101–18.

27 See Table 3.1 above for details, as well as Bevan, 'The strikes of the past ten years'; Howell, 'Great strikes', and the *Report on Strikes and Lockouts in 1888* (London, 1889). On the iron and steel workers, see N. P. Howard, 'Cooling the heat: a history of the rise of trade unionism in the South Yorkshire iron and steel industry, from the origins to the First World War', in S. Pollard and C. Holmes (eds), *Essays in the Economic and Social History of South Yorkshire* (Sheffield, 1976), 59–73.

28 On shipbuilding, see J. F. Clarke, 'Workers in the Tyneside shipyards in the nineteenth century', in N. McCord (ed.), *Essays in Tyneside Labour History* (Newcastle upon Tyne, 1977), 109–31; on agricultural workers, see Howell, 'Great strikes', 301–3; and R. Groves, *Sharpen the Sickle! The History of the Farm Workers Union* (London, 1949) 39–92.

29 G. Howell, *Labour Legislation, Labour Movements, and Labour Leaders* (London, 1902). More generally, see Hunt, *British Labour History*, 304–15, where the contrast between the New Unionism and the old is reviewed. Hunt generally opts for the 'revisionist' perspective which minimizes the difference between the two, but the evidence he marshalls nevertheless makes clear that the labour movement was very different after 1889 than before.

30 See S. Lewenhak, *Women and Trade Unions* (London, 1977); and Hunt, *British Labour History*, 299–300.

31 See E. Wigham, *Power to Manage* (London, 1973), 29–62 on the Engineering Employers' Federation; and J. Saville, 'Trade unions and free labour: the background of the Taff Vale decision', in A. Briggs and J. Saville (eds), *Essays in Labour History* (London, 1967), 317–50, more generally.

32 Buxton, quoted in C. J. Wrigley, *The Government and Industrial Relations in Britain* (Loughborough, 1979), 5. On rank-and-file movements and syndicalism, see B. Holton, *British Syndicalism, 1900–1914* (London, 1976), and R. Price, *Masters, Unions and Men* (Cambridge, 1980), 238–67. For the view that the unrest was a matter of the trade cycle and

little else, see H. Pelling, 'The labour unrest, 1911–1914', in *Popular Politics and Society in Late Victorian Britain* (London, 1968), 147–64. See also E. H. Phelps Brown, *The Growth of British Industrial Relations, 1906–1914* (London, 1959).

33 The general pattern of strikes is most clearly described in G. R. Askwith, *Industrial Problems and Disputes* (London, 1920). Evidence of collaboration between skilled and semi-skilled in the engineering industry can be found in W. Lewchuck, 'Technology, pay systems, and the motor companies', paper presented to the SSRC Conference on Business and Labour History, March 1981, at the London School of Economics.

34 Wrigley, *The Government and Industrial Relations*.

35 For a useful introduction to industrial relations after 1918, see W. R. Garside, 'Management and men: aspects of British industrial relations in the inter-war period', in B. Supple (ed.), *Essays in British Business History* (Oxford, 1977), 244–67.

36 Data in these tables were derived from several sources. Most of the French data came from E. Shorter and C. Tilly, *Strikes in France, 1830–1968* (Cambridge, 1974), Appendix B, 360–76. They relied upon the official statistics and on M. Perrot, *Les ouvriers en grève*, 2 vols (Paris, 1974), for the years 1871–90. A discussion on the merits and deficiencies of these statistics is contained in Appendix B, pp. 351–9. See also their comments on the differences between the strike statistics of various countries, p. 334.

For Germany, no such general survey exists, but the relevant information can be extracted from J. Kuczynski, *Die Geschichte der Lage der Arbeiter unter dem Kapitalismus*, Part I, Vol. 3 (Berlin, 1962), 205, and Vol. 4 (Berlin, 1967), 155; and from D. Fricke, *Die deutsche Arbeiterbewegung, 1869 bis 1914* (Berlin, 1976), 757–70. Both Fricke and Kuczynski derived their material from the various reports of the government and the General Commission of the Free Trade Unions. For a discussion of the lengthy political controversy over strike statistics, and the differences between the series produced by the unions and the state, see Fricke. The series for 1864–80 is based upon the lengthy list of strikes discovered, checked and organized by Walter Steglich and is included here simply to show trends, not to suggest the actual dimensions of strike activity. See W. Steglich, 'Eine Streiktabelle für Deutschland 1864 bis 1880', *Jahrbuch für Wirtschaftsgeschichte* (1960/II): 235–83. cf. also the data recently published in K. Tenfelde and H. Volkmann (eds), *Streik. Zur Geschichte des Arbeitskampfes in Deutschland während der Industrialisierung* (Munich, 1981).

37 Shorter and Tilly, *Strikes in France*, 164–5.

38 J. Scott, 'Social history and the history of socialism: French municipalities in the 1890s', *Movement Social* 65 (1968): 71–80.

39 The classic texts are G. Roth, *The Social Democrats in Imperial Germany* (Totowa, N.J., 1963); and D. Groh, *Negative Integration und Revolutionärer Attentismus* (Frankfurt a.M., 1973).

40 J. Cronin, 'Labor insurgency' is a first attempt at such a reinterpretation.

41 Though David Englander's pioneering PhD. thesis begins to chart these interrelationships. See D. Englander, 'Landlord and tenant in urban Britain: the politics of housing reform, 1838–1924' (PhD. thesis, Warwick, 1979).

42 D. Crew, 'Steel, sabotage and socialism: the strike at the Dortmund "Union" steelworks in 1911', in R. J. Evans (ed.), *The German Working Class, 1889–1933. The Politics of Everyday Life* (London, 1982), 108–41. In this essay, Crew disputes the arguments about the revolutionary potential of the 'Massenarbeiter' in the new industries and the argument that the Free Trade Unions and the SPD were unsympathetic and uninvolved with these new recruits to industry. For the original position, see E. Brockhaus, *Zusammensetzung und Neustrukturierung der Arbeiterklasse vor dem ersten Weltkrieg. Zur Krise der professionellen Arbeiterbewegung* (Munich, 1975). For accounts of the relationship between new technologies and worker resistance that follow rather different approaches, see H. Homburg, 'Anfänge des Taylorsystems in Deutschland vor dem ersten Weltkrieg. Eine Problemskizze unter besonderer Berücksichtigung der Arbeiterskämpfe bei Bosch 1913', *Geschichte und Gesellschaft* 4 (1978): 170–94; and D. Groh, 'Intensification of work and industrial conflict in Germany, 1896–1914', *Politics and Society* 8 (1979): 349–97.

43 Fricke, *Die deutsche Arbeiterbewegung*, 764–5; P. Stearns, *Lives of Labour. Work in a Maturing Industrial Society* (London, 1975), Appendix; D. Geary, *European Labour Protest, 1848–1939* (London, 1981), ch. 3.

44 This dip in strikes and temporary stabilization of union membership has been noted by

Perrot and by Shorter and Tilly. The former sees it as due to a turn towards other forms of collective action by workers after 1910, while the latter see it as a mere aberration along the general trend of development. Obviously, I disagree somewhat with both accounts. See Shorter and Tilly, *Strikes in France*, 380.

45 B. Moss, *The Origins of the French Labor Movement, 1830–1914. The Socialism of Skilled Workers* (Berkeley, Calif., 1976), 159; V. J. Knapp, 'Popular participation in the European general strikes prior to 1914', *Studies in History and Society* 5 (Fall 1973): 18; G. Cross, 'Productivity and French labor, 1910–1931' (MA thesis, Wisconsin, 1973).

46 P. Stearns, 'Against the strike threat: employer policy toward labor agitation in France, 1900–1914', *Journal of Modern History* 40 (1968): 474–500, provides evidence for paternalist attitudes even if his argument fails to account for them fully; and Moss, *The Origins of the French Labor Movement*, 148, documents the government repression of strikes from 1906.

47 On the transformation of strike strategy, see Brockhaus, *Zusammensetzung und Neustrukturierung*, 69–71.

48 C. Schorske, *German Social Democracy, 1905–1917. The Development of the Great Schisma* (Cambridge, Mass., 1955); E. G. Spencer, 'Employer response to unionism: Ruhr coal industrialists before 1914', *Journal of Modern History* 48 (1976): 397–412.

49 Kaelble and Volkmann, 'Konjunktur und Streik', 529–39.

50 Stearns, *Lives of Labour*, Appendix; D. Geary, 'Radicalism and the worker: metalworkers and revolution, 1914–23', in R. J. Evans (ed.), *Society and Politics in Wilhelmine Germany* (London, 1978), 267–86. The absence of sustained militancy or organization is brought out quite starkly in D. Crew, *Town in the Ruhr* (New York, 1979), 162–3; and in B. Moore, *Injustice: The Social Bases of Obedience and Revolt* (White Plains, N.Y., 1978).

51 On France, see Moss, *The Origins of the French Labor Movement, passim*; on Germany, see D. Fricke, *Zur Organisation und Tätigkeit der deutschen Arbeiterbewegung (1890–1914)* (Leipzig, 1962), 225 and *passim*; H. Grebing, *The History of the German Labour Movement* (London, 1969), 84; and for a detailed local study, R. Comfort, *Revolutionary Hamburg* (Stanford, Calif., 1966).

52 See A. Mayer, 'Political crisis and partial modernization: the outcomes in Germany, Austria, Hungary and Italy after World War I', in C. Bertrand (ed.), *Revolutionary Situations in Europe 1917–1922* (Montreal, 1977), 119–31.

53 G. Haupt, *Socialism and the Great War* (Oxford, 1972), 216–49.

4 International Strike Waves: a Critical Assessment

FRIEDHELM BOLL

I

The analytical approach of comparing patterns of workers' behaviour during strikes on an international basis has remained, not unexpectedly, the domain of sociologists and economists since they have had the long-term data available.[1] After a critical survey of quantitive strike research undertaken so far, Erich Weede (as J. E. Snyder before him) distinguishes between two models of interpretation which could help our understanding of the subject.[2] The 'economic-psychological model' tries to explain the readiness to strike by using indicators of the social conditions, the labour market (relative unemployment), the development of real wages and the rising dissatisfaction as a result of these factors. Those most frequently discussed on this model are the deterioration of the economic situation through decreasing real wages (inflation, a sudden stop to real wage increases) and an improving labour market when the economy is picking up.[3] In the German-speaking world the work of Heinrich Volkmann in particular is connected with this model. His special interest focuses on the increasing rationalization of industrial conflict through the organization of the conflicting parties. He regards this not only as strengthening the position of workers on the labour market but as a trend towards changing forms of labour conflict. Spontaneous, suddenly erupting, isolated, long-lasting and ineffective strikes are substituted by 'rationalized' industrial conflicts[4] which are strongly supported, short and well organized, taking into account the strength of the workers and the economic situation. This line of interpretation has rendered its best results in the German context but also with regard to Scandinavia where frequent industrial conflicts during the first half of the century were followed by a period after the Second World War when strikes and lock-outs decreased drastically. At the same time, an increasing degree of organization of the two sides of industry could be observed.[5] This research concentrated on identifying long-term tendencies and largely ignored the wave effects in this development.

Underlying this area of research are certain basic assumptions on modernization and rationalization of industrial conflict. They contradict the basic assumptions of the second model, which could be called the 'protest model'. This model emphasizes the discontinuities in the industrialization process and sees the unstable nature of economic growth clearly reflected in the wave-like development of industrial conflicts.[6] Continuous economic fluctuations require new positive answers from the labour movement, which provides them in cyclical strike waves. James E. Cronin, demonstrating his model with the British example, expressed these preconditions much more clearly than Edward Shorter and Charles Tilly had done using the history of strikes in France.[7] Without denying the influence of the trade cycle, they regarded the history of industrial conflict there as being mainly characterized by coming in waves. They thought this was due, on the one hand, to the changing organizational strength of the workers (in the sense that they were capable of solidarity, not in the sense of a stricter giant organization) and, on the other hand, to political developments such as an election year, government crises, or even the participation of workers' representatives in a government.

Cronin thought it necessary to advocate a fundamental change of paradigm, thus taking a polemical counter-position vis-à-vis merely economic or sociological strike research. The determining factors were those which caused the cyclical economic development,[8] not the repercussions of the trade cycle. His approach regards the strength of the workers as an important precondition too. However, this is not in terms of a collective control of working conditions on the level of established organizations but as a precondition for spontaneous and inventive action in solidarity against employers. Special emphasis is given to the continuous change in the structure of the labour force due to technological development. And the change in the structure of working conditions is thus followed by new conflicts. After periods of stagnation these conflicts erupt in new forms of struggle encompassing new and usually less qualified workers. The argument in favour of a history of industrial conflict developing in the context of strike waves will be explained in more detail using the French and the British examples.

II

Shorter and Tilly made a fundamental observation, namely, that the development of strikes in France during the past 150 years has been characterized by the outbreak of major strike action which had little to do with the trade cycle but a lot to do with the sudden strengthening of labour organizations and political events. The years 1936 and 1968 were the most outstanding dates in this chain of strike waves. A look at the national strike tables shows that, apart from France and Britain, the eruptive character of strike waves is a general hallmark in industrial countries and these strike waves often peak at the same time or follow each other very closely (Table 4.1). Figures 4.1 and 4.2 provide an even clearer picture of the peaks in strike activity for the period 1890–1914. However, they only show the figures for three countries for which strike statistics are readily available.

III

The peaks in strike activity shown in the diagrams have been calculated by different methods and are thus not fully comparable. Even after 1920,

Table 4.1   *Peaks of National Strike Activity, 1870–1921*

France	1870	1880	1890	1899	1904	1910	1919
		1882	1893	1900	1906	1911	1920
Britain	1872		1890			1910	1918
	1873		1893			1913	1921
Germany	1870		1889	1898	1904	1910	1919
	1873		1890	1900	1906	1912	1920
Italy		1885		1900	1906	1911	1919
				1902	1907		1920
United States		1886	1890	1899	1906	1910	1916
		1887	1891	1903	1907		1919
Russia					1905	1912	1917
					1906	1914	

Sources: France – E. Shorter and C. Tilly, *Strikes in France, 1830–1968* (Cambridge, 1974), 107. Because of their purely quantitative method the strikes of 1910–11 were not included by these authors. Great Britain – J. E. Cronin, *Industrial Conflict in Modern Britain* (London, 1979), 39. German Reich, Italy, United States and Russia – own calculations using the strike tables published by B. R. Mitchell, *European Historical Statistics, 1750–1970* (London, 1975).

parallel waves of strikes can be observed, especially around 1936, 1948 and 1968. In the 1920s, however, the picture is less uniform. Moreover, the amplitudes of the waves drastically decreased at the same time. (This does not refer to the exceptional years of 1926 in Britain and 1936 and 1968 in France.) For the purposes of this essay, it seems reasonable, therefore, to limit the survey of strike waves to the period ending with the years 1918–1920. Further comparability of national developments depends in the first place on what is regarded as a strike wave.

Before going into detail it should be mentioned that different types of strike waves can be distinguished. Apart from the waves covering several years, which will be the subject here exclusively, there are strike waves depending on the seasonal cycle of economic activities. Some authors even refer to monthly and weekly cycles.[9]

The waves of strikes dealt with here are based on annual statistics. They can only reasonably be described since the main industrial countries started to collect and publish the relevant data in the 1880s and 1890s.[10] The simplest criterion for describing the wave-like development of strike activity would be the minimum and maximum numbers of annual strikes and of those on strike. As shown in the diagrams, in the case of Germany this would result in a relatively regular shape of wave every five to ten years. Such a definition, however, is insufficient because it does not indicate anything about the intensity of strike activities. It would also be inadequate in such cases in Britain, France, or Italy where strike frequency and extension (that is, the number of strikes and of those involved) are vastly incongruent and/or develop in a rather inconsistent curve. Shorter and Tilly, therefore, based their analysis of strike waves on an arbitrary but plausible quantitative definition. According to them a strike wave occurs whenever the number of

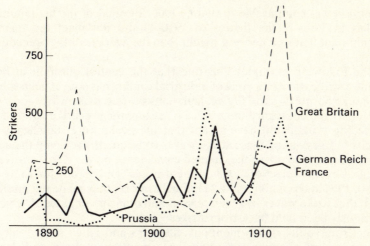

Figure 4.1   *Number of Striking Workers (in thousands)*

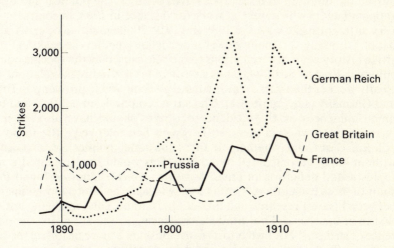

Figure 4.2   *Number of Strikes*

strikes and of striking workers during one year exceed those of the preceding five years by at least 50 per cent.[11] The annual figures for France shown above are based on this method. In contrast to the period after 1920, when the above condition was only met in 1936, 1948 and 1968, the peaks in strike activity before 1920 closely followed each other usually within two years (see Table 4.1). This indicates that these waves of strikes took place in cycles of several years, which is confirmed by developments in other countries.[12]

Unfortunately, Shorter and Tilly did not concern themselves with this question and were only interested in including quantifiable data. They thus stuck far too closely to their statistical definition. They did not regard the increase in strike activity in 1910–11 as a strike wave, although its spread and extension was comparable to that of 1906. Because of the high number of strikes in 1906–7, the figures of 1910–11 did not meet the quantitive definition of being 50 per cent higher than the average of the preceding five years.

The following examples illustrate that the central question of how to define a strike wave or a cycle of industrial conflict has not yet been solved.[13] Although Shorter's and Tilly's calculations showed strike waves in 1890 and 1904, they did not regard them as such because the low strike figures for the preceding years could have meant that the peaks were statistically freak results.[14] Eliminating these strike waves consequently relieved the authors of the necessity to prove the claimed coincidence between strike waves and political events (elections, government crises, and so on) for these years (1890, 1904 and possibly 1910–11). Furthermore, they made the interesting point that strike waves involved regions and branches of industry which had previously been held back from strikes.

As Cronin quite rightly mentions, Shorter's and Tilly's study really does not go beyond showing the coincidence mentioned above and does not pursue the question of how strike waves occur.[15] The political and organizational factors which were at work for instance in 1968, in contrast to the very different strike waves of 1936 and 1919–20, have still to be explained in detail.[16] Equally, it remains open for discussion whether the peaks in French strike history were just exceptions to the rule caused by the specific political culture in France. Strike waves as a result of French industrial relations were clearly weaker than strike waves caused by comparable problems in Britain and Germany (see Figure 4.1). The strong emphasis on political and trade union influences on the incidence of strikes should have also led to the question as to whether some strike waves had relatively little to do with political crises and whether, at the same time, political crises occurred without being accompanied by strikes. This would have required a more sophisticated definition of crisis, however, which cannot be found in the study of these two authors. Cronin too, who made an interesting comparison between his own research and that of Shorter and Tilly, made the criticism that their analysis did not produce convincing explanations for the occurrence of strikes.[17] His own efforts in establishing a more historical theory of British strike history, however, are only convincing where he goes beyond the merely quantitative results and relies on historical research, especially on that of Eric Hobsbawm.[18]

IV

The very distinct cyclical occurrence of industrial conflict in British labour history has always attracted the attention of researchers. This may be the reason why there have been far-reaching explanatory attempts. Hobsbawm in particular has dealt with such questions, and his ideas provide us with a model for a quantitative comparison of strike waves. Hobsbawm deals particularly with the years 1889–91, 1911–13 and 1919–20, which were characterized by waves of intensive union struggles accompanied by massive industrial conflicts. Besides the strong increase in the ratio of strikes generally, he underlines the following characteristics of these cycles of conflict:[19]

(1) *doubling of trade union membership* within a period of three to four years, especially in formerly unorganized trades (mining, transport, particularly in the docks, and gasworks);

(2) *changes in trade union structures* through amalgamations and the formation of new unions mainly by those workers who had been new to the union movement (general unions during the development of the New Unionism after 1889, industrial unions after 1913); rediscovery and revaluing of strikes as a means of industrial conflict;

(3) *clear shift to the left* on the ideological level, that is, an increased influence of Marxism;

(4) the importance of large *trend-setting strikes* which decisively contributed to the development of the New Unions (London dockers' and seamen's strike in 1889, miners' strike in 1892, gasworkers' strike in 1890, glass workers' strike in 1893).[20]

Cronin made an interesting point on the basis of his own calculations, namely, that during the initial stages of these strike waves the workers achieved a disproportionately high success rate. A similar observation can be made for Germany and France.[21] The central importance of cyclical conflicts for the structural changes in the trade union movement characterized decisively the postwar wave of strikes from 1918 to 1921 in Great Britain as well (union amalgamations, founding of the General Council of the Trades Union Congress).[22]

The very clear quantitative results from Britain will now be compared with some data from France and Germany (see Figure 4.3 and Table 4.2), thus showing some marked differences which require further interpretations and questions.

The development of union membership figures in Britain (Table 4.2) shows two steep increases (1889–92 and 1910–13), when each time the number of unionized workers doubled. The years in-between were marked by a rather moderate rate of increase, which often meant a stagnation of membership. In 1905–7, however, a massive but short-lived revival took place in the same way as in France and Germany. The initial phase, around 1890, was fairly similar to developments in these two countries. After falling behind for obvious political reasons (anti-socialist legislation, the crushing of the Commune) figures trebled (in Germany from 97,000 to 294,000; in France from 139,000 to 402,000) followed by a period of stagnation and then decrease. Whilst the unions in France saw a slow but continuous increase from then on, the development in Germany (which was similar to Great Britain) led to a doubling of membership between 1904 and 1907 and again to an increase of about 40 per cent between 1909 and 1912. The figures for 1920, when membership increased by 200 per cent in Germany, by about 100 per cent in Britain but only by some 50 per cent in France, indicate that again the increases were steeper in Germany and Britain. The increase out-

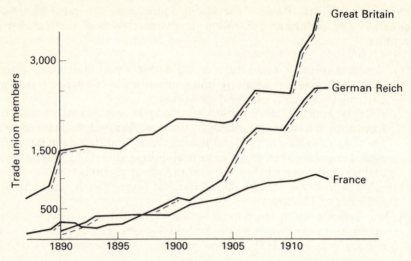

Figure 4.3   *The Development of Trade Union Membership, 1887–1913 (in thousands)*

Table 4.2   *Union Membership*

Germany		*Great Britain*		*France*	
1887	95,000	1887	674,000	1890	139,000
1890	294,000	1892	1,576,000	1893	402,000
1903	887,000	1905	1,997,000	1902	614,000
1906	1,689,000	1907	2,513,000	1906	836,000
1909	1,832,000	1910	2,565,000	1909	944,000
1912	2,553,000	1913	4,135,000	1912	1,064,000
1920	7,890,000	1920	8,348,000	1920	1,581,000

Sources: G. A. Ritter and K. Tenfelde, 'Der Durchbruch der Freien Gewerkschaften Deutschlands zur Massenbewegung im letzten Viertel des 19. Jahrhunderts', in H. O. Vetter (ed.), *Vom Sozialistengesetz zur Mitbestimmung* (Cologne, 1975), 61–120, Appendix; *Jahrbuch des ADGB 1925* (Berlin, 1926), 150 (only Free Trade Unions). For Great Britain see Cronin, *Industrial Conflict*; for France *Annuaire statistique 1936* (Paris, 1937), 58.

lined here roughly corresponds with the national strike figures. They were highest in Britain and weakest in France.

The two diagrams showing the number of strikes and the number of striking workers clearly highlight the two strike waves of 1890 and 1912 in Britain (see Figures 4.1 and 4.2). At a time (around 1890) when strike activity was restrained in France and Germany, industrial conflict in Britain reached a level which it only regained in 1911–12. Strike activity in Germany peaked four times altogether (1889, 1900, 1905, 1910), although it has to be emphasized that, in contrast to Britain, there was an increasing overall tendency. In view of the relatively low initial level in Germany during the

1880s and 1890s the wave of strike activity there must be regarded as equally strong, albeit more frequent than in Britain. Thus, developments in Germany and Britain were, in terms of numbers, quite comparable. In France, though, strike activity developed in a much steadier way. The fluctuations, especially in the number of strikes, are much less marked and follow a trend of continuous increase, similar to the figures for union membership. Doubtless these results require further explanation, particularly as different figures in view of the political positions of the union movements (*grève générale* and *syndicalisme révolutionaire* in France, trade union reformism in Britain and Germany) would have been expected. The answer to these questions is closely connected with the strike waves at the beginning and at the end of this period (1889–93 and 1910–13).

As research in Britain has dealt extensively with these problems we will briefly present its main results here before pursuing our argument further. Hobsbawm, then Cronin and Gerald Crompton emphasized that a combination of four factors was essential for causing the two waves:[23]

(1) the economic cycle;
(2) technological and consequently social change (new types of workers such as dockers, gasworkers and factory hands);
(3) political events;
(4) organizational structure, ideological orientation and strength of both sides of industry.

The damming effect which Hobsbawm emphasized was based on the craft traditions in the British trade union movement. The craft unions had refused membership to unqualified factory workers. They also disapproved of strikes as a means of struggle. After all, they saw their most important success in the establishment of conciliation boards and sliding wage scales, which tied wages to prices. The influence of these unions, however, decreased gradually during the 1870s and 1880s when technological changes and the increasing number of unskilled and semi-skilled workers endangered the position of the skilled craftsmen. Thus, the wave of strikes 1889–93 was the result of structural changes and adjustments by the trade unions. The same cannot necessarily be said about the years 1912–14. After the turn of the century the British economy continued to be weak and British employers were capable of undermining the organizational success of the New Unions in particular.[24] This counter-offensive by employers even led in some cases to the breaking up of a New Union. Thus, the wave of strikes and organizational activities between 1910 and 1914 served to reorganize these workers and this time on a more permanent basis.[25] In contrast to the continent, industrial growth in Britain slowed down after 1900 and at the same time technological modernization progressed. These two factors, in combination with the peculiar habit of British employers first to reject and even to destroy unions until massive industrial unrest enforced union recognition, contributed decisively to the damming effect so typical for Britain and to the ensuing wave of strikes.[26]

V

Before we compare national strike waves it has to be asked whether strikes as a means in industrial conflict were sufficiently spread in these countries to make such a comparison really viable. As the diagrams above demonstrate, strikes and lock-outs had become common events in these three countries before 1914. If the available data are categorized according to the number of strikes, the rate of participation, the duration of strike actions and the frequency per employed person, typical national strike patterns emerge for the period from 1890 to 1914 quite independently of the strike waves (see Table 4.3).[27]

According to these figures, the annual average between 1899 and 1914 was the lowest in Britain (640) while the highest number of strikes was recorded for Germany. However, if one looks at the extension of the strikes the picture is reversed. On average only 109 workers were involved in a strike in Germany, in France about double the number (215) and in Britain more than four times as many (456). Even taking into account that the statistical methods employed differed vastly, these figures indicate the underlying tendency for the strike weapon in France and Britain to be used more often in large-scale industry than in Germany. The available data on the size of companies involved in industrial disputes confirm this view. In Germany firms had on average forty-seven employees and in France they had fifty-nine. Furthermore, taking into account that the degree of industrial concentration, measured by the size of companies, was larger in Germany than in Britain not to speak of France, the relatively small extension of strikes in Germany becomes obvious. This can only be explained by a comparatively lower involvement of large companies and a stronger involvement of medium-sized and small firms in strikes. This conclusion is also partly based on the distribution of strikes across the various branches of industry.

In Britain and France the highly concentrated industrial sectors of mining, textiles and transport account for the largest number of striking workers (76·6 per cent and 50·1 per cent respectively). In Germany these industries account for only 29 per cent. Strike activity in Germany was clearly higher in

Table 4.3 *Industrial Conflicts* per Country (Annual Average)*

| | Britain | | France | | Germany | |
	F	E	F	E	F	E
1888–1914	725	286,000	767	164,000	—	—
1899–1914	640	291,000	975	210,000	2,058	225,000

Working days lost per year in thousands.
F = frequency (number of strikes) *E* = extension (number of striking workers)
  *Strikes and lock-outs combined. Lay-offs and indirectly involved workers are not included.
  Sources: Great Britain – calculated according to B. R. Mitchell and P. Deane, *Abstract of British Historical Statistics* (Cambridge, 1971), 171–2, and Cronin, *Industrial Conflict*, 206, 209. France – E. Andreani, *Grèves et fluctuation. La France de 1890 à 1914* (Paris, 1968), 106. Germany – *Statistik des Deutschen Reiches*, Vol. 280 (Berlin, 1916), 8.

Table 4.4 *Relative Frequency of Strikes per Year (1899–1914)*

	Strike per 100,000 employed	Striking workers per 1,000 employed	Working days lost per year and employed	per year and industrial worker
Great Britain	3·8	17·4	0·45	1·5
France	8·3	18·1	0·30	0·8
Germany	12·2	13·3	0·45	0·9

Note: These figures include striking and locked-out workers, not, however, laid-off workers. The number of employed does not include those working in agriculture, forestry, or fishing. This also applies to the following Tables 4.5 to 4.8.

Sources: Population – P. Bairoch, *La population active et sa structure* (Brussels, 1968), 136–7, 167, 187–92. Strike figures – see Table 4.3.

areas in which medium-sized and small firms predominated, such as the building industry (25·8 per cent of striking workers), the metalworking industry (9·3 per cent), engineering (12·2 per cent), the earth and stone moving industry (4·2 per cent), woodworkers (5·8 per cent), food industry (1·4 per cent). The comparatively large-scale strikes in France suggest that the then still strong small craft industry was relatively unaffected by strikes. In view of the very different degrees of industrialization in the countries under comparison the absolute figures are not sufficient. One has to include the frequency of strikes in relation to the number of workers employed or – if at all possible – in relation to the number of workers in manufacturing industry. Although this kind of calculation results in a starkly distorted picture because of the varying statistical methods used for counting crafts and professions, it is shown here as a rough indicator. On this basis Britain has the lowest rate of strikes with about four strikes per 100,000 employed. France has double this figure and Germany three times as many strikes. These differences are reversed, though, when looking at the number of workers directly involved in strikes. British strikes were by far the most extensive. (See Table 4.3).

According to the calculation shown in Table 4.4, the relative frequency of strikes per worker was as high in Britain as in Germany at 0·45 working days. In France, though, it was one-third lower. These figures, however, are not very telling as the number of people employed does not include those working in agriculture but does include white-collar employees, civil servants and the self-employed. Particularly in France the percentage of these groups was much higher than in the other two countries because of the strength of the small craft industry and its isolated workers. Once the average number of working days lost is related only to those workers in manufacturing industry the German and French figures become much closer: France 0·8 working days lost per industrial worker and year,[28] Germany 0·9 and Britain 1·5. In summary, Britain lost most working days through strikes, while France and Germany lost about the same. The longer duration of strikes in Germany is offset by the higher rate of participation in French strikes.

Table 4.5   *Working Days Lost per Strike and Year, 1899–1914*

Great Britain	France	Germany
11,816	3,649	3,735

Number of direct participants per Strike and Year, 1899–1914

291	215	109

Sources: As Table 4.3.

Table 4.6   *Working Days Lost per Direct Participant per Year, 1899–1914*

Great Britain	France	Germany
26	17	34

Sources: As Table 4.3.

There is no doubt that the very high number of working days lost in Britain (11,816) is due to the massive participation of the workforce and not to the length of strikes. Strikes in France and Germany caused about the same number of working days lost (3,649 and 3,735). In the case of France, though, the participation was higher while in Germany strikes lasted longer. (See Table 4.5.)

The longer duration of strikes in Germany (thirty-four days per striking worker: see Table 4.6) should be regarded as an expression of the particularly tense industrial relations in this country. In contrast, the extremely high rate of participation which characterized strike action in Britain indicates the comparatively well-developed union organization which made such actions of solidarity possible in the first place. The relatively short duration of strikes in France and the high proportion of one-day strikes (19 per cent on average during 1890–1914) points, on the one hand, to the demonstrative character of these conflicts (May Day). On the other hand, it shows the more locally and regionally organized union system which did not provide financial support such as payments during strikes.[29]

VI

As can be seen from Figures 4.1 and 4.2, strike activity in Britain and Germany developed with steeper fluctuations than in France. Taking up suggestions made by Shorter and Tilly, the following figures were calculated for those four years between 1899 and 1914 when participation was strongest. During these four years (out of sixteen years, which means that they covered 25 per cent of that period) the percentage of workers directly involved in strikes was: France 35·6 per cent, Germany 47·8 per cent and Britain 63·6 per cent. The concentration of strike activity within a few years, thus, was highest in Britain and lowest in France. This result is surprising in

Table 4.7 *Number of Striking Workers (in thousands) during Four Years with Peak Participation*

	Britain 1899–1914	*1910–13* absolute figures	%
All trades	4,663	2,965	64
Miners	2,193	1,354	62
Textile workers	634	424	67
Tailoring industry	97	55	57
Metalworkers	473	273	58
Transport workers	747	678	91

	Germany 1899–1914	*1905, 1906, 1910, 1912* absolute figures	%
All trades	3,614	1,727	48
Miners (including steel workers)	671	499	74
Metalworkers	334	202	60
Engineers	470	208	48
Textile	280	113	40
Wood manufacture	210	72	34
Building	931	413	44
Transport	86	32	37

	France 1899–1914	*1904, 1906, 1910, 1912* absolute figures	%
All trades	3,359	1,258	38
Miners	644	235	37
Textile	534	171	32
Wood	110	44	40
Steel	76	30	39
Metalworkers	281	127	45
Building	547	213	39
Transport	502	199	40

Sources: As Table 4.3.

so far as Shorter and Tilly emphasized the wave movement of strike activity in France. So the (according to Shorter and Tilly) highly politically motivated strikes in France were comparatively less pronounced, while strikes in Britain, which were little influenced by the government or by politics, were characterized by the deepest eruptions of labour unrest. These figures beg the question of whether Shorter and Tilly overestimated the influence of the state and politics in general and underestimated the peculiarities of the French economy, the labour relations in individual branches of industry and the system of trade unions. A brief look at the development of strikes by industrial sectors will support this cautiously proposed preliminary thesis (see Table 4.7).

The four years with the highest rate of participation in Britain coincided with the strike wave of 1910–13. Of all transport workers going on strike between 1889 and 1914, 91 per cent chose to do so during these four years. Apart from them, it was mainly the textile workers who contributed to this strike wave. Their participation in strikes was 67 per cent during this period. Other trades with intensive strike activity were below average. Of the mining and quarry workers' strikes, 62 per cent took place during 1910–13. The figure for the metalworkers was 58 per cent, and for the workers in the tailoring industry 57 per cent. In Germany the years 1905, 1906, 1910 and 1912 showed peak participation. The most prominent contribution was made by the weakly organized miners, steel workers and engineers. The most strike-prone group of workers, those in the building industry, only participated below the general average in these strike waves. Without much doubt this is due to the fact that the building cycle differs from the general economic cycle. The behaviour of the building workers was also influenced by the special labour relations in their industry.[30]

Strike participation according to industrial sectors was markedly different in France. The highly unionized metal, wood and building workers in particular, but also the railway workers and post office workers, contributed disproportionately to the strike peaks of 1904, 1906, 1910 and 1912. The strike activity of the usually very militant miners and textile workers, however, reached its peak in years different to those four upswings in the general number of strikes. This observation leads to a further explanation of the relatively weak French strike waves. The fluctuations of individual branches of industry did not follow the general trend but their own particular rhythm. In other words, they coincided less than in the other two countries and thus produced weaker strike waves altogether.

Figure 4.4 shows how much the peaks of strike extension (that is, the number of striking and locked-out workers) coincided in Germany and Britain within a few years whilst in France they were much more evenly spread. Looking at the four most intensive strike years per industry (measured by the number of striking workers) then, in Britain, seventeen industries experienced their peaks at the same time as the strike waves took place, eleven at other times. The situation in Germany was similar. Strike maxima in twenty-one industries coincided with the general peaks for all industry, while in fifteen branches they did not. In France the reverse was true. The peaks for fifteen individual industries took place at the general peaks whilst in twenty-one industries they differed.

This result requires more detailed explanation for each industrial sector. First, however, a surprising conclusion can be reached. In France, where the idea of a general strike was most widely spread, the main problem was to co-ordinate the strike activity in different industries and, as will be shown, in the regions. In Britain, by contrast, where the concept of a general strike was not particularly popular, the reality of strike activity was closest to a general strike. The strong political influence on the formation of strike waves which,

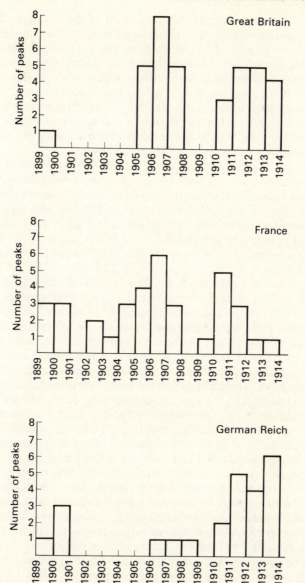

Figure 4.4 *Peaks of Strike Participation in Major Industrial Sectors*

according to Shorter and Tilly, existed in France, appears to have had far less effect than the cumulation of factors which were so important for the development of strike activity in Britain and, to a lesser extent, in Germany. These factors were a strongly concentrated economy, highly centralized organizations on both sides of industry, the structure of trade unions and the fluctuations of the economic cycle. The strong divisions between various industries in France suggest that as a result of the obviously decentralized economy and the equally diverse union movement, each industry developed its own rhythm rather than followed the general trend.[31] This is not to say that political events such as elections, government intervention, appeals to M.P.s and to Parliament as a whole did not play a role. Such events, though, appear to have been more affected by the importance and the economic cycle of particular industries and by the social relations within these industries rather than the other way round. In order to explain these differences a more detailed examination of the developments during the last decades of the nineteenth century needs to be carried out.

In spite of the lack of knowledge about the 1889 strikes in Germany it can be assumed that during the first years of the *Sozialistengesetz* (Anti-Socialist Law), which coincided with a depressed economy, union and strike activity drastically decreased. This view is supported by the table compiled by Wilfried Strenz and Heinzpeter Thümmler. Their table shows on average 102 strikes per year for the period 1884–8 but 390 strikes in 1890.[32] Their general picture is confirmed by sources for the Westphalian industrial area which recorded three strikes for the period 1872 to 1889: 1878, 1885 (the sewing machine manufacturer Koch in Bielefeld) and 1886 (the pipe-casting company Hüllen, near Gelsenkirchen).[33] Then a sudden increase can be noticed. Between 1 January 1889 and 30 April 1890 the records of the *Regierungsbezirke* (governmental districts) on Arnsberg, Münster and Minden show 104, 18 and 7 strikes respectively with 92,969, 11,384 and 339 workers involved. Taking into account that these strike figures are somewhat exaggerated as the Prussian records counted every factory involved as a separate strike, the fact remains that in the district of Arnsberg alone there were fifteen strikes by workers, other than those employed in the coal industry. Because of the predominance of the coalmining industry in this area these figures appear particularly impressive; after all, according to Prussian records, one-third of all workers on strike in Prussia during this period were counted in this district. Nevertheless, the miners' strike had a strong impact on other occupational groups, including chain smiths, coopers, construction workers and coachmen as well as on miners dispersed throughout the Sauerland. The repercussions of the great miners' strike of 1889, setting the trend for the whole period, and the reactions they provoked from the government and employers can be seen most clearly in the centres of the German trade union movement. In Hamburg, the number of strikes rose from ten (involving 5,000 strikers) in 1887 to thirty-six (involving 22,000 strikers) in 1890; in Berlin there was an increase from nine strikes (involving 1,500 strikers) in 1887 to thirty (involving 40,000 strikers) in 1890. The spectacular defeats associated with the issue of May Day in 1890 were the result of a series of lock-outs. They brought this euphoric period of struggle to an abrupt end and hastened the process of concentration in German trade unionism.[34]

Important institutional differences in the trade union movements of the three countries under comparison also influenced the patterns of strike activity. Here let it suffice to suggest that the peculiarities in the case of Germany may be seen as originating in the strong tendency towards centralization displayed by German trade unionism. This tendency characterized German trade unionism right from the beginning – deriving from the tradition of national unity in the 1848 revolution – and it was strengthened by experiences under the *Sozialistengesetz*, by the general atmosphere of optimism towards the end of the 1880s and also by the reaction which followed. In Germany, the events of these years were accompanied by the spread of socialist ideas, the appearance of a literature critical of social conditions and a temporary increase in the influence of left-wing liberalism, all of which can also be observed in neighbouring countries.[35] During the next decade the forming of centralized union organizations was instrumental in diminishing the influence of local subscription offices on calling and organizing strikes. Strike discipline was improved and the strength of the central organizations was increased essentially by large central strike funds.[36]

The influence of the German unions on strikes should not be overrated. In contrast to the French unions, however, they were strong enough to resist the demands for a revolutionary general strike – demands put to them from political quarters.[37] Major changes of union structures or a radicalization of their ideological position as a result of strike waves, a typical observation in Britain, remained marginal in the German case, at least until 1918.

The French unions' view on strikes was an entirely different one due to political events (the commune), political structure and culture. There was an unbroken tradition of strikes at least in the most important branches of the building industry, in mining and in the textile industry,[38] although the union organizations gradually had to be rebuilt, since in 1884 they had been freed from most of the legal restrictions.[39] The development of the number of strikes and of union membership largely followed the same rhythm, yet the figures conceal the fact that there were far-reaching differences in comparison with German and British unions. Until the turn of the century, there was no tendency towards centralization, as mentioned above. The *syndicats* and *bourses du travail* were mainly local or regional organizations. Any move towards centralization, as far as there was any, remained extremely weak and did not lead to the creation of strike funds, or if so, only minor ones.[40] The financial backing of labour conflicts and other supportive efforts remained the prerogative of local organizations which in many cases were helped by left-wing liberal communities. A very decisive difference to the situation in Germany was the way strikes were called, namely, by the workers themselves in their plant rather than by the organizations. Financial support for strikes was often left to spontaneous collections and was thus far less predictable than the saving of membership contributions for strike and other supportive funds. These differences explain the relative brevity and somewhat greater extension of strikes in France.

The strong regional and local powers of French unions were another factor explaining the comparatively low profile of strike waves in France. This can be seen most clearly in a comparison of the miners'. strikes. The miners were by far the most conflict-prone group of workers in all three countries.[41] Their strike actions were concentrated in particular years and thus left their mark on the era. In this respect the years 1889, 1905 and 1912 were as significant for the German labour movement as the years 1893 and

1910–12 were for the British.[42] It was different in France. Here too the miners' strikes were historical milestones.[43] But their strike sequence always stretched over several years and never led to general strikes as in Germany or Britain.[44] This pattern seemed to be the result of large distances between the coalfields in the north, middle and south of the country, the accordingly isolated labour markets and the autonomy of regional union organizations.[45]

The conflict behaviour of miners was characterized by many common features reaching beyond national boundaries. Willingness to go on strike was generally high. Strike action (outbreak and course) was marked by a large degree of spontaneity. The change to violent tactics was quick. The strike objectives were reformist. These characteristics were closely connected with the agricultural origin and the specific working and living conditions of miners.[46] They indicate that the differences mentioned were mainly due to union organization and politics which cannot be further gauged here.

VII

Cyclical waves of strikes in the major industrial countries appeared regularly during the period starting in the 1870s and lasting at least well into the 1920s. Despite the differences described it must be emphasized that an upswing in the economy was the decisive precondition for the eruption of industrial conflicts. Their extension, development and result, however, depended on national conditions. Nevertheless differences in this respect should not deflect from common denominators. The fact that the organizations developed at the same time cannot be sufficiently explained by the parallel economic development alone. The eruption of conflicts, the significance of lead-strikes, the prominent role of certain professions and the participation, for the first time, of new regions and sectors of industry were all common features. This is also true for the infectious character of strikes beyond national boundaries, the intensifying critique of society (mainly in a socialist fashion), the utopian outlook and common objectives (May Day and the eight-hour day).

The purpose of this preliminary and brief comparison was to clarify national characteristics and peculiarities. For Britain, apart from the especially strong strike waves, one additional fact is obvious. These waves of industrial conflict were always connected with a reform or restructuring of the trade union organization. The strike wave of 1870–3, which has not been dealt with here, brought about state and employers' recognition of the unions involved, mainly groups of skilled craftsmen. The creation of conciliation boards and the tying of wages to prices were the results of this recognition. The new mass unions of dockers, gasworkers, miners and cotton workers emerged between 1889 and 1893. This New Unionism was strongly socialist oriented and propagated strikes as a means of industrial conflict. It forced the older craft unions and the amalgamated unions gradually to open up their ranks for new groups of workers and to restructure their organization.[47] After many serious setbacks during the years of economic crisis in the 1890s, the New Unionism culminated in the strike wave of 1910–14 and was finally recognized.[48]

The French and German strike waves did not result in similarly far-reaching changes in union organization because the inclusion of new groups of workers into the unions had started much earlier. Yet the strike waves did lead to some important changes in union strategy, such as the breakthrough of *syndicalisme révolutionaire* around 1900, and the trend towards reformism in France after 1907.[49] In Germany the strike waves of 1889–90 and 1919–20 probably marked the most important changes. The former resulted in the breakthrough of the principle of central organization and the foundation of the *Generalkommission* (General Commission of the Free Trade Unions), the latter to a revival of syndicalism and – similar to France – the splitting up of the socialist workers' movement.

The German case shows a conspicuous contrast. On the one hand, there were relatively modern trade unions, well rooted in the working class, with central organizations, each catering for a whole group of professions or even one industrial sector, and with strong supportive resources. On the other hand, the successes achieved in large-scale industries (iron, coal, steel, chemicals, electrical and partly engineering) were rather minor.[50] This also explains the large number of small strikes which can be regarded as evasive action by the organized union giants concentrated on small and medium-sized firms. A comparison of the strike waves after 1906 indicates an element of the strong political and ideological class antagonism in the Kaiserreich, that is, the massive use of lock-outs rather than strikes.[51] This tactic was much stronger in Germany than elsewhere. The strikes of 1910–12 in particular lost their impetus for that reason and ended with a series of defeats in large-scale industries. The success of the employers in combination with the rapid growth of the 'yellow' trade union associations characterized the strikes of 1910–12 as the initial stage of renewed industrial conflict which was expected sooner or later but was deferred because of the war. Not only in this respect but also with regard to the criticism inside the unions themselves, the postwar crisis of the German trade unions had already begun in 1912.

If we compare the two models of interpretation initially mentioned, they do not appear to be mutually exclusive but complementary. If one model emphasizes the protest character of the eruptions of collective labour unrest such as was the case in Britain, where conflicts took place exactly at the same time disregarding the boundaries of industries, then the other model underlines long-term trends which continue beyond such phases of increased union struggle. It seems to be necessary to distinguish between the various industrial sectors because, in the German case, it was strikes mainly in the mining and foundry industries, the large engineering companies and the docks that followed the model of strike waves, whereas developments in the building and printing industry and in the medium-sized and small firms of the wood and metalworking industries coincided with the continuity model. More precise conclusions will presumably only emerge after a more detailed analysis of one or several strike waves which combines the statistical results with those of a case study.

Notes: Chapter 4

1 E. Weede provides a good survey of the state of international research on the macro-sociological aspects of strikes in 'Der Streik in den westlichen Industriegesellschaften. Eine kritische Übersicht der international vergleichenden und quantitativen Streikforschung', *Zeitschrift für die gesamte Staatswissenschaft* 135 (1979): 1–16. W. Spöhring, *Streiks im internationalen Vergleich* (Cologne, 1983), is more broadly based and thus equally important. J. E. Cronin, 'Theories of strikes: why can't they explain the British experience?', *Journal of Social History* 12 (1978/9): 194–220, should also be mentioned. He also discusses the British bargaining theory. Theories of long and short strike waves are the subject of P. Boomgaard, 'Methodological problems in comparing strike incidence with long and short waves', in D. Petzina and G. von Roon (eds), *Konjunktur, Krise, Gesellschaft. Wirtschaftliche Wechsellagen und soziale Entwicklung im 19. und 20. Jahrhundert* (Stuttgart, 1981), 256–9. The most important literature is mentioned in K. Tenfelde and H. Volkmann (eds), *Streik. Zur Geschichte des Arbeitskampfes in Deutschland während der Industrialisierung* (Munich, 1982), 323–5.

2 Weede, 'Der Streik', 8.

3 With regard to France one has to mention in particular E. Andréani, *Grèves et fluctuation. La France de 1890 à 1914* (Paris, 1968).

4 H. Volkmann, 'Modernisierung des Arbeitskampfes? Zum Formwandel von Streik und Aussperrung in Deutschland 1864–1975', in H. Kaelble *et al.*, *Probleme der Modernisierung in Deutschland* (Opladen, 1978), 110–70; by the same author, 'Organisation und Konflikt. Gewerkschaften, Arbeitgeberverbände und die Entwicklung des Arbeitskonflikts im späten Kaiserreich', in W. Conze and U. Engelhardt (eds), *Arbeiter im Industrialisierungsprozess. Herkunft, Lage und Verhalten* (Stuttgart, 1979), 422–38; and the somewhat earlier essay by H. Kaelble and H. Volkmann, 'Konjunktur und Streik während des Übergangs zum Organisierten Kapitalismus in Deutschland', *Zeitschrift für Wirtschafts- und Sozialwissenschaften* 92 (1972): 513–44.

5 Weede, 'Der Streik', 12 quotes the relevant literature.

6 J. E. Cronin is the main proponent of this line of argument. See his 'Theories of strikes', 211.

7 E. Shorter and C. Tilly, *Strikes in France 1830–1968* (Cambridge, 1974), rely almost exclusively on statistics. They mainly emphasize the degree of workers' organization and favourable political developments as factors which decisively determine strike waves. Cronin, in 'Theories of strikes', further underlines quite rightly the importance of technological and consequently social-structural changes.

8 Cronin, 'Theories of strikes', 199. The same interpretative models are used by G. D. Feldman, 'Streiks in Deutschland 1914–1933: Probleme und Forschungsaufgaben', in Tenfelde and Volkmann, *Streik*, 271–87 (274).

9 M. Perrot, *Les ouvriers en grève. La France 1871–1890*, 2 vols (Paris, 1974), 103–5.

10 V. Mataja, 'Die Statistik der Arbeitseinstellungen', *Jahrbuch für Nationalökonomie und Statistik*, Vol. 13 (Jena, 1897); *Handwörterbuch für Staatswissenschaften*, 3rd edn (Jena, 1909) – including, amongst others, K. Oldenberg, 'Arbeitseinstellungen'.

11 Shorter and Tilly, *Strikes*, 106–7.

12 J. E. Cronin, *Industrial Conflict in Modern Britain* (London, 1979), 48.

13 It is very difficult to find a statistically satisfactory definition of strike waves. If, however, the term 'strike wave' is used to mean a merely statistically calculated strike peak, it would seem reasonable to use the term 'cycle of conflict' for such phases covering several years and which are characterized by other features (change in the means of conflict, in objectives, involvement of other groups of workers in strike conflicts, and so on).

14 Shorter and Tilly, *Strikes*, 107.

15 Cronin, 'Theories of strikes', 208.

16 cf. the important contribution by H. Lagrange, 'Etiologie du mouvement des grèves en France' (PhD. thesis, Paris, 1980), esp. 788–90, who sees the strike waves of 1936 and 1968 as political crises, and those of 1919–20 and 1947–8 as a form of industrial conflict.

17 Cronin, 'Theories of strikes', 208.

18 E. J. Hobsbawm, *Labouring Men* (London, 1964); and by the same author, 'Considérations sur le nouveau syndicalisme 1889–1926', *Le Mouvement Social* 65 (1968): 71–80.

19 ibid., 73–5.

20 See H. A. Clegg *et al.*, *A History of British Trade Unionism since 1889*, Vol. 1 (Oxford, 1964), 55; G. Brandt, *Gewerkschaftliche Interessenvertretung und sozialer Wandel. Eine soziologische Untersuchung über die Entwicklung der Gewerkschaften in der britischen Eisen- und Stahlindustrie 1886–1917* (Frankfurt, 1975), 24; G. Crompton, 'Issues in British trade union organization 1890–1914', *Archiv für Sozialgeschichte* 20 (1980): 219–65 (221). Crompton describes the dockers' march through the City of London and the scenes of violence during the Cambrian coal strike in the Rhondda Valley in 1910 as the initiating strikes of each wave of strikes. Thus, the 1910–14 wave of strikes was also characterized by strikes signalling the pending wave of conflicts. In addition to the miners, the dockers and cotton workers, the railway workers should be mentioned. Crompton's essay is of particular relevance to the question tackled here because he relies on Cronin's statistics but describes the development of individual industries in a more differentiating fashion. As for Germany, see Volkmann's essay, 'Organisation und Konflikt', which, however, follows strongly his rationalization concept. For the London dockers' strike of 1889 see D. Wasp and A. Davis, *The Great Dock Strike 1889* (London, 1974), and J. Lovell, 'The significance of the great dock strike of 1889 in British labour history' in this volume, pp. 100–103.

21 ibid., and Crompton, 'Issues in British trade union organisation', 220. For France: Andréani, *Grèves et fluctuation*, 108; Perrot, *Les ouvriers en grève*, 66–7. For Germany: own calculations.

22 An interesting comparison between strike waves in postwar Germany and Britain is made by B.-J. Wendt, '"Deutsche Revolution" – "Labour Unrest". Systembedingungen der Streikbewegungen in Deutschland und England 1918–1921', *Archiv für Sozialgeschichte* 20 (1980): 1–56.

23 Hobsbawm, 'Considérations', 73–5; Cronin, *Industrial Conflict*, 45–7; Crompton, 'Issues in British trade union organisation', 219–21.

24 ibid., 222.

25 loc. cit.

26 A more detailed analysis of social conditions prior to and during the strike waves cannot be given here. However, there was a greater awareness of social conflicts, a fact which was reflected in literary works critical of social conditions, in socialist educational efforts, political reactions, and so on. For such analysis see B. Webb and S. Webb, *The History of Trade Unionism* (London, 1894). For Germany, H.-U. Wehler, *Bismarck und der Imperialismus* (Cologne, 1969). The general atmosphere of crisis is also emphasized by Blackbourne, in D. Blackbourne and G. Eley, *Mythen deutscher Geschichtsschreibung* (Frankfurt, 1980), 136 n. 76.

27 National patterns of strike activity are also described by Shorter and Tilly, *Strikes*, 306. A summary of the discussion on national strike patterns can be found in Spöhring, *Streiks*, 93–5.

28 Calculation of the number of industrial workers – France: J. C. Toutain, *La population de la France de 1700 à 1959*, Cahiers de l'Institut de Science économique appliquée, 133 (Paris, 1963), Table 63; Germany: G. Hohorst *et al.*, *Sozialgeschichtliches Arbeitsbuch II*, 2nd edn (Munich, 1978), 67; Britain: number of economically active people in industry according to P. Deane and W. A. Cole, *British Economic Growth 1688–1959*, 2nd edn (Cambridge, 1967), 143, less 33 per cent for employers and white-collar employees. Working days as in Table 4.3.

29 Shorter and Tilly, *Strikes*, 55.

30 This has been pointed out once more by Boomgaard, 'Methodological problems', 258.

31 The statistical comparison presented here seems to contradict the results of Shorter and Tilly in line with the view of P. N. Stearns, *Lives of Labour* (London, 1975), 310, who maintained that there were no strike waves in France. The purpose of the comparison here is only to bring the problem into the open once more and to suggest a more differentiated approach proceeding industry by industry and region by region. What appears to be particularly necessary is a precise analysis of the political, economic/structural and union influences on the development of strike intensity. It cannot be ignored that the strike waves, as Shorter and Tilly described them, were politically caused. Perrot, *Les ouvriers en grève*, 96, for example, has been able to prove that the significant increase in strike activity in 1890 was due to May Day agitation. Should Shorter and Tilly's theory be confirmed that French strike waves had mainly political causes another question arises as to why the wave movements of strike activity in the various industries and regions did not coincide more

closely? Such a question begs for more rigorous analyses of the low degree of organization of the French economy, of the comparatively weak organization of the two sides of industry, of the relatively liberal strike legislation and the influence of local social and union policies. The idea of a general strike having been a substitute for a lack of unity in the political and trade union sphere should be taken into account.

32 W. Strenz and H. Thümmler, 'Zur Problematik der Erarbeitung von Streikkarten', *Jahrbuch für Wirtschaftsgeschichte* 4/II (1974): 179–99. We shall not list details of all the documents consulted, but the following are the most important collections: Deutsches Zentralarchiv Merseberg: Preussisches Ministerium für Handel und Gewerbe; Deutsches Zentralarchiv Potsdam: Polizeipräsidium Berlin; Staatsarchiv Hamburg: Sensatsakten; Staatsarchiv Münster: Oberpräsidium Münster, Regierung Münster, Regierung Arnsberg; Staatsarchiv Detmold: Regierung Minden; Staatsarchiv Düsseldorf: Regierung Düsseldorf, Regierung Köln.

33 Staatsarchiv Münster, Regierung Arnsberg I Nr. 59, Nr. 24; Oberpräsident 2762. This also applies to the following. The files quoted here are by no means a reflection of the true picture of the number of strikes during this period. Compare the strike table for the Ruhr miners 1838–87, in K. Tenfelde, *Sozialgeschichte der Bergarbeiterschaft an der Ruhr im 19. Jahrhundert*, 2nd edn (Bonn, 1981), 629–33. The fact that the number of strikes in Germany suddenly increased from 1889 onwards remains, however, beyond any doubt.

34 For Hamburg: Staatsarchiv Hamburg, S 1907; for Berlin: calculated from Deutsches Zentralarchiv Potsdam, Rep. 30 Bln C Tit. 94 Nr. 8552 (1886–9); Deutsches Zentralarchiv Merseburg, Rep. 120 BB VI Nr. 172 (for 1890). Essential reading for the process of centralization are: W. Albrecht, *Fachverein – Berufsgewerkschaft – Zentralverband. Organisationsprobleme der deutschen Gewerkschaften in der Zeit von 1870–1890* (Bonn, 1982); G. A. Ritter and K. Tenfelde, 'Der Durchbruch der Freien Gewerkschaften Deutschlands zur Massenbewegung im letzten Viertel des 19. Jahrhunderts', in H. O. Vetter (ed.), *Vom Sozialistengesetz zur Mitbestimmung* (Cologne, 1975), 61–120; K. Schönhoven, *Expansion und Konzentration. Studien zur Entwicklung der Freien Gewerkschaften im Wilhelminischen Deutschland 1890 bis 1914* (Stuttgart, 1980), 264–6.

35 See note 25.

36 K. Schönhoven, 'Selbsthilfe als Form der Solidarität. Das gewerkschaftliche Unterstützungswesen im Deutschen Kaiserreich bis 1914', *Archiv für Sozialgeschichte* 20 (1980): 147–93, as well as Ritter and Tenfelde, 'Durchbruch der Freien Gewerkschaften', 90–2.

37 A. Grunenberg (ed.), *Die Massenstreikdebatte* (Frankfurt, 1970).

38 Perrot, *Les ouvriers en grève*, 396–8.

39 E. Dolléans, *Histoire du mouvement ouvrier*, 6th edn, Vol. 2 (Paris, 1967).

40 Andréani, *Grèves et fluctuation*, 252–3.

41 Stearns, *Lives of Labour*, 316, with a very interesting table listing the readiness to strike in different industrial sectors. There is a comparatively large amount of literature available on the strike behaviour of miners. It cannot be discussed in detail here, but one title of many is G. V. Rimlinger, 'International differences in the strike propensity of coal miners. Experience in four countries', *Industrial and Labor Relations Review* 12 (1959): 389–405.

42 K. Tenfelde, 'Gewalt und Konfliktregelung in den Arbeitskämpfen der Ruhrbergleute bis 1918', in F. Engel-Janosi *et al.* (eds), *Gewalt und Gewaltlosigkeit. Probleme des 20. Jahrhunderts* (Munich, 1977), 185–236. A. Gladen, 'Die Streiks der Bergarbeiter im Ruhrgebiet in den Jahren 1889, 1905 und 1922', in J. Reulecke (ed.), *Arbeiterbewegung an Rhein und Ruhr* (Wuppertal, 1974), 111–48.

43 Andréani, *Grèves et fluctuation*, 51–3; R. Trempé, 'Le réformisme des mineurs français à la fin du XIXᵉ siècle', *Le Mouvement Social* 65 (1968): 93–108; D. Cooper-Richet, 'La Fédération National des Mineurs' (PhD. thesis, Paris, 1980).

44 A list of the precise distribution of individual strikes by miners in each *département* is planned. A co-ordinated strike action of all or even the majority of coalmining areas did not occur before 1914.

45 Trémpe, 'Le réformisme', shows the distribution of the coalfields in the same way as Cooper-Richet, 'La Fédération'. Neither of them, however, deals with the fact at any great length that strike behaviour was relatively little co-ordinated, if at all.

46 Trémpe, 'Le réformisme', 101–3.

47 Webb and Webb, *History of Trade Unionism*, ch. 7; Brandt, *Gewerkschaftliche Interessenvertretung*.

48 Crompton, 'Issues in British trade union organisation', 220.
49 J. Julliard, 'Théorie syndicaliste révolutionaire et pratique grèviste', *Le Mouvement Social* 65 (1968): 55–69.
50 E. Domansky-Davidsohn, 'Der Grossbetrieb als Organisationsproblem des Deutschen Metallarbeiterverbandes vor dem Ersten Weltkrieg', in H. Mommsen (ed.), *Arbeiterbewegung und sozialer Wandel* (Wuppertal, 1980), 95–116.
51 Volkmann, 'Modernisierung des Arbeitskampfes', 136–7. An important book, particularly with regard to the strategies of employers, is M. Schneider, *Aussperrung. Ihre Geschichte und Funktion vom Kaiserreich bis heute* (Cologne, 1980).

5 The Significance of the Great Dock Strike of 1889 in British Labour History

JOHN LOVELL

I

The 1889 London dock strike began on 12 August with a dispute over the method of piece-work payment at one of the port's dock systems. Owing to a variety of circumstances the stoppage spread outwards from this sector until by 22 August the entire port was affected. Despite attempts by the employers to break the strike its effectiveness was maintained. By 5 September a number of employers were prepared to make concessions to the men, and on this basis a very limited return to work took place. The main body of port workers, however, remained on strike until a comprehensive settlement had been reached. This was finally achieved on 14 September. By this date the port had been at a virtual standstill for the best part of four weeks. No previous stoppage in the British shipping and dock industries had been of this magnitude.

The shut-down of the country's largest port was a major event by any standards, but the interest the strike aroused in the nation at large did not derive solely or even mainly from its magnitude. The strike appeared as an extraordinary phenomenon to contemporaries because dock workers were believed to be so poverty-stricken and demoralized as to be incapable of collective action. This view had been well expressed in the editorial columns of an East End newspaper back in 1871, at a time when a section of London dockers were protesting against a wage reduction: 'The men are comparatively helpless in the matter. They are so poor that a strike or even a combination with a view to joint action is not to be thought of. They can only appeal to the companies to reconsider the whole question, and ask the public to sustain that appeal.'[1] Events in 1872 in fact cast a good deal of doubt on this judgement, but it would nonetheless have found general acceptance in the 1880s. The Select Committee on the Sweating System, that reported in 1888, included dockers in its investigations, and Charles Booth's private inquiry into poverty in London, begun in the 1880s, focused upon dock workers at an early stage. Because of the generally casual nature of employment at the waterside, dock work was regarded by the public less as a genuine industrial occupation than as a residual employment for the 'refuse' and unemployed of society at large. When a man reached the dock gates in search of work it was felt that his fortunes had sunk low indeed. Given this view, and given the assumption that this was an area definitely beyond the reach of trade unionism, the solidarity and discipline displayed by the mass of port workers in the strike of 1889 appeared as a staggering phenomenon. Its impact upon the public mind was all the greater in view of the location of the stoppage in the nation's capital, a factor that ensured the maximum degree of publicity.

The dockers' strike was thus a spectacular struggle, and it was also of course a victorious one, in that most of the strikers' demands were conceded. It is hardly surprising that it had a major impact upon trade unionism. The strike has acquired a special significance for historians in the context of the emergence of the New Unionism of the late 1880s. Quite what New Unionism really amounted to in practice is a matter for some debate, but since the term was one used by contemporaries we will not quibble about its use here. New Unionism enters the history of the great dock strike both as cause and consequence. So far as the causal connection is concerned, the formation of Will Thorne's Gasworkers' Union at Beckton in March 1889, and its success in June in securing its objective of an eight-hour day, played a vital part in stimulating action amongst the dockers. The connections between the two sectors were very close. The great gasworks at Beckton were in close proximity to the major dock systems of the port of London, many gasworkers turned to the docks for employment in summer when work was slack at the gas plants, and finally the circle of London socialists encompassed a number of individuals who had been active in attempts to organize both the gasworkers and the dockers. Thus the three men who emerged as leaders of the great strike – John Burns, Tom Mann and Ben Tillett – had all been involved in the establishment of the Gasworkers' Union, while Thorne for his part had been a member of Tillett's unsuccessful Tea Operatives' Union. There appears to have been some rivalry between Thorne and Tillett and this played its part in the launching of the dock strike. Tillett stood against Thorne in the election for the secretary of the Gasworkers' Union, while Thorne subsequently became involved in the setting up of a rival organization to Tillett's Tea Operatives' Union. It was in connection with this latter development that Thorne turned up at the dock gates on 12 August 1889 and exhorted the dockers to strike. The links between the movements of gasworkers and dockers could thus hardly have been closer.[2]

II

The main concern in this essay, however, is with New Unionism seen as a consequence of the great dock strike. The dockers' victory made its impact on the extension of unionism to semi- and unskilled workers in two ways – direct and indirect. The indirect way stemmed simply from the force of the dockers' example. If the London dockers, of all groups, could strike successfully for better conditions, then all workers could hope to improve their position through collective action. The great publicity that the strike received ensured that the dockers' achievement was well known. Furthermore, the high level of demand for labour in the boom of 1889–90 gave to the mass of workers – as it had given to the London dockers and gasworkers – a bargaining power that they did not normally possess. This indirect impact of the dock strike upon union growth is of course hard to measure, but there is every reason to assume that it was considerable. In the early 1870s the movement among agricultural labourers had had a similar effect in stimulating organization generally. At that period there are even examples of domestic servants attempting to follow the lead given by agrarian workers.[3] It would be possible to pursue this matter of indirect impact further, in order to trace more precisely the connections between the London dockers' movement and those of other workers. Instead, however, it is proposed in this chapter to focus on the direct impact of the strike upon unionism, since in this field the strike's consequences are much more clearly evident.

Mass strikes have often functioned as agents of mass unionization. In Britain this tendency was perhaps most apparent in the years 1911–13, when spontaneous strike action in a whole range of industries triggered off a phase of explosive union growth. Mass memberships achieved in this way tended to lack stability, not least because the sectors of employment involved were usually those that proved most resistant to organization in normal circumstances. The 1889 dock strike provides a classic case of mass unionism springing directly from mass strike action, and possessing as a consequence an inherent instability. The strike's impact on the level of union membership in the port of London was dramatic. On the eve of the stoppage the port was not entirely devoid of organization. There were two societies of stevedores, numbering between them about 2,500 members, and a society of corn porters on the south side of the Thames with a mere 150 members. These groups were all that remained of the great all-grade organization of 1872, the Labour Protection League, a body that had claimed as many as 30,000 members at its peak. In addition to the stevedores and corn porters, there was some organization of lightermen and coal porters, and a few hundred dockers and warehousemen were enrolled in Tillett's Tea Operatives' Union (established in 1887). The total of all organized port workers would have been about 5,000, with only the stevedores and lightermen possessing societies of any significance. By contrast, in the immediate aftermath of the strike the various organizations laid claim to a combined total of over 25,000 members. During the winter of 1889–90 organization on the London waterfront was virtually complete; without a union card a man could not get work. The major part in this transformation had been played by Tillett's hitherto unsuccessful Tea Operatives. By linking relief during the strike to membership in a union the strike leaders boosted Tillett's union from a few hundred to 18,000 members. However, not all newly organized port workers enrolled in this union. The existing societies of stevedores, lightermen and coal porters all experienced a notable expansion, and on the south side of the river the existing corn porters' society played its part in an attempt to revive the Labour Protection League of the 1870s. Out of this attempt there emerged the South Side Labour Protection League, an organization that claimed a membership of about 5,000 in the period just after the strike. All the above organizations had existed in some form before the strike commenced, but the stoppage also resulted in the creation of a cluster of new sectional associations. Leaving aside the seafaring and ship-repairing sectors, there were probably nine of these small societies in existence in the autumn of 1889. Thus, while the strike had resulted in the complete unionization of the port, it had certainly not had the effect of drawing all port workers together in a single mass organization.[4]

The direct impact of the strike extended beyond the London waterfront narrowly defined. There was, to begin with, a direct connection between the organization of dockers and carters. The delivery of goods to and from docks and warehouses made for constant contact between the two groups and many carters struck along with the dockers in August 1889. Road transport was not an easy sector to organize and the London Carmen's Trade Union that emerged during this period was by no means a strong body. However, Tillett's union, having established its position at the docks and wharves, threw its weight behind the carters' society. Members were instructed to refuse to load vans driven by non-unionists, and this decision played a significant part in launching the Carmen's Union into a phase of rapid expansion.[5] Seamen too possessed close ties with port workers. A national seamen's union had of course emerged some time before August 1889, but it had made little progress in London. Inevitably, however, seamen were involved in the great strike, and indeed played a major part on the picket lines. The success of the strike, and the emergence of strong dockers' unions in its aftermath, were important factors in establishing the national union in London. The union was to play a major part in events in the port during the years 1890 and 1891. In addition to its impact upon groups whose work was closely connected with the docks, the strike exerted a direct influence upon organization in one further important way. The strike, as has been outlined, established the Tea Operatives' Union as a mass organization on the London waterfront. At a delegate meeting held in the East End in late September 1889 Tom Mann was elected as full-time President and the union changed its title to Dock, Wharf, Riverside and General Labourers' Union of Great Britain and Ireland (Dockers' Union being the abbreviated version). At the same time the union set about establishing a branch and district structure that would enable it both to consolidate its membership on the London waterfront and to expand into other sectors. The leadership, the new title and the emerging structure of the union all indicated a commitment to a national and general, rather than a local and occupational, form of unionism. Under the leadership of Mann and Tillett – who continued as secretary of the organization – the Dockers' Union thus became an instrument for the extension of mass unionism well beyond the confines of the London waterfront.

This wider impact of the strike, exerted through the Dockers' Union, is a point of some importance. In the period between September 1889 and July 1890 organization expanded rapidly. By the early summer of 1890 the union had achieved a membership of 25,500, organized in seven districts and sixty branches, in the Thames area alone. While the vast majority of these members were of course London port workers, one district was composed entirely of workers in the Thameside cement and paper industries and there were also branches of oil millers and brewery workers in the dockland districts. It was, nonetheless, the ports that attracted the union's organizers. By July it was represented in Hull, Cardiff, Newport, Swansea, Bristol, Gloucester, Plymouth, Southampton, Portsmouth, Ipswich, Dundee and even Amsterdam and Rotterdam. In areas outside London the great strike had given to the union and its leaders a prestige that enabled them to make rapid headway. In cases where other organizations had established footholds in provincial ports the Dockers' Union was usually able to sweep these aside without difficulty. Sometimes this was done with a degree of ruthlessness, as happened at Swansea where the National Amalgamated Labourers' Union was virtually driven out of the port.[6] Given situations of this kind not all the Dockers' provincial membership gains can be regarded as net additions to the total of unionists, but even so it can hardly be doubted that the pace and scale of unionization in the country's southern and eastern ports owed everything to the intervention of the London union. The Dockers' progress at Hull was particularly noteworthy. The union moved in at the end of November 1889, Tillett visited the port in December, in January there were 4,000 members in fourteen branches, and by September this had risen to 12,000 in thirty-one branches. At the end of the year the port was completely unionized and constituted the union's most important provincial district.[7] Despite some setbacks, and despite its exclusion from the north-western ports by the National Union of Dock Labourers (formed before the great strike), the Dockers' Union pushed its total membership well beyond the 50,000 mark during the course of 1890.

Reviewing the direct impact of the strike it can be seen that its principal result was the extension of unionism to port workers in London and various towns in the south and east. The extension was achieved mainly through the Dockers' Union, the only union involved in the strike (apart from the Sailors) that aimed at a more than merely local membership – and in this sense the only New Union to emerge out of the stoppage. Outside the sphere of port employment relatively few workers were organized as a direct consequence of the strike. The South Side Labour Protection League, although local in character, was regarded as a 'general' union by Harry Quelch its socialist General Secretary, and in the early days after the strike a number of different occupations were included in its ranks.[8] Many of these subsequently seceded to form societies of their own, but the union retained two branches composed of workers outside the port industry – one of labourers at Woolwich Arsenal and the other of labourers at engineering works in Deptford. The Labour Protection League of 1872 had also included a variety of trades based in the waterside districts. The Dockers' Union of course enrolled a range of trades. The enthusiasm at the time of the great strike affected all workers in the waterside districts of London, whatever their occupation. In the provinces too the union pulled in a range of occupations; copper workers were organized at Swansea and bricklayers' labourers and mill workers at Hull. The fact was, however, that while the union's footholds outside the port industry were to make a vital contribution to its survival in the years ahead, in 1889–92 they were only of minor importance. Organization of such groups had been merely incidental to the union's main effort at the waterside. Finally, there were the seamen and carmen. Organization of these groups in London had been stimulated by the dockers' movement, but seamen and carmen had unions of their own. None the less, the links between the three sectors were very close, and the fortunes of the seamen's and dockers' unions in particular were closely interwoven.

III

In the preceding paragraphs the direct consequences of the great strike have been discussed simply in terms of the numerical expansion of union membership in certain sectors of employment. The form taken by this extension of unionism has, however, a qualitative as well as a quantitative dimension, and this qualitative aspect must receive consideration in any attempt to evaluate the contribution of the great strike to the development of New Unionism. It was noticed above that the union growth directly attributable to the strike occurred mainly in the sphere of port employment. There is of course a certain logic in this – a dock strike resulting in the organization of dockers. None the less, two of the organizations to emerge out of the strike – the Dockers' Union and the South Side Union – possessed socialist leaderships apparently committed to the spread of unionism to all unskilled workers. Given this fact, was the actual preponderance of port workers in these unions after all a more or less accidental development? Or was it the case that the policies of union leaders were modified as their organizations developed?

The South Side Union is not really a problem. Despite its socialist leader, it represented in fact an attempt to revive an earlier form of organization, and its highly decentralized structure allowed little scope for expansive recruitment policies. The position of the Dockers' Union is more complex. At the outset the commitment to general unionism was clear enough. Thus, in October 1889 the union executive announced 'that Labourers of all kinds are eligible to join the Union', and the first rules of the union stated that it was to cater not only for port workers but also for 'any unskilled labourers in other trades'. By the summer of 1890, however, a change appears to have taken place. In the August issue of the union journal the executive announced its intention 'to forbid the enrolling of any men as members of our Union, unless they belong to some one of the departments of trade already covered by the organisation'. The reason given for this new depart-ure was the lack of resources to extend organization beyond the limits of those trades already covered by the union. It was claimed that the union needed 'not extension, but solidification'. This explanation is not entirely satisfactory. The union was still in a relatively strong position at this time, and further evidence suggests that the executive – composed of London dockers plus the full-time officers – embarked on this policy as a matter of choice. In the same month it announced: 'Our special work lies at the ports and such other places as directly affect them.' Two months later the title of the union journal was changed from the *Monthly Record* to the *Dockers' Record*, the reason given being that the new title conveyed 'a much clearer notion as to whose interests our Paper represents'. These were signs that the

Dockers' Union was beginning to regard itself more as a union of port workers – akin to the National Union of Dock Labourers – than as a general union on the model of the Gasworkers. One further development at the end of 1890 reinforces this picture. Despite the statement earlier in the year that lack of resources prevented expansion into new occupations, in December the union decided to launch a recruitment campaign among agricultural labourers. The executive launched the campaign in January 1891 and by the end of the year it was reported that fifty-eight agricultural branches were in existence. It may be doubted whether these branches were very securely established, but that is not an issue for present discussion. The point is that the rules laid down for the establishment of agricultural branches make it clear that they were regarded as a special sector of the union. The rural counties were seen as the major source of strike-breaking labour on the waterfront, and there can be little doubt that it was this perception that lay behind the union's agricultural campaign. So far from conflicting with the view that the Dockers' Union was retreating from general unionism, the campaign in the counties reinforces such a view. Agriculture was singled out as a sector for recruitment because of its particular relevance to organization on the waterfront. The campaign followed naturally from the executive's statement of August 1890, to the effect that the union's special work lay at the ports 'and such other places as directly affect them'.[9]

In itself this shift in policy by the Dockers' Union may not appear to be of great significance. The retreat from general unionism acquires some importance, however, if it is seen as a reflection of the basic strategy of the organization. The basic strategy of the Dockers' Union derived less from any new concept of unionism expounded by socialist leaders and advisers than from the union's origins in the waterfront labour market. The strategy in question was geared to the interests of dock and wharf workers and had two main elements. The first was the exclusion from waterside employment of all but union members; only when this was achieved was it possible to introduce the second element. This entailed the restriction of entry to the union, and therefore to dock employment as a whole. The strategy of course represented a response to the chronic underemployment of waterside workers that was associated with the casual system of employment. More specifically, it was designed to maximize the amount of work obtained by men who relied on the docks for a living by excluding marginal workers. In London the Dockers' Union actually put this policy into effect. It was forced to accept the job monopolies established by the other similarly exclusive unions operating in the port, but outside their respective spheres it set out to establish a monopoly of waterside employment for its own members. This was achieved in November 1889 through union control of hiring procedures. Although this control came under increasing attack from the employers from Janaury 1890 onwards, the union maintained its monopoly for a whole year. It was broken by the employers in November 1890. During the period of its operation the union was able to implement the second element in its strategy. On two occasions the organization closed its membership in London completely. The first was in December 1889. After a month membership was reopened and branch committees were given discretionary power to admit new members. In August 1890, however, the union closed its books for a second time and it is to be presumed that they remained closed until November, although district committees were given power to admit members in cases where the state of local organization warranted such action.[10] In the period to November 1890 the policy of closing the membership of the union was applied only in London, and in the provinces recruitment was proceeding rapidly. In the autumn, however, the restrictive strategy pursued by the London districts began to impinge on the whole organization.

At the first Annual Delegate Conference of the union, in September 1890, the leadership proposed a fourfold increase in the entrance fee, to be applied throughout the organization. Unlike closure of books, high entrance charges did not entail absolute restriction of entry, but represented instead a selective method of control that discriminated against marginal workers. The proposal met with substantial opposition, not because of any objection in principle to exclusive policies, but because of the varying levels of organization in the different districts. Thus the metropolitan districts, where the organization of regular workers was complete, were in favour of the increase. Hull, where organization was nearly complete, was also in favour. Bristol was the only other district to support the new fee and here again unionization of the port had reached an advanced stage. In the other districts, where organization had often begun later than in London, Hull and Bristol, and where it was still incomplete, opinion favoured no more than a twofold increase. The delegate from Portsmouth put the position clearly enough: 'It was all very well for the branches in the metropolitan area, who wanted to keep out the "scum", but it was very different with the unorganised in the provincial towns, where a high entrance fee would keep out men they really wanted in their ranks.' The outcome was that the fee was doubled, but discretionary powers were given to district committees to increase it further if necessary.[11]

This debate illustrates the truth of a view expressed by Tom Mann in an interview given at this period in connection with the Booth London survey.[12] He had remarked that a union's overt policy was something that was relative to its powers of enforcement, and that in order to get a true picture of the real aims of a society one should view it in a district where it was strong. Thus it was that waterside unions tolerated non-unionists only where they could not achieve a union shop (perhaps this is true of unions in most sectors) and were expansionist in their recruitment policies only where the organization of regular workers was incomplete. Once a monopoly of employment for unionists had been obtained entrance fees were raised and books were closed. Unions of port workers were thus, potentially at any rate, closed unions. The limitation of the supply of labour on the waterfront formed their main objective. In the case of the Dockers' Union, which had begun its life with a commitment to recruit unskilled labour generally, the dominant position of waterside workers within the organization ensured that the union would in practice tend to narrow its field of recruitment. There was a simple logic to this situation. In ports where the union was successful in enforcing a monopoly of employment for its members at the waterside, an extension of organization to other industrial groups threatened to inflate a labour force that the union was seeking to restrict, since members in other trades might turn to the waterfront when work in their own spheres was slack. The retreat from general unionism was not therefore a product simply of accident or ordinary sectional bias: it stemmed in large part from the basic strategy of the union.

IV

The strategy adopted by the Dockers' Union has a significance that extends beyond that union's own recruitment policies. Its implementation had consequences for the union's relations with other organizations, both in London and in the provinces. The commitment to general unionism, characteristic of many of the New Unions established at the end of the 1880s, resulted in part from the view taken by their founders concerning the nature of the labour market. In this view unskilled workers were regarded as an undifferentiated mass, a body of men constantly moving across industrial boundaries because they possessed no roots in any particular occupation. The great objective of unskilled workers' unions was thus to enrol all labourers irrespective of industry, and so eliminate the blackleg by creating a vast closed shop. Under this scheme the various general unions would join together, if not to create One Big Union, then at least to bring about universal interchangeability of union cards – the 'one man, one ticket' principle. In practice, however, as Eric J. Hobsbawm has shown, general unions came to depend upon footholds they obtained in certain sectors of employment, where workers were in fact more or less permanently identified with particular branches of trade.[13] This circumstance modified the policy and character of all the general unions at an early stage in their history. The case of the Dockers' Union was, however, a special one. Because of its essential character as a waterside union it had, almost from the outset, rejected the 'one man, one ticket' principle. The monopoly of employment that it obtained for its members on the London waterfront was enforced against non-unionists and members of other unions alike. Such a policy followed from the union's attempt to limit the labour supply. Other general labour organizations in London, favouring the interchangeability of union cards, inevitably found themselves in conflict with the Dockers. The South Side Union attempted to reach an understanding on this issue in the immediate aftermath of the great strike, but it was not until November 1890, when the Dockers' Union's position in the upstream sectors of the port had been seriously weakened, that an agreement was finally reached.[14] The dispute with the Gasworkers lasted longer, for two reasons. First, there was the fact that the monopoly of the Dockers' Union survived at the Victoria docks long after it had been broken elsewhere in the port. These docks were close to the Beckton gasworks so that the exclusive policies of the Dockers' Union in this area affected gasworkers who had been accustomed to work at the waterside in their own slack season. Secondly, and of much greater significance, there was the strong commitment of the Gasworkers' Union to the 'one man, one ticket' principle, a commitment that remained despite the emergence of general unionism in a form different from that originally envisaged.

The conflict between the two unions persisted for a number of years after 1889. The attitude of the Dockers' Union was that, in sectors where it was in control, no other unionists should be taken on for work while any of its own members remained unemployed. It was a policy the union enforced on numerous occasions by blocking gasworkers from port employment. In retaliation gasworkers threatened to block dockers from the gasworks of the East End, and on a number of occasions strikes on this issue were narrowly averted. At the end of 1892 a crisis was reached. The Gasworkers withdrew their support from a federal organization in which they were associated with the Dockers, and eventually the long-standing dispute was referred to an arbitration committee composed of representatives from various allied unions. This did not, however, finally resolve the matter. It was clear that as long as the Dockers were able to influence hiring procedures in any important sector of the port, so long would they refuse to depart from their resolution 'that members of our union maintain and claim the right to be taken on for work at the docks before any other union men'. They had modified this claim with respect to the South Side Union when their position was threatened in the upstream sectors of the port. The Gasworkers' Union was different, however, for it clashed with the union in a district where its monopoly was still intact. Furthermore, unlike the South Side Union, the Gasworkers' Union in London was in no sense a waterside organization; from the Dockers' standpoint, it was a union of outsiders. As the Gasworkers' and Dockers' organizations extended beyond the metropolis, so too did the conflict between them. In Hull, where the Dockers' Union established itself in strength, relations were particularly bad. In the early 1890s the local Gasworkers' secretary in that port complained that the Dockers were not satisfied unless they completely 'bossed the show'. He regarded the dispute as a conflict of principle, and expressed the view that the great work of the Gasworkers' Union all over the country was to outstrip the Dockers and all similar societies and become powerful enough to enforce the recognition of the principle of 'one man, one ticket'.[15] The conflict was not without its irony, for the organization of the gasworkers in London in the spring of 1889 had been one of the factors that had brought about the great strike and the subsequent unionization of the dockers.

The strategy pursued by the Dockers not only divided the forces of the New Unionism on an important issue of principle, it also played a part in undermining the unity of London port workers. The most serious consequences of this process were reaped by the Dockers' Union itself. The labour force of the port was not composed of an undifferentiated mass of workers but was divided into numerous sections. Some of these groups, such as the quay labourers of the north bank docks, were absolutely unskilled, but others were specialists in particular types of work, and of these latter some possessed considerable skill and bargaining power. Victory in the great strike had been achieved because all these groups acted together; had the unskilled workers who began the dispute been left to fight alone the strike would quickly have petered out. The unity of London port workers during the strike was, however, of a somewhat fragile kind. Of the more specialist groups, only the stevedores had struck simply on grounds of sympathy, and their early intervention on the dockers' side was undoubtedly the major factor in transforming a localized dispute into something approaching a port-wide stoppage. The other specialized groups, who followed the lead of the stevedores and finally brought the whole port to a standstill, all had demands of their own to make, and it was in fact the demands of these groups that prolonged the stoppage beyond the point at which a settlement had been reached for the ordinary north bank dockers. The simultaneous action of the various groups, each pursuing sectional demands, was largely attributable to two factors: first, the high level of activity in the port in the summer of 1889, and secondly, the fact that a number of these groups had received wage reductions in the months immediately preceding the stoppage.[16] While allowing that the general level of enthusiasm played an important part in spreading the strike, it is also true that the above factors provided many workers with both a motive and an opportunity to take action on their own behalf.

However it was attained, unity brought gains to all London port workers in 1889, and it was in the interests of all to preserve it. The task was not easy. The unionization of port workers that occurred during the strike and its immediate aftermath had the effect of institutionalizing sectional divisions. The least skilled groups were swept into the Dockers' Union, but the more specialized and skilled groups were enrolled in numerous small occupational organizations. In addition to already existing societies of lightermen, stevedores and coal porters there emerged the South Side Union, which organized a variety of waterside and other groups, and – as mentioned earlier – as many as nine other societies. These latter included some groups of considerable strategic importance, such as crane-drivers, tugboatmen and shipworkers in the short sea trades. Most of these organizations pursued the same policy as the Dockers' Union, in attempting to control the labour supply in their own particular spheres of employment. Despite this fragmentation of London waterside unionism, there existed in the aftermath of the strike a movement to maintain and institutionalize the united front of port workers. The instrument that lay to hand for this purpose was the Central Strike Committee. During the stoppage this body had acted on behalf of all those involved, although it had been forced to delegate its authority on the south bank to a separate committee whose members were more familiar with the special interests of the grain and timber workers of the district. The translation of this south side committee into the independent South Side Union undoubtedly detracted from the Central Committee's authority in the period immediately following the resumption of work, but the latter body none the less decided to remain in existence. In January 1890 it called a conference with a view to establishing a proper federal organization representative of all the various London waterside societies, and out of this gathering there emerged the United Labour Council of the Port of London.[17]

As an instrument for maintaining the united front of London port workers the council proved a failure, and by 1900 waterfront workers in the metropolis could only look back upon a decade of bitterness and crippling disunity. There were, of course, various reasons for this, but one of them concerned the strategy pursued by the Dockers' Union. When the United Council was formed in January 1890 the Stevedores, Lightermen, Coal Porters, Seamen and most other waterside (including ship-repairing) societies affiliated to it. The Dockers' Union, however, did not affiliate, and until the autumn of 1890 showed no interest in associating with other waterside unions in London. That autumn, however, the union's attitude began to change and by the spring of 1891 it had become the principal force behind a movement to create an all-inclusive waterside federation. The timing of the change is significant. It coincided almost exactly with the successful counter-attack by the London dock companies against the union's control of employment. This occurred in November 1890. By the time the Dockers' Union changed its policy, however, the smaller unions in the port had begun to change their views. There was now a marked reluctance to associate with the Dockers' Union, and the Stevedores in particular had reached a position by the end of 1891 in which they absolutely refused to participate with the Dockers in a federal organization.[18] In London the Dockers were isolated, and when their membership at the Victoria and Albert docks went on strike in 1900 they went down to defeat alone. By 1906 the union was virtually extinct in London.

The refusal of the Dockers' Union to associate with other London waterside societies when it was in a position of strength contributed much to this disastrous sequence of events. As implied above, the refusal stemmed in part from the union's general strategy. At one level this may appear puzzling, since the Dockers' objective of limiting the labour supply through the enforcement of a union monopoly was no different from that of many of the societies affiliated to the United Council. An issue of principle, such as that which separated the Dockers from the Gasworkers, was not at stake. What was at stake was something different: namely, the extent of the union monopoly that the Dockers sought to establish. Other waterside organizations in the port sought to restrict entry to a particular occupation, but the Dockers differed from these in that it aimed to extend its monopoly to cover the entire area of port employment. It did not, in short, recognize the job monopolies of the sectional societies, and was not therefore inclined to co-operate with these organizations on the United Council. Referring to the smaller occupational unions in the port, one Dockers' district secretary remarked: 'We may have little petty things that I will not take note of.'[19] Relations between the Dockers' Union and other waterside societies were thus bad from the outset, and in particular the former body's attempt to contest the Stevedores' sphere of influence produced much bitterness. The Dockers were encouraged in the pursuit of this ambitious policy by their numerical predominance in London and by the great growth of their organization in the provinces. The sheer size of the union, however, masked what was in reality a position of weakness in the metropolis. Most of the more skilled and specialized workers were of course organized in separate unions, and these could not be coerced into an amalgamation. Furthermore, the union's membership in London confronted an employer of unusual power in the Joint Committee that managed the great dock systems on the north bank. It was the counter-attack of this body in November 1890 that so weakened the union's position in the port. Its survival in strength at the Victoria and Albert docks beyond this date owed much to the fact that the work in this sphere was transferred to the shipowners. The latter, however, joined together in the Shipping Federation, became in time even more formidable adversaries than the Joint Committee. It was of course the Federation that broke the hold of the union in Hull in 1893 and the Victoria and Albert Docks in 1900. As the fundamental weakness of the union was increasingly exposed after 1890, so it turned to the sectional waterfront societies, hoping to use the strategic position of their members in the working of the port as a lever with which to revive its fortunes. The attitude of these bodies towards the Dockers had, however, been moulded when that union was in a position of strength; now that its fortunes were failing, they were not inclined to place their own positions at risk by coming to its assistance.

V

In the above paragraphs the great strike has been considered in terms of its direct impact upon the development of mass trade unionism. Viewed in this way, the strike's significance was less than might at first be imagined. Its immediate result was the extension of unionism to port workers in the south and east of the country. For reasons that have been examined, the unions that emerged from the strike were not greatly interested in expanding much beyond the boundaries of port employment. As potentially, and sometimes actually, closed organizations their policies also conflicted with those of other more expansive New Unions of the period. The conflict between the Dockers and Gasworkers was particularly notable in this respect, since it assumed national rather than merely local proportions. The restrictive policies pursued by waterside organizations also affected their relations with each other. In London especially, as has been shown above, the various waterfront unions were unable to maintain a united front once the strike was over.

   The organization of waterside workers presented special problems given the casual basis of employment in this sector.[20] The fact that the direct impact of the great strike was largely confined to the waterfront meant that its contribution to the expansion of unionism was of a rather impermanent nature. The last bastion of the Dockers' Union in London collapsed in 1900, and between that year and 1911 the union was only enabled to preserve any sort of presence in the port because of the resources provided by its provincial footholds. After 1893 the latter did not include Hull, the union's influence in that port having been completely destroyed by the Shipping Federation. Organization perished in other ports also, Southampton and Grimsby being examples. The union survived as an institution because it remained established in the Bristol Channel area, and it is significant that in this region non-waterside workers made up an important section of the membership. Of the smaller waterfront unions involved in the great strike some survived, and even prospered after 1900, but a number passed out of existence. The truth was that in the great movement of 1911 the waterfronts of London, Hull and various other southern and eastern ports had to be organized afresh, almost as if the great strike had never been. Tradition must, however, be allowed its place in labour history, and just as the tradition of 1872 had its impact on the movement of 1889, so the memory of the great strike must have played its part in 1911. Tom Mann and Ben Tillett, leaders in 1889 and again in 1911, ensured that the memory of the earlier triumph was kept alive.

Notes: Chapter 5

1 *Eastern Post*, 4 November 1871.
2 See the account in H. A. Clegg *et al.*, *A History of British Trade Unions since 1889*, Vol. 1 (Oxford, 1964), 57–9. Also J. Lovell, *Stevedores and Dockers* (London, 1969), 99–101.
3 See S. M. Norton, The Growth and Development of Trade Unionism amongst Previously Unorganised Workers in the Early 1870s (M.Phil. thesis, Kent, 1976).
4 Lovell, *Stevedores and Dockers*, 112–20.
5 *Labour Elector*, 14 December 1889, 4 January 1890 and 25 January 1890.
6 British Library of Economics and Political Science, Webb Trade Union Collection, Section A, Vol. XLII, 205.
7 R. Brown, *Waterfront Organisation in Hull 1870–1900* (Hull, 1972), 45.
8 Webb Trade Union Collection, Section A, Vol. XLII, 144.
9 *Labour Elector*, 5 October 1889; Dockers' Union, Rules (1889), Rule 1; *Monthly Record*, August and September 1890; *Dockers' Record*, October 1890 and January 1891; Dockers' Union, Annual Report for 1891.
10 *Labour Elector*, 4 January 1890; *Monthly Record*, September 1890. See also evidence of Clement Edwards in Royal Commission on Labour, 1892, C. 6708, Group B, Minutes of Evidence, Vol. 1, q. 8764.
11 Dockers' Union, Minutes of Annual Delegate Meeting, 30 September – 4 October 1890.
12 British Library of Economics and Political Science, Booth Collection, Group B, Vol. 140. Interview dated 15 September 1891.
13 E. J. Hobsbawm, 'General labour unions in Britain, 1889–1914', in idem, *Labouring Men* (London, 1964), 179–203 (187).
14 *Seafaring*, 8 November 1890.
15 Webb Trade Union Collection, Section A, Vol. XLII, 46–7 and 119–22. See also Brown, *Waterfront Organisation*, 49–50 and 64.
16 Lovell, *Stevedores and Dockers*, 93.
17 *Labour Elector*, 11 January 1890 and 18 January 1890.
18 Stevedores' Union Minutes, Executive Council Meeting, 24 December 1891.
19 Royal Commission on Labour, 1892, C. 6708, Group B, Minutes of Evidence, Vol. 1, q. 289.
20 See Lovell, *Stevedores and Dockers*, esp. ch. 5; also E. J. Hobsbawm, 'National unions on the waterside', in idem, *Labouring Men*, 204–20.

6 The Rank-and-File Movements and the Trade Unions in the Hamburg Docks from 1896–7

MICHAEL GRÜTTNER

I

Comparative research into the European labour movement going beyond issues relating to organizational sociology and ideological history is still in its teething stages. Social history has not come up with obvious reasons to explain why organizations and movements, so different in form and content, prevailed in different countries. The incontestable impact of German labour organizations on other countries and the staunch self-assurance with which their leaders put forward their organization as an international standard and model tend to hide the fact that in many respects the German labour movement was as much of an 'oddity' as for example French syndicalism.

This comparative perspective should be borne in mind in the following reflections on the situation of workers and unions from the time of the great Hamburg dock strike in 1896–7. What common experience did a Hamburg dock worker organized in a Social Democratic union share with a French docker who identified with revolutionary syndicalism or a docker in London whose union was steering a rather pragmatic course outside the realms of 'high politics'? Or, to put it more precisely, to what extent did similar conditions of employment produce similar forms of self-assertion and social conflict despite different political backgrounds? Behind this question lies a more general methodological problem: the question of the legitimacy of an analytical approach based on social history, which starts from the working and living conditions of the historical actors themselves and seeks to understand their awareness and behaviour on this basis. A comparative study on an international level would seem to provide a favourable framework to define both the possibilities and limits of an approach of this kind.

The following material on these questions is presented under three main headings. First of all a brief comparison is made between the 1896–7 strike in the Hamburg docks and the great dock strike of 1889 in London. This is followed by an examination of the syndicalist potential among the German dock workers which became apparent precisely during the Hamburg strike. Thirdly, an attempt is made to answer the question as to why this syndicalist undercurrent never really gained momentum in Germany in contrast to other countries – France, Spain and to a certain extent also Britain from 1910.

II

A comparison of the strikes in London in 1889 and in Hamburg in 1896–7[1] presents a number of striking similarities. Both industrial disputes played an important role in the fresh impetus gained by the organized and unorganized labour movement in each country. Both marked the spectacular mobilization of a group of workers which in fact played only a secondary role within the established labour organizations – the unskilled and casual workers. Although the divide between skilled and unskilled workers seems to have been wider in Britain than in Germany, the organization of the unions in both countries at that time was to a large extent limited to skilled workers and craftsmen. In both London and Hamburg a type of worker regarded as 'indifferent' within the organized labour movement and in whose ranks a lengthy period of economic crisis, wage cuts and general despondency had left visible traces, now proceeded to take action. In both cities the strikes were sparked off by the mass of unskilled and casual workers. However, the strikes only became an impressive demonstration of proletarian solidarity when the privileged minority of workers in full employment, including to a certain extent the skilled workers, joined in the strike action, albeit with some hesitation and in an inconsistent manner. It was precisely this group of worker, however, which prior to the outbreak of the strikes had formed the backbone of the generally weak dockers' unions. In the years of crisis union activity was almost exclusively limited to the dock workers with relatively secure jobs who saw their long-term prospects of employment in the docks. In view of the weakness of their organizations the strikers in both cities were dependent on material solidarity from outside which grew into exemplary trials of strength and endurance, attracting national attention. Moreover, both the London and Hamburg strikes went down in the history of dockers' unions as turning-points: in both countries the strikes marked the union's breakthrough to a mass organization, this despite the fact that the major dockers' federations had played no decisive role in the early stages of either strike. And a final important parallel can be seen in the reaction of the opposite camp. Following the strike, employers in both London and Hamburg began to restructure the organization of work in the docks, systematically introducing a process of 'decasualization'. There is evidence to show that in Hamburg at least this policy was a direct reaction of the shipping companies to the fact that the casual dock workers had not only initiated the strike action but had also been its main protagonists for over eleven weeks.

Unlike their colleagues in London, the Hamburg dock workers were forced to end their action in defeat, despite the great demonstration of solidarity. The reasons for this are to be found mainly in the employers' camp. Whereas the London dockers found themselves up against the employers directly concerned – the owners of the local docks and shipping companies – the strikers in Hamburg were confronted with the *Arbeitgeber-verband Hamburg-Altona* (Hamburg-Altona Employers' Association) in which the owners of the docks and shipping companies constituted a minority. Although after some time the representatives of a number of the major Hamburg shipping companies showed a will to compromise and interest in a swift end to the dispute, they were overruled by the hardliners in the employers' association.[2] The majority of the organized Hamburg employers were totally opposed to negotiating with the strikers, granting concessions of any sort, or accepting any offer of mediation. The mediation of prominent members of the middle classes and the church had been an important element in the success of the London dockers' action in 1889. In Hamburg personalities such as the Police Senator and the President of the *Bürgerschaft* (the city-state parliament) offered their services as mediator but whereas the workers agreed to this proposal, the employers' reaction was a definite 'no'. Although in 1896–7 the employers' intransigence brought the workers increasing public sympathy, even from the middle classes, it nevertheless became apparent that public opinion was not a decisive factor in a clash in industrial relations. In any case, despite some internal differences, the employers maintained their position to the very end.

To turn to the strikers, the main difference between the London and Hamburg strikes was the militancy of the conflict in Hamburg. Whereas only twenty dock workers were summonsed to court in 1889, the Hamburg strike led to the prosecution of more than 500 workers.[3] On the other hand it would be misleading to conclude from this that the workers in London were basically peaceful and the Hamburg dockers, in contrast, militant. Only a few years earlier, in 1886 and 1887, the very same workers who brought the London docks to a standstill in 1889 without major incident had created a state of social panic among the middle classes of the city with their militant street demonstrations.[4] Considering the chronological course of events of the 1896–7 strike it becomes obvious that the frequent clashes with 'black-legs' and the police were mainly concentrated in the final stage of the strike. The first three weeks passed by virtually without incident.[5] This seems to imply that the 1889 strike was relatively peaceful mainly because it was a success for the workers, whereas the militancy of the Hamburg strikers was largely an expression of imminent defeat. At the same time the contrasting reaction of the authorities and the police forces to the respective strikes is probably another reason. Whereas in London the public authorities were conspicuous in refraining from intervening in the dispute, in Hamburg the Senate and the police authorities clearly sided with the employers.[6]

III

Following the Hamburg strike a hotly debated process of 'taking stock' took place within the German labour movement. As the SPD party newspaper *Vorwärts* pointed out, the strike had been 'the mightiest union strike we have ever fought in Germany'.[7] At the same time, however, it was evident that neither the outbreak of the strike nor its course of action coincided with the unions' ideas and principles on the appropriate and effective way of settling an industrial dispute. The unions had repeatedly stressed that a high degree of organization was absolutely essential if a strike were to have any hope of success. However, in the docks of Hamburg a primarily unorganized workforce had come out on strike. The union leaders' words of warning had fallen on deaf ears. Moreover, the decision to go on strike had not been taken at union meetings but at mass gatherings open to all dock workers, whether organized or not. This form of decision-making was to be maintained throughout the strike and led to two consecutive decisions to prolong the strike against the leaders' advice at public mass gatherings. This grass-roots democracy in the form of ad hoc decision and policy-making was at odds with the claim of the unions to be the only legitimate representative of workers' interests in a wage dispute: 'If the outcome of a strike is to reflect the interests of the worker, it must be prepared. The call for strike action must come from the organisation and not from unorganised masses.'[8]

In practice, however, events had taken the opposite course. The union members had followed in the wake of the unorganized workers and the organizations had been forced to move with the tide. To avoid being caught 'off their guard' in the future wide-ranging measures would have to be taken, as *Vorwärts* in particular recommended. In the first place a decision in favour of strike action was in future to be 'in the hands of a restricted circle which was fully familiar with all the circumstances'. Secondly, rather than giving their unconditional support to spontaneous strike action, the unions would 'just have to see and if necessary let a strike which had not been prepared in the appropriate manner fall flat on its face from the very outset'.[9] Although this line of thinking was to gain increasing momentum in the years to come, it was an extremely controversial opinion in 1897. For example, the national 'Trade Union Committee' subsequently declared in public that it would have been 'completely misjudged' to have forced the dock workers to give up their strike by denying them financial support:

> Such a venture would have led to a split in the closed ranks of the strikers. It would have meant years of dissent among the dock workers and seamen and made any form of organizational work impossible. To maintain the solidarity among the strikers and win them over for the organization after the strike it was necessary to let the strikers themselves bring their action to an end.[10]

The strikers' militancy was also clearly at odds with the union's ideas and principles. The constant and increasingly bitter clashes with strike-breakers and the police was only one aspect of the warfare which virtually dominated the scene in the final weeks of the strike. Alongside this the dock workers used another weapon, about which little research has been done in Germany: sabotage. The sinking of a steamer rigged out to accommodate strike-breakers and the demolition of an inn used by a dock employer as a recruitment office are cases which created a particular stir. In both instances the strike leaders rebutted all attempts to link these incidents with the strike. However, the continued repetition of certain forms of action gives a clear picture of the real situation. For example, loaded barges or launches were frequently let loose from their moorings at night and left to drift on the Elbe. Within two months the Hamburg harbour police salvaged more than a hundred drifting vessels.[11]

After the strike this hostile atmosphere escalated into a series of virtual street battles. In the quarters where the dockers lived violent clashes with 'blacklegs' broke out. The latter finally resorted to using their revolvers. As the police advanced they were greeted with showers of stones. Most of the adjacent residents, apparently including many women, participated in the ensuing fighting on the streets and barricades from their own houses. As was the case on many similar occasions, the reaction of the Social Democratic Party and the unions was above all determined by their fear of being identified with this type of incident. In fact in the official union account of the strike Carl Legien went so far as to maintain that none of the striking workers had been involved in the 'scandalous scenes', although the lists of the arrests prove otherwise.[12]

Many dockers clearly distanced themselves from the ideas and principles of the dock workers' federation. This can be seen not only in the form of the strike action but also in the establishment of a breakaway group, the 'Association of the 1892 Stevedores'.[13] Although numerically speaking this group, like its rival, remained weak, it nevertheless had a decisive impact on the process of fermentation among the workers in the weeks leading up to the strike. In the summer of 1896 it organized two partial strikes, both of which were swiftly concluded with a victory for the workers. As a result of the hopes and expectations thereby awakened the association began to press for higher wages for all the stevedores. This was what set the ball rolling.

Characteristic of the '1892 Association' was its disdain of formal organization. Strike funds were generally rejected on the grounds that 'the capitalists cannot be fought with money'. The programmatic declarations of this splinter group were coloured by a basic aversion to the centralist structures of the large union federations and the employment of paid officials. It had been shaped by experience of the often high-handed style of leadership in the upper ranks of the dock workers' federation and the intermittent influence of some of its anarchist members. The supporters of this group aimed at wringing concessions from the employers using their own methods: unexpected and short-term stoppages. The success they achieved in the vanguard of the great strike seemed to confirm this tactic.

IV

These essential features of the 1896–7 strike are in many respects clearly more reminiscent of syndicalism in southern Europe or Latin American countries than of a labour movement with a social democratic tradition. Militant strike action outside the control of the union was of course by no means totally unfamiliar to Germany. The so-called 'localists' – union associations which on principle rejected the trend towards a nationally organized federation and the ensuing bureaucratic structures – were also to be found in other sectors of the economy. And despite its fundamental rejection by social democracy, even sabotage seems to have been more widespread in Germany than is generally assumed. For example, in 1911 alone the police authorities in Hamburg recorded some forty cases of wilful damage in the course of various strikes.[14] Seen in themselves the different aspects of the strikes pinpointed here were indeed not so unusual. It was rather the accumulation of moments of activist militancy that gave the conflict its syndicalist traits. The leaders of the dock workers' federation saw this as a basic disposition of their members. In 1910 Johannes Döring, the federation's president of many years' standing, was still complaining that 'syndicalistic ideas' could not be knocked out of the dockers' heads: 'Our colleagues are still too prone to direct action. No matter what, the first thought that enters their heads is to throw in their job!'[15]

Döring's perception of syndicalism is surprisingly 'pragmatic'. He does not refer to the influence of given ideologies or organizations but has a specific disposition in mind: the tendency to react directly, to attack at once, to stop work with no regard to the rules of controlled, institutionalized forms of action on which the unions laid such great store. Nevertheless, his definition certainly seems to hit the nail on the head. For there is much evidence to suggest that, for example, the labour movement in France remained relatively unaffected by organizational or ideological influences and that the syndicalist theory tended to reflect the 'natural' behavioural pattern of these workers in a situation of conflict.[16]

That the dock workers' affinity with syndicalist forms of militant action was neither incidental nor the result of the influence of outstanding leaders is emphasized by the fact that similar situations were witnessed in the docks of other cities and countries as well. At the seventh international congress of transport workers in 1910 it was said that 'dock workers in all countries are more or less inclined towards direct action. It is a widespread opinion ... that a sudden strike can force the employers into yielding concessions. The result is that little importance is attached to the payment of high union dues since this form of action does not require a high reserve of funds.'[17]

All this implies that the dock workers' inclination towards 'direct action' was apparently closely linked to their occupational status and their general way of life. One point which seems to be of particular importance is that for most of the labourers in the docks strikes had a lesser risk factor than for other groups of workers. Most dockers were casual workers, frequently only hired for the loading and unloading of a ship so that when the work was completed they found themselves on the streets again on the look-out for a job. The results were material insecurity, a high rate of fluctuation and frequent periods of prolonged unemployment. Yet these specific labour market structures had a further effect. Since the dockers were in any case continually switching jobs they had little to lose by going on strike. An essential card which an employer generally had up his sleeve to enforce discipline among his workforce was thus deprived of much of its impact. Moreover, in these circumstances workers could scarcely identify with their work or with a specific plant or firm. Another element which fostered 'direct action' was the relatively egalitarian structure of Hamburg dock labour, basically characterized by a majority of unskilled labourers with a few thousand skilled workers. The decisive point, however, was that in contrast to many sectors of productive industry, the unskilled labourers did not merely do the skilled workers' 'donkey-work'. Both groups of workers worked side by side with no formal pattern of hierarchy. Furthermore, the fact that the skilled workers' wages were not generally higher than the rates for unskilled labourers presumably also fostered feelings of solidarity and tended to prevent sectionalism among the workers.

Whereas the unions' means of settling disputes and preventing strikes generally gained ground for the very reason that they provided the opportunity of wringing concessions from the employers without any great risk involved, the situation in the docks was a different one. Precisely since the risks involved in a stoppage were less serious in the docks than elsewhere the workers for a long time had little incentive to resort to the unions to mediate in a dispute. Of the approximately 200 stoppages and lock-outs in the Hamburg docks on record for the years 1886–1914, spontaneous strikes, launched without the prior knowledge or participation of the union leaders, were in a clear majority. Although there is insufficient comparative evidence for the assumption that dock workers were more susceptible to strike action than other groups of the German working class, this theory has nevertheless been corroborated by other research at international level.[18]

V

This readiness to back up their own demands by coming out on strike with little regard for the unions' considerations on strategy and tactics found its most spectacular expression in the strike of 1896–7. But at the same time the eleven weeks of strike marked a turning-point. Despite the impressive show of solidarity among the strikers and despite the unexpected measure of support from public opinion, the highly organised Hamburg employers had proved a better match. The tactic of wringing concessions by sudden short-term stoppages had obviously met its limits. On the other hand, the social democratic labour movement had proved its merit during the strike, for the unconditional support from the SPD and the union press and the funds raised by the workers' organizations had formed its very backbone. In these circumstances the reasoning of the dock workers' federation that the only way to stand up successfully to the employers was through a strong organization, backed up by ample funds, obviously began to convince many dockers. As a result, the federation, extremely weak prior to the strike, now witnessed a rapid rise in its membership and for the first time became a significant force in the docks; not least for the reason that in view of the turn of events the '1892 Association of Stevedores' also affiliated itself to the federation. The strike of 1896–7 subsequently went down in history as the 'actual birth of our central organization'.[19] The way in which the defeat seemed to discipline the dockers also became evident in the following years –

the federation leaders were now much more successful in warding off strikes which seemed beyond their capacity. After the warehouse workers had pressed for higher wages in 1898 – to no avail – the SPD press reported that it was 'thanks only to the level-headed reaction of the organized workers that a strike had not yet again raged within the city walls of Hamburg'.[20] A similar pattern followed a year later when the dockers' wage demands were turned down: according to official union sources 'there was such a stir among the dockers that it was only with a great struggle that the members of the steering committee could hold their colleagues back from rashly calling for a stoppage'.[21] And finally, in 1907, during a lock-out of the stevedores, a call for a general strike was only prevented, according to a union report, by the 'firm line of the steering committee and the Hamburg officials who made no concessions to craving for popularity'.[22] The fact that a strike of similar dimensions to that of 1896–7 did not break out again in the following years was not so much due to a relaxation of tension in the docks as to the increased influence of the unions. So it is hardly surprising that years later the defeat of 1896–7 was bluntly apostrophized by the union press as 'a blessing' for the organization in that 'it crushed the indisputable presence of syndicalist trends among the Hamburg dock workers whereas a victory might have reinforced these trends to the detriment of the movement'.[23] Although this assessment was essentially true, it was doubtless rather premature. From 1897 onwards a kind of 'division of labour' began to develop. Large-scale wage disputes and strikes now tended to be carried out within the framework of the union; strikes of a lesser degree, however, continued to be fought independently by the workers – here the union did not succeed in substantially extending its influence.

This newly found strength of the dock workers' federation and the resulting discipline of the workers also had a spill-over effect within the union itself. On this point the constant amendments to the strike regulations are of particular note. This development was primarily characterized by a progressive extension of the authority of the steering committee. Whereas after the end of the great strike it had been decided that only offensive strikes needed the approval of the committee, its powers were continually extended in the coming years. From 1906 onwards all wage disputes and both offensive and defensive strikes could as a rule only be carried out with the previous approval of the federation leaders. And later a further provision was added that in 'particularly critical situations' the steering committee could even break off a strike over the heads of the members. Coupled with this was the total exclusion of the unorganized workforce from all essential decision-making.[24] This was the organization's way of formally safeguarding itself as far as possible from being caught 'off its guard' by spontaneous stoppages. However, the more and more elaborate strike regulations for some time existed only on paper; and on repeated occasions, perhaps in other ports more so than Hamburg, strikes broke out without the previous knowledge of the steering committee. Its attempts to enforce the statutes were often countered by threats to split off into a local organization. In 1904 the president of the federation, Döring, recounted that the strike regulations 'were applied in only few cases'.[25] Strike pay was nevertheless paid in all the larger-scale strikes whether the strikers respected the statutes or not. It was not until around 1908 that the steering committee felt it was in a strong enough position to deny material support in such cases in the future.[26] This development was part of a general trend towards a shift in power within the federation which went hand in hand with the advancing professionalization of the federation officials, apparent in more or less all union federations. As long as the steering committee could convince its members that these measures made the union's fighting strength more effective, there was next to no protest at grass-roots level. However, at the same time members began to dissociate themselves from the unions on an emotional level, thinking more and more in the cool terms of cost and benefit. In 1904 this was described by Heinrich Schleef, one of the leading officials in the Hamburg docks, as follows:

> In the past it was considered by everyone his duty to do as much as possible; you could see your colleagues active and getting things done. But now things have changed. If you ask for anything nowadays the reaction is always 'What do I get out of it then?' You don't get the impression that they're acting on their own behalf but for an employer – which in this case is the federation.[27]

Two years later Schleef was even more explicit:

> It's like an epidemic going through the whole organization: everyone wants to be paid for his work. . . . Ten years ago colleagues would go through thick and thin for their opinion, but now that's all in the past. Nowadays members say: I elect the steering committee and pay my dues but don't bother me with anything else.[28]

A satisfactory explanation for the union leadership's continuous efforts to prevent the outbreak of a large-scale conflict, its ever shriller campaign against 'wildcat' strikes and its determination to concentrate all important decisions in its own hands cannot be found in the contrast between a reformist leadership and a revolutionary workforce or in the growth of union bureaucracy. And the general aversion towards grass-roots activity cannot be appropriately explained by a desire to achieve greater rationality and effectiveness in union action. In actual fact the success rate of union-led strikes in Imperial Germany was not significantly higher than that of spontaneous, informal stoppages.[29]

The reluctance of the dock workers' union to enter into a conflict was on the one hand the result of the heavy defeats the workers had suffered in May 1890 and in the 1896–7 strike. Moreover, the unions' efforts to stifle independent grass-root movements and their marked mistrust of all forms of the workers 'acting on their own initiative' were basically a fully consistent expression of strategic guidelines which had determined the self-image of the social democratic labour movement from a very early stage: the opinion that the strength and authority of the workers was expressed above all in terms of the numerical development of their own organization; the conviction that decisive improvements in the proletarian 'lot' could only be achieved through the recognition of the unions by the employers and finally, from 1899, the assumption that collective agreements were the only means of guaranteeing that success achieved could be secured in the long term. For recognition of the labour organizations was only of interest to the employers if the unions could in practice demonstrate their hegemony over the workers. The Hamburg employers' association regarded the conclusion of collective agreements as above all an opportunity to 'interrupt the perpetual declared war in industry by periods of truce, at least for a time'.[30] But of course it was absolutely essential for the union to be in a position to guarantee the 'truce' within its own ranks. To a certain extent this enforcement of discipline was the price the unions had to pay for their own recognition.

Most of the union leaders were aware of this situation and the consequences it implied. Thus the spontaneous mass strikes of the English dock and transport workers in 1911 which were accompanied by militant clashes, once again gave the German transport workers' union (to which the dockers had been affiliated since 1910) occasion to present itself to middle-class public opinion as a force of appeasement:

This time the sparks of strike have not caught fire in Germany. The employers in the German transport sector owe this, not to their own power or tactics, but solely to the workers' organization, the hated German transport workers' federation. Let us make that clear to the gentlemen. Our association has absolutely no interest in bringing the whole of the economy to a standstill as has happened in England.

However, it was also stressed, and with equal emphasis, that in the long term these aims could only be fulfilled by the unions if both the state and free enterprise were prepared to accept the organization and meet its demands:

While the German Transport Workers' Federation will do all in its power to spare Germany from the economic catastrophes England has had to face, neither will it shy from defending the interests of its members effectively and fearlessly and with all its might if need be. . . . And should the transport workers' federation ever be deprived of its role of disciplining the masses in the organisation, then the inevitable outcome will be, as Schiller says in *Das Lied der Glocke*: 'Woe, if 'ere in the bosom of the towns/the kindled faggots silently heaped/the masses, breaking their fetters,/should take their fate into their own terrible hands.'[31]

VI

The willingness of the dock employers only to recognize workers' organizations in control of their own rank and file was forcefully demonstrated in 1907. Then the Hamburg docks witnessed the climax of a wave of strikes and lock-outs which after a lengthy period of 'wait and see' had once again set all groups of workers astir. For the first time since 1896–7 the boom in the shipping sector seemed to provide the dock workers, faced with an almost general depreciation in real wages since the great strike,[32] with another opportunity of launching a vehement offensive to improve their situation. In the years 1905–7 there were more than fifty stoppages and lock-outs in the harbour area. Simultaneously the dock workers' union doubled its membership within a relatively short period and for the first time succeeded in concluding collective agreements on a large scale in key sectors of the docks. Many of the companies in the harbour area became closed shops. But this success could not prevent the outbreak of a number of uncontrolled stoppages in 1906. The surge in union membership obviously did not imply that members were now prepared to renounce independent and spontaneous action. At the beginning of 1907 the *Schiffahrtszeitung*, an employers' newspaper, commented as follows:

> These strikes which have been repeatedly staged in such a malicious manner prove that the workers in the Hamburg docks are in a state of depraved disorganization and social unruliness. Two things have become quite clear. First, the union federation, which one is supposed to consider as the thinking and leading force among the workers, has precious little influence on the will of the workers, at least as far as Hamburg is concerned. Secondly, the union organization itself has not nearly enough political and economic maturity and strength of will to act against the will of its members at the critical moment.[33]

This was a remarkable commentary from a press which otherwise continued to portray the workers as basically content but artificially incited by agitators. When it was realized that the dock workers' federation could not live up to its allotted role as keeper of the peace, the consequences were soon to follow. In February 1907 the Docks' Association, a recently established employers' association, refused to recognize the status quo that had been arrived at with the union. The Association publically declared that since the dockers' union was not in a position to prevent 'wild-cat' strikes it 'no longer intended to have recourse' to the 'mediation of the organization of the dock workers' to settle disputes.[34]

The wave of strikes ended with a six-week lock-out of more than 5,000 stevedores, which was on the whole successful for the employers. At the same time it marked the beginning of a fundamental restructuring of conditions of employment. The Docks' Association eliminated the traditional informal structures of the labour market and replaced them by their own highly centralized recruitment system which was expanded into an effective means of controlling the labour force. For the first time they were now in a position to totally exclude undesirable workers from the docks in either the short or long term. This not only reinforced the employers' position in strikes and lock-outs but it also became an instrument applied against all the patterns of behaviour traditionally closely linked with the lives of casual workers: heavy consumption of alcohol even at the workplace, the frequent refusal to accept unpopular work and the high rate of pilfering.[35]

At the same time changes in the organization of labour, begun after the 1896–7 strike, continued to be forced through: short-term employment of casual workers was cut back and replaced by the recruitment of an increasing number of permanent employees with long-term contracts. The explicit objective behind this measure was to create a privileged class of 'contract workers' with material security, thus reducing the potential for conflict in the docks.[36] This strategy was reinforced by a shrewdly devised network of 'welfare facilities' for this group of workers linked with a draconian penal system and rounded off by the establishment of 'yellow' unions.

All this led to decisive changes in the power structures of the Hamburg docks. The dock workers' federation had to face the greatest crisis in its history. When the union became affiliated to the German Transport Workers' federation in 1910 its membership had dropped by 50 per cent since 1907.[37] This was of course also to be attributed to the slump which had set in at the end of 1907. Times of material instability were traditionally linked with a decline in membership of the dock workers' federation.[38] But even more decisive was the discontent of many of the members with the outcome of the 1907 lock-out and the ensuing employers' offensive. Their disappointment gave vent to massive accusations that they had been 'betrayed' by the union leaders. Although obviously quite unfounded these charges continued to be made for some time. This was the other side of the coin as far as the shift of power within the union was concerned. The more responsibility union leaders assumed in decision-making in industrial disputes, the more they became a scapegoat in the case of defeat. Although union membership increased in the years immediately before the outbreak of the First World War the high level of organization of the years 1906–7 was never again reached, not even following the 1912 wage dispute when for the first time central collective agreements were concluded for the docks as a whole.

Within the union this development helped to reinforce the line adopted in previous years which had aimed at avoiding conflict and steering clear of risks. At the union conference in 1908 the steering committee had already announced that more stringent measures would be taken against 'wild-cat' strikes. A clear majority of the delegates present supported the new line, as is illustrated by the vote against granting material support to the Mannheim coal workers who were on strike at that time without committee approval. This was obviously seen as a good opportunity to set an example since the town of Mannheim had the reputation of being a centre of syndicalist insubordination.[39] Indeed in the previous years the Mannheim coal-loaders had gone on strike on three occasions without waiting for the go-ahead from the steering committee; nevertheless in each case they had been more or less successful. All in all the shift in power between workers and employers resulted in the union itself rigorously confining its own sphere of activity. At company level its action was now almost exclusively concentrated on issues concerning wages and working hours. Other disputes resulting from conditions of employment and related subjects were now considered taboo. Thus strikes against the dismissal of individual colleagues, as the union leaders also declared in 1908, were now to be a thing of the past.[40] And as the Docks' Association prepared to extend the measures of discipline and control (certificates of employment, the contract system) developed for stevedores to the other sectors in the docks from 1907 onwards, the leading union bodies reacted with admittedly sharp criticism but failed to launch any action whatsoever in retaliation. The few groups of workers who neverthe- less walked out, more or less on their own initiative, received either no more than the half-hearted support of the organization or none at all.

However, the weakness of the workers' organizations also coincided with the weakness of the spontaneous labour movement. The employers' offens- ive from 1907, the impressive increase in their organization and power and their highly perfected control of the labour market limited the workers' scope for 'acting off their own bats' even more than in the post-1896–7 period. In disputes with individual companies the workers now found themselves more and more up against a united front of dock companies. So from 1908 the number of strikes dropped sharply. More and more fre- quently stoppages ended in defeat. Until 1914 the situation was char- acterized by the fortified position of the employers on the one hand and a union increasingly cut off from the spontaneous initiatives at grass-root level on the other. So the fact that there was a drop in the number of disputes was not so much due to a relaxation of the tension between the two sides of industry but rather on account of the fact that the employers had strength- ened their position of power. Friction had at best been alleviated for the permanent employees who continued to be a minority.

To sum up, the main argument developed here is that with the growing organizational strength of private enterprise, the development of the labour market into an instrument of discipline and the decline in the traditional groups of casual workers, the conditions for successful independent and spontaneous action at grass-root level became more and more unfavour- able. The union's problem was that it could only partially fill the resulting gap. While its leaders had stressed to the workers time and again that only a strong organization would guarantee success, in the years after 1907 it became evident that the employers had gained ground on the same territory much more swiftly. All attempts to harness the workers' discontent with this development as a point of departure for sparking off renewed activity had only modest success. However, the dwindling readiness to launch into 'direct action' was not an irreversible process. Following the revolution of 1918–19 the casual dock workers in particular fell back on the traditional strategies of the period of high industrialization, although in different circumstances and in a different form. During the postwar revolutionary crisis they formed the reservoir of syndicalist and left-wing, radical workers' unions which, as in the case of miners, were for a time a serious rival to the social democratic unions in the large German ports.[41]

Finally, returning to the questions raised at the beginning, it can indeed be stated that similar conditions of employment in the docks of various countries – the system of casual labour – seem to have produced forms of conflict which are of startling similarity. In his study of the London dock workers' unions John Lovell concludes that the 'port workers have devel- oped a great capacity for spontaneous and militant industrial action', whereas the unions remained 'weak and unstable'. He adds that 'the extent to which trade unions have been able to harness, direct and control these forces has remained limited'.[42] This is largely true of the situation in the Hamburg docks too. As has been done in many other studies, the fact should be emphasized here too that the pattern of workers' behaviour with respect to conflict was also determined and transformed by a combination of factors other than those of the workplace. These included experience gained from previous disputes, the level of organization achieved by either side and state intervention. While this comparative attempt therefore confirms the useful-ness of an analytical approach based on the direct experience of wage-earners on the shop floor, it also shows the need for research looking beyond the factory gates.

Notes: Chapter 6

1 On the London strike, apart from J. Lovell, 'The significance of the great dock strike of 1889 in British labour history', in this volume, pp. 100–103, cf. H. L. Smith and V. Nash, *The Story of the Dockers' Strike* (London, 1889); J. Lovell, *Stevedores and Dockers* (London, 1969), 92–120 and *passim*; G. Stedman Jones, *Outcast London. A Study in the Relationship between Classes in Victorian Society* (Oxford, 1971), 315–21. Apart from contemporary publications by F. Tönnies, E. Francke, C. Legien and R. Ehrenberg, two further studies have recently been published on the Hamburg strike: H. J. Bieber, 'Der Hamburger Hafenarbeiterstreik 1896/97', in A. Herzig *et al.* (eds), *Arbeiter in Hamburg* (Hamburg, 1983), 229–45; M. Grüttner, 'Mobilität und Konfliktverhalten. Der Hamburger Hafenar-beiterstreik 1896/97', in K. Tenfelde and H. Volkmann (eds), *Streik. Zur Geschichte des Arbeitskampfes in Deutschland während der Industrialisierung* (Munich, 1981), 143–61.

2 For detailed information on the internal dissent among the employers cf. the unpublished manuscript of R. Ehrenberg in Zentrales Staatsarchiv Merseburg, Nachlaß F. Althoff, Rep. 92 A II No. 62a. Bl.31–44 and *passim*. The published version of this work in which the author describes the strike from the employers' point of view is not as informative. R. Ehrenberg, *Der Ausstand der Hamburger Hafenarbeiter 1896/97* (Jena, 1897).

3 cf. Smith and Nash, *Dockers' Strike*, 108; *Bericht über die Tätigkeit des Hamburger Gewerkschaftskartells für die Zeit von 1895–1897* (Hamburg, 1898), 18–20.

4 cf. Stedman Jones, *Outcast London*, 291–300.

5 cf. *Bericht über die Tätigkeit des Gewerkschaftskartells*, 19.

6 The official union account of the incidents in Hamburg states as follows: 'In consideration of the support given by the Hamburg police authorities to the strike breakers and their conduct towards the strikers, which was frequently no less than disgraceful . . . it must seem strange that in its report the London dock committee felt bound to express its gratitude to the authorities for their support of the strikers. . . . The Hamburg dock-workers have not the slightest reason to express even the faintest gratitude to the police authorities of Hamburg.' C. Legien, *Der Streik der Hafenarbeiter und Seeleute in Hamburg-Altona* (Hamburg, 1897), pp. VI–VII. On state intervention in labour disputes in Imperial Germany in general, cf. K. Saul, *Staat, Industrie, Arbeiterbewegung im Kaiserreich* (Düsseldorf, 1974), and idem, 'Repression or integration? The state, trade unions and industrial disputes in Imperial Germany', in this volume, pp. 338–56.

7 *Vorwärts* 46 (24 February 1897).

8 Legien, *Der Streik der Hafenarbeiter*, 93.

9 *Vorwärts* 45 (23 February 1897); and 46 (24 February 1897).

10 *Correspondenzblatt der Generalkommission der Gewerkschaften Deutschlands* 11 (15 March 1897). The Trades Union Committee was comprised of representatives from each of the various social democratic unions. It both assisted and supervised the general com-mission.

11 On acts of sabotage in Hamburg cf. Staatsarchiv Hamburg (StA H), Politische Polizei (PP) S 5310–29 UA 23; StA H, Deputation für Handel, Schiffahrt und Gewerbe II Spezialakten

XXX A 8.1.2.9.; *Vossische Zeitung* (10 December 1896); *Hamburger Echo* 52 (3 March 1897).

12 cf. Legien, *Der Streik der Hafenarbeiter*, 87. On the trade and profession of those arrested see StA H, PP S 5310–29 UA 22.

13 cf. the material compiled by the *Politische Polizei* (Political Police) in StA H, PP, V 477, and PP, S 3543.

14 For example, during a stoppage by joiners, doors or windows were sawn through on building sites and floors burned with acid. Electricians tried to back up their demands by breaking pipes and wires or cutting through installed cables. cf. the police records: 'Streiksachen 1911' in StA H, PP S 2505–3 and the large collection of newspaper cuttings about spectacular cases of sabotage in StA H, PP S 2505–8 Vol. II. The problem with research into alleged or actual cases of sabotage is that it is often virtually impossible to exactly reconstruct the incidents and determine the persons responsible.

15 *Verband der Hafenarbeiter und verwandten Berufsgenossen Deutschlands, Protokoll des 11. Verbandstages*, abgehalten am 9./10.5.1910 in Hamburg (Hamburg, 1910), 91.

16 This is at least implied by the fact that with regard to strikes the behaviour of workers with an anarcho-syndicalist tradition barely differed from that of other groups of French workers. cf. D. Geary, *European Labour Protest* (London, 1981), 50–1.

17 *Courier* 37 (11 September 1910). The *Courier* was the newspaper of the German Transport Workers' Federation to which the dockers' federation was affiliated from 1910. On syndicalist tendencies among the London dockers from 1911 see Lovell, *Stevedores and Dockers*, 156.

18 cf. C. Kerr and A. J. Siegel, 'The interindustry propensity to strike – an international comparison', in C. Kerr, *Labor and Management in Industrial Society* (New York, 1964), 105–47. According to this comparative study on statistics from eleven countries, miners, seamen and dock workers went on strike most frequently. It has not been possible to go into the explanations given by Kerr and Siegel at this point.

19 *Der Hafenarbeiter* 24 (24 November 1906).

20 *Hamburger Echo* 29 (4 February 1900).

21 *Verband der Hafenarbeiter Deutschlands, Generalversammlung am 26.1.1902 und folgende Tage in Hamburg* (Hamburg, n.d.), 11. (The delegates' internal material) StA H, PP S 2296 Vol. II.

22 Deutscher Transportarbeiterverband, *25 Jahre Gewerkschaftsarbeit* (Berlin, 1922), 87.

23 *Courier* 37 (15 September 1913).

24 For the statutes with strike regulations see StA H, PP S 2296 Vol. II; PP V 478.

25 *Verband der Hafenarbeiter und verwandten Berufsgenossen Deutschlands, Protokoll des 8. Verbandstages*, abgehalten in Hamburg am 22–26.2.1904 (Hamburg, 1904), 33.

26 cf. *Verband der Hafenarbeiter und verwandten Berufsgenossen Deutschlands, Protokoll des 10. Verbandstages*, abgehalten am 11.5.1908 und folgende Tage in Hamburg (Hamburg, 1908), 80–1, 116–17.

27 *Protokoll des 8. Verbandstages 1904*, 83.

28 *Verband der Hafenarbeiter und verwandten Berufsgenossen Deutschlands, Protokoll des 9. Verbandstages*, abgehalten in Stettin am 26–2.–2.3.1906 (Hamburg, n.d.), 68.

29 cf. H. Volkmann, 'Modernisierung des Arbeitskampfes? Zum Formwandel von Streik und Aussperrung in Deutschland 1864–1975', in H. Kaelble *et al.*, *Probleme der Modernisierung in Deutschland* (Opladen, 1978), 110–70; on this point pp. 144–5.

30 The quotation is from the director of the Hamburg-Altona employers' association: W. G. H. von Reiswitz, *Die Organisation des Unternehmertums im Unterelbe-Bezirk* (Hamburg, 1906), 18.

31 *Courier* 36 (3 September 1911). It may be of interest to point out that the strike movement which the German Transport Workers' Federation apostrophized as an 'economic disaster' nevertheless ended with considerable concessions from the employers. On the dock workers cf. Lovell, *Stevedores and Dockers*, 150–2.

32 M. Grüttner, *Arbeitswelt an der Wasserkante. Sozialgeschichte der Hamburger Hafenarbeiter 1886–1914* (Göttingen, 1984), 48–56.

33 *Allgemeine Schiffahrts-Zeitung* 6 (9 February 1907).

34 ibid.

35 cf. M. Grüttner, 'Working-class crime and the labour movement. Pilfering in the Hamburg

docks 1888–1923', in R. J. Evans (ed.), *The German Working Class 1888–1933. The Politics of Everyday Life* (London, 1982), 54–79.

36 cf. A. Haas, 'Les grèves dans les ports européens et la situation des armateurs', *Revue économique internationale* S/I (1908): 41–61; on this point 54–6.

37 cf. Deutscher Transportarbeiterverband, Verwaltungsstelle Hamburg I, *Jahresbericht der Ortsverwaltung pro 1910* (Hamburg, 1911), 125.

38 This applied in general to the union organization of unskilled workers. cf. K. Schönhoven, *Expansion und Konzentration. Studien zur Entwicklung der Freien Gewerkschaften im Wilhelminischen Deutschland 1890 bis 1914* (Stuttgart, 1980), 55 and 153–62.

39 cf. *Verband der Hafenarbeiter, Protokoll des 10. Verbandstages 1908*, 62–5.

40 cf. ibid., 81, 101, 106.

41 Research on syndicalist trends in German ports from 1918, also widespread among seamen, has so far only been conducted with respect to Bremen. cf. C. Niermann, 'Auswirkungen der Weltwirtschaftskrise auf die Hafenarbeiter in Bremen vor 1933' (unpublished MS., Bremen, 1977), 42–62. The contemporary press also shows that largely similar developments were to be found in Hamburg and other ports.

42 Lovell, *Stevedores and Dockers*, 218.

Part Three

Industrial Modernization, Politics and Trade Union Organization

7   The New Unionism and the Labour Process

RICHARD PRICE

I

The first generation of labour historians had no trouble identifying the causes and significance of the New Unionism. To the Webbs, as to G. D. H. Cole, it represented the 'superior attractiveness' of a newly propagated socialism over the discredited prescriptions of a quiescent liberalism whose political sphere possessed no remedies for the distress of the Great Depression and whose trade union adherents had lost sight of the aggression that Tom Mann believed should characterize the true policy of trade unions. This view, that the New Unionism may be explained primarily by political categories of analysis, remains of continued influence as the most viable explanation of a phenomenon that Hugh A. Clegg, Alan Fox and A. F. Thompson, for example, found 'colourful and baffling'.[1] A recent history of British labour appears to give prime explanatory weight to the immediate timing of the trade cycle and the dramatic example of the match girls with changed attitudes to poverty and socialism as the long-term factors. And although a side glance is often given to the forces creating a semi-skilled division of labour, this uncertainty as to how we are to explain the New Unionism is quite typical.[2] Thus, Clegg, Fox and Thompson, staggering under the weight of the empirical model, wavered between an explanation that focused alternately on the trade cycle, the socialists and upon the structure of union government. Ultimately, they admitted, none of these variables either singly or together explained the phenomenon. The trade buoyancy was not enough to explain the massive surge in union membership because an upswing in 1882 had failed to provide a similar revival; socialism provided an 'important context' and politically astute leadership but here, too, that influence was 'probably not a major cause of the upsurge in trade union membership'. At this point, the authors beat a rapid retreat into an industrial relations analysis of union structure and government where they felt much more at home.[3]

Contemporary historians, then, have felt far less certain than the earlier generation about how we are to explain, conceptualize and interpret the New Unionism. The conventional emphasis upon the new articulation and recognition of economic grievances is insufficiently reflective of the complex relations between 'economics' and 'politics', let alone of the active role of those recipients of the political missionaries who advised, led and stimulated the New Unionism. Nor, of course, does that emphasis explain anything beyond a most general context. It would be foolish to deny any role to that

context, but it seems a bit simplistic to ascribe it primacy. A more sophisticated framework of analysis is suggested by a series of essays Eric J.
Hobsbawm published in *Labouring Men* where three elements might be
distinguished as of particular importance.

First, that the New Unionism reflected an initial response to a slowly
gathering and fractured shift in economic development from competitive
to monopoly capitalism whose most visible manifestation was the collection of 'inflammable material' at the workplace waiting to be set alight by
trade cycle movements or the pressure of work intensity. This line of
argument has been most fruitfully developed by James E. Cronin who
explicitly sees the New Unionism as the response to the heightened sense
of insecurity, and especially of unemployment, wrought by the employers'
need to increase exploitation and restore the falling profit margins of the
Great Depression. For Cronin, the New Unionism signified the workers'
search for new organizational and strategic weapons to cope with these
changing economic circumstances.[4]

Secondly, Hobsbawm pointed to the necessity for some kind of relative
occupational stability within the division of labour if the New Unionism
was to survive. And there is the clear suggestion that the New Unionism
was part of a process that required a readjustment of social relations of
production perhaps because of a general rearrangement of the 'productive
apparatus'. Thus, in an essay on the gas stokers, Hobsbawm shows how
their key role in the production process gave them a bargaining power
that depended more upon the inconvenience they could cause than upon
any possession of 'craft' skill. Like modern process workers in flow-line
production, the stokers were able to block a crucial point in the supply of
the product with potentially serious consequences for the capital expense
of the companies and the comfort and safety of the public. Just why they
were better able to do that in 1889 than in 1872 remains unclear, but what
Hobsbawm is pointing to is one aspect of a wider series of changes in the
division of labour during these years that was fracturing the mid-Victorian
distinctions between 'craft' and 'labourer' to foment the creation of a
complex semi-skilled strata whose specialized work technique endowed
them with a certain power and whose bargaining ability depended most
generally upon favourable labour markets and trade cycle opportunities.[5]

Third, in his essay on waterside unions, Hobsbawm shows the importance of changing social relations of production (and especially in respect
of employer recognition and government action) in the stabilization of the
New Unions. Thus, in an earlier essay, he had remarked upon the significance of employer recognition as a protection against membership
collapse during downswings, and in the case of the docks there is a very
noticeable coincidence between the permanence of the unionization of
1911 and 1912 and the adoption of standardized wages and recognition by
the Shipping Federation. It should be remembered, however, that the
initiatives for recognition and standardization derived not from the
employers but, in both phases of the movement, from the rank and file
themselves. The difference was that in 1911–12 the movement was more
truly national – and in this the socialist leadership was important – and

there was a clearer advantage for the employers to stabilize competitive conditions.[6]

An implication that might be drawn from these arguments, then, is that the emergence of the New Unionism has to be seen in a context that focuses more upon changing social relations both in and of production than upon the immediate conjuncture of trade cycle economies and the presence of socialist politics and personnel. Such a context would at least allow us to understand why political and trade cycle explanations can only illuminate the moment of explosion rather than the deeper structural shifts that conditioned the emergence and subsequent history of the New Unionism as a general phenomenon. Social relations of production alter in a fractured, uneven way and it is a mistake to concentrate purely on the peculiarities of the immediate timing of 1888–91. Thus, it adds nothing to interpretation, for example, merely to push the date of the New Unionism back to 1886 or to argue that London was not its only focal point.[7] Indeed, that knowledge is useful only in so far as it suggests the need to take a broad view both of the process of New Unionism's emergence and its significance within the wider history of the period. This necessity is reinforced by two obvious and well-known facts. In the first place, the New Unionism properly understood marked the breakthrough to permanent unionism on a wider front than the previously unorganized alone. Between 1890 and 1910 the unionized male workforce increased from around 10 per cent to 30 per cent and as the semi-skilled were struggling to find a viable basis for organization, the established unions were experiencing a qualitative expansion and there were the first stirrings of white-collar unionism which by the First World War had been firmly established, if at a fairly low level of inclusiveness. Thus, any account of the New Unionism has to be capable of explaining more than just one segment of the problem and should focus upon the general forces that lay behind these parallel developments. Secondly, and as a corollary, both the organizational and strategic tendencies that first appeared in the late 1880s and early 1890s were common to the period 1888 to the early 1920s as a whole and did not reach a decisive conclusion until the opening of the interwar years. The efforts to find ways of overcoming sectionalism, for example, clearly evident in the early aspirations of the general unions and a growing tendency in the skilled unions, may be said to have been resolved by the early 1920s. Not that this meant that sectionalism was no longer to be a problem, but rather that the mid-Victorian demarcations had been replaced by a more complex set of distinctions requiring a different set of organizational structures. On a more prosaic level, if the 1889 dock strike failed to create effective dockside unionism, it cannot be divorced from the realization of that possibility following the strike of 1912 and the experiences of the First World War. And, to take a very different example, but one which illustrates the unity of the period, the freedom over manning arrangements secured by the engineering employers in 1898 was not fully attained until the defeats of the early 1920s were sealed by the depression.[8]

It is suggested here that the essential unity of the period lies in the direction of change to be found within the sphere of the social relations of production. There were two things that were important in this respect, two elements that usually, but not necessarily, went together. The first was the very real technical and organizational alterations in the labour process (that is, of relations in production) that occurred during these years, and the second element was the new style of managerial assertiveness which sometimes rested upon the former but equally could be unaccompanied by any dynamic changes in the organization of production. Together these alterations were pervasive and general in their effects, and because organized as well as unorganized labour was affected, it is necessary to begin by making some very broad statements about the general development of relations in the labour process in the nineteenth century.

In the first place, and most decisively, the period saw a shift in the balance of social relations of production away from formal techniques of subordination towards a closer approximation of what Marx termed the real subsumption of labour.[9] Until the late nineteenth century the essential peculiarity of British capitalism lay precisely in the failure of industrialization to recompose social relations of production in its own mirror image. The result was a hybrid, mongrelized creation that was reflected in the contradictory character of mid-Victorian society and culture. The fractured reality of industrial capitalism was expressed, for example, in the continued predominance of the methods of formal subordination in social relationships. Thus, the terminology of master and servant law remained rooted in the sixteenth-century Statute of Apprentices until 1875. Similarly, profits continued to be derived from the extraction of absolute surplus value through methods of extensive labour utilization. Hence the central significance of hours limitation to the early and mid-Victorian labour movement. In the later part of the century, the adoption of intensive labour utilization to secure relative surplus value was revealed by the emergence of a Taylorist division of labour in the boot and shoe industry, the premium bonus system in the engineering industry, new forms of subcontracting in the non-factory trades, even the mechanization of certain areas of dock work. Furthermore, and unsurprisingly, managerial strategies began to move away from relative autonomy in the skilled trades and paternal aloofness in the unskilled, towards a more direct and bureaucratized supervision. Thus, in his chocolate factory in 1899 Edward Cadbury replaced power of punishment by foremen with a formal disciplinary code administered by a managerial committee. A similar example would be the bureaucratic accompaniments to the adoption of premium bonus system in engineering.[10]

The second feature of this restructuring of the labour process was its generality. Although not every individual trade was affected equally, the main elements were to be found in sectors as diverse as engineering, boot and shoe, gas work, the railways and clerical labour. This, too, sets it apart from the initial period of industrialization whose impact outside textiles and some areas of metalworking involved more an expansion of customary modes of production. In the later nineteenth century, it was the broad convergence of the tendency towards increased subordination which underlay the often noted confluence between industrial militancy and political consciousness as the period nears its climax in the 1920s.

But, finally, if the general experience of restructuring served to inaugurate a heightened sense of class solidarity, the differences in the social, economic and cultural formations upon which it impacted explain the particular variations in organizational and other responses. To take a very simple example. The demise of the genteel work environment of clerical labour and its increasingly specialized, insecure and even mechanized nature, led initially to an aggressive reassertion of middle-class status aspirations one of whose forms was expressed through patriotic conservatism. Only gradually did this begin to give way to an acceptance of proletarianization and its concomitant of white-collar unionism.[11]

II

In somewhat more detail, the restructuring of the labour process of the skilled industrial worker was conditioned by two factors not generally present amongst those workers who had previously remained unorganized. On the one hand, the most completely organized trades were those directly exposed to the competitive pressure that emanated from the emergent multilateral world economy. The challenge to Britain's market position from the United States and Germany was not confined to exports; a major reason for the reorganization of the boot and shoe industry was the temporary invasion of the domestic market by American footwear. On the other hand, the market imperative towards reorganization was unevenly distributed both between and within various sectors: iron and steel was sufficiently buoyant to resist the adoption of the Gilchrist-Thomas process, textiles resisted the adoption of ring spinning; but boot and shoe was sufficiently threatened to rationalize. In addition, although foreign competition as such was not present in every case – the railways are evidence of this – there was a widespread recognition (which clearly had to do with the general efficiency of the nation) of the need to place relations in production on a new basis to secure more complete productivity gains. The central domestic impediment to such reorganization as was necessary lay in the networks of resistance to capitalist control of the production process that the skilled trades had managed to erect. The paradox of the British case at this time, then, lay in the fact that although the drive to rationalize was much weaker than it was in the United States or Germany, the response occasioned from this fractured imperative was far stronger and more serious than elsewhere. Trade unionism was the institutional base and symbol of that impediment and although the situation varied both between and within trades, there is very good evidence to suggest that for much of the 1890s the balance of power at work was swinging in favour of the men as employers attempted to bargain the introduction of new techniques and methods of organization. Where attempts to renegotiate the basis of subordination failed, united and determined assaults were mounted on the protective bastions of the men, as was the case in engineering, boot and shoe and less critically in cotton-spinning.

The point, however, is that these factors dictated that the restructuring of the labour process in these trades was bound to be the product both of a sense of urgency as it was expressed in trade journals quite often, and of a direct managerial intervention. It was likely to be characterized by a relatively coherent and complete managerial strategy rather than simply confined, for example, to smashing the men in order to secure the introduction of a particular piece of machinery. The networks of resistance – such as the restrictions on machine-manning in printing and engineering – posed the central obstacles for employers engaged in reorganizing the labour process. Thus, even if employers chose to increase subordination and productivity by an expanded use of 'traditional' modes of work organization, they could not do so without acquiring an explicitly recognized freedom to intervene where necessary in work execution. Thus, the general character of the struggles of these years was not an attempt to destroy unionism but rather to enlist its disciplinary assistance in the crucial battle to remove or diminish the extent of worker control at the point of production. There was no contradiction, for example, between the introduction of the premium bonus system on the very day that the engineering lock-out of 1898 was ended and the general strengthening of union authority that resulted from the Terms of Settlement. In addition, the subsequent expansion of premium bonus was always accompanied by a thorough-going reorganization of the actual work process and also by a tightening of the formal rules of behaviour in the factories.[12] The intensity of the great conflicts of the 1890s in the skilled trades reflected the fact that fundamental issues of authority and control over the work process were at stake.

Furthermore, it was usually the case that the desired changes in the labour process were associated with – and a product of – the availability of new technology. Whether the threats to craft skill were real or imagined, there is no doubting their potency – the literature is full of complaints about technological unemployment and the destruction of skill – and whatever their actual effects on the division of labour, they clearly served to emphasize the general experience of increased subordination and vulnerability. In a profound sense, these workers were right to be fearful. The purpose and result of the new technology in this sector was not merely to intensify the work, but also to fracture and undermine established craft boundaries both within and between trades. The growing frequency of demarcation disputes from the late 1870s was one reflection of this. The recomposition of craft frontiers varied from place to place and the ability of different trades to cope with the organizational problems it raised depended largely upon the prior history of the trades. Boot and shoe workers and printers, for example, found it easier to adapt than did engineers partly because they had a more continuous experience of labour process changes. But, nevertheless, the overall impact of these changes in the skilled sector was to disrupt the structure of work and social relations of production in a way that had not been seen since the early nineteenth century. The main effect of this disruption was to create a new stratum of semi-skilled workers; or, as in shipbuilding, to provide those of previously uncertain occupational status like drillers, holers and helpers with a new sense of skill security. In this respect, the structural results of alterations in the labour process were not so different from what was happening in those sectors without a tradition of craft skill and organization.

But compared to the skilled workers, the restructuring of the labour process amongst the semi-skilled – as they were to become – was qualitatively different in three basic ways.

In the first place, it was far more a product of the gradual accretion of changes, often minor in themselves, which occurred within the context of a managerial strategy that remained paternally distant from the workforce. Generally absent was the dramatic intervention of new technology and any concerted change of direction in managerial attitudes or policies. In the gasworks, the 1880s saw continual experimentation with improved techniques. George Livesey of the South Metropolitan Gas Company and a prime actor in the events of 1889, for example, had always been an avid innovator. As early as 1883 he had proudly reported on a new machine at Beckton which improved the ratio of output to labour costs. This may have been the 'iron man' retort charger Will Thorne wrote about in his memoirs as increasing the work and reducing the gang size, but in spite of Thorne's socialist proselytizing among his mates it inspired no reaction from the men.[13] Although it is worth noting that the two major centres of experimentation in gaswork – Beckton and Manchester – were also to be the original centres of stokers' unionism in the late 1880s, the previous history of subservience to managerial change points to the second difference in the labour process changes as they affected the semi-skilled.

This lay in the fact that the latter possessed no traditional networks of resistance to capitalist control of the labour process. And it was just this that allowed changes in the organization and structure of work to accrue gradually and smoothly throughout the 1880s. Equally, it was precisely this acquiesence that explains the stunned managerial response to the strike wave of 1888–90, for there had been nothing in previous experience to anticipate such an outburst. This is not to say that there were no prior traditions of militancy amongst these groups. In both Hull and Liverpool – but particularly the former – there is evidence of work group type union activity from the 1870s and it is not without significance that Hull was to become the stronghold of the dockers' New Unionism until smashed by the concerted offensive of 1893. More usually, the evidence suggests spasmodic activity such as the London gas stokers' strike of 1872 which plunged the capital into darkness for several days. Similarly, the match girls whose strike of 1888 has been dubbed the 'first victory of the New Unionism' had always possessed a reputation for belligerent independence.[14] But the unenduring nature of this militancy before 1889, and, in the case the match girls, its continued failure to deposit any organizational residue, reflected in a large part the inadequate footholds within the labour process for permanent unionism to survive.

This leads on to the third, and most significant, difference in the nature of labour process restructuring between the skilled and semi-skilled. Whereas in the former case, the changes in the organization and technology of work threatened either the disruption of traditional craft boundaries and/or the displacement of labour, the more gradual and less dramatic changes in semi-skilled work did neither of these things. Indeed, the bias of change pointed in a more favourable direction for the men. Whilst the cumulative effects were to markedly intensify the work, and thus provide the immediate issue of 1889, they did not imply a new division of labour. In fact, the effect of the restructuring of semi-skilled work was to accentuate the pre-existing division of labour and emphasize the viability of task differentiation in such a way as to open up the potential for permanent collective action. In the late 1880s that potential was often only latent and it was the relative levels and strengths of these various forces that determined the permanence or discontinuity of the New Unionism in its initial phase of the late 1880s and early 1890s.

Thus, in the docks the seemingly spontaneous outburst of 1889 was the product of an intensified pace of work whose essential conditions had been created in the reorganization of the port of London in the early 1870s. The increasingly precarious financial position of the dock companies encouraged the expansion of various methods of subcontracting to maintain profit margins, and the centre of strike activity in 1889 – the East and West India Dock – was also the stronghold of the notorious 'plus' system.[15] But the susceptibility to organizational collapse after 1889 reflected a basically unaltered and unaccentuated division of labour. Only where the division of labour had shifted to provide some extra value to labour specialization could unionism secure a foothold. Thus, in Liverpool the mechanization of grain-loading in the early 1880s created a key group of semi-skilled workers whose expertise differed from casualized specialization in that it rested upon the ability of a fairly small number of men to handle complex machinery. This enhanced their strategic power in the work process but also provided enough occupational identity to support union activity. The same combination of circumstances applied to the coal trimmers of Cardiff who also unionized at this time.[16] But elsewhere these possibilities did not obtain, and effective unions do not appear until after the extensive mechanization and rationalization of tasks of the early 1900s. By the second decade of the century, employers were beginning to see the advantages of a stable, organized labour force and permanent dock unionism, and the implantation of a network of restrictive practices can be dated from the strikes of 1912.

On the railways, changes in work organization and managerial strategies of control in the late 1880s combined to dissolve the edifice of paternal authority which hitherto had assured subservient union attitudes. New electrical switching systems which now were required by government legislation made signal work a particular focus of change.[17] Thus, on the Midland Railway in the 1890s, to allow the passing of one train an average of fifty signals were received, twelve entries made in the train book, safety checks observed as the train passed and the frame levers – which were harder to work than the old, hung loose points – pulled. But as the complexity of the work increased, so did the skill. Previously, 'anyone could be a signalman but now you require a man of some education and good sound judgement . . . a signalman in former times had no responsibility compared with what he has now'.[18] 'Profession' was the word the men used to describe the attributes necessary for signal work. At the same time, the companies were entering a period of squeezed profit margins, due to the refusal of the government to allow carrying rates to be raised and the increasing pressure of wage demands. Pay and promotion systems began to be altered to call into question the trade off between paternal subserviences and the stability of wages, status and job tenure. Thus, the trip system of payment was introduced for goods guards and new classes of casualized guards created who were required to be on hand in case they were needed. It is within this context that the expansion of union and all-grades activity must be seen. Signalmen, in particular, had been noted for the moderation of their demands and their general lack of interest in union membership. Their workplace isolation combined with such privileges as company housing had traditionally confined their industrial relations within a purely sectionalist mould. Their transformation from peaceable servants into a body of men who provided the leadership and core support of militant all-grades movements was the product of a growing disjunction between paternal ideology and exploitative reality. The intensification of work and the concentration of interlocked signals into the block system undermined their separation both from each other and other grades.[19]

III

In response to this increased and new militancy, the period from the early 1890s to the establishment of a conciliation system in 1907 was marked by determined efforts to reassert the unilateral authority of management. The Taff Vale Railway under its martinet general manager, Ammon Beasley, exemplified the hardening of managerial control. Efforts to achieve greater subordination included the abrogation of traditional promotion and task differentiation procedures, instant dismissals with no recourse to appeal, the requirement that drivers maintain a detailed record of their movements, the refusal to recognize a system of negotiation set up in 1890 and excessive demands for overtime.[20] Beasley's methods transformed the Taff Vale Railway into the most profitable and most densely unionized in the country and its locus as the climacteric conflict of labour law reflected a decade of tension over discipline and authority.

From about 1906 the logic of this managerial strategy was rationalized by the adoption of the control system of administration which had originated in the United States and required a tightly centralized hierarchy of responsibility and supervision. Designed to ensure greater efficiency and work intensity, the system represented a further intrusion into the work autonomy of drivers, guards and signalmen and their subordination to an absolute bureaucratic authority. From 1908, for example, the responsibility for loading mineral trains on the Midland line was removed from the control of guards and transferred to office controllers. Thus, in 1913, it was claimed that 'at no time in our experience have we received so many complaints . . . concerning bullying abuse [by] minor officials . . . [of] busy signalmen in important boxes'.[21] The most significant conflicts of the period revolved around the companies' demand for complete obedience and the men's rejection of this paternalist assumption. Thus, the strikes caused by the dismissal of a driver for allegedly being drunk off duty, and the firing of a guard in February 1913 for refusing to obey a controller's order which he believed contravened the safety rules, signified a deep resentment at the subordinating demands of the control system. The nature of the conciliation system only served to reinforce these pressures: its slow-working, sectionalist structure and denial of collective bargaining merely emphasized the desirability of extended union organization. It is within the context of these changes in the structure of work and authority relations of production that the growing syndicalist sentiment amongst railway workers and the pressure from below that created the amalgamated National Union of Railwaymen in 1911 must be viewed.[22]

In gas stoking, the role of managerial discipline was far less significant in the labour process changes than it was on the railways, but the same kind of relationship existed between the changing organization of work and the division of labour. Since the late 1870s, new kinds of retorts which burned at a fiercer heat, demanded more fuel and required a constant attention and effort had decisively modified the rhythm and intensity of stoking work. Work routine shifted from unevenly fluctuating activity, punctuated by long periods of rest, to a continuous confinement within the overheated atmosphere of the retort house. Scoops and shovels increased in size, as did the numbers of retorts to be attended by each gang. As early as 1880 Livesey claimed that these regenerator and inclined furnaces had increased output by more than 20 per cent and in 1889 he admitted to shareholders that 'the work of the stokers has been somewhat increased of late years'. In addition, there was the anticipation of imminent mechanization and, indeed, by 1888 over 130 of West's retort-charging machines were in operation. The Manchester and Salford gas corporation completely mechanized stoking in 1886 with the result that the eight-hour day enjoyed for the previous decade was replaced by the twelve-hour shift.[23]

But the effects of these kinds of changes were to intensify the pre-existing division of labour rather than to suggest its recomposition. The distinctiveness of stoking work had long been a reality and the key position of the stokers in the production process had already endowed them with a certain degree of power. It is significant, for example, that the strike of 1872 in London had been sparked off by the attempt to put a navvy to do stoking work and this strike may be seen as prefiguring the efforts of the late 1880s to formalize the stoker's place within the division of labour. But this distinctiveness could not form the basis for a viable unionism until the organizational changes of the succeeding twenty years had reinforced that key position by intensifying the work and, therefore, accentuating the required skill. When the Manchester gasworks were mechanized the labour force was cut in half, but those who remained possessed security of employment and were no longer liable to be laid off in the summer. In addition, new classes of work were created which removed the responsibility of wheeling the fuel from the stokers and thus freed them to carbonize an extra 50 per cent of coal per shift. The same forces that allowed intensified work also demanded a sharper differentiation of tasks and acting together these developments both created the need for and the viability of stokers' unionism. The demands of the men in 1889 reflected this duality. On the one hand there were efforts to restrict and control the pace and extent of work requirements through limitations on the numbers of retorts to be charged by each gang, on the hours of work and on the composition of the gangs. At Beckton there were informal attempts to enforce the closed shop. On the other hand, and particularly where the labour process had been most completely reorganized, there were attempts to secure a formal recognition of the skill of stoking. Thus, at Bradford the men demanded the creation of separate classes of yardmen to haul the fuel and to scurf the retorts; in Leeds they demanded that attending to the fires be handed over to a new class of firemen.[24] Elsewhere there were demands that the 'customary' privileges granted to stokers by paternal managements (such as the tradition of stokers replacing yardmen in the summer) be formalized into rules. The point is that the key position of the stokers had been sufficiently reinforced by these developments to provide them with that margin of strength necessary to take collective action and to create permanent organization. As the rhythm and intensity of the work changed, so did the difficulties of substituting inexperienced labour. The skill of stoking resided not in knowing what to do, but how best to do it so as to survive the hostile environment and long day. The techniques of working depended upon an acquired rhythm and strength which could be greatly affected by seemingly minor changes. This was well illustrated at Manchester in 1890 when it took over a month to restore the gas supply to its pre-strike level because the blacklegs were used to working stage house retorts with scoops whose different and less arduous series of motions were inappropriate for the shovel-filled ground house retorts of Lancashire.[25] In this respect, the enhanced skill of the men may roughly be measured by noting that whereas the London strike of 1872 had plunged the capital into darkness for only two days, it took over a week to restore sufficient lighting to the town of Halifax in 1889. Similarly, the former strike had been broken fairly easily with the use of navvies and yardmen, but the preparations Livesey made for his confrontation with the union at his Vauxhall works in the autumn of 1889 included the erection of a dormitory and the importation of 700 patrolling police to cow the men, in addition to the 3,000 stationed outside to protect the blacklegs.[26]

IV

It is clear that the shock of 1889 in areas like gas stoking lay in the realization that the structure of the labour process had altered enough to allow a serious challenge to employer authority. It was universally agreed that for several months in 1889 the balance of control over work shifted towards the stokers and as Livesey pointed out to the Royal Commission on Labour the crucial question was that 'the allegiance of the workmen . . . was fast passing away'. As noted earlier, restructuring had not initially aroused any challenge to the paternalist style of management. In fact, the presentation of grievances through petitions and the mid-Victorian moralism implicit in occasional requests for an end to Sunday labour tended to reinforce paternal authority. Certainly, the gathering restiveness of the men prompted a reconsideration of managerial methods and the first public discussions on this question occurred in 1888.[27] The issue was forced, however, by the challenge posed by the demands of 1889 for restrictions on the methods and organization of work. And, thus, as on the docks and the railways, the ultimate impact of restructuring upon the social relations of production involved the necessity to reassert managerial control. This contrasted sharply with the situation in the skilled sector where the imperative was to extend managerial control to bring the relations of production into line with the new potentialities of the labour process. In this case, therefore, the initiative derived from management; in the semi-skilled trades it was a product of the massive intervention of the working class itself.

And this difference is of some importance; for although in both sectors the struggle revolved around control of the work process, the contextual differences of promise and threats determined the variations in style between the New and old unionism. In general the restructuring of the semi-skilled labour process provided an opportunity for them to increase their control over work: indeed, more properly, to establish some control for the first time through the agency of collective action. For the skilled, however, the main direction of restructuring was to promise a diminution of their power and influence and, in fact, to even threaten the very basis upon which their collective organization rested.

The semi-skilled strike wave of 1889 represented a rebellion against paternal authority made possible by changes in the labour process. But because it marked only the beginnings of a recognition that social and authority relations at work needed to be placed upon a new basis, the achievements of this phase of New Unionism were partial rather than complete. Similarly, the efforts to reassert employer authority in the shape of a formalized paternalism attained a varied and limited success. Both Livesey and the railway companies encountered resistance to their use of profit-sharing and pension schemes as means to secure contractual obedience.[28] And in municipalized gasworks of the north of England codified rules which reflected managerial control over production and imposed definite periods of contract were combined with bargaining over the conditions of work.[29] This was also increasingly the pattern on the railways. On the docks, managerial control was reasserted through the agency of free labour organizations created and manipulated by the employers which represented, perhaps, the most ambitious attempt to formalize paternal control in this period. Of course, such efforts were ultimately only holding operations – although Livesey's profit-sharing scheme survived until the 1920s – and as the elements within the restructuring process grew more and more contradictory so the extent of union membership and collective bargaining increased. Thus, by 1912 free labour organization in the docks was virtually extinct and the railway companies had abandoned their effort to separate collective bargaining from union membership.

Social relations of production in the semi-skilled sector, then, were primarily disrupted between the men and the employers, and the basic question was to what extent their material base had altered to allow permanent organization. For the skilled, the disruption of social relations was fundamentally different, because it involved the fracturing of relations within the working class as much as with employers. The generally defensive reaction of the skilled workers to these labour process changes must be seen within the context of the threats they posed to the traditional nature and balance of social and authority relations. Thus, the celebrated differences between the New and old unionism to the legislated eight-hour day question reflected the fact that for the former it represented an expression of their new-found organizational power and potential; for the latter, it signified a confession that the old structures of resistance to capitalist control of the work process were redundant. A similar conflict was involved in the necessity to restructure their organizational bases of action. The question for the New Unionists was not so much how they were to organize, but whether they were able to organize. For the old unionists, it was more complicated: how were they to adjust their organizational structures to accommodate the new classes of semi-skilled within their trades? It would be a mistake to exaggerate the difficulties this involved. The platers in the shipyards, for example, accomplished the absorption of the newly skilled caulkers and drillers with the minimum of fuss, and after several tense episodes in the 1880s they even managed to come to terms with their own helpers who had long struggled against their subordination to the craft boilermakers. The boot and shoe workers, threatened by Taylorism, the mechanization of lasting and the recrudescence of outworking in the Midlands, simply organized downwards, changing their union name in 1890 to signify the fact and dispatching recruiters out into the 'basket' working villages around Leicester and Northampton.[30] Others, most notably the engineers, found this process much more difficult to accept, perhaps because their labour process had remained relatively unaltered since the 1840s. But it was also the case that the speed and scope of restructuring was much slower in engineering than it was in boot and shoe or printing and not until the First World War did it climax in the kinds of tensions James Hinton has analysed. Certainly the tendency for militants to press for amalgamation in the years before 1914 reflected the appreciation that the boundaries of collective action needed to be expanded, if subordination was to be effectively resisted.

What is more, the defensiveness generally characteristic of the skilled sectors was also conditioned by the intimate connection between the reassertion of employer authority and the extension and expansion of collective bargaining procedures and institutions. It was the universal feature of these developments to secure a greater disciplinary power over the men by denying the legitimacy of unilateral action and undermining the autonomy of the local units of union organization. Thus, in addition to the threats of de-skilling posed by the labour process changes and the imperative to rethink the boundaries of union membership, there was the necessity to readjust the balance of internal union authority. No skilled union remained free of this tension during these years; indeed, the period marks the beginnings of modern forms of rank-and-file militancy.

Of course, this latter problem of union discipline and authority quickly emerged in the New Unions of the semi-skilled. And it provides but one instance of the often noticed convergence between New and old unionism in terms of organizational structures and issues. By the mid-1890s, for example, the eight-hour day had been adopted by old unionism and Hobsbawm has pointed to the shift in the New Unions between 1892 and 1912 from the inclusive notion of 'one man, one ticket' to the more exclusive 'one ticket, one job'.[31] The basis of this shift lay, of course, in the division of labour itself. It became clear to the gas stokers that their original hope to organize yardmen was doomed to failure when the latter eagerly accepted the paternalist offerings of Livesey's profit-sharing scheme. Their actions are not hard to understand: the promise of security to the seasonally employed yardmen and the stipulation that any man could be ordered to any job offered more to these unskilled labourers than the stokers' insistence that task differentiation be clearly demarcated. If the stokers and others began as industrial unionists they very quickly learned its irrelevancy to the character of the labour process in Britain. Compared especially to the United States and perhaps also to Germany and France, where a similar process of restructuring was in progress, there was less opportunity in Britain for the thorough-going transformation of the labour process associated with such names as Henry Ford and Andrew Carnegie. The full technological and organizational logic of real subordination was feasible only where the labour process was being freshly constructed with malleable workers. With its older industrial base and its deeply entrenched traditions of managerial and worker behaviour, restructuring in Britain was bound to be more closely confined by the past than elsewhere. Thus, the only place where industrial unionism may be said to have secured a mass base was at the new Singer sewing machine factory at Kilbowie in Glasgow where a thoroughly Taylorist labour process had been erected at the very beginning of the factory's operation.[32]

But to return to the main point, the tendency of New and old unionism to converge both in organizational form, in demands and in their styles of militancy – socialist and syndicalist sentiment was to be found in both sectors – is hardly surprising. At bottom both confronted the same general question: how best to resist the increased subordination promised by the restructuring of the labour process. The differences in detailed responses was a reflection of the different social formations upon which restructuring impacted. But the commonality of the experience is also fundamental explanation of growing political convergences and particularly in the spread or relevance of socialism.

V

The conventional explanation of the New Unionism typically conflates cause and effect. It attributes the ability of the New Unionism to emerge at the end of the 1880s to the arrival of socialist propagandists from outside the group in question to show them the tricks of the trade. In fact, socialism must be seen not as a prior category to these developments but as consequent upon the restructuring itself. That ought not to mean to imply a vulgar base-superstructure model, but more what Raymond Williams and Edward P. Thompson have called the metaphoric or mediating relationship. To put it very boldly, socialism and socialists could be received where and when the impact of restructuring had most completely undermined the viability of the previous structure of authority relations at work. Thus, not only did the match girls fail to maintain a union after 1888, but they also failed to absorb any socialist doctrine, whereas the stokers did. The reasons for this – or, at least, a partial reason – surely lay in the fact that the labour process of match-making did not undergo any change to alter the dimensions and vocabulary of the social relations of production, but in stoking and railway work it did. Thus, the match girls quickly reverted to the behaviour expected of paternal work relations; they failed, for example, to respond to the efforts of social reformers in the 1890s to mount a campaign against the employers' arbitrary handling of compensation for cases of phossy jaw. The same patterns were visible in the skilled trades. In boot and shoe, it was precisely those locations (London, Bristol and Northampton) where the reorganization of production was most advanced that rank-and-file militancy was expressed within a socialist vocabulary. Similarly, it was totally appropriate that the motion for the formation of the Labour Representation Committee in 1899 should have been moved by James Holmes, the ASRS organiser of the Taff Vale Railway.

Thus, in general terms socialism emerged as a response to the restructuring of the labour process. For both the skilled and semi-skilled, socialism provided a vocabulary which enabled the tensions, conflicts and promise of restructuring to be understood and interpreted. The dialectic involved in this process binds together the industrial and political developments of the period. Socialism attained a new-found significance in the 1890s as restructuring began to impact upon the skilled and semi-skilled; equally, by 1910, as the evidence mounted of a growing complexity of the problems of industrial and political power, the syndicalist spirit made its appearance. The events of the war years and, particularly, the increasingly coercive role of the state in the process of restructuring, transformed this syndicalist impulse into a new kind of rank-and-file militancy and organization which began to explore the possibilities of workers' control and which remained the most enduring legacy of the period.

The New Unionism has to be seen as integral to this historical dialectic. The tendency of the labour process to shift the status of labour from formal to real subordination produced New Unionism as both a structural result and a political response. That same tendency underlay the dynamic of the whole period. And in so far as the labour process was successfully restructured, it was equally the case that the drive to achieve a more complete subordination of labour produced strategies and politics which defined and contained the limits to real subordination. The New Unionism was one instance of this; it represented the initial phase of a process that was to end with the industrial radicalism of the early 1920s.

Notes: Chapter 7

1   S. Webb and B. Webb, *The History of Trade Unionism* (London, 1902), 370–3, 388–95; G. D. H. Cole and R. Postgate, *The Common People 1746–1946* (London, 1961), 425–6; see also E. M. Carus-Wilson, 'Some notes on British trade unions in the third quarter of the nineteenth century', in idem, *Essays in Economic History*, Vol. 3 (London, 1962), 219 for the suggestion of a slightly more complicated analysis; H. A. Clegg *et al.*, *A History of British Trade Unions since 1889*, Vol. 1 (Oxford, 1964), 55.
2   E. H. Hunt, *British Labour History 1815–1914* (London, 1981), 304–5. See also H. Pelling, *The Origins of the Labour Party* (Oxford, 1954) for the most complete statement of the conventional interpretation.
3   Clegg *et al.*, *History of British Trade Unions*, 87–96.
4   E. J. Hobsbawm, 'Economic fluctuations and some social movements', in idem, *Labouring Men* (London, 1964), 126–57 (140–2); J. Cronin, *Industrial Conflict in Modern Britain* (London, 1979), 93–6.
5   E. J. Hobsbawm, 'British gas-workers, 1873–1914', in idem, *Labouring Men*, 158–78; idem, 'General labour unions in Britain, 1889–1914', in ibid., 179–203 (187).
6   idem, 'National unions on the waterside', in ibid., 204–30 (222–7). Also B. Moggeridge, 'Militancy and inter-union rivalries in British shipping 1911–29', *International Review of Social History* 6 (1961): 375–412 (382–3, 409).
7   A. E. P. Duffy, 'New Unionism in Britain 1889–1890: a reappraisal', *Economic History Review* 14 (1961): 306–19.
8   Amalgamated Society of Engineers (ASE), *Monthly Journal*, May 1920, p. 31; Amalgamated Engineering Union (AEU), *Monthly Journal*, August 1925, p. 34; April 1934, p. 18.
9   K. Marx, *Grundrisse* (New York, 1973), 693; idem, *Capital*, Vol. 1 (Harmondsworth, 1976), Appendix: Results of the Immediate Process of Production, pp. 1019–38.
10 E. Cadbury, *Experiments in Industrial Growth* (London, 1912), 69–71; ASE, *Monthly Journal*, June 1902, p. 75; J. Rowan, 'A premium system applied to engineering works', in Institute of Mechanical Engineers, *Proceedings*, March 1903.
11 R. Price, 'Society, status and jingoism: the social roots of lower middle-class patriotism', in G. Crossick (ed.), *The Lower Middle Class in Britain 1870–1914* (London, 1977), 89–112.
12 J. Zeitlin, 'Industrial structure, employer strategy and the diffusion of job control in Britain, 1880–1920', in this volume, pp. 325–37; K. Burgess, 'New Unionism for old? The Amalgamated Society of Engineers in Britain', in ibid., pp. 166–84; W. Rowan Thompson, *The Rowan Premium Bonus System of Payments by Results* (Glasgow, 1917); ASE, *Monthly Report*, December 1902, p. 68.
13 *Journal of Gas Lighting*, 26 June 1883, pp. 1192–4, for a detailed report on the productivity of West's retort-charging machines. W. Thorne, *My Life's Battles* (London, 1925), 64–5.
14 R. Brown, *Waterfront Organisation in Hull 1870–1900* (Hull, 1972); E. L. Taplin, *Liverpool Dockers and Seamen 1870–1900* (Hull, 1974); Pelling, *Origins of the Labour Party*, 60.
15 J. Lovell, *Stevedores and Dockers* (London, 1969), 100–1.
16 J. Samuelson, *Labour-Saving Machinery* (London, 1893), 66–71; R. Bean, 'The Liverpool dock strike of 1890', in *International Review of Social History* 18 (1973): 51–68; Taplin, *Liverpool Dockers*, 73; Hobsbawm, 'National unions on the waterside', 214.
17 J. Simmons, *The Railway in England and Wales 1830–1914* (Leicester, 1978), 218; W. J. Gordon, *Every-Day Life on the Railroad* (London, 1898), 127; G. Alderman, 'The railway companies and the growth of trade unionism in the late nineteenth and early twentieth centuries', *Historical Journal* 14 (1971): 129–52.
18 Royal Commission on Labour, 1893–4 C. 4181, Group B, Minutes of Evidence, XXXIII, qs 26,384–5, 26,517, 27,628.
19 ibid., q. 28,037.
20 *Railway Review*, 22 September 1893, p. 1; 8 December 1893, p. 5; 15 December 1893, p. 4; 22 December 1893, p. 5; 31 May 1895, p. 1.
21 ibid., 7 March 1913, p. 3; 20 June 1913, p. 8; P. S. Bagwell, *The Railwaymen* (London, 1963), 333, 339.
22 *Railway Review*, 28 February 1913, p. 1; 7 March 1913, p. 3.
23 F. Popplewell, 'The gas industry', in S. Webb and A. Freeman (eds), *Seasonal Trades* (London, 1912), 148–209; Thorne, *Life's Battles*; Hobsbawm, 'British gas-workers';

Journal of Gas Lighting, 19 October 1880, p. 607; 26 June 1883, p. 1192; 10 November 1885, p. 830; 15 June 1886, p. 1108; 8 May 1888, p. 824; 2 July 1889, p. 9.

24 ibid., 22 October 1889, p. 793; 1 July 1890, p. 39.
25 ibid., 7 January 1890, p. 14; 21 January 1890, p. 99.
26 ibid., 17 December 1872, pp. 1033–5; Royal Commission on Labour, Group B, Minutes of Evidence, XXIV, qs 26,879–85.
27 ibid., qs 26,926–43; *Journal of Gas Lighting*, 7 August 1888, 14 August 1888, 21 August 1888.
28 Royal Commission on Labour, Group B, Minutes of Evidence, XXXIII, q. 23,839; *Railway Review*, 15 March 1889, pp. 121–4.
29 *Journal of Gas Lighting*, 17 June 1890, p. 1115; 1 July 1890, pp. 11, 39.
30 A. Fox, *National Union of Boot and Shoe Operatives 1874–1957* (Oxford, 1958), 85–99, 135–6.
31 Duffy, 'New Unionism', 314; Hobsbawm, 'General labour unions', 190.
32 *Journal of Gas Lighting*, 31 December 1889, p. 1256; Royal Commission on Labour, Group B, Minutes of Evidence, XXXIII, qs 26,877–9; *The Socialist* (Edinburgh), October 1910, p. 11; April 1911, p. 60, for industrial syndicalism at the Singer factory.

8 The Division of Labour and Politics in Britain, 1880–1920

ALASTAIR REID

I

The period of British history from the middle of the nineteenth century until the end of the First World War was marked by three main phases in popular politics. From the 1850s until the 1880s and 1890s there was fairly solid support for Gladstonian Liberalism, followed in the three decades before the war by the gradual emergence of a separate Labour Party functioning largely as a trade union pressure group. Then during and immediately after the First World War there was a marked increase in popular mobilization and in support for more radical socialist policies. The standard explanation of these shifts has been strongly influenced by Marxism, in particular by the work of Eric Hobsbawm, and has emphasized the material position of skilled workers: prosperous and secure in the mid-nineteenth-century boom years, coming under increasing pressure with the intensification of foreign competition from the 1870s onwards, and finally undermined by industrial changes which reached their peak during the war years.[1] The elaboration of this interpretation has always involved a combination of arguments about incomes and skills, but in recent years the emphasis has shifted strongly towards the latter with the use of references to changes in the division of labour as a key pivot in the accounts of the mid-nineteenth-century 'labour aristocracy' by John Foster and Robert Gray, in James Hinton's analysis of the First World War and, more recently, in Richard Price's book on the building industry.[2]

However, despite this accelerating tendency to explain popular politics in terms of the positions of certain groups of workers in the division of labour,[3] there has been little sustained analysis of the economic structures of the industries concerned and even less of the actual jobs performed and the relationships between different groups of wage labourers.

This essay therefore begins with the main characteristics of British industry in the second half of the nineteenth century, arguing for a more differentiated account of economic processes and the changing patterns of the division of labour. Then an analysis of trade unionism in the period points out the variations in the form of organization of different types of workers and argues that the construction of these institutional defences was crucial for the maintenance of their positions in the division of labour. The central thrust of this account is that the working class was economically fragmented and did not experience a major structural transformation increasing the degree of its homogeneity in this period, nor did such a process occur in the area of 'culture', as is suggested in a brief discussion of the issues of residential settlement and urban subcultures. Finally, the paper deals with the area where more fruitful explanations are to be found, that is in the changing nature of the state, focusing here on the effects of increased intervention in the economy during the First World War.

II

Most of the recently published accounts of these problems have been based on one industry and, while understandably attempting to draw broader conclusions, have generally done this in an oversimplified way. Thus the authors have either argued that the industry under study was typical, in a straightforward fashion, of other industries at the time,[4] or that it was the leading sector in a trajectory of development which all other industries were bound to follow.[5] Even when more than one industry has been studied, the variations between the cases have been subordinated to one uniform model of economic processes and changes in the organization of production.[6] Some general statements about the British economy in the nineteenth and early twentieth centuries are possible. For example, that it had a highly fragmented pattern of ownership, that it was subject to intense fluctuations in output and that it was labour intensive rather than capital intensive. However, these were exactly the kind of general features which, when worked out in particular cases, gave rise to wide variations of conditions between sectors.

There was a long persistence of small, frequently family-owned firms, a reluctance to seek outside finance and comparatively weak tendencies towards the centralization of ownership even in sectors dominated by very large companies.[7] Relations between employers were therefore characterized by competition rather than co-ordination, and frequently also by quite separate interests even within industries when firms were involved in diverse product markets. If the absence of monopolies made it hard for any one firm or group of firms to impose its will on an industry, the high levels of diversity and competition meant that employers' associations were slow to develop, and even when they did, often found it difficult to maintain coherent labour policies.[8] There was a significant degree of collusion over price-fixing in some sectors, usually in combination with collective bargaining procedures to regulate wages.[9] However, in contrast to the formation of aggressive cartels in other countries, this defensive policy did not generally lead to amalgamations and when it did they usually retained a federated rather than a centralized structure.[10]

One major distinction that can be made is that between capital goods and consumer goods industries which, in the British case, roughly corresponded to the distinction between sectors oriented to the export market and those oriented towards the home market. Most capital goods industries, being both heavily dependent on the state of world trade and having a relatively elastic demand for their products from one year to the next, were subject to intense cyclical fluctuations.[11] On the other hand, the consumer goods sectors were protected in varying degrees from the trade cycle by the relative inelasticity of demand for their products from year to year, but were subject to intense seasonal fluctuations of both supply and demand.[12] One important industry which escapes this distinction was building which, while mainly dependent on the home market and strongly affected by seasonal fluctuations, was also heavily affected by shifts in population size and distribution and by the movement of interest rates. By the late nineteenth century it had begun to fluctuate counter to the trade cycle, but was also characterized by significant divergences of patterns of activity between regions.[13] This regional unevenness in building activity was both a result of, and a good index of, the way in which specific combinations of other sectors of production gave rise to market differences in the nature and timing of regional economic development.

As a result of these high levels of fluctuation of production and the absence of tariff protection or state investment subsidies, British employers were understandably reluctant to bear the heavy overheads implied by large-scale mechanization. This was especially true of sectors, like shipbuilding and heavy engineering, in which stockpiling during depressions was not viable because of the customer-specificity of the orders.[14] Given the relatively plentiful supplies of skilled male labour available, the pursuit of labour-intensive strategies was viable even in industries which had highly sophisticated end-products.[15] This preference for manual skills, some of which were of a very long-standing nature, gave rise to a wide variety of work practices and conditions across industry and also to more or less serious demarcation disputes between groups of skilled workers anxious to protect their occupational territory against interlopers. Moreover, once such a strategy had been embarked upon it was hard to break away from it because of the growing restraints imposed by the emergence of strong occupationally based trade unions, especially when taken in conjunction with the relative weakness of employers' organizations. While British businessmen frequently greeted the development of new machinery with enthusiasm (and this was no new phenomenon in the late nineteenth century), they were often reluctant to face the lost production required to break union restraints through lock-outs.[16] Even if they did so, they were usually then unwilling to undertake the plant reorganizations required to maximize the cost-reducing potential of the new equipment.[17] It is therefore quite possible to be misled by management hopes and union fears voiced during the first discussions and skirmishes over new machinery.

These characteristics of fragmentation of ownership, intensity of fluctuation and dependence on skilled labour, combined with significant variations in market conditions, meant that British industry in the late nineteenth and early twentieth centuries manifested a high degree of regional and sectoral diversity. Within this context it makes little sense to regard British employers in any particular case as acting according to the ideal types of either neo-classical or Marxist economic theory. They were not motivated primarily by the desire to introduce the most advanced technology or by the desire to deskill and subordinate labour completely. Rather they were motivated by the desire to make profits under given economic conditions, which varied from case to case. When faced with foreign competition they

did not necessarily respond by reorganizing and modernizing their production bases – indeed, that may well have been the last thing they thought
of. In the first place, starting from a position of world domination, any given
market was relatively less important to British businessmen than the same
market was to their emerging competitors who had far more restricted
export opportunities. Even when loss of markets did have serious effects on
overall performance it was always possible to shift into the production of
more specialized and elaborate products or into other, relatively protected,
markets within the formal empire. And, of course, there was also the
well-known shift in the emphasis of economic activity within the economy as
a whole away from domestic industry and towards the provision of financial
and commercial services to the rest of the world.[18] This preference for
evasion rather than direct competition was bound to lead eventually to
increasingly poor productivity in manufacturing. However, it was a strategy
which was extremely hard to avoid and, moreover, one which did not imply
an immediate decline in profits.[19] It is indeed possible that in some important sectors the years before the First World War were ones of high
manufacturing profits based on the use of plant which was completely
covered for depreciation out of previous revenue. Though it was out of date
and rates of productivity were beginning to fall, it was in a sense free and
therefore profitable to keep in use.

When the question of labour productivity in British industry was confronted, it was likely that the first avenue of attack would have been through
the intensification of long-standing pressures within the existing structures
of production. These pressures took three major forms: first, attempts to
increase the length of the working day by the introduction of more and more
overtime work; secondly, the introduction of systems of payment which
were linked more directly to output, either in the form of traditional
piece-rates, or more recently developed, and more elaborate, bonus
systems; thirdly, attempts to reduce labour costs and weaken skilled
workers' long-term position on the labour market by increasing the employment of 'apprentices', or by bringing in less expensive grades of adult
tradesmen.[20] These methods had the advantage to the employer of avoiding
full-scale reorganization and confrontation with the unions and, moreover,
were cheaper to operate once established. It is significant in this respect that
British employers were generally unwilling to pay the high costs of supervisory labour implied by full-scale 'scientific management' and only adopted
its payment schemes.[21] In so far as there was an employers' counter-attack
after the expansion of union organization in the early 1890s, its impact on the
division of labour generally took this form. And, as a result of the piecemeal
nature of the attack and the attempts to introduce cheaper grades of skilled
labour, the workers' response was usually a sectional one, frequently
involving fierce demarcation disputes between occupations. There were
some cases in which a more systematic confrontation with the unions was
attempted and new equipment introduced on a wide scale, but even here it
did not usually lead to simple unilinear deskilling. The one significant
example of a major and unambiguous erosion of a skilled group in this
period is that of the boot and shoemakers,[22] but in the other cases skilled

men managed to retain a grip on their functions and status. In printing the unions were able more or less to capture the machinery, while in engineering a substantial number of tradesmen were upgraded to work-setting, tool-setting and tool-repairing positions and varying degrees of informal control were maintained.[23] After all, even in the archetypal case of intensive mechanization, cotton spinners had been able to retain a real purchase on the new division of labour because of an increase in their directive functions.[24] Such an outcome was even more likely in other sectors as most equipment introduced before the First World War did not take the form of interconnected machines effectively linked to a central power source (as in textiles), but rather of isolated tools which could raise productivity in one section of the production process but had no built-in pace-setting effect.

The usual emphasis in accounts of the late nineteenth and early twentieth centuries on foreign competition, increasing monopoly, the emergence of employers' associations and the extensive introduction of machinery is therefore inadequate. Some of these features were evident in some sectors, but if they had been as widespread as is often implied it would be hard to account for the continuing relative decline of British industry. Foreign competition did not affect all sectors equally: some capital goods industries, like shipbuilding and textile machine making, remained highly competitive, the expansion of state armaments contracts protected others and large sections of domestic market oriented industry were immune. Even when pressure from foreign competition was felt, the preferred employers' response was not necessarily to co-operate with their domestic competitors in an effort to reorganize ownership and production. Even when machinery was introduced it was not necessarily an unambiguous threat to skilled labour and, as a result of effective union opposition, rarely resulted in straightforward deskilling.

III

It does not seem, then, that there were economic changes in these years of such a kind as to alter the basic structure of the working population. To present the late nineteenth century as a period of decisive erosion of traditional skills and the creation of an increasingly homogeneous 'semi-skilled' factory proletariat is at best an oversimplification.[25] However, it is equally inadequate to present skilled workers in the late nineteenth century simply as 'traditional craftsmen' or 'artisans'. They were clearly wage labourers subordinated to capital, increasingly dependent on employers for the provision of their tools, and increasingly unable to regulate their working conditions by informal means alone. Indeed, the long-standing limitation of the categories available for the analysis of the working class to the polarity 'craftsman' versus 'proletarian' has been responsible for many serious misinterpretations. Instead of relying on these ideal types, and the movement from one to the other, we should see modern manufacturing production as being based on a wide spectrum of skills and work aptitudes which shade into each other. Within this spectrum there can be important changes in the levels and types of skill of particular groups without this leading to a greater degree of structural homogeneity.

At one end of this spectrum there were some groups which we might call 'craftsmen' in late nineteenth-century British industry. Some building and engineering trades had all-round skills, while other occupations had retained, or even increased, their technical indispensability even though they only performed a specialized part of the former craft tasks. Because of their relatively high levels of skill, the large amount of knowledge they passed on to their apprentices and their expensive sets of personally owned tools, such occupational groups were able to maintain a large amount of informal unilateral control within the workplace. This was often aided by the difficulty of exercising managerial control over them as a result of their concentration in single-occupation workshops or, at the other extreme, their very wide dispersal across many production sites. Moreover, such workers were generally *not* assisted by large gangs of less skilled helpers and therefore less troubled by the problems of directing the labour of other workers and less threatened by the possibility of encroachment on their work tasks by the unskilled.[26]

Though significant and interesting, such autonomous groups of technically indispensable workers were a minority by the late nineteenth century. For most 'craft' occupations increasing specialization had led to a marked erosion of technical aptitude and indispensability and for these occupations the maintenance of control over apprenticeship ratios and working conditions came to depend on varying degrees of formal organization at district and national level. The 'New Model' union structure of centralized social security funds and local or workshop trade policies which had still been suitable for the early and mid-nineteenth century was gradually being replaced by more institutionalized defences against pressures from employers, and this transition led to a series of conflicts between union members and union leaderships. On some occasions this was over the degree of representativeness of the national executive which had frequently been drawn from only one region in the period in which its tasks primarily involved financial administration.[27] On other occasions grievances over internal democracy were combined with conflicts over the nature of the policies of regulation to be adopted by the union.[28] There was therefore a widespread struggle among the specialized tradesmen in such industries as building, shipbuilding and engineering, to establish institutions which combined a degree of central regulation with a degree of membership participation appropriate to each instance, but this was not always directly accompanied by increases in the scope and permanence of formal collective bargaining structures. As the movement of rates of pay was more and more accepted to be an inevitable consequence of industrial fluctuations, more or less sporadic bargaining took place between employers and unions at district and national level and wages strikes were avoided. But the regulation of basic working conditions like machine manning and apprenticeship was still more commonly done by unilateral regulation on both sides of industry. When highly structured conciliation and arbitration procedures were established to deal with work control issues they were generally imposed by the employers in the context of a defeat for the unions' attempts at unilateral regulation. However, since the unions were not actually broken up but continued to function in the pursuit of their members' interest, they were frequently able to make significant gains within these structures, as procedural rules bound the employers too, and collective agreements restricted the sphere of managerial prerogative in individual companies. Particularly in boom years, when the demand for labour was high and their funds and organization strong, these unions were able either to take over, modify, or unilaterally abandon conciliation procedures which did not suit them.[29]

For other groups of skilled workers, however, there was a close interconnection of formal union organization and collective bargaining procedures. These were the groups frequently referred to as 'operatives', notably in the iron and steel, coal and cotton industries. In some cases these unions could only exist at all on the basis of employer toleration, either because there was no tradition of sustained worker organization or because of decisive defeats at an early stage in union development. In other cases they could only exercise control over the organization of work through the channels of collective bargaining because developments in the methods of production had either evaded or completely displaced craft regulation.[30] These sectors were characterized by their heavy dependence on export markets and their susceptibility to intense fluctuations in prices, so it was in the employers' interests to remove wage costs from domestic competition and create instead a reliable average wage linked to price levels.[31] In some other sectors, like shipbuilding, similar economic conditions prevailed and employers would have liked an automatic sliding scale of wages but they were impeded by the ability of the trade unions to exist independently of recognition and procedure. Even in the steel, coal and cotton cases the unions were by no means passive transmitters of employers' policies but were able to win for their members a large share of the benefits of increasing productivity and rising prices. Moreover, they exercised considerable degrees of control over the organization of the work on behalf of their members, regulating the allocation of labour under the seniority system in the steel industry and influencing the conditions under which new technology was introduced in the cotton industry.[32]

Developments among the 'unskilled' bore many similar features to those among the 'operatives'. In the first place, those groups which were able to build organizations in the late nineteenth century actually had significant degrees of task-specific aptitude. But their technical knowledge was not great enough nor their traditions of organization strong enough for them to sustain effective union organization without employer recognition.[33] In contrast to the 'operatives', however, many of the 'unskilled' groups which were successful in establishing unions in this period worked in sectors which had already existing trade unions of the higher skilled grades. In many cases this was a short-run disadvantage as they had initially to struggle for existence against the stronger organizations of the skilled, which wished to either destroy them or incorporate them. However, in the long run it was probably an advantage as the existence of relatively high levels of organization, and often of collective bargaining procedures, provided a supportive

structure to slot into. Given their occupational specificity and their significant levels of skill, it seems likely that the 'unskilled' attempted to exercise
control over the organization of their work by means similar to those used by
the skilled, though this remains an area requiring more investigation.[34]

It is certainly the case that the well-established schools of thought in both
labour history and industrial relations tended to ignore almost entirely the
question of the organization of work and presented events as an inevitable
evolution towards institutionalized, and peaceful, collective bargaining.[35]
The reaction evident in the politically more radical studies since the late
1960s and early 1970s, by such authors as James Hinton, Keith Burgess and
Richard Price, is therefore understandable but nevertheless inadequate.
Just because it had traditionally been said that formal institutions were an
advantage since they promoted industrial peace is not a sound basis for
simply inverting the assumption and arguing that they were a disadvantage
because they channelled grievances away from direct control and strike
action.[36] Similarly, because the role of informal unilateral regulation in the
workshop had either been overlooked or devalued is an inadequate ground
for assuming that it contained the only genuine dynamic of labour resistance.[37] It would obviously be naïve to assume that unions were straightforwardly democratic institutions, but whatever their internal structure, it is
clear that leaderships which pursued policies radically divergent from their
members' interests could be, and would be, removed. Patrick Joyce's
picture of union leaders pursuing the same goals as the majority of their
members is therefore more accurate, though significantly his oversimplified
approach to changes in work organization leads him to see the attitudes of
both members and leaders as mere reflections of employer-controlled
technical change.[38]

What is now required is a more sophisticated reinterpretation of the
development of unions as institutions and of the relationship between this
development and the changing patterns of the division of labour. As
indicated above, a useful typology would consist of the informal and
unilateral regulation exercised by the technically indispensable minority,
the formal and mixed unilateral-and-bargaining form of organization
required by the specialized tradesmen with a strong 'craft' heritage, and the
formal and dependent-on-recognition pattern of the 'operative' sectors,
which probably also applied in a modified form to the 'unskilled'. This would
begin to lead away from the crude polarization of internal union politics into
'rank and file' versus national 'bureaucracy', and point towards the complexity of interaction of the many intervening layers of trade union structure. Not only should shop stewards be seen as union officials as much as
shop floor delegates, more attention also needs to be paid to the important
role of district committees and local officials in the regulation of working
conditions.

Finally, it is important to remember that most unions did not represent
only one occupational group but rather were alliances of different groups
with distinct interests in the workplace and in the labour market. Not only
were there sometimes demarcation issues between groups of workers
organized in the same trade union, there were also disputes over the equity

of distribution of the central benefit fund between different sections of the membership. Holding a national union together was a difficult undertaking and one which required a great deal of careful internal conciliation and arbitration. The difficulty of maintaining a united front was magnified greatly when it consisted of more than one organization and it would therefore be misleading to see there being an inevitable 'rise of the labour movement' in the late nineteenth century. Rather there were only extremely precarious and internally divided alliances which ultimately had limited success in promoting united action in the industrial sphere.

IV

This interpretation of economic processes, changes in the division of labour and the forms of trade union activity presents a picture of significant diversity and variation between regions, sectors and occupational groups. Even the occupationally based organizations of labour were usually in fact based on several distinct groups and their policies were a result of attempts to balance and harmonize the different concerns of their members rather than a direct reflection of one economic interest. Clearly this must have been even more the case at the level of national political institutions and behaviour which had a dynamic of their own, independent of shifts in the economic structure of sections of the working class. However, most of the available accounts of late nineteenth- and early twentieth-century popular politics have either assumed that changes in political attitudes were a direct reflection of transformations in the material conditions of working-class life or, where such an economic explanation has been seen as insufficient or inadequate, 'culture' has been called in to provide the necessary social cement.

With reference to the literature of social criticism begun by George Orwell and forcefully developed after the setback to socialist hopes in the late 1940s, the Labour Party has been seen by authors as diverse as Perry Anderson, Eric Hobsbawm and Henry Pelling as an expression of the strengths and weakness of 'traditional' working-class culture rooted in segregated, stable and homogeneous communities.[39] At first glance this view has much of the force of common sense: it is only natural to assume that, after a significant reorganization of the economy and massive migrations from rural to urban areas, the working population would settle down and participate in increasingly shared ways of life. However, like that other common-sense assumption, that the progressive development of the division of labour and technology would reduce all workers to the lowest common denominator of skill, this view begins to seem increasingly implausible the closer it is inspected.

First, it is important to remember that in a labour-intensive economy subject to severe fluctuations in output there was a long persistence of local and interregional migration of both skilled and unskilled labour. There were also major disruptions in the process of residential stabilization, whether temporary, as in the case of the massive dislocations of the life of families and localities caused by the two world wars, or structural, as in the case of the forced migrations to the Midlands and the south-east which took place in the 1930s and after the Second World War. It is not entirely safe, then, to assume that there was an inevitable evolutionary process in operation in residential terms any more than in terms of the division of labour, and even if there was it too was marked by substantial unevenness. For example, the Lancashire textile areas and the older mining areas seem to have been settled by the middle of the nineteenth century,[40] at a time when what were to become steel, shipbuilding and heavy engineering centres were in many cases still small rural towns. Furthermore, when one of these regional industrial stereotypes is analysed more closely, as in Alan Campbell's excellent study of Lanarkshire mining, even more complex divergences between localities become apparent in both the timing and the pattern of settlement.[41]

Of course, quantitative indices of segregation and stabilization of residence would not be sufficient on their own for an adequate analysis of 'culture', as there could be strong and persistent world views and self-images prevalent across different types of locality, and continuous even in the face of residential dislocation. However, to raise this issue is to open up further complexities, for rather than one homogeneous working-class self-image there was a plurality continually reproducing itself. While the serious historical analysis of this area has scarcely begun, some of the major issues may be briefly indicated. First, there was a persistence of more or less clearly demarcated occupational communities, most obvious in the case of the miners, but also evident in distinctions even between interconnected and residentially contingent groups of metalworkers like the boilermakers and the engineers. Such occupational cultures were strengthened and maintained by a marked tendency for sons to follow their fathers into the trade, though here we would also need to consider the possible cross-cutting effects of the perennial conflict between generations. Another obvious issue is the nature of ethnic communities, frequently overlapping with that of religious denomination. This is clearest in the case of the Irish Catholic immigrants of the mid-nineteenth century, but can also be seen in the case of later overseas immigrants into London, most notably the Jews.[42] Even in cases where none of these forms of marked subculture was in evidence there would usually have been some form of straightforward localism, whether in broad terms of the region or the city, or in more intimate terms of the borough, the locality, or even the street. It does seem that in the late nineteenth century there was a consolidation of a nationwide network of commercialized leisure: public houses, sport, working-class holidays, the popular press and to a lesser extent the music hall.[43] However, this did not necessarily imply a homogeneity of content. On the contrary, it would be more accurate to emphasize the persistence of long-standing subcultures within the new institutional frameworks. Thus football, for example, should be seen as a condensation of ethnic, religious, local and occupational conflicts as much as an expression of cultural homogeneity. Finally, it is important to remember that the preceding discussion, like the subcultures to which it refers, has largely left out women who had their own parallel and more obscure world of subcultures, often in conflict with those of the men over the organization and reproduction of family life.

Just as workers were constantly engaged in struggles to define the boundaries and nature of their tasks in the workplace, so they were constantly striving to establish and define their 'communities', not only against the upper classes but also against each other. And, again in parallel with conflicts over the division of labour, none of the struggles or their outcomes had any necessary connection with a particular kind of politics. On the contrary, they were profoundly ambiguous: 'frontier' conditions could be a source either of division and demoralization or of vigorous militancy; stability could be a source of apathy as much as of collective strength; local, ethnic and occupational pride could be given a radical or a conservative interpretation. The culturally subordinate position of the British working class was not the result of its having been indelibly moulded by the values of the dominant classes but was rather due to the diversity of ambiguous and conflicting subcultures and the difficulties of establishing an effective majority counter-culture.

V

The economic, organizational and cultural fragmentation of the working class meant that it was neither inherently oppositional nor inherently incorporated, but was rather a constantly shifting mix of limitations and possibilities which could be mobilized into different configurations. Many of the most remarkable of such mobilizations in modern Britain took place during and immediately after the First World War, and the most influential account of them is to be found in Hinton's stimulating study of the engineering industry.[44]

Some of the problems with his interpretation have already been indicated. For example, he argues that the constant tensions within the unions, between 'rank and file' and 'bureaucracy', came to a head during the war as a result of trade union leaders' involvement with state labour policy. Hinton also argues that skilled engineers were faced with a traumatic challenge to their previously secure position at work as a result of mechanization and the introduction of female labour into the industry. However, although the war clearly did alter many of the pressures operating on the economy, it did not remove British employers' dislike of full-scale industrial transformation. Even in engineering the main impact of machinery and dilution was in newly established, and quite distinct, shell shops: though there was a temporary feeling of insecurity among the skilled men, it passed relatively quickly and there was no major structural change in their economic position.[45] Moreover, such sectors as shipbuilding and mining were even less affected than engineering by changes in the division of labour yet manifested similar levels of industrial and political mobilization during and after the war. While in all three cases there were tensions between members and leaders of unions these were of the same order as in the prewar years and, on the whole, the main defences of workers' interests were conducted by various combinations of workshop and institutional organization.

The explanation of the upsurge of militancy among British workers during the war is not, then, to be found in a major change either in the structure of the working class or in the internal dynamics of trade unions, but rather in the third area of Hinton's argument: the nature of state intervention in industry. However, rather than seeing the Ministry of Munitions and other government departments as coming under the influence of leading industrialists, it is important to realize that employers were increasingly excluded from the formulation of labour policy. Certainly there were many industrialists who had posts in wartime ministries, but these were generally in the 'production departments' where their expertise on technical and commercial matters was indispensable. As the war proceeded it became standard practice to separate labour policy from the production departments which tended to be too short-sighted and self-interested to see the benefits of changes in the organization of work. Indeed this policy had been pioneered by the Ministry of Munitions itself during its most dynamic period in 1915 and 1916. As a result its labour administration became the preserve of a group of progressive Liberal civil servants and ex-trade unionists who had run the Board of Trade Labour Department before the war, and who were able to develop policies which were favourable to the unions.[46]

One of the main influences on this outcome was the gradual suspension of market mechanisms and the substitution of national security for private profit as the main goal of industrial activity. In the first months of the war state intervention was limited to the expansion of armaments contracts, but as the international conflict dragged on and the mechanisms of the world economy were destabilized, it became necessary for governments to take over many of the functions of the free market: for example, the importation and distribution of raw materials. Simultaneously, the state gradually took over many of the functions of private management in key sectors: prioritizing certain types of product, allocating labour supplies and bargaining with workers' organizations. By 1918 transport and coal had been effectively nationalized; engineering, shipbuilding, steel and agriculture were subject to extensive governmental controls; prices were regulated and 90 per cent of imports and 80 per cent of domestic food consumption were handled by the state.[47]

With the emergence of this type of 'war collectivism' the subordination of the interests of private capital to those of the nation was inevitable, but the emergence of labour policies favourable to the unions was not. Indeed, especially in 1915, it had seemed possible that labour might have become subject to martial law or at least to interpretations of the Munitions Act which would have severely weakened workers' ability to organize. That this did not happen was a result of the increasing strength of trade unions in a very tight labour market, the ability of their leaders to convince key officials that 'industrial compulsion' in such a context would lead to disastrous conflicts, and the successes of local protest campaigns over rents, wages and the regulation of the labour market. As a result, the strength of organized labour was further increased and its influence on government policy, whether by permanent inclusion on committees or by ad hoc mobilization when necessary, became substantially greater than before the war.

This sense of the increasing strength of labour in bargains with the state was particularly strong among organized workers in heavy industry who were often literally bargaining with government ministries as their employers, and usually getting better results than before the war. But even among the unorganized, and those outside the munitions areas, there were some increases in strength in these years of full employment, and some perceptions of the intervention of the state in the economy and the benefits it was bringing to labour. This would seem to be a more convincing explanation of the growth of trade union and electoral support for socialist policies in these years[48] than arguments which rest on changes in the division of labour.

A similar case could be made for the years before 1914 when the emergence of pockets of support for socialism, particularly over local issues, could be explored in relation to the expansion of municipally owned enterprises. As with the wartime developments important aspects of this process were independent of popular pressures: local governments began to provide gas, electricity, tramways and telephones because their operation often involved the use of what was already public property, like the city streets, and because they wished to prevent possible damage to the local business community from private monopolies charging excessive prices.[49] At the same time, once the question of public enterprise had thus been opened up, the precise form which it took would partly depend on the reaction of the trade unions and their ability to affect policy-making at the local level. And, just as in the case of the 'war collectivism', continuing trade union and electoral support for prewar municipal projects would have depended on their success in practice.[50]

Rather than explaining shifts in popular politics in terms of irreversible transformations in the structure and culture of the working class, it is therefore proposed that they be seen in terms of changes in the nature of state intervention in the economy and changes in the relationship between government agencies and popular organizations, particularly trade unions. Such an approach could be compatible with different theories of the state, though in the interpretation presented here it is implicitly assumed that there was not a 'capitalist state' which straightforwardly pursued the interests of British employers. On the contrary, there is substantial evidence indicating that industrialists were frustrated by what they saw as their exclusion from influence over government policy, especially during the war. After all, even from a Marxist perspective there would be no reason to assume that the industrial 'fraction of capital' would always effectively dominate the state. In fact the owning class, like the working class, has a highly fragmented internal structure which cannot adequately be contained even within a sophisticated model of 'fractions of capital', each with their interests and ideologies derived from their economic functions. Rather than interpreting government policies as simple reflections of the interests of dominant economic groups they should be seen as prioritizing social stability at almost any cost, especially during such a serious crisis as the First World War. This is not to say that governments acted as neutral arbitrators free from the influence of domestic conflicts, for they were themselves subject to competing pressures to influence the shape of their policies. From this point of view it might be said that state activity represented the balance of forces in particular political situations, where the drawing of that line of balance was an active process conducted by various government agencies with their own internal histories, and often their own conceptions of the 'national interest'.

VI

The main aim in this essay has been to challenge a marked tendency of the recent literature to explain popular politics in terms of changes in the division of labour. The problem in such equations is not so much that there are other mediating influences as that the sphere of the 'economic', whether defined in terms of wages or skills, is far too uneven and ambiguous to provide an explanation for ideology and politics. Far from implying that we should therefore abandon inquiries into the organization of work and the forms of popular culture, this conclusion emphasizes the need for even more scrupulous investigations of such issues in order to map out more accurately the complex formation of the working class. The immediate economic experiences and cultural values of particular groups of workers may not be the explanation of national political changes, but any successful popular political movement will have had to take them into account in drawing up its programmes and constructing effective alliances between its potential supporters.

Moreover, the detailed study of the division of labour is highly relevant for an analysis of a particular industry or occupation, but only if it does not exclude other issues, for example, fluctuations in the labour market and the ability of workers' organizations to influence the nature of the tasks their members performed. One other issue which has often been overlooked as a result of an overemphasis on the division of labour is the impact of government regulation of labour markets, methods of production and trade union organization, the importance of which becomes particularly obvious when comparing different countries. If government policy had a significant impact on trade unionism, an area in which economic pressures would obviously have been very strong, it would have had an even greater impact on the formation of popular political attitudes and parties. More attention must therefore be paid to the internal dynamics of the state, and of politics in general, in the expectation that such an inquiry will not simply answer the old questions but rather re-pose them in significantly new ways.

Notes: Chapter 8

My thanks to Jonathan Zeitlin for his close collaboration during the preparation of this essay and to David Crew, Eric Hobsbawm, Keith McClelland, Joseph Melling, Susan Pennybacker and Gareth Stedman Jones for valuable comments on an earlier draft.

1 E. J. Hobsbawm, 'The labour aristocracy in nineteenth century Britain'; idem, 'Trends in the British labour movement since 1850', in idem, *Labouring Men* (London, 1964), 272–315, 316–43.

2   J. Foster, *Class Struggle and the Industrial Revolution* (London, 1974); R. Q. Gray, *The Labour Aristocracy in Victorian Edinburgh* (London, 1976); J. Hinton, *The First Shop Stewards' Movement* (Oxford, 1973); R. Price, *Masters, Unions and Men* (Cambridge, 1980).

3   See also P. Joyce, *Work, Society and Politics* (Brighton, 1980).

4   Price, *Masters, Unions and Men*.

5   Hinton, *Shop Stewards' Movement*; Joyce, *Work, Society and Politics*.

6   Foster, *Class Struggle*; Gray, *Labour Aristocracy*.

7   H. Levy, *Monopolies, Cartels and Trusts in British Industry* (London, 1927); P. L. Payne, 'The emergence of the large-scale company in Great Britain 1870–1914', *Economic History Review* 20 (1967): 519–42; S. Tolliday, 'Industry, finance and the state – an analysis of the British steel industry in the inter-war years' (PhD. thesis, Cambridge, 1979).

8   H. A. Clegg *et al., A History of British Trade Unions since 1899*, Vol. 1 (Oxford, 1964), 362–3; E. H. Phelps Brown and M. Browne, *A Century of Pay* (London, 1968), 174–95; J. Zeitlin, 'Industrial structure, employer strategy and the diffusion of job control in Britain, 1880–1920', in this volume, pp. 325–37.

9   See below, p. 328.

10 L. Hannah, 'Managerial innovation and the rise of the large-scale company in inter-war Britain', *Economic History Review* 27 (1974): 252–70.

11 A. C. Pigou, *Industrial Fluctuation* (London, 1927).

12 G. Stedman Jones, 'Working class culture and working class politics in London, 1870–1900', *Journal of Social History* 7 (1974): 460–509.

13 S. B. Saul, 'House building in England 1890–1914', *Economic History Review* 15 (1962/3): 119–37; J. Parry Lewis, *Building Cycles and Britain's Growth* (London, 1965).

14 S. Pollard and P. Robertson, *The British Shipbuilding Industry 1870–1914* (Cambridge, 1979); A. Reid, 'The division of labour in the British shipbuilding industry 1880–1920' (PhD. thesis, Cambridge, 1980).

15 H. J. Habakkuk, *American and British Technology in the Nineteenth Century* (Cambridge, 1967); C. K. Harley, 'Skilled labour and the choice of technique in Edwardian industry', *Explorations in Economic History* 11 (1973–4): 211–59; R. Samuel, 'The workshop of the world: steampower and hand technology in mid-Victorian Britain', *History Workshop Journal 3* (1977): 6–72.

16 W. Lazonick, 'Industrial relations and technical change: the case of the self-acting mule', *Cambridge Journal of Economics* 3 (1979): 231–62.

17 Zeitlin, 'Industrial structure, employer strategy'.

18 E. J. Hobsbawm, *Industry and Empire* (London, 1969).

19 Phelps Brown and Browne, *Century of Pay*, 174–95; D. N. McCloskey, 'Did Victorian Britain fail?', *Economic History Review* 23 (1970): 446–59; D. H. Aldcroft, 'McCloskey on Victorian growth: a comment', *Economic History Review* 27 (1974): 271–4; W. A. Lewis, *Growth and Fluctuations 1870–1913* (London, 1978).

20 J. Melling, '"Non-commissioned officers": British employers and their supervisory workers, 1880–1920', *Social History* 5 (1980): 183–221; Reid, *Division of Labour*; J. Zeitlin, 'Craft regulation and the division of labour: engineers and compositors in Britain 1890–1914' (PhD. thesis, Warwick, 1981).

21 Melling, '"Non-commissioned officers"'.

22 R. A. Church, 'The effect of the American export invasion on the British boot and shoe industry, 1885–1914', *Journal of Economic History* 28 (1968): 223–54.

23 Zeitlin, 'Craft regulation'.

24 Lazonick, 'Industrial relations'.

25 H. Pelling, *The Origins of the Labour Party 1880–1900* (London, 1965); Gray, *Labour Aristocracy*; J. E. Cronin, 'Labour insurgency and class formation: comparative perspectives on the crisis of 1917–1920 in Europe', *Social Science History* 4 (1980): 125–52.

26 Reid, 'Division of labour'.

27 ibid., 227–30.

28 B. C. M. Weekes, 'The Amalgamated Society of Engineers 1880–1914. A study of trade union government, politics and industrial policy' (PhD. thesis, Warwick, 1970); Zeitlin, 'Craft regulation'.

29 Reid, 'Division of labour'; Zeitlin, 'Craft regulation'.

30 Clegg *et al., History of British Trade Unions*, 15–31, 202–12.

31 J. H. Porter, 'Wage bargaining under conciliation agreements, 1860–1914', *Economic History Review* 23 (1970): 460–75; F. Wilkinson, 'The development of collective bargaining in Britain to the 1920s' (unpublished paper, Cambridge, 1981).
32 Porter, 'Wage bargaining'; F. Wilkinson, 'Collective bargaining in the steel industry in the 1920s', in A. Briggs and J. Saville (eds), *Essays in Labour History 1918–1939* (London, 1977), 102–32; Lazonick, 'Industrial relations'.
33 E. J. Hobsbawm, 'General labour unions in Britain 1889–1914', in idem, *Labouring Men*, 179–203; Clegg *et al., History of British Trade Unions*, 87–96.
34 E. J. Hobsbawm, 'British gas-workers, 1873–1914', in idem, *Labouring Men*, 158–78.
35 S. Webb and B. Webb, *A History of Trade Unionism* (London, 1920); Clegg *et al., History of British Trade Unions*.
36 K. Burgess, *The Origins of British Industrial Relations* (London, 1975); Price, *Masters, Unions and Men*.
37 Hinton, *Shop Stewards' Movement*; Price, *Masters, Unions and Men*.
38 Joyce, *Work, Society and Politics*.
39 P. Anderson, 'Origins of the present crisis', *New Left Review* 23 (1964): 26–54; Pelling, *Origins*; Hobsbawm, *Industry and Empire*.
40 Joyce, *Work, Society and Politics*.
41 A. Campbell, *The Lanarkshire Miners* (Edinburgh, 1979).
42 E. H. Hunt, *British Labour History 1815–1914* (London, 1981), 158–87.
43 Stedman Jones, 'Working class culture'; Joyce, *Work, Society and Politics*.
44 Hinton, *Shop Stewards' Movement*.
45 Zeitlin, 'Industrial structure, employer strategy'.
46 R. Davidson, 'The myth of the "servile state"', *Bulletin of the Society for the Study of Labour History* 19 (1974): 62–7; idem, 'The Board of Trade and industrial relations 1896–1914', *Historical Journal* 21 (1978): 571–91; Reid, 'Division of labour'.
47 R. H. Tawney, 'The abolition of economic controls, 1918–1921', *Economic History Review* 13 (1943): 1–30; S. Pollard, *The Development of the British Economy* (London, 1969), 42–53.
48 J. M. Winter, *Socialism and the Challenge of War* (London, 1974).
49 J. H. Muir, *Glasgow in 1901* (Glasgow, 1901).
50 W. H. Fraser, 'Municipal socialism and social policy' (unpublished paper, Strathclyde, 1978); S. Pennybacker, 'Municipal socialism and municipal labour in London 1889–1914' (unpublished MS. Cambridge, 1980).

9 New Unionism for Old? The Amalgamated Society of Engineers in Britain

KEITH BURGESS

I

The dramatic upsurge in labour unrest signalled by the famous London dock strike of 1889 has justifiably continued to attract the attention of labour historians as well as, more generally, students of British industrial relations.[1] Yet the wider significance of this New Unionism remains far from clear.[2] Did it, for example, mark a major discontinuity or decisive 'turning-point' in the history of labour in Britain? If so, to what extent was this New Unionism primarily an institutional development, reflecting the extension of union organization to previously unorganized and mostly unskilled workers; *or*, was this latter phenomenon only one manifestation of a wider change in mood that also affected workers having prior experience of trade unionism? Moreover, how justified is the New Unionism's reputation for militancy, its preference for confrontation rather than negotiation with employers, and its close association with independent labour if not identifiably 'socialist' politics, which distinguished it sharply from older forms of trade unionism? The purpose of this essay is to examine some of these suppositions with reference to the workplace organization and industrial policies of what the Webbs regarded as the model for 'old-style' trade unionism – the Amalgamated Society of Engineers (ASE).

Much of the difficulty in specifying what the New Unionism actually is arises from the fact that there has been a tendency to define it in terms of a *contrast* to earlier forms of trade unionism. The latter has often assumed an a priori typology which has been accepted too uncritically and without reservation. In the British case, for example, the ostensibly 'moderate' industrial and political stance of the ASE has been associated with the relatively privileged sectional or craft elite of engineering workers, whose strong bargaining position gave rise to a centralized trade union organization, able to win and secure uniform conditions in respect to wages, hours of work, apprenticeship ratios, and other 'customs of the trade'.[3] The 'spontaneous' upsurges of militancy associated with the New Unionism of semi-skilled and unskilled workers clearly do not fit this paradigm, but does the latter in fact typify accurately the ASE during the formative years of its development – say, before 1880? By and large it does not. The ASE was never an 'old-style' trade union in a way that the latter has often been defined.[4] This then raises an initial objection to the novelty of the so-called

New Unionism in Britain, which is to be clarified further by a brief discussion of the workplace organization and industrial policies of the ASE in the period before 1880.

II

The circumstances surrounding the very inception of the ASE during 1850–1 cast most obvious doubt on the traditionally Webbian characterization of the Society as a 'successful' new-model trade union, with the capacity to implement a centralized and uniform trade policy for skilled workers in the engineering industry. Amidst increasing hostility to the employers' efforts to exploit the skill-saving potential of new machinery, the ASE suffered a humiliating defeat in the lock-out of 1852, organized by the larger and more progressive firms in the industry.[5] Opposition to piece-work and 'systematic' overtime, which had been the principal planks of the Society's trade policy, was defeated as a result of the lock-out, whilst those Society members who were able to regain their employment after the dispute were forced to sign a declaration pledging not 'to interfere with or control the conditions of employment in any establishment'. What enabled the ASE to maintain its existence and slowly build its membership during the 1850s and 1860s owed little to the efficacy of its 'centralized' official organization. Rather, it was the slowing down in the rate of change in the labour process of the engineering industry that allowed the new skilled groups of fitters and turners created during the 1830s and 1840s to consolidate a steadily improving bargaining position within the ASE after 1850. This was made possible by the 'export' of British industrialization around the world during the third quarter of the century, when Britain's lead in the application of machine tool technology meant that increasing investment in now-established techniques continued to yield a rising rate of profit. The impact of innovation became increasingly marginal, tending to minor improvements rather than major changes, whilst the rapid expansion of the industry rested upon labour-using rather than labour-saving investment that consolidated the position of the fitters and turners as the largest single category of engineering labour, as well as the most numerous category of admissions to the ASE, during the period between the 1860s and the 1880s.[6]

It was thus the relatively greater stability of the labour process in the British engineering industry during these years that permitted the resolution of such thorny industrial relations issues like overtime and piece-work. With the capital-labour ratio in comparative equilibrium, there was less pressure on firms to work 'systematic overtime' except during booms when the inducement was the flood of orders rather than the cost-push effect of rising capital overheads, whilst the labour-using effect of new investment in the industry led to a steadily increasing demand for the labour of fitters and turners.[7] Similarly, the spread of piece-work that had accompanied the diffusion of new machine techniques during the 1830s and 1840s slowed down after 1850, as production methods became more routinized and it became less necessary for employers to delegate the burden of supervision by expedients like the piece master system.[8] Piece-work required a degree of standardization and repetition production that was absent in most sectors of the industry, particularly since the growing importance of overseas markets created a multiplicity of different customer needs.[9]

What contribution did the ASE thus make to the resolution of these contentious issues? This was quite marginal in so far as the Society's Executive Committee was responsible for implementing trade policy. The failure of its leadership to ban systematic overtime and piece-work during 1851–2 had led to the abandonment of co-ordinated policy-making from the centre, and increasingly the content of Society policy came to be determined at district level. Its Executive Committee became more and more involved in the administration of the Society's comprehensive system of friendly society benefits, and the reputed 'caution' and 'moderation' of the views expressed on industrial questions by its leaders like William Allan to government inquiries were probably more a reflection of the weakness of the union's leadership in determining trade policy than a sign of self-conscious 'bourgeois-mindedness'.[10] Thus there was no attempt to impose any uniform code of trade rules for the Society as a whole. For example, the executive refused to make the abolition of piece-work an official Society objective. Although it yielded to pressure from some branches when instead it introduced a bye-law setting out the conditions where the Society was opposed to it, and this was to be read to every candidate before he was admitted into a branch, its implementation was left very much to the discretion of local branches which in Swansea, Newcastle upon Tyne and Glasgow actually enrolled piece masters as members, although this was officially 'illegal', and whilst some Glasgow branches of the Society, for example, admitted piece masters, Glasgow Govan branch wanted a member from Bradford sent home because he had started on piece-work.[11] Moreover, the ASE executive even left the branches to decide whether or not the admissions rule that candidates for membership must have worked continuously for five years at their trade necessarily implied having served a formal apprenticeship.[12] Gradually, as district wage rates were recognized by employers, what became more important than proof of apprenticeship was whether prospective members were able to earn the district wage rate.[13]

What strengthened further the extent of local autonomy in the ASE was the rise of the Society's district committees during the 1850s and 1860s, representing a number of adjacent branches, and authorization was also given to the setting up of central district committees to connect together a number of districts for 'all general purposes'.[14] Although these had to be approved beforehand by the executive, control over policy was steadily concentrated in the hands of the district and central district committees, and their authority was protected by the provision in the Society's constitution that made the Delegate Meeting, composed of lay members elected by the branches, the court of final appeal; whilst the executive itself consisted of representatives elected only by the Society's London branches, and thus was hardly in a position to implement policy for the membership as a whole. The capacity of the district committees, in particular, to establish considerable control over 'the conditions of the trade' stemmed ultimately from the growing bargaining strength of the fitters and turners who dominated the Society's membership. Whilst generally careful not to attack overtly employers' 'prerogatives', the ASE at branch and district level sought an ad hoc understanding with firms over minimum rates of pay and working conditions for skilled tradesmen. The employers, on the other hand, usually preferred in the context of an expanding market to pass on to consumers the cost of concessions to labour, rather than risk disputes with so indispensable a group of employees, especially since the latter also performed supervisory and training functions that saved firms much expense and trouble.[15]

There were, of course, disputes during this period but these were localized and confined normally to periods coinciding with the beginning of an upturn or downturn in the trade cycle. Thus the struggle for the nine-hour day on Wearside and Tyneside during 1870-1 was initiated without executive approval, if not in the face of its expressed hostility, and the extent to which this movement's subsequent victory was generalized throughout the industry depended on the bargaining strength and degree of organization prevailing in the various districts.[16] The motives for executive intervention in disputes were largely defensive in character, occasioned by a threat to the trade privileges of members, when in 1866, for example, it lobbied the Manchester locomotive firm of Beyer, Peacock & Co. after a strike of ASE members who claimed that a recently appointed foreman was 'not qualified'.[17] The firm tried to get tradesmen from elsewhere but was forced to dismiss the foreman and take back the strikers after the stoppage had lasted almost two months. Thus the character of labour relations in the British engineering industry before 1880 had much of the 'spontaneity' associated traditionally with the later upsurges of New Unionism, where the initiative for policy-making was usually local and often 'unofficial', and where there is little evidence to support a case for co-ordinated and centralized control.

III

The commercial crisis of 1873 initiated a new phase in the development of world capitalism and this had a profound effect on labour in Britain generally, including workers in the engineering industry. The Great Depression of 1873-96, in particular, and the consequent changes in the labour process led to an upsurge in militancy among engineering workers that has been often overlooked as a result of the attention paid to the 'novelty' of striking gasworkers, dockers and others. What is clear, in the first instance, is that this period was not one of depression in the conventional sense of a downturn in the trade cycle. If any one factor gives these years unity it is the massive and almost continuous decline in prices, and in accounting for this, the changing character and direction of investment flows seems to have been particularly important. The boom preceding the crisis of 1873 had led to rapidly rising production costs, especially labour costs, and brought to an end the period marked by almost continuous labour-using investment that had caused a sustained growth in demand for skilled workers like the fitters and turners in the engineering industry, who had benefited from the way

capital exports from Britain had created markets abroad for British industry. The crisis of 1873 was essentially one of confidence in the continuing
capacity of overseas markets to absorb the huge amounts of capital and
goods the British economy was generating, at a rate of profit sufficiently high
to offset the steep rise in production costs, and when the extent of industrialization in Western Europe and the United States was now creating greater
self-sufficiency and even competition for British industry. The latter was
encouraged further by the spread of railways and steam shipping around the
world, which had opened up new and cheaper sources of supply abroad and
significantly reduced freight rates. British firms took advantage of cheaper
raw materials to cut their own prices, in an effort to maximize their share of a
more competitive world market, and this was the initial signal for the
subsequent downward spiral of prices throughout the British economy.
What then accelerated this process was the disenchantment of British
investors with overseas issues following the crisis of 1873, which led to a
decline in calls for new portfolio investment abroad and cheapened considerably the cost of raising capital in Britain.[18] Yet the effect of cheaper
credit was to persuade manufacturers to expand production in order to
reduce their unit costs during a period when prices generally, including the
prices of their own manufactures, were moving lower, and this had a further
depressing effect not only on prices but also on profits.[19] In short, the
opportunities for continually extending productive capacity as a means of
reducing unit costs began to be limited by the problems associated with a
rising capital–labour ratio – the organic composition of capital – and the
consequent falling rate of profit.

At first, the firms sought to adopt the characteristic capitalist response to
falling profitability by increasing the productivity of existing capitals, since
particularly in the engineering industry lower profits and the ready availability of skilled labour did not encourage the substitution of labour by new
capital-intensive techniques.[20] Many engineering employers were drawn to
widely based organizations like the Iron Trades Employers' Association
(ITEA), or strong regional groupings like the Clyde Shipbuilders and
Engineers' Association, in their efforts to manipulate prices as well as assist
in the intensification of labour exploitation. By 1879, for example, the ITEA
claimed that the ten-hour day had been reintroduced in place of the nine
hours in seventeen districts without a dispute, where it estimated that 30 per
cent of skilled men were unemployed.[21] New forms of piece-work or
payment by results were introduced to increase labour productivity,
although one leading engineering firm acknowledged that this diminished
employment, and engineering workers complained of 'more vigilant supervision' and the spread of 'task work', as well as the increasing employment of
adult 'apprentices' as cheap labour.[22] In this economic climate, workers in
many districts were forced to accept weekly earnings far below the wage
rates nominally recognized by employers. Thus in the summer of 1878 some
engineering firms in Glasgow were paying their men only 22s 4d per week,
although the negotiated minimum rate two years earlier had been 27s 6d per
week.[23]

As the depression of prices and profits continued to deepen, however, firms began to discover that there were limits to productivity growth by increasing the rate of labour exploitation in conjunction with existing manufacturing techniques. With the ready availability of new, more capital-intensive production methods in Britain by the 1880s, reflecting the pre-cocious application of high-speed steels and more 'automatic' machine tools in American and German industry,[24] enterprising employers found that this latest generation of engineering technology enabled an augmented minority of highly skilled workers to set up production routines for a growing body of semi-skilled 'machinists', who became the most numerous category of labour in some British engineering firms.[25] But this implied that there was less demand for skilled men with average ability, especially the large army of fitters and turners that had come to dominate the ASE prior to the 1880s.[26] John Price, the general manager of Palmer Shipbuilding Co. in Jarrow, noted in 1886 that the substitution of unskilled for skilled labour on drilling, slotting and planing machines was creating a new hierarchy of skilled and unskilled jobs in the engineering industry, and this view was corroborated by ASE officials in some districts.[27] These changes in the labour process were clearly to pose serious problems for the ASE's workplace organization. An immediate problem, for example, was that the Society remained largely a trade union of fitters, yet its branch and district structure had to take into account the growing number of 'machine men' who were mostly not organized in trade unions and thus not effectively represented in nego-tiations with employers. With the publication of the 1901 census, when the job description 'metal machinist' first appeared, the various categories of engineering labour accounted for almost 360,000 workers, whilst ASE membership in 1901 stood at 90,000 and most of the latter were fitters and turners.[28]

By the late 1880s, therefore, it was becoming apparent to some progress-ive engineering employers that management control of labour, in its formal unitary sense, was not sufficient in itself to maintain their competitive edge. The introduction of the latest generation of machine tool technology required firms to rethink the terms of reference for the 'optimal' utilization of labour, which had to include the actual mode of working adopted by the operative as this affected the character and sequence of decisions made during the course of his work, and in effect dissociated the aptitude and skill of the operative from any wider control he may have had in the labour process. Of course, the extent to which engineering labour was uniformly deskilled in Britain should not be exaggerated. Only a minority of relatively large firms had the benefit of economies of scale that justified massive labour-saving investment, and a core of highly skilled tradesmen was still required even in these establishments to 'set up', maintain and superintend the new machinery, whilst its manufacture remained a heavily skill-intensive occupation. In fact, it was precisely this double-edged effect of the so-called 'scientific-technical' revolution that has to be understood, especially in Britain where before 1880, if not later as well, the ASE's district committees had sought with some success to maintain 'the privileges of the trade'. Thus, whilst it is admitted that perhaps a majority of engineering tradesmen with average levels of aptitude were exposed to some form of deskilling where new techniques were introduced, a significant minority also acquired greater responsibility even where progressive employers pursued aggressive management strategies. This arose not only from the need to superintend the work of semi-skilled machinists, but also resulted from the necessity of maintaining the safety of the equipment, the product and, above all, of the other workers involved.[29] Thus the changes in the labour process threw up a new contradiction that juxtaposed, on the one hand, greater management control and, on the other, additional responsibility for a highly skilled minority.

One kind of workers' response to this development was to take the form of a narrowly conceived defensive struggle to maintain craft or sectional privileges. This meant initially that many of the ASE's district committees tried to withdraw members from working the new machinery – a policy that was to be reversed during the 1890s when the Society sought to 'follow the machines' in the interests of sectional exclusiveness. An alternative response involved a fundamental shift in attitude from craft or trade solidarity to class solidarity and class action.[30] This was encouraged by a new awareness of the wider social needs served by the organization of production, which grew as the workers' responsibility for organizing production increased. The latter helps explain why a new 'forward' faction began to emerge within the ASE after 1880, including leaders of the calibre of Tom Mann and George Barnes, who argued for the transformation of the Society into a genuinely 'industrial' union, recruiting from all grades of skill, and whose outlook was closely identified with the New Unionism. The problem was that this faction was unsuccessful in converting the ASE as a whole to its policies, despite some partial victories, and the intransigence of the 'old guard' in the Society made the years 1880–1914 a period of internal dissension over its constitution and industrial policies.

It was the long-established district committee structure of the ASE that was to provide the focus for the opposition within the Society to 'forward' policies, and which implied at first the withdrawal of members from working the new machinery. One of the first instances of the dissension this could provoke came to light in August 1886 when a conflict arose between Glasgow South Branch and the Glasgow District Committee over the manning of new machinery.[31] A member of Glasgow South Branch was summoned before the Glasgow District Committee and asked to leave his job at the Howe Sewing Machine Works in Bridgeton where he had agreed to operate two slotting machines. His branch had granted him permission to take this employment because of his 'circumstances' and 'the state of trade', but Glasgow District Committee ruled that his action was 'contrary to the interests of the Society' and he subsequently left his employment. Yet this was not the end of the matter as he lodged a protest against the District Committee's ruling to the ASE executive, which upheld the original decision of the branch. But Glasgow District Committee refused to accept the executive's judgement, and in retaliation it excluded the delegate of Glasgow South Branch from its meetings. There ensued a protracted struggle between Glasgow District Committee and the ASE executive. The latter tried to stop the former from meeting, instructing its Vacant Book

Keeper not to pay delegates their expenses. The dispute was not settled until September 1888 when negotiations ended in the election of a new Glasgow District Committee.

The logic of Glasgow District Committee's position over this affair clearly implied that in seeking to defend the 'privileges of the trade' the ASE should withdraw its members from working the latest generation of machine tools, with the result that the Society would eventually be reduced to a rump of fitters and turners isolated from some of the most rapidly expanding areas of employment in the industry. This also implied the abandonment of new techniques to non-union labour, particularly the 'machine men' whom the Society made little attempt to organize, but who represented a growing army of strike-breakers at the disposal of employers. Thus after a strike at Armstrong's Elswick plant, for example, 24 per cent of the fitters and turners who had left their employment failed to get their jobs back because they had been replaced at machines by boys at reduced wages.[32] Even for those ASE members who were not so directly threatened, 'more vigilant supervision' by managers and supervisors and the spread of piece-work, in particular, imposed growing strain on the Society's district committee structure of collective bargaining. The renewed extension of piece-work stemmed directly from the employers' efforts to maximize the productivity of new machinery where there were more opportunities for repetition work, and where the advent of high-speed steel made possible rising machinery speeds. By 1891 piece-work had become the prevailing system of wage payment in districts like the Eastern Counties, and by 1906, 35 per cent of all skilled workers in the industry were paid in this way, compared with 10·5 per cent of ASE members who had been piece-workers in 1861.[33] The introduction of piece-work often provoked bitter resistance. During 1889–90 there was a lengthy strike of ASE members employed at Maxim-Nordenfelt, the Erith and Crayford firm of armaments-makers, when management tried to extend piece-work to the fitters and turners on grounds that their 'almost automatic' machine tools made it the best method of increasing efficiency.[34] Yet the strikers complained that the system encouraged skilled labour substitution and 'systematic' overtime, and gave rise to a situation where semi-skilled machinists paid by results often earned as much as many fitters and turners who also had the additional responsibility of training, 'setting up' and supervision. There was also the argument that piece-work enabled employers to adjust rates of pay individually and at will, without regard to collective agreements negotiated by the Society's district committees. The dispute ended when the strikers' places were filled by non-unionists.

This steady erosion of the ASE's position of sectional privilege, together with the increasing militancy of unskilled workers and the spread of socialist ideas, had by the early 1890s convinced some members that fundamental changes were necessary in the organization and policies of the Society. This 'forward' faction wished to see the ASE transformed into a genuinely industrial union, recruiting workers from every grade of skill, and its growing influence within the Society was part of the wider change in mood in the British trade union movement that has merited the term New Unionism. Yet the 'old guard' who wanted no major changes in either organization or policy remained entrenched in many of the ASE's district committees, whilst the experience of internal disputes like the Glasgow episode mentioned above made its executive reluctant to provide a lead. The latter refused to support, for example, the numerous strikes of unskilled or semi-skilled non-unionists during the late 1880s and early 1890s, although these workers frequently laboured side by side with ASE members, and were a potential source of strike-breakers in technologically progressive firms. Thus during the Silvertown strike of unskilled workers in London during 1889–90, the ASE executive refused to call out its members in support, which led to criticism from 'forward' members, and it also gave no support to the unorganized machine men thrown out of work during the Maxim-Nordenfelt dispute.[35] The dissension within the Society came to a head in 1891 when the death of Robert Austin required the election of a new General Secretary. John Anderson who had been Assistant Secretary since 1883 was the nominee of the 'old guard', whilst Tom Mann was put forward as the candidate for change, and there were also several other candidates that was indicative of the amount of interest generated by the election. Anderson was elected by 18,102 votes, compared with 17,152 for Mann who was second despite the fact that the latter's campaign had suffered as a result of personal rivalry with John Burns.[36] The strength of Mann's showing in this election was sufficient to bring about a major reorganization of the ASE.

An especially elected Delegate Meeting assembled at Leeds in 1892 to undertake this task.[37] A conscious attempt was made to broaden the base of the Society's membership by making the latter open to electrical engineers, roll turners, machinists and apprentices could be recruited as probationers; whilst special sections of membership were created for workers between the ages of 30 and 55 who were not eligible for full inclusion because of infirmity or low wages. The composition of the union's executive was also changed. The practice of working representatives of the Society's London branches serving together with the full-time officials to form the executive was replaced by a new Executive Council consisting entirely of full-time officials. The ASE was divided into eight districts, each electing one full-time official who together with the customary officers now made up the executive. This provision for voting by electoral districts was intended to bridge the gulf separating the leadership at the centre from the rank-and-file member. The autonomy of the Society's district organization that had been the bastion of sectional exclusiveness was also curtailed. The Central District Committees, representing several district committees, were abolished. In their place, six full-time Organizing District Delegates were to be elected to liaise between the district committees and the executive. The increase in the number of full-time officials from four to seventeen was clearly designed to improve the prospects for concerted leadership, co-ordinated from the centre, whilst in theory the district committees were no longer as free to initiate policy as they pleased. It would appear, therefore, that the Webbian view of the ASE as a 'centralized' prototype for the craft unions of the 1850s and 1860s was not fully realized even on paper until the 1890s, when the impetus for greater executive control came from advocates of 'forward' policies who identified themselves with the outlook of the New Unionism.

In practice, however, the branch and district officials retained considerable power, especially in energetic hands. They had regular contact with members and this gave them a powerful influence over the election of full-time officials, particularly since only a minority of members usually voted. It was they who remained responsible for implementing the policy of 'comprehension' when recruiting as members workers other than the fitters and turners, and the evidence shows that the latter continued to comprise the most numerous category of members, although the ASE was now open in theory to a much larger body of workers.[38] Local autonomy was protected further since branches continued to grant 'out-of-work' benefits to members, without executive approval, when seeking to protect the customary 'privileges of the trade'. ASE members thus remained divided in their attitudes, despite the changes in the rulebook. The pattern of voting in the 1891 election showed, for example, that although John Anderson won by only a narrow margin he had consistent support from all branches, whilst Tom Mann scored well in London, Yorkshire, Manchester, Tyneside and Glasgow, but he got little support elsewhere where the voting for Anderson was almost unanimous.[39] Society members who were distant from areas of socialist ferment like London, or who felt less threatened by the effects of technological change that was confined largely to a small number of big firms in the industry, probably accepted the prospect of Anderson's victory with equanimity if not indifference. After the Delegate Meeting of 1892 had increased the ASE's complement of full-time officials, four Swindon branches circulated a petition throughout the Society protesting against the additional expense, which they claimed served no useful purpose.[40]

The split among ASE members was particularly evident in their attitude to piece-work, the eight hours issue and the 'machine question'. This impeded the development of a coherent policy for the Society as a whole, and contributed directly to its humiliating defeat in the lock-out of 1897–8. No co-ordinated action was taken on the piece-work issue, for example, where the district committees retained the initiative in policy-making and the Executive seems to have had little influence. Thus, whilst well-organized districts like Manchester were successful in subjecting piece-work to collective bargaining by persuading employers to accept the principle that piece-work earnings should approximate the standard recognized time-rate, the relative weakness of the ASE in other districts prevented its adoption as an officially recognized one throughout the Society.[41] In areas like Clydeside and Nottingham, for example, where the spread of piece-work during the 1890s was a relative novelty, the district committees sought to use their discretionary powers to prohibit the system altogether, which meant that the growing army of non-union 'machine men' in these areas were excluded from the benefits of collective bargaining as these applied only to ASE members on time-rates. The Society's lack of a unified policy was confirmed by an executive ruling that piece-work prices had to be regulated voluntarily by those members engaged in the system and could not be guaranteed by members on time-work wages.[42] This had the effect not only of isolating piece-workers from time-work men within the ASE, but also excluded the increasing majority of non-union operatives in the industry from any protection that the Society was able to obtain for its members. This was contrary to the spirit if not the letter of the ASE's policy of 'comprehension' embodied in the constitutional changes of 1892, and intensified its sectional isolation that lay behind the defeat of 1897–8.

The split among ASE members was even more serious on the issue of the eight-hour day. During the 1880s the spread of socialist ideas and the increasing militancy of the unskilled had given rise to the demand for a legally enacted Eight-Hour Day, and this also found support among 'forward' members of the ASE. They argued that a reduction in hours would lead generally to more regular employment, as well as lessen the incidence of physical and 'moral' deterioration associated with more intensive labour exploitation in the industry, although the experience of some employers who found that the adoption of the eight hours actually led to higher labour productivity cast doubt on the credibility of the demand as a means of increasing employment.[43] Within the ASE, there was considerable opposition to state interference with the 'natural liberties' of 'free adult males', and the executive was able to resist proposals to ballot members on the question until 1890–1, despite pressure from some districts.[44] In 1890 it was agreed at last to ballot members on the issue but only seventeen branches returned their vote, and although a second ballot in 1891 produced a larger poll, there was a two to one majority in support of the eight hours to be achieved by voluntary trade union action rather than by legislation.[45] Support for legal enactment was confined largely to London, Yorkshire and the West of Scotland, where the attitude of members conformed most closely to the outlook of the New Unionism, and letters from branches show the diversity of viewpoints on the question.[46] Leeds fifth branch, for example, complained that the eight hours demand was 'inappropriate' when systematic overtime was widespread and its members were still struggling to protect the nine-hour day, and this feeling was echoed by a number of branches. Birmingham fourth branch used the argument, much loved by employers, that it was the wrong time to press for the demand given rising tariffs and increasing competition abroad, and four other branches also subscribed to this view. Birkenhead opposed the eight hours because it might disrupt the 'good relations' that existed between the Society and employers, whilst Hull in a most interesting reply was hostile on the grounds that 'it would be dangerous to trust our liberty in the hands of capitalists such as represent us in the present Parliament'. This rather remarkable anticipation of working-class resentment aimed at the 'Servile State' that was subsequently created by the Liberal welfare reforms emphasizes that class-consciousness among engineering workers did not always conform to the New Unionism's identification with demands for state intervention to tackle grievances.

The deep divisions within the ASE on the eight hours issue were used by its executive to justify its refusal to grasp the nettle and put forward a 'Society view'. John Anderson, the General Secretary, reported 'serious internal differences', but he revealed his true position when he attacked those 'forward' members who 'tried to throttle the opinions of old, tried and trusted branch and district officers'.[47] The question remained whether either the employers or the 'forward' members would allow them enough time to get to grips with changing conditions. The latter began to take control of trade policy in districts where they had strong support, like London, Yorkshire and Clydeside, and they concentrated on the eight hours issue, although this was often linked to other questions, especially the contentious issue as to whether Society men should operate new machinery. It was argued that the eight-hour limit would increase the demand for labour and reduce the number of unemployed at a time of renewed labour-saving investment in the industry. The initiative behind this agitation fell generally to 'unofficial' organizing committees that often bypassed the ASE's branch and district structure. In March 1894, for example, a 'Voluntary Organizing Committee' of Society members was active in south-east London holding meetings for non-union engineering workers. One of its pamphlets observed that 'class divisions are ever getting more sharply defined' and its audience was urged to join the ASE and campaign for the Eight-Hour-Day, the 'abolition of compulsory idleness' and, perhaps most interesting of all, 'a right to a voice in determining the conditions under which Industry should be conducted'.[48] During 1893 the 'forward' members secured an important victory when they won the Eight-Hour-Day in government factories and dockyards, and by early 1897 the Society claimed that 25 per cent of its members had secured the demand.[49]

The growing influence of the left within the ASE was put to the test in August 1896 when its executive found it necessary to dismiss John Anderson as General Secretary for 'wilful neglect of duty'.[50] With the leading representative of the 'old guard' thus discredited, the way was clear for the 'forward' members to get one of their number elected as General Secretary. This time they were successful with George Barnes, a member of the Independent Labour Party who had helped Tom Mann's campaign for election in 1892. In his successful campaign, Barnes advocated a policy of militancy on issues like the Eight-Hour-Day, to be directed by the executive. This marked a major break with the institutionalized caution and sectional exclusiveness of Anderson, yet subsequent events were to show that Barnes was unable to heal the serious divisions within the Society that existed over almost all the important aspects of its trade policy, particularly its attitude towards the employment of unionists and non-unionists on new machinery. And, moreover, the ASE was clearly in no position to meet the new aggressiveness of employers in resisting the Society's demands. In 1896 the latter had established a powerful new Employers' Federation of Engineering Associations, whose 'power to manage' doctrine referred to unjustified workers' 'interference' with hours of work, the employment of apprentices and especially the authority of foremen over the employment of union and non-union labour on new machinery.[51] In short, the basic point of contention was whether new machine tools were to be introduced in ways beneficial to ASE members, or were the employers to have complete freedom to use machinery as they saw fit.

The intention here is not to recount in detail the engineering lock-out of 1897–8, which has been the subject of systematic study in both published and unpublished form.[52] What is self-evidently clear, in the first instance, is that the Engineering Employers' Federation was not set on 'smashing' the ASE, not least because most firms realized that efficient production still depended on the co-operation of the highly skilled minority of Society members with their new responsibilities for training and supervising the growing army of 'machine men' in the industry. What employers sought, above all, was to redefine the shifting 'frontier of control' at the workplace, in a way that would restore 'orderly' collective bargaining on terms favourable to themselves. Firms were especially concerned about the increasing influence of unofficial plant committees of 'shop stewards' that were regarded initially as representatives of the ASE's district committees, elected to deal particularly with the problems arising from the machine question, but which were becoming a complementary if not rival source of authority to the district committees; and unlike the latter's approach to the introduction of new machinery during the 1880s, the unofficial plant committees were not trying to ensure that ASE members should have first choice in the manning of new machinery, rather than abandoning it to non-union labour. The employers maintained, on the other hand, that the responsibility for selecting workers to do various tasks rested ultimately with themselves, and they rejected outright what amounted to the a priori claim of ASE members as a whole to man new machinery.[53]

During 1896–7 there was a mounting number of disputes over the control of machinery. Thus one employer claiming that he had long respected the ASE complained about unofficial Society 'agents' who sought to get the speed of tools reduced after these had been set by foremen, and he cited another instance where a shop committee had summoned 'a foreman of works to explain why no fresh Society men had been taken on although output had been increased by 30 per cent'.[54] Thus although the eight hours issue was the ostensible cause of the 1897–8 lock-out, the employers made it clear from the very beginning that they regarded it as a test case for the enforcement of their 'power to manage' doctrine.[55] And the ASE's humiliating defeat in this struggle highlights how dearly it paid for its failure to pursue systematically the policy of 'comprehension' instigated at the 1892 delegate meeting. It was an impossible task for what remained a trade union of mostly fitters and turners to wage industrial warfare on behalf of the non-unionist majority, particularly since with the exception of a highly skilled minority of ASE members non-unionists and unionists alike were competing increasingly for similar kinds of work.[56] The left faction within the ASE, including its new General Secretary George Barnes, was left too little time by the employers to build a New Unionism on the bedrock of the craft conservatism of many members.[57]

The terms of settlement of the 1897–8 lock-out illustrate how the employers sought to re-establish the 'shifting frontier of control' at the workplace in their favour.[58] In a statement of 'General Principles' the text of the settlement was prefaced by a disclaimer that the employers had any intention of interfering with the 'proper' functions of trade unions, but it admitted 'no interference with the management of business', and the six points that followed included an affirmation of the right of employers to hire any worker, unionist or non-unionist, with the implication that the ASE had no right to interfere with the wages or conditions of employment pertaining to non-unionists. Thus the ASE could only negotiate on behalf of its own members, and since the majority of the industry's labour force were non-unionists where bargaining was conducted individually, the terms of employment negotiated by the Society on behalf of its members were under constant threat because of the very unequal bargains that employers were able to conclude with these unorganized workers. The terms of settlement also had a section on 'Provisions for Avoiding Disputes' where the employers recognized the growing disarray of collective bargaining at local level, with unofficial shop committees increasingly eroding the authority of the ASE's district committees. A procedure was established designed to discourage unofficial 'wildcat' strikes led by these shop committees, which specified that grievances had to be discussed by representatives of the ASE and the employers at plant, district and national levels before either a general or partial stoppage of work could take place. This serves to illustrate the more widespread change in strategy by British employers generally in response to the upsurge in labour unrest associated with the New Unionism, which has been typified as marking a shift from the strategy of 'the bribe through the market' to one of 'the bribe through the organization'.[59]

IV

During the period between the end of the 1897–8 lock-out and the First World War, the ASE failed to resolve its internal divisions and sectional isolation. The Engineering Employers' Federation emerged from the lock-out in a powerful position, and it tried to consolidate managerial control further by setting up a client trade union for foremen – the Foremen's Mutual Benefit Society. This was aimed at securing the untrammelled loyalty of foremen to their employers by providing them with friendly society benefits on a scale that it was hoped would wean them away from their long-established membership of the ASE.[60] The latter had also suffered losses in membership, morale and funds as a result of its defeat, and there is evidence of likely victimization of Society members by employers in the aftermath of the lock-out.[61] The executive of the Employers' Federation noted that there was not a single strike against any member firm during the years 1902–3, whilst in the case of two 'minor stoppages of work' they had successfully brought in non-union labour to replace recalcitrant ASE members.[62] The continuing technological dynamism of the engineering industry, taking place during a period when the labour supply available generally to British employers was still growing relatively fast, implied that the multi-functional expertise of the ASE's rank and file of fitters and turners became steadily confined to the specialist 'setting up' responsibilities of the toolroom, at least in the more progressive firms. Thus one leading employer – Sir Andrew Noble who was chairman of Armstrong Whitworth & Co. – claimed in 1906 that he was introducing 'hundreds' of milling machines at his works, requiring the employment of no turners or 'high class' machinists to operate them since this was 'not at all necessary'.[63]

These developments had significant implications for the workplace organization and policies of the ASE. The 'forward' faction within the Society that had been increasing its influence prior to the 1897–8 dispute continued its agitation for the transformation of the Society into a genuinely industrial union, recruiting from all grades of skill, which might forge stronger links with the New Unions of the unskilled and semi-skilled. At the 1899 Manchester TUC, for example, the ASE's membership was persuaded by a large majority to agree to join the recently formed General Federation of Trade Unions, which had an initial membership of 350,000 and elected a leading ASE left-winger as its General Secretary. This might be taken to reflect increasing socialist influence in the Society, especially since schemes for the creation of a federation of trade unions had been actively canvassed in journals like the *Clarion*, yet the Federation's provision of a small measure of financial assistance to affiliated unions whose members were involved in disputes has been described as 'a small strike insurance fund and little else'.[64]

At the same time, the left wing within the ASE was able to persuade its sympathetic General Secretary, George Barnes, to call a special Delegate Meeting in another attempt to broaden its membership.[65] This met in 1901 and decided to create a new category of membership, open to any operative who had been working not less than two years on one type of machine and received not less than 70 per cent of the standard wage rate for turners. Yet despite this change the fitters and turners continued to dominate the class of members enjoying the full benefits and privileges of the Society. The 1901 amendments to the ASE's admissions policy also laid down only minimum conditions for entry and the branches retained the power to raise these at their discretion. In practice, therefore, all the efforts that had been made to broaden the Society's membership since the late 1880s had led to only very limited results, and as late as 1909 the socialist journal *Forward* felt justified in the context of this continuing inertia to publish a series of articles written by one ASE left-winger, Frank Rose, entitled 'The Machine Monster: Warning to Skilled Workmen', which was an impassioned plea for industrial unionism.[66]

The relative failure of the ASE's 'forward' militants to convert the Society's membership as a whole to the cause of industrial unionism was in part a consequence of the way in which the changes in the industry's labour process gave impetus to the trend towards plant bargaining by unofficial shop committees. The latter often came to represent both union and non-union labour, especially where only a minority of the labour force might be ASE members, and this implied that Society membership was less relevant to the day-to-day conduct of collective bargaining. This development was rooted in the changing character of production itself, particularly in rapidly growing sectors of the industry like motor vehicle and cycle making where 78,000 workers were employed by 1912 – equivalent to 40 per cent of Britain's labour force in shipbuilding.[67] Even in sectors of the industry where opportunities for repetition work in combination with the latest generation of machine tools were limited, the introduction of new high-speed cutting tools was leading to more precise managerial control over the pace of production, and this triggered disputes that were not amenable to settlement by the ASE's traditional structure of branch and district committees. The ubiquity of jobbing or 'one-off' production in the British engineering industry, where the lack of standardization implied almost continuous bargaining over the 'rate for the job', encouraged the growth of plant committees that sought to limit managerial control of the pace of production.[68]

This development created serious problems for the ASE during the decade or so before the First World War. Not only did the rise of plant bargaining begin to establish a parallel if not rival structure of negotiations to the procedures set up in 1898, which had been comparatively favourable to the interests of employers, but the official leadership of the ASE became increasingly committed to and identified with the 1898 terms of settlement, particularly the avoidance of disputes clause stipulating that grievances had to pass through the entire procedure up to national level whilst the rank and file remained at work. The resulting delays were especially resented because rapidly changing conditions at the workplace, particularly the fixing of job prices, strengthened managerial prerogatives since workers were deprived, at least officially, of the flexible and immediate use of the strike weapon. Discontent began to mount over the employers' introduction of the premium bonus system, for example, which in combination with new processes like high-speed cutting tools was used to reduce the time allowed for jobs and encouraged persistent rate-cutting. There was the further complaint that the premium bonus system undermined collective bargaining and trade union discipline.[69] These problems were compounded since the ASE executive had been persuaded by the employers to give its official approval to the introduction of the system in 1902. What followed was a steady weakening of the executive's authority and an increasing number of 'violations' of the 1898 terms of settlement, especially during the years 1910–14, with the result that on the eve of the First World War the terms for collective bargaining in the industry had become all but inoperative.[70]

The ASE had thus clearly not succeeded in reconciling the upsurge of 'spontaneous' labour unrest in the engineering industry since the late 1880s, which was very much in the mainstream of the New Unionism, with the resulting centralization of industrial relations that was imposed subsequently by employers to curtail this unrest. It is noteworthy that this latter development was also typical of the employers' response to labour unrest elsewhere in sectors of employment regarded traditionally as foci for the New Unionism, at least where the employers had been forced to concede collective bargaining rights to the unions.[71] In this respect, therefore, the experience of the ASE cannot be isolated from the wider developments in trade unionism and industrial relations in Britain as a whole. And in regard to political questions, the evidence would suggest that ASE members had become no less 'socialistic' than those of some of the newer unions. A local study of the membership of the Independent Labour Party, for example, shows that engineering workers comprised the single largest occupational category holding shares in the *Woolwich Pioneer*, which was a leading socialist newspaper in east London during the period 1904–10.[72] At the

ASE's Delegate Meeting in 1912 more than 50 per cent of the delegates present have been identified from their speeches as not only strong supporters of independent labour politics but also advocates of 'collectivism' to be achieved by 'class war'.[73] Yet the persistent divisions within the Society's membership over major industrial as well as political questions came to a head during the labour unrest of the First World War, when the ambiguities attached to slogans like 'workers' control' reflected the vastly different conceptions that craft conservatives and revolutionary socialists inside the ASE had of 'militant' policies. The regional and sectoral *unevenness* of the changes in the labour process of the engineering industry prior to the war accounts in large part for these divisions and ambiguities in the attitudes of ASE members.[74]

Notes: Chapter 9

1 Recent surveys that have focused on the upsurge of labour unrest in Britain during the late 1880s include J. E. Cronin, *Industrial Conflict in Modern Britain* (London, 1979); and K. Burgess, *The Challenge of Labour. Shaping British Society, 1850–1930* (London, 1980).

2 An influential critique of the 'novelty' of the New Unionism is contained in A. E. P. Duffy, 'New Unionism in Britain, 1889–90: a reappraisal', *Economic History Review* 14, (1961–2): 306–14.

3 For early critiques of the reputed 'moderation' of the ASE see G. D. H. Cole, 'Some notes on British trade unionism during the third quarter of the nineteenth century', *International Review of Social History* 2 (1937): 1–27; and R. V. Clements, 'British trade unions and popular political economy, 1850–1875', *Economic History Review* 14 (1961–2): 93–104.

4 See H. A. Clegg, 'The Webbs as historians of trade unionism, 1874–1894', *Bulletin of Society for the Study of Labour History* 4 (1962): 8–9.

5 K. Burgess, 'Technological change and the 1852 lock-out in the British engineering industry', *International Review of Social History* 14 (1969): 215–36.

6 Parliamentary Papers (1891 Census), 1893–4, CVI, v. III, table 5; J. B. Jefferys, *The Story of the Engineers* (London, 1946), 59.

7 Amalgamated Union of Engineering Workers (AUEW) Offices, London: ASE General Information Schedule, 1876, found that only 15 per cent and 17 per cent of skilled engineering workers respectively were on 'systematic' overtime and piece-work.

8 This was a system of sub-contracting where employers put out jobs to intermediaries or piece masters at a negotiated price, and the latter were then responsible for hiring, supervising and paying labour in return for a lump sum of money they received in advance from the employer who provided the plant and machinery.

9 S. B. Saul, 'The market and the development of the mechanical engineering industries in Britain, 1860–1914', *Economic History Review* 20 (1967): 111–30.

10 See, for example, the Royal Commission on Trade Unions, 1867, Cd 3873, XXXII, Minutes of Evidence, p. 40.

11 ASE General Information Schedule (1876); ASE Pollokshaws (Glasgow) Branch Minute Book (1876–84), meeting of 11 October 1883, pp. 91–2.

12 Royal Commission on Trade Unions, 1867–8, Cd 3980–VI, XXXIX, Minutes of Evidence, pp. 44–5, evidence of William Allan; and in 1868–9, Cd 4123–I, XXXI, Vol. II, pp. 252–3.

13 ibid., Cd 3980–VI, p. 41; and in 1867, Cd 3873, XXXII, p. 39.

14 British Library of Economics and Political Science, Webb Trade Union Collection, Section E, Minutes of the First Delegate Meeting of the ASE (1852), pp. 18–19, 38–9.

15 For a more detailed discussion see K. Burgess, *The Origins of British Industrial Relations: The Nineteenth Century Experience* (London, 1975), ch. 1.

16 loc. cit.

17 Royal Commission on Trade Unions, 1867–8, Cd 3980–VI, XXXIX, p. 41.

18 W. W. Rostow, 'Investment and the Great Depression', *Economic History Review* 8 (1938): 136–58 (144).

19 Royal Commission on the Depression of Trade and Industry, 1886, Cd 4715, XXI, p. 83; and in Cd 4794, XXIII, p. 133.
20 Rostow, 'Investment and the Great Depression', 147; from a different theoretical perspective, see also E. J. Hobsbawm, 'Custom, wages and work-load in nineteenth-century industry', in idem, *Labouring Men* (London, 1968), 344–70.
21 *Capital and Labour*, 21 May 1879, p. 166.
22 B. C. M. Weekes, 'The Amalgamated Society of Engineers, 1880–1914: a study of trade union government, politics and industrial policy' (PhD. thesis, Warwick, 1970), 71–2.
23 *Capital and Labour*, 31 July 1978, p. 470.
24 S. B. Saul, 'The machine tool industry in Britain to 1914', *Business History* 10 (1968): 22–43.
25 A. L. Bowley and G. H. Wood, 'The statistics of wages in the United Kingdom in the nineteenth century: engineering and shipbuilding', *Journal of the Royal Statistical Society* 69 (1906): 148–92 (179).
26 loc. cit. See also Royal Commission on the Depression of Trade and Industry, 1886, Cd 4794, XXIII, for contemporary evidence of John Scott, Greenock shipbuilders and engineers.
27 ibid., Cd 4715, XXI, Part II, Appendix D, pp. 8–9.
28 Parliamentary Papers (1901 Census), 1904, Cd 2174, table 34; Jefferys, *The Story of the Engineers*, 292.
29 For contemporary evidence see Bowley and Wood, 'Statistics of wages'.
30 A. Touraine *et al.*, *Workers' Attitudes to Technical Change* (Paris, 1965), 41–2.
31 ASE Glasgow District Committee Minute Book, meetings of August 1886–September 1888.
32 Royal Commission on Labour, 1893, Cd 6894–VII, III, *Minutes of Evidence*, p. 322, evidence of Captain Andrew Noble.
33 Jefferys, *The Story of the Engineers*, 43–4.
34 *ASE Monthly Report*, December 1889.
35 Weekes, 'The Amalgamated Society of Engineers', 15.
36 ibid., 30.
37 Jefferys, *The Story of the Engineers*, 136–7.
38 S. and B. Webb, *Industrial Democracy* (London, 1897), 1:297.
39 Webb Collection, Section E, Nomination Returns for the Office of General Secretary (ASE), 22 January 1892.
40 ASE Pollokshaws (Glasgow) Branch Minute Book (1892–7), 10 November 1892, p. 10.
41 Webb and Webb, *Industrial Democracy*, 1:297; Jefferys, *The Story of the Engineers*, 139.
42 loc. cit.
43 Weekes, 'The Amalgamated Society of Engineers', 71–2.
44 ASE Glasgow District Committee Minute Book (1884–9), 3 September 1889, p. 109, for a resolution to the executive in support of the eight hours by legislation.
45 *ASE Monthly Report* (June 1891).
46 Webb Collection, Section E, Abstract Report of the General and Local Council's Proceedings (ASE) (1 January – 30 June 1891), pp. 95–103.
47 Cited in Jefferys, *The Story of the Engineers*, 139.
48 Webb Collection, Section E, 'To unorganised engineers' (ASE leaflet, 1894).
49 *ASE Monthly Report* (February 1894, January 1897).
50 Weekes, 'The Amalgamated Society of Engineers', 59; Anderson seems to have been an habitual drunkard.
51 For a detailed analysis of this body's organization and policies see E. Wigham, *The Power to Manage. A History of the Engineering Employers' Federation* (London, 1973); Burgess, *The Challenge of Labour*, ch. 1.
52 See, for example, Jefferys, *The Story of the Engineers*; R. O. Clarke, 'The dispute in the British engineering industry 1897–98: an evaluation', *Economica* 24 (1957): 127–37; Weekes, 'The Amalgamated Society of Engineers', 144–7; Burgess, *The Challenge of Labour*, 60–71.
53 Webb Collection, Section E, Engineering Conference 1897.
54 Webb Collection, Section E, 'The skilled labour question', letter by Edward Elder, engineering employer.

55 This is clear from the trade journals of the period. See, for example, *Engineering*, 5 November 1897; *Textile Mercury*, 27 November 1897.

56 In April 1897, for example, the General Secretary of the United Machine Workers' Association claimed that the ASE was trying to displace his members from jobs in Hull, Sunderland and London: see Weekes, 'The Amalgamated Society of Engineers', 88.

57 Thus John Anderson was again nominated for the post of General Secretary in 1898 by several branches, despite his dismissal from office two years earlier.

58 Webb Collection, Section E, 'Allied Engineering Trades' lock-out: Conditions for a return to work', published 21 January 1898.

59 J. Foster, 'British imperialism and the labour aristocracy', in J. Skelley (ed.), *The General Strike 1926* (London, 1976), 21–2.

60 J. Melling, '"Non-commissioned officers": British employers and their supervisory workers, 1880–1920', *Social History* 5 (1980): 183–221.

61 Thus in March 1899, for example, some 200 ASE members in Oldham were still without work despite prosperous trading conditions: see *Textile Mercury*, 11 March 1899, p. 187.

62 Wigham, *The Power to Manage*, 78.

63 Royal Commission on Trade Disputes and Trade Combinations, 1906, Cd 2826, LVI, Minutes of Evidence, p. 311.

64 Weekes, 'The Amalgamated Society of Engineers', 149.

65 This was in part a consequence of Tom Mann's initiative in setting up the Workers' Union during April–May 1898, open to engineering workers who could not find berths in the ASE: see R. Hyman, *The Workers' Union* (Oxford, 1971), 3–4 and 6. The details of the changes subsequently made in admissions procedures can be found in J. W. F. Rowe, *Wages in Practice and Theory* (London, 1928), 110.

66 *Forward*, 16 January 1909 and next four issues.

67 Weekes, 'The Amalgamated Society of Engineers', 154n.

68 G. D. H. Cole, *Workshop Organization* (Oxford, 1923), 13.

69 Weekes, 'The Amalgamated Society of Engineers', 205 and 253–5. See also Appendix V for the extent of the spread of the premium bonus system as early as 1906.

70 For a retrospective observation on this state of affairs made from the employers' point of view see J. R. Richmond, *Some Aspects of Labour and its Claims in the Engineering Industry*, Presidential Address to the Glasgow University Engineering Society, Session 1916–17, p. 6.

71 See, for example, R. Bean, 'Employers' associations in the Port of Liverpool, 1890–1914', *International Review of Social History* 21 (1976): 358–82.

72 D. Hopkin, 'The membership of the Independent Labour Party, 1904–10: a spatial and occupational analysis', *International Review of Social History* 20 (1975): 175–94 (193–4).

73 Weekes, 'The Amalgamated Society of Engineers', 318–20, 322.

74 Of the criticisms that can be made of J. Hinton's book, *The First Shop Stewards' Movement* (London, 1973), one of the most telling is his underestimation of the changes in the labour process of the British engineering industry *before* the First World War, and this probably leads him to exaggerate the impact of technological change as the primary cause of labour unrest in the industry during the war itself.

10 The New Unionism in Britain: the Railway Industry

PHILIP S. BAGWELL

I

In the years before 1914 the British railway industry was highly labour intensive. Between 1884 and 1913 the workforce grew from 367,793 to 643,135, an increase of 75 per cent.[1] By comparison, between the censuses of 1881 and 1911 the total occupied labour force of Great Britain rose by only 45 per cent.[2] Throughout the entire period well over 40 per cent of the railway labour force could be described as completely unskilled. The 52,977 porters, 22,914 carmen and van guards, 55,001 labourers, 18,857 engine-cleaners, 6,193 carriage-cleaners and most of the 66,812 permanentway men included in a return of 1904 all used the most primitive equipment. By contrast the skilled grades, such as the 28,282 engine-drivers and firemen and 27,971 signalmen, formed a small proportion of the total numbers employed.[3]

The success of the labour management policies of the railway companies during the half century following the opening of the Liverpool and Manchester Railway in 1830 was reflected in the extremely weak state of trade union organization in those years. In 1880 fewer than one in twenty railwaymen held a union card. The Amalgamated Society of Railway Servants (ASRS), which was established in the boom conditions of 1871–2, was confined largely to the traffic grades and had a precarious existence until 1882, when its membership sank to an all-time low of 6,000 before staging a slow recovery. Recruitment into the Associated Society of Locomotive Engineers and Fireman (ASLEF), founded in 1880, was confined to the footplate grades. Another group of men in the traffic departments formed a second craft union, the United Pointsmen's and Signalmen's Society (UPSS) in 1890. The General Railway Workers' Union (GRWU) founded in 1889–90 reflected the impact of the New Unionism on the railway industry. Its birth was helped by Tom Mann; it gained most of its members from the goods and cartage departments of the railway companies and from the unskilled labourers in the railway workshops; it placed less emphasis on friendly society benefits and more on industrial muscle and on state intervention to limit hours of work. It was not until 1897, a year of intensive union activity on British (and German) railways,[4] that the Railway Clerks' Association (RCA) was formed to recruit those employed in the clerical and supervisory grades. Despite the subsequent wooing of railway employees by no less than five trade unions, a majority continued to remain unorganized until the upsurge in industrial strife in 1911–14.

II

It was the failure of the staff to organize which enabled the chairmen and general managers of the great railway companies to cling with impunity to their policy of non-recognition of the unions. In 1907 Mr. Cosmo Bonsor, chairman of the South Eastern Railway Company, expressed the 'power to manage' viewpoint, often associated with employers in the engineering industry, but also characteristic of the majority of his contemporaries in railway management: 'The company had refused, and would continue to refuse to permit a third party to come to their Board Room to discuss with them how they were to carry on their business.'[5] The railway companies used a variety of arguments to justify their refusal to negotiate with the unions. In common with the shipowners, railway general managers maintained that trade unionism was incompatible with the strict military-style discipline which it was necessary to enforce if the safety of the travelling public and the staff was to be assured. Sir George Findlay, general manager of Britain's 'senior' railway, the London and North Western, declared in 1892: 'If a railway company were to deal with the Amalgamated Society on questions affecting matters of discipline and good order, I say no discipline or good order would be maintained.'[6] Those who charged the railway companies with authoritarianism in their dealings with labour were assured that the directors were always ready to hear complaints on an individual basis. The Railway Companies' Association, established (under a different name) in 1867, asserted that 'there was no substantial grievance among the men that could not be remedied by personal negotiation'.[7] The general manager of the Great Eastern Railway maintained that it was 'considered a great privilege to get a son into the service' and that he knew of many instances of his company employing members of three generations of the same family.[8] His chairman agreed. 'But for the activities of members of the ASRS', he claimed, they would be 'a fairly happy and contented family on the Great Eastern'.[9]

Since the volume of business on the railways fluctuated less severely than it did in other industries, such as building construction or the merchant marine, most jobs on the railway were more regular and dependable than were jobs elsewhere. Furthermore, the railway network and the volume of traffic were both expanding, providing sober and loyal servants of the companies with opportunities for promotion. Cautions, suspensions, fines and, in extreme cases, sackings were ever-present reminders of the all-seeing eye of management; but for the dedicated man a job on the railways was a job for life. Accident-prone Peter Lythgoe, of the Chester locomotive depot of the London and North Western Railway, exemplifies the hold that railway employment had on men of his generation. He started work in 1864 as a cleaner earning 12s a week and rose to become a main-line driver at the top rate of 7s 6d a day in 1869. He was kept on in the service until 1914 when he reached the age of 69. In the course of his fifty-year-long career on the footplate he was fined ten times, cautioned fourteen times, suspended thirteen times and reprimanded twice. His case was untypical only in respect of the number of punishments he received.[10]

A further attraction of the railway service was the existence of company-based friendly societies, providing sickness and retirement benefits. The first of these, the Great Western Railway Provident Society, was founded as early as 1838. By 1870 there were sixty similar organizations.[11] Sir George Findlay believed that his company's policy of contributing to the various benevolent funds for different grades of staff had been well worth while since 'it prevented the servants of the North Western to any considerable extent joining the Trades Union Association, that is the Amalgamated Society'.[12]

Encouraged by the divisive tactics of the companies, many railwaymen were more concerned with conditions of employment in their particular grade and with the prospects of promotion within the grade hierarchy, that is, from engine-cleaner to fireman to driver, than they were about joining forces with men in other grades to advance the welfare of the whole. A long campaign of education by leaders of the ASRS and the GRWU was needed before rank-and-file railwaymen recognized the advantages of working together to wring concessions from the companies.

III

Although the ASRS enrolled only a small proportion of the workforce its strength varied from region to region and from grade to grade. In the late 1880s it was strongest in the territory of the North Eastern Railway and in South Wales, both regions in which there was an established tradition of trade unionism, and had more success in recruiting among the better-paid traffic grades than it did among the less well-paid shunters, platelayers and porters or among the casually employed carters. It is not surprising, therefore, that before the union's officers launched the first national All Grades Campaign in 1896–7, initiatives in formulating demands for improved working conditions came from the best-organized regions. In July 1888 branches in the north-east drew up the Darlington Programme for reduced working hours and higher pay for the principal grades of railwaymen. The campaign, organized jointly by the Tyneside and National Labour Union and the ASRS, persuaded the railway directors to agree to arbitration. The award of Robert Spence Watson, announced early in January 1890, granted a reduction in working hours to some, though not all the North Eastern Railway's wages grades. When they were faced with further demands for reduced hours nearly a year later, the North Eastern Railway Board, on 18 December 1890, resolved 'to meet any committee of the men either alone or associated with any advisors whom they ... select to accompany them'. Although the officers of the ASRS attending a conference with the members of the Board two days later were reminded that they were only there as 'advisers', their presence may be seen as a significant milestone in the development of collective bargaining on the railways. An important reason for the concession having been made was the fact that the North Eastern Railway directors were 'drawn from the region's leading trades' and were 'men who were well used to dealing with organised labour'.[13]

In August 1890 the directors of the Taff Vale, Rhymney and Barry Docks railways, confronted with similar demands for a reduction in the working day, at first refused to allow William Harford, General Secretary of the ASRS, to accompany a deputation of the men. However, after an eight-day-long railway strike had thoroughly disrupted the industry and commerce of South Wales, J. Inskip, the chairman of the Taff Vale Railway and spokesman for all three companies, negotiated a settlement with Harford.[14]

Nevertheless, the concessions made by the railway companies in the north-east and in South Wales were untypical. The large majority of the companies steadfastly refused to negotiate with the trade unions. Furthermore, from the late 1880s the profitability of the railway industry was declining, a development which highlighted the conflicting claims of shareholders and wage-earners.

IV

The effects of government intervention in the running of the railways were cumulative and resulted in an upward trend of the proportion of working expenses to passenger and freight receipts which eroded profit margins. Between 1890 and 1908 the proportion of working expenses to receipts rose from 54 to 65 per cent. At the same time the rate of return on paid-up capital fell from a peak of 4·41 per cent in 1870 to an annual average of 3·42 per cent between 1905 and 1909.[15] The Railway Regulation Act 1889 obliged all companies to introduce expensive systems of interlocking signals and points and to install continuous brakes on passenger trains. The Cheap Trains Act 1883 made obligatory the issuance of workmen's tickets at exceptionally low rates and the Railway and Canal Traffic Act 1894 severely limited the power of railway companies to increase their charges to their customers. Caught between the upper millstone of the limitation of their revenue-earning powers and the nether millstone of more expensive methods of operation, the railway directors sought an escape by increasing the productivity of labour. Nevertheless, the survival of the competitive system severely limited any improvement in the efficiency of the workforce. It is true that competition between British railway companies in the period 1880–1914 was restricted to only a few areas of operation. In 1911 a Board of Trade Departmental Committee concluded that 'the era of competition between the railway companies was passing away'. Already by 1880 wide-ranging pooling agreements had largely eliminated competition in freight charges and in passenger fares for comparable distances, and had contributed to the stability of employment of the main traffic grades – the footplatemen, guards and signalmen. There was, however, brisk competition in the collection and delivery of goods from the railheads where, according to the same Departmental Committee, 'there was an unnecessary number of carts to collect and deliver'.[16] The main-line companies serving the London terminals boasted of the frequency of their collections and deliveries; but their vans were rarely more than half loaded and the traffic did not earn sufficient revenue to pay the carters decent wages. The number of men employed in the 'goods and cartage' departments of the railway companies rose from 18,985 in 1884 to

40,969 in 1913.[17] In contrast with most other railway workers, men in this category were casually employed and job opportunities fluctuated more sensitively to movements in the trade cycle than they did in the case of the traffic grades. Thus numbers employed fell from a peak of 46,358 in the boom year 1907 to 38,753 three years later, a decline of 16 per cent, at the same time as total railway employment fell from 631,341 to 608,750, or by less than 2 per cent.[18]

The increased productivity of the traffic grades was achieved mainly by the more intensive use of existing equipment rather than by the introduction of more capital-intensive methods of operation.[19] The one important exception to this generalization was to be found in main-line signalling.

In the busiest signalboxes of the 1890s electronic devices were providing additional information for the signalman to absorb while the new levers which controlled the interlocking signals and points required a greater physical effort to move than was needed for the simpler devices they replaced.[20] William Forman, an ASRS organizer, assured the Labour Commission in 1892 that the responsibilities of a signalman were 'altogether different from what they were' – a view endorsed by his General Secretary, William Harford, who said in 1893 that 'the signalman of a quarter of a century ago would now be no more use on a railway than a boy taken out of a field'.[21] However, signalmen and switchmen taken together only accounted for 5·17 per cent of the railway workforce in 1884 and the transformation of their working environment was in sharp contrast to the situation of the vast majority of their contemporaries. Booking clerks, who greatly outnumbered the signalmen, were still using the Edmondson ticket-issuing machine, patented in 1841;[22] the permanentway men, who were nearly twice as numerous as the signalmen, used the same primitive tools to align the rails and adjust the ballast as their fathers had used before them – and their sons were to use in their turn.

The backwardness of British railways capital equipment before 1914 was particularly manifest in the character of the wagon fleet. In 1886 the average British freight car had a maximum loading of 8 tons, compared with the average United States box car's capacity of over 32 tons.[23] Actual amounts carried on British railways were well below the capacity figure. As late as 1920 the average wagon load was only 5·41 tons. Nearly one-third of the wagons on the rails at any one time were running empty.[24] By 1913 the British railway network was clutterd up with no less than 1,330,000 wagons of which 734,000 were owned by the railway companies while the remainder belonged to private firms.[25] Automatic coupling of wagons, imposed by law in the United States from 1893, was virtually absent from British railways and freight trains were not fitted with continuous brakes. In 1886 a leading English technical journal commented: 'If the English railways will persist in carrying train loads of 50 to 100 tons where they might just as well carry three or four times that load with very little increase in the main items of working cost, they must expect not only a low range of train-mile receipts but a low range of dividends as well.'[26] The writer might have added that the consequences for the railway staff were a dampening of their hopes for shorter working hours and any improvement in their meagre pay. A Ministry of

Reconstruction report in 1918 noted that British railways suffered from 'a riot of individuality' in its wagon designs, there being forty different types of hand brakes and 200 different types of axle boxes.[27] In the absence of rolling stock standardization, further burdens were placed on shunters and guards who were involved in extra, highly dangerous duties coupling and uncoupling wagons and passing from side to side of a freight train to apply or release the hand brakes.

Only in the case of the North Eastern Railway was a serious attempt made before 1914 to increase the carrying capacity of wagons and to reduce empty running. In 1900 the first experimental high capacity wagons were ordered. That there was room for improvement was shown by the fact that at the end of 1902, out of a total stock of 44,056 company-owned goods wagons only two were of 12 tons capacity or more, while 38,776 were of 8 tons capacity only. By contrast, at the end of 1913 there were 18,000 wagons, or nearly one-third of the total possessed by the company, whose carrying capacity exceeded 12 tons.[28] The achievements of the North Eastern Railway, however, were most exceptional by comparison with all other major British companies.

Thus, although in the case of signalling, management depended on the new technologies to bring about an intensification of labour and a reduction in unit costs, with other grades in the railway service the consequences of the profit squeeze experienced by the companies were felt through the imposition of a stricter labour discipline and excessive overtime working. Both these elements combined to bring about the bitterly fought Scottish railway strike from 21 December 1890 to 29 January 1891. The opening of new railway bridges across the Tay (1887) and the Forth (1890) concentrated more freight traffic in the Edinburgh district just at a time when the volume of freight being moved by rail was already increasing because of the trade boom. After the strike the main complaint of Henry Tait, General Secretary of the Amalgamated Society of Railway Servants (Scotland), was that overwork was 'becoming systematic on our railways' and that it was 'most prevalent among drivers, firemen and guards'.[29] Thomas Ballantyne, Assistant Secretary of the ASRS, informed the Royal Commission on Labour that in the month of December 1890 each of the 609 goods guards, drivers and firemen employed by the Glasgow and South Western Railway worked an average of four hours forty-eight minutes daily overtime in excess of his normal ten-hour day.[30] In times of brisk trade such overtime working was common on many railways, south as well as north of the Scottish border. The companies made sure they escaped paying the cost – in overtime rates of pay – of their mismanagement of labour by employing footplatemen and guards on the 'Trip System', described by Henry Tait as 'task work'. Under this plan, staff were allowed so much paid time to complete a round trip, but were not paid a penny more when traffic congestion or a breakdown on the line caused delays which obliged them to be on duty beyond the allocated hours.

Among the labour economies effected in the railway workshops were reductions in piece-work rates and the employment of boys instead of men. Andrew Clark, the General Secretary of the GRWU, recalled that in the machine shops at Derby a notice of reduced piece-work rates 'was posted up after the men started work in the morning'.[31]

V

Up to the early 1890s it was largely the traffic grades who made the running in union organization. But the intensification of labour described above persuaded many railwaymen, including for the first time many of those in the unskilled grades, to abandon their antipathy to union membership. After 1890 it was impolitic of the ASRS to ignore the casually employed and poorly paid who were being recruited into the GRWU. The initial response of the ASRS to the formation of the rival organization was to introduce a new, lower, rate of subscription of 3*d* a week to match that of the New Union, while keeping the 5*d* a week membership for the skilled grades. The existence of the GRWU, catering primarily for the unskilled, obliged the older union to make a bid for the support of these hitherto largely neglected members of the workforce. The ASRS's All Grades Campaigns of 1896–7 and 1907 may be seen, at least in part, as its response to the New Unionism of the GRWU.

On 24 October 1897 the general managers of all the principal railway companies in the UK received copies of the All Grades demands of the ASRS with a request from Richard Bell, the union's General Secretary, to negotiate. Hitherto each company had felt perfectly competent to manage its own labour problems. Now, with narrowing profit margins, the chairmen and general managers felt the need to stand together. Two hundred of them met at Euston on 4 November 1897 to plan a concerted riposte to the union. A fortnight later an informal sub-committee of the general managers of six of the largest companies drew up a four-point plan to beat the ASRS in the event of it calling a strike. None of the companies, with the one important exception of the North Eastern Railway, would agree to negotiate. Faced with the determined opposition of the overwhelming majority of companies the ASRS did not press its programme to the point of a strike. However, it could claim one success. The Board of the North Eastern not only discussed the union's demands with its officers but also agreed to submit the entire All Grades Programme to arbitration and to allow Richard Bell to be the spokesman for the staff. The award of the arbitrator, Lord James of Hereford, presented in August 1897, shortened hours and improved overtime rates and Sunday payments.[32]

VI

Until 1889 the Taff Vale Railway could lay claim to being the most prosperous railway company in Britain. From its foundation in 1841 it exploited an ever-expanding and highly lucrative trade in coal from the Welsh valleys down to its docks at Cardiff and Penarth. In 1888 it paid a dividend of 15 per cent on its ordinary stock. However, following the opening of the Barry docks by the rival Barry Railway on 18 July 1889, a significant proportion of its coal traffic was syphoned off. The halcyon days of the Taff Vale Company were over. Its dividend slumped to 9·5 per cent in 1889 and to a mere 3 per cent in 1890.[33] This catastrophe led George White, a shareholding agitator, to wage a crusade against the directors whom he accused of extravagance and incompetence. The appointment in 1891 of Ammon Beasley, a well-known martinet in matters of labour discipline, to the post of general manager marked the success of the agitation; but at the same time it ushered in a decade of steadily worsening industrial relations.[34]

Beasley gradually withdrew a number of the concessions made to the ASRS negotiators in 1890. When a coal strike disrupted mineral traffic in the summer of 1893 he was quick to withdraw the railwaymen's guaranteed week and was slow to reinstate it when the miners returned to work. A speaker at an ASRS meeting in Cardiff on 17 September 1893 drew applause from his audience when he declared that the 1890 agreement 'had been much violated of late'. In a discussion about uniforms which took place at the same meeting, a railwayman complained that the issue of clothing had become scandalous. 'The men look like a lot of scarecrows', he said. He was supported by another speaker who maintained that 'their corduroy suits were worse than the uniforms worn by the paupers in any workhouse in the United Kingdom'.[35] A few weeks later the editor of the *Railway Review* complained of the draconian policies of the company's management. They had

> inflicted the maximum punishment in their power, videlicet instant dismissal, without any investigation at all and also without the legal term of notice. The workmen in question included a number of drivers, firemen, guards and signalmen – good and faithful servants some of whom had been in the company's service nearly forty years, and have ... been dismissed for the most trivial irregularities of all.[36]

A fortnight later a meeting of the company's drivers and firemen protested against the new policy of requiring drivers to fill in 'train bills' each day, giving more details of how they occupied their working hours.[37]

Thus there was 'combustible material ready to hand'[38] when a spark ignited the famous Taff Vale strike which began on 20 August 1900. The spark was the victimization of a signalman for being a delegate on behalf of the men in a movement for improved minimum rates of pay. Early that month a mass meeting of 'several hundred' railwaymen in Cardiff combined a demand for his reinstatement with a claim for an additional ½d an hour in wages. An inflated demand for the bituminous coal of the South Wales pits, to fuel the ships of the Royal Navy during the progress of the Boer War, brought some benefit to colliers in the form of enhanced earnings. But a twenty-one-year contract between the Rhymney Railway Company and the principal collieries for the carriage of coal to the docks, signed before the outbreak of hostilities, prevented the Taff Vale Railway from raising its freight charges and provided it with an excuse to resist the demands of the railwaymen.[39]

The strike was fought with great determination on both sides. Ammon Beasley worked energetically to replace the strikers, depending mainly on men supplied through William Collison's National Free Labour Association, but even going to the extent of posting notices for volunteers in the locomotive sheds of the far-off County Down Railway in Ireland.[40]

Richard Bell, General Secretary of the ASRS, was at first reluctant to support the strike, but after the union's executive gave it official backing on 19 August he endeavoured to control the activities of the pickets from his temporary headquarters in the Colbourn Hotel, Cardiff. During the twelve days of the strike he received over a hundred telegrams, most of which were from branch officers reporting the movement of blackleg labour to Cardiff from all parts of the country.[41] Early in the morning of 23 August, prompted by telegraphic information received from Paddington Station, Bell and a large contingent of union pickets met forty blacklegs who had come down on the mail train from London. By offering them refreshments and their return tickets to Paddington they persuaded twenty-eight of the party to return to London on the next train. It was incidents such as this which persuaded Ammon Beasley to apply for an injunction in the High Court to restrain Bell and the local organizing secretary, James Holmes, from picketing the Great Western Railway station at Cardiff.

Although Justice Farwell's judgment in the High Court in favour of the company was overturned by the Court of Appeal, the Law Lords, in the famous Taff Vale judgment of 22 July 1901, upheld Farwell's opinion. Damages of £23,000 and costs were eventually payable by the ASRS. The case was of great significance, for ever since the passing of the Trade Union Act in 1871 it had been assured that a trade union could not be sued and mulcted in damages for wrongs done – that is, the loss of business arising from strikes – by its agents. After the Lords' judgment it was clear that any trade union that conducted a strike might have to face crippling damages.

The experience of the Taff Vale case had a decisive influence on the policy of the ASRS and on that of the wider labour movement concerning the representation of working men in Parliament. In the case of the ASRS, the union was already committed to independent labour representation in Parliament some months before the fateful struggle with the Taff Vale Railway. At the annual conference of the TUC held in Plymouth in September 1899 a resolution, drafted by one of its members, Thomas Steels of Doncaster, and calling for co-operators, trade unionists and members of socialist and other working-class bodies 'to convene a special congress to devise ways and means of securing the return of an increased number of labour members to the next Parliament', was carried by 546,000 votes to 434,000. The conference held at the Farringdon Hall, London on 27–8 February 1900 which established the Labour Representation Committee (LRC) – the forerunner of the Labour Party – was the outcome of this decision. But although the ASRS had committed itself to the cause of independent labour representation in Parliament and was among the first of the unions to affiliate to the LRC, most trade unions continued to support the Liberal Party and the election of Lib-Lab MPs – working men who were elected to the House of Commons as Liberals. Philip Snowden, who became Chancellor of the Exchequer in the first two Labour governments (1924 and 1929–31), noted that at the first annual conference of the LRC, held in Manchester in February 1901, a 'feeling of despondency' prevailed because of the very limited number of trade union affiliations to the new organization.[42]

Two years later despondency gave way to optimism as the delegates attending the third annual conference of the LRC at Newcastle in February 1903 learned that affiliated membership had shot up from the original 375,931 to 861,150. It was the Lords' Taff Vale judgment which had brought about the transformation.

Within the ASRS the immediate reaction of the union's executive was to show circumspection. Meeting within two months of the delivery of the judgment it resolved, with only one dissentient,

> that after a careful consideration of the decision of the House of Lords on the Taff Vale Railway Company versus ASRS case, we are of the opinion that the position of trade unions, as defined by the judgment is one which requires the utmost caution and deliberation before proceeding to make any alteration either in the rules or constitution of the society. We therefore decide to wait until we have before us the proposals of the Parliamentary Committee of the TUC before deciding to take definite steps in the matter.[43]

This resolution, no doubt, reflected the view of Richard Bell that the Lords' decision was now wholly unwelcome. In common with Sidney Webb, the ASRS General Secretary believed that it would have the beneficial effect of strengthening union executives' authority over hot-headed members of the rank and file whilst at the same time reinforcing the case for legislation establishing compulsory arbitration.[44]

However, the rank and file at branch meetings took a less complacent view. They inclined to the opinion expressed in the popular Sunday newspaper, *Reynolds News*, that the Lords' decision was 'judge made law in the interests of the employing classes'.[45] They had little interest in Richard Bell's hobby horse of compulsory arbitration but rather wanted the right to strike restored by Parliament. To achieve this the number of independent Labour MPs in the Commons would have to be increased. A resolution passed at the union's Annual General Meeting on 4 October 1901 reflected this rank-and-file opinion:

> That in the opinion of this Congress the recent decision of the House of Lords, based on the Taff Vale case, rendering the funds of trade societies liable in damages for the illegal acts of their agents, was a distinct reading of the law which did not previously exist; and the delegates were convinced that the remedy could only be found in electing as their law-makers and administrators those who had a practical knowledge of industrial work, and who were in sympathy with the reasonable aspirations for industrial freedom and advancement.

In December 1901 the executive acceded to the demands of numerous branches that a ballot of the membership should be held on the question of raising a voluntary levy of 1*s* per member per year for the purpose of financing the return of independent Labour members to the House of Commons. The result of the ballot was disappointing to the socialists in that only 29 per cent of the membership voted, but regarded as very satisfactory in so far as 89 per cent of those voting favoured the levy. In June 1902 therefore the executive decided to introduce the levy on a voluntary basis.[46] But in the latter part of 1902, as the full implications of the Taff Vale judgment became more widely appreciated, opinions in the branches hardened and an adjourned Annual General Meeting in January 1903 decided to amend the union's rules to make a 1*s* a year political levy obligatory on all members.[47] The rule came into force in July 1903, was declared to be legally valid by one of the most eminent Liberal lawyers, Sir Robert Reid, M.P., and by an equally eminent Conservative lawyer, Sir Edward Clarke, Q.C., and was endorsed in a ballot of the union membership in September 1905 when 50 per cent of those eligible voted and 81 per cent of those voting agreed to the compulsory levy.[48] Thus, within the six years 1899–1905 the ASRS had played a major part in bringing the LRC into being and had committed itself to support the new organization financially by introducing a compulsory annual levy of the membership.

Within the TUC the importance of the Taff Vale judgment was understood at an early date. In his presidential address to the annual congress at Swansea in September 1901, Charles William Bowerman described the Lords' decision as 'the most notable event during the year' which marked 'a crisis in the trade union movement'. He concluded that there was 'an imperative and absolute necessity' to secure increased representation of labour in the House of Commons. A delegate of the enginemen and cranemen, J. Baker, underlined the president's message when he said 'it was absurd for the people's leaders to allow the laws of the land to be made by their enemies'. James Sexton, the dockers' leader, reminding delegates that two years earlier Congress had taken the first steps towards the creation of the LRC, advocated that 'a numerically strong section of direct labour members should be sent to the House of Commons'. Delegates then proceeded to carry the following resolution: 'That this Congress expresses its gratification with the success of the LRC and further appeals to all trade unions to become affiliated with the movement.'[49]

The other influence tilting the balance in favour of affiliation was the blank refusal of James Balfour from the Conservative front benches of the House of Commons to promise any amending legislation and the Liberal leaders' equivocation on the same issue.[50] By the end of 1903 the adhesion of the engineers and the textile workers had been secured and by the end of 1905 the LRC had an affiliated membership of 921,000.[51]

When David Shackleton, M.P., chaired a meeting in the Queen's Hall, London on 16 February 1906 to celebrate the return of twenty-nine LRC candidates to Parliament in the recent general election, he was sure that 'the chief reason which influenced the trade unionists in the country in deciding to join hands with their comrades in the Independent Labour Party and other societies to form the united Labour Party was that the organised workers in the country had had a serious set back in the Taff Vale and the other decisions affecting the right of combination.'[52] Clearly the railwaymen who picketed the arrival platforms at Cardiff early in the morning of 23 August 1900 had set in motion a train of events of immense significance for the future of the British Labour movement.

VII

If it is accepted that in the years 1899–1906 the railwaymen played a major part in altering the balance of political forces in Britain, in the ensuing seven years, 1907–13, this role was to make a significant contribution to the development of industrial unionism. The undercurrent of forces which transformed the bargaining strength of the railway unions in this period was the growth in organization of those unskilled grades which for many decades had remained largely outside the scope of trade union membership.

On 18 January 1907 all railway company general managers received a copy of the ASRS's new All Grades Programme which included demands for an Eight-Hour Day for traffic grades, a ten hour maximum for other railwaymen and a 2*s* a week rise in pay. Although Richard Bell's three separate appeals for negotiation were fruitless, the times were more propitious for the unions than they had been ten years earlier. The rise in food prices helped to generate militancy and to boost ASRS membership which rose from 57,462 in 1905 to 97,561 in 1907. In October 1907 a members' ballot vote of 76,925 to 8,773 in favour of strike action hardened the resolve of the union's executive which met to fix the date for a national stoppage.

At this point Lloyd George, President of the Board of Trade, intervened by inviting the union's officers to a meeting with representatives of the companies in Whitehall on 6 November 1907. The invitation was accepted by both parties. Early on the day of the meeting the directors met separately at Euston and resolved unanimously 'not to yield in the slightest degree' in their resolve to deal direct with their men 'without intervention by the unions'.[53] As a sign of that resolve they refused to meet in the same room as the union leaders and Lloyd George was obliged to flit between the two parties as the discussions proceeded. That the negotiations did not break down was due to Lloyd George's persuasiveness and charm and to the union's abandonment of the claim – the one dearest to Richard Bell's heart – for recognition by the companies, in return for its acceptance of the companies' offer to submit to arbitration all questions concerning pay and hours of work which could not be settled in the Sectional and Central Conciliation Boards, which were established under the agreement.[54] The die-hard directors objected to yielding to arbitrators the right to decide important questions about the conditions of service of railwaymen but were consoled by the decision to exclude from membership of the boards all full time officers of the union. In their public statements they stressed that the conciliation scheme was a substitute for union recognition, not a stage in its progress. The moderates on the management side, notably Sam Fay, general manager of the Great Central Railway, were relieved that a national railway strike had been averted, were less hostile to the unions and were therefore prepared to accept the settlement with equanimity, especially since they believed it was to be of a minimum duration of seven years.[55]

By August 1911 rank-and-file railwaymen, caught up in the wave of industrial unrest that hot summer, were disillusioned with the working of the conciliation scheme. In 1907, when the scheme was initiated, conditions of prosperity prevailed; but in 1908 'trade went down with a bang' and the somewhat niggardly settlements reached in the conciliation boards or awarded by arbitrators reflected the depressed state of the companies' revenues.[56] The railwayman's average weekly wage in 1910, at 25*s* 9*d* was 5½*d* less than it had been in 1906.[57]

The national railway strike of 1911 began unofficially on 5 August when men employed by the Lancashire and Yorkshire Railway came out with a demand for a 2*s* a week increase in their wages. Its spread was rapid. In an endeavour to keep it under control, the executives of all the railway unions except the RCA met in Liverpool on 15 August and decided to offer the companies twenty-four hours in which to open negotiations, failing which a national railway strike would be called. In the belief that 'the government had undertaken to put at the service of the railway companies every soldier in the country', the directors stood firm, confident that the strike would be ineffective. Winston Churchill, as Home Secretary, did indeed dispatch no less than 50,000 troops to trouble spots and even to places, such as Manchester, where the civic authorities had not requested the intervention of the armed forces. In the House of Commons he declared he had sent in the troops solely in order to ensure the movement of food supplies, but the unpredictable state of international relations arising from the *Panther* incident at Agadir may also have influenced his bellicose reaction to the strike.[58] The events of 15–20 August when much of the industrial life of the north and of South Wales was paralysed, revealed the extent of the railway directors' miscalculations.

With the threat of war over the Moroccan crisis overshadowing the scene, Lloyd George succeeded in bringing together in one room, for the first time, the representatives of the companies and the leaders of the railway unions. The companies agreed to reinstate the strikers without penalties and both sides agreed to resume negotiations in the conciliation boards and to participate in the work of a Royal Commission on the working of the 1907 conciliation scheme. After the unions' rejection of the Royal Commission's report the threat of a further strike and the passing of a Commons' resolution urging the resumption of negotiations, there was a renewal of discussions between the two sides on 7 December. Four days later a revised conciliation scheme was agreed. It was noteworthy in that for the first time the companies conceded the right of full-time trade union officials to represent the men in the conciliation boards.

Meanwhile the union leaders who had co-operated in prosecuting the strike of 1911 considered the question of a more permanent fusion of forces. The outcome of their labours was the merging of ASRS, GRWU and UPSS to establish the National Union of Railwaymen (NUR) on 29 March 1913.

Albert Fox, General Secretary of ASLEF, left the discussions after his scheme for a federation, rather than a merger, had been rejected. The RCA did not participate. Nevertheless, the enthusiasm for the 'New Model' NUR based on the concept of industrial unionism was immense. The combined membership of the three merging unions in 1913 was 141,000. By the end of 1914 NUR membership was 273,000, equal to 44·3 per cent of the workforce. With ASLEF's 32,900 and the RCA's 29,394 the percentage unionized was now 56·0. This transformation broadly coincided with railway management's acceptance of the need to negotiate regularly with union leaders.[59]

Notes: Chapter 10

1 Return relating to the number of persons employed on the railways, Parliamentary Papers, 1884, C. 242, LXX pp. 307–17. D. L. Munby, *Inland Transport Statistics Great Britain 1900–1970* (Oxford, 1978), 46–7, Table A8.1.

2 Department of Employment, *British Labour Statistics: Historical Abstract 1886–1968* (London, 1971), 195, Table 102.

3 General Report to the Board of Trade upon Accidents that have occurred on the Railways of the U.K. during 1904, 1905, Cd 2605, LXIX, p. 57.

4 The *Verband der Eisenbahner Deutschlands* was formed in Hamburg in January 1897. H.-J. Buss, *Dreimal Stunde Null* (Frankfurt a.M., 1973), 7–8.

5 *The Times*, 31 July 1907.

6 Royal Commission on Labour, 1893–4, C. 6894, VIII, Group B, Minutes of Evidence, q. 25, 949.

7 Railway Companies' Association, *Conditions of Railway Service and the National Programme*, reprinted from *Railway News*, 19 October 1907.

8 Select Committee on Railway Servants' Hours of Labour, 1890–1, C. 6327, XVI, Minutes of Evidence, qs 9,449–56.

9 Royal Commission on the Railway Conciliation and Arbitration Scheme of 1907, 1912–13, Cd 6014, XLV, q. 10,011.

10 Public Record Office, *British Transport Archives*, LNW 15/175, Staff Register, Chester Locomotive Depot.

11 P. W. Kingsford, *Victorian Railwaymen* (London, 1970), 194–7.

12 Royal Commission on Labour, 1893–4, XXXIII, Group B, Minutes of Evidence, q. 25, 953.

13 R. J. Irving, *The North Eastern Railway Company 1870–1914* (Leicester, 1976), p. 59.

14 P. S. Bagwell, *The Railwaymen* (London, 1963), 137–9.

15 H. J. Dyos and C. H. Aldcroft, *British Transport* (Leicester, 1969), 172. D. H. Aldcroft, *Studies in British Transport History 1870–1970* (Newton Abbot, 1974), 32.

16 Departmental Committee on Railway Agreements and Amalgamations, Report, 1912, Cd 5631, XXIX, pp. 7, 10.

17 Railways: Number of Persons Employed, 1884, C 242 LXX, p. 307. Returns of Accidents and Casualties, 1914, Cd 7405, LXXVII, p. 105.

18 Reports on Railway Accidents, 1908, Cd 4287, XCIV, p. 45, and 1911, Cd 5628, LXX, p. 23.

19 'In the case of railways ... there was no revolutionary change in the techniques of operation.' D. H. Aldcroft, *British Railways in Transition* (London, 1968), 7.

20 W. J. Gordon, *Every-Day Life on the Railroad* (London, 1898), 127.

21 Royal Commission on Labour, 1893–4, XXXIII, Minutes of Evidence, Group B, qs 26,384–5. *Railway Review*, 4 August 1893, reporting a signalmen's meeting in Derby on 28 July 1893.

22 Gordon, *Every-Day Life on the Railroad*, wrote: 'The year 1891 was the jubilee of the railway ticket. . . . Unlike most inventions, the ticket remains much as it was at first. It is still numbered and dated as it was then, and its only changes have been in colour and the words

printed on it.' These comments would have been as valid for the situation in 1951 as they were for 1891.

23　E. B. Dorsey, *British and American Railroads Compared* (New York, 1887), 10.

24　Return relating to the Standard Gauge Railways of Great Britain for the Year 1920, 1921, Cmd 1256, XXX, p. 307.

25　Munby, *Inland Transport Statistics*, 122–3 and 126, Tables A25.1 and A25.2.

26　*Engineering*, 20 August 1886, p. 187.

27　Ministry of Reconstruction Advisory Council, *Reporting on the Standardisation of Railway Equipment* (4 July 1918), 1918, Cmd 9193, XIII, p. 16.

28　Irving, *North Eastern Railway*, 250–1.

29　The Report of the Select Committee on Railway Servants (Hours of Labour), 1892, C. 342, XVI, p. 126, noted that 'as a rule excessive hours appear most frequent on lines with heavy goods or mineral traffic; and, so far as regards running staff, they occur on goods, mineral and cattle trains to a much greater extent than on passenger trains'.

30　ibid., qs 25,182–6. The fullest account of the struggle in Scotland is to be found in J. Mavor, *The Scottish Railway Strike 1891* (Edinburgh, 1891).

31　Royal Commission on Labour, 1893–4, XXXIII, Minutes of Evidence, Group B, qs 23,964–8 and 23,450.

32　Bagwell, *The Railwaymen*, 141–9.

33　D. S. Barrie, *The Taff Vale Railway*, 2nd edn (South Godstone, 1950), 26–30.

34　*Railway Review*, 31 August 1900.

35　*Railway Review*, 22 September 1893.

36　*Railway Review*, 8 December 1893.

37　*Railway Review*, 22 December 1893.

38　The phrase was that of the editor of the *Railway Review*, 31 August 1900.

39　*South Wales Daily News*, 22 August 1900.

40　*Railway Review*, 30 August 1900. W. Collison, *Apostle of Free Labour* (London, 1913), 152.

41　A box file containing the telegrams was found at the back of a cupboard in Unity House, headquarters of the National Union of Railwaymen, in 1980 on the occasion of the head office move to new premises in Euston Road. The file must have remained undisturbed for sixty years.

42　P. Snowden, *An Autobiography*, 2 vols (London, 1934), 1:94.

43　ASRS, *Proceedings and Reports*, Executive Committee (September 1901), Resolution 18.

44　F. Bealey and H. Pelling, *Labour and Politics 1900–1906* (London, 1958), 74–5. H. A. Clegg *et al.*, *A History of British Trade Unions since 1889* (Oxford, 1964), 317.

45　Quoted in *Railway Review*, 2 August 1901.

46　ASRS, Executive Committee Minutes (March 1902), p. 3.

47　ASRS, Adjourned Annual General Meeting (January 1903), Resolutions 42 and 43.

48　For the legal opinions see Bagwell, *The Railwaymen*, 244–5. The result of the ballot was reported in ASRS, Executive Committee Minutes (September 1905), p. 8.

49　TUC, *Annual Report* (1901), 31, 62, 74.

50　Bealy and Pelling, *Labour and Politics*, 77.

51　H. Pelling, *A Short History of the Labour Party*, 3rd edn (London, 1968), 12.

52　Labour Party, *Annual Conference Report* (1906), 68.

53　C. Wrigley, *David Lloyd George and the British Labour Movement* (Hassocks, 1976), 55–6.

54　G. Alderman, 'The railway companies and the growth of trade unionism in the late nineteenth and early twentieth centuries', *Historical Journal* 24 (1971): 309–36.

55　Sir Guy Granet, general manager of the Midland Railway, told the Royal Commission on the Railway Conciliation Scheme (1907) that 'a solemn bargain was made that for seven years from 1907 the question of recognition should not be pressed upon the companies'. 1912–13, Cd 6014, XLV, q. 12,912.

56　The assessment of trade conditions in 1908 was Sam Fay's. Royal Commission on the Railway Conciliation Scheme, 1907, 1912–13, XLV, q. 11,813.

57　Munby, *Inland Transport Statistics*, 59, Table A9.1, 'Railways earnings and wage bill'.

58　*Hansard*, 5th Series, Vol. XXIX (22 August 1911), cols. 2,323–31.

59　The British railway unions did not attempt a merger with other transport workers' unions such as was achieved in Germany in 1908 between the Hamburger Verband der Eisenbahner Deutschlands and the Transportarbeiter Verband. Buss, *Dreimal Stunde Null*, 84–5. The NUR did, however, help to form a Triple Industrial Alliance with the National Transport Workers' Federation and the Miners' Federation of Great Britain in 1913. P. S. Bagwell, 'The triple industrial alliance 1913–22', in A. Briggs and J. Saville (eds), *Essays in Labour History 1886–1923*, Vol. 1 (London, 1971), 96–128.

11 Conflict and Organization in the Early History of the German Trade Union Movement

KLAUS TENFELDE

I

The German trade unions experienced at least four decades of changing fortunes and of dogged struggle for the survival of their organizations before the demise of the *Sozialistengesetz* (Anti-Socialist Law) allowed them, within a matter of months, to arrive at a lasting organizational structure which, in its essentials, remains unchanged to this day. Opposition to the organized expression of trade union interests stemmed not solely from uncompromising industrialists nor from the ranks of the bureaucratic authorities, but was primarily of a structural nature and resulted from the extremely varied experiences of wide sectors of the population, and in particular the working classes during the industrial revolution.

Those least affected by change after the middle of the century were the rural labourers working on the manorial estates: in this sector the great reorganization had already been brought about by the agrarian reforms at the beginning of the century and in the final analysis industrialization had little effect on the character of rural work and rural life – little, that is, at least in comparison with the effects of the concentration of industrial workers in the capitals and large cities. At the most, it was the rural employment market which was affected by the vortex of industry. The craft trades, however, present a different picture. Here the most conflicting experiences confronted one another: for some, big business confirmed developments already signalized with the introduction of freedom of trade and the ensuing overcrowding of individual trades – that is, falling family income, falling expectations of adequate opportunities for self-employment, downward social mobility and impoverishment. Cobblers and tailors were among the most severely affected. Other groups of artisans, even where they were able to survive in the long run, had to cope with far-reaching structural changes in methods of production and marketing as a result of pressure from growing factory competition. Others, for example the supply trades, benefited from rapid population growth and the development of mass consumption; as a rule, this group was actually able to expand its share of the market. Finally, for one last group of traditional trades, including, for example, the building trades, the extraordinary investment boom led to an unparalleled economic upswing. In this connection those new trades should not be overlooked which owed their existence to new opportunities as suppliers and repairers to prospering factories and large-scale industry.

Developments in the predominantly textile-oriented cottage industry were equally complex: some regions continued to find sales outlets in spite of pressures from competitors because of their remote location and poor communications; mechanization was only a very gradual process in some branches of production, and craft still remained in demand in others. The railway brought totally new conditions of employment for commercial and transport workers, and even factory workers faced an uncertain future in view of constantly alternating booms and slumps in the business cycle. Hardly had a worker transferred from a declining trade, or from the country, to what he hoped would be permanent employment in the flourishing textile trade – perhaps after a short interval in railway construction – than the industrial revolution brought about a renewed structural shift in favour of employment opportunities in heavy industry, in mining, in iron and steel works and increasingly in the engineering industry as well.

This morass of the most conflicting experiences which befell the labour force could not have been greater, more oppressive, or more misleading. For example, hardly anyone from the working class, the middle class, or the traditional social elites had realized immediately that the new developments were irreversible, had not balked at them and occasionally tried to resist them. As a rule, some form of reaction was the first response; for what was more natural than initially to look back with nostalgia to the traditional and to the familiar in the face of social change that was, though gradual, yet manifest in the life of everyone? And for this reason, the early protests of artisans in cottage industries, railway navvies, other groups of day labourers, including those in rural areas, and finally the early industrial factory workers appear more than a little ambivalent to a modern-day observer: their form seems quite modern on account of its collectivism. Their content and objectives, however, appear to a great extent reactionary in so far as they strive to re-establish conditions irretrievably lost. Thus to attribute early industrial protest movements, including the machine-breakings, which were admittedly of minor importance in Germany, to a new, trend-setting self-consciousness amongst the emerging proletariat is open to the objection that the revolt against the forms and consequences of an unwanted change was in many cases still the main motivation.[1] This is hardly surprising in view of the wide variety of activities to which workers resorted in the first instance, such as formal appeals to the authorities, the lodging of complaints and filing of petitions right up to the supreme courts of appeal, in spite of some spectacular rebellions such as machine-breaking, hunger revolts, demonstrations and mass actions on the part of railway workers, employees in cottage industry and occasionally by agricultural labourers. The code of conduct laid down for early industrial workers still provided detailed stipulations on the possibilities of appeal and their various accepted forms as a rule.[2] Since the peasants' wars at the outset of the modern period, agricultural labourers and small-holders had followed the tradition of petition to the authorities, particularly during the period of agrarian reform;

their example was followed by the miners who were indeed still strongly bound up in the reciprocal class relationships of legality and public welfare on the one hand, and of duty and obedience on the other.[3] Even artisans and domestic workers issued countless appeals and complaints right up to the throne itself, based on the illusion of a 'just' king presiding over conflicting interests. With the temporary suspension of repression during the revolutionary months of 1848–9 an absolute flood of petitions was unleashed on the newly installed authorities, the Frankfurt Parliament and its economic committee.[4]

II

Viewing the process of trade union formation in Germany from the perspective of such varying and conflicting experiences and patterns of conflict regulation, it is therefore hardly surprising that the development of a stable trade union structure took at least three decades, and was by no means completed even by the mid-1870s on account of renewed authoritarian and administrative repression. On the other hand, in comparison with Britain and in view of the difficult circumstances this was actually a relatively rapid process which depended on the specific forms of the later and therefore more rapid industrialization of Germany. It was not only the middle-class German social reformers at the forefront in the *Verein für Socialpolitik* (Association for Social Policy)[5] who closely observed the course of events in Britain but also in particular the early trade union central associations;[6] and in this way they prepared the German public for the acceptance in principle of the inevitability of open conflict between capital and labour.[7]

Although strikes had been known for centuries as a form of protest on the part of journeymen within the guilds, their increasingly frequent occurrence since the onset of industrialisation was met, at best, with suspicious mistrust, predominantly however with an attitude of sharpest condemnation. In part, this related to the inconsistent experiences mentioned above, that is, to the fact that the emerging labour force first had to make this method of conflict resolution its own, as they had yet to learn the most appropriate method of realizing their interests. For workers not incorporated in traditions of internal trade and guild bonds the primary means of expressing their interests, beyond petitioning the authorities, were generally riots and relatively disorderly demonstrations. Furthermore, one should not overlook the fact that the onset of social change in the early phases of industrialization threw up a wide range of new problems of adaptation which could not, or at least not primarily, identify the work process and the capitalist economic order as the primary cause of conflict. The strike, therefore, emerged only gradually and by a roundabout route as the appropriate method of resolving conflicts from amongst a host of diversely motivated and quite varying forms of protest. On the other hand, Germany had a long tradition of authoritarian laws against combination which actually reached a new peak in the repressive measures against the journeymen's movements at the turn of the eighteenth and nineteenth centuries.[8] Unlike France and

Britain, where early laws against combination had even been partly implemented by the comparatively strong and self-conscious middle classes, in
Germany it was predominantly the bureaucratic, late-absolutist authoritarian state which challenged and fought against the legality of any collective
articulation of interests, above all those arising from the lower classes.
Class-motivated and official repression was thus inherent in the development of the constitutional state of Prussian Germany in modern times. It
therefore comes as no surprise that, under the conditions of capitalist
industrialization, the survival of traditional social and political elites and
their renewed establishment in a position of power with the founding of the
German Empire and in its constitutional system soon became associated
with anti-emancipatory traditions of thought and behaviour directed solely
against the working class and that these traditions could be made to serve
particular interests. This is the root of the uncompromising authoritarian
Herr-im-Hause attitude to any kind of workers' movement which was
prevalent amongst employers in heavy industry.[9] As far as the state and
industrial conflict is concerned,[10] there is a further important point: the
traditionally repressive patterns of thought and behaviour which found
expression in the actions of the state disrupted the process of trade union
formation at its most vulnerable point, at, as it were, the 'natural' relationship between conflict and organization.

If the constitutive character of social conflict in the development of the
trade unions[11] is taken as a serious factor, an endless array of examples from
early trade union history must be considered, which without exception
demonstrate the extent to which contemporary conflicts aroused and stimulated the establishment of stable organizational structures. Wherever work
processes and forms of industrial organization, communal conditions, circumstances of origin and trade-specific traditions presented themselves as
favourable starting-points for the formation of groups and stimulated the
exchange of ideas and experiences, learning processes leading to relatively
regulated patterns of conflict were instigated and considerably accelerated
by the current conflict. On the other hand, however, the strike as a special
form of social conflict[12] was a relatively late achievement in branches and
regions where communications were underdeveloped. Thus, the comparatively complicated instrument of the strike is generally the result of an
interlinking network of communications, often acquired and rehearsed over
a period of years and which has gained embryonic organizational structures:
in provident funds, educational and social clubs, as in residual elements of
guild organizations and, finally, in rather loose networks including working-
men's associations and other small-scale friendship societies, in which the
antagonism between capital and labour had been experienced for years as a
degrading, debasing conflict of interests on which the basis of wealth and
poverty are founded. From this viewpoint, there were to all intents and
purposes no 'spontaneous' strikes, unless that spontaneity is taken to denote
simply the relationship between an unexpected event and a specific reaction.

For example, before the first great Ruhr miners' strike broke out in 1872[13]
a network of miners' societies, mostly affiliated to the Catholic parishes,
existed in Essen – the focal point of the strike – which, in addition to pastoral

duties, also pursued educational and social aims. In 1867 the workers in Essen had already presented wide-ranging petitions to the Prussian Ministry of Commerce[14] strongly condemning certain practices of colliery management and had demanded higher wages and regulated working hours. This last great action of petitioning was already accompanied by the revolt of individual workforces under threat of violence. It was unsuccessful. Strike activities at individual nearby collieries followed in 1868 and yielded partial successes, although no permanent organization of the movement was achieved in spite of the efforts of a newly formed local branch of Ferdinand Lassalle's *Allgemeine Deutsche Arbeiterverein* (ADAV – General German Workers' Association). In fact, the miners, as had already been apparent in the early actions and as remained customary until after the turn of the century, preferred to rely on a special internal workers' organization for dealing with conflict: the election of normally three delegates per mine mandated to represent the workers' ideas to the pit management, that is, the workers reserved the right to examine and approve any negotiated results. Within a few years the deficiency of this method of interest-articulation had become apparent in the face of the already long-established, regionally organized power of the employers. Thus the pit delegations once again formed the basis of strike organization in the dispute of 1872, though there was a characteristic further development already evident in the first days of the strike: the several dozen delegates elected from amongst their own numbers a strike committee to organize the conflict and to negotiate. The committee was carefully selected so as to remain free of political influences and was subsequently highly successful with regard to its organizational tasks, although as far as the actual strike demands were concerned it was unsuccessful. The defeat of the strike demonstrated the necessity for some permanent formulation of the miners' interests, at least on a regional basis. For this committee, which consisted above all of representatives of local miners' clubs (*Knappenvereine*), combined in permanent session – a frequent aspect of union formation in all trades – and threw itself enthusiastically into the task of founding a regional miners' union. It actually got as far as drafting the statutes and even probably establishing the first payment offices, usually within the existing miners' clubs. The trade union, however, foundered on the legally required approbation of the statutes by the responsible authorities, the royal regional government in Düsseldorf.

The conduct of the strike itself displayed a marked intensification of the network of communication between the strikers. Badges allowed mutual recognition between those on strike, a regular programme of meetings was attended, the local press was carefully studied, an effective organization for the maintenance of public order – a type of strike police – was set up, and attempts were probably also made to control the news and rumours which circulated so rapidly during periods of strike. Contrary to expectations and contrary to the natural fears of contemporaries, the strike in no way opened the door to all manner of excesses by the striking miners; in fact quite the reverse was the case for the strike leaders were well aware of the negative effect of such excesses on public opinion, which was basically sympathetic. The strike organizers therefore issued a constant stream of appeals for good conduct which had widespread disciplinary effect, as had been characteristic of the history of the strike for a long time: as early as 1866 Friedrich Albert Lange had noted that work stoppages were not now degenerating into the rough brutality of former times and were better organized.[15] Decades later another writer confirmed that the factor of fortuitousness and elemental force characteristic of the strike as an economic phenomenon was gradually diminishing and giving way to a regulative standardization; and that this was the progressive aspect of the right to strike,[16] which the trade union movement had actually only just achieved at the time of the Ruhr strike, after the years of sacrifice and conflict in the 1860s.

Under pressure to succeed, the dispute gave rise to highly efficient organizational forms which were able to take into account the interests of individual workforces and the miners as a whole, as well as the power of the employers. The strike organization fulfilled a primarily internal function with an explicitly disciplinary objective. For in 1872 political neutrality was the dictate of the hour in view of the opprobrium attached to the Social Democrats and of the *Kulturkampf* which Bismarck was just beginning to fight against the Catholic Church and its bishops and priests as well as the Catholic community in Prussia. Such a marked striving for autonomy is also exhibited in the history of a number of trade union central associations in this period; this must also be seen as a response to the competition among the workers' parties and, in the case of Lassalle's adherents, their contradictory attempts to affiliate the trade unions.[17]

Furthermore, the strike had demonstrated the unsuitability of organizations consisting simply of delegates and representatives of the traditional *Knappenvereine*, and had underlined the need for a permanent presence representing trade union interests. Thus, a new element was introduced into the existing, more or less formalized organizational structure which led to an increased differentiation of the earlier variety of functions that the societies and associations had performed: pressure group politics came to be their dominant concern. From the original fragmentation of organizational forms and functions a more rational centralization was born which, had it been crowned with success, would have led on to other and new tasks.

It is always tempting to provide a traditional interpretation of the working and social behaviour of the German miners in terms of the centuries of class-specific experience which lasted formally up to the 1860s, that is, to suspect the miners of a certain backwardness particularly as far as the articulation of their interests is concerned, as compared, that is, with other more advanced trades and organizations. This interpretation is only partially correct. The example given here shows how rapidly the miners actually achieved a completely appropriate form of conflict as a result of a learning process that set out from a traditional form of protest, the 1867 appeal, and was favoured by a group culture already based on the traditions of their class and little affected by migration. Therefore, though the miners can, to a certain extent, be regarded as a special case, it is clear that an experience in their history at the time of the formation of the empire broadened into solidaristic action, which took decades of protracted conflict to achieve and be translated into action in other trades. It is thus possible to trace simultaneous and absolutely identical learning experiences in other German mining areas which parallel the experiences of the miners of the Ruhr.[18] What had been concentrated into a few short years in the case of the miners had long since begun in other trades, for example in the 1850s during a powerful and lengthy economic upswing. While the concentration of miners in large-scale industry and in towns and their large numbers had certainly played a part in accelerating the learning process, barriers to learning had a greater effect on other areas as a result of a decentralized market or partriarchal working conditions amongst much smaller groups of workers or craftsmen. Even the general transport facilities and communications in out-of-the-way areas and similar factors could have a parallel effect – as in the case of the rural lower classes who had been deprived of their decisive potential for protest by the establishment of peasant ownership under the agrarian reforms.

The basic features of workers' conduct developed for example in the course of a labour dispute amongst the textile workers in the Lennep district in 1850, which has been thoroughly researched. They were quite similar to those displayed in the Essen strike of 1872, which with approximately 21,000 strikers was apparently the first mass strike in Germany.[19] During the Lennep dispute the workers at the forefront of the strike had been making efforts to obtain legal representation of their interests, stating that they 'had petitioned their masters for an improvement in their condition but had been refused, had approached the government in confidence and begged for help, had believed, had had faith and had bided their time all in vain; their destitution and desolation had remained unchanged'.[20] It was from this unsuccessful experience that the already long-established workers' society drew its persuasiveness and staying-power for a long, unsuccessful labour dispute which, after mediatory action by the authorities, even led to military intervention. In other areas too state intervention was still a characteristic feature of conflicts, on the one hand in the form of mediation, sometimes successful, by local authorities and regional governments after a strike had already been called, as well as in the form of military intervention during a strike; and on the other hand and in a much more important sense for the argument developed here, through repressive intervention in the initial stages of disputes – through permanent and suspicious surveillance of all collective activities among the workers. Considering that any collective conflict depends on a prior process of opinion formation and the articulation of demands in meetings, a process which has often taken a number of years before it ever reaches the stage of translation into action, police intervention at meetings, which was generally arbitrary though legitimized by the continuing laws against combination, affected the relationship between conflict and the formation of an organization probably at the most vulnerable point. In particular, the strike movement of the 1850s, which culminated in the currently still insufficiently researched 1857 wave of strikes, provides clear examples of the prevention of trade union organization by means of police opposition at the earliest possible point of conflict.[21] Even after admittedly limited rights of combination had been conceded, police surveillance measures – though varying widely from area to area – had the same effect.

As a result the history of conflict in Germany right up to the First World War took the form of a constant coexistence between differing stages of development:[22] again and again groups of workers capable of conflict in principle had to resort to outdated and inadequate methods of settling conflicts; time after time the same learning process had to be run through – from the practice of old forms of protest through appeals and petitions, on the one hand, and collective disobedience to a regulated settlement by strike on the other – and over and over again state intervention threatened to repress the trend towards organizational consolidation which had been tremendously accelerated by the conflict. Such action in fact favoured radical forms of protest on occasion.

During the *Vormärz* this was also the case for the miners of Saxony who, after years of petitioning, were forced to draw 'certain political conclusions';[23] it had been the case for the textile workers of Lennep in 1850 and, for example, in 1870 for the printers whose organizational development was otherwise in an advanced stage: 'imbued with enthusiasm for the concept of workers' rights' they were 'no longer prepared humbly to present their requests and desires to the throne or to leave it to the mercy of the capitalists to decide whether their miserable lot was to be improved'.[24] It was even more the case during the years of the *Sozialistengesetz*, 1878–90, when the mainly confessional workers' associations, committed to articulating their views within the system, flourished and gave birth to great petition movements, and even those workers of free trade union persuasion also saw themselves thrown back on petitions. What characterized the situation was the fight by means of pleas and appeals – as in the case of the shipwrights of Hamburg in the 1880s[25] – initially simply to win the right of assembly, and in this way to attain a regulated means of expressing their interests. After the miners of the Ruhr had already developed full union potential in 1872 and, in the subsequent years up to 1877–8, had made repeated attempts to form an association which invariably foundered on administrative opposition, even they saw themselves reduced to falling back on pre-union ways to formulate their objectives during the period of the *Sozialistengesetz*; and again they had to free themselves from the ballast of earlier forms of protest during the great strike wave of 1889–90.[26] Even shortly before the outbreak of the First World War attempts by individual labour forces to improve their lot by the method of appeal were still by no means rare. Sometimes the companies were effectively able to control and channel this particular method of expressing protest through workers' commissions and similar institutions.[27]

III

Such traditional, legitimist methods of channelling conflict were of course overtaken by events, in particular where democratic assembly was feasible and resulted in collectively organizing for industrial conflict. From the mid-1860s this had already been the case in Saxony due to the earlier lifting of the laws against combination there, but subsequently spread over a wide area, particularly during the increasingly international wave of strikes and unionization between 1864 and 1872.[28] Subsequent histories of the trade union associations have all too frequently emphasized aspects of organizational traditions while overlooking the trigger function of industrial conflicts in the formation of union organizations;[29] they have persistently tended to see the strike as an organizational weapon rather than primarily as an instrument of the workers themselves. Thus, the movement for the right to strike and combine of the mid-1860s basically provided considerable impetus for the formation of the first three central trade union associations (cigar workers, printers and tailors) and, for the first time, provoked a reaction from the political parties. Although the printers in particular had strong and established organizational traditions, it was the so-called *Dreigroschenstreik* in Leipzig in the spring of 1865 which gave clear demonstration of the necessity and efficiency of a tighter trade organization.[30] In other trades the strike was at least a factor in consolidating union organization[31] – mainly, that is, where workers' provident funds and educational societies had already united workers of a particular trade for decades. In such cases, class antagonism regularly manifested itself during the course of the strike. The strike wave of the 1850s triggered off extensive unionization amongst workers from widely varying branches in a traditional trade union stronghold such as Hamburg.[32] If in times of economic upswing the strike failed to spark off collective action in other trades, observation of neighbouring industrial disputes nevertheless provided insights and eventually led to the consolidation of organizations with trade union objectives. For example, with reference to the organization of the carpenters Ulrich Engelhardt noted that this was probably the first instance of dispensing with spontaneous means of conflict and giving priority to achieving a base for conflict built on viable organizational conditions.[33] In the case of Germany not one of the three 'national' waves of strikes and unionization in the 1850s, 1865–73 and 1888–90 remained exempt from interference in the right to democratic assembly; in each case the authorities exerted their influence, prohibited or restricted the learning process. It was also the case during the years of the foundation of the empire, that attempts to affiliate the unions to the political parties presented a further intervening factor that could either consolidate or divide potential loyalties.

The stimulating effect of conflict on organization was confirmed repeatedly by contemporary observers, starting with the Communist Manifesto.[34] Carl Stegmann and C. Hugo stated in 1897 that it was clear that antagonism was generally increased by strikes and that all workers in factories and works had acquired a clear awareness;[35] and that it could therefore be observed that the formation of a trade union was often the outcome of a strike – an observation, incidentally, which Stegmann and Hugo may have picked up from the Webbs[36] and which has been rather euphorically summarized by Richard Seidel, a former authority on the historiography of the German trade unions, on the basis of an analysis of the strike movements of the 1860s:

> The strike unites those of equal social rank. It proceeds from a vague notion of joint interests. The arrangement of the strike, the cooperation

of the workers during the strike gradually intensifies this notion to a first fleeting perception, provides the first experiences of joint action. The strike thus becomes a generating elemental force of the movement and, in individual cases, frequently the immediate source of a permanent alliance. However, as soon as the original forms of strike lose their effectiveness such forms must give way to improved and permanently viable methods of labour dispute. It is the first vital task of the organisation to find and elaborate such methods.[37]

An analysis of the history of industrial conflict in later decades would provide more detailed evidence that the existence and effectiveness of such trade unions born out of conflict situations considerably accelerated the process of structural differentiation between the interests of the two sides of the class struggle, again and always in the context of real confrontations. However, the history of the German employers' associations can certainly not be said to date only from the early 1890s and certainly not only from the well-known strike of the textile workers of Crimmitschau in 1903.[38] In addition to their economic and marketing concerns, the earliest interest groups of employers, including even the local employers' societies of the early industrial revolution, already performed employer functions in the sense of intervention in labour matters, though it seems likely that the earliest evidence of the organizational consolidation of such functions in their own societies is to be found in the building industry as a result of the specific market conditions of this branch. This development naturally did not imply any recognition of the trade unions as partners for negotiation and wage agreement in their own right, although as time went by collective industrial agreements became more and more unavoidable.[39]

Seidel's observation on the bunching of learning experiences in situations of conflict also ties in well with some widely known insights of the more recent sociology of conflict from Georg Simmel to Lewis A. Coser.[40] Simmel has already emphasized that new norms are created in the course of conflict and old norms are modified, while more recent investigations attribute decisive importance to 'the phenomenon of communication as the specific motivating principle of social consciousness'[41] and for 'the comprehension of conflict situations'.[42]

In the wake of escalating class antagonism communication networks are greatly stimulated and partly established anew within the framework of the existing way of exchanging experiences at the workplace, in the community, in associations and elsewhere. The framework is generally determined by the market situation in the various affected trades. An indispensable role is then assigned to the available channels of communication which spread knowledge of the conflict beyond the local area. This is why the early labour and trade union press was so important, as described in 1869 as follows: 'As speech is to sociable people, so the press organ is to a movement spread over towns and the countryside. There is no possibility of effective opposition against the enemy, no enduring enlightenment of the masses, in a word no progress is possible, without the mighty sword of the press.'[43]

A whole array of evidence demonstrating the huge increase in importance of the labour press as a channel of information and as the means by which an exchange of experiences extends across different regions during times of dispute can be presented, based, for example, on increased subscriber figures, the type of reporting, or the organization of collection campaigns.[44] Although such an intensification of the network of communication may have been stimulated by current strikes in some cases, it was obviously also based on a more far-reaching process which not only found expression in the press but stemmed from the rhythm of economic growth. Earlier studies of strikes[45] have already indicated that collective conflicts over wages and working conditions reveal a clear numerical increase in times of economic upswing, if not in terms of the numbers of actual participants and their duration. More recent investigations have confirmed and further differentiated this observation, even going so far as to establish regular time-lags between economy rhythms and strike movements.[46] It must further be noted, as Eric J. Hobsbawm has shown,[47] that there are marked peaks even in the seasonal variation of labour disputes, as in spring and, to a lesser extent, in October, which are typified by increased mobility amongst wide sectors of the population. The origin of this mobility is controversial. However, the general consensus tends towards an economic interpretation related to the labour market and which can be most easily traced in the case of servants, agricultural labourers and workers in the building trade. More importantly it seems that an existing strike propensity is not solely achieved by a network of regulated exchanges of information and ideas but also by psychological developments which tend to activate the links and relationship between those affected in the same way.

On the other hand, once created and accepted by at least a nucleus of members and sympathizers, stable trade union organizations have a basically new influence on the original relationship between conflict and organization. The trade union movement did not simply form and stimulate organizational potential by its example, but also and primarily by its active influence, particularly after central organization had evolved, so that the development of organizations out of a conflict situation received a different emphasis. On the other hand, the conflict situations retained their original function of stimulating organization in spite of the inherent union tendency to substitute for potentially damaging disputes a permanent presence. Thus, those local organizations of individual trades which had previously kept their distance from the appropriate trade union central associations tended to join existing associations in the course of current disputes, albeit often only for financial reasons. Where trade union organization demonstrably stemmed from former provident funds and educational institutions, collective conflicts more or less impelled the organization towards adequate techniques of struggle and forms of organization, as can be observed, for example, in the development of strike regulations.[48] In addition, successful strikes generally confirmed and strengthened existing organizations, whereas strike defeats could jeopardize the existence of local societies and whole associations. Such experiences were the main reason for the tendency of the trade unions to avoid strikes, often at all costs – quite contrary to the prevalent slanderous public opinion.[49] This attitude obviously provoked internal disputes. One could even go so far as to postulate that the formation of a union actually allowed the potential for conflict outside the union to be tamed. In addition, existing capacity for conflict in individual trades was channelled and rationalized by the formation of a trade union organization, for example by calculating the chances of success with special reference to the market and the economic climate. The organization also tended to utilize a sluggish economic climate to extend and consolidate its structure. From the early 1890s Carl Legien, who had almost alone recognized the hidden rhythm underlying the development of the trade unions, thus developed a masterly technique of leadership,[50] in which he was aided by the formation of the *Generalkommission*, the umbrella executive of the Free Trade Unions. Thus the trade union organizations provided the network and the means for the workers to look to the future.

IV

However, this takes us beyond the phase of development of the German trade union movement under discussion here. During this phase in which the unions were founded, that is, up to about 1890, trade union formation was most strongly stimulated by disputes which increasingly arose from the central conflict of interests within the capitalist mode of production. A focal point of the argument pursued here has been that this phase was disrupted by practices of state intervention in a particularly sensitive area, namely, where potential for conflict was built up by a network of communication. The state acted against democratic processes of decision-making by any assembly of the workers concerned and, in addition, against all burgeoning local and central trade union organizations. This phase was thus prolonged artificially. There is no doubt that, freed from continued state repression, the German trade union movement would have developed fully as early as the 1870s, and would have created a mass organization of the most important branches of industry and an efficient federation, as has been clearly demonstrated by the example of the Essen strike of 1872. The emerging trade union central associations had already broken free from the clutches of party politics at an early point in the case of the printers, and in other branches, at the latest after the notorious 'coup' of Johann Baptist von Schweitzer, the 'dictator' of the ADAV, in 1869, when Lassalleanism returned to the straight and narrow orthodoxy on trade union questions. By then neutrality and trade union autonomy had become a centre-piece of their policies.[51]

The concept of organization had been spread and firmly established as a result of rapidly assimilated learning processes, not only in the tightly organized central associations of craft workers, but also in the case of factory workers and, as already mentioned, the miners, though naturally there were important regional variations. Furthermore, from 1871 onwards there were attempts, closely associated with the names of August Geib and Theodor York, to found a trade union federation. These attempts, which were finally to be realized in 1890, naturally met with widespread opposition, including that from an older generation of artisans, but would none the less almost have been crowned with success before the *Sozialistengesetz* was passed, had they not, on the other hand, been thwarted by the police state, that is, the behaviour the German Empire displayed in questions concerning the workers.[52] And finally, a word about the *Sozialistengesetz* after 1878. After the enforced 'quiet of the graveyard'[53] during the early years the law was in force, the state had scarcely begun to introduce 'positive' recompense in the period of 'mild practice' in the form of the famous welfare legislation[54] and the granting of some latitude for trade union activity, when the basic connection between conflict and organization associated with the business cycle re-established itself, a factor which motivated the notorious 1886 strike decree of the Prussian minister Robert von Puttkamer and once again brought an end to any willingness to make concessions, at least as far as Prussia was concerned.[55] Once again, it was the blow aimed against the rights of assembly and combination which was to strike at the very heart of emancipation. Thus, during the last years of the *Sozialistengesetz* the readiness for conflict remained dammed up and the formation of trade unions had to walk a tight-rope of legal restrictions on association until the floodgates were opened after 1888 to release a strike wave of unprecedented dimensions. The pressure to organize could no longer be contained. This clearly demonstrated the failure of repression by means of emergency legislation and the indomitability of the labour movement.

This artificial prolongation and postponement of the process of trade union formation as a result of state intervention must be considered as one of the many aspects of a Prusso-German *Sonderweg* towards the modern industrial state which, in part, had its origin in the discrepancy between socio-economic and socio-political developments. Those social historians who consider trade union formation to display a relatively extensive autonomy within the framework of the structural changes of an industrial society will thus, in the end, have to look to the formative influence of the socio-political system in the case of Germany. In fact the Prusso-German constitutional system was no mere constitutional form but far rather a social reality.[56] This was revealed not only in substantial obstacles to political participation but extended to the class-specific processes of socialization in a society determined by pre-industrial status allocation, into the conflict-ridden daily life of the worker in the factory and into the community. What was fatal about this situation was that it was only too easy in the end to cover and disguise economic interests with apparently non-economic aspirations and objectives. To take just one example: the mutually beneficial protectionism of industrialists and the large landowners after the introduction of protective tariffs in the late 1870s actually concealed a type of second, secret anti-socialist law, which was intended to consolidate conservatism against the forces of reform.

V

The early history of the German labour movement displays certain decisive characteristics which can only be attributed to the specific development of modern Germany. This applies, for example to the 'premature' foundation of a labour party, as it has been described, even before any basic structure of trade union organization had evolved,[57] and to the specifically state-oriented position of this party.[58] It also applies to its theoretical radicalism and its fear of practical politics in spite of its growing appeal to the working class. It applies to the form in which the process of structural differentiation between the middle classes and the working classes expressed itself at a time of belated and enforced unification into a nation state;[59] and it applies, perhaps to an even greater extent, to the political and intellectual predilections of the class adversary, the capitalist middle classes, since their retreat from democracy after the unsuccessful revolution of 1848–9. The early, pre-industrial development of a well-planned bureaucracy, which soon involved large numbers of civil servants and was highly efficient, had an impact on the values and the behaviour even of the working class. This impact can hardly be overrated. It can also be seen in the industrial bureaucracy of the 'constitutional factories' of the Wilhelmine period.[60]

The belief that the foundation of the German Social Democratic Party was 'premature' is based on the concept of a so-called 'normal' pattern of development in the labour movement: structural change, conflict, trade unions, political party. In fact, as can be demonstrated simply by regional comparisons within the empire, without the critical disruption of the process of trade union formation by the authoritarian state, the labour force would hardly have been likely to resort to methods of political influence, for example through the suffrage agitation inspired by Lassalle, quite so rapidly in its attempt to achieve a minimum of legal preconditions for the undisturbed development of trade unions. It is hardly surprising that an appeal to the state in a country where Manchester liberalism and its regulating social implications remained, in the long run, a mere politico-economic episode and had little effect on the traditional high esteem in which state action was held, was also a prevalent attitude among the early trade unions, in spite, and also because of constant daily experiences of repression.

The artificial delay in the initial phase was of course not always a disadvantage for the German trade unions. Thus they were able to rely on well-developed self-confidence and class-consciousness amongst the industrial workers when the modern trade union structure was established within a few months in 1889–90, and after it had survived its first real test in the subsequent years of crisis. It was a class-consciousness whose thirst for action had been dammed up in the years of oppression and had burst the bounds of traditional trade exclusivity long ago. It was the state which, in its ignorance, had stimulated the rapid conquest of elitist guild traditions and had accelerated the development of modern means of interest articulation which transcended individual trades and involved modern, centralist inter-industrial forms of organization. The disputes of the 1890s about the principles of trade union organization and the localist challenge appear as rearguard actions whose long-term effect may be considered of little importance. In the same way the German trade unions were able to hold their own against syndicalist concepts right up to the postwar era.[61] The British example shows that a decision in favour of an organizational structure closely related to the shop, which would have been quite possible in Germany, would have left its mark and would, in the long term, certainly have restricted the capacity for struggle. In passing, it is interesting to note the specific modernity of political objectives in the German trade unions which is evident, for example, in reactions to the deskilling of organized trade union members – although the problem was probably of less importance in Germany – and in the continued positive acceptance of technological progress up to the present day.[62] Under these circumstances, it is perfectly legitimate to argue that it was actually the very backwardness of the socio-political system which impelled the German trade unions and the forms and methods of pressure group struggle in general towards a relatively modern route at the turn of the century.[63]

Notes: Chapter 11

1 E. J. Hobsbawm, 'The machine breakers', in idem, *Labouring Men* (London, 1964), 5–22; M. Henkel and R. Taubert, *Maschinenstürmer. Ein Kapitel aus der Sozialgeschichte des technischen Fortschritts* (Frankfurt a.M., 1979).

2 cf. B. Flohr, *Arbeiter nach Mass. Die Disziplinierung der Fabrikarbeiterschaft während der Industrialisierung Deutschlands im Spiegel von Arbeitsordnungen* (Frankfurt a.M., 1981), 96.

3 cf. inter alia H. Hübner and H. Kathe (eds), *Lage und Kampf der Landarbeiter im ostelbischen Preussen. Vom Anfang des 19. Jahrhunderts bis zur Novemberrevolution 1918–19*, 2 vols (Berlin, 1977); P. Borscheid, *Textilarbeiterschaft in der Industrialisierung. Soziale Lage und Mobilität in Württemberg (19. Jahrhundert)* (Stuttgart, 1978); see also K. Tenfelde, 'Bis vor die Stufen des Throns. Bittschriften und Beschwerden der Ruhrbergleute 1830 bis 1900', in K. Bergmann and R. Schörken (eds), *Geschichte im Alltag – Alltag in der Geschichte* (Düsseldorf, 1982), 30–56.

4 H. Bleiber, *Zwischen Reform und Revolution. Lage und Kämpfe der schlesischen Bauern und Landarbeiter im Vormärz 1840–1847* (Berlin, 1966), 160; R. Moldenhauer, 'Die Petitionen aus Kreis und Stadt Wetzlar an die Deutsche Nationalversammlung 1848/49', *Mitteilungen des Wetzlarer Geschichtsvereins* 23 (1967); B. Moore, *Injustice. The Social Bases of Obedience and Revolt* (London, 1979), 124, 471.

5 e.g. V. A. Huber, *Reisebriefe aus England im Sommer 1854* (Hamburg, 1855); L. Brentano, *Die Arbeitergilden der Gegenwart* 2 vols (Leipzig, 1872–73).

6 Numerous references in U. Engelhardt, *'Nur vereinigt sind wir stark'. Die Anfänge der deutschen Gewerkschaftsbewegung 1862/63 bis 1869/70*, 2 vols (Stuttgart, 1977), *passim*.

7 cf. G. Schmoller, 'Arbeitseinstellungen und Gewerkvereine', *Jahrbücher für Nationalökonomie und Statistik* 19 (1872): 293–320.

8 A. Griessinger, *Das symbolische Kapital der Ehre. Streikbewegungen und kollektives Bewusstsein deutscher Handwerksgesellen im 18. Jahrhundert* (Frankfurt a.M., 1981), 255–85; on earlier strikes see also R. Lison, 'Produktion – Proletariat – Protest. Zum Konstitutionszusammenhang von Streik und Gewerkschaft', in *Entstehung der Arbeiterbewegung* (Berlin, 1981), 152–78.

9 Still the most comprehensive discussion of Prussian authoritarian repression is H. Rosenberg, *Grosse Depression und Bismarckzeit. Wirtschaftsablauf, Gesellschaft und Politik in Mitteleuropa* (Berlin, 1967), 204, 206. Repression is accentuated differently, for example in the form of an employers' patriarchalism that adapted the authoritarian attitudes of the state authorities, by the 'Sonderweg' critics. cf. for example D. G. Crew, *Town in the Ruhr. A Social History of Bochum, 1860–1914* (New York, 1979), 2–5, but see p. 156. See esp. J. Kocka, 'Capitalism and bureaucracy in German industrialization before 1914', *Economic History Review* 33 (1981): 453–68.

10 K. Saul, 'Zwischen Repression und Integration. Staat, Gewerkschaften und Arbeitskampf

im kaiserlichen Deutschland, 1884–1914', in K. Tenfelde and H. Volkmann (eds), *Streik. Zur Geschichte des Arbeitskampfes in Deutschland während der Industrialisierung* (Munich, 1981), 209–36.

11 Engelhardt, '*Nur vereinigt sind wir stark*', 2:1006; cf. my review: *Archiv für Sozialgeschichte* 21 (1981): 702–8.

12 For details on the problem of definition (social conflict, social protest, labour struggle): Tenfelde and Volkmann, *Streik*, Introduction, pp. 12–14.

13 On the following, K. Tenfelde, *Sozialgeschichte der Bergarbeiterschaft an der Ruhr im 19. Jahrhundert*, 2nd edn (Bonn, 1981), 470–86.

14 Printed: H. Imbusch, *Arbeitsverhältnis und Arbeiterorganisation im deutschen Bergbau. Eine geschichtliche Darstellung* (Essen, 1908). Reprinted with an introduction by K. Tenfelde (Berlin, 1980), 685–8.

15 *Der Bote vom Niederrhein*, 25–28 February 1866.

16 G. Schwittau, *Die Formen wirtschaftlichen Kampfes (Streik, Boykott, Aussperrung usw.). Eine volkswirtschaftliche Untersuchung auf dem Gebiete der gegenwärtigen Arbeiterpolitik* (Berlin, 1912), 69.

17 Numerous references in Engelhardt, '*Nur vereinigt sind wir stark*', esp. 1:310–12, 472–4.

18 cf. K. Tenfelde, 'Konflikt und Organisation in einigen deutschen Bergbaugebieten 1867–1872', *Geschichte und Gesellschaft* 3 (1977): 212–35.

19 E. Schmidt, 'Erster Massenstreik der Bergleute. Essen im Jahre 1872', *Das Münster am Hellweg* 25 (1972): 107–28.

20 D. Dowe, 'Legale Interessenvertretung und Streik. Der Arbeitskampf in den Tuchfabriken des Kreises Lennep (Bergisches Land) 1850', in Tenfelde and Volkmann, *Streik*, 31–51, quotation p. 31, from an appeal by the strikers to the public (*Trier'sche Zeitung*, no. 285/1850) a few days after the start of the strike.

21 cf. esp. T. Offermann, *Arbeiterbewegung und liberales Bürgertum in Deutschland 1850–1963* (Bonn, 1979), 146–53; on earlier research E. Todt, *Die gewerkschaftliche Betätigung in Deutschland von 1850 bis 1859* (Berlin, 1950), 166.

22 H. Volkmann, 'Modernisierung des Arbeitskampfes? Zum Formwandel von Streik und Aussperrung in Deutschland 1864–1972', in H. Kaelble *et al.*, *Probleme der Modernisierung in Deutschland. Sozialhistorische Studien zum 19. und 20. Jahrhundert* (Opladen, 1978), 110–70 (140).

23 H. Schlechte (ed.) *Die Allgemeine Deutsche Arbeiterverbrüderung 1848–1850. Dokumente des Zentralkomitees für die deutschen Arbeiter in Leipzig* (Weimar, 1979), 174–82, 330–1.

24 U. Engelhardt, 'Arbeitskämpfe als Instrument der Lageverbesserung? Zur Motivation, Zielsetzung und Effizienz von Streikbewegungen in der Vorbereitungs- und Konstituierungsphase der Gewerkschaftsbewegung', in W. Conze and U. Engelhardt (eds), *Arbeiterexistenz im 19. Jahrhundert. Lebensstandard und Lebensgestaltung deutscher Arbeiter und Handwerker* (Stuttgart, 1981), 385–409 (393).

25 Documented in detail: Staatsarchiv Hamburg, Politische Polizei V 142a, 265.

26 cf. G. A. Ritter, *Arbeiterbewegung, Parteien und Parlamentarismus. Aufsätze zur Sozial- und Verfassungsgeschichte des 19. und 20. Jahrhunderts* (Göttingen, 1976), 71–4.

27 An example in G. Schulz, *Die Arbeiter und Angestellten bei Felten & Guilleaume. Sozialgeschichtliche Untersuchung eines Kölner Industrieunternehmens im 19. und beginnenden 20. Jahrhundert* (Wiesbaden, 1979), 331; for the activity of a workers' commission see esp. R. Vetterli, *Industriearbeit, Arbeiterbewußtsein und gewerkschaftliche Organisation. Dargestellt am Beispiel der Georg Fischer AG (1890–1930)* (Göttingen, 1978), 147–9; cf. also Flohr, *Arbeiter nach Mass*, 68–70.

28 cf. esp. E. Gruner, 'Der Klassenkampf als formendes Element der neuesten Geschichte', *Schweizer Beiträge zur Allgemeinen Geschichte* 18/19 (1960–1): 475–506; more precise causes of individual strike waves are examined by E. J. Hobsbawm, 'Economic fluctuations and some social movements since 1800', in idem, *Labouring Men*, 126–57; for a comparison see for example E. Flow and M. Katauka (eds), *1868 – Year of the Unions. A Documentary Survey* (London, 1968).

29 As examples see H. Müller, *Die Organisationen der Lithographen, Steindrucker und verwandten Berufe* (Berlin, 1917); reprinted with an introduction by W. Albrecht (Berlin, 1978), 482–4; A. Bringmann, *Geschichte der deutschen Zimmerer-Bewegung*, Vol. 2 (Hamburg, 1905); reprinted with an introduction by G. Beier (Berlin, 1981), 4–6 and

passim; F. Paeplow, *Zur Geschichte der deutschen Bauarbeiterbewegung. Werden des deutschen Bauwerkbundes* (n.p., n.d. [1932]), 263–5 and *passim*. See also G. Beier, *Schwarze Kunst und Klassenkampf*, Vol. 1 (Frankfurt a.M., 1966), who stimulated historiography on trade unions. He separates his analysis of the famous *Dreigroschenstreik* (pp. 346–8) from his treatment of the unions' foundation (pp. 376–8).

30 ibid., 376. cf. also U. Engelhardt, 'Zur Entwicklung der Streikbewegungen in der ersten Industrialisierungsphase und zur Funktion von Streiks bei der Konstituierung der Gewerkschaftsbewegung in Deutschland', *Internationale Wissenschaftliche Korrespondenz zur Geschichte der deutschen Arbeiterbewegung* 15 (1979): 547–69 (557–9).

31 Engelhardt, '*Nur vereinigt sind wir stark*', 1:379–81.

32 cf. H. Laufenberg, *Geschichte der Arbeiterbewegung in Hamburg, Altona und Umgegend*, Vol. 1 (Hamburg, 1911; reprinted Berlin, 1977), 182; using the example of the dock workers in 1864, briefly on this topic D. Geary, *European Labour Protest 1848–1939* (London, 1981), 40.

33 Engelhardt, '*Nur vereinigt sind wir stark*', 1:495. For the influence of the trade unions on strike behaviour in general see D. Snyder, 'Determinants of industrial conflict. Historical models of strikes in France, Italy and the United States' (PhD. thesis, University of Michigan, 1974), 73ff.

34 cf. *Marx-Engels-Werke*, Vol. 4 (Berlin, 1974), 471; further references in W. Ettelt and W. Schröder, 'Zur Rolle der Gewerkschaftsbewegung bei der Herausbildung der "Eisenacher" Partei', in H. Bartel and E. Engelberg (eds.), *Die grosspreussisch-militaristische Reichsgründung 1871. Voraussetzungen und Folgen*, Vol. 1 (Berlin, 1971), 552–97 (560–4); also W. Ettelt and H.-D. Krause, *Der Kampf um eine marxistische Gewerkschaftspolitik in der deutschen Arbeiterbewegung 1868 bis 1878* (Berlin, 1975), 28–37.

35 C. Stegmann and C. Hugo, *Handbuch des Socialismus* (Zürich, 1897), reprinted Leipzig, 1972, 786.

36 cf. S. Webb and B. Webb, *The History of Trade Unionism* (London, 1894), 22.

37 'Streiks als Wegbereiter der Gewerkschaften' in *Die Arbeit* 7 (1930): 396–405. There is occasional criticism of this interpretation in Engelhardt, '*Nur vereinigt sind wir stark*', 1:107–9, 367.

38 cf. H.-P. Ullmann, 'Unternehmerschaft, Arbeitgeberverbände und Streikbewegung 1890–1914', in Tenfelde and Volkmann, *Streik*, 194–208.

39 cf. esp. K. Megerle, 'Zur Entstehung von Arbeitgebervereinigungen. Überlegungen am Beispiel des Heidenheimer Fabrikantenvereins von 1835', *Geschichte und Gesellschaft* 6 (1980): 189–219; on the building trade see W. Renzsch, *Handwerker und Lohnarbeiter in der frühen Arbeiterbewegung. Zur sozialen Basis von Gewerkschaften und Sozialdemokratie im Reichsgründungsjahrzehnt* (Göttingen, 1980), 46–63; on mining see Tenfelde, *Sozialgeschichte der Bergarbeiterschaft* 217 and *passim*.

40 cf. L. A. Coser, *Theorie sozialer Konflikte* (Neuwied, 1972), 142–4.

41 H. J. Krysmanski, *Soziologie des Konflikts. Materialien und Modelle* (Reinbek b. Hamburg, 1975), 113.

42 W. M. Esser, *Individuelles Konfliktverhalten in Organisationen* (Stuttgart, 1975), 82.

43 Quoted in Engelhardt, '*Nur vereinigt sind wir stark*', 2:873.

44 cf. for example the collection campaign on the occasion of the Waldenburg miners' strike in 1869: ibid., 1146–60.

45 cf. the contributions by K. Oldenberg in the various editions of the *Handwörterbuch der Staatswissenschaften*, esp.: *Die Arbeitseinstellungen in den einzelnen Staaten*, Vol. 1, 3rd edn (Jena, 1909), 927–64.

46 cf. J. Bouvier, 'Arbeiterbewegung und Wirtschaftskonjunkturen', in G. Ziebura (ed.), *Wirtschaft und Gesellschaft in Frankreich seit 1789* (Cologne, 1975), 250–65 (257); H. Kaelble and H. Volkmann, 'Konjunktur und Streik während des Übergangs zum organisierten Kapitalismus in Deutschland', *Zeitschrift für Wirtschafts- und Sozialwissenschaften* 92/II (1972): 513–44 (516–18).

47 Hobsbawm, 'Economic fluctuations', 131.

48 cf. e. g. J. Schmöle, *Die sozialdemokratischen Gewerkschaften in Deutschland seit dem Erlasse des Sozialisten-Gesetzes*, Vol. II/1, *Der Zimmererverband* (Jena, 1898), 74–5, 156, 178–80.

49 See Tenfelde and Volkmann, *Streik*, Introduction, p. 21.

50 cf. Ritter, *Arbeiterbewegung, Parteien und Parlamentarismus*, 75–7, with numerous references to Legien's original call for organization in the *Correspondenzblatt*.

51 cf. as well as the numerous references in Engelhardt, '*Nur vereinigt sind wir stark*', *passim*, the source collection by U. Borsdorf *et al.* (eds), *Grundlagen der Einheitsgewerkschaft. Historische Dokumente und Materialien* (Cologne, 1977), 15–17.

52 cf. for example Bringmann, *Zimmerer-Bewegung*, 1:194–6 and *passim*.

53 E. Basner, *Geschichte der deutschen Schmiedebewegung*, Vol. 1 (Hamburg, 1912), 60.

54 cf. G. A. Ritter, *Sozialversicherung in Deutschland und England. Entstehung und Grundzüge im Vergleich* (Munich, 1982).

55 cf. the synopsis by Ritter, *Arbeiterbewegung, Parteien und Parlamentarismus*, 60–71; see also *Die Lohnbewegung der Tischler in Hannover-Linden in den Jahren 1883 und 1884 nebst Bericht und Abrechnung der Kommission*, ed. J. Riedmann (Hanover, n.d. [1884]), which stresses the importance of the workers' statistics for a long-term calculation of the struggle; see also H. Bürger, *Die Hamburger Gewerkschaften und deren Kämpfe von 1865 bis 1890* (Hamburg, 1898); H. Müller, 'Der Rathenower Bauarbeiterstreik von 1885 und die Berliner Politische Polizei', *Jahrbuch für Wirtschaftsgeschichte* (1972/III): 63–76; for the strike edict see for example I. Auer, *Nach zehn Jahren. Material und Glossen zur Geschichte des Sozialistengesetzes*, 2nd edn (Nuremberg, 1913), pp. 146–8.

56 cf. G. A. Ritter, 'Entwicklungsprobleme des deutschen Parlamentarismus', in idem (ed.), *Gesellschaft, Parlament und Regierung. Zur Geschichte des Parlamentarismus in Deutschland* (Düsseldorf, 1974), 11–54.

57 cf. W. Schieder, 'Das Scheitern des bürgerlichen Radikalismus und die sozialdemokratische Parteibildung in Deutschland', in H. Mommsen (ed.), *Sozialdemokratie zwischen Klassenbewegung und Volkspartei* (Frankfurt a.M., 1974), 17–34.

58 G. A. Ritter, *Staat, Arbeiterschaft und Arbeiterbewegung in Deutschland. Vom Vormärz bis zum Ende der Weimarer Republik* (Berlin, 1980), 69–71.

59 cf. G. Mayer, 'Die Trennung der proletarischen von der bürgerlichen Demokratie in Deutschland 1863–1870', in idem, *Radikalismus, Sozialismus und bürgerliche Demokratie*, ed. by H.-U. Wehler (Frankfurt a.M., 1969), 108–78; H. A. Winkler, 'Wandlungen des deutschen Nationalismus', *Merkur* 33 (1979): 963–73; J. J. Sheehan, 'What is German history? Reflections on the role of the nation in German history and historiography', *Journal of Modern History* 53 (1981): 1–23.

60 cf. esp. Kocka, *Capitalism and Bureaucracy*; idem, *Die Angestellten in der deutschen Geschichte. Vom Privatbeamten zum angestellten Arbeitnehmer* (Göttingen, 1981), 64–6.

61 cf. esp. K. Schönhoven, *Expansion und Konzentration. Studien zur Entwicklung der Freien Gewerkschaften im Wilhelminischen Deutschland 1890 bis 1914* (Stuttgart, 1980).

62 cf. J. Kocka, 'Gewerkschaftliche Interessenvertretung und gesellschaftlicher Fortschritt. Historische Überlegungen zur deutschen Entwicklung im 19. und 20. Jahrhundert', *Gewerkschaftliche Monatshefte* 32 (1981): 319–36.

63 cf. G. D. Feldman, 'German interest group alliances in war and inflation, 1914–1923', in S. Berger (ed.), *Organizing Interests in Western Europe: Pluralism, Corporatism and the Transformation of Politics* (Cambridge, 1981), 159–84 (162); see also G. Beier, 'Kontinuität und Diskontinuität gewerkschaftlicher Organisationen unter dem "Sozialistengesetz",' in D. Döring and O. E. Kempen (eds), *Arbeiterbewegung und Demokratie* (Cologne, 1979), 76–95, esp. 92–4.

12 Localism – Craft Union – Industrial Union: Organizational Patterns in German Trade Unionism

KLAUS SCHÖNHOVEN

I

The quarter century between the abolition of the *Sozialistengesetz* (Anti-Socialist Law) in the autumn of 1890 and the beginning of the First World War in the summer of 1914 was a period which determined the long-term development of the German trade union movement. During these two-and-a-half decades the unions became a movement of millions of people and the largest mass organization of the German working class. The unions extended beyond their craft base and expanded their regional foundations. They changed their internal institutions and developed self-help institutions. They became financially stronger and stabilized their organizational structure. The rapid increase in membership made a bureaucratic structure and full-time officials necessary. Thus, vertically structured administrative districts had to be created and formal statutes had to be drawn up specifying the various levels of delegation and leadership. A trade union constitution developed which remained valid during the Weimar Republic and, in its essential features, also determined the reorganization of the trade union movement after 1945.

The extension of the organizational power of the union movement during the Wilhelmine Empire also strengthened the position of individual unions in the labour market. Their weight as negotiating partners of employers during labour disputes increased. They consolidated their position as collective representatives of the workers' interests during conflicts over wage agreements. It was, therefore, not without pride that a jubilee publication in 1915 referred to the 'victorious breakthrough' of the concept of unionism, emphasizing that, during the twenty-five years from 1890 onwards, the unions had achieved an impressive size.[1]

Some light will be shed on the background to the organizational structure of union expansion below. We will also ask what organizational form the collective consciousness of labour took, and how working-class solidarity was strengthened. At the same time the difficulties of decision-making inside the mass organizations will be outlined. These organizations had centralized decision-making responsibilities and introduced various stages of representative participation for members while abolishing models of

direct democracy to determine the wishes of the rank and file. The centralization of the trade union organizations in Germany began comparatively
early. Therefore, this analysis has to start with a brief review of the phase in
which the trade union movement was reconstructed during the special legal
situation created by the *Sozialistengesetz*. Then we will deal with the internal
debates and the organizational principles of the years immediately after
1890. And finally, the individual stages of consolidation and concentration
of trade union organizational structures will be examined. The Free Trade
Unions are the main subject of the essay. Their membership and importance
was not even nearly matched by the other two German trade union
organizations, the Hirsch-Duncker Trades Associations and the Christian
Trade Unions. But our concentration on the social democratic trade union
movement is also justifiable because the non-socialist union associations did
not experience any comparable internal controversies; nor did they face
decisions of such fundamental importance for the shape and structure of
their organisations.

II

At the beginning of October 1890, when the shackles of the *Sozialistengesetz*
were removed and the social democratic unions regained their freedom to
manoeuvre, the existing associations presented a colourful picture. During
the twelve years of state repression a network of various organizations had
gradually developed. These organizations had taken on trade union tasks
and served the working class as vehicles for articulating their protests and
interests. Partly the result of improvisation, they had been founded without
central guidance. They included a wide range of associations, from isolated
local clubs, which met only sporadically, to craft associations on a national
scale, which maintained regular communications through confidential
agents, or had at least created informal communication channels through
their own trade papers. In addition there were local support funds for the
sick, for intinerant workers and for dependents of those who died. These
funds served as social self-help institutions for the working class and as cover
organizations for the union movement while it was under police surveillance. The most widespread organizations were the local craft associations,
based on the traditional artisans. The close local ties of these clubs had a
twofold advantage. On the one hand, clubs at local level were more
manageable and easier to protect against state prosecution. On the other
hand, a more lasting feeling of solidarity could develop within a circle of
familiar colleagues because the workers continued social traditions and
mutual welfare provisions dating back to the time of the guilds. Furthermore, they accepted the same values and norms developed during their
common working life, which facilitated organization.

The statistical data available for the period show that the crafts predominated among the trade union organizations in the 1880s. At the end of 1882
in Hamburg, for example, there were independent craft associations for
engravers, brushmakers, basket-makers, cartwrights, masons, ships' car-

penters, blacksmiths, shoemakers, ropemakers and twisters, decorators, goldplaters, dockers, cigar and cigarette makers.[2] These clubs which concentrated their organization on narrowly defined, specific crafts formed the new local cores for the reconstruction of the trade union movement. They also continued the traditions interrupted by the *Sozialistengesetz* when it came into force in the autumn of 1878.

The reconstruction and development of the central organizations took a similar course. These organizations went beyond local level, but the creation of their structures was based on rather informal procedures. The thirteen organizations listed by the Berlin police authorities at the end of 1884 included eleven associations of craft-trades, in part highly skilled. Only the tobacco workers' associations, whose roots went back to the revolution of 1848–9, and the association of manufacturing workers, the predecessor of the textile workers' union, did not concentrate their recruitment on the crafts. Both associations looked after the employees of a whole industrial branch and took in unskilled workers and women as members, an unusual organizational concept for the German unions of this period.

Craft unions remained the favoured form of union organization even at a time when a great number of new unions were formed as a result of widespread strikes during the last years of the *Sozialistengesetz*. Of the fifty-eight central organizations of the Free Trade Unions which existed in 1890,[3] the vast majority confined themselves to a particular trade. And the handicraft trades remained predominant. However, from the size of membership, it is evident that in addition to craft workers, important centres of union organization had evolved in raw material production, transport and the processing industries. In particular the unions of the miners, dockers and metalworkers should be mentioned. Together with the older tobacco workers' association and the organizations of the unskilled factory workers and building labourers, they contained one-third of the almost 300,000 union members at the end of 1890.

It was already obvious at this time that the trade union movement was shifting towards previously unorganized industrial branches and occupations. But the majority of union members still came from small and medium-sized firms, in which the employees had been through an apprenticeship of several years. These highly skilled workers had scarcely been affected by industrialization. They worked mainly in branches of production hardly touched by mechanization and in which manual skills were in particular demand. Despite the fact that industrial reality with its deskilling effects had not yet reached them personally, they decided to break with old guild traditions and journeymen's associations and opted for unionization. This is particularly true of the urban workers, who were the backbone of the union movement and showed much greater interest in union organization than their colleagues in rural areas. These urban groups had quickly recognized the dynamism of industrial development and the social and economic changes deriving from it, and their consciousness changed. This was shown in the fact that they turned away from guild-oriented behaviour and organizations and accepted the principle of union representation.

However, this change did not take the form of a radical break with craft traditions. Rather it was a learning process of variable duration, depending on each individual trade association. Initially the associations founded towards the end of the *Sozialistengesetz* departed from their familiar craft orientation only in exceptional cases. The majority of organizations upheld their craft tradition and accepted only skilled workers as members. During the 1890s and shortly after the turn of the century virtually all associations dropped this narrow definition of a trade. Only some organizations, such as the printers' associations, retained their exclusive position until 1914. In the majority of cases, however, the extension of unionization to include semi-skilled and unskilled workers of the same industrial sector was forced upon the organizations by the further division of labour. The increasing mechanization of the working process, the introduction of production methods based on the division of labour and the continuous expansion of industrial factories changed traditional skills and crafts. Distinctions between groups of workers according to their qualifications disappeared. The number of semi-skilled and unskilled workers in the expanding old industrial sectors increased in the same way as in the new large factories of the chemical and electrical industry. Therefore, extending recruitment to those groups of workers who had no apprenticeship or artisans' certificate was practically a question of survival for many trade unions.

III

In the years immediately after 1890, however, the main question was what organizational structure the unions should take. A debate was conducted which sometimes took passionate forms. The future of the craft unions and the possibility of institutionalized co-operation between central union organizations of similar occupations were discussed. An argument also developed over the principle of centralization and whether it actually could provide a working basis for the German trade union movement. Ostensibly, the subject of this discussion was whether independent local unions could exist beside the centralized trade unions without being strictly organized and without centralized bureaucracies and decision-making structures. But behind the argument about centralism and localism lay far-reaching differences about the ideology, the concept, the character and the tasks of trade unions. These debates were superseded by the controversy about organization. A decision had to be taken on the extent of the representative principle within the unions, that is, on internal union democracy, and also on the role of trade union interest-politics with regard to the emancipation of the working class.

The local clubs which had been formed during the first years of the *Sozialistengesetz* had often functioned both as trade union offices and as secret meeting places for the outlawed socialists. This double role of economic and political centres of the labour movement went unchallenged where neither the party nor the unions had superior local channels of communication or organizational structures. But from the mid-1880s the local clubs gradually lost this unrivalled key position because by then numerous national trade union organizations had been set up which incorporated existing craft associations and, at the same time, tried to restrict the autonomous tendencies of local groups. The continued existence of an independent local movement was even more threatened when the *Sozialistengesetz* expired and the Social Democratic Party was able to rebuild its own local organization in the autumn of 1890.

The localists had internal differences, and developed contradictory strategies in their various urban strongholds.[4] In Berlin, in particular, a movement opposed to the liquidation of localism emerged which stubbornly fought to retain local self-determination within the unions and strongly rejected submission to a central leadership. The localist groups there drew strong support from the building industry, where the degree of mechanization was low and small companies were dominant. In addition, there were some specialized crafts which employed a small number of people (tile-setters, instrument-makers, piano-makers, basket-makers, box-makers, cane workers, potters, pewterers). They catered exclusively for urban demands, and their conditions of work and wages depended entirely on the local situation. They simply had no interest in a national organization because they could hardly organize the members of their occupation, who were dispersed all over the country. They were thus not even in a position to form their own powerful organization. But they had serious doubts about joining a larger union representing a similar occupation, because these specialist workers feared that their particular interests would not be sufficiently taken into account.

The Berlin metalworkers, carriers working in commerce and transport, domestic servants, coal workers, packers, storehands and market labourers had different reasons for opting for a local union organization. Until 1896 there was no central union organization for the heterogeneous groups of workers in the service industries which they could have joined. There was no common professional interest amongst those workers, and union solidarity beyond their immediate occupational sphere had to be developed gradually. After an initial struggle against localist competition the union which was founded in 1896 successfully managed to integrate these groups in Berlin within ten years. The metalworkers of the capital defended their local autonomy until 1897, although the first industrial union in Germany, the *Deutsche Metallarbeiterverband* (German Metalworkers' Union), had been founded in their branch of industry in the summer of 1891. For many years they refused to co-operate with the central union. The reasons were partly personal rivalries and partly mutual prejudices between the local union leaders in Berlin and the national executive of the metalworkers in Stuttgart. Only when the national executive took the initiative and opened its own administrative office in Berlin, which quickly enrolled a large number of new members, did local union leaders decide to negotiate a merger. The national executive made an unusual number of concessions and the Berlin section was conceded a special status within the metalworkers' union.[5]

At the end of 1895 45 per cent of the free union members in Berlin were still members of independent local unions. However, the fact that the workers in Berlin preferred local union organizations and maintained a clearly localist consciousness for years did not involve only an organizational dimension. With their autonomous union structure the proponents of localism subscribed to a concept of unionism which could not be realized through a centralized union organization. They questioned the division of labour within the labour movement which reserved the political sphere of action for the Social Democratic Party and the representation of economic interests for the unions. Their fundamental objection to centralization was that this form of union organization had to be paid for by the unions' 'renunciation of politics'.[6] But they did not want to abandon political agitation within the union movement because, in their view, the struggle for the improvement of the workers' plight could not be separated from the socialist vision and the programme of the party.

They pleaded for a united labour movement whose internal and anti-capitalist functions should be entwined in terms of personnel and institutions. This organizational concept was strongly favoured by the Berlin working class because it had been practised during the years of the *Sozialistengesetz*. After 1890 the supporters of localism in Berlin only hesitantly gave up the strategic concept of a united organization comprising both trade union and political activities. But the leadership of the Free Trade Unions and the Social Democratic Party unanimously rejected the localist model, even though they themselves could not quickly agree on the delimitation of their respective spheres of action. In fact until the First World War conflicts and controversies broke out time and again between the party and the unions over their respective areas of responsibility and over the form that co-operation between them should take. During the 1890s the *Generalkommission* (the General Commission of the Free Trade Unions) under Carl Legien became the official representative of the social democratic union movement.[7] It rejected localist ideas for two reasons, emphasizing the need for union centralization in the capitalist economy and the role of the unions as a training ground for solidarity.

As far as Legien was concerned, the localists lived in a world dominated by old-fashioned guild traditions. In a developing capitalist industry, this world was doomed. As long as artisanally organized companies produced for the local market, Legien held, local union organizations had been in a position to influence local working conditions. But even when methods of production were developed based on craft skills but still aiming at mass output, the inescapable necessity arose to 'contact colleagues in neighbouring towns in order not to damage their income by flooding the market with goods'. But at a time when companies produced for the world market, supra-regional co-ordination of union activities was even more important. Legien rounded off his argument by pointing out that industrial working conditions were unstable and labour extremely mobile. Local unions could control the supply of labour when artisans still tramped slowly from town to town. Since then, however, trains and steamers transported 'thousands of workers to a town within one day, and alas if the arriving masses did not understand the cultural needs of the workers'. For this reason alone, a comprehensive union organization was necessary to cover the remotest parts of the country. Such an organization could only be financed and controlled by a centralized union.[8]

This line of argument was based on the dynamics of the industrialization process. Legien supplemented it by directing some points against the accusation of the localists that confining the unions to bread and butter policies would necessarily lead to the 'stupefaction of the workers'. The representation of the wage interests of the workers within the existing state and continuous union work towards their betterment had a very high priority for Legien in the struggle against capitalism. And he thought this fight to be strategically important for the realization of social democratic goals. In his view, the workers could not be won over by merely verbal appeals to their class consciousness, but only by collective actions in the fundamental conflict with the owners of capital, where these actions led to an experience of solidarity. Time and again he argued that the political education of the workers began in the reality of their everyday life, and that the party and the unions had to further this process interdependently but in different roles. He thus justified the existence of two organizational structures for the labour movement. To him the division of labour within the working-class movement was necessary and it made sense. He did not deny, though, 'that a final betterment of the position of the working class, the abolition of labour for wages and the complete recovery of the value of their work would only be possible via the political route'. Against this primacy of the party in the realization of the future society, he added in the same breath the equally important tasks of the unions within the existing state:

On the other hand, the mass of the workers had to be won over to this idea, won over by the economic struggle in today's bourgeois society. This is because it is this struggle for a better standard of living, the struggle against the encroachments of the employers, against their abuse of economic power, it is this struggle which provides the worker, who has not yet been won over to political action, with an insight into the evils of today's mode of production. This struggle shows him what little he can expect of the wealthy classes and how much he can achieve for himself if he increases his own power by joining forces with his comrades in misery.[9]

Legien's organizational model of partnership, based on a division of labour between the party and the unions and their equal rights within the movement of proletarian emancipation, was supported by most delegates at the first union congress after the fall of the *Sozialistengesetz*. 'By a substantial majority' the congress in Halberstadt decided in favour of the centralist organization of the Free Trade Unions and against localist autonomy.[10] Thus a very important decision was taken on a principle which paved the way for the centralist development of the German trade union movement and henceforth forced the independent local organizations into an increasingly unimportant existence on the sidelines.[11] But the final verdict had not yet been given on localism as a direct form of democracy and thus an alternative. During the syndicalist tendencies of the First World War and the revolution of 1918–19 these ideas and concepts, which had been buried for more than two decades after the decisive decision in Halberstadt, re-emerged. The Halberstadt congress carried the second resolution on the organizational structure of the Free Trade Unions far less decisively than it had rejected the localist ideas. Whether central unions founded on the basis of occupation or industry sectors should become the core of the trade union movement was not resolved. On this issue there were unresolvable differences between the delegates from the various industrial branches. In the end a compromise was reached which maintained the organizational independence of the existing central unions – from the barbers' union with 500 members to the metalworkers' union with 26,000. Unions covering similar occupations were asked only to co-operate, and this co-operation was to be institutionalized through cartel agreements. Thus the concentration of unions into a few large and strong industrial organizations, which the metalworkers in particular favoured, was blocked. The congress's recommendation that supra-regional ties at industrial level should be formed was non-obligatory. It was left to the future, and to the individual unions, to decide whether co-operation would develop or whether the occupational orientation would be maintained.[12]

IV

Despite various attempts to strengthen the institutional ties between the existing unions – fifty-five central organizations were represented in Halberstadt – occupation remained the decisive criterion for the organization of the Free Trade Unions in the following years. Nearly all unions initially concentrated on consolidating their position within one occupational area and refrained from merging with similar organizations within their industry. This behaviour certainly reflected the craftsman-like solidarity between skilled workers who still represented the majority of union members. This preference for an occupational type of organization should not be denounced by the use of terms such as professional arrogance or caste spirit because there were a number of obstacles which had nothing to do with guild traditionalism and yet prevented a concentration of union organization beyond occupational delimitations.

For example, the financial strength of individual unions varied considerably. And the local and regional areas which they covered did not match. Their self-help and social support institutions were based on differing contributions and offered different services when changing jobs, in case of unemployment, illness or for invalids, during strikes and when disciplined by an employer. Their statutes, the responsibilities of the executives and the participation of members also varied widely. The degree of organization had developed unequally in individual occupational areas. Their chances of succeeding in the labour market could be good or bad even within one and the same industrial sector. This meant that one union was able regularly to conclude collective agreements whilst a similar union still had to pursue its wage policy through strikes.[13]

Therefore, the Halberstadt congress and all those which followed until 1914 avoided imposing a common organizational structure on the Free Trade Unions. Had they done so without taking into account the internal structures of the unions they would have been more likely to damage than to improve union solidarity. This cautious approach by the general union congresses and the *Generalkommission* was based on the recognition that to change organizational structures required an intense opinion-forming process amongst the members concerned and depended, furthermore, on commercial and technological changes within individual occupations. After 1892 they confined themselves to recommending an intensification of voluntary co-operation on the part of the unions and to encouraging mergers but without enforcing them by decrees.[14]

For the proponents of a union system cutting across occupational boundaries, one based on a few industrial unions, this reticence was unsatisfactory and disappointing. The metalworkers had spoken out in favour of the industrial principle in Halberstadt, a principle largely realized in their branch after 1891.[15] From their point of view, those unions which did not want to extend beyond occupational boundaries lagged behind the employers in terms of their organizational policy. In the last analysis this would diminish the chances of union success. In view of the rapid concentration of production and the formation of cartels in the metal-producing and manufacturing industry, this was an undeniably strong line of argument. But it did not apply to industries with mainly small and medium-sized companies where production methods were craft-oriented and employers' associations were not very powerful. Apart from the case of the timber industry the example of the metalworkers was not followed by other unions.

But even the metalworkers' union and the woodworkers' union, which was founded in 1893,[16] could not incorporate all the existing professional unions of their respective industry-wide union organization. Apart from the Berlin localists, the unions of the blacksmiths and the moulders did not join the new type of union, the industry-wide union of the metalworkers. Neither was it possible to incorporate the gold and silversmiths, the engravers and chasers, the dockers, machinists and stokers. These groups continued with their familiar central organizations. Only after the turn of the century did they hesitantly give up their organizational independence. This was partly because the metalworkers' union with its large number of members was exercising strong pressure to further the mergers.[17] In addition, the organizational power of the employers in the vertically and horizontally integrated companies of the metal industry was so great and their willingness to make concessions in wage disputes so small, that the merger of rival free central union organizations was practically unavoidable.

In the timber industry the formation of an industry-wide union took place through a merger of the joiners' union and the turners' union, as well as some other groups of skilled workers which did not represent a large number. The organizations of the engravers, barrel-makers, glaziers and gold-platers refused to join. Only the gold-platers joined later, in 1906. The joiners had been the strongest group in this branch, and their decision to bring together all occupations of the timber industry into one union started the process of union mergers. After it had been founded the industry-wide union made little progress in expanding its organization to include other skilled groups in the industry. But the expansion of its membership proved that the grouping together of craft-oriented workers with specific skills into one union did not diminish the emergence and strengthening of union solidarity. Thus, those opponents of industry-wide unions were proved wrong who had maintained that the organizational success of the unions was rooted in the concept of skilled occupations, and who, therefore, had prophesied the failure of the industrial unions.[18]

The workers in other industrial branches followed the example of the metalworkers and the woodworkers only hesitantly, if at all. After the 1892 congress in Halberstadt, the process of union concentration stagnated in most industries until the turn of the century. The occupationally oriented trade union remained the predominant organizational form within the Free Trade Unions. But, as mentioned already, the term 'occupation' in most unions now covered also the semi-skilled and unskilled, and all employees of one occupational area were admitted as members. After the turn of the century the problem of a stronger concentration of the fragmented individual unions again assumed importance in the internal discussions of the Free Trade Unions. But the metalworkers' demand for an organizational clear-out and the concentration of occupationally oriented unions in one large industry-wide organization was not accepted. A number of smaller unions abandoned their organizational independence by joining a bigger union; but at the same time a number of small new unions for specialist occupations were founded (specialist engravers, xylographers, civilian musicians). Decisive progress in the merger of existing unions was made mainly in the construction industry. In 1911 a new big union was formed, the construction workers' union, in which bricklayers, unskilled building workers and, from 1912 onwards, also stucco workers co-operated. But even in the construction industry hopes of a unitary organization within the industry were not fulfilled. The carpenters, painters, stone-layers and asphalt-layers did not join the construction workers' union.

V

If the absolute number of central union organizations is taken as a yardstick for the progress of union concentration during the two-and-a-half decades before 1914, one might get the impression that not much had changed between 1892 and 1914. Fifty-seven central organizations were represented in Halberstadt. At the beginning of the First World War forty-six such organizations still existed. But behind these figures lies a fundamental transformation which had not been completed by 1914 but was stopped suddenly by the beginning of the war.[19] More than half of the organizations represented at the first union congress had been dissolved or merged with others by 1914. Some of the newly founded organizations, for example the workers in local government and the transport workers, joined the group of unions with the largest membership. Also, the relative weight of individual organizations within the movement as a whole had completely changed. Of the forty-six organizations which existed at the beginning of the war, thirty-nine were limited to one or very few similar occupations. Besides that, there were seven big organizations (metalworkers, construction workers, transport workers, factory workers, woodworkers, textile workers, miners) which all had more than 100,000 members and comprised 70 per cent of the total membership of the Free Trade Unions.

These seven multi-occupational mass unions represented the modern trend in German trade unionism. They reduced the existing differences between skilled, semi-skilled and unskilled workers by opening their organization to all employees in their industrial sector. They also admitted women, which was expressly forbidden by the statutes of several craft-oriented unions. They had a dense network of administrative offices covering the whole of the Reich through which they could systematically recruit members and look after them. The mass unions could finance a full-time administration and did not have to rely on honorary part-time officials. They had enough money to see through even prolonged strikes without endangering the existence of the union and were better equipped for the continuous conflict between the trade unions and the owners of capital than the small unions with a low membership.

But the undeniable advantages of mass organizations should not obscure the difficulties which occurred in the bureaucratic and centralized trade union structures. The large union organizations were not in a position to let their membership participate in forming an opinion on all relevant union questions and in internal decision-making, which might have been achieved through direct democratic processes. The statutes of most unions provided for ballots only in a few narrowly defined exceptional cases, for example the dissolution of the union. Therefore, problems of internal union democracy were bound to develop. The change-over from a localist movement based on members' meetings, where interests were articulated spontaneously, to a centralized union organization with statutes and several levels of delegates, led to a reduction in the direct decision-making power. But as the unions were forced to centralize if they wanted to remain active in the national labour market, they could not avoid the problems which arose from the dismantling of local autonomy. Including workers with widely differing skill levels within one union, and even more the merger of heterogeneous union organizations into one industrial union, was bound to cause internal tensions. The central leadership could neither represent the various interests of specialized groups of workers without restriction nor always properly evaluate the different working conditions of their members. Equally, there was no way in which they could have levelled out the wage differentials which existed locally and regionally as long as there was no national collective agreement enabling them to smooth out the worst distortions in the national wage structure. Thus internal union conflicts were inevitable. They arose particularly often in the most important area of union policy, that is, in the struggle for higher wages and better working conditions for the workers.

Over the years, all union organizations had precisely regulated this area of union activity by statute. Strikes were led by the national executive which before the start of a strike required local union offices to provide comprehensive surveys indicating whether the strike was actually necessary and its chances of success.[20] Of course, this kind of statutory rule significantly reduced the autonomy of local members to decide on a strike. Also, the decision whether a strike was approved or not depended on considerations which were plausible to the national leadership but not always to the rank-and-file members. Therefore, the centralist regimentation and control of strike movements often caused strong controversies at national union congresses and internal opposition groups were formed, which, however, usually did not survive very long. In the last years before the outbreak of the war, when the unions' room to manoeuvre was reduced and the confrontation between labour and capital became more embittered, nearly every major strike caused tensions between rank and file and the union leadership. Under the heading 'Leaders and Masses' this became an important subject of the union papers.[21]

These tensions were often caused by the strategies followed by national executives to reduce labour conflicts and their costs. The repercussions of internal tensions on the organizational unity of the central organizations, however, should not be overestimated. There was no general crisis of confidence between leaders and led in any of the unions, apart from temporary opposition groups. But there were a number of indications that workers and union members became critical of the representative policies of the union leaders. These indications included lack of interest in unionization as such, a reluctance to attend meetings or to pay membership dues, and spontaneous wild-cat strikes by the rank and file which were an expression of protest against the discipline imposed by statute from above. Open resistance by members, though, was an exception. The most spectacular example was the dockers' strike in 1913. But such rebellions usually ended either with an internal union compromise or the failure of the spontaneous strike action. One does not have to go so far as to say that the German trade unionists had a special disposition to bow to authority to explain their surprisingly high discipline compared to other countries. But one cannot deny that the German labour movement, that is, the unions and the Social Democratic Party, had strongly hierarchical organizational structures. The authority which accrued to officials by virtue of their office was respected. Their orders were followed, albeit sometimes unwillingly. And their leadership was accepted. Internal union opposition remained in the minority at national union congresses. The chairmen, once elected, could claim by common practice to be re-elected. Their monopoly of the leadership was not endangered.[22]

VI

The continuity of union leadership and the highly formalized institutional life was sharply castigated by contemporary critics as oligarchic and bureaucratic.[23] But their polemically formulated prejudices often prevented them from recognizing the real situation. Thus, for example, it was not sufficiently appreciated that the mobilization of workers through the unions was accompanied by an immense fluctuation in membership. This sometimes made the organizational work of the unions a Sisyphean task, with gains and losses in membership nearly balancing out during the course of an average year. But in order to stabilize the fluctuating membership a rapid expansion of union administration was required. Its main task was to persuade new members to become permanently involved with the union.[24]

Nor did the critics take sufficiently into account the hostility towards the unions which existed in the Kaiserreich and its repercussions on internal union policies. There was a strategy of conflict, a 'class struggle imposed from above', which safeguarded the autocratic tyranny of the kings of industry by arbitrary police bullying and partisan court rulings.[25] The social-political climate which developed in the Wilhelmine era was perceived by the unions as the climate of war. Trade union papers published a plethora of articles which not only gave expression to the feeling of being threatened but also called the unions the 'armies of the penniless' whose fight against the state and against capital had to be organized in military style. From this point of view the officials were officers and sergeants, and the members had to obey them.[26] But even authors who used less military language called the unions 'fighting formations' which could only be successful as 'united collectives'.[27] This was why they demanded from their members 'integration or greater subordination of the individual to the common interest' as required when 'conducting a social war'.[28]

The strong emphasis on the fighting character of the unions 'in a world of enemies'[29] certainly had an internal function too. By appeals to union discipline the dissatisfaction of members with the policy of the leadership could be muted. But the trade union officials also had responsibility for the continued existence of their organization. They were, therefore, less inclined to take risks and enter conflicts than some members expected them to be. This attitude of the union officials was attacked as organizational fetishism. In view of the historical context of their behaviour this accusation must be qualified. The paid officials lived off the 'workers' pennies' and they did, of course, have a personal material interest in keeping their union employer solvent. At the same time, though, they were accountable to the members to see that income from subscriptions and the concentrated financial power of the union was used in the most effective way for the purposes of the union organization. The unions were always to be in a position in which they could go on strike, and their negotiating power was not to be weakened, but rather strengthened, by a continuous extension of organizational power. Under the Kaiserreich the unions were not only in permanent conflict with the owners of capital but at the same time had to fight against trade union legislation which weakened their negotiating position. Time and again they were confronted with the threat of being outlawed.

For the trade union leaders of the Wilhelmine period who belonged to the generation which founded the unions, the twelve years of persecution and illegality under the *Sozialistengesetz* were still real to them and not simply part of a long-gone past. Against the background of their own political socialization during the period of the *Sozialistengesetz* they were particularly strongly impressed by the anti-union climate in state and society which continued even after the turn of the century. Therefore they steered their unions' policies along a tightrope between shying away from risks and being prepared to fight. To the next generation of members, those born after 1880, who were strongly represented amongst the rank and file, the caution of the leadership at times of internal tension appeared to be exaggerated. The leadership, for their part, criticized the impetuous eagerness of their young colleagues. The union leaders' reasons were not primarily to secure the material basis on which their livelihood depended, as some vicious critics maintained, but to safeguard the existence of the unions. They did not want carelessly to subject them to a renewed period of illegality after having gone through all the trouble of founding and stabilizing them.

The main priority of the full-time officials, in thought and action, was without any doubt the preservation of the union organization. Therefore, they tried to avoid, if possible, strike actions with unpredictable results. This attitude was geared towards securing the existence and present form of the unions which demanded self-discipline and solidarity from members and restricted their spontaneity. But during times of revolutionary change this could lead to the dead end of stagnation. Even in the prewar period the social democratic left, which criticized the unions, pointed this out. These critics vehemently attacked the organizational pride and the caution of the union leaders.[30] The controversies within the unions were thus not merely the expression of a conflict between the founder generation and the generation of members who had joined after the turn of the century. There were also genuine differences of opinion about the leeway available for negotiation and the objectives of union policies.

At the core of the argument was the question of the degree to which the authoritarian Wilhelmine state could be reformed. Views within the labour movement as a whole differed widely. The unions could not provide a clear answer as to the future strategy and tactics of the labour movement, nor could the Social Democratic Party. The unions, therefore, concentrated on their tasks within the existing capitalist system, that is, the wage struggle and the betterment of the social conditions under which the workers had to live. This decision in favour of continuous reform of the existing state was approved by the majority of trade union members. They thought the realization of the future society to be the responsibility of the Social Democratic Party. This was entirely in the spirit of the division of labour between the party and the unions. This self-imposed limitation of the unions to the socio-economic field within the existing system protected their organizational structure during the First World War. The division of the party was not followed by a split within the unions, in spite of the fact that the division of the German labour movement, which had occurred during the war, reached far into the union movement and increased internal tensions. The unions tried to cope with the new situation after the break-up of the old Social Democratic Party into rival parties by declaring their political neutrality at the first postwar congress in 1919. This step was meant to secure at least the unity of the union side of the labour movement and the continued existence of the organizations which had been founded at great sacrifice.

Notes: Chapter 12

1 P. Umbreit, *25 Jahre deutscher Gewerkschaftsbewegung 1890–1915. Erinnerungsschrift zum fünfundzwanzigsten Jubiläum der Begründung der Generalkommission der Gewerkschaften Deutschlands* (Berlin, 1915), Foreword.

2 Information from: D. Fricke, *Die deutsche Arbeiterbewegung 1869 bis 1914. Ein Handbuch über ihre Organisation und Tätigkeit im Klassenkampf* (Berlin, 1976), 654. Also W. Albrecht, *Fachverein–Berufsgewerkschaft–Zentralverband. Organisationsprobleme der deutschen Gewerkschaften 1870–1890* (Bonn, 1982); an informative survey is provided by G. A. Ritter and K. Tenfelde, 'Der Durchbruch der Freien Gewerkschaften Deutschlands zur Massenbewegung im letzten Viertel des 19. Jahrhunderts', in H. O. Vetter (ed.), *Vom Sozialistengesetz zur Mitbestimmung* (Düsseldorf, 1975), 61–120. Apart from that, one should also mention the contemporary presentation by J. Schmöle, *Die sozialdemokratischen Gewerkschaften in Deutschland seit dem Erlasse des Sozialisten-Gesetzes* (Jena, 1896).

3 For the membership development of the individual unions cf. Ritter and Tenfelde, 'Der Durchbruch der Freien Gewerkschaften', appendix of tables. The lines of organizational development sketched briefly here are dealt with in detail by K. Schönhoven, *Expansion und Konzentration. Studien zur Entwicklung der Freien Gewerkschaften im Wilhelminischen Deutschland 1890 bis 1914* (Stuttgart, 1980).

4 There is still no study which summarizes the local trends in the German labour movement; important insights are provided by D. H. Müller, *Idealismus und Revolution. Zur Opposition der Jungen gegen den sozialdemokratischen Parteivorstand 1890 bis 1914* (Berlin, 1975); idem, 'Probleme gewerkschaftlicher Organisation und Perspektiven im Rahmen eines arbeitsteiligen Organisationskonzeptes', *Internationale Wissenschaftliche Korrespondenz zur Geschichte der deutschen Arbeiterbewegung* 15 (1979): 569–80; idem, 'Syndicalism and localism in the German trade union movement', in this volume, pp.239–49; cf. also G. A. Ritter, *Die Arbeiterbewegung im Wilhelminischen Reich. Die Sozialdemokratische Partei und die Freien Gewerkschaften 1890–1900* 2nd edn (Berlin, 1963), 113–15; Fricke, *Arbeiterbewegung*, 746–8.

5 cf. for the history of the *Deutsche Transportarbeiterverband* and the development of the *Deutsche Metallarbeiterverband* Schönhoven, *Expansion und Konzentration*, 357–9.

6 Thus one of the founders of the localist movement in Berlin, G. Kessler, in an article on 6 February 1887, quoted from Fricke, *Arbeiterbewegung*, 746; cf. also Müller, 'Probleme gewerkschaftlicher Organisation', 574–5.

7 cf. Schönhoven, *Expansion und Konzentration*, 283–306.

8 Thus wrote Legien in an article on 21 February 1891 in the *Correspondenzblatt der Generalkommission der Gewerkschaften Deutschlands*, which he published. This article appeared as the forerunner to a series of essays on the internal organizational problems of the trade unions, which was then published separately by the *Generalkommission* as a pamphlet: *Die Organisationsfrage. Ein Beitrag zur Entwicklung der deutschen Gewerkschafts-Bewegung* (Hamburg, 1891).

9 From an article in the *Correspondenzblatt* (23 May, 1891).

10 cf. 'Protokoll der Verhandlungen des ersten Kongresses der Gewerkschaften Deutschlands, abgehalten zu Halberstadt vom 14. bis 18. März 1892', in *Protokolle der Verhandlungen der Kongresse der Gewerkschaften Deutschlands*, Vol. 1 (Bonn, 1980) (reprint), 61. After this decision thirteen delegates from locally oriented unions left the congress under protest. Amongst them were the representatives of the Berlin metalworkers and masons. Twenty-three other delegates, also representing local unions, did not associate themselves with this protest.

11 In 1897 the local unions founded their own umbrella union which from 1901 onwards was known as the *Freie Vereinigung deutscher Gewerkschaften*. The membership of this union, which was strongly represented above all in the building trade, never exceeded 20,000. After anarcho-syndicalist forces had become dominant in the *Freie Vereinigung*, the Mannheim party conference of the SPD in 1906 passed a resolution which 'strengthened the unity of the trade union organizations', condemned their 'Sonderbündelei' and encouraged the locally organized Social Democrats to affiliate to the *Freie Gewerkschaften*. Thereupon 10,000 localists went over to the Free Unions; the *Freie Vereinigung* itself had a mere 7,133 members in 1912. cf. the statistics in Fricke, *Arbeiterbewegung*, 746–8.

12 On the course of the congress cf. Schönhoven, *Expansion und Konzentration*, 276–9.
13 The significance of these factors, listed only briefly here, in the individual branches, and where forms of co-operation and concentration movements can be discerned, is dealt with in detail by Schönhoven, ibid., 331–76; cf. also idem, 'Selbsthilfe als Form von Solidarität. Das gewerkschaftliche Unterstützungswesen im Deutschen Kaiserreich bis 1914', *Archiv für Sozialgeschichte* 20 (1980): 147–93.
14 See, for example, the 'Resolution zur Vermeidung von Grenzstreitigkeiten', passed by the Hamburg trade union congress, in *Protokolle*, Vol. 3 (Berlin, 1980), 46. Further resolutions on the question of organization in U. Borsdorf *et al.* (eds), *Grundlagen der Einheitsgewerkschaft. Historische Dokumente und Materialien* (Cologne, 1977), 106–8.
15 cf. on the prelude to the founding Schönhoven, *Expansion und Konzentration*, 308–10.
16 cf. ibid., 320–2.
17 cf. ibid., 357–9.
18 This interpretation is also represented to some degree in scholarly essays: A. Dissinger, *Das freigewerkschaftliche Organisationsproblem. Eine soziologische Studie* (Jena, 1929).
19 The last trade union congress before the outbreak of war in June 1914 dealt once more in detail with problems of organization, after the factory workers' unions and those of the community workers had presented motions demanding that 'the way be opened for a factory-based organization'. However, these ideas, which sought to realize the principle of 'one shop, one trade union', in order to prevent demarcation disputes in large companies with heterogeneous occupational structures, were rejected by the congress. cf. details of the debates in *Protokolle*, Vol. 5 (Berlin, 1980), 249–51, 371–3. During the First World War the organizational debates were not continued and a silent agreement was reached between the unions, which prohibited members from joining other organisations of the Free Trade Unions.
20 It also became necessary to pass strike statutes for financial reasons. Since the unions often incurred considerable costs during labour struggles because of strike support for their members, some sort of regulation in this sector was urgently needed. cf. Schönhoven, 'Selbsthilfe als Form der Solidarität', 159–61.
21 cf. for details of this idem, 'Arbeitskonflikte in Konjunktur und Rezession. Gewerkschaftliche Streikpolitik und Streikverhalten der Arbeiterschaft vor 1914', in K. Tenfelde and H. Volkmann (eds), *Streik. Zur Geschichte des Arbeitskampfes in Deutschland während der Industrialisierung* (Munich, 1981), 177–93. The reinforcement of the powerful position of the employers in the labour struggles during the late empire is stressed emphatically by D. Groh, 'Intensification of work and industrial conflict in Germany, 1896–1914', *Politics and Society* 8 (1978): 329–97. A concrete strike pattern, marked by tensions between the trade union grass roots and its leaders, is revealed by H. Homburg, 'Anfänge des Taylorsystems in Deutschland vor dem Ersten Weltkrieg unter besonderer Berücksichtigung der Arbeitskämpfe bei Bosch 1913', *Geschichte und Gesellschaft* 4 (1978): 170–94.
22 cf. Schönhoven, *Expansion und Konzentration*, 221–60.
23 The most prominent critic was Robert Michels, who in his work published in 1911, *Zur Soziologie des Parteiwesens in der modernen Demokratie*, reprint of 2nd edn (Stuttgart, 1970), dealt above all with the internal structures of social democratic workers' organizations and reached numerous polemically exaggerated judgements. cf. for a more recent and less prejudiced discussion using as examples the trade unions in Germany, J. Bergmann, 'Organisationsstruktur und innergewerkschaftliche Demokratie', in *Beiträge zur Soziologie der Gewerkschaften* (Frankfurt, 1979), 210–39.
24 For the degree of membership fluctuation cf. Schönhoven, *Expansion und Konzentration*, 150–98.
25 There are numerous examples in the two memoranda by the *Generalkommission*: *Das Koalitionsrecht der deutschen Arbeiter in Theorie und Praxis. Denkschrift der Generalkommission der Gewerkschaften Deutschlands*, edited on behalf of the *Generalkommission* by Carl Legien (Hamburg, 1899); S. Nestriepke, *Das Koalitionrecht in Deutschland. Gesetz und Praxis. Im Auftrag der Generalkommission der Gewerkschaften Deutschlands* (Berlin, 1912); see also K. Saul, *Staat, Industrie, Arbeiterbewegung im Kaiserreich. Zur Innen- und Sozialpolitik des Wilhelminischen Deutschlands 1903–1914* (Düsseldorf, 1974); Schönhoven, *Expansion und Konzentration*, 74–6.
26 Thus wrote the chairman of the community workers' union in an article in the union's newspaper: *Die Gewerkschaft*, no. 3 (7 February 1898).

27 Thus argued the Nuremberg workers' secretary Adolf Braun in an article published in 1910: 'Gewerkschaftliche Verfassungsfragen', in idem, *Die Gewerkschaften, ihre Entwicklung und Kämpfe. Eine Sammlung von Abhandlungen* (Nuremberg, 1914), 75–84, quotation p. 80.
28 Thus stated the editor of the carpenters' union newspaper August Bringmann in his much-read organizational handbook, *Praktische Winke*, 3rd edn (Berlin, 1909), 46–7.
29 Braun, *Die Gewerkschaften*, 83.
30 cf. esp. K. Kautsky, *Der Weg zur Macht*, ed. and introd. by G. Fülberth (Frankfurt, 1972); see also idem, 'Die Aktion der Masse', *Die neue Zeit* 30/1 (1911); A. Pannekoek, 'Massenaktion und Revolution', *ibid.*, 30/2 (1912), and the various attitudes of R. Luxemburg, *Gesammelte Werke*, Vols. 1–3 (Berlin, 1970–3).

Part Four

Syndicalism, Christian Unionism and 'Free' Labour

13 Syndicalism and Localism in the German Trade Union Movement

DIRK H. MÜLLER

I

The undercurrent of syndicalist sympathies in the German trade union movement arose out of strong opposition to the centralization of local unions. This localist opposition was opposed to the loss of local autonomy, particularly the right to initiate strikes that centralization would mean. The centralists believed, with some justification, that local struggles could be won more easily with regional or national support. The localists realized this of course, but preferred to trust the 'spontaneous solidarity'[1] of other workers who would themselves decide whether to support a particular struggle. The centralists, on the other hand, wanted to set up a central strike fund, properly financed by the local groups, so that the movement could use its limited resources to concentrate on those areas of greatest need and where the most use could be made of them.

There were two reasons why the controversy between the proponents of the two different organizational concepts raged for so long. First, in many industrial disputes union members were in a minority and had to form a temporary alliance with unorganized workers;[2] and secondly, for a long time the employers would only negotiate with spokesmen elected from the strikers themselves and were not willing to enter into negotiations with the representatives of the unions.[3]

The localists did not want any formal code of conduct imposed from above, which in the event of a strike means the executive of the union in question. They insisted rather that the general meeting[4] of those directly involved in a conflict was to be the sovereign body. In addition to this body, which was at all times responsible to itself alone, this early form of trade union organization (also known as the *Versammlungsbewegung*) had developed formalized subsidiary oganizations, although their role was purely administrative and technical.[5] The strike and negotiating committees, for example, were supposed to brief the area meetings. In the workplace similar tasks were undertaken by the elected spokesmen of the workforce.[6] In those branches of industry still organized mainly along craft lines most of the unions representing one trade only were supporters of this localist movement. The usual procedure involved the election by his colleagues of a spokesman or shop steward in the workplace. This spokesman negotiated with the employer on their behalf. He would also collect the money for the local strike fund and deliver it to the negotiating committee, at the same time attending area meetings of all shop stewards in his particular trade, intended to assess the local situation.[7] Where this shop steward system was not common practice the necessary information was gathered by particular committees or even by elected individuals.[8] Likewise in the branches of industry where many trades were involved in the same workplace a similar system prevailed, as for instance in the Berlin metal industry. Here again, the shop steward of a workplace was elected by his colleagues, and he functioned simultaneously as the representative of the predominant trade in that workplace. The obvious weaknesses of this form of organization were the lengthy and public discussion about tactics, organizational discontinuity and uncertain financial resources.[9]

After the *Sozialistengesetz* (Anti-Socialist Law) had interrupted the process of centralization in the trade union movement, the *Versammlungsbewegung* experienced a renaissance, as under the terms of the repressive legislation its more informal character made it more immune from attack than its more centralized counterparts,[10] while at the same time the workplace-based organizational structure afforded a higher degree of internal social control than the associational type of organization. It was only after the *Sozialistengesetz* had been repealed that small craft unions of skilled (industrial) artisans ceased to be the dominant type of trade union organization.[11]

Berlin became the centre of trade union localism after the *Sozialistengesetz* not only because the workers in this industrial complex were desperately fighting for their independence, but also because the Berlin trade unions were better able to manage the interplay between the different forms of union organization, namely, the craft union, the general meeting and the shop steward system. This flexibility, so essential for survival, was all the more necessary as they had to confront the Royal Prussian police rather than a local force.

II

However, the question of the retention of local autonomy for those directly involved in a conflict was not the only basis of trade union localism. In 1891 the Berlin metalworkers refused to join the newly founded *Deutscher Metallarbeiterverband* (DMV – German Metalworkers' Union) because, among other reasons, they did not want to sacrifice their dual structure. The organization of the workplace allowed them to form institutions representing the interests of either a particular trade or workers in a particular industry according to the situation. The shop steward functioned in the one instance as the spokesman of his trade in a particular factory, and in another as the representative spokesman for his workplace within a particular industry. Then he met with fellow spokesmen beyond the factory boundaries, thus forming comprehensive committees of the same trade.[12] Through this flexible arrangement the Berlin metal trades union and the similarly organized public metalworkers' organizations managed to avoid the continual conflicts about spheres of responsibility that plagued the Free Trade Union movement. In comparison with the trade unions organized purely on trade and geographical lines, the Berlin organizations based on workplace structures were better placed to adapt themselves to the constant structural changes in industries which spanned several trades.[13] A shop steward elected by all his colleagues in a workplace could successfully bridge the gap between the organized and unorganized workers. Through his double function as a spokesman of both his workplace and his trade, opportunities for dividing these two spheres of interest were avoided and the shop stewards' movement in both the shopfloor and more general meetings remained united.[14]

However, conflicts between the various committees and the union organizations on the one hand and between individual trade groups and the whole of the metalworkers in Berlin on the other, made it clear that the retention of local autonomy by those groups directly involved in a conflict, whether defined by a factory or trade, was not by any means without problems on a local level. During the moulders' strike in 1897, which began at the Borsig works, and which led to a lock-out in all of the Berlin metalworking plants with own moulding shops, a general meeting of the Berlin metalworkers directed the moulders to accept the judgement of the industrial arbitration court with the argument that 'individual branches should not have the power to decide the fate of many thousands'.[15]

The umbrella organization of the localists, the *Freie Vereinigung deutscher Gewerkschaften* (Free Alliance of German Trade Unions), founded in 1897, had similar problems. However, the Berlin metalworkers preferred to join the DMV in the same year, after their local autonomy had been guaranteed.[16] As before, the *Berliner Metallarbeiterverband* (Berlin Metalworkers' Union) defined local autonomy as the right of those directly involved to determine the course of events. Even after the dissolution of the metalworkers' public organization in 1900 this autonomy remained intact until 1907 when the Berlin branch of the DMV found itself unable to bear the financial burden of mass lock-outs without massive support from the central executive. The employers had resorted to this measure in response to wage demands of small local groups of workers, and in the end the general assembly of the DMV imposed its national strike code on the metalworkers in the imperial capital.[17] However, it was not simply the financial consequences of local autonomy that brought the Berlin workers into line. The centralists in the DMV saw a connection between political localism – supported by the radical faction of the Social Democratic Party that were in favour of a political mass strike – and the proponents of trade union local autonomy.[18] To the executive of the DMV it seemed as if the radical Social Democrats amongst the Berlin metalworkers had tried to use the strike of the 150 turners at Siemens & Halske in 1905 to prove that the necessary level of consciousness for a general strike had been reached: as, unlike the strike of the Berlin moulders in 1897 which had also been accompanied by mass lock-outs, the lock-out victims, 8,000 at first, then later 30,000, did not attack the autonomy of the strikers.[19] Thus the general meeting of the DMV responded by abolishing the autonomy of the Berlin workers' groups as defined by trade or workshop, prohibiting the DMV shop stewards from accepting any mandate from whatever assembly to call and lead a strike and leaving it to union branches to hold general meetings not as members' meetings but as delegates' meetings.[20] From 1908 this happened in Berlin.[21] Thus the organizational development of the DMV was not completed until 1907 at the earliest. One important precondition for this had been the acceptance by employers of union officials as negotiating partners. Previously they had only been willing to recognize spokesmen for 'their' workers: the spokesmen elected from amongst the workers in an individual firm. The Berlin metalworkers' strike of 1905 which had begun in a turning shop was of considerable importance in changing the attitude of the employers. This strike had been the result of opposition to a compromise formula worked out jointly by the management and a workers' committee to resolve conflicts about piece-work rates. After mass lock-outs lasting many weeks the employers' federation and the Berlin DMV negotiated,[22] and the results were laid before an autonomous general meeting of workers. A decision was reached by a simple majority vote. This was the last time before the First World War that such a public decision-making process took place in the DMV.[23] The employers realized that it was more rational to recognize and negotiate with a trade union than with small groups of hostile workers, who were able, as in the case of the turners, to exploit the lack of standardization in industry. Their refusal to work meant that even without the lock-outs the whole plant would have ground to a halt in a few days as they produced the vital nuts and bolts unobtainable elsewhere.[24]

III

In contrast to the metalworkers, the workers in the building trades in Berlin were not integrated gradually into the Free Trade Unions. The localism of the building trades had constituted itself as an industrial and political opposition during the years of the *Sozialistengesetz*, after the non-social opponents (the carpenters) had manoeuvred their Social Democratic colleagues out of union administrative positions in order to minimize the government's opportunities to attack them.[25] This secession meant for the outlawed Social Democratic Party that the new local building trades societies could continue to function as legal substitute organizations for the party. As political organizations were not allowed to combine beyond the locality, the localism of the building trades was reinforced by a combination of political and trade unionist motives that made an integrative development analogous to the metalworkers very difficult.

There were also a number of technological and economic characteristics which fuelled the localism of the bricklayers and the carpenters. Highly qualified bricklayers and carpenters could not easily be replaced by other workers.[26] A building simply could not be moved to another area for other workers to build it. The vast majority of contractors were small firms with very little capital, and a long strike could entail legal penalties for them.[27] Finally, until the turn of the century there was no single association of employers in the construction industry in Berlin.[28] Therefore, it was possible for workers to conclude wage agreements with individual contractors very speedily during a strike. In the 1880s and 1890s approximately one-third[29] of the bricklayers and carpenters in Berlin migrated to the capital only during the building season. Whenever in conflict with employers the localists in Berlin used the medieval technique of blacking the town. Thus their strikes were usually accompanied by a great exodus of building workers. During the Berlin bricklayers' strike of 1889 about two-thirds of the 19,000 workers in this sector left the area.[30] They received only travelling costs and a small amount for expenses from the strike fund, although all paid the same contribution. However, this tactic had serious drawbacks: the blacking technique caused a surplus of labour in the vicinity of Berlin, for example in Potsdam, resulting in wage cuts there.[31]

The strikes of the Berlin bricklayers and carpenters in the mid-1890s led by negotiating committees can no longer be analysed in terms of the economic *Versammlungsbewegung* of craft workers. In time these had changed into a seasonal, open trade union which integrated not only the seasonal workers but also those who were organized in local craft associations or branches of the centralized trade unions. The members of this open union were issued with membership cards bearing their names. Stamps recording their union dues were affixed to these cards and during a strike they were stamped by the negotiating committee to show the amount of financial support received.[32]

The workers assembled in workplace, area, or general meetings. During strike actions special committees and their paid assistants policed the buildings and placarded those building sites where all the union's demands had been met. The workers there had to pay an extra supplement to the strike funds. In winter, when building work ceased and about 30 per cent of the migrant bricklayers and carpenters left the town,[33] large sections of this loosely structured open trade union and its shop steward organization along with the differentiated wage structure in Berlin regularly collapsed.[34] During winter months the centralists and localists fought out their organizational struggles[35] which were then publicly banned on the decision of one of the first full meetings of the new season.[36] The opponents were usually appointed to the negotiating committees on the basis of parity, and the division of labour within the committees was decided by lot.[37] However, as the wage demanded was never paid by all employers and concessions won did not even apply to all the building sites run by a particular contractor, but only to the one where a conflict had taken place, and it was then often gradually eroded, a permanent state of war existed, in which individual sites were blacked. Nor were the building trades and their subsidiaries entirely free from lengthy disputes, which often ended in stalemate. It seemed reasonable to both employers and workers to replace the loosely organized code of conduct which had existed until then by a more organized, stricter, more binding kind of strike code. Thus the Berlin bricklayers' strike of 1899 was ended by a tariff proposal put forward by the joint negotiating committee, which was ratified in two separate general meetings, once by the centralists and once by the localists, and then countersigned by the union negotiators.[38] The localists had to overcome their fundamental opposition to tariff agreements in order to retain some influence over the Berlin bricklayers' wage negotiations.

IV

The *Freie Vereinigung* (Free Alliance), the umbrella organization of the localists from 1897, had to formulate this principle more moderately.[39] At their congress in 1900 the cornerstone of 'spontaneous solidarity' was removed and a strike code introduced.[40] This memorable fourth congress of the Free Alliance not only had two last-minute resolutions to debate, one tactical, the other organizational, but on top of this had to come to terms with the removal from the statute-book of a law opposition to which had formed the political justification for their localism.[41] In December 1899 the law which forbade political groups to combine was rescinded. Although legislation governing the right to combine had been the province of the imperial government since 1871, it was not until 1908 that legislation governing combination for the whole empire was introduced. Until that point the situation had been regulated by a mishmash of sometimes contradictory laws passed by the different states stemming from the period of reaction in the 1850s. Their common content was the prohibition of political groups to combine, which remained in effect until December 1899. 'Political' was defined by the relation of the citizen or an association of like-minded people towards the state and its laws. Even the discussion of 'political' questions counted as political activity. Local political groupings were not allowed to form alliances with each other and regional or national organizations were not allowed to set up local branches in Prussia and thus to develop an infrastructure. Furthermore, until 1908 women were not allowed access to political meetings and organizations or unions. All of this had a considerable impact on trade union organization as the unions did not want to exclude the discussion of social questions from their agenda and women from their membership. Although these laws on combination had no direct consequence for the localism of the building trade, whose main strength lay in the exclusively male trades of the carpenters and bricklayers, the Free Alliance did not become centralized after the combination laws were rescinded. For it the loss of local autonomy meant not only the strengthening of the process of centralization but also that of the trade union movement as a whole. From its point of view the gradual improvement in wages had an integrative effect on the workers which considerably weakened the revolutionary potential of the social democratic movement. Thus for the Free Alliance the question of organizational structure was to be decided on the basis of political effectiveness rather than in the interests of trade union efficacy. In fact for it trade union ineffectiveness was the means to a political end:

> If the trade union movement succeeds, if it brings the worker what he hopes for . . . this would show him that he can hope to build a better life on the basis of the present order, and the necessity for a social revolution

would seem less real, the present state would be protected . . . the trade union movement has a revolutionary effect when it demonstrates the practical impossibility of its aims. It has arisen only to fade away: it can never be an end in itself, only a means. It is only revolutionary in the sense that it awakens hopes that it can never fulfil. It enlightens. Its defeats are its propaganda. . . . Whoever expects great things from the trade union movement quite rightly wants to build it into as powerful and effective a weapon as possible. Those who regard it as of secondary importance will not.[42]

The following passage from an article written eleven years later by the mentor of the localists, Gustav Kessler, proves that we are not dealing with a transitory attitude: 'We are of the opinion that the trade union . . . is at best a hindrance to Social Democracy that must unfortunately be tolerated.'[43]

For the localists criticism of a tactic that was aimed simply at improving wages in a particular situation was not as serious as the refusal to contemplate any social reform. At the beginning of the 1890s they had formed a building workers' cartel in Berlin modelled on the lines of the one in Paris. This organization campaigned in vain for recognition as a general contractor for all public buildings. But it never developed into anything more than a short-lived propaganda agency. This cartel was to include in its prices, instead of the usual calculations of profit for shareholders, the costs of meeting all union demands. Only up to 10 per cent of the cartel's wage-workers would be bricklayers, carpenters, or other building workers from outside Berlin.[44] The level of a 'fair wage' was to be determined by productivity – for the skilled jobs this meant according to the level of self-exploitation. Gustav Kessler's concept of using capital for the general good rather than abolishing it lay behind this enterprise.[45] How effective self-exploitation might be in hastening the process of the development of social responsibility will not be discussed here. There was a second possibility: to attempt to divide the public and private building markets, in order to realize union demands and increase the level of organizational consciousness at least in one sphere, in fact a significant one in the imperial capital. The building workers' cartel was apparently founded for this purpose. Although it aimed at becoming the general contractor for all public works in Berlin it was never really more than a transitory propaganda exercise. The self-administered building workers' cartel was supposed to be a model for future socialist production, which was, of course, the ultimate aim of the localists. Next to the defence of local autonomy this was the second similarity of the localists to the French syndicalists, and they regarded themselves as the German counterpart to that movement even after theoretical considerations had divided it. This oversight was later rectified, and the name 'revolutionary syndicalism' adopted.

The localist concept of organization was also directed against the social heterogeneity of the Social Democratic movement. The Free Alliance, like the Social Democratic Party, was a centralized organization of *Vertrauensmänner* (elected stewards). At public meetings the local branches of the Free Alliance, similarly to the local Social Democratic Party, elected delegates to its national congress. An executive was elected from amongst the delegates. The link between the national executive and the local branch was maintained by the spokesman, who was also elected openly. The parallel nature of the trade union and political organizations was a conscious move to facilitate the combination of both into one economic and political body whose members were exclusively workers. Here the localists, on the other hand, modelled themselves on the organizational proposals put forward by Becker at the initial founding congress of the *Sozialdemokrati-sche Arbeiterpartei* (SDAP – Social Democratic Workers' Party) in 1869, but which he had immediately withdrawn. These proposals saw both workers' political groups and the trade unions as the organizational nuclei of a socialist workers' party. After the turn of the century the localists pointed to similar developments in England.[46]

As the balance of power within the SPD changed, so too did the nature of the localist trade union opposition to the party. The localists gave up their earlier idea of the primacy of the political struggle, at the latest during the debate about the mass strike, and turned to anti-parliamentary ideas. They saw direct (revolutionary) action as the major means of achieving a social transformation, for which psychological rather than organizational pre-conditions had to be created.[47] The autonomous individual became the necessary precondition for the socialist economy and egalitarian administration of the future society. With the adoption of this view, the so-called *historische Psychismus* propounded by Raphael Friedberg,[48] who, after the death of Gustav Kessler in 1903, had become the chief ideologue of the localists, this undercurrent of ideas in the trade union movement incorporated some elements from the left wing of the party known as *Junge*. After their secession from the party they propagated certain syndicalist concepts of trade union organization.[49] As the localists turned against the Social Democrats the party moved from its position of neutrality in the debate about trade union organization. This was made easier as the localists' political significance had declined, even in Berlin, after the strongest of the localist organizations had pulled out of the Berlin bricklayers' tariff commission and thus refrained from further trade union activity.

The end of localism both within the Free Trade Unions and the Social Democratic Party was marked by two events. In 1907 a centralized strike code was imposed on the metalworkers of Berlin, and the Nuremberg party congress of 1908 made membership of the SPD incompatible with member-ship of the *Freie Vereinigung*.[50] The impossibility of being a member both of the SPD and a localist union decimated the membership of the localist organizations, which had reached their zenith in 1900 with a membership of 20,000. Their numbers steadily declined thereafter.[51] Until the First World War the *Freie Vereinigung* remained an ineffective organization of craft and inter-craft discussion groups for diverse anarchist, anarcho-syndicalist, anti-trade union and anti-militarist ideas. After the November Revolution of 1918 some veterans continued the tradition and called the twelfth congress of the *Freie Vereinigung deutscher Gewerkschaften* for December 1919. At this congress the *Freie Arbeiter-Union Deutschlands (Syndikalisten)* (Free Workers' Union of Germany/Syndicalists) was founded. Its basic programme was composed of various theoretical and organizational resolutions that had been passed in the prewar years. The 'Declaration of Principles' contained elements of both the German workers' councils' movement and the French revolutionary syndicalists.[52] Fritz Kater, long-serving chairman in the Wilhelmine era, was reinstated and he only retired from this post shortly before the demise of the Weimar Republic after forty years at the head of the movement.[53] Rudolf Rocker, recently returned from internment in an English prisoner-of-war camp, was the intellectual leader of postwar syndicalism in Germany. In 1890–1 he had belonged to the radical left opposition in the Social Democratic Party in Mainz.[54]

This continuity in personalities and organizational concepts helps to explain why, after the November Revolution, this particular undercurrent within the German working-class movement, which aimed at egalitarian rather than representative organizational and social structures, remained divided. The urban artisan socialism of the localists in the building trades may have differed in technological and geographical ways, but historically it was not incompatible with the concept of workers' councils developed by the metalworkers. However, their ideas for a future society remained insular. The 'chimney-socialism' of those who built the chimneys and that of those who worked in their shadows stayed apart. Not even repression both were subjected to could serve to unite them without any reservation.

Notes: Chapter 13

1 *Protokoll über die Verhandlungen vom 6. Kongreß der Freien Vereinigung deutscher Gewerkschaften*, abgehalten am 13., 14., 15. und 16. September 1903 (Berlin, 1903), 141.
2 The public funds of the Berlin metalworkers were only dissolved in 1900. cf. *Deutsche Metallarbeiter Zeitung (DMZ)* 10 (10 March 1900).
3 ibid., 34 (23 August 1902).
4 *Berliner Volkstribüne* 42 (20 October 1888).
5 Staatsarchiv Potsdam (StAP), 15301, Bl. 368.
6 StAP 15582, Bl. 96.
7 StAP 15299, Bl. 48, and 15301, Bl. 31.
8 StAP 15585, Bl. 27–9, and 15299, Bl. 514.
9 L. Neuberger, 'Die Geschichte des Streikreglements der freien Gewerkschaften Deutschlands' (PhD. thesis, Heidelberg, 1923), 28–30.
10 *DMZ* 22 (9 July 1887).
11 G. A. Ritter and K. Tenfelde, 'Der Durchbruch der Freien Gewerkschaften zur Massenorganisation im letzten Viertel des 19. Jahrhunderts', in H. O. Vetter (ed.), *Vom Sozialistengesetz zur Mitbestimmung* (Cologne, 1975), 61–130 (82).
12 StAP 15237, Bl. 400 and Bl. 592.
13 The smiths, for example; cf. K. Schönhoven, *Expansion und Konzentration. Studien zur Entwicklung der Freien Gewerkschaften im Wilhelminischen Deutschland 1890–1914* (Stuttgart, 1980), 361.
14 This dual system was looked on as a model and was later incorporated into the administrative system of the DMV. cf. *Die sechste ordentliche General-Versammlung des Deutschen Metallarbeiter-Verbandes*, abgehalten vom 1. bis 6. Juni 1903 im Saale des Gewerkschaftshauses zu Berlin (Stuttgart, n.d. [1903]), 147–8.
15 *DMZ* 42 (16 October 1897).
16 *Protokoll der dritten ordentlichen General-Versammlung des Deutschen Metallarbeiter-Verbandes zu Braunschweig ...*, abgehalten vom 20. bis 24. April 1897 (Stuttgart, n.d. [1897]), 109–11.

17 *Protokoll der achten ordentlichen General-Versammlung des Deutschen Metallarbeiter-Verbandes*, abgehalten vom 20. bis 25. Mai 1907 in den Zentralsälen in München (Stuttgart, n.d.) (1907), pp. 39 and 240.

18 *DMZ* 44 (4 November 1905).

19 These two conflicts did not only differ in respect to their duration and the attitude of the lock-out victims. On the day before the strike the local union administration had, against all previous practice and without ratification, authorized the shop stewards of the workshop concerned to enter into binding agreements with the employers. The shop stewards, however, remained true to their standards and left the ratification of their proposals to a general strike meeting. (cf. *Die Aussperrung in der Berliner Elektrizitäts-Industrie 1905*, published by Ortsverwaltung Berlin of the DMV, Berlin 1905, p. 8.) The local union administration was not pleased with the shop stewards' behaviour as this form of democracy was no longer practised generally by the branch. For many years only a small number of the membership had been able to attend general meetings of the branch as a whole for geographical reasons, and the shop stewards as 'representatives' had long been recognised as the 'heart' of the organization. (cf. *Protokoll der siebenten ordentlichen General-Versammlung des Deutschen Metallarbeiter-Verbandes*, abgehalten vom 12. bis 17. Juni 1905, Stuttgart, n.d. [1905], p. 154.

20 *Protokoll der achten ordentlichen General-Versammlung*, 25, 39, 192, 220–1, 240, 260.

21 Deutscher Metallarbeiter-Verband, Verwaltungstelle Berlin, *Jahres-Bericht der Ortsverwaltung Berlin pro 1908* (Berlin, 1909), 95–6.

22 *Die Aussperrung in der Berliner Elektrizitäts-Industrie 1905*, 17–18.

23 ibid., 20.

24 J. Kocka, *Unternehmensverwaltung und Angestelltenschaft am Beispiel Siemens 1847–1914* (Stuttgart, 1969), 355.

25 J. Schmöle, *Die sozialdemokratischen Gewerkschaften in Deutschland seit dem Erlasse des Sozialisten-Gesetzes*, Part II: *Einzelne Organisationen*, Section I: *Der Zimmererverband* (Jena, 1898), 42–3.

26 K. Oldenberg, 'Das deutsche Bauhandwerk der Gegenwart' (PhD. thesis, Berlin, 1888), 24–5.

27 Schmöle, *Die sozialdemokratischen Gewerkschaften*, 5.

28 K. Werner, *Organisation und Politik der Gewerkschaften und Arbeitgeberverbände in der deutschen Bauwirtschaft* (Berlin, 1968), 12.

29 Oldenberg, *Das deutsche Bauhandwerk*, 7.

30 StAP 15295, Bl. 91 and Bl. 103.

31 StAP 15295, Bl. 81.

32 *Vorwärts* 69 (21 March 1896).

33 Oldenberg, *Das deutsche Bauhandwerk*, 7.

34 StAP 15584, Bl. 244 and 15585, Bl. 279.

35 StAP 15297, Bl. 9–10, 15–16 and 23.

36 *Vorwärts* 69 (21 March 1896).

37 *Vorwärts* 69 (21 March 1896).

38 *Vorwärts* 151 (1 July 1899).

39 *Einigkeit* 28 (15 July 1900) and *Protokoll über die Verhandlungen vom siebenten Kongress der Freien Vereinigung Deutscher Gewerkschaften*, abgehalten vom 10. bis 19. April 1906 (Berlin, 1906), 23.

40 *Protokoll über die Verhandlungen vom vierten Kongre der Vertrauensmänner-Zentralisation Deutschlands vom 24. bis 26. Mai 1900* (Berlin, 1900), 95.

41 *Protokoll des ersten Kongresses der lokal organisierten oder aufgrund des Vertrauensmännersystems zentralisierten Gewerkschaften Deutschlands zu Halle a. S. 1897* (Berlin, n.d. [1897], 5, 8, and *Protokoll über die Verhandlungen vom vierten Kongreß der Vertrauensmänner-Zentralisation*, 53.

42 *Der Bauhandwerker* 37 (16 September 1893).

43 *Einigkeit* 26 (25 June 1904).

44 StAP 15583, Bl. 269, and *Der Bauhandwerker* 22 (3 June 1893).

45 *Protokoll des ersten Kongresses der lokal organisierten oder aufgrund des Vertrauensmännersystems Zentrolisation Gewerkschaften Deutschlands*, 5.

46 ibid., 6, and *Protokoll über die Verhandlungen vom vierten Kongress der Vertrauensmänner-Zentralisation*, 53–5.

47 *Einigkeit* 37 (16 September 1905).
48 loc. cit.
49 D. H. Müller, *Idealismus und Revolution. Zur Opposition der Jungen gegen den Sozialde-mokratischen Parteivorstand 1890 bis 1914* (Berlin, 1975), 160–3.
50 *Protokoll über die Verhandlungen des Parteitages der Sozialdemokratischen Partei Deutsch-lands*, abgehalten in Nürnberg vom 13. bis 19. September 1908 (Berlin, 1908), 546.
51 *Protokoll über die Verhandlungen vom sechsten Kongress der Freien Vereinigung deutscher Gewerkschaften*, 133–5.
52 *Protokoll über die Verhandlungen vom zwölften Kongress der Freien Vereinigung deutscher Gewerkschaften*, abgehalten am 27., 28., 29. und 30. Dezember 1919 (Berlin, n.d. [1920], 3–6.
53 International Instituut voor Sociale Geschiedenis, Amsterdam, Nachlass Rocker: Rudolf Rocker, Fritz Kater (Ms.).
54 H. M. Bock, *Syndikalismus und Linkskommunismus von 1918–1923. Zur Geschichte und Soziologie der Freien Arbeiter-Union Deutschlands (Syndikalisten), der Allgemeinen Arbeiter-Union Deutschlands und der Kommunistischen Arbeiter-Partei Deutschlands* (Meisenheim a. G., 1969), 439.

14 Mass Organization and Militancy in Britain: Contrasts and Continuities

RICHARD HYMAN

This essay attempts to sustain a dual focus upon the two phases of explosive growth in union membership and collective militancy in 1888–91 and 1911–14; to trace the processes of transition over the intervening decades; and to outline some of the parallels and divergences between the two periods of upsurge. Collective organization among 'general labour' provides a central but not exclusive theme. Since Eric J. Hobsbawm's classic study in 1949[1] there has appeared a voluminous literature on the New Unionism and on the 'labour unrest', on the history of individual unions and on specific aspects of the working class and the labour movement in the three pre-war decades. But there has been no comparable attempt to offer a synoptic assessment, in the light of recent research, of the character and significance of general unionism from its eruption in 1888–90 to the outbreak of war, let alone to locate this within a conspectus of the changing structure and orientations of British trade unionism as a whole. Such an ambitious exercise cannot be seriously contemplated within the constraints of the present chapter, which is intended more modestly to outline some issues relevant to such a task.

The discussion which follows is in three parts. The first surveys current views on the struggles and organizations of 'general labour', traditionally symbolized by the London dock strike of 1889. It examines the debate on the nature and significance of the New Unionism in the light of the broader patterns of unionization and strike activity in the late 1880s. The second summarizes the decline and transformation of the New Unions after their brief initial successes, again relating their experience to the wider context of British unionism. The third assesses the sources and implications of the 'Labour unrest' of the immediate prewar years, considering in particular how far these events may be regarded as a repeat of the earlier experience. A brief conclusion seeks to draw some of the arguments together.

I

The traditional stereotype of New Unionism is a familiar story, centred around the struggles and victories of such groups as match girls, gasworkers and dockers; the rise of militant new organizations unencumbered by friendly benefits and committed to the recruitment of the poor and oppressed regardless of occupation; the powerful challenge to the complacency and exclusiveness of established labour leaders by socialists and advocates of independent political action. The contrast between 'old' and 'new' trade unionism fuelled the polemics of the time, acquired scholarly credentials with the publication of the Webbs' *History of Trade Unionism* in 1894[2] and informed the historical consciousness of subsequent generations of trade unionists.

The 'revolutionist' critique of the traditional account is by now familiar to historians.[3] Dramatic upsurges in unionization have been a common feature of periods of favourable trade, as existed in 1889–91. The New Unions which burst upon the labour scene were part of a broader and longer-term expansion, and did not fall into any single pattern: not all were socialist-led or universalistic in their recruitment aspirations. Low subscriptions and few benefits were inevitable accompaniments of unions which appealed to low-paid workers; those leaders who proclaimed a doctrine of 'fighting unionism' were making a virtue of necessity. And in any event, whatever the rhetoric of the heady days of 1889 such leaders soon became preoccupied with the mundane tasks of routine administration and the cultivation of bargaining relationships with employers.

It is possible to accept many of the recent qualifications to the earlier conception of New Unionism yet still insist that 1888–91 marked a radical turning-point for British trade unionism. Total union membership before the upsurge was roughly three-quarters of a million out of a labour force of some 12 million. Unions were, in the main, tiny and fragmented; at the start of 1888 only a dozen claimed a membership of over 10,000 while the largest, the Amalgamated Society of Engineers (ASE), had less than 52,000 members including a number overseas. Though the traditional crafts by now contributed only a minority of unionists, their ethos continued to dominate: the sectionalism and parochialism associated with a narrow occupational and typically local basis of recruitment being characteristically reflected in the organizations of cotton workers and coalminers which with the crafts now constituted the bulk of the movement.[4]

Against this background, the mushroom growth of the 'general labour' unions necessarily created a profound impact. At the peak in 1890 the National Amalgamated Union of Sailors and Firemen officially reported 60,000 members and the Dock, Wharf, Riverside and General Labourers' Union 57,000. The other main waterside organization, the National Union of Dock Labourers, affiliated to the TUC on the basis of 40,000 members. For their part the (unregistered) National Union of Gasworkers and General Labourers claimed 60,000, as did the National Labour Federation, while the Tyneside and National Labour Union recorded 40,000.[5] While such figures must be regarded with considerable scepticism, what was popularly defined as the New Unionism may have achieved a maximum membership of some 300,000, or roughly a fifth of all trade unionists.

Yet if the global figure of trade unionists doubled over the three years 1888–90, much of the expansion must be located in the 'old' unions and in those which, while newly formed, were not stereotypical New Unions. The most notable example was the reconstruction of mining unionism, which for much of the 1880s had been in disarray. At the start of the decade the Miners' National Union, always a loosely structured organization, was largely ineffectual, and the county unions on which it was based were – with the notable exception of Durham and Northumberland – in serious decline; in Yorkshire, one of the largest coalfields, membership had fallen to 2,800.[6] In the early 1880s some success had been achieved in consolidating organization and co-ordinating action within the central coalfields, but the sharp recession of 1885–7 and major conflicts with the employers caused a severe setback. The subsequent economic recovery facilitated new moves towards national co-operation, culminating in the formal constitution of the Miners' Federation of Great Britain (MFGB) in 1889, and reflected in the negotiation of four successive increases of 10 per cent in wages between 1888 and 1890. These achievements ran in parallel with the revival of membership in the localities. The most dramatic expansion was in the Yorkshire Miners' Association; from a claimed membership of 8,000 in 1887 it increased to 50,000 in 1890 and 55,000 in 1892, overtaking the long-dominant Durham Miners' Association which held aloof from the MFGB. The total membership reported in mining unions in the latter year was 315,000, well over half being affiliated to the MFGB. This was probably three or four times the total membership of district and county unions a mere five years earlier, and outside Durham and Northumberland represented perhaps a tenfold expansion. This rise in unionization must have involved a shift in membership composition from the relative elite of face-workers towards the lower-paid day-wage men; and the platform of the MFGB involved commitment to a statutory eight-hour day for miners and rejection of sliding scale agreements which tied wages to the fluctuating price of coal. But in other respects the MFGB – with its close and enduring association with Liberal politics, its roots in the stable and cohesive communities of the pit villages, and its explicit commitment to conciliatory relations with employers – had little in common with the New Unions which shared its year of birth.

On the railways the parallels were somewhat closer. In 1889 the General Railway Workers' Union (GRWU) was formed with the explicit aim of organizing the lower-paid and often casual grades of employees who were neglected by the Amalgamated Society of Railway Servants (ASRS). The GRWU declared itself a 'fighting union' unencumbered by friendly benefits, and espoused the goal of the legal eight-hour day. Recruitment was rapid, even if claims of 45,000 members in nine months[7] are viewed with disbelief.[8] Certainly its longer established rival ASRS was helped by this competition to a more vigorous stance; its membership (which in 1882 had fallen to 6,321) reached 10,000 in 1887, almost 20,000 in 1889 and 30,000 in 1892. Moreover, the 'old' railway union was still expanding while its 'new' challenger was near collapse. Even more successful was another 'old' union with some 'new' characteristics, the National Union of Operative Boot and Shoe Riveters and Finishers. Formed in 1874 as a breakaway from a traditional society dominated by skilled hand-workers, the union primarily recruited operatives in the expanding mechanized section of the footwear industry. Its membership of only 3,000 in 1880 rose to

13,000 by 1889, almost doubled the following year and reached 42,500 in 1892 – making this probably the fourth largest union in the country.

Nor was craft unionism itself stagnant in this period. In the metal trades between 1888 and 1892 the ASE increased its membership by a third, the United Society of Boilermakers and Iron and Steel Shipbuilders by a half, while the Associated Society of Shipwrights more than doubled. Among the building trades both the Amalgamated Society of Carpenters and Joiners and the Friendly Society of Operative Stonemasons grew by a half, while the United Operative Bricklayers' Trade Society expanded from under 7,000 to over 22,000. In printing the National Typographical Association increased by a half, the London Society of Compositors by a fifth.

The extensive character of union growth in a context of favourable labour market conditions cannot realistically be assimilated to the experience of the Dockers or Gasworkers. The same is true of strikes, the number of which reached a peak in 1889–91. Transport and 'miscellaneous' trades, responsible for only twenty-three of the 517 recorded stoppages in 1888, accounted for 323 out of 1,211 in 1889, 290 out of 1,040 in 1890 and 159 out of 906 in 1891.[9] But the aggregate figures are sufficient to indicate that the explosive upsurge of New Unionism contributed only a minority of the increase in industrial conflict, even though in 1889 seamen and dockers represented almost half the recorded number of strikers. The traditionally unionized trades of building, mining, metals and textiles, which provided over 90 per cent of recorded stoppages in 1888, were still responsible for almost two-thirds in the peak years of 1889 and 1890, and their share rose again to three-quarters in the following two years.

II

The years 1888–92, then, were a period of general and rapid increases in union membership and of high levels of collective struggle. The facilitating condition – as so often with explosions of militancy and unionization – was a sharp turn in the labour market in workers' favour after a phase of heavy unemployment. The precipitating causes were almost certainly varied: in some cases an intensification of work pressure,[10] in others a reaction against employer encroachments on traditional worker prerogatives, elsewhere an effort to restore wage reductions imposed in less favourable times, in yet other contexts a novel awareness of ability to fight collectively for shorter hours, higher pay, or more tolerable working conditions. Radical political ideologies and more vigorous organizational principles clearly provided an additional stimulus; but its impact was decisive only in a minority of situations. New Unionism, if the term is to be applied with any kind of precision, was only one specific element in a far broader process.

The limits of New Unionism were also temporal: the ephemeral character of the qualitative and quantitative achievements of 1888–90 is a familiar argument. Groups of workers, often without prior experience of collective militancy, had taken employers by surprise in the first dramatic struggles. But a counter-attack quickly developed, particularly in the face of attempts to build on the initial victories through such demands as the closed shop, and even before economic conditions turned the unions suffered a series of damaging defeats. In the summer of 1890 the Dockers' Union had claimed over 25,000 members in the Thames area, but concerted opposition by the major companies quickly confined effective organization to the Victoria and Albert Docks. This stronghold survived until a disastrous strike defeat in 1900, and 'by 1906 the Dockers' Union was virtually extinct in London'.[11] Total membership in the union fell by well over half between 1890 and 1892, and in another two years was down to 10,000 – a level around which it was to fluctuate for over a decade. The northern-based National Union of Dock Labourers declined to similar numbers. Other New Unions fared even worse. In the north-east, the National Labour Federation collapsed: membership fell to 6,000 in 1892, and the union dissolved two years later. Its local rival, which became the National Amalgamated Union of Labour, managed to hold a membership of around 20,000, though it declined somewhat after the turn of the century. The most successful of the New Unions was the Gasworkers, though its fortunes too were volatile; membeship fell to 23,532 by 1895 but more than doubled in the following four years. It soon lost most of these new gains but then stabilized at around 30,000 members.

Associated with this process of decline was a substantial dilution in the 'general' character of the New Unions. Hugh A. Clegg, Alan Fox and A. F. Thompson have claimed that those organizations with the most hetero-geneous membership 'adopted this form unintentionally', either because the core sectors recruited were occupationally mobile, or because the successes of a particular group of workers encouraged others to join in.[12] In any event, it was the more miscellaneous categories of labourer who proved most vulnerable when the phase of growth was halted. As Hobsbawm has shown, it was those New Unions whose organization was confined to a homo-geneous occupational or industrial constituency which weathered the 1890s most successfully, and which did best during the following decade. Within the 'general' unions themselves it was largely the mixed branches which collapsed and the specialist branches which survived and expanded. Hence his conclusion that 'the General Unions, at any rate between 1892 and 1911, depended far more on their foothold in certain industries and large works than on their ability to recruit indiscriminately'.[13]

The transition from (in some cases) aspiring all-inclusive organizations of 'general labour' to combinations of workers with specialized abilities and bargaining potential was closely connected to a shift in policies and prior-ities. 'Recognition' from employers was quickly perceived by New Union leaders as the means to stabilize the gains of the initial militancy. Thus the officers of the Dockers' Union were concerned from the outset to persuade employers that unionization entailed a reliable and disciplined workforce, and to establish machinery for conciliation and negotiation which would prevent a repeat of the confrontation of 1889; a central preoccupation was to restrain their own members from 'restrictive practices' and spontaneous sectional militancy.[14] The experience of the employers' counter-attack served to reinforce, in many unions, the concern to establish orderly industrial relations and stable bargaining units; and indeed it was precisely where such strategies won the goodwill or at least tolerance of employers that viable organization was most commonly sustained through the lean years. With the retreat – implicit or explicit – from the ideology of 'fighting unionism', those unions which had initially proclaimed their opposition to sickness and funeral benefits were soon, in the main, to change their position: not least because such friendly benefits could be seen as an important method of inhibiting the decline in membership. In many respects, then, 'the "new unionism" of 1889 thus became uncomfortably like the "old unionism" it had once fought'.[15]

Finally, it is of some importance that the organizational continuity of those unions which survived did not reflect a similar continuity of worker collectivities. Hobsbawm has remarked that the general unions acted 'as a convenient "banker" for a multiplicity of local and sectional bargaining units';[16] but it is necessary to add that the composition of these units was constantly changing. The 'London Dockers' survived despite the destruction of organization in the London docks – and the loss of other groups such as farm labourers whose recruitment had been a notable feature of 1889–90 – because of compensating successes in Bristol and South Wales, which in 1910 provided two-thirds of the branches in the whole union.[17] More specifically, the decision of Welsh tinplate workers to join the Dockers' Union at the turn of the century may well have saved it from extinction. The other main dockers' union, first established in Glasgow, soon launched its main stronghold on Merseyside, and later built up substantial membership in Ireland. In the Gasworkers, two-thirds of the membership in 1891–2 was located in the London District; four years later the region provided little more than a quarter of a smaller membership, with expansion in the Midlands and Yorkshire contributing substantially to the union's continued viability. Further development in Lancashire and on Tyneside helped keep the union going in the new century, as the original membership base dwindled further. Geographical and occupational shifts in membership composition went together, the diversification being finally signified by a change of name to National Union of General Workers.[18] The National Amalgamated Union of Labour, which until 1893 retained 'Tyneside' as part of its title, was still at that date overwhelmingly rooted on the north-east coast. But changed economic conditions subsequently ravaged the original base among shipyard labourers, and the union was saved by its recruitment in such areas as Sheffield, Liverpool, Belfast and the Medway. Most striking, however, is the example of the Workers' Union, formed with grandiose objectives in 1898. Its early years were marked by rapid rise and decline of branches in a variety of areas and industries; miscellaneous trades in London, farm workers in Shropshire, council employees in Yorkshire, metalworkers in South Wales, semi-skilled engineers in Birmingham; for more than a decade it was only the constant succession of such points of temporary organization which kept the union alive. What survived was thus a name, a rulebook, a small cadre of officers, rather than any stable body of unionized workers. In large measure this encapsulates the story of New Unionism as a whole during these years.

On Clegg's assessment, 'on the most generous interpretation the new unions of 1889 did not include as much as 10 per cent of total trade union membership in 1910, and probably the figure should be nearer 7 per cent'.[19] This diminished significance reflected not only the losses which have been described, but also the expansion of unionism elsewhere. Most notable was the continued process of consolidation in coalmining. In 1893 the MFGB survived a four-month lock-out of 300,000 miners, suffering only a temporary loss of membership. At the turn of the century, strengthened by the adhesion of the newly constituted South Wales Miners' Federation, it claimed 360,000 members out of half a million trade unionists in the industry as a whole. By 1910, after the affiliation of the major districts which had hitherto held aloof, its membership was 600,000 with an additional 125,000 coalminers in separate organizations. Although union membership in many of these years had merely kept in line with expanding employment in the industry, the 1910 figure represented a substantial rise in the proportion unionized (over 70 per cent).

Important advances were also made by the unions in the cotton industry. Among spinners, quasi-craft unionism was already so strongly entrenched by the 1880s that there was virtually no scope for expansion; though the two decades after 1890 saw the growing (and often coercive) recruitment of the spinners' assistants (the 'piecers') to subordinate membership. In 1910 the Spinners' Amalgamation recorded 23,000 spinners and over 31,000 piecers in membership. On the weaving side of the industry, by contrast, unionism in the early 1880s was in disarray; and the reconstruction of industry-wide organization in 1884 brought only gradual recovery; in particular there was little reflection of the general expansion of British union membership associated with New Unionism. But from 1892, with the consolidation of industry-level collective bargaining and the negotiation of a uniform piece-work list, growth was rapid: by the turn of the century the Amalgamated Weavers' Association claimed 81,000 members, and in 1910 112,000. Including unions outside the 'Amalgamated Association of Card and Blowing Room Operatives, formed in 1886 for workers in the preparatory processes in the spinning industry, displayed a similar trajectory. By 1910 its membership had reached 45,000, encompassing almost all the unions in the relevant trades. In the cotton industry as a whole, union membership had stood at some 90,000 in 1888, was double this number at the turn of the century and three times in 1910.[20]

The craft-dominated industries – with coal and cotton the third major component of British trade unionism – provided overall a record of expansion, though experience varied considerably between industries, and as a proportion of total union membership the aggregate strength declined. In the metal, engineering and shipbuilding industries, numbers rose gradually from 280,000 in 1892 to 370,000 in 1910 – failing to keep pace with the expansion in employment. In building the record was even worse: from a membership of 158,000 in 1892 the total rose to 254,000 in 1900; but the next decade was disastrous, with numbers falling back to 157,000. By contrast the printing unions fared well, membership increasing steadily from 45,000 in 1892 to 74,000 in 1910: more than matching the growth in the industry's employment.

Other areas of expanding employment saw union growth which was often a harbinger of dramatic advances in the immediate prewar years. On the railways, ASRS recruitment was boosted by major campaigns for recognition and improved conditions in 1897 and 1907; and though some of the membership gains were short-lived it could claim 75,000 in 1910, while the other railway unions together held 40,000 members. In the public service sector generally progress was registered, most notably among postal workers, schoolteachers and a range of municipal employees.

Across the economy as a whole, union membership passed 2·5 million during 1910 – the equivalent of one worker in every seven. Quantitative expansion was accompanied by qualitative shifts of perhaps far greater significance. The first was the emergence of formal machinery of industry-wide collective bargaining, at times the result of union pursuit of uniformity of conditions, more often the achievement of new and combative employers' associations seeking to contain grass-roots challenges to management control. In cotton, the weavers' uniform list of 1892 was followed a year later by the Brooklands Agreement terminating the spinners' lock-out. In shipbuilding, a series of national agreements on substantive conditions commenced in 1893. The bitter engineering lock-out of 1897–8 concluded with Terms of Settlement prescribing a system of local and national conferences on disputed issues. In building, machinery of local and national conciliation boards was agreed more amicably in 1905. In mining – where the owners insisted on the principle of local autonomy – conciliation machinery at coalfield level became firmly established after the 1893 lock-out.

Secondly, and partly in consequence, there was a growing centralization of authority within national trade unions. Headquarters officials rapidly displayed a commitment to the smooth operation of national bargaining procedures, even when these had been imposed by the employers, and as a corollary sought increased discipline over union branches and districts. Concern with financial stability provided an additional incentive to impose central authority over the initiation of strikes, and over the pursuit of local demands which might result in conflict: it was in the two decades around the turn of the century that the term 'unofficial strike' acquired widespread currency. Such centralizing tendencies, particularly in unions with a tradition of locally enforced autonomous craft controls, were a fertile source of internal contention.[21]

A third and again associated trend was the growth in the numbers of full-time union officials. In their *History of Trade Unionism* the Webbs noted that 'this Civil Service of the Trade Union world, non-existent in 1850, numbered, in 1892, between six and seven hundred'.[22] Three years later, in *Industrial Democracy*, they argued that extension of the level of collective bargaining was of necessity accelerating this process.[23] This was particularly evident in the 'piece-work trades': cotton and shipbuilding unions were among the pioneers of the professional negotiator. But around the turn of the century there was a general movement within the larger 'old unions' toward structural reforms involving the appointment of new officials; while the New Unions depended from the outset on a comparatively large corps of organizers. Overall, suggest Clegg, Fox and Thompson, 'the number of officials grew faster than total union membership'.[24] By modern standards of elaborate administrative machinery, official hierarchies and detailed rulebook specifications of executive powers, it may seem far-fetched to speak of a 'union bureaucracy' emerging in this period. Nevertheless, in these years it became possible for the first time to view the position of trade union official as a distinctive career, and to associate with the position a set of social perspectives and material interests divergent from – and even antagonistic to – those of the membership. Significantly, it was in this period that the notion of 'rank and file' came to be regularly counterposed to that of 'officials'.[25]

III

The years immediately preceding the outbreak of the war saw industrial struggle on a scale well in excess of the upsurge a quarter of a century earlier. In 1912, in particular, there were 1·2 million strikers, far in excess of the total recorded in any previous year; and an aggregate of 40 million strike-days, substantially above the previous record in 1893. The figure of 1,500 stoppages recorded in 1913 was well above the previous peak in 1889, and was indeed to be exceeded in only one subsequent year before the 1940s. The 'labour unrest' was accompanied by an accession of new trade unionists surpassing (in absolute if not relative terms) the achievements of 1888–91: by 1914 there were over 4·1 million union members, an increase of roughly three-fifths in the space of three years. Qualitatively, these years were viewed as involving a transformation as profound as that conventionally attributed to New Unionism.

There is a familiar interpretation, enunciated by Élie Halévy[26] and developed in more lurid tones by George Dangerfield: that the 'labour unrest' was part of a general disintegration of the established social and political order, and would – but for the war – have culminated in a more or less insurrectionary general strike.[27] Subsequent historians have responded sceptically. E. H. Phelps Brown has insisted that militancy was far from universal. 'It was in fact confined to two sectors: unskilled and low-paid labour generally; and all grades of wage-earners in two industries, coal-mining and the railways. Of the great trade union stronghold that had stood in 1906 singularly little was engaged.'[28] Others have sought to deflate the supposed impact of syndicalism, emphasizing the weakness of the movement in Britain, and stressing that the Triple Alliance of miners, railwaymen and transport workers was far from a potential vehicle of a revolutionary general strike.[29] For Henry M. Pelling, indeed, the collective struggles of 1911–13 were 'very much what we would expect in view of the comparatively full employment of the period'.[30] More recently, however, there has been something of a reaction against the 'revisionist' account. Standish Meacham (1972) has suggested that economic grievances were compounded by a growing sense of class division and antagonism, lending a distinctive and unprecedented character to the prewar militancy.[31] Robert Holton has challenged the picture of British syndicalism as feeble and short-lived, stressing the wide industrial base of workers' militancy and exploring its development among groups ignored by Phelps Brown. For Holton, their struggles can appropriately be understood as 'proto-syndicalist'.[32] And for Richard Price, Dangerfield was basically correct in linking the 'industrial unrest' to 'the reality of a society in crisis'.[33]

This persistent controversy reflects the unique but elusive quality of the prewar turbulence. The 'romantic' interpretation in its entirety can scarcely bear close scrutiny. 'Liberal England' was in many respects a highly resilient social formation, and was able to accommodate the discrete challenges from workers, feminists and Irish precisely because they did *not* constitute an integrated revolt. Nor is there a convincing case that syndicalism – on any precise definition – was more than marginally connected with the conflicts in industry: to speak of 'proto-syndicalism' or 'a sense of an impending clash' is to restate rather than elucidate the thesis of an intangible mood of social dissension.

Yet the modern 'industrial relations' reading is itself unsatisfactory: the controversies and engagements of 1911–14 embodied aspirations and discontents which transcended the frame of reference of routine collective bargaining. Pelling's argument, treating the trade cycle as a sufficient explanation of workers' actions in these years, is particularly inadequate.[34] Certainly it is true that 'men could more readily defy their employers when the supply of potential blacklegs was at its lowest'; but what moved them to defiance, and on such a scale?[35] Analysis in terms of trade union bargaining strategy simply will not do, for one of the distinctive features of the unrest was precisely that the initiative came so often from rank-and-file members or non-unionized workers, with union officers typically seeking to exert restraint.[36] In many cases, indeed, struggles were explicitly directed against conditions agreed between employers and trade union negotiators.

To comprehend the specificity of the period it is first necessary to transcend the superficial parallels with 1888–91. Like the earlier period, the pattern of activity was complex, spread unevenly over a wide range of industries and occupations (far wider, certainly, than Phelps Brown assumed), whose forms of struggle varied significantly and which rose to prominence at different times. But the prewar strikes were larger and more protracted, on average, than those of the earlier period, often because they bore, at least implicitly, on intractable issues of management and discipline.[37]

The unionization process also displayed important contrasts to the experience of New Unionism. In 1888–91, as has already been seen, the major – and certainly the most lasting – gains were registered in sectors with strong traditions of trade unionism; whereas in 1911–14, paradoxically, the New Unions of a quarter of a century earlier really came into their own. Almost every existing union shared in the massive growth in aggregate union membership; but those most firmly entrenched – partly because their coverage was already much more comprehensive than in 1888 – expanded comparatively little. Coal and cotton began to lose their pre-eminence, with over 40 per cent of total union membership in 1910 but only 30 per cent by the outbreak of war. Unions in building, metals and printing expanded proportionately faster, but their contribution to aggregate membership fell from roughly a quarter to a fifth. By 1914 they had been overhauled by the transport and 'general labour' groups – for the most part the heirs of 1889 – which with well over a million members were approaching 30 per cent of the total. And in clear contrast to their earlier advance, the gains were permanent: even in the depths of the interwar depression, British union membership did not drop more than marginally below its 1914 level; and by then the general unions, reconstructed through amalgamation, had more than consolidated their position.

Yet it would be wrong to conclude, with Phelps Brown, that 'of the unskilled we may say that the three years beginning with 1911 were the second wave of the surge that had risen first in 1888';[38] for the 'New Unionism' had many distinctive features. In 1911, as in 1889, seamen and dockers played an important part in the initial upsurge; but they were soon eclipsed, particularly after the fiasco of the 1912 London strike; and over the whole period of the 'unrest', the Dockers' Union was the least successful of the 'general labour' unions. Among transport workers, indeed, it is the achievements of the railwaymen which stand out, with the national strike of 1911 generating a sustained advance. The merger which formed the National Union of Railwaymen in 1913 drew the bulk of its membership from the old ASRS, but embraced something of the New Unionist spirit of the GRWU. By the outbreak of war the new organization had recruited half the employees in the industry, winning effective recognition from the hitherto bitterly anti-union railway companies.

What sharply differentiates the 'general' unionism of this period from its predecessor is its substantial basis in manufacturing industries which were only marginally affected by the earlier upsurge. In some cases this involved establishing organization in mass production operations with little or no trade union tradition: chemicals, rubber and paints; breweries, flour-mills and food-processing; building materials; and a wide range of other, often new factory-based industries. Elsewhere – most notably in the metal trades – the advance depended on recruitment of the growing categories of 'semi-skilled' workers neglected by established craft societies. This locus of organization is most sharply exemplified by the most successful of all the general unions, the Workers' Union, with 5,000 members in 1910 and almost 160,000 by the end of 1914. Its achievement was rooted in the transition of engineering from a craft-based to a mass production industry.[39] From a tiny nucleus in a Birmingham small arms factory, a series of strike victories – culminating in mass stoppages throughout Birmingham and the Black Country in the summer of 1913 – and imaginative organizing strategies were to yield dramatic results. By 1914 half of the union's hundred largest branches were based on engineering firms, and almost half the remainder drew part of their membership from the industry.[40]

This factory-based composition of membership expansion – shared, to a lesser degree, by all the fastest-growing 'general unions' of the period – reflects important changes in the structure of capital and the working class. By the end of the nineteenth century, as Hobsbawm has lucidly argued, the traditional dichotomy between 'craftsman' and 'labourer' had become eroded in practice, even if it still dominated workers' perceptions of each other and of themselves. But by 1911 – far more than in 1889 – there had become established a growing body of 'mass workers' in production industries, committed to a particular line of employment[41] and possessing strategic 'skills' which were neither craft-based nor transferable outside their specific area of production. In many cases it seems probable (much more research is needed before firm generalization becomes possible) that the intensity of production pressures and managerial control increased during the early years of the century, while pay remained at or near the level of 'general labourers' and was of course declining in purchasing power. Certainly it is evident that the size of employing units was increasing, rendering management more remote from the shop floor, while the direct agents of supervision were often oppressive in their conduct. More cautiously still, one may speculate on the impact of the increasingly overt intervention of the state in working-class life; of the encroachment of the 'universal market'[42] into ever wider areas of working-class leisure and consumption; of changes in the social structure of working-class communities.[43] In any event, by 1911 there existed new categories of employment with solid potential for unionization; ample grievances relating to pay, the production relationship, and more diffuse social discontents; labour market conditions favourable for collective struggle; and a cadre of union organizers and activists – the survivors of 1889 and their successors – ready to provide an institutional framework for the new upsurge.

The very complexity of the factors underlying the rise of 'general unionism' necessitates a cautious assessment of the even more heterogeneous phenomenon of the 'labour unrest'. Thus it is impossible to accept, as a universal explanation, Price's view that 'the revolt of labour [can be] seen as a response to the corporatist society that was being erected. . . . The labour militancy grew out of the historical struggle for work control.'[44] A more nuanced analysis would need to situate this specific dimension of the 'unrest' within a broader framework. Those who participated in the struggles of these years may be divided into three basic categories. The first element in the 'unrest' involved the rise of the 'unorganised'[45] or of workers in hitherto weakly unionized industries. As well as the mass production workers discussed in the previous paragraphs, the railwaymen constitute an obvious example. The second element involved non-craft workers in strongly unionized industries, such as coalminers and cotton-weavers, often reacting against the constraints and disciplines of collective agreements and bargaining arrangements which were the sedimented product of the struggles of previous decades.[46] The third element involved the resistance, by cohesive groups accustomed to considerable unilateral control over the labour process and over broader conditions of employment, to a dual attempt by managements and by union leaderships to impose new forms of discipline. It is the experience of this type of struggle – and specifically as conducted by building craftsmen – which frames Price's interpretation of the 'unrest'. But however qualitatively significant this dimension of the conflicts, in quantitative terms it was very much a minority factor. Most strikers were not fighting to defend traditions of control and autonomy within the labour process – for they had never enjoyed such benefits – but were wage-slaves struggling for subsistence. And to the extent that many had never experienced the (double-edged) products of collective bargaining, they were striking for rather than against trade union controls. And despite the extent of the prewar militancy and the remarkable advances in unionization, the point must still be made that the large majority of British workers did *not* revolt during these turbulent years, and that by 1914 three-quarters of them remained outside the ranks of trade unionists. A balanced appraisal of 1911–14 must accommodate this salient, if negative fact.

IV

One may conclude with a sense of paradox. The ephemeral successes of the New Unions of 1889 must be considered of less direct significance than the sustained consolidation which occurred in the previously unionized sectors. The main historical importance of those struggles which are traditionally emphasized is the *indirect* outcome of these unions' brief flowering: the survival of an organizational framework within which could be integrated the post-1910 expansion, even though this second upsurge primarily involved very different categories of workers. In this way, modern British trade unionism acquired its exceptional structural character, with the massive general unions straddling a multiplicity of industrial and occupational boundaries.

Ironically, two of the most explosive phases of structural transformation in the past century thus illustrate the remarkable evolutionary adaptability of the machinery of British unionism. This constitutes a not inconsiderable reason to view sceptically the belief that – but for events in Sarajevo – the prewar struggles would have escalated to a momentous climax. Certainly the strike wave was not subsiding by August 1914: the number of stoppages remained at the level of the previous year, and their duration was increasing. But the evidence suggests that, for many of the groups involved in the 'unrest', the very process of unionization and negotiation over conditions of employment served to alleviate the material grievances which had helped inspire the upsurge. The revolts of those protesting against the discipline of established bargaining arrangements were less easily palliated; but here too there were already signs that modest institutional adjustments could fragment and deflate much of the disruptive potential. The absence of a coherent political challenge to the established social order is underlined by the jingoistic enthusiasm with which the outbreak of war was generally received by even militant workers. Hence the scope for compromise and accommodation inherent in even dramatic forms of trade union struggle must be a central lesson of the experience of these turbulent years.

Notes: Chapter 14

1 E. J. Hobsbawm, 'General labour unions in Britain 1889–1914', in idem, *Labouring Men* (London, 1964), 179–203.
2 While the Webbs' discussion of 'The old unionism and the New' was more nuanced than

some contemporary treatment – they stressed the parallels with earlier upsurges of mass unionism, and noted the transience of 'some of the secondary characteristics of the New Unionism of 1889' (S. Webb and B. Webb, *The History of Trade Unionism*, London, 1920 edn, p. 420) – their own involvement in many of the controversies of the time encouraged a somewhat idealized presentation of many of its features.

3 A. E. P. Duffy, 'New Unionism in Britain, 1889–90: a reappraisal', *Economic History Review* 14 (1961): 303–19, provided an early reassessment, though his criticisms of the Webbs were somewhat misplaced; H. A. Clegg *et al., A History of British Trade Unions since 1889*, Vol. 1 (Oxford, 1964), developed a more extensive critique. For recent surveys of the state of debate see J. Lovell, *British Trade Unions 1875–1933* (London, 1977), and E. Hunt, *British Labour History 1815–1914* (London, 1981).

4 The Board of Trade commenced the compilation of labour statistics in 1886, and the first of a series of Reports on Trade Unions appeared the following year. But only eighteen organizations were covered; and though the reports became progressively more extensive, it was only with the creation of a specialized Labour Department in 1893 (when the monthly *Labour Gazette* was launched) that a relatively comprehensive set of statistical data commenced. For discussion of union membership at the end of the 1880s see Clegg *et al., History of British Trade Unions*, 1–2.

5 In 1891, when the Gasworkers' Union made its first official membership report (and when numbers were already falling), the figure was 35,719. The 1890 membership of the Engineers was 67,928 – only a little above the claims of the largest (or at least the most immodest) New Unions. For comments on the membership of the major New Unions see Clegg *et al., History of British Trade Unions*, 82–3.

6 R. P. Arnot, *The Miners* (London, 1949), 61. The figure of 2,800 was recorded by the Board of Trade as the membership of the South Yorkshire Miners' Association, which merged in 1881 with the West Yorkshire Association; the membership of the latter is unknown. In coalmining there was a persistent tradition of the collective organization at pit level (particularly after 1860 when a statutory right to elect a 'checkweighman' was established), even in the absence of formal trade unionism. District and county organization was more vulnerable to collapse, while unity at national level had rarely endured unbroken for any substantial period.

7 T. Mann and B. Tillett, *The 'New' Trade Unionism* (London, 1890), 8.

8 Clegg *et al., History of British Trade Unions*, 83, note that the GRWU nationally recorded 20,000 members at the 1890 TUC, but 'their Liverpool branch was separately affiliated on the incredible figure of 40,000'.

9 As with trade union statistics, the early Reports on Strikes and Lock-outs are of questionable reliability; but the broad evidence of trends and industrial distribution may reasonably be accepted. The detailed report for the peak year of 1889 listed 1,145 stoppages, of which seamen and dockers accounted for 131, road transport workers for 48 and gasworkers only 7.

10 As for example among gasworkers: see E. J. Hobsbawm, 'British gas-workers, 1873–1914', in idem, *Labouring Men*, 158–78.

11 J. Lovell, *Stevedores and Dockers* (London, 1969), 146.

12 Clegg *et al., History of British Trade Unions*, 91–2.

13 Hobsbawm, 'General labour unions', 187.

14 In a well-known passage, the Webbs argued the similarity between Mann's work as Dockers' Union president and that of William Allan as secretary of the Engineers several decades earlier: see Webb and Webb, *History of Trade Unionism*, 419.

15 Hobsbawm, 'General labour unions', 191.

16 ibid., 192.

17 Clegg *et al., History of British Trade Unions*, 85; A. Bullock, *The Life and Times of Ernest Bevin* (London, 1960), 29.

18 Though this did not occur until 1916. For membership details see H. A. Clegg, *General Union in a Changing Society* (Oxford, 1964).

19 ibid., 32.

20 The 'amalgamations' which constituted the industry-wide units in the main branches of the cotton trade were in fact federations of local associations which for many purposes were autonomous. For further details see H. A. Turner, *Trade Union Growth, Structure and*

Policy (London, 1962); Clegg *et al., History of British Trade Unions*; K. Burgess, *The Origins of British Industrial Relations* (London, 1975).

21 The most detailed discussion of such tendencies is to be found in the context of building trade unionism, in R. Price, *Masters, Unions and Men* (Cambridge, 1980); but the most famous conflicts were in the Engineers: see J. B. Jeffery's *The Story of the Engineers* (London, 1945); J. S. Hinton, *The First Shop Stewards' Movement* (London, 1973); Burgess, *Origins of British Industrial Relations*.

22 Webb and Webb, *History of Trade Unionism*, 466.

23 S. Webb and B. Webb, *Industrial Democracy* (London, 1897), 179–81.

24 Clegg *et al., History of British Trade Unions*, 478.

25 The illustrative account quoted by the Webbs (*History of Trade Unionism*, 469–71) is justly famous.

26 E. Halévy, *The Rule of Democracy* (London, 1934).

27 G. Dangerfield, *The Strange Death of Liberal England* (London, 1936).

28 E. H. Phelps Brown, *The Growth of British Industrial Relations* (London, 1959), 333–4.

29 See for example B. C. Roberts, *The Trades Union Congress 1868–1921* (London, 1958); G. A. Phillips, 'The triple industrial alliance in 1914', *Economic History Review* 24 (1971): 55–67.

30 H. Pelling, *Popular Politics and Society in Late Victorian England* (London, 1968), 155.

31 S. Meacham, '"The sense of an impending clash": English working-class unrest before the First World War', *American Historical Review* 77 (1972): 1343–64.

32 R. Holton, *British Syndicalism 1900–14* (London, 1976).

33 Price, *Masters, Unions and Men*, 236–8.

34 Pelling, *Popular Politics and Society*, 150.

35 Moreover, unemployment was at an even lower level in 1898–1900, yet the number of strikes declined during these years. Pelling's account is also notable in dismissing falling real wages – a factor emphasized by almost every other historian – as a cause of the 'unrest': 'There was probably still confusion in the minds of working men about the relationship between money wages and real wages.' This patronizing comment assumes that workers (and male workers' wives), often struggling to maintain a weekly balance between income and expenditure (see for example M. P. Reeves, *Round About a Pound a Week*, London, 1913), failed to notice that prices were rising sharply while wages stagnated.

36 Most notably, the railway strike of 1911 and the miners' minimum wage strikes of 1911 and 1912 fell into this category.

37 For more detailed comments see J. E. Cronin, *Industrial Conflict in Modern Britain* (London, 1979), 51–2.

38 Phelps Brown, *Growth of British Industrial Relations*, 334.

39 More has argued (C. More, *Skill and the English Working Class*, London, 1980, p. 185) that in British engineering 'if skill is adequately defined either by labels – turner, fitter etc. – or in the case of some unlabelled groups by pay, then the decline between the 1880s and the 1900s was extremely slow'. But a key feature of these decades was the success of craft unionism in preserving traditional job categories and pay relationships despite substantial changes in technology and the labour process; another significant factor was the geographical location of the 'new' sectors of engineering (in the south and the midlands) outside the northern strongholds of the ASE.

40 The Workers' Union has suffered from a large measure of historical neglect; for a detailed account of its development see R. Hyman, *The Workers' Union* (Oxford, 1971).

41 Hobsbawm's reference ('General labour unions', 202) to the fluid career of one Workers' Union activist, presented as typical of semi-skilled engineering workers, is somewhat misleading: the case constitutes one extreme from a spectrum of biographical studies, many of which demonstrate remarkable stability of employment. See R. Hyman, 'The Workers' Union 1889–1929' (D.Phil. thesis, Oxford, 1968), 175.

42 H. Braverman, *Labor and Monopoly Capital* (New York, 1974), ch. 13.

43 For a stimulating attempt to explore such themes in a comparative dimension see P. N. Stearns, *Lives of Labour* (London, 1975).

44 Price, *Masters, Unions and Men*, 239–41.

45 The conventional equation of 'unionized' with 'organized' implies a dangerous illusion.

Capital itself organizes workers, whose collective actions commonly take place without the formal sanction of trade unionism.

46 There are obvious parallels with Gramsci's analysis, a few years later, of the 'industrial legality' established by trade union action (A. Gramsci, *Political Writings 1910–1920*, London, 1977, p. 265). For militancy in mining see H. Francis and D. Smith, *The Feds* (London, 1980), and for cotton see J. L. White, *The Limits of Trade Union Militancy* (London, 1978). It should be noted that while intensified work pressure was an important factor in some of the disputes in this category, more straightforward wages issues predominated. Indeed the tendency for some unions to negotiate long-term wage agreements, at the very time when prices were rising substantially, was a potent factor behind some of the conflicts.

15 Revolutionary Syndicalism and the British Labour Movement

ROBERT J. HOLTON

I

It is customary to characterize the various European labour movements in terms of national stereotypes.[1] In this way British labour history is often seen in terms of Fabian reformism and parliamentary pragmatism, French labour history in terms of periodic revolutionary upsurges presaging a new social order, and German labour history in terms of the systematic construction of mass organization. From this perspective, the historic impact of revolutionary syndicalism is seen as concentrated mainly in France, and in 'Mediterranean' societies like Spain and Italy where anarchist anti-state traditions were important. In the case of Britain, it has often been assumed that revolutionary syndicalism remained a relatively insignificant current, an alien import which crossed the English channel from France only to find an inhospitable terrain dominated by trade unionists engaged in orderly collective bargaining, and Labour Members of Parliament earnestly absorbed in the respectable pursuit of political reform. One recent historian has likened the scholarly investigation of revolutionary syndicalism in Britain to the vain search for a *revolution manquée*.[2]

The use of such national stereotypes has of course come under challenge from several directions.[3] In the first place it is argued that occupation rather than nation state is the most salient unit of analysis in the explanation of labour movement behaviour. French, German, or British miners, for example, may be seen as sharing more behavioural characteristics in common than the various components of each individual national labour movement, for example British miners, British printers, British metal-workers, share between them. While earlier research on the inter-industry propensity to strike provided impressive backing for such claims,[4] more recent findings have stressed significant variations in behaviour between workers engaged in the same occupation.[5] This has stimulated some interest in distinctive regional patterning of labour movement behaviour, socio-economic region appearing as a third possible unit of analysis distinct from nation state and occupation.[6] At the same time it is doubtful whether accounts of the various national labour movements can simply be built up from an agglomeration of regional or occupational components. This is partly because the formation of increasingly centralized and democratic nation states during the history of Western capitalist development has involved a parallel process of labour movement centralization and bureau-cratization in both the political and trade union fields. Such processes of incorporation into the national polity have a certain autonomy of their own, requiring some kind of 'national' rather than a purely 'regional' or 'occupational' level of analysis.

A second cogent objection to the practice of labelling labour movements in terms of national stereotypes claims that such labels tend to be static and ahistorical. As such they fail to reveal the significant shifts in the dominant mode of labour movement behaviour over time, shifts dependent perhaps on alternating patterns – or 'long-waves' – of economic expansion and economic crisis. From this perspective, the characterization of British Labour as 'reformist' or 'Fabian' provides a misleading overgeneralization incapable of distinguishing phases of militancy, that is, 1825–48, 1910–26, 1968–80, from periods of relative labour quiescence such as 1850–80, 1950–68. Much recent debate on British labour history has simply assumed the 'reformist' stereotype as a given, and proceeded very quickly to rehearse certain global explanations of this supposed phenomena,[7] notably the theory of the Labour aristocracy.

This essay rejects the presupposition that British labour history may be read in terms of predominant tendency to reformism and pragmatism. On the contrary it accepts that considerable shifts in attitude and behaviour are evident over time. The main purpose here is to explore the early phases of one such shift away from parliamentarism and conciliatory trade unionism towards militant direct action and social confrontation that occurred between 1910 and the defeat of the General Strike of 1926. The aim is to assess how far these developments represented the development of revolutionary syndicalism in Britain. The central thrust of the argument will be that revolutionary syndicalism did represent a significant part within the labour movement in this period, but that its impact stemmed from indigenous pressures within British society, rather than the external stimulus of revolutionary ideologies imported from overseas.

II

Certain methodological problems are posed by any attempt to conceptualize revolutionary syndicalism as a mode of labour movement activity. The most conventional approach is to assume that one is dealing with a body of doctrinal principles. In this respect there are many advantages to a broad generic definition which embraces all those movements known variously as 'revolutionary syndicalist', 'anarcho-syndicalist', 'Industrial Unionist', and so on. What this group has in common is first of all the objective of emancipating the working class from capitalist society through revolutionary industrial contestation (direct action and the General Strike) rather than political means, that is, the agency of a revolutionary party or parliamentary politics. Such objectives are further linked to the notion of workers' control over post-capitalist society through industrial rather than political organization, namely, by the direct producers themselves rather than some kind of state. Consequently when such a definition is applied to empirical analysis, any evaluation of the impact of revolutionary syndicalism becomes a matter of establishing how many people supported such doctrines and how successful they were in implementing them.

This procedure has obvious analytical advantages in pinning down the scale of formally committed revolutionary syndicalist opinion, which may then be compared with alternative doctrinal currents within the labour movement (for example, parliamentary socialism, orthodox Marxism, and so on). At the same time it has the serious disadvantage of neglecting layers of working-class consciousness and behaviour which approximate to the formal doctrinal principles, but yet are not explicitly affiliated to any tangible revolutionary syndicalist organization. Such a neglect is especially serious in the case of syndicalism, since it was a movement which placed such a great stress on ouvrierism, that is, working-class self-reliance and the distrust of middle-class leadership. 'It is not the Sorels ... and such figures who count the most – it is the obscure Bill Jones on the firing line, with stink in his clothes, rebellion in his brain, hope in his heart, determination in his eye, and direct action in his gnarled fist.'[8]

An alternative method of conceptualizing revolutionary syndicalism taking such characteristics into account is to regard it as a social movement operating on both formal and informal levels. As Joseph Gusfield has persuasively argued:

There is a mixture of formal association and informal diffuse behaviour encompassed in the concept of a [social] movement. A significant distinction can be made between the 'directed' and 'undirected' ... segments of movements. The directed sense of a movement is characterised by organised and structured groups with specific programs, a formal leadership structure, definitive ideology and stated objectives. Its followers are members of an organisation as well as partisans to a belief. The undirected segment of a movement is characterised by the reshaping of perspectives, norms and values [outside] ... a specific vocational context. The followers are partisans but need not be members of any association which advocates the change being studied.[9]

Such a conceptualization certainly preserves the conventional identification of a particular labour movement current with formal adherence to a set of principles. But what it adds to this is a serious injunction to examine the 'reshaping of perspectives, norms and values' within less explicitly committed modes of action. Such a procedure encourages us to move beyond the crude dualistic conception of labour movement activity as either 'revolutionary' or 'reformist', thereby directing attention to complex layers of consciousness which seem not to fit either category very well. In other words, assessment of the 'mentality' or 'mood' of workers engaged in strike action or mass demonstrations is just as important to the exploration of revolutionary syndicalist impact as the investigation of theoretical debates among professional revolutionaries.

III

The history of prewar British syndicalism can be divided into two phases.[10] The first, stretching from around 1900 to 1910, saw the emergence of a very small hard core of revolutionary propagandists together with a proliferation of tiny organizations. Such groupings were influenced to a considerable extent by the international context of revolutionary syndicalist, industrial unionist and anarcho-syndicalist developments. Scattered contacts were made between British militants and European anarcho-syndicalists or the newly formed American Industrial Workers of the World (IWW). These often depended on internationally mobile working-men, whether seamen, migrant workers, or political refugees. In a British seaport like Liverpool links were forged between local militants, Spanish anarcho-syndicalists, the American supporters of the IWW and Jewish political refugees.[11] At the same time it is clear that anti-state revolutionary traditions more indigenous to Britain also played a significant part in this phase of diffuse debate and unspectacular propaganda work. The leading influence of this kind was probably that of William Morris and the Socialist League active in the late 1880s and early 1890s.

Compared with the 2 million or so workers organized in orthodox trade unions or the thousands of voters who were beginning to support the newly formed Labour Party, the scale and organizational coherence of revolutionary syndicalism in this first phase was extremely limited. At this stage the main impact of revolutionary syndicalism was restricted to a vigorous propaganda challenge mounted against the small British Marxist party, the Social Democratic Federation (SDF). This was especially evident in the campaign mounted by supporters of Daniel de Leon and reflected in the formation of the Socialist Labour Party in 1903, and the Industrial Workers of Great Britain in 1909 on the model of the American IWW. This thrust represented widespread disquiet with the increasing parliamentary orientation of European Social Democracy, and a leaning towards revolutionary industrial organization rather than the state as the nucleus for a new social order. Such de Leonite emphases were especially important in the development of a revolutionary industrial movement in the important industrial region of Clydeside and were reflected in the wartime shop stewards' movement among metalworkers.

The second phase of British revolutionary syndicalism began around 1910 and was not finally brought to an end until the failure of the General Strike of 1926. The years 1910–14, with which this essay is mainly concerned, were however crucial to this phase of militancy. For it was during this immediate prewar period that revolutionary syndicalism became gradually transformed from a tiny propagandist current to a militant labour mentality capable of actively challenging (ultimately unsuccessfully) both the structures of managerial authority within the capitalist enterprise, and the legitimacy of existing state power.

The period from 1910 to 1914 represents one of those periodic 'upsurges' of labour movement activity which characterize the labour history of industrial capitalist societies. The two immediate characteristics of the unrest were mass strikes and rapid trade union recruitment. From 1910 until the outbreak of war, working days lost rose to an annual total of 10 million or more, while trade union membership increased from 2·1 million to 4·1 million over the same period. Such developments were unparalleled since the early 'explosions' of unrest in 1871–3 and the New Unionism of 1889–91.

There were, however, some important contrasts between 1910–14 and the earlier phases of unrest. The most striking was the high degree of aggressive, sometimes violent and often unofficial industrial militancy during the latter 'explosion' compared with the rather more peaceable official action on the earlier occasions. There is a particularly vivid contrast between the London dock strike of 1889, when dockers marched peacefully through the City of London to gain public sympathy, and the 1910 Welsh miners' strike when miners clashed violently with civil power at Tonypandy and elsewhere. This comparison indicates the more general contrast between what Eric J. Hobsbawm has called 'the evangelistic organising campaigns of the dock strike period' and the 'mass rebellions' of the latter explosion.[12] Such contrasts are clearly evident in the labels New Unionism as against 'labour unrest' which have become attached to the two phases of labour activity.

What most disturbed middle-class interests about the 'labour unrest' was undoubtedly its violent, unofficial and insurgent character. It was not simply that episodes of industrial confrontation and defiance of civil or military authority posed awkward problems of public order, though this, in the context of parallel unrest over women's suffrage and Irish Home Rule, was serious enough. What was even more disconcerting, however, was the apparent failure of the trade union movement to channel industrial grievances through the increasingly acceptable institutions of collective bargaining and conciliation. The Cabinet's leading advisers on industrial relations including George Askwith (Board of Trade), R. Redmayne (Chief Inspector of Mines) and David Shackleton (Home Office) all warned that the older generation of conciliatory union leaders were rapidly losing their authority to younger, more militant men. The spirit of compromise fostered within collective bargaining mechanisms was being challenged by direct action.

Another aspect of the unrest detected by many observers was the implicit challenge to the parliamentary system posed by the 'explosion' of mass discontent in the streets and workplaces. The periodic defiance of police, magistrates and the military, coupled with a sensed failure of the existing political parties to deal effectively with working-class grievances, persuaded many that the whole structure of parliamentary democracy and party politics was under threat. Diagnoses ranged from H. G. Wells's and Hilaire Belloc's condemnation of the unrepresentative basis of existing political parties, through Graham Wallas's belief that politicians through their manipulation of labels and slogans were breeding an increasing cynicism and disaffection, to Norman Angell's contention that unrest reflected awareness of the lack of necessary social and political qualifications among the leading decision-makers.

If we apply the conceptualization of revolutionary syndicalism as a two-layer social movement to the British labour unrest of 1910–14, there is considerable evidence of syndicalist mood or mentality at work during the strike wave. Evidence drawn from police intelligence reports, testimony by employers and detailed accounts of strike action in the local press illuminate the main components of this mood.

In the first place much strike action was local, unofficial and hostile to the existing labour leadership. This is especially evident in the genesis of the South Wales miners' strike of 1910, the national waterside and railwaymen's strikes of 1911 and the London building workers' reaction to the employers' lock-out of 1914. Second, and in conjunction with these unofficial characteristics, was the considerable amount of collective violence associated with strike action. Violence is of course a notoriously difficult indicator to use in support of any particular hypothesis about motivation.[13] This is partly because collective violence is not the outcome of some unilateral assertion of will, but arises during a relationship between two or more social forces. The character of intervention by the state during labour disputes, for example, is as much if not more responsible for actual numbers of dead or injured as is the policy or intention of strikers. It is also partly because collective violence by itself is an ideologically unspecific category equally compatible with conservative as revolutionary intentions.

When one examines the specific character and targets of strike crowd violence during the labour unrest, however, there is significant evidence of violence directed at capitalist managers, and plant and installations, as well as the violence against strike-breaking workers generally found during most trade union recognition disputes. In South Wales attacks were made on the homes of mine managers and the property of magistrates, as well as on pit-head installations. In Yorkshire, railway track was torn up and communication disrupted. In London, transport workers fought a revolver battle with blacklegs in the docks. In general terms such episodes show a marked similarity with many of the instances of sabotage and violent direct action found in French or Italian labour history, and often taken to be evidence of revolutionary syndicalist inclinations. The only significant difference in comparative levels of violence between British and French strikes seems to be the lower level of fatalities in the former. This may, however, be a product of the less physically repressive policies of the British state as compared with its European counterparts.

It may still be argued that such violent direct action remains compatible with trade union objectives – a kind of latter-day 'collective bargaining by riot' – rather than any explicit revolutionary feeling. Such an objection carries a certain force since we are at this stage dealing more with an implicit mood or mentality rather than any conscious plan to reconstruct society. At the same time, there is further empirical evidence to suggest that the strike wave differed in certain respects from the more orthodox sectional procedures of trade unionism, geared to purely economistic objectives.

A fourth important aspect of the labour unrest was the periodic suspension of internal sectional divisions within the working class. This took several forms. In the first place internal occupational divisions within industries were sometimes transcended during the course of disputes. Significant examples occurred among seamen, where status-conscious ships' cooks and catering staff allied during the course of waterfront militancy with manual grades such as firemen and seamen. There is also some evidence of a parallel breakdown of the traditional status barriers on the railways between 'skilled' drivers and unskilled labourers, enabling the construction of a common front in some episodes of unrest.

In the second place, there is evidence of occupational unity between trades during strikes, notably between miners and railwaymen, dockers and carters, and metalworkers and miners. Thirdly, there is an important case of suspended ethnic and religious hostility between Protestants and Catholics in Liverpool during the strike unrest of 1911 in that city. At the very least such instances of trans-occupational unity foreshadowed a new era of labour movement organization, based on organization by industry rather than organization by sectional trades. In a few areas such as Liverpool or South Wales, however, the suspension of purely sectional consciousness went further than that, creating moments of class unity. This sense of unity, based upon class rather than sectional mobilization, was further combined with the awakening of a sense of class power in opposition to capital and state. This was expressed not only in direct action but also organizationally through strike committees and mass demonstrations. It is at this point that the committed revolutionary syndicalist militants found it possible to take on a leadership role in trying to transform the aggressive mentality of proto-syndicalistic class unity into a more purposeful projection of a new social order.

What, then, of the second layer of the revolutionary syndicalist movement – the committed activists? Leaders like Tom Mann and Jim Larkin certainly became national household figures during the labour unrest, and worked alongside local militants like Noah Ablett, A. J. Cook, Jack Wills, Charles Watkins and Fred Bower. How far was this small cadre successful in transforming the syndicalist mentality into a more explicit revolutionary movement capable of effective action?

In the first place, it must be stressed that in only a very few cases, for example the South Wales miners' strike of 1910, did committed syndicalists make any input into industrial action at the outset of strikes. This suggests that the doctrines of revolutionary syndicalism were not the underlying cause of the labour unrest. There is, however, considerable evidence that committee syndicalist activities did have a significant impact on labour opinion and action during and after particular phases of strike action. As far as strike policy is concerned, the ubiquitous Tom Mann, leader of the Industrial Syndicalist Education League (ISEL), was centrally involved during the course of a number of disputes. The most important of these was the Liverpool transport strike of 1911 where he headed the strike com-mittee.[14] This body probably represented the greatest challenge to capitalist authority during the strike wave. Not only did it act as an organ of class unity transcending differences of occupation and religion among the working class but it also began to act as an organ of class power through its control over the city's transport system. Any employer wishing to move goods had to obtain a strike permit from the committee. Even the state-controlled Post Office had to ask for this permission. At the same time no attempt was made by Tom Mann or the committee to seize power and declare the revolution.

In general terms it was only as a result of a pre-existing syndicalist mood of direct action and aggression that committed syndicalists gained an audience during strikes. Their aims were moreover quite modest, aiming at education and organizational consolidation of the forces of labour rather than immediate revolutionary change. In such respects syndicalists played an important part in broadening the basis of original strike demands. In the mining industry, for example, a local dispute over local wage payments in South Wales was transformed largely under syndicalist auspices into a national campaign for a minimum wage, involving the first ever national miners' strike. This was associated with an influential pamphlet *The Miners' Next Step* which sold many tens of thousands of copies. This built on the syndicalists' reputation as rank-and-file strike leaders to advance the case for workers' control of the mines independent of state intervention and distinct from schemes for nationalization advocated by the socialists.

The organizational consolidation of labour was also promoted by revolutionary syndicalists through the notion of industrial unionism. This campaign was designed to match the increasing concentration of capital in the years before the First World War. But it also drew much of its support from the successful experience of co-operation between different occupational groupings that had occurred during the strike wave. Important instances of consolidation at around this time included the formation of the National Union of Railwaymen, and a regrouping of builders' unions into the Amalgamated Union of Building Trade Workers.

Although revolutionary syndicalists were often leading advocates for such schemes, their successful adoption cannot be solely attributed to syndicalist influence. This is because many non-revolutionary union leaders saw in federation or industrial unionism a means of making collective bargaining more viable in the face of federated capital. This in turn would undermine unofficial rank-and-file initiative and lead to fewer strikes. The ambivalent character of such schemes is further evident in the project for a triple alliance of miners, railwaymen and transport workers. Revolutionary syndicalists advocated such an alliance, as a means of promoting class unity through a combined general strike of the three sectors. Orthodox trade union leaders by contrast saw this large co-ordinated body as a means of forcing employers to the conference table, thereby avoiding strikes.[15] Such ambivalences were to become fully evident after the First World War – especially in the General Strike of 1926 organized around an extended version of the alliance. While this was seen by some activists as the beginning of a radicalization process leading to the subversion of the capitalist system, most others (including trade union leaders) saw it as a bargaining move well within the ambit of the British Constitution.

If prewar syndicalists made only a limited contribution to the success of union amalgamation schemes, their contribution to certain other spheres of labour movement development was far greater. In the case of the movement for independent working-men's education, for example, syndicalists with their emphasis on working-class self-reliance played a leading part in the establishment of the Plebs League and the Central Labour College (CLC). The Plebs League was an organization which supported local study classes in the various provincial centres where workers studied such questions as Marxist economics and industrial history. The CLC was a residential college whereby unions supported a limited number of full-time students taking similar courses. Syndicalist propaganda was also to be found in a number of other papers and pamphlets, including the new 'rebel' daily – the *Daily Herald* – launched in 1912 after an earlier strike of printers.[16] This paper had a circulation of around 200,000 at its peak before the onset of the First World War. Alongside the *Herald* were a number of smaller monthly syndicalist papers, none with a large circulation, but each stressing various aspects of the revolutionary syndicalist critique of capital and state. Typical themes included anti-militarism, industrial unionism and the critique of welfare capitalism based on state-sponsored social reform. Such activities continued right up to the disruption of the labour movement engendered by the First World War, but were recovered within a few years to form much of the basis of the wartime shop stewards' movement.

Overall, then, revolutionary syndicalism scarcely came close to the seizure of power. It did on the other hand contribute a good deal to the institutional development of the British labour movement in terms of union reorganization, workers' education and the establishment of a radical labour daily press. Above all, perhaps, the appeal of workers' control and direct action at the point of production continued to exert a considerable influence on British labour history, even after the spread of Leninist revolutionary politics throughout Europe in the aftermath of the Russian Revolution of 1917.

IV

One of the most significant features of this analysis is that the doctrines of revolutionary syndicalism only began to make significant headway after the outbreak of rank-and-file strike unrest in 1910. This indicates that revolutionary syndicalism, whether imported from abroad or home grown, was not the underlying cause of the labour unrest. How, then, are the sudden prominence and modest successes that revolutionary syndicalist activists were able to make in the years after 1910 to be explained.

The economic origins of syndicalism can be traced back to the increasingly precarious condition of British capitalism in the years leading up to 1914. Although this period has often been seen as the 'heyday of empire' and the epoch of a quiescent working class dominated by a comfortable labour aristocracy, this rosy picture conceals some quite adverse economic trends which had important implications for the position of labour. Such trends included a slowing down in rates of growth of industrial productivity and a worsening of Britain's terms of trade with other countries, especially those producing food and raw materials. These two developments combined to hold down the level of real wages after 1900. While profits, rents and prices increased significantly between 1900 and 1914 money wages did not keep pace. Average real wages probably fell by 10 per cent between 1900 and 1912. Furthermore, while pressure on wages was general in this period, its impact was greatest in industries where productivity levels were falling fastest and where price increases were ruled out by market conditions or institutional limitations. The coal industry and the railways, both scenes of industrial unrest, fall into this category. Economic trends of this kind produced a massive build up of material grievance among workers. Mass unrest developed because the long-term trend of rising spending power was now checked, and because of the sharp contrast between working-class living standards and the conspicuous luxury consumption of Edwardian rentiers and manufacturers. Economic unrest of this kind did not by itself stimulate syndicalism, but it did provide a general sense of material deprivation on which revolutionary industrial movements might build. For grievances over wages inevitably created great pressure on orthodox trade unionism and on parliamentary socialism to bring improvement and reform. Any failure here led the disaffected to look further afield, in particular to the direct action philosophy of syndicalism which bypassed collective bargaining and parliament altogether.

Changes in industrial structure and capitalist industrial power also played an important part in the growth of British syndicalism. Of particular significance was the development of business amalgamation into larger units of production, which led to a high degree of concentration in patterns of ownership and control. While the actual pace of amalgamation and merger was less rapid in Britain than in the USA or Germany, its extension was still significant in a number of sectors like railways and transportation. Greater industrial cohesion was also developed through various informal groupings of producers, as well as more formal arrangements like employers' associations. Such changes greatly strengthened capitalist industrial power in the face of foreign competition and domestic labour unrest, both of which had been intensifying in the last quarter of the nineteenth century. The growth of big business and 'federated capital' only produced further industrial unrest, however, since it undermined the prevailing local or sectional basis of trade union organization. Consequently, organized labour now began to shift away from localism towards industry-wide organization. Industrial unionism was increasingly seen as an essential means of consolidating labour's strength in the face of concentrated capitalist power. Support for this policy depended not only on direct experience of structural changes in British industry, but also on workers' anticipation of future industrial concentration on the model of the aggressive American trusts and business combines.

Industrial unionism was by no means equivalent to syndicalism, being quite compatible as already indicated with a more efficient reformism. Nevertheless, organizational changes of this kind were increasingly linked with militant policies. This was because the concentration of capitalist power was often associated with aggressive employer policies against organized labour. Where this was so industrial unionism, combined with direct action methods, brought militants much closer to syndicalist affiliation. Once more the American experience of big business anti-unionism made many British observers anticipate similar attacks in their own country.

The industrial unionist aspect of syndicalism developed not only in response to the growing concentration of capitalist industrial power but also to the sometimes associated process of technological innovation. The latter was important in industries like engineering and building. Here technological change usually resulted in the displacement or downgrading of craft skills to semi-skilled status. The effect was to jeopardize the traditional bargaining strength of craftsmen, whose skilled labour had previously been relatively scarce. While many craftsmen clung desperately to hopes of retaining their previous, privileged status, a growing number looked instead to trade union amalgamation as a means of creating a new bargaining strength. Technological change could only be combated by the joint organization of skilled, semi-skilled and unskilled in one industrial union. Industrial unionism of this kind did not tend automatically towards syndicalism, being compatible (once again) with a more efficient reformism. It was none the less quite often associated with industrial aggression towards employers. Many disaffected craftsmen sought to combat the power of capital not simply by organizational reform, but also by developing the craftsman's traditional resistance to managerial interference within the workshop in new directions. The gap between 'job control' aspirations of this kind and the syndicalist emphasis on workers' control of industry was not a large one. As economic grievances mounted and technological dislocation increased, a growing number of militant craftsmen were inclined to bridge the gap. The acceptability of syndicalism to radical craftsmen was also increased through the revolutionary industrial emphasis on direct action at the point of production. This accorded well with the craftsman's customary assertion of local autonomy in determining policy free from interference by management or by full-time union officials.

A further set of origins of British syndicalism related to the failure of employer and state policies designed to contain the expansion of labour militancy since the 1880s. The trebling of union membership between 1888 and 1910, coupled with the development of independent labour representation, produced a significant sense of threat amongst many employers. Militant industrial action also created considerable alarm, particularly from the 1890s onwards when 'socialistic' ideas were detected at work amongst trade union activists. Industrial unrest and 'indiscipline' were attacked, not simply as problems of public order but more fundamentally as challenges to capitalist authority in the workplace and as threats to Britain's competitive position in world markets. As economic and social pressures such as these became intensified during the 1890s, so the policy of employers and the state towards organized labour evolved in search of some new solution. A new configuration of attitudes and policies now emerged, which placed relatively less stress than hitherto on overt repression and somewhat greater emphasis on measures which acted as more subtle forms of social control. Increasingly between 1890 and 1914 the attempt was made to defuse unrest by incorporating labour representatives within limited bargaining institutions, and by the development of state-sponsored social welfare policies.

Extensions of union recognition and collective bargaining, often the outcome of intense struggle, did of course represent a significant advance for organized labour. Nor was progress as steady and easily achieved as the expansion of union membership from 750,000 in 1888 to 2·5 million in 1910 may imply. However, in spite of the partial success of the counter-attack by anti-union employers, it was increasingly agreed that trade union demands could be more effectively defused by bargaining and in particular by utilizing union officials as a mediating influence between labour and capital.

British syndicalism drew considerable strength from pools of dissatisfaction with the fruits of collective bargaining and conciliation machinery in the years between 1890 and 1910. Grievances centred on the growing remoteness of officials from shop floor problems as bargaining machinery, increasingly national in scope, was extended through a wide range of industries. Unrest also arose because the machinery moved at a slow pace, however urgent grievances might be. To some it appeared that the incorporation of union officials within bargaining institutions had succeeded in defusing their earlier radicalism. Official policies tended to become more cautious and conservative, as the consolidation of the union's bureaucratic strength took precedence over demands for radical social change. Whether this process of 'goal displacement' occurred 'spontaneously' or by conscious employer design, it is clear that union expansion in this period led not only to greater bureaucratization, but also to a greater resistance to militant industrial policies. Officials relished their recently expanded bargaining status in respect of management and were increasingly unwilling to jeopardize collective bargaining recognition by agreeing to direct action. Rank-and-file dissatisfaction with the process flared up periodically over the years in response to particular local grievances, but became more generalized in the early twentieth century as real wages declined. Such unrest led to a greater incidence of unofficial strikes, and also to a search for alternative policies to those adopted by conciliatory trade union leaders. Revolutionary syndicalism made sense in this atmosphere as a movement which emphasized direct action and shunned orthodox bargaining and conciliation machinery.

The emphasis on incorporation as a form of social control was evident not only among employers but also in the activities of the state. While retaining the option of physical repression as a means of containing threats to 'public order', government also began to develop less overtly hostile forms of containment in response to the extension of labour movement strength. Many of these were associated with the expanding labour functions of the Board of Trade. Thus by the Industrial Conciliation Act of 1896, conciliation facilities were offered to back up recent initiatives by employers in the direction of bargaining and conciliation machinery. This policy was further expanded in the years of unrest after 1900 when George Askwith of the Board of Trade acted as industrial trouble-shooter during protracted strikes. The Board also encouraged the incorporation of labour officials within its activities through their appointment as Labour Correspondents sending information into a central statistical office. More fundamental schemes of corporatism were attempted in 1911 when the Industrial Council was set up to create permanent institutional links between capital and labour. A major concern of the council was an investigation of the best ways to gain workers' acceptance of agreements entered into by employers and union officials.

It is probable that state-sponsored conciliation policies made some contribution towards syndicalist support. This was partly because workers were sceptical of the supposedly 'neutral' role of the state in this context and were often convinced that it was acting instead in the interest of employers. The attractions of revolutionary syndicalism as a movement which rejected the existing state as an organ of class rule are therefore obvious. The incorporation of union officials into government-sponsored conciliation machinery also stimulated syndicalist adherence, in so far as leaders became less responsive to rank-and-file agitation, and direct action seemed the only alternative.

Outside the sphere of conciliation, state-sponsored incorporation policies were also reflected in the Trade Disputes Act of 1906. This measure was in many ways a most significant concession to organized labour, since it reversed the hostile Taff Vale judgment. Picketing was made viable once more, by giving union funds immunity from persecution for damages caused by dislocation during a dispute. Yet in other respects the legislation was intended as a means of control. Protection was given only to 'responsible' trade union activity, since only peaceful picketing was allowable. Employers were the first to point out, however, that the new legal situation failed to prevent peaceful picketing escalating into more aggressive industrial conflict. Some observers like Cuthbert Laws of the Shipping Federation even claimed that 'this history of syndicalism was contemporaneous with the Trade Disputes Act'.[17] This is undoubtedly an exaggeration. Given the mounting economic and social pressures on working-class conditions already discussed, it is doubtful whether failure to reverse Taff Vale would have retarded syndicalist advance for very long. The less restrictive trade union law that resulted from the 1906 legislation did, however, remove one obstacle to strike mobilization. This made the task of syndicalist strike leadership rather easier than it might otherwise have been.

An area of state social control with far greater bearings on the origins of syndicalism was the social welfare programme enacted by the Liberals between 1906 and 1914.[18] Whatever their progressive 'Welfare State' reputation, such policies were also designed to discipline labour and make it more efficient. By these means it was hoped to ease both the problem of overseas competition and domestic inefficiency, and the challenge of an increasingly powerful labour movement. Legislation creating labour exchanges and the national insurance system, for example, should not be interpreted simply as reform to alleviate unemployment and ill health. It was also designed to promote industrial efficiency and social discipline. By regulating unemployment benefit and the labour market, for example, it was hoped to protect the 'honest' working man 'willing to work' from demoralizing contact with 'wastrels', or from critics of the capitalist system. Many of the social control functions of Liberal social policy are reflected in the provisions of the legislation itself. Unemployment benefit, for example, was not to be paid to those previously dismissed for 'industrial misconduct', a category including many militants and aggressive individuals 'guilty' of insubordination towards the employer. While much of the legislation contained coercive sanctions against anti-capitalist behaviour, it was also hoped that measures of social protection would underwrite and stimulate existing elements of moral consensus of attitude between labour and capital. By alleviating the problem of unemployment it was hoped that working-men and their representatives would more easily internalize and enthusiastically promote bourgeois ideals of 'proper' and 'responsible' behaviour, without the need for legislative intervention. The Liberal objective was the creation of an upright sense of individual 'independence' among workers, whereby no man felt he had to call anyone 'master' even though he was actually being constrained within a system of authority. To help in this process, Liberal politicians hoped that trade union officials and parliamentary leaders would co-operate with the implementation and administration of the legislation.

The development of social control through state welfare policy was a particularly important stimulus for syndicalist expansion. The anti-state aspect of revolutionary industrial thought was the most attractive socialist option available to those who perceived the social discipline implications of welfare policy. By emphasizing the coercive role of the state as an organ of class rule, syndicalists may have tapped indigenous traditions of working-class hostility to state intervention. These included day-to-day resistance by working-class families to the Poor Law system or law courts. This kind of conflict was probably rarely socialist in inspiration but rather an attempt to assert working-class independence from agencies of control. Yet it did provide an anti-state mentality on which syndicalism could try to build.

The failure of the Labour Party to set out a viable alternative to welfare capitalism reflected a wider loss of radical momentum within the parliamentary area. Although the 1906 general election successes had been greeted with genuine enthusiasm by many working-class militants, the subsequent erosion of the party's independent reforming zeal reflected a rapid process of political incorporation. Liberal strategists clearly recognized this, particularly Lloyd George who by 1912 regarded the parliamentary socialists as the best policemen for the syndicalist. The pre-1914 Labour Party certainly continued to expand its mass base right up to the outbreak of war. This is reflected in the support of many trade unionists for a political levy on their union subscriptions to finance the party, and in the establishment of an 'orthodox' labour daily, the *Daily Citizen*, to rival the 'rebel' *Daily Herald*. Yet for all this, the 'policing' effect of parliamentary socialism failed to prevent a polarization of attitudes within the labour movement. Over time many labour activists became disillusioned with the parliamentary politics of gradualist reform. Some hoped for a more radical version of political socialism; for others, however, the clear-cut, non-parliamentary message of revolutionary syndicalism proved more attractive, since it avoided the problems of political incorporation which increasingly beset the Labour Party in parliament.

British syndicalism drew support not only from the revolt against parliamentary labourism, but also from disaffection within the ranks of the Marxist wing of the socialist movement organized within the Social Democratic Federation (SDF). This disaffection was related to the Federation's increasing loss of revolutionary dynamism by the first decade of the twentieth century. Like many other sections of the Second International, the dominant SDF strategy rested on a crude form of economic determinism in which the collapse of capitalism was regarded as inevitable. While waiting for this collapse, the most that could be done was to struggle for desirable 'palliative' reforms which might act as 'stepping-stones' to revolution. Contrary to some existing stereotypes about the SDF's revolutionary 'purism', therefore, the reality was one of increasing involvement in the local politics of municipal reform.

Syndicalism proved an attractive alternative to SDF orthodoxy in two senses. First, its emphasis on revolutionary activism and the aggressive élan of direct action was far more acceptable to many militants than the sterile economic determinism which assumed that capitalist collapse was inevitable. Thus instead of the effective separation of the maximum programme of revolution from the minimum programme of reform, syndicalism offered a strategy which invested day-to-day struggles in the workplace with revolutionary significance. Direct action methods built up the sense of aggressive confidence necessary for a revolutionary seizure of power. A second reason for the appeal of syndicalism was its emphasis on the potential of industrial conflict for revolutionary change. This potential had been consistently neglected by the SDF leadership which saw wage militancy and strikes as both ineffective and irrelevant to the creation of a socialist society.

V

While it is possible to show that the revolutionary syndicalist impact in Britain depended to a great extent on social and political developments indigenous to British society, there still remains the more general problem as to why revolutionary syndicalist movements should have emerged in such a wide range of Western industrial capitalist societies (France, Italy, Spain, the United States, Britain) in the years between the 1890s and the 1930s. What this concurrence suggests is that there were perhaps some features common to this whole range of societies during the years in question, features creating a propensity to syndicalist action.

It used to be thought that revolutionary syndicalism was very much a backward-looking movement seeking to restore elements of producer control over the workplace which had been lost with the advance of capitalism and the destruction of a peasantry. Such an argument was often buttressed by the belief that revolutionary syndicalism movements were concentrated in areas of economic 'backwardness' as in southern Europe. This whole argument is, however, very dubious. It is, for example, quite simple to show that revolutionary syndicalism, in its adoption of industrial rather than craft unionism, and in its critique of welfare capitalism, contained important elements of a forward-looking struggle against some of the more modern elements of capitalist development. Moreover, the concept of workers' control of industry was quite distinct from the attempt to restore some kind of idealized medieval world of independent peasant producers. Rather it represented an acceptance of the case for the socialization of control over the products of labour, products created in the first place by the wage-worker's labour.

What, then, may be specific about the 1890s–1930s is first of all that this period represented an important epoch of Western capitalist advance beyond the original industrial heartlands of Britain, to include France and the United States. Such an advance was not, however, without its internal crises and contradictions, not least among which was the capitalist attempt to continue to secure managerial authority in the workplace in the face of a working class growing in size and organizational strength. Such conflicts may of course be endemic in a capitalist system, as may be workers' resistance in some shape or form. What, however, turned certain workers' resistance in a revolutionary syndicalist direction at this time may have something to do with the fact that to a great extent the workforce such as miners, craftsmen, dockers and migrant agricultural workers was yet incompletely trained in routine capitalist factory discipline. What is certainly evident in the British case is how few syndicalist-inclined workers before 1914 were located within the factory system. Even the militant metalworkers of the wartime shop stewards' movement generally represented craftsmen threatened with skill-displacing technological change rather than labourers or machine-minders.

The hypothesis being advanced here, therefore, is that revolutionary syndicalism was not a backward-looking movement, nor yet a movement appropriate to the deadening social disciplines of the contemporary machine-technology factory-based workforce. Rather it represented a transitional form of labour movement activity, transitional between earlier capitalist craft methods and a second phase of factory-based mass production.[19] As such it is possible to admit that the particular causes of the revolutionary syndicalist impact in Britain were indigenous to that society, while at the same time indicating a more general comparative framework for the analysis of revolutionary syndicalism in terms of stages of capitalist development.

Notes: Chapter 15

1 The use of national stereotypes seems especially prevalent among sociologists. See for example M. Mann, *Consciousness and Action among the Western Working Class* (London, 1973), chs 4–6; A. Giddens, *The Class Structure of the Advanced Societies* (London, 1973), ch. 11.

2 G. A. Philips, 'The triple industrial alliance in 1914', *Economic History Review* 24 (1971): 55–67 (67).

3 For an able general survey see P. Stearns, 'National character and European labor history', *Journal of Social History* 4 (1970–1): 95–124.

4 C. Kerr and A. Siegel, 'The inter-industry propensity to strike – an international comparison', in A. Kornhauser *et al.*, *Industrial Conflict* (New York, 1954), 189–204.

5 See for example G. Rimlinger, 'The legitimation of protest; a comparative study in labour history', *Comparative Studies in Society and History* 2 (1960): 329–43.

6 The work of John Laslett on the comparative study of mining regions is a case in point.

7 The most blatant example of this procedure is the Perry Anderson–Tom Nairn approach to British social history. See for example T. Nairn, 'The anatomy of labor', *New Left Review* 27 (1964): 38–65, and 28 (1964): 33–62.

8 *Industrial Worker*, 8 May 1913.

9 J. Gusfield, 'Social movements', in D. Sills (ed.), *International Encyclopaedia of the Social Sciences*, Vol. 14 (Drayton, 1968), 445.

10 A more detailed survey of the empirical data on which this argument is based may be found in R. Holton, *British Syndicalism 1900–14* (London, 1976).

11 A detailed study of the local syndicalist organizations is available in R. Holton, 'Syndicalism and labour on Merseyside 1906–14', in H. Hikins (ed.), *Building the Union* (Liverpool, 1973), 121–50.

12 E. J. Hobsbawm, review of H. Pelling, 'Popular politics and society in late Victorian Britain', *Bulletin of the Society for the Study of Labour History* 18 (1969): 49–54 (51).

13 E. J. Hobsbawm has suggested some methodological problems in the use of 'violence' as a social indicator in 'Labour history and ideology', *Journal of Social History* 7 (1974): 371–81 (378–9).

14 There is a very detailed account of the strike available in H. Hikins, 'The Liverpool general transport strike of 1911', *Transactions of the Historic Society of Lancashire and Cheshire* 113 (1961): 169–95, esp. 171–8.

15 Philips, 'Triple industrial alliance', *passim*.

16 R. Holton, 'Daily Herald v. Daily Citizen 1912–15', *International Review of Social History* 19 (1974): 347–76.

17 Statement to the Employers' Parliamentary Council Inquiry into the Trade Disputes Act, *The Times*, 19 February 1914.

18 For a stimulating discussion of this legislation see J. R. Hay, *The Origins of the Liberal Welfare Reforms 1906–14* (London, 1975).

19 This hypothesis has been powerfully advanced as an explanation of French syndicalism in E. Shorter and C. Tilly, *Strikes in France 1830–1968* (Cambridge, 1974), 75.

16   The Christian Trade Unions and Strike Activity

MICHAEL SCHNEIDER

The subject of this essay does not need much justification in view of the diverse opinions and prejudices held about the Christian Trade Unions. They were called 'yellow' or 'black', 'economic pacifists', 'blacklegs', to mention only those descriptions which refer directly to behaviour during labour conflicts. However, it must be said at the beginning that the Christian Trade Unions did not show a very specific behaviour during industrial conflicts which could be described as *the* Christian union's attitude in these matters. The control of labour conflicts lay in the hands of the individual union concerned. Thus the strike activity clearly differed among the Christian unions depending on the development of branches or trades, the degree of organization, the relative strength, and so forth. Therefore behaviour during labour conflicts can only be discussed at the level of individual unions. However, space does not allow us to do this here. Research into the major industrial conflicts of individual unions also indicates that it is not possible to generalize about the 'usual' behaviour of Christian Trade Unions during such conflicts. In connection with the *Geschichte der Christlichen Gewerkschaften 1894–1933*[1] research was done on the associations of miners, textile workers, metal and engineering workers, construction workers, tobacco and cigar workers, stone workers, painters and decorators, woodworkers and the *Gutenbergbund* (the Christian printers' association). Precisely because analysis of the major strikes of these unions did not reveal one or more common denominators, no 'representative' survey can be given here.

What can be attempted, however, is a characterization of the behaviour of Christian Trade Unions during strikes by comparing statistical evidence about them and their social democratic counterpart, the Free Trade Unions. In the first section of this essay basic views about strikes common to all Christian unions will be outlined. The second section attempts to arrive at a general statistical approximation of the Christian unions' strike practices, the peculiarities of which will then be summarized in the third part. In the final section some examples will be discussed.

I

Although the intention is to outline the ideological background common to all Christian unions, the debate about their programme cannot be dealt with in detail here. Neither can the problems of a 'wage theory' supported by the

Christian unions, that is, the demand for a 'family wage', be discussed. We shall deal briefly only with statements referring to their policy on collective wage agreements and labour conflicts. The *Gewerkverein Christlicher Bergarbeiter* (The Association of Christian Miners), founded in October 1894 and initially covering the *Oberbergamtsbezirk* (administrative district of the mining industry) Dortmund, provided a model for most of the other Christian Trade Union organizations founded later. Its model character was expressed mainly in the objective laid down in paragraph 2 of its statute: 'It is the objective of the *Gewerkverein* to raise the moral and social position of miners on the basis of Christianity and the law and to promote and maintain peaceful understanding between employers and workers.' Furthermore, it was emphasized that 'the union faithfully supports the Kaiser and the Reich and rules out any discussion of a religous and party political nature'.[2] The 1899 congress in Mainz, the first joint congress of the Christian unions, adopted these principles of party political neutrality and of interdenominationalism in its Guiding Principles. It also adopted the social partnership approach of the *Gewerkverein*:

> You cannot forget that workers and employers have common interests; based on the fact that both, as inseparable factors of labour, not only have to see to the right of appropriate remuneration for the latter vis-à-vis capital but most of all that they represent the interests of the production of goods vis-à-vis the consumption of them.
>
> Both sides quite rightly claim the right to the highest possible reward for their investment in the production of goods – the employer for his capital, the worker for his labour. Without both, capital and labour, there can be no production. Therefore, all the efforts of the trade unions should be pervaded and carried by the spirit of reconciliation. Demands have to be measured, but presented firmly and with determination.
>
> A strike must be the last resort and should only be applied when it promises to be successful.[3]

The leaders of the Christian Trade Unions must have noted with real bitterness that the employers, particularly in the mining industry of the Ruhr, but also in the textile industry, were not prepared to accommodate their idea of a social partnership. Petitions remained unanswered, offers to negotiate were rejected. The Christian Trade Union movement was thus by no means regarded in a better light than the Free Trade Unions. On the contrary, it was seen by many employers as a particularly sophisticated variant of the labour movement, which would lead the workers into the arms of social democracy anyway. Even in their initial phase the Christian Trade Unions were involved in numerous labour conflicts which in some cases, for instance when lock-outs occurred, nearly led to the breakdown of these young organizations. However, the Christian unions took part in these strikes largely to counter their reputation as 'lackeys of the employers and the Church' who were not likely to strike.[4]

After the Frankfurt congress (1900) had recommended that the unions conclude 'firm wage agreements' to secure the results of their wage struggle in a lasting way,[5] the Krefeld congress (1901) once more emphasized in a resolution: 'The Christian Trade Unions do not reject strikes on principle, but they regard them as the last resort in the pursuit of their objectives.' One could hardly express the acceptance of strikes more hesitantly. Also, strike action was not to be mistaken for 'class struggle', as a strike was only the expression of 'justified efforts by the workers to sell their labour for a favourable price', and that was to be achieved, 'if possible, by peaceful settlement with the employers. In order to avoid unplanned and unprepared strikes the unions have to introduce certain strike rules which make the support of a strike dependent on the approval of the union executive.'[6]

With formulations such as these the Christian Trade Unions attempted to cope with the competition from the Free Trade Unions, and with the distrust shown by some quarters of the Catholic Church. Finally they hoped to serve their own interests by maintaining and stabilizing their organization. The latter was characteristic of their strike regulations, in which the central executive took only a very reticent part, for one 'cannot establish rules for the conduct of strikes valid for all cases'.[7] Generally these regulations required two-thirds of the affected workers to be in favour of a strike, yet the union executive also reserved for itself a right of veto. On the other hand, a vote of one-third of the membership was regarded as sufficient to end a strike. Furthermore, strike action was to be taken only if it promised to be successful.

The Christian Trade Unions thus acknowledged the necessity for strikes. But for economic as well as moral reasons, they regarded them as a 'last resort', in line with their social partnership approach. The *Zentralblatt* provided a summary of the ideas of the Christian Trade Unions in 1906: 'The level of wages and the conditions of work depend to a large extent on a sense of justice, but partly also on supply and demand, and finally on the influence which the workers are able to exercise through their organization.'[8] This single sentence combined the traditional 'Christian social' ideas – justice, a reference to the economic cycle (supply and demand) and thinking in terms of organizational power – all of which presumably reflected the experience of the first few years of Christian Trade Union work. However, whether there was in fact a special 'Christian' behaviour in labour conflicts remains to be seen.

II

A first approximation of the characteristic behaviour of Christian Trade Unions during labour conflicts can be arrived at by looking at the structure of their expense accounts. It is noticeable from Table 16.1 that in the early years of the Christian unions the support they paid to striking and disciplined workers represents an unusually high share of the total support payments compared with that paid by the Free Trade Unions. This indicates that the Christian unions, whose fees were kept low until 1905–6 in order to attract new members, felt it necessary to keep strike pay at a level comparable with that paid by the Free unions, presumably again to attract and hold members.

Table 16.1 *Payments Made to Workers on Strike and Disciplined as a Percentage of Total Expenditure for Support Measures by the Christian and the Free Trade Unions, 1900–13*

Year	Christian unions	Free unions
1900	83·7	57·5
1901	75·6	40·6
1902	69·1	37·7
1903	76·4	57·9
1904	63·1	57·6
1905	81·1	62·8
1906	62·5	62·9
1907	51·1	52·2
1908	30·3	23·8
1909	28·7	27·4
1910	51·7	52·1
1911	49·1	47·0
1912	32·7	37·0
1913	39·6	36·7

Sources: Data for the Christian Trade Unions calculated from *Jahrbuch der Christlichen Gewerkschaften für 1910* (Cologne, 1910), 23, 25; and *Jahrbuch der Christlichen Gewerkschaften für 1915* (Cologne, 1915), 20, 22–3. The data for the Free Trade Unions are from *Correspondenzblatt der Generalkommission der Gewerkschaften Deutschlands*, Statistischer Anhang 1913, p. 195, and 1914, p. 203.

Table 16.2 *Payments Made during Strikes and Lock-outs as a Percentage of the Total Expenditure of the Christian Trade Unions, the Free Trade Unions and the Hirsch-Duncker Trades Associations, 1905–14*

Year	Christian unions	Free unions	Hirsch-Duncker Associations
1905	46·5	36·6	24·5
1906	31·5	36·2	32·9
1907	23·3	30·1	8·5
1908	12·0	11·3	5·5
1909	12·7	13·7	6·3
1910	25·2	32·9	13·4
1911	22·7	27·8	14·4
1912	12·5	19·7	14·9
1913	16·2	21·4	17·5
1914	5·8	6·5	11·9
average 1905–14	20·8	23·6	15·0

Source: Compiled from L. Heyde (ed.), *Internationales Handwörterbuch des Gewerkschaftswesens* (1930–1), 1617–19.

Only from 1906 onwards did the percentage shares of the two organizations become roughly the same.

If, however, the expenditure on strike support and lock-outs is related to the total expenditure of the Christian and Free unions another picture emerges. Table 16.2 shows that in relation to total expenditure the payments made by the Christian unions for strike action were nearly always lower than those made by the Free unions from 1906 onwards. During the period 1905–14 the Christian unions made 20·8 per cent of their total expenditure available for strike support payments. This was clearly higher than corresponding payments made by the Hirsch-Duncker Trades Associations (15 per cent) but did not reach the level paid by the Free unions (23·6 per cent). The annual fluctuations in these shares cannot be discussed here.

The trend suggested here emerges even more clearly when one looks at the respective strike participation by members of the Christian and Free unions. There is a significant difference between the Christian and the Free Trade Unions if one looks at the number of participants in strikes as a percentage of total membership (see Table 16.3). During the period 1903–12 this percentage with one exception is consistently lower for the Christian unions than for the Free unions. Strike participation was initially comparatively high, as for example in 1905 when the miners' union played an important part in the overall organization. However, this levels out if the average for the period 1903–13 is calculated. The annual average of strike participation for the whole period is 9·2 per cent for the Christian and 12·9 per cent for the Free unions. The average for the years 1903–6 is 16·9 per cent for the Christian and 14·7 per cent for the Free unions, while for the years 1907–13 the average is 4·8 per cent for the Christian and 11·9 per cent for the Free unions.

However difficult it is to determine whether a strike is aggressive or defensive, it must nevertheless be noted that for the total period reviewed here aggressive actions clearly represent a higher proportion of the total number of strikes for the Christian unions than for the Free unions (Table 16.4). This could be due to a difference in the yardsticks for evaluating strikes. However, the gap is striking because these statistics do not tally with the view the Christian unions had of themselves. One would expect them to emphasize their defensive character. The feud between sections of the Catholic Church and the Christian Trade Unions, which is known as *Gewerkschaftsstreit*, could have also promoted this tendency.

The participation of Christian trade unionists in labour conflicts decreased as their involvement in 'peaceful wage campaigns' increased (Table 16.5) , which statistically also included negotiations on working hours, safety at work and 'grievances of all kinds'. This development was reflected in the number of wage campaigns generally, but mainly in the ratio between the number of members of the Christian Trade Unions taking part in strikes and those who were involved in wage campaigns. Apart from some fluctuations, the overall tendency clearly shows a decline in strikes as a proportion of all campaigns.

A survey of trade union 'co-operation' does not provide a clear-cut picture which would amount to a trend. Although varying greatly, the proportion of

Table 16.3 Participation in Strikes by the Christian and Free Trade Unions, 1903–1913

Year	Aggressive strikes		Defensive strikes		Strike costs		Number of participants			
	Christian unions	Free unions	Christian unions	Free unions	Christian unions	Free unions	Christian unions		Free unions	
							actual	%	actual	%
1903	47	597	26	582	155,030	3,218,681	4,713	5·2	74,981	8·4
1904	92	867	25	608	133,362	3,256,785	8,019	7·5	98,831	9·3
1905	181	1,366	35	837	1,000,320	5,942,716	80,602	42·5	381,296	28·3
1906	345	2,012	52	996	853,435	7,176,299	30,049	12·2	215,415	12·7
1907	189	1,605	35	799	743,270	5,904,801	17,171	6·0	173,094	9·2
1908	82	678	81	1,117	424,992	4,477,039	6,809	2·6	126,883	6·9
1909	112	832	74	1,007	489,023	5,934,453	7,210	2·6	131,244	7·1
1910	182	1,514	55	906	1,239,500	18,457,769	22,366	7·1	369,011	18·2
1911	247	1,863	65	1,044	1,199,598	16,062,906	18,490	5·3	325,253	13·9
1912	250	1,676	77	949	654,323	1,733,749	13,124	3·7	479,589	18·7
1913	234	1,425	72	899	989,631	14,825,881	21,036	6·2	248,986	9·6

Sources: Figures for the Christian Trade Unions compiled and calculated from Jahrbuch der Christlichen Gewerkschaften für 1914 (Cologne, 1914), 27–8, and Jahrbuch der Christlichen Gewerkschaften für 1915 (Cologne, 1915), 21–2. Figures for the Free Trade Unions compiled and calculated from Correspondenzblatt der Generalkommission der Gewerkschaften Deutschlands 1904, 542–4; 1905, 655–7; 1906, 693–5; Statistischer Anhang: 1907, 116–18; 1908, 203–5; 1909, 212–13; 1910, 204–5; 1911, 208–9; 1912, 252–3; 1913, 210–12; 1914, 256–7. The figures for the number of people participating in strikes refer to strikes and lock-outs together, except for the Free Trade Unions in the years 1903–7.

Table 16.4   *Aggressive Strikes as a Percentage of All Strikes: Christian and Free Trade Unions, 1903–13*

Year	Christian unions	Free unions
1903	64·4	50·6
1904	78·6	58·8
1905	83·8	62·0
1906	86·9	66·9
1907	84·4	66·8
1908	50·3	37·8
1909	60·2	45·2
1910	76·8	62·6
1911	79·1	64·1
1912	76·5	63·8
1913	76·5	61·3

Sources: As Table 16.3.

Table 16.5   *Participation of Christian Trade Unions in Wage Campaigns and Industrial Action, 1903–13*

Year	Wage campaigns overall Number (1)	Members involved (2)	Number of members involved in strikes (3)	Ratio of (3) to (2) %
1903	153	11,053	4,713	42·6
1904	291	14,818	8,019	54·1
1905	614	106,618	80,602	75·6
1906	1,024	68,768	30,049	43·7
1907	1,089	59,718	17,171	28·8
1908	683	43,238	6,809	15·7
1909	706	26,046	7,010	26·0
1910	951	73,112	22,366	30·6
1911	1,181	52,139	18,490	35·5
1912	1,184	53,623	13,124	24·5
1913	1,506	95,529	21,036	22·0

Sources: As Table 16.4.

Table 16.6   *Campaigns Initiated by the Christian Trade Unions Alone as a Percentage of Total Wage Campaigns*

Year	% of total	Year	% of total
1903	31·2	1908	43·8
1904	25·4	1909	33·0
1905	38·4	1910	26·7
1906	38·9	1911	35·1
1907	55·5	1912	33·4
		1913	34·1

Sources: As Table 16.4.

Table 16.7   *Reasons for Labour Conflicts as Given by the Christian Trade Unions*

Year	Reasons: higher wages	shorter hours	both	defensive actions
1903	17	—	20	14
1904	41	—	44	28
1905	81	—	99	38
1906	143	27	204	30
1907	126	8	96	26
1908	42	1	37	86
1909	70	2	53	89
1910	117	3	89	51
1911	109	8	109	49
1912	155	11	94	53
1913	503	14	309	142

Source: A. Siegler, *Die Lohnpolitik der Christlichen Gewerkschaften Deutschlands (1894–1933)* (Mannheim, 1978), 116.

wage changes initiated by the Christian unions alone averaged around one-third of all campaigns (Table 16.6). On the basis of these data it is hardly possible to arrive at any far-reaching conclusions, taking into account for instance the impact of the *Gewerkschaftsstreit* at various stages.

Table 16.7 illustrates not only that the vast majority of the strikes by the Christian unions dealt with wages and working hours, but together with Table 16.4 also emphasizes that the unions pursued a predominantly offensive policy on labour disputes.

The statistics for individual Christian unions bring the reality of labour conflicts more clearly into focus (Table 16.8). However, these statistics are not complete. The differences in the number of participants from individual unions involved in wage campaigns allow only a cautious judgement on policy differences. A more detailed analysis at industrial branch and factory level is required in order to be more conclusive. On the basis of the data in Table 16.8 only a very general confirmation of a connection between economic cycles and wage changes on the one hand and the Christian unions' attitudes towards strikes on the other hand is possible. The state of the economy in particular was one factor taken into account by Christian unions when deciding on the timing of strikes.[9] All in all, the only conclusion to be drawn here is that participation in wage campaigns decreased in 1907–8 in accordance with the stagnation of the economy. This applies particularly to the textile, wood and engineering industries, as well as to the consumer goods, tin foods, china, glass and toy industries. A. Siegler concludes that in contrast to this trend, the end of the boom in 1913 'seemed to have indirectly caused only metal and engineering workers, the woodworkers and tailors to be more reticent in their wage policies'.[10]

III

In summarising the data on the strike activities of the Christian Trade Unions before the First World War, it must be pointed out that they were not 'yellow', 'economic-pacifist' organizations. On the other hand, one cannot overlook the fact that they took part in strikes less often than could be expected statistically on the grounds of their share of the total union membership. This reluctance to take industrial action was a result first of their ideology which was geared towards negotiations, secondly of the threat to their existence posed by the *Gewerkschaftsstreit* and thirdly of their organizational weakness. The last factor in particular often made it more advisable to rely on petitions, presentations, and so on – courses of peaceful action, incidentally, which were not also unusual for the Free unions.

Time and again the Christian unions defined their exact attitude towards strikes. These statements found their most precise interpretation in the unions' actions. Indeed, a strike was regarded by the Christian Trade Unions as the last resort for solving a conflict of interests. The catalogue of preconditions for strike action was so comprehensive that it was fulfilled only in very rare cases. These preconditions had to be met in order for strike action to be regarded as a successful means. In fact, if the outcome of a labour conflict in favour of the unions was as certain as the Christian unions demanded, a strike would have been unnecessary right from the beginning for the simple reason that the employers would have known that they did not have a chance of successfully pressing their demands. Assuming that, as a rule, strikes in fact occurred only when the outcome was not absolutely certain right from the beginning, it must be said that the Christian unions were often over-cautious. This is confirmed by the detailed analysis of individual strikes mentioned above which cannot be discussed here.

However, one can understand why the Christian unions insisted on being treated as equal partners according to their strength during negotiations as well as during the preparation of strikes. And one cannot blame them for being embittered when this was not the case, or for their view that they should not be regarded as blacklegs because they were working during a strike which they did not agree with from the start. On the other hand, the Free Trade Unions could often rightly complain about a lack of solidarity from the Christian Trade Unions who on several occasions prematurely and unilaterally ended strikes which had started as joint actions.

IV

How difficult it was for the Christian and the Free unions to find a common or merely co-ordinated approach to labour conflicts is most clearly illustrated by the *Prinzipienkampf* in the Cologne timber industry. This conflict resulted in the Christian unions' fundamentally rethinking 'co-operation between the Christian and the social democratic trade unions during wage campaigns and strikes'.[11]

'The contradictions on questions of principle between the Christian and

Table 16.8 Participation of Christian Trade Unions in Strikes and Wage Campaigns, 1902–13

		1902	1903	1904	1905	1906	1907	1908	1909	1910	1911	1912	1913
Miners	(a)	–	–	–	61,200	2,059	1,012	–	–	–	800	–	1,053
	(b)	–	–	–	60,000	2,059	800	–	–	–	615	–	639
Construction workers	(a)	578	4,045	5,996	12,034	14,881	17,770	25,585	6,762	33,271	4,785	3,885	42,136
	(b)	426	1,790	2,998	8,058	4,043	5,112	1,570	2,761	14,613	2,759	3,885	2,739
Textile workers	(a)	1,226	2,202	2,982	11,720	14,055	11,162	4,579	5,506	6,739	13,046	9,419	12,975
	(b)	852	1,241	393	2,755	8,817	2,434	1,071	811	1,454	4,883	478	8,180
Metal and engineering workers	(a)	64	1,222	1,521	10,384	9,333	6,223	2,152	2,657	9,951	10,944	13,488	9,792
	(b)	64	860	530	5,488	5,404	2,032	1,002	374	3,369	2,855	2,009	2,072
Unskilled and transport workers, factory workers	(a)	476	790	328	3,230	10,053	5,918	–	–	–	–	–	3,913
	(b)	–	27	51	1,338	5,016	1,070	–	–	–	–	–	322
Woodworkers	(a)	817	1,373	2,750	2,820	6,409	4,755	2,355	2,786	5,485	4,674	4,629	6,575
	(b)	209	414	830	1,296	1,727	965	507	1,018	815	1,540	829	800
Ceramics workers	(a)	–	61	114	2,412	3,708	3,655	1,245	911	2,675	2,198	3,083	4,337
	(b)	–	–	–	451	1,018	957	802	430	465	627	–	649
Tobacco workers	(a)	268	284	345	497	4,269	2,419	429	392	1,814	4,166	3,898	1,296
	(b)	70	–	50	–	829	285	24	62	296	2,796	2,120	24
Shoe and leather workers	(a)	330	471	319	422	743	1,422	656	789	2,474	2,055	673	1,204
	(b)	140	296	98	30	141	864	321	286	462	388	185	522

	1903	1904	1905	1906	1907	1908	1909	1910	1911	1912	1913	1914
Tailors and dressmakers (a)	443	261	82	794	1,136	1,902	882	607	750	1,761	1,874	1,270
(b)	390	11	48	621	486	1,506	91	41	175	423	1,574	198
Painters and decorators (a)	–	344	–	806	1,850	1,500	642	105	2,821	394	198	3,829
(b)	–	74	–	290	482	1,025	167	64	117	176	38	3,661
Gutenbergbund (printers) (a)	–	–	–	–	16	52	60	–	–	–	–	–
(b)	–	–	–	–	16	52	–	–	–	24	–	–
Workers in the graphical industry (a)	–	–	81	300	256	339	325	378	549	699	564	1,030
(b)	–	–	–	275	11	19	85	82	32	40	57	728
Public service workers (a)	–	–	–	–	–	–	4,388	5,307	6,525	4,774	10,782	3,115
(b)	–	–	–	–	–	–	1,109	1,011	536	701	1,023	–
Home workers (a)	–	–	–	–	–	–	–	–	–	636	199	50
(b)	–	–	–	–	–	–	–	–	–	500	–	50
Provisions and fine foods industry workers (a)	–	–	–	–	–	–	–	–	–	1,059	455	1,195
(b)	–	–	–	–	–	–	–	–	–	109	124	365

(a) participants in wage campaigns
(b) participants in strikes
Sources: Compiled from the annual surveys and statistics of the *Mitteilungen* and the *Zentralblatt* 1903 to 1914 respectively.

the Social Democratic trade unions' would not exclude 'a common approach by both movements, where the solution of mere trade union tasks is concerned'. But some preconditions had to be fulfilled. The Christian unions demanded mainly 'that they should be offered an early opportunity to evaluate the facts in order to share in the decision-making before wage campaigns or strikes are initiated. The same applies to the tactics to be pursued during wage campaigns or strikes.' Thus, the position of the Christian woodworkers was recommended to the entire Christian union movement:

(1) If an organization wants to initiate a wage campaign and a second union organization has to be taken into account, the latter has to be informed as soon as possible so that it can also make all the necessary preparations.
(2) Before initiating any campaign mentioned under point 1, the organizations involved must agree on the demands and also on the timing and the planned tactics.
(3) If other organizations do not fulfill the preconditions mentioned under 1 and 2, the members of our union have to determine through a decision of a meeting the tactics they want to pursue and ask the Central Executive for their approval.

As mentioned above, this 'regulation' was the result of a conflict in the Cologne timber industry which had led to controversies between the two large trade union movements of different ideological persuasion (*Richtungs-gewerkschaften*) since 1903. In 1903 and 1904 the point at stake was that the *(Freie) Deutsche Holzarbeiterverband* ((Free) German Woodworkers' Union) had formulated its demands at its own meetings to which the representatives of the *Christliche Holzarbeiterverband* (Christian Wood-workers' Union) were not admitted. Also, in 1904 tools were downed in some workshops without any consultations with the Christian union. The main bone of contention, however, was the fact that the Free unions insisted that no representatives of the Christian unions were to take part in negotiations with the employers.

After strikes had taken place in the rail carriage works in 1904, the situation was brought to a head in 1905. Although the two unions had consulted regarding the demands of the carpenters, differences remained on whether it was advisable at this point to press these demands through strike action. While the Christian union was against striking, the Free union decided in favour of it. In some works, therefore, strike action was taken from 1 April. A meeting of the Cologne section of the *Christliche Holzar-beiterverband* decided, by a margin of twelve votes against, not to participate in the strike. About 600 of its 800 members were present at that meeting. In a resolution passed by the assembly, the strike was characterized as 'a frivolous game with the workers' interests by the social democratic union leaders', designed to force the Christian union in a 'dictatorial way' into fighting. 'For the members of the *Christliche Holzarbeiterverband*', read the resolution, 'this campaign is to be regarded as non-existent'. This meant that the Christian unionists continued to work. 'The Christian union', the resolution continued, 'will also continue to run its employment office.' Thus, the plans of the social democratic union would be foiled.

According to the Christian union, this was followed by 'terrorist measures' against the Christian woodworkers, a claim which the Christian union used for propaganda purposes. The strike was lost after several weeks, not least because new labour came to the area. What remained though, especially amongst the members of the Free Trade Unions, was an unusually strong feeling of bitterness.[12] Meanwhile, the Christian unions rejected the accusation of having broken the strike, not least by pointing to their behaviour in the mining industry on the Ruhr in the same year.

The fact that there were several layers of motivations contributing to the willingness to strike or to support a strike is most clearly demonstrated by the history of the most influential Christian union, the *Gewerkverein Christlicher Bergarbeiter*. In 1905 it let itself be drawn into a labour conflict, in the same way as the other unions. In 1912, however, it maintained its opposition to strike action. Party political motives, the increasing bitterness of the *Gewerkschaftsstreit* and the assumption that, at that point, a strike did not have much chance of success all contributed to forming the association's policy, as will be briefly described below.[13]

The Association of Christian Miners decided at its meeting of local chairmen on 27 November 1910 under no circumstances to co-operate with the *Alte Verband* (the social democratic miners' union). Therefore, separate wage claims were formulated. However, this did not mean a rejection of a strike as a matter of principle. They simply considered that there was little point in striking at that time. It was precisely this ambivalence in rejecting a strike which triggered a press controversy with the *Germania*, once again highlighting the opposing views in the *Gewerkschaftsstreit*. The demands of the Association were rejected by the *Bergbauliche Verein*, the mining employers' organization, which pointed out that wages had gradually increased anyway. Nevertheless, at its executive meeting on 5 October 1911, the *Gewerkverein Christlicher Bergarbeiter* committed itself to rejecting co-operation with the other mining unions. It also rejected any attempt to push through wage demands by directly approaching the company-owners. The Association wanted instead to restrict its actions to a *Teuerungsinter-pellation* (interpellation asking that wages should keep up with prices) in the Reichstag and to informing the public. It further decided to draw up petitions to the Reichstag, the government and the local authorities high-lighting the plight of the miners. A police observer reported from 'reliable sources' that this decision was due to the fact 'that the *Gewerkverein* wanted to avoid anything that could have offended the state authorities, the company-owners and the patriotically minded workers in view of the conflict between itself and the *Alte Verband* and of the forthcoming elections'. The members of the executive, the report remarked approvingly, 'honestly intended to make a determined effort to wrest the Reichstag's seats of Dortmund and Gelsenkirchen-Bochum from the Social Democrats'.

During the extraordinary general meeting of the *Gewerkverein* of the Ruhr district in Essen on 8 October 1911 the behaviour of the pit authorities was condemned because it had not satisfactorily fulfilled a promise to increase wages made by the mining owners' association in December 1910. Yet the matter was left with an appeal to honour this commitment. Then, on 12 October, a joint meeting of the four miners' unions took place which – according to the police report – unanimously criticized the situation regarding wages, but did not come to any decision on a joint approach; opinions differed widely between the *Gewerkverein* and the other unions on the chances of success of a strike, the dangers of which were illustrated in a statement made by the Christian union. The police observer gained the impression that the decision – as far as the Ruhr district was concerned – was seen in connection with developments in England, as it was emphasized 'that a strike in England would cause a strike by the Ruhr miners should wages not have been improved by then'. Otto Hue from the *Alte Verband* had conceded at the meeting that he too could hardly foresee a victory over the pit-owners. But he thought they could be forced into a compromise because the miners were better organized than in 1905 and also because the economic situation was favourable.

No agreement on concerted action could be reached during the joint meeting of the central executives of the four unions in October 1911, and opinions clashed again violently at their meeting on 5 February 1912. The bitterness of the debates was presumably due not least to the result of the Reichstag elections of January 1912. The Social Democrats had gained votes, but – because of the co-operation between the *Zentrum* (Catholic Centre Party) and the *Nationalliberalen* (National Liberal Party) on the second ballot – they lost seats in Bochum and Duisburg. The *Alte Verband*, the *Hirsch-Dunckersche Gewerkverein* and the *Polnische Berufsvereinigung* (the Polish miners' union) urged an immediate wage initiative, whilst the representatives of the Christian association flatly rejected this; they preferred to wait for the wage negotiations which the employers had announced for March/April 1912. The three other unions, now joined in the 'Dreibund' (triple alliance), consequently asked the pit-owners' association for higher wages on 6 February 1912 without the *Gewerkverein*. The answer on 13 February held out the prospect of higher wages but rejected negotiations. On 19 February the union demands were not only formulated more precisely but also extended. The 'Dreibund' asked for a wage increase of 15 per cent and, in addition, demanded the introduction of an eight-hour shift as well as a further reduction in working hours to seven, and six hours where working conditions were particularly difficult and hot, the establishment of non-discriminatory labour exchanges and of arbitration courts with equal representation. An answer to this catalogue of demands was expected by 5 March 1912. In view of the good economic situation the timing for aggressive action by the miners seemed to be favourable, and the predictable miners' strike in England, which actually started on 1 March 1912, seemed to improve the situation even further.

Even before the employers rejected these demands, work had already stopped in some pits. When the rejection came, a meeting of district representatives on 7 March recommended a strike from 11 March. The 'Dreibund' accepted this recommendation and, on 10 March, issued its own call to strike.

The position of the *Gewerkverein* was a complicated one. On the one hand, the necessity of wage increases was accepted; on the other hand, as the *Gewerkschaftsstreit* was coming to a head, reticence seemed advisable. A further consideration was that participation in an unsuccessful strike would lead to the disappointment of members and corresponding losses in membership. Participation in a successful strike would bring the *Gewerkverein* closer to the *Alte Verband* and possibly tie them together permanently. The reaction to this dilemma was ferociously to criticize the *Alte Verband*, which – so it was said – was looking for a trial of strength, seeking to destroy the *Gewerkverein* and would lead a sympathy strike with the English miners without any regard for the dangers of such a course for the German workers. The 'national' interest especially was pushed to the foreground in the arguments put forward. The intention was not only to dissociate themselves from the 'internationalist' Social Democrats, but also to recommend themselves to potential sympathizers in the government and church as a responsible 'national force'. The *Gewerkverein* was also clearly attempting to avoid an accusation of strike-mongering by the Catholic workers' associations in Berlin, which could endanger support which might come from some quarters of the church, as had happened in 1905.

The extraordinary general meeting of the *Gewerkverein* for the Ruhr district took place on 6 March. The position of the executive, and thus the rejection of the strike, was unanimously supported. Further, it was demanded that the Minister of the Interior provide military protection, if required, for those willing to work, because the police forces were insufficient. This request was put to the Secretary of State Clemens von Delbrück on 11 March.

While the miners' strike of 1905 had the sympathy of large parts of the public, the labour conflict of 1912 was generally regarded as an arbitrary action, which possibly even had the objective of manoeuvring the *Gewerkverein* into a difficult if not impossible situation. Well over 190,000 miners took part in the initial stages of the strike, that is, about half of all miners in the Ruhr district. By 13 March their number had increased to 235,000 (61 per cent of the workforce). However, after the army was sent in on 14 March numbers decreased rapidly. Estimates of the degree of participation in the strike vary enormously. They range from between 34 and 75 per cent of all miners, without any indication of the dates to which they apply. The Free Trade Unions especially pointed out that many Christian trade unionists took part in the strike action – despite the unequivocal rejection of the strike not only by the *Gewerkverein* but also by the religiously oriented workers' associations and *Knappenvereine* (miners' guilds). By 19 March work was back to normal. Widespread disciplinary action was subsequently taken – both for breach of contract and because of excesses which had occurred.

It is not surprising that the Christian Trade Unions regarded the unsuccessful end of the strike as a vindication of their position. Greater caution was necessary, it was said, because the option of negotiating had not been exhausted, and the degree of union organization and the unions' financial position were too weak. Furthermore, the English miners' strike had actually decreased pressure on the German pit-owners because they did not have any competition to fear. All this had been overlooked by the Free Trade Unions because they had only been aiming to force the *Gewerkverein* to its knees. This was a goal particularly close to the heart of the Free unions, so the argument continued, because they were embittered about the election results especially as Hue had lost his parliamentary seat. In any case, the *Alte Verband* and the *Gewerkverein* blamed each other for the hapless end of the strike. Whilst the latter regarded the strike as a mistake right from the beginning, the former accused the Christian unionists of being blacklegs.

Although the doubts of the Christian miners' union appear to have been vindicated by the course of the strike, one must ask whether a united approach of all four miners' unions would not have considerably improved the chances of success. This, at least, was the view taken by the Free unions which – after the strike – felt very bitter towards the *Gewerkverein*. This bitterness was also noticeable at rank-and-file level. To give an example: during the discussion at a public meeting of 350 to 400 miners in Datteln on 12 December 1913, the Christian miners were branded as 'blacklegs', who had called for the military, and as a 'festering boil on the neck of the workers', which had to be burnt out 'by a redhot iron'. The 'yellow' unions at least were no hypocrites. The strike of 1905 also leant support to the view that a common front could have been successful.

However, if one accepted that this strike was 'a wrestling match between the social democratic and the Christian union movement', it was entirely clear by now that, at least in the centres of the Christian union movement, successful strikes were hardly possible without them and certainly not against them. The *Gewerkverein* had used this description of the strike in a skilful propaganda campaign to prove the economic and political importance of Christian Trade Unions.

The attitude of the Christian unions was noted by the Reichstag on 14, 15 and 16 March. On 14 March the Secretary of State for Internal Affairs, Delbrück, commented that the strike was unnecessary as far as wage increases were concerned, and that it was started before all possibilities for a peaceful solution had been exhausted. And on 14 and 16 March respectively the M.P.s Carl Matthias Schiffer (Christian textile workers' union) and Johannes Giesberts took the opportunity to highlight the economic and political responsibility which the Christian unions had shown. Hermann Imbusch too propounded this thesis in the Prussian Chamber of Deputies on 18 March. In addition the Christian unions condemned the 'terrorism' of the striking workers in order to show themselves as a force of law and order.

The accusation of strike-breaking was indeed of central importance. According to Giesberts, speaking on 16 March, the Christian unions had tried to undermine this argument by pointing out that it could hardly be called strike-breaking if the second largest union did not participate in a strike which it regarded as hopeless. The *Gewerkverein* was not taking any orders from the *Alte Verband*. This was in fact also the tenor of statements made on this subject at the Christian unions' congress in October 1912. The assembly, however, was uncertain about whether the 'national and economic responsibility' demonstrated had paid off. The Ruhr strike was characterized as a harbinger of mass strikes with which one had to reckon at all times. But the

Christian unions had evidently shown themselves to be a bulwark against such a development.

The controversies about the strike behaviour of the Christian and the Free unions should not make one forget the numerous examples of co-operation – from the Ruhr miners' strike in 1905 to several conflicts in the Krefeld textile industry between 1906 and 1909 and the construction workers' struggle in 1910. However, one can summarize that the conflicts caused greater interest than the co-operation. Controversies determined the relationship between the Christian and the Free unions, usually in connection with labour conflicts such as those in the Cologne joinery trade, the Munich engineering industry in 1905, the conflict in Badisch-Rheinfelden in 1909, or the dyers' strike in Krefeld in 1913.

Both large ideologically oriented union movements had one thing in common, the belief that a growing degree of organization would result in increased strength, and that labour conflicts would also strengthen the organization. The second aspect was emphasized by the Free Trade Unions, the former by the Christian unions which aimed at making actual strikes largely superfluous by impressive threatening gestures. However, both aspects were taken into account by the two competing movements. It should not be overlooked that the Christian unions were in a position to forgo actual strikes because the actions of the Free Trade Unions increased the credibility of their threats.

Their real influence on wage movements cannot be calculated in precise money terms. It is certain, however, that even before the First World War it was virtually impossible to conduct a successful strike against the wishes of the Christian unions in areas and industrial branches where these organizations were strong. The realization of this fact should have had a moderating influence on the Free Trade Unions. The Christian unions liked to point this out time and again, not least as a sign of their responsible attitude in the 'national' context. The Free unions, for their part, in order to legitimize their position vis-à-vis 'more radical' workers, if necessary, used the argument that the Christian organizations were reluctant to go on strike. Thus, whilst the Christian unions thought they had a moderating influence on the Free unions, the Free unions hoped to 'educate' their Christian counterparts and turn them into instruments of the class struggle through everyday work, the hostility of the employers and, most of all, through labour conflicts.

The fundamental difference in the two large ideologically orientated union movements in their view of themselves cannot be overlooked. However, this difference was not as visible in practice as it was in statements of principle and calls to action. The Free unions expressly used such statements to differentiate themselves from the *Hirsch-Dunkersche Gewerkvereine* and the Christian competition. In contrast to the Christian unions, the Free unions emphasized that the struggle for higher wages and shorter working hours was led by the unions 'in the knowledge that there was an insurmountable contradiction between capital and labour, but that the union struggle will make the working class stronger in its resistance and thus more prepared for the final solution of the social question'. Carl Legien too expected the Christian unions to be forced into co-operation with the Free unions by the reality of labour conflicts, as demonstrated by the miners and construction workers in 1905 and 1910.[14]

However, time and again the Christian unions distanced themselves from precisely this 'fighting mentality' of the Free unions. They criticized the Free unions for leading their members unprepared into hopeless situations; for being irresponsible and frivolous; for not seizing the hand of the Christian unions when the objective was to force through demands by a joint approach in negotiations. Finally, they concluded, the often meagre results achieved by strike action could have been obtained peacefully at less cost. In their written statements, the Christian unions insisted that in contrast to the Free unions, they alone really regarded strike action as the last resort in a conflict. In view of the overlapping factors influencing the unions – competition, organizational structure, politics, religion and finally *Weltanschauung* – it is hardly possible to speak of a specifically 'Christian' behaviour in labour conflicts. Yet precisely by their strike behaviour the Christian Trade Unions proved themselves to be a clearly independent branch of the German labour movement.

Appendix

Membership of the Christian Unions, 1900–31

	Total	Female
1900	(76,744)	?
1901	84,497	?
1902	84,667	?
1903	91,440	5,465
1904	107,556	7,624
1905	188,106	11,991
1906	247,116	21,646
1907	284,649	24,122
1908	260,767	22,087
1909	280,061	20,182
1910	316,115	21,833
1911	350,574	27,152
1912	350,930	28,008
1913	341,735	27,623
1914	218,197	25,624
1915	162,425	24,242
1916	178,907	28,764
1917	293,187	44,416
1918	538,559	72,409
1919	1,000,770	160,024

Source: M. Schneider, *Die Christlichen Gewerkschaften, 1894–1933* (Bonn, 1982), 767–71.

Notes: Chapter 16

1 M. Schneider, *Die Christlichen Gewerkschaften 1894 bis 1933* (Bonn, 1982), esp. 281–321. There you will also find further literature which is not listed here. Only the economic dissertation by A. Siegler has to be named: *Die Lohnpolitik der Christlichen Gewerkschaften Deutschlands (1894–1933)* (Mannheim, 1978), which has provided many an inspiration.

2 *Jahrbuch der Christlichen Gewerkschaften 1908* (Cologne, 1908), 71.

3 *Geschichte und Entwicklung der Christlichen Gewerkschaften Deutschlands nebst Protokoll des III. christlichen Gewerkschaftskongresses zu Krefeld (26.–29. Mai 1901)* (Mönchengladbach, 1901), 10–11,

4 See O. Müller, *Die christliche Gewerkschaftsbewegung Deutschlands, mit besonderer Berücksichtigung der Bergarbeiter- und Textilarbeiterorganisationen* (Karlsruhe, 1905), 167.

5 *Geschichte und Entwicklung der christlichen Gewerkschaften*, 16.

6 ibid., 17.

7 See 'Zur Streiktaktik I', in *Mitteilungen des Gesamtverbandes der christlichen Gewerkschaften Deutschlands* 15 (11 November 1901): 137–9 (137).

8 'Einordnung der neuzeitlichen Arbeiterbewegung in die bestehende Gesellschaft', in *Zentralblatt der christlichen Gewerkschaften Deutschlands* 4 (26 February 1906): 49–52 (49).

9 See for example 'Verminderung der Streiks während der Krise', in *Mitteilungen* 19 (23 December 1901): 173–4.

10 Siegler, *Die Lohnpolitik der Christlichen Gewerkschaften*, 112.

11 For the following see *Sozialdemokratische Streik-Taktik, insbesondere gegenüber christlichen Gewerkschaften, mit vorzugsweiser Berücksichtigung einiger Vorgänge im Kölner Schreinergewerbe*, edited by the Christliche Holzarbeiterverband (Cologne, 1905).

12 cf. *Ein Denkmal dem Christlichen Holzarbeiterverband. Aus Anlass seiner Heldentaten im Schreinerstreik in Köln 1905*, edited by the Deutsche Holzarbeiterverband (Stuttgart, 1905), e.g. p. 3.

13 cf. Schneider, *Christliche Gewerkschaften*, 281–321, and H. Imbusch, *Bergarbeiterstreik im Ruhrgebiet im Frühjahr 1912*, 8th edn (Cologne, 1912).

14 C. Legien, *Die deutsche Gewerkschaftsbewegung (1900)*, 2nd edn (Berlin, 1911), 15–16.

17 The National Free Labour Association: Working-Class Opposition to New Unionism in Britain

GEOFFREY ALDERMAN

I

The history of British industrial relations is dominated by the history of trade unions. There are several reasons why this should be so. There was a time when only trade union historians were interested in industrial relations history. In those industries where trade unions dominate, such as mining, there seems very little else to write about, as far as industrial relations are concerned, which is not covered by the chronicles of the mining unions. Even in industries where trade union domination has never been so great, such as clothing, the tendency is to tell the story in terms of the strengths and weaknesses of such trade unions as have been formed. There is also a practical consideration. Usually the archives of trade unions are accessible and compact. Try to trace the history of industrial relations in an industry where there never was a trade union, or even a trade newspaper or periodical, and one is faced at once with the daunting prospect of having to search hither and thither, in all sorts of byways, for archival material.

New Unionism in Britain is very much a case in point. The history of New Unionism is dominated by the history of those trade unions whose emergence was vividly associated with it. The role of socialists is, rightly, given prominence, for they alone saw the potentialities of the new mood of industrial militancy for the project dearest to their hearts: the formation of a socialist political party with working-class backing. 'The unions', Keir Hardie declared, 'must be won.'[1] And won they were. But it took a decade or so for the Trades Union Congress to accept the idea of separate Labour representation in Parliament (1899), and the Labour Party did not adopt even lukewarm socialism until 1918.

How did the events of this period 1889–1914 strike ordinary working-men in Britain? By 'ordinary working-men' those are meant, as this was the vast majority, whose main concern was to earn enough each week for the essentials of life for their families and themselves, whose politics (assuming they had the vote) were of the simplest, and for whom being unemployed was the greatest tragedy that could befall a man. It is worth remembering in this context that in 1901, when the size of the labour force in Great Britain was about 16·3 million, the total number of trade union members was only just over 2 million.[2] And when we examine the impact of socialism, the contrast becomes even starker. In his brilliant essay on 'The Working Class and the Origins of the Welfare State', Henry Pelling has reminded us that the British working classes at the turn of the century were not merely apathetic about social reform; they were overtly hostile.[3] They viewed with the utmost suspicion any encroachments by the apparatus of the central government into the way they organized their lives. They objected to state interference in industry if this resulted – as it often did – in the restriction of hours of work and/or the size of wage packets.[4] They viewed 'the state' as 'an organisation run by and for the benefit of the wealthy'.[5] The majority of working-men were in consequence staunch advocates of laissez-faire; an additional justification for this view was the fear that the reintroduction of tariffs would lead to higher food prices.

Socialism in the 1880s and 1890s was very much a middle-class movement. Those trade union leaders who joined the Labour Representation Committee were not in the main socialists.[6] If they had any religious faith they were likely to be anti-socialist, because for many at this time socialism was still synonymous with atheism. The alliance between socialists and trade unionists, which found expression in the Labour Representation Committee, was indeed a marriage of convenience. Those trade unions which affiliated to the new organization did so for one purpose only: to reverse, through parliamentary means, the anti-union trend of judge-made law in the 1890s, of which the final judgment of the House of Lords in the Taff Vale case (July 1901) was seen as the culmination.

It is clear, therefore, that the study of trade unions and of socialism at this time is not going to get us very far in an understanding of working-class ideas and motivations. In particular, we need to pay much closer attention to those working-men and women who were not socialists, and who did not join trade unions. And, in the context of New Unionism, our understanding of industrial relations is going to be very incomplete if we concentrate merely on the rise and fall of the New Unions. It is not enough to study those who joined the New Unions. We must pay some attention to those – the vast majority – who did not do so. That is not an easy thing to do, because for the most part these people have left no record of their thoughts and actions. But we know that in some cases there was not merely indifference to New Unionism, there was active hostility. The National Free Labour Association (NFLA) was one outcome of this hostility.

The NFLA was the premier strike-breaking organization which operated in Great Britain between 1893 and 1914. It was not the only such organization, but whereas others, such as the Shipping Federation,[7] were employers' organizations, the NFLA was founded by working-men and was not a capitalist tool. To understand why it was founded, and what were the motives of its founders, we need to remember that the advent of New Unionism, symbolized in the London dock strike of 1889, gave an entirely new twist to the meaning of collective bargaining, for it represented a challenge not only to employers but also to the more traditionally minded trade union leaders. These men, liberal in spirit and often Liberal in political conviction, objected both to the socialist views of Ben Tillet, Tom Mann and their supporters, and to the tactics of the New Unionism – 'an aggressive, militant unionism', the veteran trade union leader and former Liberal M.P. George Howell called it in 1892, 'which said, not *let them* all come, but *you must* all come, into the union'.[8]

Howell belonged to a generation for whom trade unionism had much less to do with strikes and much more to do with mutual aid between working-men. Picketing and the closed shop were concepts from which they instinctively shied away, for such concepts, and the enforcement of them by means of strikes, had no place in a laissez-faire society. The fluctuations of wages and employment were part of the natural order of things; to regulate such matters by means of industrial action and (worse still) to use trade union power to bring about socialist ends, as it seemed many of the New Union leaders were trying to do, was to fly in the face of nature, to flout the freedom of the individual and to flirt with revolution.

William Collison was one who found in these sentiments much with which he could agree. Collison was born on 22 June 1865 in London's East End, the son of a policeman. After a spell in the army he became a bricklayer's labourer, and joined the Amalgamated Labourers' Union in 1884. Then he took a succession of casual waterfront jobs, and in 1886 was elected a delegate for the Mansion House Unemployed Relief Committee. The experience of relief work in the East End proved a turning-point in Collison's life. Not only was he brought into contact with poverty in the raw; he also had first-hand experience of the way in which, as it seemed to him, socialists were exploiting London's unemployed for their own ends. He became an omnibus driver, and in 1889 helped form the London and County Tramway and Omnibus Employees' Trade Union, of which, for a time, he was a paid official. But he disliked the union's president, and could not stomach the union's headstrong militancy. He left the union, and omnibus work, in 1890, tried to find casual work in the docks, but was refused employment 'because I could not show my Trade Union ticket':

> I felt I was being pursued and dominated by a tyranny. . . . I was a pariah among workmen, because I did not belong to a certain Union of which I knew nothing and cared less. . . . It flitted into my mind at that time that there must be thousands of other men as capable as myself . . . who shared my state of rejection. I thought then that were it possible for us to meet and hold council together we might well arrive at some common grounds of defence and retaliation. This was my first vague thought towards Free Labour.[9]

Collison determined 'that the best retreat from Trade Unionism lies in attack'.[10] He took up the struggle in the firm belief that 'the partial conversion of the Unions to Socialism, with its destructive and confiscatory tendencies, transformed them into a despotism for the enforcement of . . . false and subversive doctrines'. But it was not merely socialism to which Collison objected; he abhorred equally the modus operandi of New Union-ism – 'strikes, intimidation, boycotting, and unlawful picketing' – examples of which he claimed to have found in abundance in the London riverside unions created by John Burns, Ben Tillett and Tom Mann.[11] Nor was

Collison the only trade unionist to have reached such conclusions. John Chandler, one of the founders of the Amalgamated Riverside Labourers' Union in 1883, had actually joined in the 1889 dock strike. Joseph Penrose was founder and first president of the Dock Foremen and Permanent Coopers' Trade Union.[12] In these men Collison found like-minded individualists prepared to join him in challenging New Unionism. With their help, on 16 May 1893, he called a 'General Conference of men interested in Free Labour' at Aldgate, in the City of London. At this meeting the National Free Labour Association was formed.[13]

II

The NFLA was methodically organized. It had a printed constitution which stated its objects, the first of which was declared to be 'to maintain Freedom of Labour, based on the right possessed by every man to pursue his Trade or Employment without dictation, molestation or obstruction'. Financial members, who originally paid 2s 6d per annum, were entitled to take part in the elective and, if elected to office, the administrative work of the organization. Non-financial members merely registered with the Association to obtain employment. Chandler was first president of the NFLA, but real power lay with Collison. He was both General Secretary and manager; the constitution of 1902 gave him a salary of £300 per annum plus expenses. He continued to guide the fortunes of the NFLA until its disappearance at the end of the 1920s.

The NFLA had an executive committee but, more important from the point of view of credibility, it boasted an annual congress, open to the press and lavishly advertised. The first such congress was held in London on 31 October and 1 November 1893. Attended by 160 delegates said to come from all parts of the country, the meeting heard messages of support from politicians and other public figures. A resolution was passed against 'the recent senseless and abortive strikes which ... have had a most disastrous effect upon the living of the wage-earning classes' and unlawful picketing was condemned.[14] Congresses such as this marked the high point of the Association's work each year; the deliberate aim was to ape the methods of the Trades Union Congress. By the time of the third congress, in 1895, held at Newcastle upon Tyne, socialists had become sufficiently alarmed to feel the need to send Tillett, and other like-minded trade unionists, northward to denounce Collison and his association. But this strategy backfired. Collison offered to debate collective bargaining with the Newcastle Trades Council; the offer was refused. Tillett and his friends had already suffered a reverse at the Cardiff Trades Union Congress, where new procedures had been adopted designed to deplete socialist representation at future congresses.[15] Now Tillett's further discomfiture at Newcastle added fuel to Collison's anti-socialist campaign. Worse was to follow. Collison published a deliberate libel on Havelock Wilson, the sailors' leader. Wilson sued him, but when the trial took place, in March 1896, he refused to go into the witness box on his own behalf. He obtained one farthing damages, without costs.[16]

Collison obviously enjoyed these interludes, but the serious work of the NFLA lay in other directions, and fell into three distinct parts. First there was propaganda on behalf of 'free labour' and against New Unionism. The NFLA had its own newspaper, the *Free Labour Gazette*, which appeared (under several changes of title) between 7 November 1894 and 27 April 1907. Until April 1896 Collison was named as its proprietor and publisher. Thereafter the editor and proprietor was John Charles Manning, an experienced journalist and later private secretary to the millionaire coal-owner Lord Joicey.[17] Manning's death in the spring of 1907 led to the demise of the free labour organ, for Collison had neither the money nor the journalistic expertise to run it himself.

The newspaper was the main vehicle for attacks on socialist organizations. Attempts by Keir Hardie's Independent Labour Party, and other bodies, to secure the eight-hour day were condemned as 'tyrannical'. Character assassinations of socialist leaders were frequently indulged in. The alliance between the Liberal and Labour parties, and the Liberal government's reversal of the Taff Vale decision in 1906, was bitterly attacked. The Eight Hours Act for miners (1908) was likewise condemned by the NFLA, as was the Liberal scheme setting up labour exchanges (1909). In 1911 the congress of the NFLA pointed with alarm to the growing tendency of employers to enter into closed shop agreements with trade unions.[18]

Secondly, the NFLA did engage in a certain amount of parliamentary and election activity. In 1894 it organized a campaign against the prohibition of 'contracting-out' in the Liberal government's Employers' Liability Bill, which never became law. The following year, at the general election, the Association campaigned against those parliamentary candidates in London whose views on the restriction of alien (largely Jewish) immigration were suspect; four of the candidates were defeated. The restriction of alien immigration was very popular in working-class circles at the time, and the Trades Union Congress had itself called for such restriction on more than one occasion. In January 1897 the NFLA campaigned on behalf of the Conservative candidate, Louis Sinclair, in the Romford by-election; Sinclair won.[19] But Collison's own efforts, in 1898 and 1899, to enter municipal politics met with failure.[20] And it is clear that the tariff reform controversy which split the Unionist Party had repercussions also within the NFLA.[21]

After 1906 the political targets of the Association were beyond doubt: in the long run, the entire apparatus of the compact between the Liberal and Labour parties; in the short run, the 'preposterous piece of class legislation' embodied in the 1906 Trade Disputes Act, which had reversed Taff Vale.[22] To understand why the NFLA was so opposed to the 1906 Act it is necessary to dwell in some detail upon the third, and most important sphere of its activities, the battle against New Unionism.

III

Collison knew enough about New Unionism to realize that ultimately it could only be fought at grass-roots level. He also knew that there were many working-men who wished for nothing better than to be able to get on with the task of earning a livelihood without having to bother about unions, collective bargaining, closed shops, or picketing. He knew too that, especially in dockland areas, there was an army of unemployed waiting desperately for the chance of a job, and willing to do almost anything to earn a few shillings. All that was needed was organization. This was provided by the NFLA, which maintained a network of 'Free Labour Exchanges' in London and the major provincial centres. Their purpose was to break strikes by keeping a register of men, who could be transported if necessary from one part of the country to another. An employer who wished to call upon the services of the Association was obliged to enter into a contract specifying the daily rate of pay for each man's services for the duration of the strike. No man could be registered as a free labourer unless he signed a pledge, agreeing 'to work in harmony with any other man engaged, whether he is a member of a trade union or not'.[23]

Estimates of the success of this strike-breaking organization varied greatly. Collison boasted that between 1893 and 1913 the NFLA had 'fought and been successful in no less than 682 pitched battles with aggressive Trade Unions in different parts of the United Kingdom', and that during that time 850,000 workmen had been registered.[24] If these figures are accurate, it is clear that the bulk of the disputes in which the NFLA were involved were small-scale affairs, mainly involving unskilled or semi-skilled workers in dockland; Collison's value to the craft industries was very limited, and the use of his men by engineering firms during the great lock-out of 1897 had a minimal impact on the dispute.[25]

But Collison's greatest success, which even the trade union movement acknowledged, was on the railways. In 1900 he had been asked to organize a supply of railwaymen for a strike anticipated by the directors of the Great Eastern Railway. Then the Taff Vale Railway dispute began, and the free labourers were transferred to South Wales instead. Collison had made certain that every man sent to the Taff Vale Company had signed a contract to enter into its service. The company was thus able to sue the Amalgamated Society of Railway Servants for inducing breaches of contract. The momentous legal judgement consequent upon that dispute, and the victory of the company in obtaining damages in December 1902, not only left the premier railway union £42,000 the poorer; it deprived trade unions of immunity at law for their industrial actions, and so dealt a fatal blow to the strike weapon, and also to the right of peaceful picketing, within the then existing legal code.[26]

Collison was quick to publicize the victory. Yet the Taff Vale judgment proved to be something of an anticlimax. There is no evidence that the NFLA was busier after 1902 than before. In January of that year the Association boasted that 'upwards of 500 senseless strikes' had been defeated. If Collison's figure, quoted earlier, of a total of 682 strikes defeated between 1893 and 1913 is believed, then clearly the bulk of his victories came in the period *before* Taff Vale. The truth was that Collison could never hope to supply skilled or semi-skilled workmen in numbers large enough to defeat strikes outright. What he could hope to do was to provide gangs of men to maintain a workforce of some sort, and so wear down the morale of strikers. The period of relative peace under Taff Vale was due less to the impact of the judgment than to the fact that the majority of employers preferred collective bargaining to industrial warfare.[27]

Collison's last success of any magnitude was in April 1905, when the NFLA was called upon to intervene in the shipsmiths' strike at Sunderland. Then, in December, came the downfall of the Unionist government, the advent of a Liberal ministry and, in 1906, the Trade Disputes Act. Collison's industrial world fell about him. He was deserted even by his traditional customers. During the railway crisis of 1907 his offer of '20,000 ex-railwaymen and others' was brushed aside by the companies; nor did he play any part in the 1911 national railway strike. The NFLA could still hope for some successes where unskilled workers were concerned, and in the summer of 1912 free labourers supplied by it helped defeat the London dock strike.[28] But the major part in the defeat of that strike was certainly played by the Shipping Federation; and in 1912 the government announced that it would no longer give 'blacklegs' (that is, free labourers) unconditional protection.[29]

The golden age of strike-breaking, at least in the pre-1914 period, was well and truly over. Yet somehow the NFLA survived. During the Great War Collison maintained as best he could the attack upon trade unions. But there is no evidence that he did more than issue leaflets and engage in anti-union propaganda. At the general election of 1923 the Association urged voters to support the Conservative Party; and three years later it claimed to have played a part in preventing the pilfering of coal supplies during the miners' strike.[30]

Perhaps Collison hoped that, in the wake of the government's defeat of the 1926 'General Strike', the 1906 Act would be repealed; it wasn't. Prime Minister Baldwin was able to thwart the aims of the Conservative right wing in this respect, in the interests of national reconciliation. Although the NFLA still existed, it played no part in strike-breaking and its network of free labour exchanges vanished.[31] After 1928, however, it ceased to be listed in the *Post Office London Directory*. The exact date of its demise is uncertain. Collison himself died at his home in Essex on 8 March 1938; evidently many secrets of the NFLA died with him.

IV

It is very easy to dismiss Collison as a crank, and the NFLA as just one of many 'front' organizations invented by employers to supply non-union labour as part of the counter-attack against New Unionism. Collison was certainly prone to vanity, and his autobiography, *The Apostle of Free Labour*, published in 1913, is full of absurd exaggerations, a few lies and many half-truths. Although the NFLA was formally founded in 1893, it had a precursor, the 'Free Labour Association', formed by the Shipping Federation in 1892, and of which Collison had been chairman.[32] That association, which had flourished in London's dockland since the mid-1880s, was in turn descended from a number of groups of men who were willing to hire out their services for political demonstrations, strike-breaking, or more general 'protection' duties. These organizations, though allegedly working-class, were actually funded by Conservative politicians.[33]

Collison's sources of funds are less clear. The French writers Paul Mantoux and Maurice Alfassa, who came to Great Britain in 1902 to undertake a survey of British trade unions, accepted the accounts given to them by Sidney Webb and by the extreme anti-socialist Earl of Wemyss that the NFLA was an artificial association funded by the Employer's Parliamentary Council, which Wemyss and others had established in 1898.[34] But it has been proved elsewhere that this is altogether too simplistic, and ignores the fact that influential employers at that time disliked physical-force methods, while others, such as the railway companies, gave sums too small to finance more than a fraction of the NFLA's activities.[35] The Employers' Parliamentary Council was absorbed into the Federation of British Industries in 1916. The NFLA thus not only predated the council, but outlived it too.

The truth probably is that Collison was prepared to receive money and facilities from whichever source happened to be the easiest available at any particular time: in the early days the shipowners; later the railway companies; then the Employers' Parliamentary Council; from time to time engineering and building employers, and gas and tramway companies. The NFLA's existence was very much one from hand to mouth.

But other charges levelled against Collison have greater conviction. In 1895 the *Musée Social* of Paris sent over groups of observers to British trade unionism. One of their number, Paul de Rousiers, was present at the NFLA's Newcastle congress and actually addressed it. Two years later he revealed that decisions at the congress, even though they had been opposed, had been declared unanimous, that the delegates had in fact represented nonexistent groups, or towns they had been told to represent, and he strongly hinted that the whole charade had been stage-managed by Collison himself.[36] This damning indictment was subsequently reinforced by the testimony of two of Collison's former colleagues: John Sennett, a stevedore who had been secretary of the Free Labour Association in 1892; and William Ellis, who, until dismissed by Collison in March 1904, had been an official of the NFLA in Manchester.[37]

There are indeed many discrepancies in Collison's story as he told it. At some points the relationship between Collison and the Conservative Party was closer than he himself dared admit at the time.[38] It is worth recalling that Collison was a personal friend of the mysterious Maltman Barry, through whom Conservative money was channelled into the Independent Labour Party.[39] But we must also add that working-class conservatism was a fact of political life, and that many enfranchised working-men habitually voted for the Conservative Party.[40] It is also true that membership figures for the NFLA are notoriously unreliable. In December 1895 Collison stated that there were 127,000 members; but this figure is simply not borne out in an examination of the total income of the NFLA as Collison gave it.[41] It is just conceivable that in the mid-1890s Collison had 60,000 enrolled financial members, plus an unstated number of non-financial free labourers who were simply registered with him for the purpose of obtaining employment. But in the absence of precise records we shall never know what the true state of membership actually was.

Yet Collison's achievements, exaggerated though they were, were real enough, and the trade union movement was right to be wary of him. At one level the NFLA operated unashamedly as a supplier of blackleg labour, as a 'yellow' union. At another level it was a genuine reflection of working-class hostility to, as it seemed, the rigidity of New Unionism and the disproportionate influence socialists were having upon British trade unions. On this subject Collison did not mince his words: 'Everywhere to-day [in 1913] we see signs of general revolt and social eruption. Agitation is one of the most profitable industries of the moment. Socialism has been made to pay. I found the tyranny of a self-appointed, privileged aristocracy of labour . . . and finding that tyranny intolerable, I fought it.'[42]

If the conditions implied here of the sort of industrial system envisaged seem unrealistic, it must be remembered that Collison, Chandler, Penrose and the other organizers of the NFLA could boast of origins every bit as proletarian as those of John Burns or Ben Tillett. The activities of the NFLA and the following which, however transitory, it was able to build up should serve as a reminder to historians of the period that there was no such thing as working-class solidarity, and that employers and governments were not the only people at that time who disapproved of the militancy of New Unionism, and who were intent on resisting it.

Notes: Chapter 17

1 Quoted from P. Poirier, *The Advent of the Labour Party* (Oxford, 1958), 72.
2 D. Butler and A. Sloman, *British Political Facts 1900–1975*, 4th ed. (London, 1975), 288, 299. Even in 1970 the number of trade union members (11 million) was less than half the labour force (25 million).
3 H. Pelling, *Popular Politics and Society in Late Victorian Britain* (London, 1968), 1–18.
4 ibid., 4–5, for the example of the cotton operatives. For some examination of the attitude of railwaymen towards state regulation of hours of work, see G. Alderman, *The Railway Interest* (Leicester, 1973), 137.
5 Pelling, *Popular Politics*, 5.
6 ibid., 15.
7 On the Shipping Federation see G. Alderman, 'The National Free Labour Association. A case-study of organised strike-breaking in the late nineteenth and early twentieth centuries', *International Review of Social History* 21 (1976): 309–36 (311) (cited hereafter as Alderman, 'NFLA').
8 G. Howell, *Labour Relations, Labour Movements and Labour Leaders* (London, 1902), 449.
9 W. Collison, *The Apostle of Free Labour* (London, 1913), 41–2.
10 ibid., 43–4.
11 ibid., 88–9, 91–3.
12 On Chandler and Penrose see J. C. M. (J. C. Manning), *The National Free Labour Association: its Foundations, History and Work* (London, 1898), 88–91.
13 Collison, *Apostle of Free Labour*, 93–5.
14 *Morning Post*, 31 October 1893, p. 4; 1 November 1893, p. 5; *Evening Standard*, 2 November 1893, p. 4; J. M. Ludlow, 'The National Free Labour Association', *Economic Review* 5 (1895): 110–18 (112).
15 H. A. Clegg *et al.*, *A History of British Trade Unions since 1889*, Vol. 1 (Oxford, 1964), 259.

16 Alderman, 'NFLA', 316.
17 Collison, *Apostle of Free Labour*, 106–7.
18 *The Times*, 31 October 1911, p. 10.
19 *Free Labour*, 15 February 1897, p. 59.
20 Alderman, 'NFLA', 320.
21 *The Times*, 16 October, 1906, p. 7.
22 Alderman, 'NFLA', 321.
23 *The Times*, 2 November 1893, p. 6; 22 November 1893, p. 3.
24 Collison, *Apostle of Free Labour*, 95.
25 Alderman, 'NFLA', 325.
26 ibid., 310, 324–5.
27 ibid., 325.
28 Collison, *Apostle of Free Labour*, 288–93; *Daily Graphic*, 30 May 1912, p. 4; 31 May 1912, p. 5.
29 Alderman, 'NFLA', 326.
30 ibid., 334.
31 loc. cit.
32 *The Critic*, 2 July 1898, p. 24.
33 Alderman, 'NFLA', 326–7.
34 P. Mantoux and M. Alfassa, *La crise du trade-unionisme* (Paris, 1903), *passim*.
35 Alderman, 'NFLA', 328–32.
36 R. de Rousiers, *Le trade-unionisme en Angleterre* (Paris, 1897), 353.
37 Alderman, 'NFLA', 317, 323, 327–8.
38 ibid., 320.
39 Clegg *et al.*, *History of British Trade Unions*, 276; Collison, *Apostle of Free Labour*, 235–8.
40 Clegg *et al.*, *History of British Trade Unions*, 275–6. James Mawdsley, the General Secretary of the Amalgamated Association of Operative Cotton Spinners (1878–1902), fought a by-election at Oldham in 1899 as a Conservative candidate.
41 Alderman, 'NFLA', 329.
42 Collison, *Apostle of Free Labour*, 327.

Part Five

Trade Unions, Employers and the State

18 The British State, the Business Community and the Trade Unions

JOHN SAVILLE

I

It is coming to be appreciated that British labour movement studies have paid too little attention to the attitudes and tactics of the ruling groups in society in matters related to the labour market. There has, of course, always been a statement of government policies, but far less notice has been taken of long-term strategies, or the role of the bureaucracy, or the relationships between the business community, the politicians and the government of the day.

The British state in the nineteenth century had certain special character-istics which developed out of the long evolution of Britain into a parlia-mentary democracy. The civil war and interregnum of the mid-seventeenth century, the character of the settlement of 1688, the particular and indeed unique ways in which industrialization took shape at the end of the eighteenth century all made their contribution to the emergence of the laissez-faire state of the nineteenth century; and to the understanding of the state by bourgeois thinkers in the role of night-watchman. Liberty, in the classical British sense, was the absence of restraint; and absence of restraint, as the classical economists developed the concept in economic terms, allowed the self-interest of the individual to better his condition unhindered and untrammelled by state interference or intervention.

By the middle of the nineteenth century there was in existence in Britain a state power that was remarkably unbureaucratic, and there was no standing army of any size. The internal forces of security – the police and allied bodies – had been met with immense hostility, and were growing only slowly. There was, of course, enough physical force at the disposal of governments to contain popular disturbances, riots and upheavals, as the repression against the Chartist movement of the 1840s abundantly demonstrated;[1] but by comparison with continental Europe the Britain of 1850 was remarkably unmilitaristic (the colonial situations were, of course, very different) and there was a degree of political freedom not to be found in most of the older contemporary societies. Middle-class radicalism, as well as working-class dissent, was vigorously hostile to increases in government expenditure; and in general, British society came as near to a laissez-faire economy as has ever been practicable in the modern world.

The liberty and freedom extolled by bourgeois philosophers, and practised by politicians, extended, of course, to the conditions of the market-place, and in particular to conditions in the labour market. And indeed, the coercive power of the state was continuously invoked to ensure that 'freedom', in the liberal economic sense, was always maintained. For a quarter of a century before 1825 trade unionism was illegal; the new Poor Law of 1834, whose economic implications are so often misunderstood, was a most effective agent in the labour adaptation process; the Master and Servants Laws, not finally repealed until 1875, were an effective deterrent to the industrially fractious in many small-scale enterprises.[2] The balance was heavily weighted against the labourer in terms of his bargaining power with the employer; and only very slowly did the industrial labour force succeed in offsetting, and then never more than partially, the tremendous weight and power of the property-owners. Over almost the whole range of British industry down to 1914 the contract arrived at in the open market remained the rule. The 1875 Trade Union Act was an important advance upon previous law and it offered legal equality to the unions which had not previously existed; but when the unskilled and semi-skilled began to avail themselves of their legal rights after the great union upheavals of 1889, the courts of law began to hand down judgments which in spirit and in content overthrew the declared intentions of the 1875 Act; and the anti-trade union decision in the famous case of Taff Vale was the culmination.[3] The Taff Vale judgment was reversed by Parliament in 1906; and the Trade Boards Act of 1908 established the minimum wage, but at first only for four very small industries. Down to 1914, then, there was no serious interference with the 'free' bargaining processes in which the working-men were always at a major disadvantage, and only the skilled workers were able, in certain ways and in some measure, to curb the strength of the employers' position.

There were, however, important political changes which began to alter the context within which, in the long run, decisions affecting the labour market were to operate. In the second half of the nineteenth century the successive governments which had at their command the coercive powers of the state authority were never confronted with a major crisis of any kind from the working-class majority of society. The course of political events ran smoothly; but given that manual workers did form the greater part of the social formation it became increasingly necessary to bring at least a section within the constitution, of which the franchise was the symbol. Hence the Second Reform Act of 1867, by which certain groups of working-men in the towns were given the parliamentary vote,[4] and within the next decade, as noted above, there was passed trade union legislation which provided the unions with a privileged status: political and trade union legislation which was the beginning of the long process of incorporation into the structures of bourgeois society. The key thinker in the context of these important new directions was Walter Bagehot; and it is worth reminding ourselves of his arguments for a strategy that was realistic in a society with a proletarian majority increasingly demanding certain basic rights. In the preface to the 1872 edition of his *The English Constitution* Bagehot set out his advice to the ruling groups in British society. First, the starting-point must be that in an overwhelmingly proletarian society, the supreme danger to be avoided was a 'permanent combination' of working people. There was, of course, the recognition by Bagehot that it was precisely the decline of that danger – so obvious and menacing in the Chartist years – that had brought about the willingness to extend the franchise in 1867. But the very fact that the suffrage had now been given to some working-class groups made the reality of a working-man's political party much more of a possibility in the future. To avoid this coming about, Bagehot wrote, would require 'the greatest wisdom and the greatest foresight in the higher classes'. They (the higher classes) must not only be prepared to remove every actual grievance which was articulated by the masses, they must also try to eliminate every 'supposed' grievance. What defined a 'grievance' Bagehot left unspecified, but he went on to say that as a general rule the ruling classes 'must willingly concede every claim which they can safely concede, in order that they may not have to concede unwillingly some claim which would impair the safety of the country', which was another way of saying that property rights must remain inviolable. Bagehot noted that the approach he was advocating would demand both restraint and understanding, and that in particular what must be avoided were those political struggles over questions that were not fundamental but which, if allowed to develop, could easily gain a momentum and be prolonged over time, with the result that the working classes would acquire both political experience and a social cohesion in the struggle: qualities that must be delayed as long as possible.[5]

There was never any doubt that all governments of the day were in full control during the second half of the nineteenth century. Bourgeois society was stable, and its political consciousness reflected that stability. It would be wrong to suggest that the businessmen were in any fundamental way different from the politicians, but many were obviously nearer to the point of production, and some dealt with trade unions; and their industrial attitudes were often sharper and more crude than those of the politicians. The business community was, of course, mixed in its appreciation; some, of whom Armstrong John Mundella was the acknowledged leader, were conciliators, but most, in varying degree, adopted a tougher approach. Some broad correlation, perhaps, may be made with the degree of labour intensity in any particular industry.

II

The last quarter of the century is a good period to observe the attitudes of the business community. The world was changing fast; prices began falling after 1873 and went on declining for the next twenty years; other nations began to increase the tempo of their industrialization, and Germany in the 1880s, and the United States in the 1890s, began to be encountered on the world market as serious competitors. There was considerable intellectual confusion about what was happening. Most writers on economic matters tended to offset the talk of depression with the statistics of industrial production, as far as they were available, or with the foreign trade figures in quantity terms, or with the income tax returns. Robert Giffen produced a series of tables on these lines for the Royal Commission on Depression of Trade (1885–6); and in the same month, December 1886, in which the Royal Commission's Final Report appeared, M. G. Mulhall wrote an article in the *Contemporary Review*, entitled 'Ten Years of National Growth'. His opening words, 'The progress made by the United Kingdom in the last ten years is very remarkable', set the tone of his article, and he went on to provide the statistical basis for his statement. Between 1875 and 1885 trade, at 1875 prices, had increased by 22 per cent; shipping by 67 per cent; and so on, including estimates for the increase in per capita wealth. Mulhall also showed notable declines in the rates of pauperism, and of mortality, and general increases in the statistics of social well-being; and the only unfavourable index for Mulhall was the decline in the birth-rate.

In general, it was the free trade ideologues who took the most optimistic view: John Bright among the politicians; *The Economist*, and usually *The Times*, among the journals.[6] To businessmen, however, and to those who were close to them in spirit and outlook, matters looked very different. It was falling prices and falling profits that dominated their thinking, and it was these phenomena to which they constantly returned in the evidence they gave to the Royal Commission on the Depression of Trade. And falling profits led to the business community's general agreement on the central problems that they were confronted with as entrepreneurs: that British labour had higher wages and worked shorter hours than elsewhere in Europe; and the corollary was the vigorously expressed opinion that labour costs were at such a level that in a period of falling prices nothing was left to the capitalist. The argument was not, however, limited to the 1880s. There was a spate of writing and statistical analysis which concentrated on the rise in the real earnings of the working classes in the thirty years up to the 1880s, and much of which further showed that most if not all of the increase in national wealth had gone to the labour side of national income. Moreover, this shift in labour's share in national income had been accentuated during the years of the price fall since the middle 1870s. Giffen's inaugural address to the Statistical Association in 1883 summed up the argument:

> It would not be far short of the mark to say that almost the whole of the great material improvement of the last fifty years has gone to the masses. The share of capital is a very small one ... the rich have become more numerous, but not richer individually; the 'poor' are, to some smaller extent, fewer; and those who remain 'poor' are, individually, twice as well off on the average as they were fifty years ago. The 'poor' have thus almost all the benefit of the great material advance of the last fifty years.[7]

The fact that Giffen was in large part misreading the situation (although there is no question about a rise in working-class living standards) is beside the point. His analysis was widely commented on, and generally accepted; and the same thinking was clearly demonstrated by the evidence of the businessmen who appeared before the Royal Commission on the Depression of Trade and Industry (1885–6). Whatever their differences of opinion – and they were extraordinarily confused and contradictory, as between themselves – there was almost complete unanimity on (*a*) that the rate of return on capital had declined sharply in the years since the fall in prices had begun, and (*b*) that the share of labour had increased. Their agreed conclusion was that high wages were responsible for much of their problems. The Commission restricted its investigations mainly to textiles, iron and steel, agriculture and shipbuilding. There was only one representative of chemicals. He was asked sixty-six questions: forty-three were on wages, trade unions and strikes; eight on tariffs and free trade; one on technical education. This witness for the chemical industry worked the Le Blanc process, which he admitted produced soda at a higher price than with the Solvay process; but when asked whether his firm could compete successfully with foreign competition, much of which used the Solvay process, he replied: 'I think we can compete, so far as it concerns the cost of raw materials. I think we are upon the whole upon an equality, except in regard to labour.' And he later summed up his position in these words:

I have no hesitation in saying that if the cost of labour is lessened our chance of competition will be very greatly improved. Taking the article of soda, for example, the cost is entirely composed of labour, except the royalties paid for coals and salt, and at each stage the wages are at present higher than our competitors abroad have to pay.[8]

No one on the Commission probed the technical differences between the Le Blanc and Solvay processes – the latter was certainly superior. This witness, as with the great majority of all the businessmen who gave evidence, was dominated by the wages question, and the belief that the British rates of wages were at such a level that the capitalist was left with little or no profit. General opinion in the 1880s supported the businessman. The question which immediately poses itself is that if it was the case that the conditions within the labour market had changed so unfavourably towards the capitalist, why was there so little discussion about the possibilities of abridging or economizing labour, and thereby reducing labour costs? In fact there was almost no such discussion, and again and again the discussion pivots on the matter of reducing wages, and thereby making industry more competitive (and, of course, more profitable). This would seem to be general confirmation of an argument that Hrothyur J. Habakkuk made in his comparative study of American and British industry: that by contrast with American manufacturers those in England were primarily concerned with money, rather than efficiency, wages. He suggested that in the last thirty years of the nineteenth century, labour in Britain 'was no longer as abundant as it had been earlier in the century', and that other things being equal, it could be expected that the response of employers would be in the direction of capital-deepening, that is, the substitution of capital for labour.[9] Habakkuk suggested two possible offsetting factors: the first, that except for the boom years of the early 1870s there was never a general shortage of labour; and the second, that the attitudes of British entrepreneurs were heavily conditioned by the experience of the past, in which cheap labour had been central to the processes of economic growth. But whatever the reasons, there is no doubt about the emphasis upon money wages.

But what was happening on the ground? And how did the businessmen carry through the application of their undoubtedly simplistic analysis of the economic world in which they found themselves? In what follows the statistical generalizations made have been taken from a number of sources, and these are then brought together to suggest some general comments on entrepreneurial motivation. It may be noted at the outset that the statistical facts do not, except for the first decade of depression, bear out what the businessmen thought was happening to their economic position.

The first two series are the index of productivity and the movement of money wages. The real output per occupied person in industry rose steadily from the 1860s to the end of the century with a sharp rise in the decade from 1886. At the same time there is very little rise in the average level of money wages; and putting these two series together makes it clear that unit wage costs showed a persistent and marked fall, especially in the twenty years after 1877. Between 1886 and 1896 it is estimated that there was an average fall – over the whole of manufacturing industry – of some 13 per cent in unit wage costs.[10]

The next series is the wage–income rates in industry.[11] This is the ratio of average earnings per wage-earner to value added per occupied person in industry; and the ratio thus established exhibits the movement over time in the division of the product between pay and profits. The data for the United Kingdom are interesting. From the middle 1870s to about 1886 the ratio remained high – that is to say, the share of profits in the product of British industry was exceptionally low in the decade before 1886, and contemporary opinion – which so vociferously bemoaned the fact of low levels of profit – was not exaggerating. But after 1886, with the continued and indeed sharper fall in unit wage costs, there was a gradual widening of the profit margin, illustrated by falls in the wage–income ratios. This ratio demonstrates the *share* of profits not the *rate* of profit; and what data there are on rates of profit confirm what has been stated already. Excluding agriculture, the rate of profit showed a rise from about 1883; a check between 1890 and 1893; and a further rise to a peak in 1897.

The last index is the capital–output ratio which showed a downward trend between 1881 and 1895, roughly paralleling the wage–income ratio.

Now if all these data are put together to make a connected account, the story appears like this. Prices are falling for twenty years from the mid-1870s to the mid-1890s. The share of profits would seem to have been exceptionally low in the second half of the 1870s and in the early years of the 1880s. The problem for entrepreneurs was obviously how to improve the profits share of the total product and to lift up the rate of profit. There are several ways in which this could have been done. The two most obvious are first capital investment – that is, an abridgement of labour by technical innovation; and second, economizing labour costs by increasing the work load or by a better organization of the work flow and generally improved efficiency of the enterprise. In other words, using the same capital equipment in a more productive way: what the economists call 'disembodied technical progress'.

It was, of course, this second road that the British entrepreneurs took during this last quarter of the nineteenth century. It was, that is to say, to the labour side of business organization to which businessmen directed their attention; and the question is why did they do this rather than engage in capital-deepening. It is a question, of course, that is difficult to answer, or rather, it lends itself to a number of answers. Obviously one has to look to the total environment in which the businessmen operated, and it is indeed one of the weaknesses of many versions of the theory of the firm that economic considerations alone are seriously considered. But there are good reasons for arguing that one of the central features of the period under analysis was the entrepreneurial emphasis upon money wages. To repeat Habakkuk, this emphasis upon money wages would naturally lead any entrepreneur, when confronted with a profit squeeze, to discover what could be done in the matter of reducing the costs of labour. There were no doubt other factors involved, including the structure of the capital market (that is, the ease with which capital could be raised) or the average level of entrepreneurial expectations of the future (if indeed there is an average to be determined). There was something of a parallel between the 1880s and 1890s and the 1950s, underlined by Charles P. Kindleberger in his volume on *Europe's Post-War Growth*. Kindleberger noted the perplexity of some British economists who, having documented the problems of labour short-ages and labour bottlenecks, then found it difficult to explain why British industry did not respond with capital-deepening investment. And Kindle-berger remarked that following the Lewis model, capital-deepening is more difficult to achieve than marginal expansion with improved techniques and more efficient management.[12] The comparison should not be pressed too far: in the 1880s the central feature of entrepreneurial psychology is gloom and lack of confidence in the future and no one could predict when the downward movement of prices would come to an end. To trim labour costs and to improve management would seem to many the prudent courses of action to be adopted in order to achieve a general reduction of unit costs.

III

It is time to relate some of these matters to trade union history. There were several strands to the union movement in the last quarter of the century which need first of all to be disentangled. One was the emergence of New Unionism involving the organization of the semi-skilled and the unskilled, and the sharp decline of unionization among the New Unionists in the first half of the 1890s. A second was the considerable technical change in certain industries that was occurring in the 1890s. A third was the growth of restrictive practices, and finally there was the legal attack upon the unions which culminated in the Taff Vale judgment.

Now some of these matters are commonplace. New Unionization and the court's challenges to unions have been much discussed: but technical change and restrictive practices are less analysed, and it is this last to which some brief comments may be addressed.

Restrictive practices, including the use of 'ca-canny' as a weapon in industrial relations, are talked about relatively little by labour historians.[13] But after 1900 when productivity in general was stagnant, or falling, some economists have laid great emphasis upon the relevance of restrictive practices. What is not yet available is a chronology of the development of restrictive practices. There is a great deal of the kind of information which is required for all trades in Richard Price's recent study of the building industry,[14] and until a good deal more research is carried out historians are not going to be able to answer some, at least, of the questions that are suggested here. But if the economizing of labour costs in the last quarter of the century is taken as the background, an immediate question to pose is the effect upon workers' practices. Asked more specifically, what was the effect of the entrepreneurs' pressures upon unit wage costs, 1880–1900, and of their success in reducing these costs over time? The unemployment situation for each occupation naturally affects the answer, and the 1890s, with the domestic boom developing strongly from 1894, was very different in this context from the low levels of capital investment and the unused capacity of the middle years of the 1880s. Price noted that in most branches of the building industry 'it took the Great Depression to effectively remove the final vestiges' of the restrictionism of the 1860s.[15] It is, of course, easy to understand why the practice of 'ca-canny' develops on the waterfront from about 1890 on – and why it was only partially successful, in general, or not successful at all. But there are many occupations where restrictive practices began early in craft or industrial history, and it would be illuminating to be able to trace their development in the face of hardening of management practices. One would also wish to be able to be precise about the acceptance of conciliation procedures and the extent to which agreement on the union side was the product of industrial weakness rather than strength. Certainly this is true of most sliding scale agreements.

The structures of labour markets have been largely avoided by labour historians, and their study may perhaps alter current perceptions of change. If one allied this economic analysis with a more detailed comprehension of businessmen's attitudes, together with an appreciation of the growing awareness of governments and their civil servants of the union 'problem', the student of labour history may well begin to look upon familiar events somewhat differently. It is simplistic for Hugh A. Clegg, Alan Fox and A. F. Thompson to argue that 'had British employers wished to be rid of trade unions, the depression years of 1902–05, with the Taff Vale precedent valid in every court, were as favourable an opportunity as ever presented itself. There are, however, relatively few instances of organised employers taking advantage of it to attempt to weaken or destroy the unions', and they conclude that there is much evidence to suggest that 'most employers were not "anti-union"'.[16] The argument has been widely accepted, among others by John Lovell in his book on *British Trade Unions*.[17] There was, however, no chance at all of the 'destruction' of the unions. It could not be done, even had it been desired; and most intelligent businessmen as well as politicians would certainly not have accepted the approach. There were, of course, plenty of 'unintelligent' businessmen and politicians around. But the responsible and politically sensible among the élites applied Bagehot's dicta to the unions as well as to political matters; and those who counterpose conciliation machinery to outright union opposition and union-bashing are failing to appreciate that these approaches are only different sides of the same coin – to be used, in varying degree, when and where suitable. This is not, of course, to argue that policies followed by governments, or employers' associations, or individuals are always calculated and long-sighted, full of insight and shrewdness. Sometimes they are, but just as often they represent ad hoc reactions to immediate events that are often wrongheaded. There is, however, self-interest and there is also experience and intelligence; and while many mistakes and miscalculations have been made by all those involved in political and industrial affairs, there are long-term trends that can be dissected and understood. Keith Middlemas's general argument that modern British society has witnessed the 'marginalisation' of radical protest, dissent and extra-parliamentary activity applies as much to unions as to working-class politics;[18] indeed, since the trade unions have always 'worried' the business community and their politicians much more than has the Labour Party, it is especially the unions to which the Middlemas analysis applies. It must always be remembered that there have always been, in twentieth-century Britain, many more ways of killing a pig than by drowning it in milk.

Notes: Chapter 18

1 The literature is considerable; see F. C. Mather, *Public Order in the Age of the Chartists* (Manchester, 1959).

2 D. Simon, 'Master and servant', in J. Saville (ed.), *Democracy and the Labour Movement* (London, 1954), 160–200.

3 J. Saville, 'Trade unions and Free Labour: the background to the Taff Vale decision', in A. Briggs and J. Saville (eds), *Essays in Labour History*, Vol. 1 (London, 1960), 317–20, reprinted in M. W. Flinn and T. C. Smout (eds), *Essays in Social History* (Oxford, 1974).

4 The impact of the working-class enfranchisement was much reduced by, among other things, the problems of registration; for which see N. Blewett, 'The franchise in the United Kingdom, 1885–1918', *Past and Present* 32 (1965): 27–56.

5 *The Collected Works of Walter Bagehot*, ed. N. St John-Stevas, Vol. 5, *The English Constitution* (London, 1974), 165–202, (esp. 171).

6 See, for example, the leading article in *The Times*, 17 January 1887, commenting on the Final Report of the Royal Commission on the Depression of Trade and Industry.

7 'The progress of the working classes in the last half century', *Journal of the Statistical Society* 46 IV (December 1883): 619–20.

8 Third Report of the Royal Commission on the Depression of Trade and Industry, 1886, C. 4797, XXIII, Minutes of Evidence, q. 13, 676.

9 H. J. Habakkuk, *American and British Technology in the Nineteenth Century: The Search for Labour-Saving Inventions* (Cambridge, 1962), quotation p. 195.

10 E. H. Phelps Brown and M. H. Browne, *A Century of Pay. The Course of Pay and Production in France, Germany, Sweden, the United Kingdom and the United States of America, 1860–1960* (London, 1968), 117–19.

11 ibid., 132–4.

12 C. P. Kindleberger, *Europe's Post-War Growth* (London, 1959), ch. 4, esp. p. 84.

13 See the special note on 'ca-canny' in J. M. Bellamy and J. Saville (eds.), *Dictionary of Labour Biography*, Vol. 6 (London, 1982), 98–101.

14 R. Price, *Masters, Unions and Men: Work Control in Building and the Rise of Labour 1830–1914* (Cambridge, 1980).

15 ibid., 150.
16 H. A. Clegg *et al.*, *A History of British Trade Unions since 1889*, Vol. 1 (Oxford, 1964), 362–3.
17 J. Lovell, *British Trade Unions, 1875–1933* (London, 1977).
18 K. Middlemas, *Politics in Industrial Society* (London, 1979), *passim*.

19 Industrial Structure, Employer Strategy and the Diffusion of Job Control in Britain, 1880–1920

JONATHAN ZEITLIN

Historians have long regarded the period 1880–1920 as a key turning-point in the economic, social and political history of modern Britain. In these years, it has often been argued, the erosion of British hegemony in the world economy undermined the basis of mid-Victorian stability, provoking a dramatic upsurge of industrial conflict and ultimately a realignment of the political system.[1] This line of interpretation has recently been developed further by historians such as James Hinton, Keith Burgess, Robert Gray, James E. Cronin and Richard Price, who see the late nineteenth and early twentieth centuries as a period in which the structure of industrial work and of the working class more broadly was radically transformed. Pressed by growing competition at home and abroad, employers, these authors suggest, sought to free themselves of their dependence on expensive and refractory skilled labour by reorganizing work processes, introducing new machinery and payment systems, and developing new methods of supervision and control. The resulting decline in skill levels and autonomy at work is held to have eroded existing divisions between different sections of the labour force, paving the way for the emergence of a wider class-consciousness. This purported shift in the social composition of the working class has in turn been deployed to explain changes in popular politics such as the rise of the Labour Party and the spread of socialist ideas.[2]

While each step in this analysis is questionable, this essay will concentrate primarily on its foundations in the interpretation of the division of labour and industrial relations in the period.[3] The argument of the essay is developed in three parts. In the first section, a summary presents the results of a more detailed account of developments in the engineering industry, which has often been seen as an archetypal case of mechanization and deskilling in response to foreign competition.[4] Focusing on employer strategies at the level of the enterprise and of the Engineering Employers' Federation (EEF), an attempt is made to show that despite their apparently decisive victory in a lock-out fought explicitly over managerial prerogatives, British engineering employers did not undertake a radical transformation of the division of labour during the fifteen years preceding the First World War.[5] In the second section, taking the results of this case study together with those of a wider body of recent research, it will be argued that the limits of employer labour strategies can primarily be explained by the constraints and incentives stemming from the fragmented structure of firms and markets in the late Victorian and Edwardian economy. Finally, the essay suggests that far from promoting an increase in managerial authority in the work-place during these years, such employer strategies provided the basis for a far-reaching diffusion of job control practices to new sections of the labour force, which to this day constitutes one of the salient features of British industrial relations.

I

As earlier historians have emphasized, the 1890s were a decade of growing tension between employers and unions in engineering. Employers' turn towards wider organization and confrontation with the unions in the 1890s was the result of a set of interrelated developments which were calling into question both the division of labour and the pattern of industrial relations which had been established at mid-century. These developments were of both a structural and a conjunctural character. Thus intensified foreign competition, new opportunities for mechanization and the gradual exhaustion of returns from an extensive development of the existing division of labour came together in the context of heightened conflict between employers and craft unions to precipitate a full-scale crisis in the established pattern of industrial relations.

In the first instance, the intensified industrial conflict of the early 1890s had its origins in a wide-ranging union offensive aimed at exploiting a period of boom to regain ground lost to the employers over wages and working conditions during the previous two decades of depression. Employers' efforts to cheapen and intensify skilled labour during the 1870s and 1880s had resulted in a substantial deterioration in the position of the skilled worker and in the effectiveness of craft regulation, though contrary to what certain historians have argued, these did not involve the introduction of new automatic machine tools such as the turret lathe or the milling machine, which were not used in significant numbers in Britain until the mid-1890s.[6]

In 1897–8 the EEF was effectively able to isolate the Amalgamated Society of Engineers (ASE) and to bring the union to its knees by the financial cost of a prolonged lock-out. The resulting Terms of Settlement, while conceding a certain role for collective bargaining in wage determination, extracted an explicit recognition of managerial prerogatives in the organization of work, and installed a novel disputes procedure designed to force the union to choke off local craft resistance. In the aftermath of the lock-out, employers believed that they had removed the major barrier to the rapid transformation of the division of labour in their works.

Yet by 1914 it had become clear that despite important gains, engineering employers had failed, at least in the older sectors of the industry, either fully to displace the skilled worker from his central position in the division of labour or to break the back of craft resistance as a constraint on their freedom of action in the workplace. To be sure, employers continued to introduce automatic machine tools at a rapid pace, and were able to undermine the long-term reproduction of craft regulation through increasing employment of semi-skilled labour, the extension of payment by results and the subversion of apprenticeship into cheap labour. But ASE members were increasingly able to capture control of new machinery, and 60 per cent of the workforce in Federated firms was still classified as skilled in 1914.[7] Productivity growth levelled off after 1900, and foreign producers continued to expand their share of world markets.[8] Even more striking were the successes scored by a resurgent craft militancy from 1909 onwards, and the continued dependence on skilled labour revealed by the munitions crisis of the First World War.

Why did British engineering employers fail to take full advantage of the hegemonic position they had won in 1898 to effect a thoroughgoing transformation of the division of labour in the industry? The answer lies in a combination of the broader industrial relations strategy developed by the EEF; and the responses of the ASE executive, local officials and the rank and file.

Engineering manufacturers' approach to the division of labour in their works was largely determined by their investment strategies, which in turn depended on the structure of established enterprises, on the nature of their product and on the movement of demand. A full-scale transformation of the division of labour in line with the best-practice engineering technology of the day involved extensive capital investment in new machinery, and often required a major reorganization of workshop layout or even a purpose-built plant if it was to be fully effective.

Ambitious investment programmes of this kind were discouraged in the first instance by the fragmented structure of ownership which characterized most of the older sectors of the industry. Outside of armaments and railway work, these sectors were dominated by small and medium-sized firms, often family owned and usually specializing in a particular product range, with a larger penumbra of smaller and less specialized firms comprising the bulk of the industry. The highly competitive relations among individual firms, their lack of market power, their reluctance to seek outside finance and their limited development of managerial hierarchies all combined to inhibit engineering manufacturers in the older sectors from embarking on expensive and risky programmes of investment aimed at the capture of new markets through a transformation of the division of labour in their works.

In any case, such an investment programme could be possible only where there was a sizeable and rapidly growing demand for a standardized, mass-produced product. Such a demand was weak in Edwardian Britain outside a few newer sectors such as cycles, electrical goods and certain classes of armaments. Firms in the older sectors were further discouraged from such retooling by the opportunities for maintaining adequate short- and medium-term profit levels by concentrating on their existing specialities and by shifting towards semi-protected markets in the empire and the rest of the underdeveloped world. These opportunities became especially lucrative with the export boom fuelled by the shift in the terms of trade after 1900.[9]

Hence in most engineering firms, innovation was confined to the introduction of new machine tools and work practices within a workshop organization that remained structurally unchanged. Employers' attempts to free themselves of craft regulation were more an extension of their traditional strategies for work intensification and cost-cutting than any breakthrough into a new 'Taylorist' mode. Thus the promotion of handymen on to skilled men's work, the extension of piece-work and systematic overtime, the subversion of apprenticeship into cheap labour – together with minor wage advances and reductions – dominated conflicts between skilled workers and employers after as before 1898. The principal novel element could be found in the introduction of new systems of incentive payment and supervision, and even these tended in practice to degenerate into old-fashioned rate-cutting exercises.[10]

While individual employers pressed home their piecemeal assault on craft regulation, responsibility for maintaining a favourable overall framework for managerial prerogative rested with the EEF. Strategically, the EEF remained committed to defending the 1898 settlement which guaranteed managerial freedom of action in machine-manning, payment systems and workshop organization. At the same time, it sought to deploy employers' collective strength to depress district wage rates in hopes of restoring British firms' competitive edge in world markets. The central instrument of this strategy was the new disputes procedure. Since no strike could 'constitutionally' take place until a deadlock had been reached at national level, the Federation could use its national strength to choke off local flare-ups of craft militancy, and to delay wage advances in the upturns.

Conscious of its dominant position and of the ASE executive's willingness to work within the Terms of Settlement, the EEF generally refrained from threats of a national lock-out, preferring to isolate local resistance through pressure on the union leadership while offering financial support to the firm concerned. The success of these tactics in the dozen years after the lock-out meant that the Federation could afford to offer minor concessions on procedural questions to the ASE executive while maintaining an intransigent stance on issues involving managerial prerogative.

The success of this strategy depended in large measure on the determination of the ASE executive to work within the Terms of Settlement and to convert the demands of its members from craft regulation to economistic collective bargaining, which it was hoped would prove more acceptable to the employers. In the event, however, this strategy collapsed as a result of the intense commitment of ASE members to craft regulation, of the democratic constitution of the union and of the internal contradictions within the employers' own strategy. The EEF's insistence on pressing a hard line on wages at the same time as its attack on craft regulation undermined any possible appeal of the ASE executive's strategy, and after a series of decisions by internal union bodies limiting its right to curtail benefits to unofficial strikers, the General Secretary was forced to resign.[11] The resulting upsurge of craft militancy enjoyed considerable success in the 1911–14 boom, and a new union executive committed to the defence of craft regulation repudiated the Terms of Settlement and related agreements on the eve of the First World War.

While the previous success of its cautious tactics, together with the difficulties of unifying employers behind a lock-out at the apogee of a boom, inclined the EEF to continue peaceful negotiations with the ASE, it seems probable that a major confrontation would have ensued had not the war intervened. In the event, the impetus towards a renewed confrontation was strengthened by the intensity of wartime industrial conflict, and the Federation secured a reaffirmation of managerial prerogative with its overwhelming victory in the 1922 lock-out against the backdrop of mass unemployment. By that time, however, the position of the old and new sectors had diverged still further, and opportunities for a major transformation of the division of labour were confined even more clearly to the latter.[12]

II

The engineering industry is, of course, no microcosm of British industry as a whole, and presents many specific features. But the conclusions of this case study are strongly reinforced by a burgeoning literature on other key sectors of the British economy in this period, notably cotton textiles, iron and steel and shipbuilding.[13] Taken together, these studies show remarkable similarities in the labour strategies adopted by British employers in diverse sectors of the economy which contrast sharply with those that seem to have been adopted during the same period by their principal competitors in Germany and the United States. Many areas of contrast stand out, but three require emphasis here: the limited character of British employers' investment strategies and of their efforts to transform the division of labour; their greater acceptance of trade unions, particularly in heavy industry; and the high level of job control achieved not only by skilled workers, but also by other sections of the labour force.[14] Grouped together, these characteristics form a coherent whole and go a considerable distance towards identifying the peculiar and enduring features of workplace industrial relations in Britain.

This pattern of employer and union behaviour can be explained in the first instance by the structure of firms and markets in the pre-1914 British economy. To begin with the structure of firms: most sectors were dominated by fragmented, family-owned firms: thus there were nearly a hundred major firms in shipbuilding; similar numbers in coal and iron and steel, and many more in engineering. There was little tendency towards cartelization or monopoly, and even where some centralization of capital occurred, there was little movement towards the emergence of centralized managerial control structures. Thus, as Leslie Hannah has noted, there were only twelve multi-divisional firms in the United Kingdom as late as 1948. Most large firms resembled less giant American corporations than federations of independent profit units linked by a loose financial control and employing local labour market strategies, of which the steel and precision engineering combine of Guest, Keen and Nettlefold furnishes a good example.[15]

At the same time, British firms tended to be heavily oriented towards export markets, especially in the capital and staple goods industries. These markets were in turn characterized by sharp cyclical fluctuations and were dominated by non-standard demand, especially for capital goods.[16] Secondly, British firms, by virtue of Britain's early dominance of the world economy, had the option of evading competition by shifting into semi-protected markets. In broader institutional terms, other significant inheritances from this precocious hegemony over the international economy were a sharp separation between industry and finance which discouraged the banks from seeking industrial outlets for their capital; and a national commitment to a complex multilateral trade pattern which severely restricted any move away from free trade in economic policy.[17]

These features of firm and market structure had extremely important implications for employers' labour strategies. First, they inhibited the development of a corporate infrastructure on a scale parallel to that of Germany and the United States: thus, as Joseph Melling among others has shown, firms in Britain were much less likely than their foreign competitors to develop elaborate internal schemes for training, promotion and welfare; their managerial and supervisory hierarchies likewise remained less elaborated.[18] A second consequence was the general avoidance of extensive capital-intensive investment except where this could be clearly justified by existing market conditions. Firms generally preferred to rely on relatively cheap and abundant skilled workers, who could be hired and fired according to the business cycle and who could largely be expected to supervise not only themselves but also subordinate grades of workers. Often this process developed not only within but also between enterprises, as firms came to rely on subcontracting networks to meet peaks in demand rather than extending their own capacity. That something like this occurred in engineering can be seen from the tendency for both the growth of the capital stock and of productivity to fall behind that of output from 1880 and particularly from 1900.[19]

III

It will be evident that this type of managerial strategy provided a fertile ground for the growth of craft unionism and indeed of trade unionism more generally. In America, the vast resources of the emergent corporations and the incentives provided by rapidly expanding markets for mass produced goods encouraged and enabled employers to sweep aside all internal opposition. But British employers had neither such power nor such incentives. They therefore tended to eschew frontal assaults on established trade unions in favour of other methods of restraining wages and adjusting them to the business cycle, which their short-time horizons led them to regard as the central issue in industrial relations.[20]

We can identify two central mechanisms whereby British employers' labour strategies prepared the ground for an extensive development of job control practices which would later come considerably to circumscribe managerial freedom of action in the workplace. The first emanated primarily from the craft sectors, and had its origins in skilled workers' own efforts at unilateral regulation of the production process and the labour market; while the second flowed from the unintended consequences of the collective bargaining procedures designed to secure joint regulation of wages in the so-called 'operative' trades, such as coalmining, cotton textiles and iron and steel.

In the craft sectors, British employers' dependence on skilled labour in the production process provided the foundation for an intensive development of craft institutions which then helped to rigidify the existing division of labour. A crucial dimension of this process was the capture by skilled workers of new techniques and processes which, in principle, could have been operated by non-craftsmen, and the subjection of these processes to union work rules. The best-known example of this process, common to most industrial societies at the end of the nineteenth century, was the capture of mechanized typesetting by hand compositors.[21] An example which is more peculiar to Britain is the craft status carried over by cotton-spinners from the common to the self-acting mule.[22] Shipbuilding supplies two of the more striking cases, the platers' successful defence of craft privilege despite the reduction in their skills resulting from the transition from iron to steel hull construction, and the capture of pneumatic riveting by hand riveters during the First World War.[23]

Where skilled workers were not powerful enough to capture new processes outright, a major impetus to the diffusion of job control was given by their relations with the less skilled, relations which could prove antagonistic or co-operative depending on the circumstances. Where conflicts of interest prompted craftsmen to adopt a hostile attitude towards the organization of the less skilled, the latter often found themselves forced to imitate the tactics and organizational practices of the former in self-defence. The classic example here is perhaps that of the semi-skilled workers in the printing industry, particularly the NATSOPA press hands, who began in the late nineteenth century to organize themselves into chapels, control entry to the job, maintain fixed manning levels and contest the differentials and demarcation lines of the apprenticed craftsmen above them on the job ladder.[24] In other industries such as cotton-spinning and steel, conflicts between craftsmen and underhands resulted in a compromise between the interests of the two groups. Craftsmen maintained a measure of their former privileges, particularly regarding wage differentials, but lost the right to move to top jobs in other plants as the underhands obtained plant-based seniority schemes which assured some of their number of eventual promotion to the best jobs.[25]

Craftsmen's response to the organization of the less skilled was by no means uniformly hostile. Where long-established lines of demarcation and static technology insulated skilled workers against challenges from subordinate groups, craftsmen could actively encourage the organization of the less skilled: in printing, for example, the compositors, who unlike the press managers were not threatened by the semi-skilled, played an active role in the formation of the New Unions of printing labourers in 1889 and later conducted joint strikes for the eight-hour day and the elimination of low-paid female labour with these unions in the Printing and Kindred Trades Federation.[26] In other circumstances, where lines of demarcation remained fluid, craftsmen could colonize less skilled occupations into parallel crafts in order to protect their own organizational position. Thus in the course of the United Society of Boilermakers and Iron and Steel Shipbuilders' emergence as the central union for skilled metalworkers in iron and steel shipbuilding during the second half of the nineteenth century, the union expanded its base from the highly skilled angle-iron smiths and platers to incorporate the rather less skilled riveters, caulkers and holders-up.[27]

The outcome of these patterns of conflict and co-operation between craftsmen and the less skilled in pre-1914 Britain was not merely the extension of job control to new groups, but also the subversion of the material basis for what elsewhere became the main alternative to craft organization: namely, industrial unionism. In this vein Eric J. Hobsbawm has suggested that the successful organization on a craft basis of strategic groups of workers with intermediate skill levels such as cotton-spinners and riveters discouraged the formation of industrial unions which would inevitably have relied heavily on such groups. Thus general unionism emerged as the main alternative to craft organization, not only because of the ideological preconceptions of its founders, but also because the scattered and isolated position of the remaining groups of semi-skilled workers, such as gasworkers, platers' helpers and engineering machinists, forced them to form federations of closed shops across industries in order to establish their organizations on a viable financial basis.[28]

The second mechanism for the diffusion of job control in late nineteenth-century Britain was, as it has already been suggested here, linked to the operation of the collective bargaining institutions which had by 1920 become generalized through most of British industry. As Frank Wilkinson and others have observed, these institutions had their origins in the so-called 'operative' trades such as coal, cotton, hosiery and iron and steel, and were closely bound up with the economic environment that has already been described. In these highly competitive sectors, firms were exposed to sharp fluctuations on the world market and were generally concerned both to take wages out of competition and to adjust them rapidly to changing product prices. Once in place, such institutions tended to reinforce the existing division of labour in several ways. First, joint boards and conciliation and arbitration procedures tended to permit unions to survive where workers were too weak to have forced them on employers by their own efforts; then the disputes procedures associated with them, by taking key decisions on manning and new technology out of the hands of individual employers, tended to promote compromise settlements which diluted the unilateral exercise of managerial prerogatives.[29] Finally, as Howard Gospel has argued, the existence of industry-wide wage determination procedures further discouraged individual firms from developing more formal structures for corporate personnel management.[30]

The craft sectors, on the other hand, followed a different path, as the clash between management and unions' efforts to impose their competing models of unilateral regulation overshadowed any tendency towards the emergence of joint regulation. Thus employers sought to force disputes procedures on craft unions as in building, shipbuilding and engineering, where they were introduced after lock-outs or unsuccessful strikes. Even here, though, there was a built-in tendency for these procedures to generate compromises over time; in any case, the unions tended to throw them off when they felt strong enough, as in all three industries on the eve of the First World War.[31]

In attempting to account for the distinctive features of workplace industrial relations in Britain as these had emerged by the eve of the First World War, the principal emphasis has been placed here on the constraints of firm and market structures on employers' investment and labour strategies; responding to the opportunities created by these strategies, unions were able to develop forms of job control which further restricted employers' freedom of manoeuvre in the workplace. While these constitute the principal causal links at work in this period, the argument put forward here should not be read as an attempt to develop an economic-structural determinism. Although alternative strategies were in principle available to late Victorian and Edwardian entrepreneurs, it is not proposed to reopen this notoriously vexed question here.[32] But in conclusion some remarks should focus briefly on some of the ways in which *political* and *legal* as well as economic forces helped to shape the character of workplace industrial relations in Britain during this period.[33]

To a certain extent, the spontaneous influence of economic structures on workplace bargaining can be said to have been greater in Britain than elsewhere precisely because of her 'abstentionist' or 'voluntarist' legal traditions. In most countries where an elaborate legal framework has been established for the regulation of collective bargaining, with the recent exception of Sweden, this has tended to circumscribe union inroads into managerial prerogatives. This tendency is particularly evident in those countries where legal intervention has been indispensable in overcoming employer opposition to union organization, as in the United States and Weimar Germany. It is important to remember, however, that repeated legislative interventions have been required in this country to protect unions from judges' applications of what they consider to be the more general tenets of the English common law. In the United States, where there is a written constitution which allots a major role to judicial review of legislation, a much more restricted view of the rights and responsibilities of trade unions has prevailed which owes as much to the political as to the economic differences between the two countries.[34]

The British state also contributed more directly to consolidation of the pattern of industrial relations whose origins have been sought in this essay in the structure of the late nineteenth-century economy. Thus public policy aimed from the 1890s onwards at diffusing those bargaining procedures which had come to be seen by civil servants, trade unionists and even many industrialists as the 'British model' of industrial relations into those sectors where economic forces did not encourage their spontaneous emergence, through such measures as the 1896 Conciliation Act, Trade Boards and the Whitley Councils. Similarly, the political influence of organized labour, coupled with the state's preoccupation with social peace even at the expense of capitalist conceptions of industrial efficiency, tended to contain employer aggression within more limited bounds than on the continent or in the United States.[35] Hence, despite, and in part because, of its 'voluntarist' approach to industrial relations, the British state came quite unintentionally to reinforce the economic and institutional structures constraining employers' freedom of action in the workplace.

Notes: Chapter 19

1 See for example E. J. Hobsbawm, *Industry and Empire* (Harmondsworth, 1969).

2 J. Hinton, *The First Shop Stewards' Movement* (London, 1973); K. Burgess, *The Origins of British Industrial Relations* (London, 1975); idem, *The Challenge of Labour* (London, 1980); R. Q. Gray, *The Labour Aristocracy in Victorian Edinburgh* (Oxford, 1976); idem, *The Aristocracy of Labour in Nineteenth Century Britain c. 1850–1914* (London, 1981); J. E. Cronin, *Industrial Conflict in Modern Britain* (London, 1979); R. Price, *Masters, Unions and Men: Work Control in Building and the Rise of Labour 1830–1914* (Cambridge, 1980). Much of this work builds on ideas first set out by E. J. Hobsbawm, 'Trends in the British labour movement since 1850', and idem, 'The labour aristocracy in 19th century Britain', reprinted in idem, *Labouring Men* (London, 1964), 316–43 and 272–315 respectively.

3 For a more comprehensive critique of this interpretative tradition which highlights the weaknesses of its treatment of culture and politics, and with which I am in substantial agreement, see A. Reid, 'The division of labour and politics in Britain, 1880–1920', in this volume, pp. 150–65.

4 For example, Burgess, *Origins of British Industrial Relations*, ch. 1; Hinton, *Shop Stewards' Movement*; J. B. Jefferys, *The Story of the Engineers, 1800–1945* (London, 1946); and Hobsbawm, 'Labour aristocracy', 288–9, 300–1; but for a slightly different interpretation, idem, 'British gas-workers, 1873–1914', in idem, *Labouring Men*, 158–78 (170–1). Economic historians have also emphasized the role of American competition as a spur to the introduction of labour-saving technology in the British engineering industry: see S. B. Saul, 'The American impact on British industry, 1895–1914', *Business History* 3 (1960): 19–38.

5 The evidence for the arguments in this section is drawn from a longer paper, J. Zeitlin, 'The labour strategies of British engineering employers, 1890–1922', in H. Gospel and G. Littler (eds), *Managerial Strategies and Industrial Relations: Historical and Comparative Perspectives* (London, 1982), 25–54, and J. Zeitlin, 'Craft regulation and the division of labour: engineers and compositors in Britain, 1890–1914 (PhD. thesis, Warwick, 1981). Where no citation is given in this section, the reference is to these works and the literature discussed therein. These arguments are based on the following main sources: (1) the archives of the EEF, now held at the Modern Records Centre, Warwick University, which include the case files of issues raised through the disputes procedure at local and national level; (2) the printed records of the various trade unions, which include the monthly reports of the ASE's organizing district delegates; (3) the Webb Trade Union Collection at the British Library of Economics and Political Science, which includes the manuscript sources of interviews and correspondence with local trade union officials and employers; (4) the reports of parliamentary bodies, notably the Royal Commission on Labour in the 1890s; and the trade and technical press.

6 See, for example, K. Burgess, 'New Unionism for old? The Amalgamated Society of Engineers in Britain', in this volume, pp. 166–84. For evidence of the limited introduction of the new machines see S. B. Saul, 'The market and the development of the mechanical engineering industries in Britain, 1760–1914', *Economic History Review* 20 (1967): 110–30, and idem, 'The machine-tool industry in Britain to 1914', *Business History* 10 (1968): 22–43.

7 Figures in Jefferys, *The Story of the Engineers*, 134.

8 E. H. Phelps Brown and M. Browne, *A Century of Pay* (London, 1968), 174–95, especially the figures on pp. 177, 180–1; S. B. Saul, 'Engineering', in D. H. Aldcroft (ed.), *The Development of British Industry and Foreign Competition, 1875–1914* (London, 1968),

186–237, (229); R. Floud, 'The adolescence of American engineering competition, 1860–1900', *Economic History Review* 27 (1974): 57–71.

9 On the development of firms and markets in the engineering industry, see Saul, 'Mechanical engineering industries'; idem, 'Machine-tool industry'; idem, 'Engineering'; Floud, 'American engineering competition', and idem, *The British Machine Tool Industry, 1850–1914* (Cambridge, 1976), esp. ch. 3; D. H. Aldcroft, 'The performance of the British machine-tool industry between the wars', *Business History Review* 45 (1966): 218–96; C. Trebilcock, *The Vickers Brothers: Armaments and Enterprise, 1855–1914* (London, 1977); and Board of Trade, Report of the Departmental Committee on the Position of the Engineering Trades after the War, 1918, Cd 9073, XIII. On the growth of the newer sectors and the obstacles to their development, see also S. B. Saul, 'The motor industry in Britain to 1914', *Business History* 5 (1962): 22–44; R. J. Irving, 'New industries for old? Some investment decisions of Sir W. G. Armstrong, Whitworth and Co., 1900–1914', *Business History* 17 (1975): 150–75; I. Byatt, 'Electrical products', in Aldcroft, *Development of British Industry*, 238–73; and R. E. Cotterall, 'Electrical engineering', in N. Buxton and D. H. Aldcroft (eds), *British Industry between the Wars* (London, 1979), 241–75. Before 1914 British motor cars were not made in long series, though the growing standardization of components, particularly in engine production, required a large-scale use of automatic machine tools even in the quality firms; see W. Lewchuk, 'The evolution of management techniques: the Daimler Motor Company, 1896–1914' (unpublished paper, Cambridge, 1981).

10 These remarks are based on a detailed study of the case files and correspondence on machine-manning and payment systems in the archives of the EEF, and of the monthly reports of the ASE Organizing District Delegates in the union's *Monthly Journal and Report*.

11 In addition to the material in my thesis, see B. C. M. Weekes, 'The Amalgamated Society of Engineers, 1880–1914: a study of trade union government structure and industrial policy' (PhD. thesis, Warwick, 1970); and R. Croucher, 'The ASE and local autonomy, 1898–1914' (MA thesis, Warwick, 1971).

12 For a fuller treatment of one new sector during the interwar period, see J. Zeitlin, 'The emergence of shop steward organisation and job control in the British car industry', *History Workshop Journal* 10 (1980): 118–138; and idem, 'Workplace militancy: a rejoinder', *History Workshop Journal* 16 (1983): 131–6.

13 On cotton textiles, see Lazonick, 'Industrial relations and technical change: the case of the self-acting mule', *Cambridge Journal of Economics* 3 (1979): 231–62; idem, 'Competition, specialisation and economic decline', *Journal of Economic History* 51 (1981): 31–8; idem, 'Production relations, labour productivity, and choice of technique: British and U.S. cotton spinning', ibid., 491–516; idem, 'Factor costs and the diffusion of ring spinning in Britain prior to World War I', *Quarterly Journal of Economics* 96 (1981): 89–109. On iron and steel see F. Wilkinson, 'Collective bargaining in the steel industry in the 1920s', in A. Briggs and J. Saville (eds), *Essays in Labour History* (London, 1977), 103–32; B. Elbaum and F. Wilkinson, 'Industrial relations and uneven development: a comparative study of the American and British steel industries', *Cambridge Journal of Economics* (1979): 275–303; and S. Tolliday, 'Industry, finance and the state – an analysis of the British steel industry in the inter-war years' (PhD. thesis, Cambridge, 1979). On shipbuilding, see A. Reid, 'The division of labour in the British shipbuilding industry, 1880–1920 (PhD. thesis, Cambridge, 1980); K. McClelland and A. Reid, 'Wood, iron and steel: technology, labour and trade union organisation in the shipbuilding industry, 1840–1914', in R. Harrison and J. Zeitlin (eds), *Divisions of Labour: Skilled Workers and Technological Change in Nineteenth-Century Britain* (Brighton, 1985); R. Okayama, 'Employers' labour policy and craft unions: a study of British industrial relations in shipbuilding from the 1870s to the war', *Bulletin of the Institute of Social Sciences, Meiji University* 3 (1979): 1–19; and E. H. Lorenz, 'The labour process in the British and French shipbuilding industries: two patterns of development', *Journal of European Economic History* (forthcoming).

14 Among the rapidly growing literature on the labour strategies of American management, see D. Nelson, *Managers and Workers: The Origins of the New Factory System in the United States, 1880–1920* (Madison, Wis., 1975); D. Montgomery, *Workers' Control in America* (Cambridge, 1979); J. Holt, 'Trade unionism in the British and US steel industries 1880–1914', *Labour History* 18 (1977): 5–35; A. Chandler, *The Visible Hand: The Mana-*

gerial Revolution in American Business (Cambridge, Mass., 1977). There is much less material available in English on German employers, but some useful information can be found in D. Crew, *Town in the Ruhr* (New York, 1979); H. Homburg, 'Scientific management and personnel policy in the modern German enterprise, 1918–39', in Gospel and Littler, *Managerial Strategy*, 137–56; D. Groh, 'Intensification of work and industrial conflict in Germany, 1896–1914', *Politics and Society* 8 (1978): 349–97; E. G. Spencer, 'Employer response to unionism: Ruhr coal industrialists before 1914', *Journal of Modern History* 48 (1976): 397–412. It would be a mistake, however, to overstate the similarities between German and American managerial strategies: many German firms tended to specialize less on the mass production of consumer and light capital goods than on products such as electrical machinery, optics and fine chemicals which were made in smaller batches and required a more highly skilled labour force. This specialization seems to have converged with the bureaucratic traditions of German enterprise to produce a distinctive managerial style, which emphasized training and welfare more than the decomposition of tasks, while sharing American employers' hostility to trade unions. For some hints in this direction see Homburg, 'Scientific management'; and J. Kocka, 'Entrepreneurs and managers in German industrialisation', *Cambridge Economic History of Europe*, Vol. VII, Part I (Cambridge, 1978), and idem, 'The rise of the modern industrial enterprise in Germany', in A. Chandler and H. Daems (eds), *Managerial Hierarchies: Comparative Perspectives on the Rise of the Modern Industrial Enterprise* (Cambridge, Mass., 1980), 77–116.

15 L. Hannah, *The Rise of the Corporate Economy* (London, 1976); and idem, 'Visible and invisible hands in Great Britain', in Chandler and Daems, *Managerial Hierarchies*, 41–76; P. L. Payne, 'The emergence of the large-scale company in Great Britain, 1870–1914', *Economic History Review* 20 (1967): 519–92; Reid, *Division of Labour*; Tolliday, *Industry, Finance and the State*; M. W. Kirby, *The British Coalmining Industry, 1870–1946* (London, 1977), ch. 1; R. Loveridge, 'Business strategy and community culture: manpower policy as a structured accommodation of conflict', in D. Dunkeley and G. Salomon (eds), *The International Yearbook of Organization Studies* (London, 1981).

16 Saul, 'Mechanical engineering industries'; Floud, 'American engineering competition'; Reid, 'Division of labour'; and S. Pollard and P. Robertson, *The British Shipbuilding Industry, 1870–1914* (Cambridge, Mass., 1979).

17 Hobsbawm, *Industry and Empire*; W. A. Lewis, *Growth and Fluctuations, 1870–1913* (London, 1978), chs 4–5; M. W. Kirby, *The Decline of British Economic Power since 1870* (London, 1981), ch. 1; P. L. Cotterell, *Industrial Finance, 1830–1914* (London, 1980).

18 J. Melling, '"Non-commissioned officers": British employers and their supervisory workers, 1880–1920', *Social History* 5 (1980): 199–211; and idem, 'Employers, industrial welfare and the struggle for workplace control, 1880–1920', in Gospel and Littler, *Managerial Strategies*, 55–81.

19 H. J. Habakkuk, *American and British Technology in the 19th Century. The Search for Labour-Saving Inventions* (Cambridge, 1967); C. K. Harley, 'Skilled labour and the choice of technique in Edwardian industry', *Explorations in Economic History* 11 (1973–4): 391–419; R. Samuel, 'The workshop of the world: steampower and hand technology in mid-Victorian Britain', *History Workshop Journal* 3 (1977): 6–72; Lazonick, 'Self-acting mule'; Phelps Brown and Browne, *Century of Pay*, 174–95.

20 For the explicit rejection by British employers of a high wage/high productivity strategy in the early automobile industry, see W. Lewchuk, 'Fordism and British motor car employers, 1896–1932', in Gospel and Littler, *Managerial Strategies*, 82–110.

21 In addition to my thesis, see J. Zeitlin, 'Craft control and the division of labour: engineers and compositors in Britain, 1890–1930', *Cambridge Journal of Economics* 3 (1979): 263–74.

22 Lazonick, 'Self-acting mule'.

23 Reid, 'Division of labour'; McClelland and Reid, 'Wood, iron and steel'.

24 J. Child, *Industrial relations in the British Printing Industry* (London, 1967); K. Sisson, *Industrial Relations in Fleet Street* (London, 1975).

25 Wilkinson, *Collective Bargaining*; Wilkinson and Elbaum, *Industrial Relations*; Lazonick, 'Self-acting mule'; H. A. Turner, *Trade Union Growth, Structure and Policy* (London, 1962); and J. White, *The Limits of Trade Union Militancy* (Westport, Conn., 1978).

26 Zeitlin, 'Craft control and the division of labour.'

27 Reid, 'Division of labour'; McClelland and Reid, 'Wood, iron and steel'.

28 In E. J. Hobsbawm, 'General labour unions in Britain, 1889–1914', in idem, *Labouring*

Men, 179–203; 'The aristocracy of labour reconsidered', *Proceedings of the Seventh International Economic History Conference* (Edinburgh, 1978); and in comments on a previous version of some of these ideas presented at his seminar at the Institute of Historical Research in 1980.

29 R. Tarling and F. Wilkinson, 'The movement of real wages and the development of collective bargaining in the UK, 1855–1920', *Contributions to Political Economy* 1 (1982): 1–23; J. H. Porter, 'Wage bargaining under conciliation agreements, 1860–1914', *Economic History Review*, 23 (1970): 460–75; Lazonick, 'Self-acting mule'; idem, 'Production relations'; Elbaum and Wilkinson, 'Industrial relations'.

30 H. Gospel, 'Employers' organisations: their growth and function in the British system of industrial relations in the period 1918–1939' (PhD. thesis, London, 1974).

31 On shipbuilding, see Reid, *Division of Labour*, and Okayama, 'Employers' labour policy'; on building, Price, *Masters, Unions and Men*, and Burgess, *Origins of British Industrial Relations*, ch. 2.

32 For an interesting attempt to recast the terms of the debate, see Lazonick, 'Competition'. In a paper on 'Historical alternatives to mass production' written jointly with Charles Sabel (forthcoming in *Past and Present*), I have attempted to show that the flexible production of specialized goods using skilled labour and general-purpose machinery constituted a potentially viable strategy for nineteenth-century entrepreneurs, though the implications for the British case are not developed.

33 I have deliberately avoided reference to cultural explanations of economic decline such as that advanced by M. J. Wiener, *English Culture and the Decline of the Industrial Spirit* (Cambridge, 1980). Such factors are far from irrelevant in principle, and are clearly important in explaining phenomena such as the weak links between science and industry in Britain. But in their present form, such arguments overstate the influence of southern English high culture on the rest of the country, and are rarely able to provide evidence for its direct effects on industrial behaviour.

34 On Britain, see O. Kahn-Freund, *Labour Relations* (Oxford, 1979), ch. 8. On the United States, see D. Brody, *Workers in Industrial America* (New York, 1980), chs 3 and 5; H. J. Harris, *The Right to Manage: Industrial Relations Policies of American Business in the 1940s* (Madison, Wis., 1982); and idem, 'The snares of liberalism? Politicians, bureaucrats and the shaping of federal labour relations policy in the United States ca. 1915–1947', in S. Toniday and J. Zeitlin (eds), *Shop Floor Bargaining and the State: Historical and Comparative Perspective* (forthcoming, Cambridge, 1985). On Germany, see J. Clark and R. Lewis (eds), *Labour Law and Politics in the Weimar Republic: Selected Essays of Otto Kahn-Freund* (Oxford, 1981); and B. Weisbrod, 'Economic power and political stability reconsidered: heavy industry in Weimar Germany', *Social History* 4 (1979): 241–63, who emphasizes the role of employer opposition to collective bargaining as a source of union support for compulsory arbitration.

35 Tarling and Wilkinson, 'The movement of real wages'; for a somewhat different view, see R. Davidson, 'The Board of Trade and industrial relations, 1896–1914', *Historical Journal* 21 (1978), 511–91 and idem, 'Social conflict and social administration: the Conciliation Act in British industrial relations', in T. C. Smout (ed.), *The Search for Wealth and Stability: Essays in Economic and Social History Presented to M. W. Flinn* (London, 1979), 175–97. For a conspicuous example of a Conservative administration pressuring employers to pursue a more conciliatory policy in a later period, see H. A. Clegg and R. Adams, *The Employers' Challenge: A Study of the National Shipbuilding and Engineers Disputes of 1957* (Oxford, 1957); S. Toniday, 'Government, employers and shop floor organisation in the British motor industry, 1939–1969', in idem and Zeitlin, *Shop Floor Bargaining and the State*.

20 Repression or Integration? The State, Trade Unions and Industrial Disputes in Imperial Germany

KLAUS SAUL

I

As Imperial Germany's interlude of peace came to an end on 31 July 1914 with the announcement that there was a threat of war, and a mobilization order was to be expected at any time in Berlin, members of the steering committees of the socialist labour movement, the Social Democratic Party executive and the *Generalkommission der Freien Gewerkschaften* (the General Commission of the Free Trade Unions) prepared themselves for arrest. They also feared dissolution of the party and union organizations, and considered the probability of a renewed period of illegal activity.

Two days later, following the government's call for a 'bond of trust' to guide future relations between state and unions and its assurance that their organizations would not be disbanded, the Free Trade Unions endorsed an immediate halt to all wage disputes, they agreed to co-operate with social welfare schemes during the war and enlisted the help of unemployed industrial workers with the harvest. With the vague pledge of a repeal of state emergency legislation directed against the unions, and new guidelines for administrative and judicial practices, it seemed, on the eve of war in 1914, that for the first time in the Reich's history the path of state control, harassment and containment of the socialist union movement and the obstruction of its activities in labour disputes had at last been abandoned. Moreover, it had seemed to union leaders in the summer of 1914 that daily confrontation might have been forced by the powerful employers' lobby into a 'decisive social battle' for the very existence of the unions; this danger had now apparently been averted.[1]

In the three decades between the re-establishment of an independent trade union movement in the early 1880s and the integration of the unions into the war economy, the reactions of the state to the expansion of industrial disputes and the rising unionization of the workers presented a varied picture, full of contradictions and opposites. There was malicious and often petty-minded police harassment in Prussia, in the Kingdom of Saxony and in most of the smaller north and central German states. More liberal practices prevailed in the south and south-west of Germany. On the one hand there was support for collective agreements from the Reich government, on the other hand the embittered and stubborn adherence to the ban on strikes for rural workers continued east of the Elbe. The administration of laws remained class-biased against strikers; at the same time mediation before state industrial courts towards settling industrial disputes took place. The demonstrative use of machine-guns against striking miners in Mansfeld in 1909 and in the Ruhr in 1912 was part of this varied picture, as was succcessful state mediation in the construction workers' lock-out in 1910 covering the whole area of the Reich for the first time ever. The appointment of professors of political economics sympathetic to the unions went along with the spreading of anti-socialist and anti-unionist propaganda in state schools and in state-controlled district newspapers and by means of the state-sponsored anti-socialist agitation groups, such as the *Deutsche Kriegerbund* (the association of German soldiers) and the *Reichsverband gegen die Sozialdemokratie* (Reich Association against Social Democracy). These contrasting examples give an indication of the many sides to the question. The complexity of the situation may be explained by the different political cultures north and south of the Main, the frequent lack of co-ordination in policy between the various states and the ministries in Prussia and the Reich and, in particular, the basic divide which split not only public opinion but even the bureaucrats into two opposing camps. Were trade unions structural elements of a modern social constitution which offered the opportunity of integrating the working classes into the social order of Imperial Germany and were they indispensable not only as a means of raising the socio-cultural status of the workers, but also as a counterweight to the power of the industrialists? Or, conversely, were Free Trade Unions first and foremost socialist propaganda training and cover-up organizations, to be put down if the state was to survive?

Both premises came up against the constraints imposed by the balance of power in German society. At least after the demise of the *Sozialistengesetz* (Anti-Socialist Law) it did not seem possible to find a parliamentary majority in favour of clear-cut anti-union legislation. This was due to the universal, equal and secret Reich suffrage and the ever-increasing politici-zation of working-class voters. Nor could a firm policy of reform – based on a Reichstag majority and a broadly based extra-parliamentary alliance of middle-class social reformers, together with reformist Social Democrats and all creeds of unionists – ever hope to overcome the deeply rooted influence of the Junkers from the east of the Elbe who were dominant in the Prussian administration, the army, the Prussian *Landtag* (State Parliament) and at court. The same applied to the opposition of west German heavy industry whose anti-unionist line was sure to meet with the approval of the pressure groups representing the old *Mittelstand*.[2]

Up until the outbreak of the First World War this situation of stalemate provides the background for the attempts at union depoliticization and integration, and also for the state's role as mediator, the projects and endeavours to worsen the legal position of the unions and the curbs on the voicing of union interests in both industry and trade, whether implemented by administrative or judicial or police measures. It also provides the context for the success in preventing the unionization not only of the rural workers east of the Elbe but also of the transport workers and junior officials in the large Reich and state public services, and for the extension of a powerful effective police and military deterrent force. The analysis of this situation serves to illustrate the motives, instruments, possibilities and limits of state intervention in labour disputes under Prussian administration and Reich legislation.

II

Whereas the Anti-Socialist Law had failed to break the Social Democratic Party's continuity in personnel and organization, in a period of severe economic depression the phase of harsh state persecution in the years 1878–9, rounded off by a purge in the factories, more or less completely destroyed the union organizations whose membership had amounted to some 50–60,000 immediately prior to the *Sozialistengesetz*. However, the subsequent 'almost total peace' came to an end in 1882 at the latest when a large number of *Fachvereine* (craft associations) were re-established at local level and merged into federations in the following two years. Towards the end of 1884 the Berlin Chief of Police whose department had been the central watchdog of the socialist labour movement in Germany since 1878 subsequently addressed an internal memorandum to the Prussian Minister of the Interior with an emphatic warning that the expansion of the union movement would soon force the authorities to abandon their policy of wait-and-see and adopt a firmer line of principle. The unions admittedly offered social democracy 'splendid fields of agitation' but on the other hand with the rising power of capitalism they were also a 'valuable movement, becoming more and more essential as the spokesman for specific legitimate economic interests'. Since the 'economic source of the union movement could never be cut off', a policy of pure repression would serve no purpose save to discredit state authority in the eyes of the working classes.[3]

This was in fact the dilemma faced by all state measures of repression in the decades to come. Whereas with its social policy the state endeavoured to project itself to the workers as a 'charitable institution' and therefore to win over the loyalty of the masses, its measures of persecution confirmed the social democratic theory of a class society, which in turn nourished the hate and embitterment of the working class.

In the final analysis this could only be beneficial to the Social Democratic Party since it was the only party which promised a radical change of the status quo. The only means of abolishing the Reichstag suffrage and the right of coalition would have been to openly violate the law or to stage a coup d'état. The state's measures to curb union activities could therefore only hope for limited, ad hoc success since in a period of forced industrialization the rise of the unions could simply not be averted.

In 1884 the Chief of Police hoped he had discovered another way round this dilemma. He proposed to the Minister of the Interior that unions prepared to accept a high degree of government control over their activities – including their internal administration and their finances – would be granted a sphere of activity of their own, to be guaranteed by Reich legislation; this would mark the 'beginning of the corporate structuring of the working classes'. The state's powers of control, combined with sanctions against the leaders and threats that their associations would be disbanded if they overstepped the bounds of the law, were to guard against social democratic infiltration and prevent the associations from developing into a 'kind of social democratic sub-branch and cash-office'.

However, state policy vis-à-vis the unions in Prussia did not follow this advice. Its acceptance was blocked by the conservative bureaucrats' mistrust of the endeavours of the lower classes to help themselves, by the realistic awareness of the degree of opposition to such a policy among those classes which regarded themselves as the pillars of the state, and doubtless also in the hope that a policy of social insurance which was just beginning to get off the ground would have an overall stabilizing effect on the system. Increasing strike activity and demands for state protection from the industrialists concerned led to a new wave of state harassment in 1885/6. From 1885 onwards, on instructions from the Prussian Minister of the Interior, the rigid provisions of the Prussian Law on Associations dating back to the reactionary year of 1850 which prohibited women, schoolchildren and apprentices from joining political associations, or combining in any form among themselves, were systematically applied against the unions. If any evidence could be found of even sporadic joint action in matters relating to social policy – for example, petitioning for safety provisions at work – both local associations and the federations were closed down by order of the police.

This action was quite obviously biased: the legislation on association was applied only to the *Fachvereine*. It was not enforced with respect to the liberal Hirsch-Duncker Trade Associations, which were tolerated by the state, nor to the craftsmen's guilds or the agricultural and industrial pressure groups, which were much more active than the trade unions in trying to influence legislation.

Nevertheless, from 1887 onwards the *Reichsgericht*, the supreme court of the Reich, consistently sanctioned these measures which drastically curtailed the unions' field of activity, forced them into political abstinence, even in matters of welfare policy, and reduced union affairs to no more than the regulation of material working conditions in the individual factory.[4]

The Prussian Minister of the Interior, Robert von Puttkamer, issued his famous decree on strikes on 11 April 1886. Puttkamer aimed at restricting even the limited scope the unions had enjoyed since the lifting of the state ban on combination and strikes for industrial workers in 1869 and at virtually immobilizing strike activity. Although he initially reminded the police authorities of their duty to remain impartial in labour disputes, this soon proved to be no more than a red herring. The lengthy list of possible statutory offences inevitably brought strike activity close to being considered a criminal act. Moreover, the minister gave express orders that if requested by an employer the police were to prevent strikers from putting any pressure on workers who had not come out on strike. This ban on picketing was totally without legal foundation. Even more than on the economic effects of strikes, the Minister of the Interior's suspicions were centred on their political impact. It was considered that the leaders of the revolutionary social democratic movement were not so much concerned with using a labour dispute to reach certain objectives such as a wage increase or a reduction of working time but had a different goal in mind: the gulf between employers and employees was to be widened, fuel added to the fire of 'hate against our entire political and social order'. Thus 'the minds of the working masses, victim to their wily charms, were gradually to be prepared for a violent revolt'. In these circumstances the provisions of the Anti-Socialist Law were to be applied to the letter. The 'ring leaders of the strike movement' were to be expelled from areas such as Berlin, Frankfurt and Hamburg-Altona where a 'minor state of siege' prevailed; riots resulting from strikes were to be used as a pretext to declare a 'total state of siege'.[5]

A further attempt to gain control over the union organizations added to the swelling wave of harassment which included a ban on all union gatherings in Berlin and the expulsion of leading union officials from the capital of the Reich. One of the provisions from the Reich Penal Code under which it was an offence to set up an insurance company without the prior consent of the authorities provided a lever in this case. From 1886 onwards the Prussian police authorities declared that on account of their mutual assistance funds the unions were to be considered as insurance agencies and therefore required a licence under the law. So the unions were left with the alternative of either giving in to state supervision or being closed down by the police. As he explained to the Prussian Minister of the Interior in August 1887 and February 1888, this seemed to have given the Berlin Chief of Police the opportunity of assuring state control over the raising and use of the associations' funds without specific anti-union legislation; it also meant that decision-making on the waging of labour disputes would be firmly in the hands of the state. Finally, it meant that henceforth the state would be in a position to remove Social Democrats from leading union positions. However, this strategy failed to get off the ground. The majority of the federations amended their statutes, deleting all legal rights of their members to financial support, the very principle of insurance. Although some of the *Oberlandesgerichte*, the higher regional courts, interpreted the revised statutes as no more than an attempt to bypass the law and approved sanctions against union officials and the disbanding of trade unions, the Prussian *Oberverwaltungsgericht* (the higher administrative tribunal), besieged by appeals from the unions for protection from the latest sanctions, overruled the action of the police authorities in a number of test cases in 1888–9: associations which did not guarantee members the right to financial assistance were not to be considered as insurance agencies.[6]

A few weeks after the publication of one of these test cases in the ministerial gazette of the Prussian Ministry of the Interior, which marked the withdrawal of this particular strategy, the Ruhr miners' strike in May 1889 involving over 90,000 miners demonstrated the limits of the repressive practices to date and showed that they had not checked the growth of union federations. The Ruhr miners' strike was the culmination of a prolonged wave of strikes which swept through almost all trades and industries and which coincided with the economic upturn from 1888. This was the largest strike in the history of Imperial Germany so far and, as a result of the intervention of the troops, also the bloodiest one.

However, it owes its importance in German labour history to the fact that for the first time the authorities did not simply limit themselves to maintaining public law and order but went a step further. With the support of public opinion, enormous pressure was put on the industrialists to settle the dispute by entering into negotiations between representatives of the Ruhr mining interests and a delegation of the striking miners. The authorities were fearful of any paralysation of the Reich's preparedness for war and a collapse of industrial production, railway transport and local public services as a result of the coal shortage; there was also concern that the still monarchist miners might be transformed into political radicals. Moreover, real sympathy was felt for these workers who never saw the light of day in the 'realm of everlasting night' and there was a feeling of prejudice against the 'coal magnates' and 'agitators' among the ranks of the coal-owners in the Ruhr who were regarded as responsible for the outbreak of the strike. The strike was therefore not seen as a socialist plot but as a legitimate instrument used by the workers to gain their share of the booming profits enjoyed by the Ruhr mines.[7]

Thus after the 'great strike' of 1889 was settled, the regional authorities in the Rhineland and Westphalia, the Prussian ministerial bureaucrats and Wilhelm II's informal group of social advisers set their minds to working out a strategy of 'strike prevention' for the future. Although on account of the power struggle between *Reichskanzler* Bismarck and Wilhelm II and the sluggish wheels of bureaucratic procedure, these discussions failed to bring forth administrative measures or concrete legal provisions until the years 1890–2, they revealed the bureaucrats' scepticism of the industrialists, who were only interested in profits, and their concern about the dangerous consequences the organization of the workers in the Free Trade Unions could have for the entire political system. It was hoped that the public authorities, committed only to the 'common good', could act as an impartial mediator between the classes and that in the new 'social monarchy' a better basis of legitimacy could be found for the system as a whole. On 21 January 1890 the Kaiser called for prompt reforms to ward off the danger of revolution. However, talks between the Prussian ministerial experts on social policy and the *Reichsamt* of the Interior in December 1889 and January 1890 immediately made it clear that while the scope for reform was restricted by the opposition of the 'propertied classes', a policy of intensified repression would meet with the resistance of the majority in the Reichstag. At the same time there was great pressure coming from the growth of the socialist trade unions and the spreading of social democratic influence among the industrial workers.

The aim of state intervention in this situation was therefore to relax social tension in the larger enterprises, thus removing any cause of strike. The overall situation of the workers was to be improved; the spirits of young workers eager to follow a strike call were to be dampened by greater parental control while the older, 'calmer', 'more level-headed' workers were to be given consultative rights at plant and inter-plant level in the settlement of disputes and improvement of working conditions. The intention of this state 'organization of labour' was to cut the ground from under the unions' feet. State and local police forces were to be reinforced and more effectively deployed; harsh sanctions for inciting fellow workers to break their contracts and for threatening strike-breakers were to act as a deterrent; the state railway, private industry and local public services were to be equipped with ample supplies of coal; freight charges were to be reduced to facilitate coal supplies from strike-free mining areas abroad; convicts were to be set to work in the mines and strikers replaced by soldiers or miners called up for service – these measures were designed to make a worker think twice before laying down his tools and were intended to reduce the pressure to resort to armed force, the political cost of which – the radicalization of the workers – could be very high indeed for the social and political status quo of the Wilhelmine system.[8]

These general guidelines which included discussion on the most radical possibility of all – the nationalization of the mines, giving the miners civil servant status – were only implemented in part. It was above all the amendments to the Reich Industrial Code of 1891, and the Prussian Mining Law of 1892, along with the simultaneous expansion of industrial supervision (officials were under obligation to intervene when grievances were raised and to mediate in cases of dispute), which enabled the state to strengthen its grip on working conditions and enforce minimum standards. For the first time the working regulations in factories and mines, previously usually no more than a code of discipline with a list of sanctions, now had to lay down the entire content of a contract of employment. Similarly the opportunity of faster and inexpensive legal proceedings before the new industrial courts set up in 1890 meant that at least disputes on the interpretation of existing contracts of employment could be settled peacefully. This legalization of industrial relations furthermore served to quell potential conflict in the factory. Moreover, the ministerial bureaucrats were counting upon the 'educative effects' of the co-operation between employers and employees in these special courts with parity representation.[9]

However, the material aspects of working conditions – above all wages and hours of work – remained the domain of the entrepreneur. On this point the government was pinning its hopes on the influence of public opinion and the employers' willingness to compromise: on account of the workers' legal right to a hearing and the submission of working regulations to the authorities a private relationship of employment had to a certain extent become a public matter. It was therefore hoped that potential grounds for conflict could be nipped in the bud. A procedure making working regulations subject to official approval did not however seem so politically opportune. As the *Reichsamt* of the Interior pointed out, the state would thereby be assuming responsibility for working conditions so that the 'agitation of the working class against irksome provisions of labour regulations' would then be directed at the state.[10]

One means of indirectly influencing working conditions in the private sector was however the planned development of state-owned companies into model institutions – but this project soon came up against the fiscal interest in the profitability of the companies which after all covered some 70 per cent of overall Prussian state expenditure. There were also doubts about the impact such a step might have on the national economy as a whole. Higher wages, a reduction in working hours and expanded social benefits at plant level in the nationalized sector would send up the production costs of German industry, jeopardizing its competitiveness on the world market and at the same time add fuel to the rural exodus from the east of the Elbe, further aggravating the shortage of farm labour.[11]

So in the final analysis the only door open was to appeal to the reason of the industrialists. This was the task of the semi-official central bureau for employees' welfare facilities, founded in 1891, which advocated the expansion of industrial social policy. In internal discussions at the end of 1889 and the beginning of 1890 the establishment of factory co-operatives as a means of doing away with 'living on tick' and the 'exploitation' of the workers by small business (and also to deprive them of an important financial source which kept the pot boiling during a strike), the founding of housekeeping schools for working-class girls and the construction of factory-subsidized housing all seemed particularly appropriate means of raising the standards of living of the worker without actually increasing his wages; he would thus be made 'content', his mind kept off the thought of industrial dispute and politics in general by diverting him from the tavern back into the arms of his family.[12] In contrast to the extension of factory 'welfare facilities', larger enterprises took no advantage of another door opened by the 1891 amendment to the Reich Industrial Code – increased supervision and discipline of juvenile workers who were considered as particularly susceptible to calls for a strike. Measures which could be applied included payment of juveniles' wages to their parent or guardian. Although the industrialists were generally of one mind about the growing 'unruliness' and political radicalization of working-class youngsters, they were more concerned with safeguarding their own interests and winning over productive, hard-working young workers. They therefore opted for measures such as wage incentives rather than trying to regiment the workers' private lives, for example banning them from the inns and taverns.[13]

On 24 January 1890 William II put forward a proposal on workers' participation at plant and inter-plant level. This proposal provided for mandatory workers' committees (to remove or prevent the growth of a 'social democratic rival government' in the factories), workers' chambers for individual trades and crafts in larger districts (designed as a kind of look-out post) and finally permanent arbitration boards in cases of industrial dispute. However, these proposals were blocked by the uncompromising and unyielding stance of heavy industry and the Ruhr mining lobby who refused to budge from their position of being master in their own house. In their factories and mines the establishment of the workers' committees (which was left, under the amendments to the Reich Industrial Code and the Prussian Mining Law of 1891–2, at the employers' discretion) was virtually nonexistent. This meant however that the state's strategy of strike prevention collapsed at its very foundations. It was precisely this lack of 'understanding' between employers and employees which was the main cause for union infiltration into the large enterprises and the outbreak of strikes.[14]

The offer of state assistance in settling disputes, when finally implemented, also remained relatively modest. The *Gewerbegerichtsgesetz* (Industrial Courts Law) of July 1890 laid down that the establishment of industrial courts was the responsibility of the municipal authorities with the exception of the mining sector where they fell under the jurisdiction of the central authorities of the *Land* in question. Under this law it was the presiding judge's duty, if requested to do so by both parties concerned, to form an arbitration board comprised of members from both sides of industry to settle labour disputes. This provision gave the employers an absolute right of veto. Furthermore, the award of the arbitration board was not legally binding although it could admittedly pull considerable weight through pressure from public opinion.[15]

The lessons drawn in 1889–90 by the industrialists in the mines of the Ruhr and in the west German heavy industry were the complete opposite of those drawn by the ministerial bureaucrats and Wilhelm II's advisers on social policy. In these years the state was trying to nip potential situations of conflict in the bud, settling industrial disputes in the factory either by negotiations at workers' committee level on the eve of a strike or by arbitration in state arbitration boards following the outbreak of a strike. The Ruhr mine-owners, however, utterly refused to negotiate with the miners' delegation and in the years 1890–3 followed a different course: strike insurance, closed door agreements to prevent a high fluctuation of workers, agreements on the expulsion of agitators from all the Ruhr mines and harsh sanctions against the strikers. These measures were intended to re-establish the employers' control over their workers which had been shaken by the strike, and stabilize a quasi-military relationship of subordination based on orders and unconditional obedience.

At the end of 1889, on express instructions from Bismarck, the Rhenish-Westphalian authorities had been obliged to abandon their role as mediator, a policy which had in fact been initially effective. Therefore in the early 1890s the situation described by the Essen chamber of commerce in 1889 as the normal and desirable circumstances in the case of strikes in other sectors could also be applied to industrial disputes in the Ruhr mines, namely, that the role of the state was confined to maintaining 'law and order'.[16]

Beyond the Rhineland and Westphalia the end of the *Sozialistengesetz* similarly coincided with a rigorous counter-offensive from the newly formed employers' associations and in particular from the metalworking industry, the masters' corporations and the established industrialists' organizations. To them the most effective means of strike prevention and employer protection was to crush the union organizations by mass lock-outs, the dismissal of active unionists, subsequently barred from any means of employment – for the rest of their lives ideally – by the widespread circulation of 'lists of agitators', and by 'press-ganging' their 'own' workers into leaving the trade unions and signing anti-union pledges. A final method, applied in the metalworking industry in Hamburg in 1888 and in Berlin in 1890, was to gain full control and a monopoly over labour recruitment. This was done by labour exchanges, operated by the employers themselves, a type of disciplinary office which relieved the individual industrialists of the irksome and time-consuming process of 'vetting' a worker in search of employment. The system proved an indispensable aid in labour disputes since it allowed the exclusion of workers who had a record of previous involvement in strikes or lock-outs. Notably in the campaign against the first German May Day celebrations in 1890 close co-operation was established between employers in the private and public sectors – thus blacklists of the agitators and 'contract-breakers' were exchanged between the employers' associations in the metalworking industry and the directors of the Prussian military and railway workshops. Moreover, as a means of 'defending civil order' from the 'onslaught of social democracy' this hostility could count on the broad support of 'national' public opinion. Under the conditions of the slump which continued into 1895 these measures did not remain without effect. Even in a socialist stronghold like Hamburg the number of organized workers fell by about two-thirds between 1890 and 1895.[17]

III

For the German trade union movement the decades between the expiry of the *Sozialistengesetz* on 1 October 1890 and the outbreak of the First World War were an overall period of turbulent expansion. In 1891 the Free Trade Unions had 277,659 members. After a period of decline and gradual recovery, membership soared from 1896 onwards, passing the one million mark in 1904 to reach a peak of 2,548,763 in the last year of peace, 1913. Industrial disputes became a part of everyday life. However, at the same time, as from 1905 and originating in the printing industry, 'armed peace' – regulations on collective agreements – gained increasing momentum in most of the trades and in the small and medium-sized businesses in the processing industries.

Thus by the end of 1913 the working conditions of some 1·4 million workers were guaranteed by collective agreement, over 80 per cent of whom were in addition covered by arbitration boards to settle disputes resulting from the application of the agreements. As part of an overall socialist subculture tending to cover all walks of life, the unions now began to integrate themselves into the class society of Imperial Germany. They now had new, satisfying fields of activity within the existing state system: they had a role to play in the state social insurance institutions, in particular in the autonomous local health insurance schemes, in the jurisdiction and arbitration activities of the industrial courts, in the administration of local employment bureaux with parity representation, the expansion of which had been fostered by the Prussian Ministry of Trade as a means of containing unemployment. Further, the unions had a limited degree of responsibility in municipal poor relief schemes and finally they worked in close co-operation with the trade supervisory authorities in applying the safety provisions and in the legal advisory service of the workers' secretariats.

There were, however, some very obvious clouds on the horizon. All attempts up to 1914 to organize the rural workers, the white- and blue-collar workers in the large Reich and state service industries as well as the new class of commercial and technical employees had failed, not least since the state had been pulling in the opposite direction. This ranged from a ban on strikes for agricultural labourers east of the Elbe and a prohibition for railway workers to combine in 'anti-establishment' associations to the social privileges for clerks and 'private officials' in the insurance law for white-collar employees of 1911. The combined countervailing force of legal restrictions, state administrative measures and the anti-unionist strategies of the employers in Imperial Germany is reflected in particular in the dramatic rise in membership of both the *Deutsche Landarbeiter Verband* (German Rural Workers' Association) and the *Deutsche Eisenbahner Verband* (German Railwaymen's Association) after the November Revolution of 1918: from 21,470 in the first half of 1914 to over 600,000 at the end of 1919 for the rural workers and from a mere few hundreds before the war to some 345,000 for the railwaymen. In 1914 the system of collective bargaining had not yet penetrated into those sectors which formed the backbone of the German economy: agriculture, mining, heavy industry, the large chemical industries, the electrical and engineering industries, commerce, transport, insurance and banking. From 1905 in the large metalworking, electrical and engineering factories the growth of the 'factory associations', dependent on the industrialists and committed to industrial peace, often coincided with the destruction of the union shop steward network and seemed to have cut off union access to workers in the iron works and chemical companies for ever. In certain sectors, such as the Saar and Mansfeld mining areas, in the Prussian-Hessian State Railway Company, then the world's largest employer, and on the farms and estates east of the Elbe, it was only by using the conspiratorial methods developed under the *Sozialistengesetz* that trade unionists could continue their work – at a time when printers, construction workers, carpenters, painters and tailors were all covered by national collective wage agreements. The labour market for skilled workers was still dominated by the employment bureaux biased towards the employers, although in fear of the intervention of Reich legislation they had increasingly relaxed the harassment of politically 'undesirable' union workers. At local level the three-class electoral system stood in the way of civil equality for the workers, preventing them from having an effective say in local affairs. The 'democratization of honorary offices' stopped at the point where the state's security interests seemed involved. As a rule workers were therefore not elected as lay assessors or members of a jury and up to the outbreak of war in 1914 the Prussian government denied Social Democrats recognition as members of school deputations or as town councillors in municipal authorities. As late as 1896 the Prussian Ministry of Trade in a secret decree forbade industrial supervisory officers all contact with union committees of appeal, which, in the minister's opinion, used the 'unearthing and discussion of certain grievances' for the main purpose of 'serving the interests of their party, stirring up the workers and sowing discontent far and wide'. And in 1911 the Reich government used the passing of the *Reichsversicherungsordnung* (Reich Insurance Regulation) to remove the 'rule of the reds' over the local health insurance schemes by limiting the voting rights of the workers' representatives. For the Reich leadership and the Prussian state government up to 1914 the containment of the socialist labour movement had absolute priority over the policy of furthering reform, on the basis of which middle-class social reformers gradually hoped to integrate the working class.[18]

The main target of state policy vis-à-vis the unions in particular remained the containment of the socialist labour movement and the prevention of its strike activities. To protect strike-breakers and the employers in an industrial dispute was considered the task of a policy which was to maintain the political system. Conservative bureaucrats and judicial authorities saw the pact between the authorities, the courts and the employers as a joint effort to defend the state system and the social order and therefore quite legitimate and in fact almost a matter of course. The bias against the working class in the judicial system and the war of the police against all socialist organizations including the Free Trade Unions were part and parcel of the social reality of the time. The oft repeated demand for impartiality in the judiciary and official neutrality in industrial disputes could scarcely influence the daily activities of the administration and the judges.

In Imperial Germany freedom of combination was not a basic social right but – according to the *Reichsgericht* in 1889 – 'a privilege in criminal law'. In 1869 the *Gewerbeordnung* (Industrial Code) of the North German Federation had lifted the individual states' ban on combination and strikes for industrial workers with the exception of agricultural labourers, railwaymen, sailors and apprentices. This regulation was adopted by the Reich in section 152 of the *Reichsgewerbeordnung* in 1871. In the opinion of the Supreme Court of the Reich this presented an exception to the provisions of criminal law since an act of coercion was thereby not liable to prosecution.

Stoppages were legal but not exactly legitimate. Combination was tolerated but did not merit protection. Any union member could opt out as he wished, leaving the union with no right to claim or sue for unpaid dues or the return of strike pay. In Imperial Germany every employer could prohibit his employees from joining certain trade unions. He could dismiss an employee on the grounds of union membership and, as a deterrent, he could make this sanction public; his rights of dismissal were unbounded. The employer could even place a dismissed worker's name on a blacklist, thus making it impossible for him to find a job in his profession in either the short or long term within the sphere of influence of the employers' association in question. As long as there were appropriate reasons for the blacklisting and the worker was not entirely cut off from all means of making a livelihood, the employer's act of taking the law into his own hands was not interpreted by the courts as an offence against public morality for which compensation was to be granted. The police authorities often encouraged this harassment by granting employers access to the membership lists of the local union branches or to reports on the supervision of union meetings. On occasion they even went so far as to press the employers to dismiss active unionists. The nationalized industries of the Reich and the states were out-and-out strongholds of the repression of union agitation. And in the last decades before the war the Prussian Ministry of the Interior used all the indirect means at its disposal to repress and check union influence, by giving support to the 'yellow' labour movements and purging the veterans' associations of those members who refused to leave the Free Trade Unions.[19]

Despite warnings from middle-class social reformers that it was discrediting itself as a system of class domination, the state accepted the high political costs of this failure to protect the right to free combination and of the active participation of state authorities in the harassment of organized workers. So up to the end of the Wilhelmine era the federated governments turned down every Reichstag motion to guarantee combination at least at the level of protection which had been laid down in the provisions of section 153 of the *Gewerbeordnung* in 1869 to prevent the closed shop system. Similarly, in 1908 and again in 1911, the Prussian ministries and the *Reichsämter* rejected the Reichstag proposal to grant state-sponsored contracts only to those companies which represented their employees' right of combination and accepted the principle of collective bargaining. A clause of this kind would have totally undermined the anti-unionist practices of heavy industry and the dockyards, both dependent on armament contracts.[20]

Thus outside those sectors of industry covered by agreements union membership could already imply a considerable degree of risk; this was even more true of active participation in an industrial dispute. Under a court decision approved by the *Reichsgericht* in October 1890, even the call for a strike or a boycott could lead to proceedings on charge of blackmail. To make a public call to down tools without reference to the observance of the terms of notice was considered incitement to others to break their contracts. As the *Reichsgericht* discovered at the end of 1889, such an act could lead to imprisonment on grounds of resistance to the law. If the action was considered by the court as the 'use of physical force', a 'threat', a 'slight' to someone's 'honour' or 'slander' – criminal offences under section 153 of the *Gewerbeordnung* – anyone deemed guilty of encouraging those who had not followed the strike call to come out on strike could be sentenced to prison for up to three months. These were rather hollow grounds for an offence and had nothing to do with the principles of criminal law. As a result cases of contemptuous spitting at the strike-breakers, jeering and shouts of 'blackleg' could be pursued through the official channels if the insulted worker failed to lodge a private complaint. A particularly malicious campaign was waged by the police against pickets. Following experiments in 1891–2 with police regulations which laid down a general prohibition on trespassing in the vicinity of mines and industrial installations and the proceedings against pickets from 1897 on the grounds of 'public mischief', in 1900 the Prussian Minister of the Interior finally discovered an effective way of bypassing the *Reichsgericht*'s ruling in favour of picketing. Henceforth any police officer could order off and even arrest a picket who showed resistance on the grounds that he was obstructing traffic. A mere statement from the police officer in court that the order had been made to 'maintain the safety and smooth flow of traffic on public roads' was sufficient justification of his action. In cases where despite the union leaders' warnings and steps of precaution strikers and blacklegs nevertheless came to blows in the course of a stoppage, the courts often applied the law relating to breach of the peace and imposed exemplary prison sentences.[21]

The bias in weighing up the evidence and establishing the grounds for sentence, the severity of the penalties – designed to have a deterrent effect – and the judiciary's efforts to fill in gaps in the legislation was clear evidence, not only to social democratic critics but also to middle-class social reformers, that justice was often administered with a strong class bias. In many cases the judiciary extended its interpretation of the law in such a way as retrospectively to enforce a tightening of the right of combination which had been proposed by the Reich government and had been rejected by the Reichstag with an overwhelming majority in the years 1891 and 1899. This was compatible with the subjectively sincere conviction of the judge that he was not bending the law but for reasons of state security interpreting it in such an albeit rather questionable, yet legitimate way that acts which seemed to endanger the state and social order would not remain unpunished. The judiciary moreover knew that they had the full backing of the Prussian Minister of Justice on this matter. The minister had left no doubt about the interests of the state government in rapid and 'energetic' proceedings in cases of strikes. This could be clearly seen in his instructions to the public prosecutors, public statements before the Prussian *Landtag*, the publication of test cases in the judicial ministerial gazette and his criteria for political selection when nominating and promoting judges and public prosecutors. And finally their conscience was at rest in interpreting the law in this way since they were ignorant of the modern labour movement and simply accepted the social prejudices of their environment without question. So, much to the concern of the unions, public debate on increased protection for those willing to work at the end of the 1890s and during the last few years of peace led to a considerable tightening-up of the administration of justice.[22]

Behind all the various measures implemented by the Prussian ministries and the authorities to check the expansion of the Free Trade Unions as far as possible and hinder their publicity and organizational work again lies the conviction that bourgeois society had to be guarded against the threat of socialism. The unions therefore found themselves confronted with countless forms of police harassment. Their meetings were kept under police surveillance, their officials were spied on, their younger members were reported as Social Democrats to the military authorities before call-up, their meeting rooms were seized, while open-air meetings and May Day demonstrations were banned on the flimsiest of grounds, members distributing leaflets were penalized for alleged disturbance of the Sunday peace, innkeepers lived in fear of reprisals for putting up union publicity and information posters, union speakers and editors were reported to the state prosecutors on the slightest grounds for defamation of employers or state officials.

In the state's intervention in industrial disputes this offensive against the socialist labour movement frequently blurred the distinction between the state's duty to maintain public order on the one hand and siding with the employers on the other. Actions ranged from a police officer ordering pickets off a deserted street for being an obstacle to the traffic on instructions from the employers, to the Kaiser himself who commented on the suppression of the Mansfeld miners' strike in 1909: 'Splendid indeed! If our words fall on deaf ears, action will not! Orders must be obeyed, la discipline avant tout.'[23]

Nevertheless, the Reich government and ministerial bureaucrats were always aware that the interests of the public authorities and the employers' associations in the field of union policy were not fully identical. To identify fully with the employers would be bound to lead to conflict, not only with the Christian and Hirsch-Duncker Trades Associations, but also with the majority in the Reichstag and the reformist wing of the educated middle classes. It would also accelerate the workers' alienation from the pro-establishment parties. Victory for the employers achieved by the state doing all within its power to back them up, even calling in the troops, would inevitably result in the radicalization of the beaten working class and a defeat for a monarchical system. It would moreover be a considerable strain on the loyalty of the common soldier who would be sure to feel abused as an advocate of employers' interests. So up to 1914 the Prussian Minister of the Interior firmly insisted that troops should only be called in if and when the situation had got completely out of police control; he warned the authorities not to yield too lightly to the 'employers' regular insistence on calling in the troops'.[24]

Highly distrustful of the employers' tactics, he and the Prussian Minister of Trade had in 1892 already refused to give their approval to employers' strike insurance in the Ruhr mines, insisting that they would only do so when it had been laid down in the statutes that mandatory arbitration proceedings would be opened in the case of industrial disputes.[25] In 1903 the Ministry of Trade refused the admission of the Prussian masters' corporations to the employers' federations on the grounds of their aggressive character.[26] And a year later the secretary in the *Reichsamt* of the Interior, Count Posadowsky, expressed concern that the developing concentration of power in the hands of the industrial employers' associations would increase social tension. He feared that the repercussions of this would erase the ideological differences between the 'social democratic' and the 'non-social democratic' unions which could lead to the development of strong industrial federations. And finally, it might mean that the 'labour movement would gradually become more and more oriented against capitalism'.[27] In 1905 the Prussian state government did not hesitate to enter into a hefty dispute with west German heavy industry over the Ruhr miners' strike. Against the will of the proprietors of the mines, the government tried to get arbitration proceedings off the ground in the interests of the 'national economy' and the 'common good' and despite furious protests from the heavy industrial lobby a Bill on conditions of work in the mines was introduced in the Prussian *Landtag*.[28]

All in all, however, the state's efforts to extend its influence over the settling of industrial disputes remained few and far between, even after 1890. The Reich government did admittedly reaffirm their commitment to the state's duty to 'prevent threatening labour disputes as far as possible or nip them in the bud by means of a further extension of legislation'. Therefore, contrary to the wishes of the leading industrial federations, it gave the go-ahead to the Reichstag decision to extend the powers of arbitration of the industrial courts in 1901 – although their activity in this field remained limited up to 1914.[29]

The days when state 'organization of labour' could provide a counter-weight to the unions were gone. The obligatory workers' committees in the Prussian mining industry set up in 1905 remained either completely inef-fective or were taken over by active union workers who used the limited scope of the committees to promote the interests of their unions.[30] The Reich government's Bill on *Arbeitskammern* (chambers of labour), based on parity of representation from both sides of industry and initially intro-duced in 1908, was finally rejected in 1911.

This followed years of wrangling on the issue of the eligibility of union officials. The majority in the Reichstag was of the opinion that these institutions could not possibly achieve their objectives – to promote social peace and to act as an arbitration board in industrial disputes – without the participation of experienced trade unionists.[31] Attempts to de-politicize the union movement by educating the workers and moulding them into peace-ful, down to earth representatives of the interests of their respective professions also bit the dust. When drawing up the *Bürgerliche Gesetzbuch* (Civil Code) the Reich government and the Prussian state government had already absolutely refused to further the industrial and craft associations by drawing up liberal regulations on the private right of association, to 'wrench the working population from the Utopia of social democracy and win them over for the existing state and social order'.[32] However, the Trade Union Bill, announced in January 1904 and brought before the Reichstag in November 1906, was unacceptable to unions of all creeds. Its provisions on union liability, the authorities' rights of control and intervention, the restriction of the unions' scope to no more than supporting its members and representing their direct professional interests and the ban on mutual financial assistance between the federations, indispensable in large-scale strikes, would have placed the very existence of the unions at the whim of the state supervisory authorities. In view of the strong opposition the Reich government gave up any further attempt to introduce legislation controlling the unions.[33]

In the final years before the war the Reichstag tabled a number of resolutions on the protection of the right of combination and the estab-lishment of a Reich arbitration office – all to no avail. This illustrated not only the growing influence on Parliament of the working-class voter and the middle-class social reformer, but also the Reichstag's own impotence. On the other hand, the fervent campaign of the *Centralverband Deutscher Industrieller* (Central Federation of German Industrialists) from 1910 for a greater degree of 'protection for workers willing to work' made it quite clear to the unions that wide circles of German industry had by no means come to terms with the existence of independent and powerful trade unions. Army intervention in the Ruhr miners' strike in 1912, the administration's harder line in dealing with strikers, the severity of penalties and finally the Reich government's plans to restrict the unions' publicity work and militant action within a general reform of criminal law seemed to suggest that in the summer of 1914 the time was nearly ripe for confrontation between the public authorities and the trade union movement. With mingled pessimism and optimism Ernst Francke, Secretary General of the *Gesellschaft für Soziale Reform* (Society for Social Reform), wrote in a confidential letter on 2 July 1914: 'I fear we shall have to go through another *Zuchthausvorlage* [penitentiary bill] before the road is clear for positive activity.'[34]

Notes: Chapter 20

1 cf. H.-J. Bieber, *Gewerkschaften in Krieg und Revolution*, Vol. 1 (Hamburg, 1981), 73ff. This essay is a continuation of the considerations in my article 'Zwischen Repression und Integration. Staat, Gewerkschaften und Arbeitskampf im kaiserlichen Deutschland', in K. Tenfelde and H. Volkmann (eds), *Streik. Zur Geschichte des Arbeitskampfes in Deutschland während der Industrialisierung* (Munich, 1981), 209–36.

2 cf. R. Köhne, *Nationalliberale und Koalitionsrecht* (Frankfurt a.M., 1977), 95–316; K. Saul, *Staat, Industrie und Arbeiterbewegung im Kaiserreich* (Düsseldorf, 1974), 283–394; T. Vormbaum, *Politik und Gesinderecht im 19. Jahrhundert* (Berlin, 1980), 102ff., 128ff., 372ff.

3 Memorandum dated 27 December 1884, printed in W. Schröder, 'Ein Gewerkschaftsgesetz des Bismarckstaats?', *Zeitschrift für Geschichtswissenschaft* 19 (1976): 310–21; on the development of the craft associations cf. the continuous reports of the Berlin Chief of Police, in R. Höhn, *Die vaterlandslosen Gesellen*, Vol. 1 (Opladen, 1964).

4 Judgement of 10 November 1887; for its enforcement cf. e.g. J. Schmöle, *Die sozialdemokratischen Gewerkschaften in Deutschland seit dem Erlasse des Sozialistengesetzes*, Vol. 1 (Jena, 1896), 131ff., 154ff., and W. Schultze, 'Öffentliches Vereinigungsrecht im Kaiserreich 1871–1908' (PhD. thesis, Frankfurt a.M., 1973), 407ff.

5 Printed in *Die Selbstverwaltung* 21 (22 May 1886): 165–6.

6 cf. e.g. W. Schröder, 'Buchdruckerbewegung, Kapital und Staat', *Beiträge zur Geschichte der Arbeiterbewegung* 9 (1967): 636–59; Schmöle, *Die sozialdemokratischen Gewerkschaften*, 139ff., 174ff., *Ministerialblatt für die gesamte innere Verwaltung* 50 (1889): 66ff.

7 cf. the recent publication by K. Tenfelde, *Sozialgeschichte der Bergarbeiterschaft an der Ruhr im 19. Jahrhundert*, 2nd rev. edn (Bonn, 1981), 573ff.; I. Costas, *Auswirkungen der Konzentration des Kapitals auf die Arbeiterklasse in Deutschland (1880–1914)* (Frankfurt a.M., 1981), 122ff.; W. Wittwer, 'Zur Taktik der herrschenden Klassen gegenüber dem Bergarbeiterstreik von 1889', in *Evolution und Revolution in der Weltgeschichte*, Vol. 2 (Berlin, 1976), 541–64.

8 Regional authorities: H. G. Kirchhoff, *Die staatliche Sozialpolitik im Ruhrbergbau 1871–1914* (Cologne/Opladen, 1958), 85 ff.; P. Rassow and K. E. Born, *Akten zur staatlichen Sozialpolitik in Deutschland 1890–1914* (Wiesbaden, 1959), 34ff.; G. Adelmann (ed.), *Quellensammlung zur Geschichte der sozialen Betriebsverfassung*, Vol. 1 (Bonn, 1960), 169ff., 218ff. Ministerial bureaucracy: Gamp memorandum: 'Die Ausstandsbewegung der Grubenarbeiter und die Massregeln zu ihrer Bekämpfung' and the discussions of a committee of experts from some Prussian ministries and the *Reichsamt* of the Interior, December 1889/January 1890 in Geheimes Staatsarchiv (GStA) Berlin, Rep. 84a/11 400 and 11 401; Zentrales Staatsarchiv Merseburg (ZStA II), Rep.. 120 BB VII, 1 no. 3, Vol. 8 and 9. On Wilhelm II's advisers: H. Rothfels, *Theodor Lohmann und die Kampfjahre der staatlichen Sozialpolitik* (Berlin, 1927), 96ff.; J. C. G. Röhl (ed.), *Philipp Eulenburgs Politische Korrespondenz*, Vol. 1 (Boppard, 1976), 406ff.; Wilhelm II's notes dated 21 January 1890, in *Propyläen-Weltgeschichte*, Vol. 10 (Berlin, 1933ff.), facsimile following p. 160.

9 Industrial supervision: Rothfels, *Theodor Lohmann*, 110ff., and S. Poerschke, *Die Entwicklung der Gewerbeaufsicht in Deutschland* (Jena, 1911). Industrial courts: A. v. Saldern, 'Gewerbegerichte im wilhelminischen Deutschland', in *Wissenschaft, Wirtschaft und Technik* (Munich, 1969), 190ff.

10 On 21 December 1889 (see note 8 above); on its origins: C. Koehne, *Die Arbeitsordnungen*

im deutschen Gewerberecht (Berlin, 1901), 48ff., and Kirchhoff, *Die staatliche Sozialpolitik*, 106ff.

11 cf. ibid., 118ff., and Adelmann, *Quellensammlung*, 515; in general ZStA II, Rep. 120 BB VII, 1 no. 24, Vols. 1–3 and adh. 1.

12 On the establishment and activity of the central bureau cf. ZStA II, Rep. 120 BB VII. 1, no. 38, Vols. 1–3, and *Schriften der Zentralstelle*, Vol. 1 (Berlin, 1893ff.).

13 Lengthy reports in ZStA II, Rep. 120 BB VII, 3 no. 23, Vol. 1. Interim results: M. Quarck, 'Ortsstatuten über Lohnzahlung an Minderjährige', *Blätter für soziale Praxis* 27 (5 July 1893): 3ff. Origins: GStA Berlin, Rep. 84a/11408 and 11409. Criticism: A. Bebel, 'Die Gewerbeordnungsnovelle', *Neue Zeit* 9/II (1891): 331–2.

14 Notes dated 22 January 1890, printed in G. Frhr. v. Eppstein (ed.), *Fürst Bismarcks Entlassung* (Berlin, 1920), 148ff.; on the application of this cf. I. Costas, 'Anfänge der Partizipation im Industriebetrieb. Die Arbeiterausschüsse 1889 bis 1920', in J. Bergmann *et al.* (eds), *Geschichte als politische Wissenschaft* (Stuttgart, 1979), 335–78.

15 cf. I. Jastrow, 'Die Erfahrungen mit den deutschen Gewerbegerichten', *Jahrbücher für Nationalökonomie und Statistik* 69 (1897): 374ff.

16 Quotation taken from the *Jahresbericht der Handelskammer für den Kreis Essen 1888* (Essen, 1889), 12. On the employers' tactics following the strike, see the annual reports of the mine-owners' association; P. Osthold, *Die Geschichte des Zechenverbandes* (Berlin, 1934), 26ff., and M. Kealey, 'Kampfstrategien der Unternehmerschaft im Ruhrbergbau seit dem Bergarbeiterstreik von 1889', in H. Mommsen and U. Borsdorf (eds), *Glück auf, Kameraden!* (Cologne, 1979), 175–97 (183ff.).

17 According to the extensive collection of material in Staatsarchiv Hamburg, Politische Polizei S 68100 Vol. 1 and 3, and the reports in *Der Arbeitgeber* 1 (1890–1) and the documentation in *Ein Komplott gegen die deutsche Arbeiterklasse* (London, 1891); on the May Day celebrations the recent publication by W. D. Hund, 'Der 1. Mai 1890', in J. Berlin (ed.), *Das andere Hamburg* (Cologne, 1981), 119ff.

18 On the various aspects cf. K. Schönhoven, 'Gewerkschaftliches Organisationsverhalten im Wilhelminischen Reich', in W. Conze and U. Engelhardt (eds), *Arbeiter im Industrialisierungsprozess* (Stuttgart, 1979), 403–21; H. Volkmann, 'Organisation und Konflikt', in ibid., 422–38; Costas, *Auswirkungen der Konzentration*, ch. 5; Saul, *Staat, Industrie und Arbeiterbewegung*, ch. 2; K. Mattheier, *Die Gelben* (Düsseldorf, 1973); J. Flemming, *Landwirtschaftliche Interessen und Demokratie* (Bonn, 1978), 315–36; J. Kocka, 'Vorindustrielle Faktoren in der deutschen Industrieentwicklung', in M. Stürmer (ed.), *Das kaiserliche Deutschland* (Düsseldorf, 1970), 265–86; A. v. Saldern, 'Wilhelminische Gesellschaft und Arbeiterklasse', *Internationale Wissenschaftliche Korrespondenz* 13 (1977): 469–505; idem, *Vom Einwohner zum Bürger* (Berlin, 1973), esp. 302ff.; idem, 'Sozialdemokratische Kommunalpolitik in wilhelminischer Zeit', in K.-H. Nassmacher (ed.), *Kommunalpolitik der Sozialdemokratie* (Bonn, 1977), 18–62; H. K. Weitensteiner, *Karl Flesch—Kommunalpolitik in Frankfurt am Main* (Frankfurt a.M., 1976); W. Bocks, *Die badische Fabrikinspektion* (Freiburg, 1978), 56ff., 172ff. (1896 quotation: p. 186); M. Martiny, 'Die politische Bedeutung der gewerkschaftlichen Arbeitersekretariate vor dem Ersten Weltkrieg', in H. O. Vetter (ed.), *Vom Sozialistengesetz zur Mitbestimmung* (Cologne, 1975), 153–74.

19 cf. Schultze, *Öffentliches Vereinigungsrecht*, 557ff.; Saul, *Staat, Industrie und Arbeiterbewegung*, 66ff.; idem, 'Der Staat und die "Mächte des Umsturzes"', *Archiv für Sozialgeschichte* 12 (1972): 293–350 (302ff.); idem, 'Der "Deutsche Kriegerbund"', *Militärgeschichtliche Mitteilungen* 2 (1969): 120ff., and W. Lübeck, 'Die Rolle der Kriegervereine im System des preussisch-deutschen Militarismus bis zum Ausbruch des 1. Weltkrieges' (PhD. thesis, Halle-Wittenberg, 1974), Annex, pp. 43–4.

20 cf. Saul, *Staat, Industrie und Arbeiterbewegung*, 63–4, and Costas, *Auswirkungen der Konzentration*, 225–6.

21 cf. Schultze, *Öffentliches Vereinigungsrecht*, 631–750; Saul, *Staat, Industrie und Arbeiterbewegung*, 211–69.

22 cf. ibid., 189–91, and examples on the influence of public opinion: *Die Not des vierten Standes*, by a medical doctor (Leipzig, 1894), 180ff., and *Jahresbericht der Ortsverwaltung Berlin des Deutschen Metallarbeiter-Verbandes 1913* (Berlin, 1914), 83.

23 The quotation is taken from: H. Freydank, 'Die Randbemerkungen Wilhelms II.', in *Archivalische Forschungen zur Geschichte der deutschen Arbeiterbewegung*, Vol. 1 (Berlin,

1954), 238ff.; in general: Saul, *Staat, Industrie und Arbeiterbewegung*, 293ff., and idem, 'Der Kampf um das Landproletariat', *Archiv für Sozialgeschichte* 15 (1975): 163–208 (180ff.).

24 Decree dated 30 October 1901, in ZStA I, RdI 7005; on the planning of military intervention in general: B.-F. Schulte, *Die deutsche Armee 1900–1914* (Düsseldorf, 1977), 267ff., 535ff. On the very varied density of the police forces cf. e.g. the 1912 table in M. Neefe (ed.), *Jahrbuch Deutscher Städte* 21 (Breslau, 1916): 238ff.

25 Decree dated 14 March 1892, printed in *Sozialpolitisches Centralblatt* 1 (1892): 192–3.

26 cf. Saul, *Staat, Industrie and Arbeiterbewegung*, 435, n.15.

27 Immediate report dated 17 May 1904, in ZStA II, Rep. 89 H XIII, Gen. 47, Vol. 2.

28 cf. K. Saul, 'Staatsintervention und Arbeitskampf im Wilhelminischen Reich 1905–1914', in H.-U. Wehler (ed.), *Sozialgeschichte Heute* (Göttingen, 1974), 479–94 (487ff.).

29 Posadowsky vote, dated 15 June 1901, in GStA Berlin, III, Hauptabt, no. 1744; running commentary on arbitration activity in *Das Gewerbegericht* 6 (1901–2ff.).

30 cf. Adelmann, *Quellensammlung*, 361ff., and E. Kroker, 'Arbeiterausschüsse im Ruhrbergbau zwischen 1905 und 1914', *Der Anschnitt* 6 (1978): 204–15.

31 cf. K. E. Born, *Staat und Sozialpolitik seit Bismarcks Sturz* (Wiesbaden, 1957), 226ff.

32 cf. P. Kögler, *Arbeiterbewegung und Vereinsrecht* (Berlin, 1974), 66ff. (quotation on p. 82: anonymous proposal from the second Civil Code committee 1891); cf. also T. Vormbaum, *Die Rechtsfähigkeit der Vereine im 19. Jahrhundert* (Berlin, 1976), 131ff.

33 cf. Saul, *Staat, Industrie und Arbeiterbewegung*, 33–5, and Köhne, *Nationalliberale und Koalitionsrecht*, 199–201.

34 cf. Saul, *Staat, Industrie und Arbeiterbewegung*, 269ff., 306ff., and on the middle-class social reformers: U. Ratz, *Sozialreform und Arbeiterschaft* (Berlin, 1980), 85ff., 214ff. (quotation p. 194, n. 266: letter to August Pieper).

Part Six

Trade Unions and the Political Labour Movement

21 Trade Unions and the Labour Party in Britain

JAY M. WINTER

The current state of play in the study of trade unionism and the development of the Labour Party in the years 1900–18 reflects important changes in the way British historians have come to understand the relation between working-class politics and working-class culture. Recent trends in labour history in this period may be sketched briefly in three parts: first, in terms of what we know about the organization and activity of the institutions comprising the labour movement; second, in terms of what we know, but cannot agree about, which is how to specify the political meaning of working-class consciousness; and third, in terms of what we do not yet know but hope to discover in the course of research in progress.

I

On the first level, labour historians have provided over the past two decades a clear and detailed account of the organizational history of the trade union movement in the generation prior to the First World War. As many of the essays in this volume demonstrate, we can now build on a substantial set of individual union histories which provide the essential record of the struggle for recognition, of inter- and intra-union conflict, especially over the question of the tension between craft and general unionism, and of strike activity.[1]

As yet, though, there is no complete account of the process whereby the Labour Party broke the old Liberal hold over the political allegiance of trade union leaders and rank and file. The outlines of the story can be gathered from Henry M. Pelling's study of the socialist revival and 'conversion of the unions' in the 1890s[2] and in John Saville's account of the background to the Taff Vale judgments of 1899–1901, which moved the Trades Union Congress to sponsor a Labour Representation Committee.[3] This organization's brief six-year life as the first form of the Labour Party is surveyed in Frank W. Bealey and Henry M. Pelling's *Labour and Politics 1900–1906*.[4] The local and regional character of much of the pioneering work in independent labour politics is still largely unknown or unpublished. Important exceptions are Edward P. Thompson's study of Tom Maguire and the Independent Labour Party in Yorkshire,[5] Roy G. Gregory's analysis of the recruitment of the Miners' Federation of Great Britain to the ranks of the

Labour Party,[6] and the work of P. R. Thompson, among others, on London.[7]

Invaluable work in filling in the story of the links between trade unionism and independent labour representation on the local level has been done by the editors of the indispensable *Dictionary of Labour Biography*[8] and the *Warwick Guide to British Labour Periodicals*.[9] The latter volume has opened up important areas of research fuelled by the rich mine of information to be found in the labour press.

It still remains true, though, that there are few full-length studies of the careers of the major trade union leaders of this period. Dona Torr's *Tom Mann and his Times*, published as long ago as 1956,[10] and a more recent biography of Ben Tillett[11] are the isolated exceptions that prove the rule. The dearth of archival sources on the early lives and work of men of the stature of Robert Smillie of the Miners' Federation in part accounts for this gap in the literature.

The leadership of the Labour Party in its formative years, has been much better served by biographers. Not one but three scholars have recently published book-length studies of Keir Hardie.[12] A major biography of Ramsay MacDonald appeared in 1971, but its treatment of the years before 1918 is disappointingly thin.[13] Ross McKibbin has provided a brief vignette of MacDonald in these years, which must serve until a fuller study is undertaken.[14] Arthur Henderson's life surprisingly still awaits a scholarly biography. Beyond an early portrait by Mary Agnes Hamilton, now long out of date, there is only a brief but penetrating essay (also by Ross McKibbin) on Henderson as leader of the Labour Party.[15]

Among the second order of party activists, socialist intellectuals have attracted considerable biographical attention,[16] which some believe to be far out of proportion to their significance within the Labour Party or the labour movement as a whole.[17] Still, it must be remembered that the appearance of many Fabians among the new generation of Labour Members of Parliament elected in 1945 was in part the stimulus for much of the early historical study of the Fabian Society and its articulate spokesmen and fellow travellers.[18]

With the opening fifteen years ago of the Labour Party archives in Transport House, one of Ernie Bevin's legacies to the labour movement, it became possible to reconsider in detail the question of the interaction between trade unionism and Labour politics in the early years of the Labour Party. The first historian to exploit this archive systematically and sympathetically was McKibbin, whose *Evolution of the Labour Party 1910–1924* supersedes everything previously written on the party in this period.[19] As we shall elaborate below, some of the assumptions on which this important work rests are controversial, but there is no doubt about the significance of the author's achievement in setting out the full record of the party's struggle for survival in its early years. The picture McKibbin presents of a defensive and hesitant party in the prewar period, dedicated to no objective other than the election of Labour M.P.s, is a powerful and convincing one. Does this limited outlook and strategy reflect organizational and electoral or primarily sociological and cultural constraints? Were those limits not lifted during the

First World War? These are the questions to be addressed in the second part of this essay. In sketching answers to them, we can see the lines which divide current interpretations of this important and turbulent period of labour history.

II

It is in his answers to these questions that McKibbin offers an interpretation of the political meaning of class consciousness which is completely at odds with a number of central assumptions embedded in the work of earlier labour historians. McKibbin does not for a moment deny the existence of class consciousness in early twentieth-century Britain,[20] but in his hands the concept takes on a profoundly revisionist character. Class sentiment, in his work, becomes the shoals against which socialist and progressive hopes foundered rather than the rock on which their potential or real power rested. To him, the mass support of the Labour Party in its early years was indeed based 'upon a highly developed class consciousness and intense class loyalties',[21] but these notions had no intrinsic socialist content, latent or actual, and very frequently, an anti-socialist bias. In the period of Ramsay MacDonald and Keir Hardie, then, the Labour Party was less the party of socialism than, in the French phrase, the party of ouvrierism.

Within this overall interpretation, McKibbin's view about the impact of the First World War on the Labour Party and its ideological character is clear. The growth in the power of trade unions during the war inexorably diminished their tolerance of middle-class socialists, whose organizational defeat was fixed in the form of the 1918 party constitution. So much for Clause Four of the 1918 party constitution, which committed it in principle 'To secure for the producers by hand or brain the full fruits of their industry' through 'the common ownership of the means of production'. Window-dressing at worst, stirring rhetoric at best, but inevitably made hollow by the intrinsic anti-middle-class and anti-socialist character of the class consciousness of much of the leadership (and by implication, much of the rank and file) of the trade union movement. Hence McKibbin's conclusion to this work: no one can claim that the Labour Party failed to serve the cause of socialism, because as a trade union party 'it was never designed to do so'.[22]

What McKibbin has done, in effect, is to draw us back to where we should be in the study of labour history, that is, to the questions of the nature of class consciousness and its political manifestations. Anyone who has read more than a few pages in this field will have realized that this is an area of persistent confusion and controversy, not only in terms of the definition of 'class consciousness', but also because historians rarely agree as to what constitutes valid evidence of its existence. To appreciate the extent of McKibbin's reinterpretation of labour politics in the period of the First World War, it may be useful to offer a brief sketch of four aspects or kinds of class-related sentiments, which previous historians have seen as informing militancy and radical thought within the labour movement.

The first may be termed 'craft consciousness', or the recognition of the similarity of interests shared by men in the same trade, line of work, or level of 'skill', however that last ambiguous category is defined. James Hinton has shown the explosive potential of such feelings among engineering and other metalworkers in the war years.[23] The second is 'class awareness', or a sense of the adversary nature of the interests of groups of manual labourers and the interests of those who do not work with their hands. Much of the work of E. P. Thompson has centred on the emergence of such attitudes and the conflicts which arose inevitably from them.[24] The third comes under the heading of what may be termed 'political class consciousness'. This level of understanding goes beyond (but does not eclipse completely) the first two meanings of class, in that through their struggles at the point of production and elsewhere, working-men come to sense a unity of the divisions between antagonistic groups as they are expressed in the sphere of state power as in industrial life. Much writing about the Chartist period and the later reform of the franchise identifies such ideas as powerful motive forces behind radical agitation.[25] The fourth may be termed 'revolutionary class consciousness', which describes the state of mind of those workers who can envision a different kind of society from the one in which they live, and who work to seize the moment to eradicate the barriers of property and poverty and to recast society as a whole in a new mould. In Marxist terms, 'revolutionary class consciousness' is both the means to and the outcome of the transformation of a 'class in itself' to a 'class for itself'. John Foster has identified elements of this stage of 'revolutionary class consciousness' among Oldham workers in the 1840s,[26] although his views have not gone unchallenged.[27]

This essay is not the place for a full examination of the nuances and ambiguities inherent in each of these definitions. For our purposes, what is important to note is the deep conviction of virtually all labour historians that the labour process itself breeds militancy and radicalism in the same way, in a sense, that a nuclear reactor breeds fissionable material: it may never explode, but its potential for eruption is ever-present. It is this assumption that McKibbin has challenged at its core. In his work, class consciousness is a term which need not entail any of the above notions. It is rather a term which describes attitudes which are defensive, negative, or apolitical. A class conscious stance thus becomes one of working-class suspicion of middle-class men and women arising out of a belief in the fundamental incompatability of the ideas and politics of men who do not share the same life experiences or the same way of earning a living, whether or not they are your allies or ostensible partners in the labour movement.

Let us consider just two examples of this line of reasoning as it applies to the relation between trade unions and the Labour Party in the war period. First, there is McKibbin's treatment of the antagonism between some members of the Independent Labour Party who opposed the First World War and patriotic trade unions who supported it. This conflict was resolved in the 1918 constitution in a way which was unfavourable to the ILP, a body which had attracted to its side many middle-class dissenters, previously Liberals whose 'appearance in the Labour movement', according to McKibbin, 'merely exaggerated the class-consciousness of some of the union leaders and damned the ILP even more in their eyes'.[28] Secondly, note the assumptions behind his account of trade union responses to the draft party constitution, formulated in 1917. Trade union objections are interpreted by McKibbin as 'obvious' proof that 'the class-conscious unions were preparing themselves against a putative army of middle-class socialists'.[29]

What we confront here is a profoundly revisionist interpretation of the political meaning of class consciousness under British conditions. Its fundamental premiss is that because of its working-class character, the Labour Party could not but be infused by the spirit of a defensive and politically inert working-class culture. Some objections to this argument will be raised below, but it is important to note how other recent work in the field of labour history has reinforced the view that class consciousness meant apathy and conservatism rather than militancy and socialism in early twentieth-century Britain.

In an important article, Gareth Stedman Jones has described the 'prevailing tone' of late nineteenth-century working-class culture in London as 'not one of political combativity, but of an enclosed and defensive conservatism'. This outlook was 'staunchly impervious to middle-class attempts to guide it'. The working class revealed by Charles Booth's social survey had as its 'dominant cultural institutions ... not the school, the evening class, the library, the friendly society, the church or the chapel, but the pub, the sporting paper, the race course and the music hall'.[30] By the 1880s and 1890s a distinctive working-class culture existed which was oriented towards the family and home rather than towards the trade and the workplace, which grew physically and socially much further apart. This 'culture of consolation' had as its popular spokesman the artistes of the music hall and in cinema, already an important leisure industry in 1914, the incomparable figure of Charlie Chaplin. According to Stedman Jones he is the archetypal figure of prewar working-class culture: decent, sentimental, doggedly persevering, constantly at sea in a storm not of his own creation. Frequently he is the victim of forces he does not understand or control, but despite which he manages somehow to survive. His is a world largely without politics, or in other words, without the belief that things can be different from what they are.[31]

Other studies of working-class leisure and popular entertainment reinforce the view that both ouvrierism and conservatism grew out of 'the mood and attitude of the masses'.[32] It is but a short step to the conclusion, stated by Stedman Jones, that the advent of the Labour Party 'marked not a breach but a culmination of this defensive culture'. Without a clear conception of the state or the political character of the struggle of organized labour, the labour movement in the late nineteenth century could not even begin to explore the legacy and achievements of the Chartists and working-class radicals of the pre-1850 period. Instead the emphasis

> shifted from power to welfare. Socialism, as Tom Mann defined it, meant the abolition of poverty. The founding moment of the Labour party was not revolution abroad or political upheaval at home, but a defensive solution to the employers' counter-offensive of the 1890s. The ending of

Britain's industrial monopoly did recreate an independent labour politics, as Engels had prophesied, but not in the way he had intended. The L.R.C. was the generalization of the structural role of the trade union into the form of a political party. It was not accountable directly to its constituency, but indirectly via the trade unions upon which its real power was based. Its mode of organization presumed mass passivity punctuated by occasional mobilization for the ballot box. As a form of political association it was not so much a challenge to the new working-class culture that had grown up since 1870 but an extension of it. If it sang Jerusalem it was not as a battlecry but as a hymn. De facto, it accepted not only capitalism, but monarchy, Empire, aristocracy and established religion as well. With the foundation of the Labour party, the now enclosed and defensive world of working-class culture had in effect achieved its apotheosis.[33]

From entirely different political perspectives, then, both Stedman Jones and McKibbin agree that in the Labour Party, the British working class got the party that it deserved.

The test of any historical approach to the problem of class consciousness is how well it describes the evidence of working-class attitudes and behaviour. The revisionism offered by McKibbin and other scholars does have force and substance, but when examined against the background of the war period, this kind of cultural determinism both oversimplifies events and ignores important discontinuities in the history of the British working class and the British labour movement. The first objection that needs to be raised is that these arguments reduce class consciousness to a feeling more appropriately termed class self-consciousness (or class rancour) and then imply that this particular perception of class position can be used to describe adequately the range of political loyalties and beliefs of the leadership and rank and file of both trade unions and the Labour Party. That working-class attitudes to politics have been culturally determined is probably true, in very sweeping terms, but that this determination moved in only one direction – towards caution and conservatism and against militancy and socialism – is not a plausible proposition, especially in the period of the First World War.

This is not to deny the longevity of the working-class tradition of rancorous rejection of anything tainted by contact with middle-class hands or the force of anti-intellectual sentiment in some quarters of the labour movement, then or now. It is rather to suggest that in this form the dismissal of the revolutionary romanticism implicit in the view that working-class politics must be socialist politics has gone too far. Indeed, the new interpretation is a useful corrective to the view that class consciousness always yields a socialist or militant labour movement, but it is equally true that the experience of class has never precluded that possibility.

It comes close to the Leninist argument about 'economism' when we confront the view that the limits of labour politics in the period of the First World War were set by a handful of cautious and conservative trade union 'barons' who paid the piper and thereby called the tune. But even Lenin had to revise some of his views on socialist strategy when the outbreak of the First World War transformed the political agenda. And if we leave out the possibility of revolution in a country never threatened by military defeat, what was true in the Central and Eastern European context was also true in Britain. It is this dimension of the upheaval of the war which the revisionist argument cannot accommodate.

For this reason McKibbin's interpretation of the war period must be challenged. The principal objections are in two areas. The first is that it ignores the fact that political alliances between middle-class intellectuals and trade unionists in defence of working-class interests were established during the war, worked well and became a permanent fixture of the labour movement. The second is that it underestimates the extent to which the war experience changed the conditions of working-class life in such a way as to open new possibilities for (and create new obstacles to) the realization of socialist objectives.

Consider first the supposed dichotomy between conservative trade unionists on the one hand and middle-class socialists on the other during the war. After 1914 most trade union leaders worked in effective partnership with civil servants, experts and employers in the organization of munitions production and related work. Their new managerial functions and status drew them both closer to middle-class advisers – consider G. D. H. Cole's work for the Amalgamated Society of Engineers – and further from rank-and-file members of their own unions. This was a central concern of the shop stewards' movement, a far more serious working-class threat to trade union leadership than a putative middle-class invasion of the Labour Party. To accept the modest and vague socialist commitment of the 1918 Labour Party constitution may be understood, therefore, as a way for trade unionists to head off a growing body of working-class militancy in the factories.[34] It is hard to see the shadow of ouvrierism in this context.

This concept seems unhelpful too in describing reactions to the Russian Revolution of 1917. Supporters and opponents of the revolution were not distributed simply along class lines. Ramsay MacDonald and Robert Smillie both addressed the Leeds Convention of 1917 on the need for solidarity with their Russian comrades.[35] Arthur Henderson was certainly puzzled and frightened by Bolshevism, but his support of the call of the Petrograd Soviet for a socialist conference in Stockholm cost him his place in the War Cabinet. That he then went on to join MacDonald and Sidney Webb in the reconstruction of the Labour Party is a well-known story, very hard to square with any version of the anti-middle-class class consciousness thesis.[36]

Webb's central role in the formulation of party policy grew out of his association with many leading trade unionists in the War Emergency Workers' National Committee.[37] 'Workers by hand or by brain' fashioned a successful war economy. Why should they not stay allied, Webb argued, to help mould the postwar world? Of course the function of intellectuals within the party was never clearly defined. McKibbin shows effectively how their freedom of action in relation to the party executive was circumscribed after 1918.[38] But the fact that they were there at all was a change of some importance, attributable to the war and to the political role labour's intellectuals played in it. Given the centrality of the work of Webb, Henderson and MacDonald in the reconstruction of the party, it is best to view Clause Four as a commitment by trade unionists and middle-class socialists alike to perpetuate the political gains of the war.

The second difficulty in McKibbin's treatment of the war period is that it understates the extent to which the world conflict opened new political possibilities for the labour movement precisely because the war constituted an important social and economic discontinuity in the history of the British working class. The first point which must be taken into account here is the emergence of a new relationship between the state and the economy during the war. Before 1914, the state played a relatively minor role in the economic life of the country. The impact of changes in the next four years was so profound that even after the dismantling of the war economy in 1918–21, total government expenditure as a percentage of gross national product never returned to prewar levels. This threshold effect was matched by a concentration effect, whereby the state took responsibility for certain tasks previously the province of local authorities or in private hands.[39] Wartime extensions of government expenditure on public health, education and unemployment insurance were not eliminated by postwar economies.

Some gains of the war economy were, therefore, irreversible. This is also true in terms of the elimination of much of primary poverty in Britain in the war period. A major improvement in the wage levels and conditions under which the lowest-paid and worst-off sections of the working class lived was an unintentional outcome of the working of the war economy. A reduction in the economic distance between strata of the working class and a substantial, if short-term, change in the skill composition of the labour force increased substantially the degree of homogeneity of the English working class as a whole.[40]

It was the very variegation and complexity of the Edwardian class structure matched by the subordinate economic role of the state in working-class life which explains an apparent paradox: why workers were at times intensely class conscious at the point of production and either intensely apathetic politically or prepared to let other classes represent their interests in local and national politics. What the war effort did was to alter each element in this equation. A more homogeneous working class with a deep knowledge of state intervention in most areas of life emerged from a war experience which made the logic of independent labour representation appear in a distinctly new light.

At the same time, changes within the propertied strata of the middle and upper classes helped ensure the fusion of the Liberal and Conservative parties and the appearance of the streamlined class-based political system of the period 1920–80.[41] Equally the fact must not be neglected that the war exploded many of the older attractions of liberalism to working-class voters: the great schism in the leadership of the Liberal Party and the Irish revolt damaged the Liberal Party, perhaps fatally, and could not but help garner votes for Labour. In the fields of political and economic history, few accept the view that the First World War did not matter. It is equally difficult to accept a similar argument when advanced by labour historians.

The sensible approach may be to chart a path roughly halfway between what may be called the revisionist and the orthodox interpretations of labour in the period of the Great War. The war did not demonstrate either the innate conservatism or the innate radicalism of the British working class. What it did was to change the lives of thousands of working people, and offer them a new sense of participation in the nation's affairs. It also meant better wages, conditions and dignity for thousands on the edges of what Edwardians liked to call the 'residuum', the unskilled or casually-employed urban working class. In this context, Clause Four of the 1918 Labour Party constitution touched the desire of many ordinary working people to perpetuate the advances of the war period. It should not be forgotten that what skilled workers saw as a loss in terms of privilege and differentials, the rest of the working class knew as a gain.

The effect of the postwar slump was to restore many of the pre-1914 differentials, but not to such an extent that one could equate the prewar and postwar structure of the British working class. Among workers in the major staple export trades, postwar mass unemployment was as much a leveller as was wartime full employment. Apathy in the interwar period was thus not a continuation of the reflex reactions of an inward and conservative working class. It was the natural response of disillusionment and hopelessness made worse for many by the fact that the war was, in a very real sense, a liberation. When Robert Roberts recalled Salford life in the first quarter of this century, he entitled the chapter on the war 'The Great Release', the sense of which even the dreary years of the 1920s could not erase.[42] In Salford, as in the rest of working-class Britain, a vote for the Labour Party after 1918 was a vote not to return to the prewar world.

What the war did, therefore, was to give to many working people – to those who had served in the factories as well as to those who had served in the trenches – a belief that political change was possible and that they had a right to participate in it. The enfranchisement of the unskilled male working-class voter in 1918, which McKibbin and others have argued was the key force in the rise of the Labour Party after 1918,[43] helped translate this belief into action. And while it did not produce a militant Labour Party, it did provide mass support for a largely working-class institution which hardly resembled the frail creature of the prewar period.

One of the apparent strengths of McKibbin's position is that it fits in well with the record of Labour Party cautiousness in the interwar years. But after 1918, it was not the supposed hostility of class conscious trade unionists to middle-class ideas which blocked the realization, even in small increments, of the socialist programme of 1918. Here again, the force of economic change (rather than cultural determinism) is the key element to observe. The contraction of the British economy completely undermined two key assumptions held by many within the leadership of the Labour Party and the trade union movement: first, that the economic buoyancy of the immediate prewar period would be restored shortly after the war; and second, that the continuing expansion of British capitalism would, in Robert Skidelsky's phrase, finance its supersession.[44] Clause Four of the 1918 constitution reflects these optimistic notions. Consequently over time the socialist commitment took on the character of an idea born in another and earlier age.

Similarly, the timidity of Labour's economic strategy hardly reflected a conservative working-class culture. Without a distinctive economic outlook to relate its social objectives to the structural problems and weaknesses of British industry and trade, Labour and trade union spokesmen adopted the prevailing orthodoxies of the time – monetary and fiscal restraint. It was this contradiction between social and economic policy which crippled Labour's response to the onset of scarcity in the interwar years. Of course, it is a commonplace of the economic history of the period that Labour was not alone in this failure of analysis and prescription. No one, including John Maynard Keynes, broke through the log-jam of economic ideas in the 1920s.[45] It is therefore impossible to blame trade unionists for the myopia and conservatism which were nearly universal afflictions.

None of the above argument is meant to deny the truth of much valuable work done by McKibbin and others on facets of working-class culture. Perhaps what is necessary to temper the revisionist case is the belief that political and economic events of the magnitude of the First World War must surely have had a cultural outcome as well as a cultural source. If this is a return to the 'primacy of the political', then so be it; but it will involve centrally the idea that class consciousness points in more directions than simply towards apathy or towards militancy. Indeed, in most periods it points in both directions at once; and to praise the merits of dialectical reasoning hardly seems out of place in a discussion of the historical meaning of class consciousness. The conclusion here, therefore, is that the deeper is the sense of the multiple political meanings of class consciousness, the closer labour historians will be to providing a full account of this turbulent period of labour history.

III

To do so we will need to extend our research into a number of largely uncharted areas. One concerns the question of whether the undoubted improvement in the standard of living of the working class in the second half of the nineteenth century affected the political aspirations of trade unionists and other workers. It is difficult to determine when people become aware of improvements in living conditions or in life chances, as expressed in expectancy of life at birth, for instance, which rose after the 1850s, or in infant mortality rates, which fell steeply after 1900. It is even more unclear as to how such awareness of rising real wages and improving health as existed influenced the political outlook of working people. There is some force in the view that primary poverty precluded political participation in late Victorian and Edwardian Britain. As yet no one has shown that its eradication after 1914 enabled more people to engage in active political work of even the most elementary kind, whatever its political content.

Labour politics on the local level undoubtedly showed important variations on this as on many other questions. But here too, research has not yet gone very far. There is an urgent need for many more studies like Sidney Pollard's *History of Labour in Sheffield* before systematic comparisons of different communities, their trade unions and their politics in the period under review will become possible. The effect of migration and ethnic divisions in cities like Liverpool, Glasgow and Leeds will need particular attention. So will the question of the way in which different conditions in the labour market in different regions affected the growth of trade unionism and working-class politics. A recent study of the East End of London suggested that there was no direct correlation between a change in the labour process (and consequently in the labour market) on the one hand, and the growth of socialist politics in the interwar period on the other.[46] How true this was of other cities or areas remains to be seen.

Virtually nothing is known too about the activities of working people on town councils, school boards, boards of guardians and other agencies of local government which were open to working-class participation and electoral pressure from 1889, three decades before universal manhood suffrage for parliamentary elections became law. Very little has been published on precisely how many Labour candidates stood in local elections, how many were successful and what those who won did during their terms of office.[47] The initial impression gleaned from preliminary research is that before 1918 very few working people found their way into local government and made a substantial impact on it. It is said that Oscar Wilde rejected an active political life on the grounds that 'socialism takes too many evenings'; how much more difficult it must have been for manual workers to extend the monotony of paid labour into the dreariness of unpaid committee work in their spare time. But on this as on so many other questions, the shift from the analysis of national to local conditions of political and trade union affairs will help to create the more complete and more effective portrayal of the public life of labour which is the aim of us all.

Notes: Chapter 21

1 For example, R. Page Arnot, *The Miners*, 2 vols (London, 1949, 1953); P. Bagwell, *The Railwaymen* (London, 1968); W. Garside, *The Durham Miners* (London, 1971); R. Hyman, *The Workers' Union* (Oxford, 1971); J. Lovell, *Stevedores and Dockers* (London, 1969); J. E. Williams, *The Derbyshire Miners* (London, 1961); H. Clegg *et al.*, *A History of British Trade Unions since 1889* (Oxford, 1964), Vol. 1.
2 H. M. Pelling, *The Origins of the Labour Party* (London, 1954).
3 J. Saville, 'Trade unions and free labour: the background to the Taff Vale decision', in A. Briggs and J. Saville (eds), *Essays in Labour History*, Vol. 1 (London, 1960), 317–50.
4 F. W. Bealey and H. M. Pelling, *Labour and Politics, 1900–1906* (London, 1960).
5 E. P. Thompson, 'Home to Tom Maguire', in Briggs and Saville, *Essays in Labour History*, 1:276–316.
6 R. Gregory, *The Miners and British Politics 1906–1914* (London, 1968).
7 P. R. Thompson, *Socialists, Liberals and Labour: The Struggle for London 1885–1914* (London, 1967); and G. Stedman Jones, *Outcast London* (Oxford, 1971).
8 J. Saville and J. Bellamy (eds), *The Dictionary of Labour Biography*, 6 vols (London, 1972ff.).
9 R. Harrison *et al.*, *The Warwick Guide to British Labour Periodicals* (Brighton, 1977).
10 D. Torr, *Tom Mann and his Times*, Vol. 1 (London, 1956).
11 J. Shneer, *Ben Tillett* (London, 1981).
12 I. McLean, *Keir Hardie* (London, 1975); K. Morgan, *Keir Hardie* (London, 1975); F. Reid, *Keir Hardie* (London, 1978).
13 D. Marquand, *Ramsay MacDonald* (London, 1977).

14 R. McKibbin, 'James Ramsay MacDonald and the problem of the independence of the Labour Party 1910–1914', *Journal of Modern History* 42 (1970): 216–35.

15 M. A. Hamilton, *Arthur Henderson* (London, 1938); R. McKibbin, 'Arthur Henderson as Labour leader', *International Review of Social History* 23 (1979): 79–101.

16 Among others, L. P. Carpenter, *G. D. H. Cole* (Cambridge, 1973); N. MacKenzie and J. MacKenzie, *The First Fabians* (London, 1977); and on Fabian ideas in general, A. McBriar, *Fabian Socialism and English Politics 1884–1918* (Cambridge, 1962).

17 E. J. Hobsbawm, 'The Fabians reconsidered', in idem, *Labouring Men* (London, 1964), 250–71.

18 This is reflected in Hobsbawm's own Cambridge doctoral dissertation on the Fabians (1949) as well as in the early writings of Pelling and MacBriar.

19 R. McKibbin, *The Evolution of the Labour Party 1910–1924* (London, 1974).

20 See his article 'Social class and social observation in Edwardian England', *Transactions of the Royal Historical Society*, 5th series, 28 (1978): 175–200.

21 McKibbin, *Evolution of the Labour Party*, 243.

22 ibid., 247.

23 J. Hinton, *The First Shop Stewards' Movement* (London, 1974).

24 Above all, E. P. Thompson, *The Making of the English Working Class* (London, 1963).

25 A. Briggs (ed.), *Chartist Studies* (London, 1959); R. Harrison, *Before the Socialists* (London, 1966).

26 J. Foster, *Class Struggle and the Industrial Revolution* (London, 1974).

27 G. Stedman Jones, 'Class struggle in the industrial revolution', *New Left Review* 92 (1975): 35–70.

28 McKibbin, *Evolution of the Labour Party*, 90.

29 ibid., 99.

30 G. Stedman Jones, 'Working-class culture and working-class politics in London, 1870–1900: notes on the remaking of a working class', *Journal of Social History* 7 (1974): 460–508.

31 ibid., 490–7.

32 For example, A. Mason, *Association Football and English Society 1865–1914* (Brighton, 1978).

33 Stedman Jones, 'Working-class culture', 499–500.

34 Hinton, *Shop Stewards*.

35 S. Graubard, *British Labour and the Russian Revolution 1917–1924* (Cambridge, Mass., 1956).

36 J. M. Winter, *Socialism and the Challenge of War* (London, 1974), chs 7–8.

37 R. Harrison, 'The War Emergency Workers National Committee 1914–1920', in A. Briggs and J. Saville (eds), *Essays in Labour History*, Vol. 2 (London, 1971), 211–59.

38 McKibbin, *Evolution of the Labour Party*, ch. 9.

39 A. J. Peacock and J. Wiseman, *The Growth of Public Expenditure in the United Kingdom* (London, 1961).

40 J. M. Winter, 'Some aspects of the demographic consequences of the two world wars with special reference to Western Europe', in *Proceedings of the Seventh International Economic History Conference* (Edinburgh, 1978); E. Hunt, *British Labour History 1815–1914* (London, 1981), 334.

41 W. D. Rubinstein, 'Wealth, elites, and the class structure of modern Britain', *Past and Present* 76 (1977): 99–126.

42 R. Roberts, *The Classic Slum* (Manchester, 1966).

43 R. McKibbin *et al.*, 'The franchise factor in the rise of the Labour Party', *English Historical Review* 91 (1976): 723–52.

44 R. Skidelsky, '1929–1931 revisited', *Bulletin of the Society for the Study of Labour History* 19 (1970): 4–5.

45 S. Pollard (ed.), *The Gold Standard and Employment Policies between the Wars* (London, 1970).

46 J. A. Gillespie, 'Economic and political change in the East End of London during the 1920s' (PhD. thesis, Cambridge, 1984).

47 See the preliminary assembly of data in M. G. Shepherd and J. L. Halstead, 'Labour's municipal election performance in provincial England and Wales 1901–13', *Bulletin of the Society for the Study of Labour History* 39 (1979): 39–62.

22 The Free Trade Unions and Social Democracy in Imperial Germany

HANS MOMMSEN

I

By contrast with developments in Western and Southern Europe, German trade unions tended to form industrial or central organizations, and to pursue social and political objectives beyond individual company level at a very early stage. The early associations (*Gewerkvereine*) which emerged during the revolutionary period in 1848–9 received their major impetus from the demand for human and civil rights for the working class as well as equal rights for wage-earners within society. The idea of comprehensive unionization was directed towards the creation of national trade union associations from the very start. Their task was, on the one hand, to strengthen the self-confidence of the working class and, on the other, generally to represent the workers' interest vis-à-vis the employers and the state. The tendency to organize according to trades was combined with the idea of comprehensive social reforms. These reforms were to be achieved by appealing to the public and the employers, not by social revolution. The concept of association appeared to be a sufficient means to this end. Therefore, the emphasis was immediately placed on the creation of comprehensive organizations, as is shown by the example of the first two associations, which emerged during the revolutionary period – the *Gutenbergbund* (the printers' association), and the *Association der Zigarrenarbeiter Deutschlands* (Association of the Cigar Workers in Germany).[1]

The tendency to give priority to comprehensive organization and to seek representation at national level has remained typical of the German trade union movement. In contrast, political distinctions between the unions remained of little importance, the distinction that is between the liberal *Hirsch-Dunckersche Gewerkvereine*, the trade unions associated with the emerging political labour movement and the Christian unions created during the early 1890s. The contrasting notions of self-reliance and state aid became less sharply distinguished in view of increasing resistance to the principle of union organization on the part of the employers.[2] For all branches of the trade union movement, whatever their political persuasion, direct confrontation at the workshop was subordinate to the general objective of social reform. As the industrialization of Germany was based on close links between private entrepreneurial initiative and economic measures taken by the government, the view soon prevailed that pressing social problems could not be solved locally or at company level but only through state intervention. This opinion was widespread amongst the upper echelon of the bureaucracy and amongst the socially aware representatives of the upper middle classes as was demonstrated by the foundation of the *Verein zur Förderung des Wohls der arbeitenden Klassen* (Society for the Betterment of the Working Class) shortly before the revolution.[3]

The first major attempt at unionization in Germany, the *Arbeiterverbrüderung* (Workers' Fraternization), which was founded by Stephan Born in 1848, characterizes the difference between this starting-point and that of other Western countries. The *Arbeiterverbrüderung* adopted a two-pronged approach, partly under the influence of the Chartist movement. On the one hand, it represented the interests not only of artisans and industrial workers but also those of self-employed craftsmen, and built upon traditional efforts to create welfare institutions. On the other hand, it pursued a clearly social political objective. By claiming an active role in the recruitment of labour and the right to control working conditions and wages, it would have had to become a semi-official institution in the long term. Right from the start the aim was to organize all workers and to create *one* unified central union.[4]

As we know, these attempts failed because of intervention by the police and repression in the post-revolutionary period. Only the printers' and cigar-makers' association survived this first phase of unionization at national level. Although the 1850s were also marked by many union activities and occasionally by strikes, this development was rather modest measured against the degree of industrialization in Germany. Only with the start of the New Era, when some of the high hopes which the Liberals had pinned on Prince Wilhelm seemed to be realized after he became Regent in 1858, did unionization take place on a larger scale. This was connected with the short revival of the liberal movement which ended irrevocably with Bismarck's success in the constitutional conflict. However, the unions remained confined to the craft trades for a long time and largely excluded the real factory working class.

The developing union movement was an important recruiting area for the political labour movement which came on to the scene with the founding of the *Allgemeine Deutsche Arbeiterverein* (ADAV – General German Workers' Association) in 1863, and after 1869 it found a second pillar of support in the *Sozialdemokratische Arbeiterpartei* (Social Democratic Workers' Party). In contrast to other West European countries the formation of an independent labour party in Germany took place at the same time as the upswing of union organization. Wolfgang Schieder has spoken in this context of a 'premature party-formation'.[5] Yet for the politically active groups of the German working class there was no real alternative to the formation of political parties. In view of the chronic weakness of left-wing liberalism and the still increasing narrow-mindedness of the employers in social questions, this was the only chance to create the preconditions for organizing the working class, and especially for obtaining the right to form unions. It was characteristic of the backwardness of the German constitutional situation that the leaders of the *Gewerkvereine* never really questioned the option of taking the political route, and that they largely accepted

Ferdinand Lassalle's programme, although he rejected the work of the trade unions. However, his successor, Johann Baptist von Schweitzer, quickly reversed this position vis-à-vis the unions.[6] Lassalle's popularity particularly in trade union circles was largely based on the combination of two objectives which had already been prominent within the *Arbeiterverbrüderung*: the principle of co-operatives and reliance on the state. Social equality of the working class and their economic betterment were to be achieved through state intervention and co-operatives. The low regard in which the ADAV held trade union activities became rather secondary by comparison.

The *Sozialdemokratische Arbeiterpartei* too initially showed little inclination to see union activities as a means of rectifying social grievances. It was mainly tactical considerations that led August Bebel to seek the support of the unions. The draft statue which he produced had the same aim as Lassalle's ADAV, that is, to tie the unions' efforts very closely to the programme of the socialist party. But both factions of the German labour movement were forced into tactical compromise by the upswing of union activities in the wake of the economic boom during the *Gründerjahre*. However, it was not least the union-oriented groups, including the Brunswick Committee, which pressed for a solution to the conflicts within the political wings of the labour movement.

At the *Gothaer Einigungsparteitag* (the party congress in Gotha when the two parties merged) both factions therefore formally dropped Lassalle's anti-union orientation. In contradiction to the Gotha Programme they emphasized the important role of unions in the struggle for the emancipation of the proletariat. This was in contradiction to the Gotha Programme. The programme contained a whole series of social-political demands, but did not deal with the union question. The view also prevailed that the unions were 'merely a training ground for the political movement',[7] a clearly mechanistic reinterpretation of Marx's and Engels' position. The General Committee meetings of the unions immediately following the party congress emphasized the need 'to keep politics out of the union meetings and generally not to be active in politics as a union'.[8]

The unions' recognition of the primacy of the political movement was also connected with the economic crisis following the end of the boom of the *Gründerjahre*. The unions' promising organizational development stagnated once more. It was important for the relationship between the party and the unions that union organization only started to improve again at the beginning of the 1880s when many union associations were founded. This later union movement was influenced to a large extent by the attitude of the officials, the majority of whom were members of the SPD. This did not change until the second phase of development at the beginning of the 1890s. Within the unions new leaders emerged who were, on average, markedly younger than the party leaders. They now took a much more pragmatic and self-confident position vis-à-vis the political organization.[9]

There were isolated voices, such as Ignaz Auer, who argued against the de-politicization of the unions if it went any further than simply acting in accordance with the Law of Association. The division of labour between party and unions, which seemed to exist as a result of the political abstemiousness of the unions, often disguised a feeling of rivalry on the part of party officials. Repeatedly the *Sozialdemokrat* warned against a decline into mere trade unionism. Lip-service was paid to the fact that unions were necessary, but this acknowledgement was combined with warnings not to overrate them. 'Only the workers in medium sized and small industries', read the edition of 4 October 1882, 'are still capable today of organizing themselves into unions and being successful through these organizations.'[10] Such views were accompanied by the criticism that too much strike action took place. This certainly also reflected an element of fear on the part of the union leadership that the unions could be severely weakened by insufficiently prepared strikes and strikes without hope of success. Yet behind this was also the fear that the revolutionary energies of the working class could be wasted in 'useless' strikes. It is not surprising that the primacy of the political party and the merely supportive function of the unions' 'economic struggle' was reaffirmed in the Erfurt Programme of 1891.[11]

During the period of the *Sozialistengesetz* (Anti-Socialist Law) the common interest of the party and the unions came more to the fore. After 1890, however, their particular characteristics, the result of their different societal tasks, were inevitably accentuated more strongly and led finally to a different understanding of their respective roles. The catch-phrase describing the unions as the 'recruiting schools of the party' was adopted by union leaders when they wanted to reassure the party of their loyalty. But it was also obvious that the now quickly developing union movement was trying to lose the image of being merely auxiliary to the labour movement. On the occasion of May Day 1890 the unions now took the initiative. Conflicts arose as a result of the ambiguous attitude of the party executive, which had left the decision of how to celebrate May Day to the individual organizations. Attempts to avoid the locking out of workers in Hamburg who had refused to work on May Day led to a broadly based movement towards a common policy within the unions. The first step was an initiative by the shop stewards of the German metal and engineering workers calling for a union congress to look into the implications of the defeat of the Hamburg strike. This initiative led to the founding of a supra-union commission calling itself the *Generalkommission der Freien Gewerkschaften Deutschlands* (General Commission of the Free Trade Unions) whose initial task it was to prepare the union congress in Halberstadt in March 1892.[12]

The organizational difficulties faced by the *Generalkommission*, under the circumspect leadership of Carl Legien, when attempting to centralize the union movement, have been detailed by Klaus Schönhoven.[13] There was agreement between the participating central unions and craft associations about rejecting the localists, who in turn continued to advocate close linkage between the economic and political struggle and who were giving political support to the radical left within the SPD. In Halberstadt the majority of the unions were prepared to leave the representation of political interests to the party whose objective it was to create a socialist society, while they fought for an improvement in the living conditions of the workers on the basis of the existing situation. However, this did not mean that Legien and the other members of the *Generalkommission* intended to exclude the unions from political tasks as a matter of principle, although the existing legislation on the freedom of association implied an unambiguous non-intervention. Initially it was the questions of the centralizing role played by the *Generalkommission* and its financing which were at the forefront of internal union decision-making. The 'sinister plans' of the *Generalkommission*, which had been hotly disputed, turned out to be a proposal, which it had sent round in an unpublished circular in October 1894, to hold a congress about legislation on safety regulations at the place of work, the inspection of factories, accident insurance and on problems regarding the freedom of association.[14] Without any doubt, the intent of this initiative was to influence the whole area of social policy systematically. This step by the *Generalkommission* was regarded by the union associations, not least by the highly organized printers, as an attempt to create some kind of shadow government to the leadership of the Social Democrats. They believed this could lead to an undesired politicization of union work. However, this danger seemed to have been ruled out by the loose form of co-operation between the union associations and the Social Democratic Party. It is not surprising that the party leadership in the main had similar feelings. Ignaz Auer in particular spoke for the many who distrusted Legien's attempts at centralization. Legien was successful, though, in calming criticism from the party executive and officials, which was clearly articulated even by August Bebel at the Cologne party congress in 1893, by repeated assurances that the leading role of the party was not under attack. Bebel had consciously avoided a break, and in the end he did not oppose the intention of the *Generalkommission* to look into the problems of social policy. But on the whole he remained sceptical.

Justifiably, the party looked at Bismarck's welfare legislation with distrust. Its intention was obviously to alienate the working class from the social democratic movement. Because of this experience the party leadership was lukewarm about social legislation although formally it was in favour of safeguarding and extending the freedom of association, improving safety at work and having shorter working hours. However, as shown during the May Day campaign, it was only a half-hearted approach. The experience of Bismarck's welfare legislation appeared to indicate that the unity of the political labour movement would not be affected. As Bebel explained in Cologne in 1893, he saw expanding the government's social policy as a successful method of narrowing the unions' field of activities. He thus made himself the mouthpiece of the majority who thought that the main emphasis should be on the 'political struggle'.[15] At this point it was not yet foreseeable that the policy of the New Course, which favoured the expansion of Bismarck's welfare legislation and taking account of the interests of the industrial working class, would end abruptly and subsequently be replaced by a policy of repression embodied in the *Umsturzvorlage* (Anti-Subversion Bill).

The situation thus seemed to be one in which the unions were ending their close ties with, and their subordination to, the SPD and were instead taking a more flexible political line which did not exclude co-operation with bourgeois groups as a matter of principle. It was significant that Legien's attendance at the *Freie Hochstift* Conference on the eve of the Cologne party congress in 1893 was the subject of bitter attacks.[16] There was then some hope amongst middle-class social reformers that the unions could be freed from the dominance of the SPD. They were encouraged in this view by statements of leading unionists who were arguing at the time, albeit mainly for tactical reasons, in favour of the party political neutrality of union organizations. With regard to the miners in the Ruhr, the history of their organization, the *Alte Verband* (the Old Association), had shown that too close an association with the Social Democrats was detrimental to the development of the organization. Thus Otto Hue's slogan for the party political neutrality of the unions found lively support. The *Generalkommission* also took steps in this direction, pointing out time and again, however, that the SPD was the only party in the Kaiserreich which actually represented the interests of the working class. Where this tendency would have led had the employers' attitude and government policies not hardened markedly must remain an open question.

Despite the continuing distrust in authoritative party circles, the *Generalkommission* stuck to its original line with tactical skill and tenacity. This line ultimately meant a new division of labour, giving the union movement the task of improving the conditions under which the class struggle took place by influencing government legislation, while at the same time representing the interests of the industrial working class directly. It took a few years to overcome this rivalry, especially as the left that was now emerging quickly seized on the fears of the party executive that the *Generalkommission* was developing into some kind of rival government. The party paper *Vorwärts* dropped meaningful hints about the 'sinister plans of the *Generalkommission*'. The fact that the union congress in Jena had discussed social policy issues led to the comment that it was not regarded as being in the interest of the party to have two authorities issuing directives.[17] Questions of prestige played an important part in this conflict. Thus the demand of the *Generalkommission* for equality was described as 'megalomania' at the Cologne party congress in 1893. Legien had to accept that the union organization could in no way replace the political organization.

It was mainly the change in the overall political climate which prevented these differences in opinion from escalating into a lasting conflict. The setback caused by the end of the New Course meant the Social Democrats were also forced into a position where they felt it necessary to ensure that the *Generalkommission* was an ally. However, initially this was only expressed in confidential talks, which were later leaked. Significantly, the *Generalkommission* reacted badly to the publication of the full text of the agreements made before the Mannheim party congress of 1906. The union leaders were embarrassed to have to acknowledge publicly the existence of formal agreements with the party leadership.[18] To give up the original subordination of the unions to the party in favour of equality was the consequence of a development which favoured the unions. They had a younger leadership than that of the party, in which the first signs of stagnation were beginning to show. The debate about the case of mass strikes for political ends, which necessarily implied a clarification of the relationship with the unions, only provided a long overdue opportunity for tackling this question.

The rapid rise of the union movement in the early 1890s was bound to lead to renewed questions about the relationship between the unions and the party. The idea of using a general strike for political objectives came from outside Germany. Experience gained in Belgium, the Netherlands, Sweden and Italy strengthened the belief in such a strategy, a belief particularly widespread within the Second International. A more detailed analysis of each situation, of course, would rather have given cause for scepticism.[19]

II

The concept of political strikes was alien to German Social Democrats. The decision in favour of the parliamentary route basically excluded such means, especially as it could not but lead to a permanent hardening of the parliamentary battle-lines which the majority of the party in fact hoped would soften. More important for the party leadership, though, was that mass strikes could easily get out of control and were hardly consistent with the principle of disciplined organization because the non-organized workers had also to be enticed into action. Therefore, the question arises as to why the issue of mass strikes could become a problem at all and one which moreover preoccupied the party for years. The relative popularity which the mass strike slogan temporarily achieved can be explained by the fascination of the increasingly frequent strikes in this period. Their actual success, however, remained far behind expectations.

Due to the growing prestige of the unions also within the SPD, the concept of mass strikes automatically implied the organizational participation of the unions. Thus there was a certain logic in the unions gaining in stature precisely because of the rejection of mass strikes. Ostensibly, the debate about mass strikes resulted from an analogy with Belgium where they had been used with a certain success in pressing for the right to vote. The Reichstag elections in 1903 saw a remarkable increase in the number of votes for the SPD. However, this resulted only in a limited number of additional seats, and the improved parliamentary position could not be translated into greater political influence. Without a change in Prussia's electoral system, a real shift in power in favour of the SPD was unimaginable. At the same time, the tendency to change the electoral law to the disadvantage of the SPD increased in a number of federal states. Suddenly, the party found itself on the defensive on this issue. In fact, strike action was used in Hamburg in a vain attempt to avoid a change for the worse in electoral legislation.[20]

Yet the issue of mass strikes was debated passionately within the party and the unions mainly because political strikes were seen as a chance to overcome the increasing threat of political stagnation. There was a certain disappointment about the wait and see policy of the party leadership, which was mainly concerned with expanding the organization. The debate with Eduard Bernstein and emergent revisionism must be seen in this context, otherwise the vehemence with which this ideological conflict took place can hardly be understood. Bernstein's utopian idea was rejected. He advocated moving gradually towards democracy by using more flexible tactics and working in alliance with the bourgeois left. Bernstein's defeat concealed from the party as a whole that his criticism of the attitude of the party leadership revealed the failure of the previous strategy which had left the political initiative increasingly with the class enemy.

August Bebel's anti-revisionist position may explain why he did not oppose mass strike propaganda more energetically. Indeed, the party leadership was at no point seriously considering putting such a strategy into practice. It was significant that Karl Kautsky advised against mass strikes with the argument that this would unnecessarily weaken the organization of the proletariat; although everthing should be done to be prepared for the possibility that the bourgeois parties might violate the constitution and take counter-revolutionary action.[21] Bebel articulated the view held within the party that political mass strikes should be regarded exclusively as a defensive weapon and be used for the defence of the rights of the working class. Rudolf Hilferding too wanted to see mass strikes essentially reduced to a means of defending the Reichstag suffrage. This defensive element was also present in the arguments put forward by the representatives of the left such as Clara Zetkin. 'If the ruling classes destroy the basis of legality', she said at a union rally in Berlin in August 1905, 'then the proletariat is right in saying: I position myself on the rock-hard basis of my power.'[22]

The representatives of the party's left, especially Rosa Luxemburg and Karl Liebknecht, regarded mass strikes precisely as a means of leading the party from the defensive into the offensive in the struggle for power. Thus they hoped to overcome the stagnation threatening the movement, whose political isolation had become obvious after the Reichstag elections of 1903. Mass strikes appeared to be the all-powerful formula which could provide the movement with a revolutionary perspective again by referring to the events in Russia. For tactical reasons, however, Rosa Luxemburg felt forced to support the conciliatory position which Bebel took at the party congress in Jena in 1905. But she was perfectly clear in her own mind that the resolution on mass strikes proposed by Bebel dealt with political mass strikes as a 'mechanical recipe for defensive political tactics', not as an elementary form of revolution.[23] She had hit the nail on the head.

The view is often held that it was mainly the influence of the unions which prevented the party from whole-heartedly embracing the concept of mass strikes.[24] Certainly the vast majority of the unions were opposed to mass strikes right from the beginning. They feared strikes would lead the union movement back into the 'political morass', quite apart from the fact that it was doubtful if such strikes could be organized. Equally, the *General-kommission* was determined to counter with all means the mass strike euphoria which temporarily gripped the trade unions. In 1904 at the congress of the Second International in Amsterdam, Robert Schmidt put the unions' position emphatically: 'The proletariat's struggle for political power will not be decided by the general strike but by continuous work in all sectors of economic and public life.'[25] Yet even in the party, with the exception of the rapidly emerging left wing, the view predominated that mass strikes were only the last means to be used against a counter-revolution.

The party leadership played down the issue of mass strikes and deliberately did not put it on the agenda of the party congress in Bremen in 1904. However, the *Generalkommission* tackled this question at the Cologne union congress in 1905 in order to reject the revolutionary efforts of the left and to bring the party into line with the union position. The implicit claim to a leading role in central questions of strategy led to sharp criticism in party circles. By forging ahead the *Generalkommission* placed at risk the tacit alliance between the party and the union leadership which had been formed on this issue. Bebel's compromise resolution at the Jena party congress in 1905 blunted the mass strike as a political weapon, nothing more than a threatening gesture towards the ruling classes.

The unions could accept this solution, although they regarded mass strikes as having only extremely limited chances of success, bearing in mind their experience with previous strikes, including the strike of the Crimmitschau textile workers which had ultimately failed. However, the issue of electoral reform in Prussia gave the mass strike concept a fresh impetus, and the left also managed to influence individual unions to some degree. In this situation, the party executive decided to enter into those confidential negotiations which finally led to the Mannheim agreement of 1906. After the results of these negotiations had become common knowledge through an indiscretion, a public discussion could no longer be avoided. The *Generalkommission* not only achieved agreement that in case of a decision in favour of a general strike the unions had to give approval in advance. The resolution passed by the party congress also assured the unions that agreement would have to be sought on all questions concerning the common interests of both organizations. Furthermore, it was conceded that the *Generalkommission* was responsible for the whole area of social policy.[26]

August Bebel got round Karl Kautsky's efforts in Mannheim formally to spell out the primacy of the party over the unions. His compliant attitude towards the unions derived not least from the recognition that it was impossible to tie the self-confident union movement to decisions which existed only on paper. The party executive was certainly also influenced by the rapidly growing membership of the Free Trade Unions.[27] The *Generalkommission* hoped to achieve fundamental social change through gradual successes gained step by step. However, the increasingly unified approach of the employers rendered these hopes vain. The development of the unions after 1905 was characterized rather by the contradiction between the exaggerated expectations of the members, and the growing scepticism of the leadership which tried everything to prevent organizational setbacks as a result of abortive industrial disputes.

III

The spectacular growth of union membership in the period between 1903 and 1907 led to a more balanced situation between the individual regions which had previously varied enormously in strength. The increase in membership did not continue to the same degree thereafter. Setbacks in 1907–8 could be compensated for in the following years but the growth of membership clearly slowed down and was actually reversed in 1913. The collapse of union membership which took place during the first war years was thus preceded by a union crisis during the last years before the war. As the development in individual trades and unions varied, some organizations were more severely affected than others by the setback.[28]

More decisive, however, for the unions' power was the problem of membership fluctuation. It was caused, on the one hand, by the high mobility of industrial workers and the tendency to change jobs, and often trades. This situation continued throughout the prewar period and only changed significantly in 1921. On the other hand, the high rate of fluctuation, which amounted to 100 per cent in some years in most unions, was a result of the rapid growth of unionism. During periods of economic depression, fluctuation was clearly reduced. Whilst there were marked differences between individual unions, it was characteristic that those members who had not been in the union for very long largely contributed to the fluctuations. In contrast to the early years of the union movement, strike defeats played a minor role. On the other hand, there was a clear connection between the upturn of the economy and membership growth.[29] The organization was most firmly based in the traditional, still mainly craft-oriented trades. The situation was reversed in the sphere of large-scale industry where semi-skilled workers were increasingly employed and the union had difficulties in forming any noteworthy organization.[30]

Up to and during the First World War the Free Trade Unions mainly represented the interests of largely craft-oriented workers in small and medium-sized firms. This was particularly true of the officials. Most union leaders had a craft background themselves. Many of them had learned a trade which had become less relevant or even superfluous during the process of industrialization. This explains why the leaders of the Free Trade Unions did not fully recognize the organizational problems involved in the development of large-scale industrial companies and the emergence of particular industrial regions.

Trade union organization was regionally structured. The local union cartels gained an overriding importance. They were capable of running the unions' legal advice bureaux, they could turn union centres into meeting points for the organized workers and locally co-ordinate the actions of each trade union organization. On the other hand, this form of organization had the severe disadvantage that it was not tied to the shop floor. In many of the large companies it was impossible to form a union organization because of the systematic repression of any union activity. Before the First World War it had been almost impossible to expand unionization in heavy industry, beyond a few modest beginnings.

The *Generalkommission* and central organizations devoted a substantial part of their energies to unifying and centralizing the diverse branches of the craft-oriented trade union associations. These differed greatly in size and comprised both crafts which were dying and crafts still strongly influenced by guild traditions. The principle of the industrial union which was first realized by the *Deutsche Metallarbeiterverband* (German Metalworkers' Union) and the *Deutsche Holzarbeiterverband* (German Woodworkers' Union) was idealized in this context. In practice a large degree of centralization and unification proved to be detrimental to trade union representation in several parts of the organization and led to the alienation of individual groups of workers. It was precisely the distinction between various trades and conditions of employment in large-scale industry which was used as a means of discipline within the companies, and to strengthen resistance to trade union strategies. It is thus not surprising that the *Generalkommission* by and large had to abandon the plans which it had been advocating for centralization and unification. Although it seemed feasible in the long term, the problem with this policy at the time was that it created an impression of union strength which did not in fact exist, and it often hampered the unions in making the best use of spontaneous protests.

In order to combat the instability of union membership most trade unions expanded their system of social welfare. But this did not live up to expectations and the fluctuation in membership could only be partly limited.[31] At the same time, the support system swallowed a high percentage of membership contributions, especially as some unions introduced unemployment benefits. Such expenditure often exceeded the cost of strike pay several times over. The experience of living beyond their means, especially in view of organizational setbacks, strengthened the latent tendency to leave these welfare tasks to the state and local authorities. This is yet another explanation for increasing rapprochement between the Free Trade Unions and the existing order.[32]

The fighting power of the unions depended to a large extent on the stability of the membership and the degree of union organization. The growing tendency amongst employers to organize and the formation of cartels and large industrial concerns increased the risks of entering into industrial disputes. This was even more the case as employers became less hesitant to use lock-outs. Especially after 1905 the number of lock-outs in industrial disputes increased substantially. At the same time, the unions were often forced on to the defensive. The ratio of defensive strikes to strikes of an aggressive nature continuously increased in favour of the former.[33] A growing membership did not necessarily mean a stronger position for the unions in labour conflicts.

The endeavours of the Free Trade Unions to rationalize industrial disputes and to replace them by agreements which would preserve their fighting power necessarily led to a growing interest in collective wage agreements. In collective bargaining with individual employers and industrial branches, agreements could be reached that industrial disputes would not jeopardize all existing regulations concerning wages and working conditions. This was an important advantage over individual or collective working contracts. At the same time, the system of collective bargaining offered an opportunity to increase the level of union organization. The expansion of this system implied formal equality of the workers and their organization as negotiating partners.[34]

Indeed, the *Generalkommission* spoke out very early in favour of collective bargaining. This was also true for the majority of the central union organizations. However, the implications of collective bargaining were somewhat ambivalent. On the one hand industrial disputes became more predictable. On the other hand the system could lead to unfavourable commitments, especially when collective labour contracts were agreed at local or company level without involving the union leadership. Collective agreements were more popular at local level than with the union executive. The *Deutsche Metallarbeiterverband* repeatedly warned against the light-hearted signing of collective contracts. But most importantly, it increasingly emerged that acceptable collective agreements could only be reached after previous strike action. Thus, collective agreements were no substitute for strikes. The idea that an expansion of the collective bargaining system would make the relations between labour and capital more mundane and lead to a co-operative relationship between the two sides of industry turned out to be illusory.[35]

The extent and the area covered by collective agreements was extremely limited in the prewar period. In 1913 only 13·2 per cent of all employees were covered by such agreements which were, as a rule, to be found in medium-sized and small companies and only in rudimentary form in the textile and electrical industries. Heavy industry consistently declined to conclude collective agreements until 1918. Less than 5 per cent of collective contracts covered large companies with more than a hundred employees; and in 1913 the duration of collective agreements had become rather shorter.[36] Quite apart from that, in most cases the agreements only dealt with piece-work rates, working hours and overtime and, at best, contained minimum wage regulations. Central questions of determining the level of payments were almost entirely excluded. The increase in the number of collective agreements by 1914 was thus only a qualified success. Furthermore, these agreement were not legally binding on the two sides of industry until after 1910, and even then only inadequately.[37] While the area covered by collective labour contracts was expanded in some industrial branches, it became increasingly narrower in others.

The Free Trade Unions were able to conclude collective agreements for about one-third of total membership before the outbreak of the First World War. However, their importance was qualified by the often very narrowly defined contents of the agreements and the additional fact that heavy industry was not included. Thus the relatively high percentage of workers covered by collective agreements reflected the notorious weakness of the union movement in the area of heavy industry. Hopes that the system of collective bargaining would bring about a reduction of class conflict clearly proved to be false. The fight for collective agreements, therefore, did not necessarily imply a reformist strategy, but was absolutely consistent with the objectives of the class struggle.[38] On the one hand, the *Generalkommission* pursued more sweeping aims in connection with the system of collective bargaining. Legien remarked in 1918 that the *Zentralarbeitsgemeinschaft* (Joint Industrial Alliance, which was intended to establish a framework for labour–management co-operation) represented the continuation of a trend which had begun with collective agreements. This view is characteristic of a markedly reformist attitude towards collective labour contracts and is also reflected in the statements made by the *Generalkommission* at trade union congresses dealing with this question.[39] On the other hand, the *General-kommission*, like the SPD, opposed any regulation by law of rules of collective bargaining, as the *Zentrumspartei* (Centre Party) in particular had demanded since 1905. The unions certainly must have feared that their room for manoeuvre would be noticeably limited by such legislation. Apart from the tactical consideration that in view of the relative strength of the parties in the Reichstag, any legislation on collective bargaining would fall short of the unions' expectations, confidence in the growing organizational strength of the unions played a decisive role.[40] This attitude did not amount to an option in favour of the strike weapon, although it was feared that any extension of the rules of collective bargaining would lead to a limitation of the right to strike. Rather, behind this attitude lay the long-term objective of determining the conditions of work by negotiating with the employers from a position of equality.

The strategy of the unions was characterized by efforts to avoid strikes if possible and was due not least to the experiences of the early 1890s. This approach had already been the basis for the rejection of the concept of mass strikes, albeit for tactical reasons and in an outwardly mild form. For most trade union leaders the revolutionary ideas which the left associated with this concept were unacceptable. What Rosa Luxemburg intended to achieve by unleashing the spontaneity of unorganized workers through mass strikes was exactly the opposite of their endeavours. The concept of mass strikes as a means of mobilizing resistance against deprivation and arbitrary actions by employers was increasingly alien to the pragmatists in the union movement who were the leaders of the Free Trade Unions. This often led to conflicts with the members, as in the case of the strike in the Hamburg docks in 1896–7.[41] In fact, the workers displayed unusual endurance and admirable solidarity in many conflicts. Despite unfavourable conditions their readiness to strike was exceptionally high. The element of moral protest which came to the fore particularly during hopeless strike action was regarded in a rather negative light by the union leadership and was normally not exploited to expand the organization.[42]

IV

The reasons for the German union leaders' lack of enthusiasm for engaging in industrial disputes go back to the early period of union organization. The image of the employer derived from that of the independent entrepreneur of the 1850s and 1860s, and assumed a far-reaching identity of interests between the employer and his workers. At the level of small and medium-sized companies with small labour forces this identity of interests actually existed in part. It seems to be characteristic that it was not the employers themselves, but rather the group of managers who were later active in the employers' associations, who were accused of being 'agitators'.[43] Short-comings on the part of the employer were often regarded as the result of insufficient information about the living conditions of the workers. On the one hand, this amounted to an inadmissible underestimation of the conflict of economic interests, and ultimately reduced it to a question of personality. On the other hand, trade union leaders tended to see union activities as being merely of an economic nature; they defined the role of the unions as a corrective within the capitalist mode of production.[44]

It was the leading figures of the craft unions and of the industrial unions in particular who often developed a mentality which was akin to that of the employers. Significantly, technological advances, even where they objectively put the labour force concerned at a disadvantage, were generally welcomed. Trade union officials usually held the view that industrial growth would allow the needs of the working population to be satisfied. It is noteworthy in this context that Taylorism was not rejected or opposed right from the beginning. Union members were also expected to be highly disciplined workers. This was seen as indispensable to the modern process of production which relied on the division of labour, and it was not seriously questioned. On the other hand, though, arbitrary and unwarranted disciplinary actions by the employers were sharply criticized.

Therefore, it is not correct to explain the position of the leading cadres of the Free Trade Unions in terms of 'opportunism' or ideological categories such as 'revisionism' and 'reformism'. Their attitude was based on the principle of social compromise with the employers. Their experience in heavy industry especially confirmed the view of the union leaders that union successes could only be secured permanently by state welfare legislation. The objective of unionizing the labour force as comprehensively as possible not only served the purpose of its being able to stand up to the employers with the strike weapon which was regarded as *ultima ratio*;[45] it also provided the legitimization for increased social policy demands vis-à-vis the state, local administrations and the legislature. It would require more intensive studies to determine to what extent corporatist concepts were at work. Consequently, it was not the company level and not co-determination within the company which were at the forefront of union objectives.[46] The unions' tasks were seen rather as those functions which were in the public interest and thus required state guarantees and legal protection. The unions acquired this position within the system of the war economy, based not least on the *Vaterländische Hilfsdienstgesetz* (Auxiliary Service Law).[47]

The *Generalkommission*'s expectation of gradually increasing trade union influence by extending and centralizing the unions' organization was achieved only in part before the First World War. On the contrary during the last prewar years severe setbacks were looming in the sphere of heavy industry. The miners' strike in the Ruhr in 1912 resulted in a clear defeat, despite all union efforts.[48] This conflict in the Ruhr proved that unorganized labour was an unpredictable factor and was not prepared to submit to the strike leaders of the trade unions. Their relative weakness in heavy industry and the intransigence of the employers forced the *Deutsche Metallarbeiterverband* and the miners' *Alte Verband* to appeal to the social responsibility of the state by influencing the general public and by representations to the Prussian Minister for Trade and Commerce.[49]

By contrast, the Free Trade Unions managed to develop a fruitful working relationship with the local authorities, mainly in the south German states. The local health insurance system played an important role in this because unions and local authorities had equal representation on their executive committees. Equally, by establishing *Arbeitersekretariate* (Workers' Secretariats) the unions were increasingly drawn into practical welfare tasks. In 1905 the *Generalkommission* created the *Sozialpolitische Abteilung* (Department for Social Policy) to cope with this development. Social policy initiatives by Social Democratic members of the Reichstag and the state parliaments were co-ordinated and prepared with the unions. The number of union representatives who were members of the parliamentary parties was also increasing. Working with the co-operative societies, educational union activities and participation in the work of various bodies of the welfare administration contributed to the increasing integration of the union movement into the existing political system.[50]

For this reason the view became predominant within the Free Trade Unions that the policy of small steps practised by a pragmatic union élite would be more successful in the medium term than the strategy of opposition advocated by the Social Democratic Party executive. The latter's strategy was influenced by centrist dogma but lost its inherent logic after 1913. However, it was significant that the union leaders, whose activities were to a large extent directed towards internal affairs, were to some extent fearful of contacts with the representatives of the state's welfare policy. This explains their reticence on the question of shaping the law regarding working conditions and collective bargaining. On the other hand, though, there was no shortage of ideas and suggestions for giving the unions a legal and quasi-public role. The effects of the concept of union autonomy which developed during the growth years of the union movement were still apparent in the 1920s and furthered the continuing separation of union institutions from public institutions, not least in the educational sphere.[51]

The high degree of internal union bureaucratization, of which the members actually approved, resulted in the union bureaucrats and the membership having different perspectives. The term labour aristocracy does not properly describe this situation, which was the result of an unavoidable division of roles. There was never any doubt about the solidarity of the union leaders with the ordinary members. They had, as a rule, also worked their way up from a proletarian background.[52] The bureaucratic definition of their role and the tendency to overvalue organizational questions, however, meant that they could not imagine society changing to a socialist order in any other way than by a gradual integration of union institutions into the state machine. Administrative considerations replaced political objectives to a large extent; and this has had a lasting effect on the unions' views on the gradual implementation of socialist principles in the economic area.

After August 1914 fears of contact with the bourgeois-capitalist society in its Wilhelmine form receded more and more. The markedly national view of most union representatives encouraged the union leadership to institutionalize co-operation with the state administration. It is thus entirely understandable that the Free Trade Unions agreed to the *Burgfriedenspolitik* (policy of industrial and political truce) without waiting for a statement from the Social Democratic Party executive and that they readily integrated themselves into the war economy.[53]

V

It could be asked to what degree the trade union movement in Germany reflected the specific political culture which had developed during the formation of the nation state. The insistence on organizational centralization, although many of the *Generalkommission*'s plans remained plans, the idea of an *Einheitsgewerkschaft* (unified trade union movement) and the relative lack of interest in developments at company level were not the result of the objective situation of the union struggle, but ultimately derived from an understanding of politics as a means of finding solutions at state level. The relative independence which the unions had gained from the Social Democratic Party after 1906 reinforced this development. However, there were no fundamental differences of opinion between the trade unions and the political wing of the labour movement after the party had dropped its claim to lead. As a mass organization the Free Trade Unions were a younger movement than the party. Changes taking place in the SPD shortly before the turn of the century, the loss of its character as a movement, did not affect the unions much; for they were rapidly expanding during this period. This contributed to the different theoretical position taken by the unions. Union leaders were fundamentally different from the first generation of party leaders as far as age and political experience were concerned. It was not accidental that, after Bebel's death in 1913, the party entrusted the party leadership to a man who came from the union movement, to Friedrich Ebert.

During the First World War and the early years of the Weimar Republic, party and union leaders had become an increasingly homogeneous group and there was mutual penetration of their organizations. But this served neither the *Allgemeine Deutsche Gewerkschaftsbund* (ADGB – General Confederation of German Trade Unions) nor the now divided political labour movement well. Rather it led to a mutual limitation of their room for manoeuvre. After the tactical wooing of the unions by the Lassallean and the Eisenach parties and their subordination to the status of 'recruiting schools' for the movement, their mutual relationship was determined increasingly by the party's dependence on the unions after 1906. This dependence diminished the flexibility of the reformist majority in the party vis-à-vis the growing left, which later split from the party, and it also contributed to the paralysis of the party during the break-up of Wilhelmine Germany.

Notes: Chapter 22

1 cf. U. Engelhardt, 'Gewerkschaftliches Organisationsverhalten in der ersten Industrialisierungsphase', in W. Conze and U. Engelhardt (eds), *Arbeiter im Industrialisierungsprozess. Herkunft, Lage und Verhalten* (Stuttgart, 1979), 372–402 (378–80); G. Beier,

Schwarze Kunst und Klassenkampf (Frankfurt a.M., 1966); W. H. Schröder, *Arbeiter-geschichte und Arbeiterbewegung. Industriearbeit und Organisationsverhalten im 19. und frühen 20. Jahrhundert* (Frankfurt a.M., 1978), 239–40.

2 A fundamental experience in this respect was the Waldenburg miners' strike in 1869 which was imposed on the *Hirsch-Dunker* Trades Associations. cf. U. Engelhardt, *"Nur vereinigt sind wir stark". Die Anfänge der deutschen Gewerkschaftsbewegung 1862/63 bis 1869/70*, Vol. 2 (Stuttgart, 1977), 1075 and *passim*, particularly 1196–7.

3 cf. J. Reulecke, 'Der Centralverein für das Wohl der arbeitenden Klassen', in W. Köllmann and J. Reulecke (eds), *Mitteilungen des Centralvereins für das Wohl der arbeitenden Klassen*, Vol. 1 (Hagen, 1980), 23–42.

4 cf. F. Balser, *Sozial-Demokratie 1848/49–1863* (Stuttgart, 1962), 55–65.

5 W. Schnieder, 'Das Scheitern des bürgerlichen Radikalismus und die sozialistische Partei-bildung in Deutschland', in H. Mommsen (ed.), *Sozialdemokratie zwischen Klassenbewe-gung und Volkspartei* (Frankfurt a.M., 1974), 17–34 (28–9).

6 cf. W. Schröder, *Partei und Gewerkschaften. Die Gewerkschaftsbewegung in der Konzep-tion der revolutionären Sozialdemokratie 1868/69 bis 1893* (Berlin, 1975), 41–3; H. Wachen-heim, *Die deutsche Arbeiterbewegung 1844 bis 1914* (Frankfurt a.M., 1971), 112–18.

7 Legien at the Cologne Party Congress (*Protokoll über die Verhandlungen des Parteitags der SPD in Köln 1893* (Berlin, 1893), 183–4).

8 ibid., 230.

9 cf. K. Schönhoven, *Expansion und Konzentration. Studien zur Entwicklung der freien Gewerkschaften im Wilhelminischen Deutschland 1890 bis 1914* (Stuttgart, 1980), 233–4.

10 Quoted from Schröder, *Partei und Gewerkschaften*, 224.

11 For the party's lack of interest in trade union activities cf. G. A. Ritter, *Die Arbeiterbewe-gung im Wilhelminischen Reich* (Berlin, 1959), 123–7; H.-J. Steinberg, 'Die Entwicklung des Verhältnisses von Gewerkschaften und Sozialdemokratie bis zum Ausbruch des Ersten Weltkriegs', in H. O. Vetter (ed.), *Vom Sozialistengesetz zur Mitbestimmung* (Cologne, 1975), 121–34 (128–9).

12 cf. W. Schröder, *Klassenkämpfe und Gewerkschaftseinheit* (Berlin, 1965), 130ff.

13 cf. Schönhoven, *Expansion und Konzentration*, 268ff; also cf. Ritter, *Arbeiterbewegung im Wilhelminischen Reich*, 120–2; Schröder, *Klassenkämpfe und Gewerkschaftseinheit*, 187ff.

14 cf. Schönhoven, *Expansion und Konzentration*, 290–1.

15 *Protokoll über die Verhandlungen des sozialdemokratischen Parteitags in Köln 1893*, 201: 'We may be unionized as much as we like, once capital has captured as much power as at Krupp's and Stumm's and in the Dortmunder Union, in the coal and steel districts of Rhineland and Westphalia, then the trade union movement is finished, then there is only the political struggle left.'

16 ibid., 202.

17 On this fundamental issue see the study of H. Langerhans, *Partei und Gewerkschaft. Eine Untersuchung zur Geschichte der Hegemonie der Gewerkschaft in der deutschen Arbeiter-bewegung, 1890 bis 1914* (Berlin, 1972).

18 Wachenheim, *Die deutsche Arbeiterbewegung*, 415–16; Langerhans, *Partei und Gewerk-schaft*, 14–15.

19 Wachenheim, *Die deutsche Arbeiterbewegung*, 401–2; for the genesis of the mass strike debate cf. A. Grunnenberg (ed.), *Die Massenstreikdebatte* (Frankfurt a.M., 1970); E. Georgi, *Theorie und Praxis des Gewerkschaftsstreiks in der modernen Arbeiterbewegung* (PhD. thesis, Jena, 1931).

20 cf. G. Griep, 'Sozialdemokratie und freie Gewerkschaften 1905/06', *Zeitschrift für Ge-schichtswissenschaft* 11 (1963): 915–40 (929–30).

21 K. Kautsky, 'Grundsätze oder Pläne?', *Neue Zeit* 24 (1906): 781–8; K. Kautsky, *Der politische Massenstreik* (Berlin, 1914).

22 R. Hilferding, 'Zur Frage des Generalstreiks', *Neue Zeit* 22 (1904): 134–42; *Vorwärts* (23 August 1905), quoted from Griep, 'Sozialdemokratie und freie Gewerkschaften', 925.

23 Quoted from ibid., 931 n. 85 (letter from Rosa Luxemburg to Henriette Roland-Holst, dated 2 October 1905).

24 F. Deppe *et al.*, *Geschichte der deutschen Gewerkschaftsbewegung*, 2nd edn (Cologne, 1978), 88–93; Langerhans, *Partei und Gewerkschaft*, 32–3; *Geschichte der deutschen Arbeiterbewegung*, Vol. 2 (Berlin, 1966), 2:97–9.

25 Quoted from Wachenheim, *Die deutsche Arbeiterbewegung*, 404.
26 Griep, 'Sozialdemokratie und freie Gewerkschaften', 936–8; Wachenheim, *Die deutsche Arbeiterbewegung*, 415–22.
27 Schönhoven, *Expansion und Konzentration*, 107ff.
28 ibid., survey on pp. 125–44.
29 cf. ibid., 178–98; also cf. H. Kaelble and H. Volkmann, 'Konjunktur und Streik während des Übergangs zum organisierten Kapitalismus in Deutschland', in *Zeitschrift für Wirtschafts- und Sozialwissenschaften* 92 (1972): 513–44.
30 K. Schönhoven, 'Gewerkschaftswachstum, Mitgliederintegration und bürokratische Organisation in der Zeit vor dem Ersten Weltkrieg', in H. Mommsen (ed.), *Arbeiterbewegung und industrieller Wandel. Studien zu gewerkschaftlichen Organisationsproblemen im Reich und an der Ruhr* (Wuppertal, 1980), 16–37, esp. 27ff.
31 Schönhoven, *Expansion und Konzentration*, 172.
32 cf. K. Schönhoven, 'Selbsthilfe in Form von Solidarität. Das gewerkschaftliche Unterstützungswesen im Deutschen Kaiserreich bis 1914', in *Archiv für Sozialgeschichte* 20 (1980): 147–93; cf. P. Ullmann, *Tarifverträge und Tarifpolitik in Deutschland bis 1914* (Frankfurt a.M., 1977), 142–7.
33 cf. E. Domansky, 'Arbeitskämpfe und Arbeitskampfstrategien des Deutschen Metallarbeiterverbandes von 1891 bis 1914' (PhD. thesis, Bochum, 1981), 79 and *passim*. This development indicates that the hardening of the position of the employers in heavy industry did not just have economic and organizational reasons, but that it was a reflex reaction to the situation following the first Russian revolution in 1905 when class conflict seemed to have become more pronounced. This study gives some very interesting insights into the ambivalence of trade union attempts to centralize the organizational structures.
34 Ullmann, *Tarifverträge und Tarifpolitik*, 201.
35 cf. Domansky, 'Arbeitskämpfe und Arbeitskampfstrategien', 305 and 392.
36 Ullmann, *Tarifverträge und Tarifpolitik*, 98–9.
37 ibid., 101–2; cf. M. Martiny, *Integration oder Konfrontation? Studien zur Geschichte der sozialdemokratischen Rechts- und Verfassungspolitik* (Bonn-Bad Godesberg, 1976), 75–6.
38 cf. Ullmann, *Tarifverträge und Tarifpolitik*, 200–1.
39 cf. ibid., 201 and 205; T. Leipart, *Carl Legien. Ein Gedenkbuch* (Berlin, 1929), 137.
40 Martiny, *Integration oder Konfrontation*, 78ff.
41 cf. M. Grüttner, 'Mobilität und Konfliktverhalten. Der Hamburger Hafenarbeiterstreik 1896/97' in K. Tenfelde and H. Volkmann (eds), *Streik. Zur Geschichte des Arbeitskampfes in Deutschland während der Industrialisierung* (Munich, 1981), 143–61; for the 1913 strike cf. Domansky, 'Arbeitskämpfe und Arbeitskampfstrategien', 363ff., and Wachenheim, *Die deutsche Arbeiterbewegung*, 569–72.
42 Domansky, 'Arbeitskämpfe und Arbeitskampfstrategien', 393.
43 ibid., 339ff.; the findings of M. Kealy are interesting in this context, namely, that younger managers were far less open-minded towards social considerations than older owners of companies/employers. See M. Kealy, 'Kampfstrategie der Unternehmerschaft im Ruhrbergbau seit dem Bergarbeiterstreik von 1889', in H. Mommsen and U. Borsdorf (eds), *Glück auf, Kameraden! Die Bergarbeiter und ihre Organisation in Deutschland* (Cologne, 1979), 175–97 (183–6).
44 Domansky, 'Arbeitskämpfe und Arbeitskampfstrategien', 290.
45 ibid., 64.
46 cf. H. Mommsen, *Klassenkampf oder Mitbestimmung. Zum Problem der Kontrolle wirtschaftlicher Macht in der Weimarer Republik* (Frankfurt a.M., 1980), 17ff.
47 cf. H.-J. Bieber, *Gewerkschaften in Krieg und Revolution. Arbeiterbewegung, Industrie, Staat und Militär in Deutschland*, Vol. 1 (Hamburg, 1981), 219ff., who provides an exposition using a wide range of data.
48 A. Gladen, 'Die Streiks der Bergarbeiter im Ruhrgebiet in den Jahren 1889, 1905 und 1912', in J. Reulecke (ed.), *Arbeiterbewegung an Rhein und Ruhr* (Wuppertal, 1974), 111–48 (141ff.).
49 cf. H. Mommsen, 'Soziale und politische Konflikte an der Ruhr 1905–1924', in idem, *Arbeiterbewegung und industrieller Wandel*, 62–94 (75–6).
50 cf. M. Martiny, 'Die politische Bedeutung der gewerkschaftlichen Arbeitersekretariate vor dem Ersten Weltkrieg', in Vetter, *Vom Sozialistengesetz zur Mitbestimmung*, 153–74.
51 See Martiny, *Integration oder Konfrontation*, 83–4 and 126–7.

52 cf. G. Beier, 'Das Problem der Arbeiteraristokratie im 19. und 20. Jahrhundert', in *Herkunft und Mandat. Beiträge zur Führungsproblematik in der Arbeiterbewegung* (Frankfurt a.M., 1976), 9–71 (42ff.); Schönhoven, 'Gewerkschaftswachstum, Mitgliederintegration und bürokratische Organisation', 33–4.

53 cf. S. Miller, *Burgfrieden und Klassenkampf* (Düsseldorf, 1974), 48–51.

Notes on Contributors

Wolfgang J. Mommsen is Director of the German Historical Institute, London, and Professor of Modern History at the University of Düsseldorf. He is the author of *The Age of Bureaucracy. Perspectives on the Political Sociology of Max Weber* (Oxford, 1974) and *Theories of Imperialism* (London, 1980). His many articles have made major contributions to the historical debate on Wilhelmine Germany.

Eric J. Hobsbawm is Professor Emeritus in London. Among his many contributions to labour history are *Primitive Rebels. Studies in Archaic Forms of Social Movement in the 19th and 20th Centuries* (Manchester, 1959), *Labouring Men. Studies in the History of Labour* (London, 1964) and *The Age of Capital, 1848–1875* (London, 1975).

Sidney Pollard is Professor of Economic History at the University of Bielefeld. Among his books are *The British Shipbuilding Industry 1870–1914* (Cambridge, 1979) and *Peaceful Conquest. The Industrialisation of Europe, 1760–1970* (Oxford, 1981).

James E. Cronin is Associate Professor at the University of Wisconsin, Milwaukee, and has worked extensively on the history of strikes in both Britain and Europe. His writings include *Industrial Conflict in Modern Britain* (London, 1979).

Friedhelm Boll is Reseach Fellow at the Institute for Social History, Brunswick-Bonn, and has published *Frieden ohne Revolution? Friedensstrategien der deutschen Sozialdemokratie bis zur Revolution 1918* (Bonn, 1980) and *Massenbewegungen in Niedersachsen 1906–1920* (Bonn, 1981).

John Lovell is Senior Lecturer in Economic and Social History at the University of Kent. Among his publications are *Stevedores and Dockers* (London, 1969) and *British Trade Unions 1875–1933* (London, 1977).

Michael Grüttner teaches at the Technical University of Berlin. Besides several articles on working-class culture and social conflict he has published *Arbeitswelt an der Wasserkante. Sozialgeschichte der Hamburger Hafenarbeiter 1886–1914* (Göttingen, 1984).

Richard Price is Professor of Modern History at the Northern Illinois University. He has written *An Imperial War and the British Working Class. Working Class Attitudes and Reactions to the Boer War 1899–1902* (London, 1972) and *Masters, Unions and Men. Work Control in Building and the Rise of Labour 1830–1914* (Cambridge, 1980).

Alastair Reid is a Fellow and Director of Studies in History at Girton College, Cambridge. He has written several articles dealing with important topics in British labour history.

Keith Burgess is currently head of the History Department at the Roehampton Institute of Higher Education. His major publications are *The Origins of British Industrial Relations. The 19th-Century Experience* (London, 1975) and *The Challenge of Labour. Shaping British Society 1850–1930* (London, 1980).

Philip S. Bagwell is Professor Emeritus and has published extensively on labour history. His most recent contributions are *The Railwaymen*, Vol. 2, *The Beeching Era and After* (London, 1982) and *End of the Line? The Fate of Public Transport under Thatcher* (London, 1984).

Klaus Tenfelde is at present Privat-Dozent for Modern History at the University of

Munich. His many articles mainly deal with mining and other topics of social history. He is the author of *Sozialgeschichte der Bergarbeiterschaft an der Ruhr im 19. Jahrhundert* (2nd edn, Bonn, 1981) and *Proletarische Provinz. Radikalisierung und Widerstand in Penzberg/Oberbayern 1900 bis 1945* (Munich, 1982). Together with Heinrich Volkmann he edited *Streik. Zur Geschichte des Arbeitskampfes in Deutschland während der Industrialisierung* (Munich, 1981).

Klaus Schönhoven is Professor of Political Science and Contemporary History at the University of Mannheim. Among his publications are *Die bayerische Volkspartei 1924 bis 1932* (Düsseldorf, 1972) and *Expansion und Konzentration. Studien zur Entwicklung der Freien Gewerkschaften im wilhelminischen Deutschland 1890 bis 1914* (Stuttgart, 1980). Together with Dieter Langewiesche he edited *Arbeiter in Deutschland. Studien zur Lebensweise der Arbeiterschaft im Zeitalter der Industrialisierung* (Paderborn, 1981).

Dirk H. Müller is currently working on a project on political, cultural and economic organizations of the working class in the Weimar Republic. He is the author of *Idealismus und Revolution. Zur Opposition der Jungen gegen den sozialdemokratischen Parteivorstand 1890 bis 1894* (Berlin, 1975).

Richard Hyman is Reader in Industrial Relations at Warwick University and has published extensively in the field of industrial relations and labour history. Among his major books are *The Workers' Union* (Oxford, 1971), *Strikes* (3rd edn, London, 1984) and *Industrial Relations: A Marxist Introduction* (London, 1975).

Robert J. Holton is Senior Lecturer in Sociology at Flinders University of South Australia. He is the author of *British Syndicalism 1900 to 1914* (London, 1976) and *The Transition from Feudalism to Capitalism* (London, 1984).

Michael Schneider is Fellow at the Research Institute of the Friedrich-Ebert Foundation in Bonn. Among his books are *Das Arbeitsbeschaffungsprogramm des ADGB* (Bonn, 1975), *Aussperrung. Ihre Geschichte und Funktion vom Kaiserreich bis heute* (Cologne, 1980), *Streit um Arbeitszeit: Geschichte des Kampfes um Arbeitszeitverkürzung in Deutschland* (Cologne, 1984) and *Die Christlichen Gewerkschaften 1894 bis 1933* (Bonn, 1982).

Geoffrey Alderman is Reader in Politics at Royal Holloway College, University of London. Among his publications are *The Railway Interest* (Leicester, 1973), and more recently *The Jewish Community in British Politics* (Oxford, 1983) and *Pressure Groups and Government in Great Britain* (London, 1984).

John Saville is Professor Emeritus in Hull. Among his publications are *Rural Depopulation in England and Wales, 1851–1951* (London, 1957). He is editing, together with Joyce M. Bellamy, *The Dictionary of Labour Biography* (London, 1972ff.), of which seven volumes have so far been published. In many articles he has made major contributions to British labour history.

Jonathan Zeitlin is Lecturer in Modern Social History at Birkbeck College, University of London. He has published several articles on job control and employers' strategies.

Klaus Saul is Professor for Social History at the University of Oldenburg. He is the author of the book *Staat, Industrie, Arbeiterbewegung im Kaiserreich. Zur Innen- und Sozialpolitik des Wilhelminischen Deutschland 1903–1914* (Düsseldorf, 1974), and wrote many articles dealing with the social history of the German Kaiserreich.

Jay M. Winter is Lecturer and Fellow of Pembroke College, Cambridge. He is the author of *Socialism and the Challenge of War. Ideas and Politics in Britain, 1912–1918* (London, 1974), and editor of *The Working Class in Modern British History* (Cambridge, 1983). He currently does research into the impact of nutrition on civilian health and infant mortality.

Hans Mommsen is Professor of Modern History at the University of Bochum. He is author of *The German Resistance to Hitler* (London, 1970) and *Klassenkampf oder Mitbestimmung. Zum Problem der Kontrolle wirtschaftlicher Macht in der Weimarer Republik* (Frankfurt, 1978). Some of his major articles on labour history are collected in *Arbeiterbewegung und nationale Frage* (Göttingen, 1979).

Hans-Gerhard Husung was a Research Fellow at the German Historical Institute, London. He has published *Protest und Repression im Vormärz* (Göttingen, 1983) and several related articles. He is currently working on a research project on labour during the First World War in Britain.

Index